PENGUIN BOOKS

THE LAST MILLION

David Nasaw is the author of *The Patriarch*, selected by the *New York Times* as one of the 10 Best Books of the Year and a 2013 Pulitzer Prize Finalist in Biography; *Andrew Carnegie*, a *New York Times* Notable Book of the Year, the recipient of the New-York Historical Society's American History Book Prize, and a 2007 Pulitzer Prize Finalist in Biography; and *The Chief*, which was awarded the Bancroft Prize for History and the J. Anthony Lukas Book Prize for Nonfiction. He is a past president of the Society of American Historians, and until 2019 he served as the Arthur M. Schlesinger, Jr. Professor of History at the CUNY Graduate Center.

Praise for *The Last Million*

"In *The Last Million*, Nasaw has done a real service in resurrecting this history. . . . Anyone who thinks President Trump's demonization of foreigners is an aberration should read this history."
—*The Washington Post*

"One of the many virtues of *The Last Million* is the author's ability to make vivid sense of a bewildering moment. He clarifies without oversimplifying. . . . Nasaw takes pains to avoid facile comparisons between the history he recounts and the current global moment, with its—our— own seas of refugees. As his calmly passionate book makes plain, however, one would need to be willfully covering one's eyes not to see how then bleeds into now."
—Adina Hoffman, *The New York Times Book Review*

"David Nasaw devastatingly illustrates in *The Last Million* there was widespread reluctance among the victorious Allies to confront the true nature of the Holocaust. . . . *The Last Million* describes in meticulously researched detail what happened to the [displaced persons] who felt—understandably enough—that they could not go back to the lands of their birth."
—*The Wall Street Journal*

"Insightful and eye-opening . . . Nasaw is a humane writer with a knowledge of his subject that is broad and deep." —Jim Zarroli, NPR.org

"A great contribution of Nasaw's book is that it takes the cinematic moment in which American soldiers arrive and pronounce the nightmare over—'*Shalom Aleichem, Yidden, ihr zint frei,*' a Jewish chaplain from Brooklyn announced when he drove into Buchenwald—as a starting point rather than a closing scene." —*The New Yorker*

"Based on an avalanche of research, sweeping, searching, and filled with intimate details, *The Last Million* tells the enduringly relevant and not well-known story of how political differences between the United States and the United Kingdom, Cold War calculations, ethnic and religious conflicts, and antisemitism trumped humanitarian considerations, 'turning what should have been the primary mission upside down and victimizing those who had suffered the most.'" —Glenn C. Altschuler, *The Jerusalem Post*

"Through great research, Nasaw helps the reader understand the complexity of permanently relocating refugees to a new country." —*The Seattle Times*

"Nasaw, a two-time Pulitzer Prize finalist, has once again produced an extraordinarily well-researched book that is well worth reading." —*The Christian Science Monitor*

"In his magisterial new book *The Last Million: Europe's Displaced Persons from World War to Cold War*, Nasaw describes what really happened in the years immediately after the war, when the Jewish survivors languished in the displaced persons camps in Germany." —*The Jewish Week*

"[A] tour de force of historical reckoning . . . As [*The Last Million*] so powerfully illustrates, the war in Europe did not end when the fighting stopped: the casualties mounted for years." —*Columbia Magazine*

"[A] thoughtful, panoramic study of the people who had no home to return to following World War II . . . *The Last Million* is not an easy read, filled as it is with pathos and pain, but it provides the framework, through it's extraordinary sweep of history, to begin understanding one of the most monumental consequences of war: a group of people from whom everything was stolen." —Jewish Book Council

"Breathtaking and powerful, a wholly absorbing read—and perfect for classroom use." —Dagmar Herzog, author of *Unlearning Eugenics*

"*The Last Million* shows how refugee policies are deeply enmeshed in global systems of power. No other text so clearly shows the connections linking the Cold War aftermath of World War II, the question of Palestine, and anti-Semitic immigration policies in the West." —David Scott FitzGerald, author of *Refuge Beyond Reach: How Rich Democracies Repel Asylum Seekers*

"*The Last Million* offers a stunning overview as it also dives into the daily lives and perceptions of Europe's postwar displaced persons and U.S. immigration policies and prejudices." —Marion Kaplan, author of *Hitler's Jewish Refugees: Hope and Anxiety in Portugal*

"*The Last Million* is a riveting, deeply researched, deeply humane book about a moment in history whose legacy remains with us today." —Peter Beinart, author of *The Crisis of Zionism*

"In his beautifully written and heartbreaking book, Nasaw's *The Last Million* evokes the painful plight faced by the million displaced Jews and eastern Europeans looking to start a new life in a new land after World War II." —Steven J. Ross, author of *Hitler in Los Angeles: How Jews Foiled Nazi Plots Against Hollywood and America*

"David Nasaw's *The Last Million* tells the gripping and very timely story of how the United States confronted the massive refugee problem in the aftermath of World War II."
—Frank Biess, professor of history, University of California, San Diego

"*The Last Million* is an enduring and important scholarly contribution to a historical reckoning with antisemitism and a dark chapter of nativism in American immigration policy. Especially in view of the suspicions some American politicians have cast on immigrants in recent years, it is also a timely and much-needed reminder that such sentiments have a long and disgraceful history." —Jeffrey Herf, University of Maryland, College Park

"David Nasaw's vividly written *The Last Million* is the most comprehensive history of the fate of the 'displaced persons'—Jewish Holocaust survivors and refugees from Soviet-occupied territories in eastern Europe—in the years after World War II."
—Jeremy D. Popkin, William T. Bryan Chair of History, University of Kentucky

"*The Last Million* plunges its readers into the intense national debates over the resettlement of postwar Europe's refugees—from Holocaust and slave-labor camp survivors to former Nazi collaborators—at the very point in history when Cold War pressures were dramatically reconfiguring the global map of ethnic and political identity."
—Jean-Christophe Agnew, professor emeritus of American Studies and History, Yale University

"David Nasaw gives the juxtaposition of Confederate flags and Camp Auschwitz T-shirts on January 6, 2021, its own surprising history—one deeply rooted in the years after World War II, when an unholy alliance of Southern Democrats and cold warriors, soaked with raw anti-Semitism, prevented the U.S. from offering sanctuary to Jewish survivors of the Holocaust. The story is not a pretty one, but it is a page-turner, and an important one for our own moment."
—Linda K. Kerber, author of *No Constitutional Right to Be Ladies: Women and the Obligations of Citizenship*

"A thought-provoking, highly recommended perspective on a complex and largely overlooked people and period of modern history." —*Library Journal* (starred review)

"[Nasaw] provides a characteristically thorough and impressively researched account of the roughly one million displaced persons who found themselves stranded in Germany after the end of the war. . . . While delving into the weeds of political compromise and legislation, Nasaw never loses sight of the hopes and struggles of the people at the center." —*Shelf Awareness*

"Nasaw skillfully and movingly relates a multilayered story with implications for contemporary refugee crises. This meticulously researched history is a must-read."
—*Publishers Weekly* (starred review)

"Masterful . . . A searching, vigorously written history of an unsettled time too little known to American readers." —*Kirkus Reviews* (starred review)

ALSO BY DAVID NASAW

The Patriarch:
The Remarkable Life and Turbulent Times of Joseph P. Kennedy

Andrew Carnegie

The Chief: The Life and Times of William Randolph Hearst

Going Out: The Rise and Fall of Public Amusements

Children of the City: At Work and at Play

Schooled to Order: A Social History of Public Schooling in the United States

The Last Million

Europe's Displaced Persons from
World War to Cold War

——— ✦ ———

DAVID NASAW

PENGUIN BOOKS

PENGUIN BOOKS
An imprint of Penguin Random House LLC
penguinrandomhouse.com

First published in the United States of America by Penguin Press,
an imprint of Penguin Random House LLC, 2020
Published in Penguin Books 2021

ISBN 9780143110996 (paperback)

THE LIBRARY OF CONGRESS HAS CATALOGED THE HARDCOVER EDITION AS FOLLOWS:
Names: Nasaw, David, author.
Title: The last million : Europe's displaced persons from World War
to Cold War / David Nasaw.
Other titles: Europe's displaced persons from World War to Cold War
Description: New York : Penguin Press, 2020. | Includes bibliographical
references and index.
Identifiers: LCCN 2020016888 (print) | LCCN 2020016889 (ebook) |
ISBN 9781594206733 (hardcover) | ISBN 9780698406636 (ebook)
Subjects: LCSH: World War, 1939–1945—Refugees—Europe. | United Nations
Relief and Rehabilitation Administration. | International Refugee
Organization. | Refugees—Europe—History—20th century. |
Refugees—Government policy—Europe—History—20th century. |
Jewish refugees—Europe—History—20th century. | Political
refugees—Europe—History—20th century. |
Jews—Europe—Migrations—History—20th century. |
Humanitarianism—History—20th century. | Europe—Emigration and
immigration—History—20th century. | World War,
1939–1945—Refugees—United States. | United States—Emigration and
immigration—Government policy.
Classification: LCC D809.E85 N37 2020 (print) | LCC D809.E85 (ebook) |
DDC 940.53/145—dc23
LC record available at https://lccn.loc.gov/2020016888
LC ebook record available at https://lccn.loc.gov/2020016889

Printed in the United States of America
1st Printing

Designed by Amanda Dewey
Front matter maps by Jeffrey L. Ward

This book is dedicated to those who, having lived through the most difficult moments any human can endure, affirmed their existence, their joys and suffering, their expectations and hopes, through the acts of writing, speaking, and recalling them for future generations.

CONTENTS

Part Six · THE LAST ACT

NORWAY

SWEDEN

Baltic Sea

Ventspils

Liepāja

Priekulė

Ri...

⑤

③

④

LITHUAN...

North Sea

DENMARK

Tilsit

Kovno

Danzig

◇ Stutthof

EAST PRUSSIA

④

WÖBBELIN ◇

RAVENSBRÜCK •

• Stettin

SACHSENHAUSEN

Berlin

• Poznań

TREBLINKA

Warsaw

⑧

NETH.

GERMANY

Łódź

SOBIBOR

Lublin ◇

DORA-MITTELBAU ◇

POLAND

BUNZLAU

⑥ ⑦

GROSS-ROSEN (Rogozhnica)

MAJDANEK ◇

TRAWNIKI

NORDHAUSEN ◇

BUCHENWALD ◇

THERESIENSTADT

Kielce

Breslau

BELZEC

OHRDRUF ◇

◇ TEREZÍN

AUSCHWITZ-BIRKENAU

Kraków

Lwów

BELG.

LUX.

CZECHOSLOVAKIA

FRANCE

⑥

DACHAU ◇

MAUTHAUSEN

Munich

• Salzburg

Vienna

HUNGARY

SWITZERLAND

AUSTRIA

ITALY

CROATIA

BERGEN-BELSEN ◇

① ②

© 2020 Jeffrey L. Ward

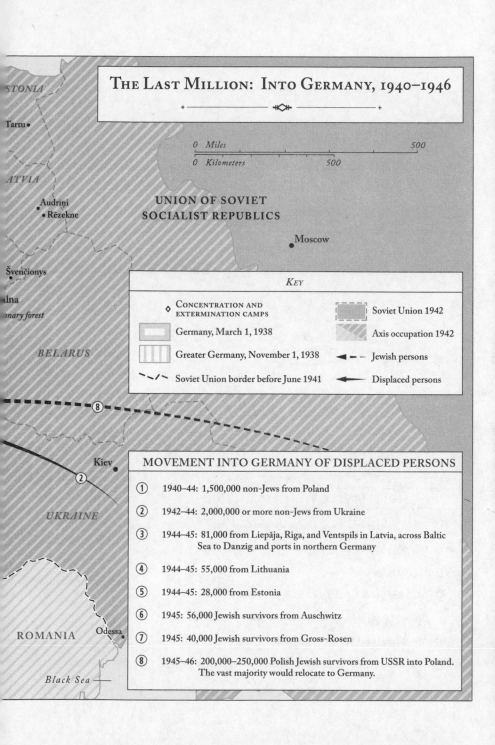

THE LAST MILLION: INTO GERMANY, 1940–1946

0	Miles		500
0	Kilometers	500	

ŠTONIA

Tartu •

ATVIA

Audriņi
• Rēzekne

**UNION OF SOVIET
SOCIALIST REPUBLICS**

• Moscow

Švenčionys

lna
nary forest

BELARUS

KEY

◇ CONCENTRATION AND
EXTERMINATION CAMPS

⬜ Germany, March 1, 1938

▥ Greater Germany, November 1, 1938

～・／～ Soviet Union border before June 1941

▦ Soviet Union 1942

▨ Axis occupation 1942

◀ − − Jewish persons

◀━━ Displaced persons

⑧

Kiev •

②

UKRAINE

MOVEMENT INTO GERMANY OF DISPLACED PERSONS

① 1940–44: 1,500,000 non-Jews from Poland

② 1942–44: 2,000,000 or more non-Jews from Ukraine

③ 1944–45: 81,000 from Liepāja, Riga, and Ventspils in Latvia, across Baltic Sea to Danzig and ports in northern Germany

④ 1944–45: 55,000 from Lithuania

⑤ 1944–45: 28,000 from Estonia

⑥ 1945: 56,000 Jewish survivors from Auschwitz

⑦ 1945: 40,000 Jewish survivors from Gross-Rosen

⑧ 1945–46: 200,000–250,000 Polish Jewish survivors from USSR into Poland. The vast majority would relocate to Germany.

ROMANIA   Odessa •

Black Sea

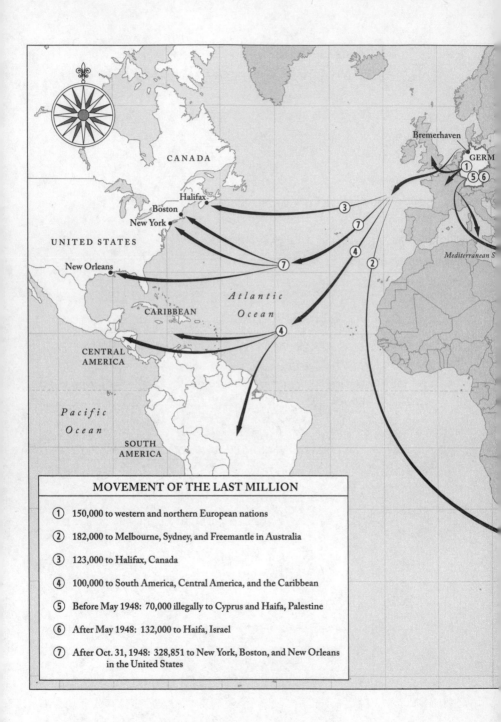

MOVEMENT OF THE LAST MILLION

① 150,000 to western and northern European nations

② 182,000 to Melbourne, Sydney, and Freemantle in Australia

③ 123,000 to Halifax, Canada

④ 100,000 to South America, Central America, and the Caribbean

⑤ Before May 1948: 70,000 illegally to Cyprus and Haifa, Palestine

⑥ After May 1948: 132,000 to Haifa, Israel

⑦ After Oct. 31, 1948: 328,851 to New York, Boston, and New Orleans
    in the United States

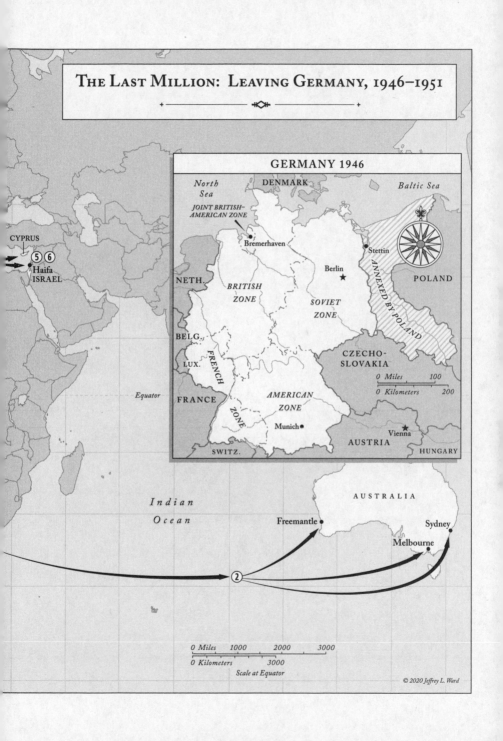

THE LAST MILLION: LEAVING GERMANY, 1946–1951

GERMANY 1946

North Sea

DENMARK

Baltic Sea

JOINT BRITISH–
AMERICAN ZONE

Bremerhaven

Stettin

Berlin ★

ANNEXED BY POLAND

POLAND

NETH.

BRITISH
ZONE

SOVIET
ZONE

BELG.

LUX.

FRENCH

ZONE

FRANCE

AMERICAN
ZONE

Munich

CZECHO-
SLOVAKIA

Vienna ★

AUSTRIA

HUNGARY

SWITZ.

0 Miles 100
0 Kilometers 200

CYPRUS

⑤ ⑥
Haifa
ISRAEL

Equator

*Indian
Ocean*

AUSTRALIA

Freemantle

Sydney

Melbourne

②

0 Miles 1000 2000 3000
0 Kilometers 3000
Scale at Equator

© 2020 Jeffrey L. Ward

The Last Million

INTRODUCTION

The War's "Living Wreckage"

THE VIOLENCE OF WAR did not end with the signing of cease-fires, truces, or peace treaties. War bled into postwar and millions of innocents who had never taken up arms continued to suffer long after the soldiers had gone home. Germany was in free fall; chaos reigned; national, regional, and local military, police, and political authorities had abandoned their posts. There was, literally, no one directing traffic, no one policing the streets, no one delivering the mail or picking up the garbage or bringing food to the shops, no one stopping the looting, the rape, the revenge-taking as millions of homeless, ill-clothed, malnourished, disoriented foreigners: Jewish survivors, Polish forced laborers, former Nazi collaborators—all displaced persons—jammed the roadways, the town squares and marketplaces, begging, threatening, desperate.

"Wandering Hordes in Reich Alarming: Allies Fear Grave Problems May Arise—Ask Liberated to Stay Where Freed," John MacCormac of the *New York Times* reported in a front-page story on April 7, 1945.[1] "Germany has become history's greatest hobo jungle since the Dark Ages," *New Yorker* writer Joel Sayre cabled home on May 2.[2]

The American and British soldiers moving east into Germany, and the reporters who accompanied them, were transfixed by what *Collier's* magazine columnist W. B. Courtney referred to as war's "living wreckage—living, moving, pallid wreckage."

> It washed up and down the margins of the autobahn in a dragging tide. It was composed of people of all sizes, ages, races and varieties or garments. A few had bicycles. Some pushed handcarts. The majority, however, rolled baby carriages. The baby carriage is the sorriest joke in Europe today, for you never see a baby in one. . . . Instead they are filled with pots and pans and tools, and all the impediments of nomads. There were shivering maids, and youths in shorts, with legs blue and raw. There were released German soldiers with their army packs and cut branches for walking sticks. You knew the displaced persons by the bulk of their clothing and the magnitude of their bundles. A man wearing two or even three suits, a woman wearing several dresses and a couple of coats and carrying more were not unusual sights. None seemed to want food. Their want lay sadly deeper, and you could not touch it with your pity but could only surmise that it was for country and home and news of loved ones. Having once seen the wandering lost millions of Europe, you could never forget them, even as you could never fully know what thoughts were in their minds or what lumps were in their hearts. In the rain and wind, they were a steamy, abject porridge of human woe.[3]

BARELY CLOTHED IN RIPPED AND RAGGED, oversized striped camp uniforms, the Jewish survivors were distinguishable by their pallor, emaciated physiques, shaved heads, lice-infested bodies, and the vacant look in their eyes. "You could see them walking down the street," Chaplain Herbert Eskin of the U.S. Army recalled, "some of them, with torn shoes, barefooted, with their long coats, the women, and the men with the pajamas, you know, dirty, very short hair looking to talk to someone for aid."[4]

The vast majority of Jewish survivors remained in the camps, too ill to leave on their own. The soldiers who encountered them tell the same stories of initial shock, then disgust, accompanied by alternating waves of pity, anger, and stomach-churning illness, followed by a body- and soul-wearying sadness that would not dissipate, a disillusionment with all things human, an enervating, pervasive disquiet that would remain with them for the rest of their lives.

Their first task was the burial of the dead and the triage of the living. Thousands of corpses littered the ground, or were stacked in sheds or uncovered graves. Among the living were those known within the camps as the *Muselmänner*,* the unworldly, ghostly walking dead, too ill, too weak, too hurting to be moved, who had to be bathed and fed in their barracks until they were strong enough to be removed on stretchers to hospital facilities. Those afflicted with or dying of typhus were quarantined and left to perish. Those who were ambulatory were moved to assembly centers to be patched together again and repatriated, as soon as possible.

On April 11, Buchenwald was liberated by the inmates, hours before the arrival of the American army, but after the Germans had evacuated some twenty-eight thousand prisoners, a third of whom had died in sealed railroad cars or on arrival at their new camps or while trying to escape. On entering the camp, American soldiers from the 6th Armored Division of the Third Army found twenty thousand inmates, four thousand of whom were Jews.[5]

Chaplain Herschel Schacter of Brooklyn, the youngest of ten children of Polish Jewish émigrés, commandeered a jeep and drove to Buchenwald the day it was liberated.

---

* According to the Shoah Resource Center at Yad Vashem, *Muselmann* was the "German term widely used among concentration camp inmates to refer to prisoners who were near death due to exhaustion, starvation, or hopelessness. The word *Muselmann* literally means 'Muslim.' Some scholars believe that the term originated from the similarity between the near-death prone state of a concentration camp *Muselmann* and the image of a Muslim prostrating himself on the ground in prayer." "Muselmann," www.yadvashem.org /odot_pdf/Microsoft%20Word%20-%206474.pdf.

As we approached the area, the first thing that struck was these huge gates. . . . I walked through. . . . I could see the huge smoke stacks and I rushed in that direction. . . . There were piles of human bodies stacked like cordwood, waiting to be shoveled into the crematorium. . . . I couldn't tarry very long there, and moved on looking for living Jews. . . . I was peering into the faces of some people who were walking around and I had no way of knowing who was a Jew and who wasn't, and I finally stopped one little guy who looked to me to be a Jew and I just asked him in Yiddish . . . whether there are any Jews here and he said of course and he quickly led me to . . . a small compound in this huge camp that was wholly reserved only for Jews. It was by far the most dilapidated and run down area. . . . There were in the first barrack a few hundred people who were obviously too weak, too sick, too bewildered to get out of the barracks. . . . They were just lying there looking out at me half dazed, half crazed, more dead than alive. I didn't know what to say, what to do. All I did was call out in a loud Yiddish "Shalom Aleichem Yidden, ihr zint frei." I was under the impression that many of the people there were not even aware of what had happened. . . . I went from barracks to barracks, and in each one repeated the "Shalom Aleichem" and explained that I am an American, that I am a rabbi, and that we have come to help them, and that the war is over, and of course I spoke in Yiddish, and they clearly understood and got the message and I was everywhere surrounded by people who looked at me and touched me to see if it was real, if I was alive.[6]

Liberation for most of the Jewish survivors arrived with the American and British soldiers who entered the gates, calling out in foreign languages they did not understand that they were free. For others, it came when their German guards stripped off their uniforms, put on civilian clothes, and fled. "The first thing I saw was the guards starting to get on their trucks or run away on foot," Henry Aizenman recalled a half century later of his escape from the Wöbbelin concentration camp. With a group of other inmates, he ran toward the armory, grabbed the rifles left behind, and chased after the guards. Henry didn't know how to shoot a rifle, but the others did. "And then we were free."[7]

For the thousands of survivors whom the Germans had moved from camp to camp in the last weeks of the war to prevent their being discovered and freed by the Allied armies, liberation came on the roads, in the forests, on boxcars, in train stations, wherever they happened to be when the SS or the Hitler Youth or the overage members of the *Volkssturm* or the local volunteers who were guarding them disappeared.

ALLIED SOLDIERS SET UP checkpoints and roadblocks at major intersections and on the main thoroughfares, gathered the endless streams of the lost and homeless, boarded them onto trucks, and transported them to assembly centers where they could be sorted out: the German soldiers hiding among them dispatched to POW camps; Nazi officers and officials and high-level collaborators to prisons to be held and then tried for their crimes; Allied POWs, slave laborers, political prisoners, and concentration camp survivors to assembly centers to be fed, clothed, shaved, sheltered, deloused, separated by nationality, and treated for typhus, tuberculosis, and venereal disease to prevent the infection of civilian populations.

The Allied bombing raids had wreaked such damage in the cities that there were few large structures intact to provide shelter for the displaced. Former military barracks, dormitories for forced laborers, airplane hangars, waiting rooms in railway stations, windowless warehouses, storage sheds, garages, apartment complexes, emptied hotels and resorts, monasteries and churches, government offices and schools, abandoned factories, and, in a few cases, entire city neighborhoods were cleared, cleansed, and converted. Roofs, walls, and plumbing were repaired, fences erected, latrines dug, military guardposts established on the perimeter, food, drugs, sanitary supplies trucked in.

The movement of multitudes of displaced persons into the assembly centers was, for the millions of forced laborers and prisoners of war from Western Europe, Italy, and the Soviet Union, the first step in their journey homeward. Trucks, air convoys, trains, all available means of transportation were requisitioned to remove them from Germany. Days after the German surrender, Albert A. Hutler, chief of the U.S. Army's Displaced Persons Office in Mannheim, was informed that "road blocks have been thrown on all the roads in our area with the purpose of picking up all people circulating." Ten 10-ton trucks would every two hours pick up the displaced and deliver them to the assembly center for processing. Three thousand would be sent home by train every day. "We will use 2 trains one ready for loading at 8 AM, and another ready at 1:30. Each train will carry 1500 passengers."[8]

The largest number of displaced persons in the American and British zones of occupation were the Soviet POWs and forced laborers, more than two million of them. The Soviets wanted them repatriated—and immediately. Their nation was devastated and they required every body and soul to be returned home to rebuild it.

The Allies had agreed at Yalta to give priority to the repatriation of Soviet POWs and civilians. Within days, never more than a week or two after their delivery to the assembly centers, they were loaded into trucks, cargo planes, and railcars for the trip east through Germany into the Soviet zone of occupation and then homeward. Because there was not enough rolling stock, only women, children, and the infirm rode the trains. Everyone else had to walk to the Soviet border where the Soviets had constructed their reception centers. "Russian displacees," wrote W. B. Courtney, "as they surge cheering across to the Red Army, are greeted with a day-long bedlam of speeches, bands, flags, placards, slogans and a myriad of loudspeakers that blare recordings of Russian folk music. And then you watch them trudge past this jolly barricade and disappear into the enigma and the great silence of the East, and you wonder how they will fare and if the back of the zone is as hospitable as its bosom."[9]

Those who were able to walk on their own did not wait for the transports. Singly, but most often in groups of five, ten, twenty, or more, the Polish Jewish survivors, who numbered in the thousands, and the French, Belgian, and Dutch POWs and forced laborers, who numbered in the millions, made their way home. They stowed away on railway cars; they hitched rides on military transports, hay wagons, motorized or horse-drawn carts, and lorries; they stole or "borrowed" bicycles, motorcycles, cars, jeeps, rowboats. They walked, limped, stumbled forward, begging for food and drink or robbing it, taking shelter when night came in bombed-out shells of buildings and warehouses, in barns and haylofts, in abandoned army barracks, in public parks and marketplaces.

Henriette Roosenburg, a Dutch resister freed from her prison in Waldheim, Germany, scrounged for rags with which to sew a Dutch flag that she and her fellow Hollanders hoped would draw to them other countrymen with whom they could begin the journey home. Dragging a child's wagon and a disabled pram filled with their belongings, Roosenburg and her newly freed friends traveled on foot and by wagon, rowboat, and ferry to Halle, where they were put on a plane to Brussels and then home.[10]

August St. André, a French prisoner of war, profiled by *Life* magazine on May 14, 1945, had spent the war as a forced laborer in a porcelain factory, four hundred miles from his home in France. Liberated, he strapped his suitcase to a bicycle, rode to the nearest rail station, boarded a freight car for France, and hitchhiked the rest of the way to his home near the Belgian border.[11]

DESPITE THE LOGISTICAL PROBLEMS—the lack of rolling stock, trucks, and cargo planes, the bombed-out roads and bridges, shortages of food and fuel, and the exhaustion of the troops who, having fought and won the war, now had to transport millions of civilians home—the repatriation campaign succeeded beyond expectations. By October 1, 1945, more than 2 million Soviets, 1.5 million Frenchmen, 586,000 Italians, 274,000 Dutch citizens, almost 300,000 Belgians and Luxembourgians, more than 200,000 Yugoslavs, 135,000 Czechs, 94,000 Poles, and tens of thousands of other European displaced persons, or DPs, had been sent home.[12]

There remained left behind in Germany more than a million displaced persons warehoused in camps, overseen by the occupying militaries and the United Nations Relief and Rehabilitation Authority (UNRRA), which had been organized in 1943 to oversee wartime recovery and the repatriation of the displaced.

The Last Million is the story of these displaced Eastern Europeans who, when the shooting stopped, refused to go home or had no homes to return to. It is the story of their confinement in refugee camps for up to five years after the war ended.*

The Polish Catholics who comprised the largest group of displaced persons had come to Germany during the war, the vast majority deported against their will as forced laborers to replace soldiers sent to the eastern front. They had homes and families to go back to and a government that welcomed their return, but hundreds of thousands preferred to remain in refugee camps in Germany. Caught up in the postwar conflict between East and West, they had been warned—and heeded those warnings—not to return to a Poland devastated by war, threatened by civil war, no longer independent but under Soviet domination, its eastern provinces ripped away and annexed by the USSR.

The Estonians, Latvians, Lithuanians, and some of the western Ukrainians had, unlike the Poles, departed their homelands voluntarily

---

* Thousands of displaced persons ended the war in Austria and Italy and were settled in camps in those countries, but the major focus of this book is on the more than 90 percent who ended the war in Germany and were placed in camps there.

in the final year of the war, in flight from the advancing Red Army. Large numbers of them had collaborated with the Nazi occupiers; some had participated in the slaughter of their Jewish neighbors; a significant number had fought in German uniforms as part of Waffen-SS units.* Even the innocent among them whose collaboration had entailed nothing more than working in a post office under German superiors feared that should they return they would be charged with treason or war crimes. They preferred to remain in the relative safety of the displaced persons camps in Germany until their nations were liberated from the Soviets or they could start their lives anew somewhere else.

A much smaller number of Jewish survivors of concentration, labor, and death camps had entered Germany in the last months of the war. As the Red Army moved westward, German officials, fearful lest the world discover the full extent of Nazi atrocities, had loaded them into boxcars or death-marched them into Germany to work them to death in the underground munitions factories that Hitler believed were going to produce the miracle weapons that would win the war for the Third Reich. Those still alive when the war ended had no families, no homes, no loved ones to return to. Their ultimate destination, they hoped, would be a Jewish homeland in Palestine or with family members in the United States, but for now they had no choice but to remain in the displaced persons camps in Germany, where they were fed, sheltered, and protected by the American and British militaries, and where they enjoyed a measure of security they had not known since the war began. They were a small minority of the Last Million, numbering under thirty thousand, until in 1946 they would be joined in the displaced persons camps in Germany by the Polish Jews who had escaped death by fleeing across the border into the Soviet Union.

The camps in which the Last Million would spend the next three to

---

* The Waffen-SS had originally been Hitler's bodyguards, but under Himmler had evolved into specialized military units. As part of their initiation, members were tattooed with their blood types under their left armpits.

five years were conceived as temporary facilities, but converted by the
displaced persons into island communities, divided by nationality, with
their own police forces, administrative committees, churches, schools,
theaters, newspapers, and medical services. Food, supplies, and security
were provided by the military; special assistance and support by accredited religious and ethnic voluntary organizations; administrative oversight by UNRRA. Black market operations connected insiders with
German civilians outside and brought into the camps luxuries and necessities not otherwise available.

The Last Million were able to exert some control over their daily
lives in the camps, but not over their futures. Those who were willing
to return home would be assisted in doing so. But those who had no
intention of going home again or had no homes to return to were marooned, with neither the resources nor permission nor the documents
they needed to leave the camps and Germany and resettle elsewhere.

Their fate was in the hands of the Allies, who remained sharply divided over what to do with them. The Americans and the British were
agreed that the Eastern Europeans whose lands had been occupied or
annexed by the Soviets had the right to refuse or delay repatriation, if
that was what they chose, and the international community had the
responsibility of caring for them until they decided to go home again or
a place was found for them to resettle.

The Soviets and the Eastern bloc of nations where the DPs had formerly lived demanded that they be repatriated. Only the Jews and
Spanish Republicans were, they argued, truly displaced; the others had
homes to return to and nations ready to welcome them. Those who
sought refuge in the camps were, they insisted, refusing repatriation
because they preferred being fed by the western Allies and UNRRA to
working to rebuild their shattered nations, or, worse yet, because they
feared punishment as quislings, Nazi collaborators, or war criminals
should they return home. Fearful that the Americans and the British,
their former allies, were under the protective cover of UNRRA
warehousing anti-Communist, anti-Soviet dissidents to later deploy in

counterrevolutionary propaganda or military campaigns not dissimilar to the ones they had launched after the Russian Revolution, the Soviet bloc nations demanded that the camps be closed and the displaced persons sent home or left to fend for themselves without Allied or UNRRA assistance.

After a year of fruitless and increasingly acrimonious debate and the obstinate refusal of the Last Million to go home, the Americans and the British concluded that, repatriation having failed, they would have to resettle the displaced persons in new homes and homelands outside Germany. UNRRA would be replaced by the International Refugee Organization (IRO), whose mandate would be resettlement, not repatriation. The Soviet bloc nations tried, without success, to block the establishment of the new organization, then refused to join or contribute to its financial support.

The IRO would succeed in removing the Last Million from the camps by marketing them as the solution to labor shortages aggravated by the recent war. Britain, France, Belgium, and then Canada, Australia, and the nations of South America and the Caribbean were encouraged to send recruiting teams to the camps to select displaced persons to fill their particular labor needs. The first choices of the recruiters were the Latvians and Estonians because they were white, Protestant, healthier than the forced laborers and concentration camp survivors, reliably anti-Communist, and with a reputation for being disciplined and diligent. Next were the Lithuanians, Ukrainians, and Polish DPs. Ignored or intentionally discounted in the recruiting nations' eagerness to gain a cheap labor force was the fact that a not insignificant proportion of the Baltic and some of the Ukrainian DPs had collaborated with the Nazi occupiers or fought alongside them.

The IRO member nations that accepted for resettlement hundreds of thousands of Protestant, Catholic, and Eastern Orthodox Eastern Europeans refused to do the same for the 200,000 to 250,000 Jewish displaced persons, who remained trapped in the camps in Germany, the land of their murderers, awaiting the opening by the British of the gates to Palestine or the offer of visas to the United States, Canada, or Australia. With no legal route out of the camps, thousands left clandestinely for ports from which they could sail to and enter Palestine.

From the moment he assumed office in April 1945, President Truman had believed that in order to remove the Last Million from Germany, he would have to pressure the British to open Palestine to Jewish immigration. Only when it became clear that the British were not going to do so did he recommend that Congress consider passing emergency legislation to admit America's "fair share" of Europe's refugees, including significant numbers of Jewish survivors.

The United States was among the last nations to welcome the Last Million for resettlement, save those whom the CIA and State Department deemed useful for clandestine Cold War campaigns at home and abroad. Though the White House; the State Department; Jewish, Catholic, and Protestant churches and voluntary organizations; distinguished citizens; and prominent politicians from both sides of the aisle supported legislation that would permit some of the displaced persons to enter the country, the pushback from midwestern Republicans and southern Democrats stalled, then transfigured the displaced persons bill introduced in Congress into something quite different from what Truman and its proponents had envisioned. The major obstacle, though never articulated as such, was the admission of the Jewish DPs, some 150,000 to 200,000 of whom had entered the camps from Poland in 1946 after surviving the war in the USSR. The opponents of DP legislation, trading in timeworn Judeo-Bolshevik conspiracy theories, suggested that those who had lived in the Soviet Union or Soviet-dominated Poland and been liberated by the Red Army were more than likely to be Communist sympathizers or clandestine operatives and, for that reason alone, should be barred from entering the United States.

Congress procrastinated, investigated, debated endlessly, as Cold War fears supplanted memories of Second World War atrocities. The displaced persons bill that was finally passed in June 1948, three years after the German surrender, was blatantly, frighteningly discriminatory.

It granted visas only to those who were reliably anti-Communist and excluded the Polish Jews who were not. Forty percent of the visas were reserved for displaced persons whose homelands had been annexed by a foreign power—that is, Estonians, Latvians, Lithuanians, and western Ukrainians, those DP populations with the largest number of collaborators, war criminals, and quislings among them. Ninety percent of the Jewish DPs from Poland who had entered Germany after December 22, 1945, were declared ineligible for admission under the legislation.

With Congress opposing the entrance of large numbers of Jewish DPs to the United States and no other nation willing to accept them, the president had only one option available to him: to relocate them to Palestine. The alternative was to compel the Jewish survivors to remain on German soil, under German law and police powers, in the nation whose leaders had attempted and nearly succeeded in exterminating them. Overriding State Department concerns, President Truman supported the UN resolution for the partition of Palestine and then recognized the independence of Israel.

With the vast majority of the Jewish displaced persons on their way to an independent Israel and the United States having opened its doors, the Last Million were, some of them after five years in the camps, removed from Germany and scattered throughout the nations of the earth. That among them were thousands who had collaborated with the Nazi occupation forces, served in German-organized and -commanded Waffen-SS units, and/or committed war crimes would not be publicly revealed for another three decades.

Part One

———————————— ◆ ————————————

INTO GERMANY

From Poland, the Baltic Nations, and the Death Camps

FROM POLAND AND UKRAINE: FORCED LABORERS, 1941–1945

"We Were Only Allowed to Work, Nothing Else"

DOLF HITLER'S AMBITIONS WERE ENORMOUS. To attain them he would have to redraw the map of Europe, murder millions, displace millions, and import onto German soil as forced and slave laborers millions more. There were, simply put, not nearly enough Aryans inside Germany to raise and harvest the crops, work in the factories and munitions plants, support the infrastructure, and feed and supply the armies that would bring into being Hitler's new world order.

In February 1933, Hitler promised "that for the next 4–5 years the main principle must be: everything for the armed forces." For the next two years, German rearmament proceeded in secret. Then, in March 1935, Hitler declared that despite the restrictions imposed by the Treaty of Versailles, Germany planned to construct an air force, reinstitute conscription, and expand the existing army to 550,000 men.[1]

By the mid-1930s, the effects of the remilitarization and rearmament were felt throughout the country. As German farm laborers entered the armed forces or moved away from the land, attracted by the promise of higher wages in rapidly and perpetually expanding war industries, labor shortages threatened agricultural production. To

alleviate these shortages, Hitler seeded the land with non-Aryan, sea-
sonal foreign workers recruited from among the *"Untermenschen"* of
Eastern Europe. By 1936–37, a quarter of the agricultural workforce
was foreign-born, by 1938–39 it was 43 percent, by 1940, after the invasion and occupation of Poland, 60 percent.[2]

The largest number of foreign workers came from Poland. They included, after 1939, prisoners of war who, despite international law, were
"stripped of their ex-combatant status, recategorized as civilian workers
and assigned to German farms," and young civilians, many of them
attracted by the promise of generous paychecks, plentiful food (certainly
more than was available at home), and, for some, the chance to be near
loved ones who had been deported to Germany as POWs.

With few, if any, German men left behind to supervise their labor,
the foreign laborers were watched over by women, young boys, and elderly men. To prevent any social or, worse yet, sexual relations between
"subhuman" Poles and Aryans, fraternization was not simply condemned, but criminalized in a series of decrees issued in March 1940.
The Poles were required to wear yellow badges with a purple border and
the letter "P" on their clothing. They were housed in separate facilities,
barred from restaurants, public spaces, and public transport, and forbidden to attend church with Germans. Polish men, but not women, engaging in sexual relations with Aryans were subject to death by hanging.
"One reason for these endless restrictions," historian Mark Mazower
has written, "was that, especially in the countryside, regulations were
often ignored. The friendly relations that existed between Poles and
Germans in the villages and on isolated farms worried the authorities,
and they called for renewed vigilance and regimentation."[3] "We were
only allowed to work, nothing else," recalled Nina Mursina, a Polish
forced laborer who had spent the war years in Germany.

> We were not fed like human beings—our provisions were
> poor and low in calories. We worked with potatoes but were not
> allowed to fry any on the fire for ourselves. If the guards smelled

the smoke they set fierce dogs on us. Everything was forbidden. In 1944 I was 19 years old. At that age you're already dreaming about love. The German women employed with us came to work with make-up on, they had done their hair in front of the mirror. And we, as *Untermenschen*, wore dreadful rags and wooden clogs that clattered when we walked.[4]

It did not take long for news to travel east of the conditions the Polish workers were encountering in Germany. As the number of volunteers decreased, the Nazis responded with threats, intimidation, violence, and kidnapping. All Poles between the ages of fourteen and twenty-five living in the area of the General Government, that part of Poland that had not been annexed to the Reich but was occupied and ruled by German officials, were conscripted into mandatory labor service. Those, girls in particular, who could not demonstrate that they were regularly and gainfully employed were designated for immediate transport to Germany. Young men and women who refused would be severely punished; parents who encouraged or tolerated such refusal would be punished as well, their lands and/or farm animals taken from them.

Hitler had anticipated that the German military would quickly defeat the Red Army and he could bring the millions of soldiers in the east home again. But not only did the German armies fail to bring the war to a speedy and triumphant conclusion, they suffered horrendous losses on the eastern front. To replace soldiers killed or incapacitated, the draft age was lowered and exemptions ended for large numbers of men employed in the armaments industry. These initiatives generated more soldiers for the front, which was the primary objective, but they also robbed the home front of laborers at a time when the industrial workforce had to be expanded to produce the tanks, guns, ammunition, and combat aircraft needed in the east.[5]

Hitler had long resisted bringing Soviet civilians or POWs to Germany as forced laborers or making use of them in any other way. He regarded Russian and Ukrainian peasants and soldiers as subhuman beasts and their officers and political commissars as savage, fanatic "Jew-ish Bolsheviks." As losses on the eastern front and an overall shortage of manpower made it impossible to fight a war in the east and maintain control over the newly occupied areas, he would have no choice, how-ever, but to employ them as prison and death camp guards in the occu-pied territories and as forced laborers in the Third Reich.

In the autumn of 1941, the Germans began recruitment in the POW camps in southern Ukraine for "volunteers" to be trained as guards in the SS camp in the Polish town of Trawniki. "Selection was based on German roots, non-Russian nationality, hatred of the Bolsheviks, and state of health." Among those selected were Ivan Demjanjuk, Feodor Fedorenko, and Jakiw Palij, who would later enter the United States as displaced persons.

At Trawniki, the former POWs and Ukrainian volunteers "learned German marching songs and received a crash course in rudimentary Command German. . . . Trawniki also maintained a slave labor camp of Jews, which provided the guards an opportunity to practice their train-ing techniques of herding, guarding, and shooting on live subjects." After two or three months of preparation, the Trawniki trainees, now rehabilitated, armed, and with SS blood-type tattoos under their left armpits, were assigned to one of several labor or death camps in Poland.[6]

On October 31, 1941, with the labor shortages in the east and on the home front growing more dire by the day, Hitler bowed to the inevita-ble and authorized the use of Soviet POWs inside Germany. Those 5 percent of the Soviet POWs healthy enough to make the journey and be put to work in the Third Reich—three million had already been starved to death—were deported to Germany.[7]

Fritz Sauckel, newly appointed as general plenipotentiary for labor mobilization, was also authorized to "recruit" Ukrainians for work in Germany. As in Poland, Sauckel and the Nazis tried at first to entice volunteers to relocate on short-term labor contracts. "The propaganda for labor in the Reich appeared mainly in newspapers; leaflets; bro-chures; large, brightly colored posters; and an itinerant exhibition. . . .

At workplaces and before feature film showings, *Come to Lovely Germany* was shown, a film that portrayed young people laughing and singing all the way to a German farmer's warm welcome." Ukrainians who migrated to Germany were told that they would "earn a good wage and receive free housing and medical care. . . . Dependent relatives in Ukraine would receive financial support as well. Moreover, the workers would learn skills that would later secure them good jobs back home. Because of all these benefits, the workers would be happy." As importantly, they would be doing their patriotic duty as Ukrainians by contributing to the war against Bolshevism.[8]

Though the campaign met with early success, if only because of near-starvation food shortages, by mid-1942, as news trickled back to Ukraine by hand-delivered letters and the testimony of "escapees" and "returnees" that the so-called guest laborers were worked harder and paid less than Germans; fed poorly; housed in leaky, overcrowded barracks; forced to wear humiliating "OST" badges; and prohibited from fraternizing or socializing with Germans or from visiting theaters, movie houses, restaurants, and other public establishments, the number of volunteers declined to near zero.

The Germans resorted to coercion, as they had in Poland. Village elders and mayors in the countryside and officials in "labor offices" were given weekly quotas of "recruits" to fill. For those selected for labor in Germany, there was no way out other than to escape into the forests to join the partisans. Few took this route, knowing full well that if they failed to appear at the station on the day and time they were instructed to, their houses and workplaces would be raided, their families harassed, in extreme cases their villages burned.

Paul Raab was the Nazi official in the Wassilkow* territory in Ukraine charged with overseeing the filling of "the district quota of workers to be delivered to Germany." Through most of 1942, as he reported to his superior, "propaganda" alone had been sufficient to

---

* Raab referred to it this way; the town in question was probably Wassylkiw.

convince Ukrainians to report for labor service. When persuasion
failed, which he claimed happened "only very rarely," force was employed to compel compliance. In August 1942, after a prominent family
had refused to supply one of its sons for labor duty, he notified his superior that he had "decided to take measures to show the increasingly re-
bellious Ukrainian youth that our orders have to be followed. I ordered
the burning down of the houses of the fugitives. The result was, that in
the future, people obeyed willingly, orders concerning labor obligations. . . . This hard punishment was accepted by the population with
satisfaction."[9]

Large numbers of Ukrainian girls and women were deported to
Germany after Sauckel in September 1942 authorized their employment as domestic servants. "Consulted on the matter, Hitler brushed
aside possible racial objections: many women in the Ukraine, he declared, were of German descent anyway, and if they were blonde and
blue eyed, they could be Germanized after a suitable period of service in
the Reich. Sauckel's decree duly required that the women, who were to
be between the ages of fifteen and thirty-five, should look as much like
German women as possible."[10]

Julia Bresinuk, who lived in the village of Novaa Salow in eastern
Ukraine, was sixteen when the Germans arrived. A short time afterward, a man on horseback rode through the village. "He was like a town
crier, and he was announcing that the Germans were recruiting workers
to go to Germany to work there to help in the war effort. I think this
news was in the paper too." Julia's older brother, Ivan, begged their father to let him and his twenty-seven-year-old unmarried sister, Helen,
volunteer. "The money we can make, Papa . . . in six months, we'd make
more than I get paid in three years at town hall!" Julia's father was
reluctant—he trusted the Germans even less than he did the Soviets—
but he gave in to his older children's request. When the day came for
Ivan and Helen's departure, Julia walked with her mother and father to
the town hall. "A lot of villagers had volunteered. They were after the
wages Germany had promised. There were eight or ten big work wag-

ons filled with hay for the people to sit on, the wagons would take them to the train station some thirty miles away." So many villagers left for Germany that summer that, come fall, the high school was closed so that the students could fill in for the workers who had been taken away.

Julia, along with everyone else in the village, anxiously awaited news from family members in Germany. They received none, nor did her brother or sister or any of the other volunteers return after their promised six-month tours had ended. The silence was worrying at first, then ominous. "People stopped volunteering," Julia remembered. The winter of 1942–43 had been a difficult one, in Ukraine and throughout the Soviet Union. Word filtered back to the village "that the Russians were driving the Germans back out of Russia. The Nazis needed more people to work their war factories back in Germany and started drafting people. No more mention of money or a short six month stay."

In the early summer of 1943, more than a year after Julia's brother and sister had left for Germany, a "Brigadier, one of the nicer ones . . . came to the house. He told Papa that shootsmen [Ukrainian auxiliary policemen working for the German occupation] were killing people who refused to go to Germany, and that I would have to go. I had to report to the train station. . . . Transportation would be supplied from the town hall. I had to leave in three days!"

Julia tried to escape into the forest with her mother. She was discovered by one of the shootsmen. "He knew me, my brother and my parents, but I somehow knew he would not hesitate the shoot me. The shootsmen were caught up in the Nazi madness; killing was simply part of his 'job.'" Julia was not shot, but taken to the railway station and put on a train for Germany. "There were a lot of parents along the tracks, pushing and shoving and bumping into one another, trying to get a last look at their children."

After an extended journey in railway boxcars, trucks, and by foot, Julia was "processed" in a labor exchange in Weimar and assigned to Apolda, about twelve miles away, where she would spend the rest of the war living in a barracks with other "guest workers" and operating a lathe in a nearby factory.[11]

Tadeusz Piotrowski and his mother, brothers, and sister, who lived in that portion of Ukraine which had been incorporated into the new Polish nation after the Great War, surrendered to the SS for forced labor to avoid the marauding bands of Ukrainian nationalists intent on clearing western Ukraine of ethnic Poles. They were transported to Essen, an industrial city on the western edge of Germany. "We were taken to a nearby heavily guarded collection camp consisting of plain wooden barracks surrounded by a high barbed-wired fence," disinfected with DDT, given new work shoes, and inspected by officials of the Foreign Workers' Camp Administration. The "ablest from among our ranks [were handed over] to the waiting industrial police for factory work. If they were chosen for the Krupp works . . . they received Krupp blankets stamped with three interlocking wheels and the firm's blue, yellow-striped prison uniforms. The next ablest were handed over to the waiting farmers for agricultural labor. Then, Germans who needed domestic help claimed whomever they wanted. Finally, those who were left (and we were among these)—the old and the young, the infirm and the feeble, the lame, and even the blind—were told to wait."

Tadeusz and his family were assigned living quarters in a classroom with six other families.

> All together, about 300 people occupied the former school-house, the Ukrainians in one wing, the Poles in the other. . . . My mother worked as a cleaning woman in the local police station. . . . My sister, Anna, worked in the disinfecting "lavatories" where new recruits were brought daily to be deloused with DDT. . . . Franek and Janek [his older brothers], who were still children themselves, worked on construction (mixing cement, assisting bricklayers, for instance), within a ten-kilometer radius of the schoolhouse. Since no transportation was provided, they had to walk both to and from the assigned work in summer and in winter.

*Displaced persons are disinfected with the chemical DDT
in Lüneburg, Germany, May 1945.*

Tadeusz, who was not yet six years old, was not given a work assignment, but spent the day with his mother as she cleaned the local police station. "Our daily regimen began at 4:30 A.M. with rising. Work started promptly at 5:00 A.M. and ended at 6:00 P.M. without any breaks."[12]

By the summer of 1943, when Tadeusz and his family arrived in Essen, there were already 6.5 million foreign workers in Germany, almost 5 million of them civilians, the remainder POWs. By the fall of 1944, there were nearly 8 million foreign workers, more than 20 percent of the total workforce.[13]

Their experiences as forced or slave laborers were as varied as the nations they had been deported from. Tadeusz Piotrowski remembered years later that in the swirl of POWs, "guest" workers, and concentration camp inmates, where every non-German suffered from malnutrition, disease, and exposure, there were "three general rules. . . . (1) The Jews were to be treated in the worst possible way; (2) the Russians in the next worst possible way; and (3) the people from the East were to be treated worse than the people from the West."

Rations for Eastern Europeans were half those given to Western Europeans, barely enough to keep workers alive and productive; overcrowding in the barracks and dormitories endemic; sanitation and hygienic conditions abysmal; clothing, blankets, and shoes in short supply and, when worn out, seldom replaced; vermin, disease, malnutrition, and corporal punishment a constant threat.[14]

The Germans exploited the foreign workers until the very end of the war. In March 1945, as the American army advanced into German territory, the Germans relocated Tadeusz and his family with thousands of others, vast numbers of them slave laborers in the Krupp factories, from Essen to the city of Meiningen in central Germany. Their train was bombed several times. "Having escaped death . . . terrified, worn out, and hungry, we finally arrived at Meiningen. . . . The wooden barracks into which we were dumped were packed with people in varying stages of decay." Tadeusz recalled, "Unbelievable as it may sound, even as people were starving and dying like flies everywhere, Germans would come looking for workers." His brothers volunteered for work. "To stay put meant certain death; perhaps they could find something in the city of Meiningen to prolong their life." They found a parcel of food stamps that kept them alive until May 1945, when the Americans arrived.[15]

FROM LATVIA, LITHUANIA, ESTONIA, AND WESTERN UKRAINE

In Flight from the Red Army

THE CITIZENS OF ESTONIA, Latvia, and Lithuania had enjoyed a brief moment of independence after World War I, only to lose it, first to the Soviets, then to the Germans.

The Soviet-German nonaggression pact signed by Vyacheslav Molotov and Joachim von Ribbentrop in August 1939 contained a secret protocol granting the Soviet Union an exclusive sphere of influence over Finland, Estonia, Latvia and that part of western Ukraine, or Galicia, that had been incorporated into the new Polish state under the Treaty of Riga of March 1921. In September, Stalin demanded that the Soviet sphere of influence be extended to include Lithuania. Hitler agreed. Stalin in return granted Germany a larger portion of the former Polish state and the right to "repatriate" ethnic Germans residing in the Baltic nations. The Soviets then annexed western Ukraine and compelled the Estonian, Latvian, and Lithuanian governments to sign "mutual assistance pacts" and agree to the establishment of Soviet military bases. When Finland refused Soviet demands to cede Finnish territory to the USSR, it was invaded by the Red Army.

On October 7, 1939, the Germans, in need of "Aryans" to settle the territories seized from Poland and incorporated in the Reich, formally invited the Baltic *Volksdeutsche** to return to their true homeland. Convinced that they would live better, richer lives, tens of thousands of Baltic Germans left the homes they had inhabited for up to seven generations to be resettled in lands the Third Reich had annexed from Poland. In early 1941, thousands more, including many who claimed to be ethnic German but were not, departed from Lithuania. Those who could prove their Aryan ancestry were offered German citizenship.[1]

In mid-June 1940, as German armies ripped through Western Europe, from Norway to the Low Countries into France, the Red Army marched into and occupied Lithuania, Latvia, and Estonia. Puppet governments were formed and bogus elections held for new parliaments that, at their first meetings, "proclaimed the three countries to be soviet socialist republics and voted to send delegations to Moscow to apply for annexation to the USSR. . . . Sovietization proceeded apace in all domains of life in each country. . . . Large industrial enterprises were nationalized, as were banks and all land. . . . Educational institutions were placed under new leadership . . . Newspapers were closed or subjected to strictest censorship. . . . By the end of 1940, all major and minor institutions, if not closed, had been purged of their former 'bourgeois' leadership."[2]

It is difficult to underestimate the selective brutality of the new Soviet regimes against their perceived enemies: the clergy, intellectuals, artists, large landowners, shopkeepers, manufacturers, professionals, former members of the military, and government officials. That brutality reached the breaking point in the spring of 1941. Stalin believed he could avoid a German invasion and war, at least for the time being, but that it was necessary nonetheless to assure that there were no anti-Soviet or pro-German pockets of resistance and no subversive elements in the Baltic states.

In mid-June 1941, Soviet officers rounded up, packed into railroad

---

* The term *Volksdeutsche* ("German folk") referred to ethnic Germans born and/or living outside of Germany.

cars, and deported tens of thousands of Latvians, Estonians, and Lithuanians whom NKVD (the Soviet Secret State Police) officers suspected
of harboring anti-Soviet or bourgeois tendencies. "The deportations,"
Romuald Misiunas and Rein Taagepera have written, "served as a massive shock to the citizens of the Baltic republics, which no doubt had
been the intention. Now it was no longer select individuals whose dis-
appearance without a trace could be explained by some system of logic,
but large groups representing various sections of the population." No
one knew how the lists had been drawn up or whether this was the first
of many deportations to come or who among one's neighbors, family,
and friends had assisted the NKVD in identifying enemies of the regime and directing Soviet officers to their homes.[3]

On June 22, 1941, a week and a day after the deportations, three
million German soldiers, thousands of trucks and tanks, and six hundred thousand horses pulling heavy artillery and supply wagons invaded
the Soviet Union in Operation Barbarossa, preceded by an overwhelming and overwhelmingly successful air campaign that virtually destroyed
the Soviet air force. Within a matter of weeks, German forces occupied
the Baltic nations and much of western Ukraine.

The Wehrmacht, on its trajectory eastward toward Leningrad, did
not leave behind sufficient soldiers, military officers, security police,
SS, or intelligence officers to police and administer the newly conquered
territories. With a large number of Baltic *Volksdeutsche* already relocated,
the German occupiers had to employ local non-Aryans to execute their
orders. Within the racial hierarchy constructed by Nazis, the Baltic peoples were afforded pride of place and more "self-rule" (or the semblance
thereof) than the Poles, the Ukrainians, or other conquered eastern peoples. In each of the Baltic nations, "Directorates" or "Self-Administrations"
were established, though as historian Valdis O. Lumans has written with
special reference to Latvia, these entities "had no power to initiate any
measures. . . . In essence the Self-Administration amounted to no more
than an administrative organ created to facilitate the German occupation and execute what the Germans wished."[4]

In western Ukraine, which had been annexed by the Soviets after the Molotov-Ribbentrop Pact, the Germans were more vigilant and discriminating. Still, lacking the manpower to govern, they recruited thousands of Ukrainians to assist them in administering and policing those areas where the ethnic German population was sparse. Appointed officials were charged with "routine administrative tasks," including submitting regular written reports "on questions such as agricultural production; budget problems; health issues; monthly birth rates; cattle diseases; the state of roads, sidewalks and bridges; housing issues."[5]

The Germans had no trouble finding people in Ukraine and the former Baltic nations to work with them. Hundreds, if not thousands, of government employees and civil servants who had resigned or been dismissed from their positions after the Soviet takeover were more than ready to return to their desks. Among the first tasks of the new district leaders, mayors, and village elders was a thorough census of the local population. This included a "nationality clause" that identified Jews. Census-takers were directed as well to report on inhabitants who had recently moved into the district or into a new house, another tool for exposing Jews who were trying to escape detection.[6]

Those Baltic nationals and western Ukrainians who collaborated with the German occupation did so for many and diverse reasons: because they believed in the Nazi mission and ideology; because they were convinced that the occupation was permanent or near-permanent; because the Nazis represented the present and the future, and there was no good reason to resist what history had ordained; because they were inclined to work for and with whatever regime happened to be in power, whether that regime was indigenous or externally imposed; because they feared for their lives and livelihoods and their families should they decline to cooperate; because they would rather live under Nazi occupation than Communist and were persuaded that the Germans would protect them from the Soviets. As long as the German military appeared to be ascendant, there were few social or material costs to collaboration. Only with the return of the Red Army would the meaning of collaboration be retroactively reconfigured from a practical working relationship with the regime in power to a moral and political crime.

The terms of collaboration were, in the Baltic nations and the western Ukraine as in every other nation occupied by the Germans, set by the occupiers. The "often quoted phrase 'certainly, Poland did not have its Quisling,'" Jan T. Gross instructs us, "is of only limited heuristic value. It merely tells us that the Germans, locally, had not made the offer."[7]

Collaboration took many forms. For some, it entailed putting on German uniforms and serving under German command in Waffen-SS or auxiliary police or paramilitary units and tracking down, torturing, herding into ghettos, and shooting Jewish civilians and other enemies of the Nazi regime. For others, the terms of engagement were more benign. Collaboration meant holding on to or taking a position in the civil service; treating German soldiers in a hospital; confiscating and redistributing property seized from Jews; tacitly or enthusiastically supporting Nazi ideological positions in school or university; feeding German soldiers or guarding their military installations; collecting taxes; delivering the mail; rationing and distributing food, fuel, and clothing; staffing the courts and penitentiaries; repairing the roadways; and managing dozens of government departments, from "Water Supply and Sewage" to "Ports and Economy," "Sea Markings," "Agricultural Buildings," and "Building Inspection."[8]

FOR THE MEN, women, and children of the Baltic nations and western Ukraine, the world had been turned upside down—again. The Soviets had fled, replaced by German invaders and occupiers.

For the millions of Jews who lived in Estonia, Latvia, Lithuania, and western Ukraine, the German invasion was the beginning of the end. Non-Jews who had feared for their lives, their families, and their fortunes under the Soviets celebrated the arrival of the German troops and blamed the Jews for their past misfortunes. "After the Soviets had gone, Jews were held responsible for the suffering. They were accused of having welcomed the Soviet occupiers and then of collaborating with their reign of terror."[9]

The association of Jews with Bolsheviks was taken almost as a matter of faith. There was no need for evidence. It was assumed that every Jew was a subversive, a Bolshevik. "The Jews displayed themselves to be very prominent in the communist period," Mrs. Vita Steinhardt, a high school student in Latvia when war broke out, recalled in an oral history in 1981.

> They very actively participated in the rise of communism. . . . And that, for Latvians, is what started this hostility against the Jews. For they with their eyes experienced what Communism meant for the Jews. And Latvians were thrown out and Jews put in their place. They, in the Communist period, began to work like masters. . . . At that time the Russians, coming into Riga with tanks took over Riga, the Jews were so happy. . . . They were so happy, so joyful, and were whispering so the whole time. . . . They were waiting, expecting the Russians, and with great enthusiasm they greeted them. . . . In every influential position there was definitely a Jew.[10]

Blaming the Judeo-Bolsheviks for all that had gone wrong under the Soviet occupation served another critical purpose as well. As Timothy Snyder has written, while the Soviets "did employ Jews in higher numbers than the prewar regimes . . . Soviet power was based everywhere in the local majorities: be they Latvian, Lithuanian, Belarusian, Ukrainian, Russian, or Polish. Insofar as the non-Jews made the claim that Jews were Soviet collaborators and that Soviet collaborators were Jews (and insofar as such claims are made today), they minimized the indispensable role that non-Jewish locals played in the Soviet regime."[11]

The war against the Soviet Union was, for tens of thousands of Eastern Europeans who greeted the Germans as liberators, a war against Bolshevism and its evil twin, Judaism. It gave license to those whose families had been deported, persecuted, or imprisoned for their "bourgeois tendencies" to turn the tables on the Jews, who they "knew" had consorted with the Soviets and encouraged if not engineered the Soviet occupation and the terrors that accompanied it.

The leaders of the Lithuanian Activist Front who had escaped to Germany after the Soviet takeover in the summer of 1940, in a published statement on the eve of the German invasion, declared that "the crucial day of reckoning has come for the Jews at last. Lithuania must be liberated not only from the Asiatic Bolshevik slavery but also from the Jewish yoke of long standing."[12]

The same dynamic was at work in western Ukraine, where a leaflet distributed in Lwów* (Lviv) from the ultranationalist OUN-B,† led by Stepan Bandera, "warned Jews that, 'You welcomed Stalin with flowers [when the Soviets occupied East Galicia in 1939]. We will lay your heads at Hitler's feet.'" Bandera loyalists determined that Jews "have to be treated harshly. . . . We must finish them off. . . . Regarding the Jews, we will adopt any methods that lead to their destruction." Jews were slaughtered not only because some had sided with or taken up leadership positions with the Soviets, but because they were perceived as the perpetual, unassimilable other that did not and could not belong to the ethnically pure Ukrainian nation the nationalists intended to establish in the foreseeable future, with or without German support.[13]

"The pulse of anti-Jewish violence in the rimlands [the lands between Germany and the USSR] did not come out of nowhere," historian Mark Levene has written. "Whether conducted by townspeople or rural folk, there were conscious revenge attacks against a part of the population which was not just deemed to have collaborated with the

---

* Place names, especially in Eastern Europe, are never stable. I have used the place-names that were in usage at the time I refer to them. In parentheses I give the place-name in use as of the writing of this book, in 2020.
† The OUN-B was the faction of the Organization of Ukrainian Nationalists loyal to and controlled by Stepan Bandera.

Soviets but was held to be directly responsible for the liquidation of national hopes and aspirations," for the destruction of that brief moment of independence that had followed the Great War.[14]

In the cities, the towns, and the rural hinterlands, as the Red Army fled and the German military approached, local people confiscated Jewish property; attacked Jews on the streetcars, the trains, and in the streets; burned synagogues; looted shops and homes and offices; and murdered men and women whose only crime was that they were Jewish. Abraham Golub, a Hebrew educationalist, kept a diary throughout the occupation and recorded the shock felt by Jews who were suddenly exposed to the fury of local mobs. The Lithuanians "did not conceal their joy at the outbreak of the war: they saw their place on the side of the Swastika and expressed this sentiment openly."[15]

Jack Arnel, who was twelve years old, remembered the chaos and terror in Vilna (Vilnius), Lithuania, with Russian soldiers running through the streets, bombs falling, and German soldiers and officers marching into the city. The morning after the German invasion, Jack went out into the courtyard to play with his Polish friends. Down the road came a motorcycle with a sidecar and three German soldiers with machine guns strapped behind them. With a finger pulled across his throat, one of the German soldiers declared, almost matter-of-factly, *"Alle Juden* will be killed." Only Jack, who spoke Yiddish, understood what the German had said. He went into his home at once and hid sobbing in his room. Why had the German said this? he asked his parents. What did it mean? "The real tragedy has begun."

Jewish males were "scooped up" wherever they might be, day or night, and put in jail. No one knew at first why or where they had been taken. The hope was that they had been sent away to work. But that was not the case. Those who could not bribe their way out of prison were herded into trucks and driven to the nearby Ponary forest, where they were shot and thrown into a mass grave. The Germans gave the orders, but the Lithuanians did the killing. "Lithuanians were the most brutal ones, they were the most cooperative with the Germans. They participated in the slaughter. They were extremely brutal." Jack's father was spared only because he was a furrier and the Wehrmacht intended to employ local practitioners of the trade to make fur vests.[16]

One hundred and eighty miles to the north, in Riga, Latvia, Yakob Basner, who was seven years old when the Germans invaded, recalled how one of his family's neighbors, a non-Jew who spoke Yiddish, pointed out to the police where Jews lived and the places where they might be hiding. When the police couldn't find Yakob's father's hiding place, they took his mother to headquarters. "They were drunk celebrating. . . . They ridiculed the Jewish people that were there, beating them up." They grabbed the Basners' landlord, "stripped him naked," and, in a frighteningly direct allusion to what they considered to be the ancestral, irremediable connection between Jews and Bolsheviks, "put on his head a Russian army hat and he had to sing Russian songs."[17]

After the first days of torturous, murderous, wanton, often public violence against Jews, the German occupying authorities moved in to organize the killing and the killers. Though the pogroms that preceded and/or accompanied the invasion had not been "an effective way to eliminate Jews . . . the production of lawlessness," as Timothy Snyder has written, "was an appropriate way to find murderers who could be recruited for organized actions."[18]

The German occupying authorities had their own security police and intelligence officers, but there were never enough of them, nor were they capable without local helpers of locating, imprisoning, ghettoizing, and liquidating Jews and Communist partisans. Former policemen, military officers, and members of neo-fascist, antisemitic,* anti-Bolshevik partisan and guerrilla units, as well as local militia, some of whom had come out of exile in Germany to march with the Wehrmacht, were recruited or volunteered for and were organized into *Schutzmannschaft*, or auxiliary police, units led by German officers. Some were assigned to "police"

---

* I have used "antisemitic" and "antisemitism" for the reasons articulated by the International Holocaust Remembrance Alliance (www.holocaustremembrance.com/sites/default/files/memo-on-spelling -of-antisemitism_final-1.pdf). I have not, however, changed citations from sources that employ other usages.

local neighborhoods, while others secured the rear against partisans, guarded military installations, Jewish ghettos, prisoner encampments, and railway stations. They identified and registered the Jews in their regions, moved them into ghettos or concentration camps, policed them there, and when ordered to do so, marched them to the killing fields or loaded them onto convoys, cordoned off the sites, raised their rifles, pulled the triggers, then supervised their countrymen as they covered over the mass graves.[19]

The recruits who joined the auxiliary police units in their local towns, cities, and districts enlisted for a variety of reasons: because the rations were good; because serving under the Germans removed any taint of suspicion from those who had worked as policemen, soldiers, or officers under the Soviet-dominated regimes; because they believed that their service in "this 'brotherhood of arms' with Nazi Germany would lead to the rebirth of a national army"; because they hoped that the Germans would reward their contribution to the war against the Bol-sheviks by granting their homeland some form of autonomy; because they believed it was their duty as well as their pleasure to take revenge against the Jews and destroy the Bolshevik-Judaic-Asiatic menace, once and for all; because they hoped to grow rich from confiscating Jewish loot; because they enjoyed the killing.[20]

In Estonia, three thousand of the country's four thousand Jews es-caped to safety in the Soviet Union before the Germans arrived. Police-men in Tartu, the second-largest city in Estonia, working under German command, located, arrested, and transported the remaining Jews to a concentration camp, where they were tried for collaborating with the Soviets, condemned to death, stripped of their clothes, their hands tied behind their backs, loaded onto trucks, driven about three miles to the execution fields where trenches and pits had been dug to receive their bodies, and shot. By the early fall of 1941, after the Estonian Jews had been liquidated, Jews from other parts of the Baltic region, then from Berlin and Theresienstadt and elsewhere, were transported to Tartu, along with POWs and political prisoners. Some twelve thousand would die there. Ervin Viks and Karl Linnas, who would escape to Germany and be resettled as displaced persons, Viks in Australia, Linnas in the United States, were camp commandants at Tartu.[21]

In Vilna, where by December 1941 forty thousand Jewish residents had been shot in the Ponary forest and thousands more imprisoned in a ghetto, Algimantas Dailide, who served in the "Communist-Jews" section of the Lithuanian Security Police, or Saugumas, located Jews in hiding and arrested and handed over to the Germans those who had attempted to escape from the ghetto. Dailide's crimes were especially heinous, as he was part of a scheme to extort money from Jews who were promised that they would be smuggled out of Vilna by truck for a fee. After paying the fees demanded, they were instead taken into custody and delivered to the Nazis for execution. When the war was over, Dailide, having escaped as the Red Army approached and relocated to Germany, applied for and was granted DP status after lying on his application. He would emigrate to the United States as a displaced person in 1950.[22]

In Švenčionys, fifty-three miles from Vilna, the chief of the Saugumas was Pranas Puronas, grandfather of the American poet and writer Rita Gabis. After years of research in several archives, traveling thousands of miles, and working with historians, researchers, and translators in several locations and multiple languages, Gabis discovered that her grandfather had played a part in the mass shooting at Poligon of eight thousand Jews. The Germans gave the orders; the Lithuanians shot and buried the victims, and, when their task was done, celebrated at a banquet on the town green "with food and drink and the local authorities, the shooters, police, [Gabis's] grandfather, eating and singing and feeling the liquor burn the back of their throats, their breath a distillery." Puronas would flee Lithuania at war's end for Germany, where he would seek and be granted DP status, and later emigrate to the United States.[23]

One hundred and seventy-five miles to the north, in Rēzekne, Latvia, Boleslavs Maikovskis served as captain of the second police precinct. In late December 1941, two Latvian police officers were killed in the nearby village of Audriņi, perhaps by Soviet partisans. Maikovskis directed the policemen under his command to join with German soldiers in arresting the residents of Audriņi, burning the village to the ground, and shooting thirty villagers in the market square. Maikovskis would also receive DP status, and eventually be relocated to the United States.[24]

Just how many Eastern Europeans took part in the torture, looting, incarceration, and murder of Jews remains unknown. In the Lithuanian provinces, where a large percentage of the Jewish population lived in shtetls that were 50 percent Jewish, "one half of the population was persecuted, robbed and eventually murdered by a significant proportion of the other half," writes Christoph Dieckmann, author of a sixteen-hundred-page study of the Holocaust in Lithuania. "Many Lithuanian regional and local officials, as well as policemen and civilians, were involved in the entire gamut of activities which aimed to identify, select, separate and isolate the victims; plunder their property; and finally participate in their murder."[25]

Historian Valdis Lumans concludes of Latvia that if we include not only those who pulled the triggers, but those who identified Jewish neighbors and hiding places, those who participated in rounding up victims, leading them to their slaughter, and covering up the evidence, and those who served in the auxiliary police battalions, the number who took part in the Jewish genocide "probably reaches well into the several thousands."[26]

The result of such collaboration was that by war's end, 90 percent of Lithuania's quarter million Jews had been murdered; Latvia, with its sixty-six thousand Jews, and Estonia, with a few thousand, had been rendered virtually *Judenfrei*. More than one and a half million Jews had been murdered in Ukraine.[27]

WHILE HITLER AND the German occupiers assigned non-Aryans to a variety of administrative duties in the occupied territories, they resisted placing them in positions that required them to carry weapons. By the spring of 1942, however, with more than three hundred thousand German soldiers dead or missing on the eastern front, and with the draft pool already enlarged to include the young, the middle-aged, and previously exempt industrial workers, the Germans had no choice but to recruit and enlist non-Aryans in armed auxiliary police units and newly established Waffen-SS legions. An intermediate racial category, the "Germanizable," was invented and deployed to legitimize the placing of weapons in non-Aryan hands. "Service in the militarized auxiliary police units, and later, in the Waffen-SS, was viewed as a way of bringing out the best racial elements and encouraging their Germanization."[28]

Fritz Sauckel, Hitler's plenipotentiary for labor, agreed in April 1943 "to exempt Latvians and Estonians from the latest labor drive" if they agreed to serve, now or at some future date, in the military. In Estonia and with slight variations in Latvia and Lithuania, young men were given the option of fulfilling their compulsory labor service requirements by serving "in the SS legion, in auxiliary units of the Wehrmacht or as factory workers in war-related industries. Those signing up for the legion were promised the immediate return of their lands" that had been taken from them during the Soviet occupation.[29]

Waffen-SS divisions were composed initially of those, including former auxiliary policemen, who had demonstrated their willingness to kill and their loyalty to the Nazi occupiers. Auxiliary policemen who had served with the Arājs Kommando, the most vicious of the Latvian auxiliary forces, joined the Latvian Legion. Karl Linnas and his colleagues from the Tartu concentration camp joined the Estonian Legion.

Only in Lithuania was there a shortage of volunteers. After attempts to recruit Lithuanians for a Waffen-SS division failed in early 1943, the

Germans, more desperate than ever for military manpower, organized
the Lithuanian Territorial Defense Force in early 1944, which they
promised would be commanded by Lithuanians and restricted to fighting Bolshevik partisans in the Baltic area. "This effort, unlike previous
mobilization efforts, enjoyed the blessing of many native notables. . . .
The actual level of volunteers exceeded expectations; some 30,000 came
forward, and the originally planned number of battalions was somewhat
increased."[30]

Some of those called up, especially the older men, refused service.
They hid in plain sight or escaped to the forests or, if they were Estonian, to Finland. Most, however, like Inara Verzemnieks's grandfather,
Emils, a Latvian economist, who was called up in the last conscription
group in late March 1944, heeded the warnings posted in the newspapers that "unconscious citizens who refrain from fulfilling their responsibility to their nation at this decisive moment and have not heeded the
instructions will not be able to live unaffected. Sooner or later they will
receive the punishment they deserve." He joined the Latvian Waffen-SS
unit, put on a German uniform with "SS bolts at the collars," and, at his
induction, pledged his loyalty to the Reich. "I swear by God this holy
oath that in the struggle against Bolshevism I will give the Commander
in Chief of the German Armed Forces, Adolf Hitler, absolute obedience and as a brave soldier I will always be ready to lay down my life for
this oath."[31]

Hitler and the German high command were able to rationalize arming Baltic nationals because according to Nazi racial theories they were,
except for some of the Lithuanians, "Germanizable." This was clearly
not the case with the vast majority of Ukrainians left behind after the
Volksdeutsche and Volga Germans had been evacuated. By the spring of
1943, having run out of other options to rectify manpower shortages at
home, on the front lines, and in the rear, Himmler approved the creation of a Ukrainian Waffen-SS horse-drawn infantry division. The division was labeled "Galician"; to call it Ukrainian, the Germans feared,
might exacerbate nationalist sentiments.

During the first month of recruitment, some eighty thousand young Ukrainian men, many of whom had previously served in auxiliary police units, stepped forward. The major incentive here, as in the Baltic nations, was the opportunity to join in the German-led antisemitic, anti-Soviet crusade. The OUN, the Organization of Ukrainian Nationalists, which had its own paramilitary units, was initially opposed to the formation of a German-organized, German-commanded Waffen-SS division, but quickly recognized the utility of arming and training ethnic Ukrainians who might one day serve as the nucleus for an independent Ukrainian national army.[32]

The majority of Ukrainians who volunteered for the Waffen-SS division were dismissed as unfit, large numbers because they did not meet the SS's rather stringent physical and height requirements, others because of ties or sympathies with the OUN. Nineteen thousand were accepted and took their oath, giving themselves "to the disposal of the Germany army," swearing "to the German Leader and Commander-in-Chief of the German Army, Adolf Hitler, unswerving loyalty and obedience," and putting on standard gray Waffen-SS uniforms, distinguished from the German uniforms by the absence of "runes on the right collar patch" and the substitution of a Galician insignia.[33]

Balts and Ukrainians served the German military and occupation forces in Waffen-SS divisions, and as members of auxiliary police, security police, paramilitary, and support units. By war's end, according to German military historian Rolf-Dieter Müller, up to 60,000 Estonians, 100,000 Latvians, 40,000 Lithuanians, and 250,000 Ukrainians, some voluntarily, some enthusiastically, some under pressure, some under compulsion, had sworn oaths of allegiance to Hitler and taken up arms against the Soviets.[34]

INTO GERMANY, 1944—45

On June 22, 1944, exactly three years to the day after the Germans had invaded the Soviet Union, the Red Army launched Operation Bagration, named for a hero of the war against Napoleon in 1812. By early 1945, the German armies had been pushed back along the fourteen-hundred-mile front that extended from Bucharest in the south to Leningrad in the north. They were on the defensive in the west as well, as the British and American armies advanced more slowly than expected but inexorably toward the Rhine. With the Luftwaffe nearly destroyed in the air battle that preceded and prepared for the Normandy landing, Allied bombers, almost unimpeded now, attacked major armament and aircraft plants, transportation networks, and urban areas.

As the Soviet reoccupied Ukraine and the Baltic nations, those who had served in the auxiliary police forces or Waffen-SS legions, those who had murdered or participated in the murder of Jews and suspected Communists, those who had held government positions or worked in the civil service under the Nazi occupation packed up their belongings, buried whatever treasures they could not take with them, assembled their extended families, and fled west toward Germany. They did so because they knew or suspected that if they remained, they would be punished for their wartime activities.

Three years earlier, when the Soviets had fled the Baltic nations and western Ukraine in advance of the German invasion, they had left behind informants, party members, and NKVD underground cells that had kept track of the activities of collaborators and war criminals. With the return of the Red Army, the NKVD, with state investigators and prosecutors, took up positions in the reoccupied towns, villages, and cities. Quislings, enemies of the state, collaborators, and war criminals were rounded up and put on trial, not to determine their innocence or guilt, but to demonstrate that those who had collaborated with the

Nazi occupiers had committed treason and would be punished accordingly.

In July 1943, the Soviets held their first war crimes trials in Krasnodar, in southern Russia, which had recently been liberated from German occupation. Eleven Soviet citizens were convicted of high treason and collaboration in the murder of seven thousand citizens, most of them Jews. The defendants pleaded guilty, and eight were condemned to death by hanging; three were given sentences of twenty years of forced labor. The proceedings and public executions were filmed; an abridged trial transcript was translated and published.[35]

In Ukraine, the NKVD, almost simultaneously with the return of the Red Army, "conducted several thousand investigations into the activities of former *Schutzmannschaft* members and local administrators. In many cases, the murder of Jews lay at the heart of the legal proceedings. Severe sentences were handed down for collaboration, especially for participating in killing operations. From 1943 to 1947, the death sentence was common; from 1948 on, twenty-five years in the Soviet labor camps was a typical sentence."

In December 1943, three Germans and a twenty-six-year-old Ukrainian who had ferried Jews from a nearby hospital to the killing fields, and may himself have taken part in the shooting of sixty children, were put on trial for the murder of fifteen thousand Soviet citizens in a ravine outside Kharkiv known as Drobitsky Yar. There was no mention of Jews in the testimony or the verdict—death by hanging. Still, it did not escape anyone's attention that the Soviet citizens murdered by the defendants had been Jews. The trial was held in a theater, the public and reporters invited inside to witness the proceedings, cameras in hand, to record it. In 1944, a full-length documentary of the trial was screened throughout the USSR and in London and New York. By then, news of the trial, the charges, and the verdict had been broadcast throughout Ukraine and the Baltic nations. This was the final signal to those who had collaborated with the Nazis to abandon their homes, their families, and their homelands at once, before the arrival of the Red Army.[36]

LARGE NUMBERS OF Latvians, Estonians, Lithuanians, and Ukrainians who had volunteered for or been conscripted into German military or paramilitary units escaped westward in advance of the Red Army, hoping to enter Germany disguised as civilians, or surrender and be incarcerated in British or American POW camps, instead of being taken by the Soviets and deported to work camps.

The 14th Waffen Grenadier Division of the SS (1st Galician), after fighting its first and only major battle at Brody in western Ukraine in July 1944, had been deployed to Slovakia, then to Slovenia to fight antifascist insurgents. At war's end, the survivors who remained with their units surrendered to the British and were relocated to POW camps, most of them in Italy. Others, abandoned by their officers, discarded their army paybooks, stripped off their uniforms, and attempted to cut away the SS blood-type tattoos under their left armpits. "A few of the more resourceful and enterprising individuals headed into the remote Austrian mountains," writes Michael James Melnyk, whose father was a Waffen-SS veteran. "They, together with a handful of others, having discarded their military apparel, made their way to camps in Germany. Claiming to be forced labourers they managed to register themselves as stateless persons and were subsequently reclassified as refugees. Thus, having obtained the appropriate paperwork they were able to maintain the status of civilians, thereby evading the fate of their comrades."[37]

Large numbers of Estonian and Latvian veterans deserted their units and, posing as civilians, crossed into Germany. Evald Mätas, who had served with an Estonian Waffen-SS division, escaped by ship from Tallinn Harbor to Liepāja in Latvia in September 1944. With a fellow Estonian soldier, he hitched a ride to Dresden, where they registered "at the Employment office," were "issued temporary passports," and were sent into German-occupied Czechoslovakia to work for the railway for the remainder of the war.[38]

Andrejs Eglitis, a Latvian, had been trained by and served in a Latvian Luftwaffe squadron.* In January 1945, he and a friend, under heavy Soviet fire, ran away from their unit, discarded their uniforms, hid their military papers in their shoes, "borrowed" discarded Latvian ration cards that they would display as evidence that they were civilians, and made their way with a group of other refugees to the Baltic coast, where they boarded a barge bound for Danzig (Gdańsk). There, they located a refugee center where they were fed and given beds by the Germans.

"We lay down and immediately fell asleep. After a while somebody kicked me in the butt. . . . There were two German policemen with rifles pointing at us. I stood up fast and pulled out [my ration book] and explained that we were refugees from Latvia escaping the Communists. They let us stay in the room with orders to report in the morning to the police building." Fearful that at the police station they would be exposed as deserters, the two men left town and followed the railroad tracks until they reached a station and "jumped on a bumper between cars. . . . We wanted to go as far west as possible, and three times we changed trains at different cities." Their final destination was the rail station outside a small farming community southwest of Berlin. "We walked inside the station and saw a man working there. We asked if he knew a farmer who needed help. He said he could find one for us and asked us to wait." The *Bürgermeister* arrived and "took us to a social hall, and about ten farmers were waiting for us. Some of them were women whose husbands had been called into the service. . . . I was picked by an older farmer, and Johan [his companion] was chosen by a woman." They would remain in the area a few months more, until "one day at the beginning of May 1945, the news was spread: the Americans are coming."[39]

Some of those who escaped to Germany did so because they had committed war crimes or taken up arms against the Soviets. Many who

---

* He would claim in his memoirs that he had been drafted by the Germans and, instead of killing himself or being sent to a concentration camp, the only other choices available, had entered flight school, where he was trained as a pilot for the Luftwaffe and given a German uniform.

were innocent of such crimes but had worked alongside or under the direction of Germans left because they feared that the Soviets on returning would tar all who had collaborated with the occupation with the same brush, as traitors who deserved punishment for their actions during the war or as potential dissidents who would resist the new regime. Many more, having experienced Soviet rule, fled rather than endure a second Soviet occupation.

The westward exodus included writers and intellectuals; members of nationalist political parties; army officers; factory and shop owners who anticipated that the Soviets would confiscate their businesses; large landowners and better-off peasants who feared collectivization; professionals who anticipated that they would be replaced in universities, the schools, and the courts by those who toed the party line; families that had been given back by the Germans what Sovietization had taken from them; women who had been left behind when their husbands or fathers were conscripted into the army; the elderly who knew they could not survive another invasion; and parents who feared for the safety of their children as the bombs fell and food and water became more and more scarce.

"Although the absolute numbers will always remain estimates," historian Andrejs Plakans has written of the Baltic nations, "most research agrees that approximately 80,000 Estonians, 160,000 Latvians, and 64,000 Lithuanians left their homeland during the final ten months of the war and headed westward." Another 120,000 western Ukrainians fled in advance of the Red Army in the summer of 1944.[40]

The Ukrainian refugees journeyed with their extended families in caravans, by foot or horse-drawn wagon, moving westward to the outer borders of Galicia, then into Slovakia and Hungary, and from there to Germany. "We were conscious," wrote Kost Pankivsky, one of the leaders of the nationalist Ukrainian Central Committee, "of the fact that the Bolsheviks would not stop at the borders of Galicia, nor would they halt in Czechoslovakia or Poland. . . . We only knew that Bavaria, agricultural and centrally located, was the most appropriate area for us."[41]

The Lithuanians traveled south and west through Poland into East Prussia, sleeping in barns when they were lucky, working to bring in the harvest, before moving on again, inching closer, day by day, until after weeks if not months of vagabondage, they arrived on German territory.

Povilas Burneikis, who had worked for Lithuania's agriculture and interior departments in Kovno (Kaunas) during the occupation, departed with his wife and two-year-old son in the fall of 1944. "Our bay horse had no trouble hauling us over the well-built German roads of East Prussia." They found refuge in Tilsit (Sovetsk), just over the border. "A week slipped by, then another, into the second half of September, 1944. The weather was pleasant, the sun shone brightly and warmed us still. The fiery warfront, having slashed through our precious homeland, paused at the Lithuania-Germany border." The Germans, more desperate than ever for laborers, separated Povilas from the rest of his family and conscripted him into a work unit to dig trenches in the wildly mistaken hope that they might hold back the Soviets. In March 1945, wounded by "Bolshevik shells," Povilas was evacuated to a German field hospital, then transported via ships, trains, ships, and more trains into Germany to recuperate sufficiently to be put back to work. He would not be reunited with his family until the spring, at war's end, when he "managed to locate my family" in a displaced persons camp in Bavaria. "My now three-year-old son no longer recognized me, explaining that his daddy was away digging trenches."[42]

Rita Gabis's grandfather, mother, aunt, and great-aunt left Lithuania, where her grandfather had been chief of the security police under the Gestapo. As the Red Army approached from the east and the Germans retreated westward, her grandfather destroyed his papers and buried his motorcycle, in the hope that when Lithuania was liberated from the Soviets he could return and retrieve it. Once across the border in Germany, the family was interned in a work camp until her grandfather, probably by bribing the commander, secured their release. They spent the rest of the war in a mountaintop village, sheltered by a priest.[43]

Latvians flee west as the Red Army approaches in October 1944.

From Estonia and Latvia, the principal routes of escape were by ship across the Baltic Sea, south to East Prussia, or southwest into Germany. Passage could be bought, bribes paid to secure space on the German ships that carried military supplies and reinforcements to Baltic ports. Fishing boats, yachts, and every other variety of vessel were available for the right price. "As the German and Latvian soldiers retreated westward and southward towards the port cities, so did much of the Latvian population, filling the roads with refugees and their belongings, often mixing with military convoys and clogging the roadways."[44]

Riga, Latvia, the capital and busiest of the Baltic ports, was by the summer of 1944 flooded with Latvian and German soldiers, civilians, officials, and dependents all vying for space on the departing military ships. The Germans, preparing for their last stand against the Red Army, encouraged Latvians and Estonians who had worked for the Reich to emigrate. Announcements on German radio proclaimed in the fall of 1944 that the Third Reich was committed to evacuating Latvians and "saving valuable Latvian blood," because "Latvians and Estonians

belonged to the Indo-European family of nations and were closely related to the German nation. Their valuable blood must therefore under
all circumstances be saved for the European community, and this high
aim must now be pursued with the greatest energy." No exit visas would
be required for the journey to Germany. Latvians were instructed to
"assemble at the dock," where they would be offered tickets on spacious
passenger steamers. Once in Germany, they would be housed, given
work, and "receive the same treatment as German evacuees."[45]

The more Baltic nationals the Germans could relocate away from
the Red Army into Germany and put to work there, the better their
chances of protecting the homeland from Soviet invasion. "Evacuation
first to safer regions within the frontiers of Latvia, and later on to Germany, became the topic of the day," the U.S. embassy in Stockholm,
which monitored German radio broadcasts from Riga, noted on September 19, 1944.

> People were asked to show kindness to the refugees who for
> the last three months had been crowding the highways, because
> no one knew when it might be his own turn for sharing their
> hard lot. . . . As the situation increased in seriousness, and it was
> realized that no part of Latvia could really be regarded as safe,
> evacuation to Germany was discussed more and more openly.
> People were told where to apply for traveling permits, and the
> address in Germany of the special bureau for Latvian refugees
> was given repeatedly.[46]

Inese Kaufman's father, a Latvian doctor and surgeon, left first with
the Wehrmacht. The family lore was that he had treated a Russian soldier who had warned him to leave because, as a professional, a large
landowner, and a doctor who had cared for Germans and run the local
hospital, he was "on a list" to be deported as soon as the Red Army returned. Inese's grandmother and the rest of the family left later, after
they had buried the family's valuables.[47]

Inara Verzemnieks's grandmother Livija, whose husband served with the Latvian Legion, boarded a ship from Riga with her sister, her infant son, and her two-year-old daughter. On landing they "began to walk" westward. "Hundreds of thousands of other people were doing the same: the displaced, deserters, war criminals, their intended victims who had managed to resist, to escape, all walking as one limping mass through the carnage." In the years to come, Livija would not say much about her final journey from home. "She would limit her account to statements such as: *'We slept in the woods during the day, and tried to keep the children quiet. Then we would walk at night.'*" She and her sister and the two babies "tried to follow the rail tracks, a common route for Europe's displaced at the time, one of the last intact paths that one could trace through the flattened landscape." They walked for nine months, stopping here and there, where a kind farmer needed an extra hand and had space in the barn for strangers to sleep. Their journey ended "in Pinneberg, on the outskirts of Hamburg."[48]

On arriving in Germany proper or East Prussia or German-occupied Czechoslovakia, often after months on the road, the Baltic refugees capable of work, including the elderly and children, male and female, were distributed to factories or farms or wherever there was a labor shortage. If there was no work where they landed, they were herded onto trains and shipped elsewhere. Able-bodied young men were separated from their families and sent to the front lines to dig trenches for the military. Those who had occupied positions at the higher levels of administration were given preference, as were the families of auxiliary policemen. Special labor exchanges were established to find positions for specially qualified professionals, engineers, physicians, pharmacists, and chemists.[49]

Those who arrived in the last year of the war did not have an easy time in a Germany devastated by aerial bombardment, with thousands of homeless civilians looking for safe shelter, with food, water, and coal in short supply. Still, they were treated better by German officials than the Eastern European forced laborers who had been deported earlier in the war. "They were regarded as Aryans by the Nazis . . . rather than Slavs. [One young Latvian woman] remembered that when she collected her rations 'there were two queues for bread. Germans and Balts went first and the Poles had to wait.'" Those whose husbands, brothers, or fathers were in the Latvian Waffen-SS legion received better treatment still.[50]

Food was always a problem—there was never enough of it. Shelter was as great a problem. Refugee families were housed in temporary barracks or farm outbuildings with émigrés from different parts of occupied Europe, or in barns, in fields, in deserted or bombed-out factories and warehouses, where they remained, sometimes for weeks, until the Germans were able to relocate them in semi-permanent housing. A few were fortunate enough to find living spaces where they could remain for months, some for the duration of the war.[51]

In the ever-changing landscapes of war and occupation, it was never easy to know where one was. Armies would come and go, advance and retreat, occupy then withdraw. Even in those parts of Germany that had been liberated by the American armies, the refugees were beset by anxieties that the Soviets would move in and take over. As the acting Lithuanian chargé d'affaires, a holdover from the state that had been annexed by the USSR in 1940, wrote the former Lithuanian minister to London, "The uncertainty as regards future, the wild rumours spread by unknown agencies about the allegedly possible extradition of the refugees to the Russians, or about the impending occupation by the Soviet Forces of the territories hitherto occupied by the British and American troops, further the agonies of our people and make their distress still greater."[52]

Vaclovas Zawkiewicz, a Lithuanian businessman, entered Germany with eight family members in October 1944. He had moved his family from Schwerin in the north to Berlin, then back north to Lübeck, which had been liberated by the British. What he didn't know was that Lübeck was within the borders of the Soviet zone of occupation. When the British army evacuated Lübeck, Zawkiewicz and his family packed their belongings again and followed the British troops out of the city. "They walked along with a Russian-speaking family whose hand cart they attached to the Zawkiewicz wagon. . . . The family walked to Hamburg in the British zone where they found refuge at the [nearby] displaced persons camp."[53]

Agate Nesaule and her family escaped on board a ship from Liepāja, Latvia. Agate, then seven years of age, remembered it was warm outside the day they left their house, with their paintings, dishes, clothes, books, and dolls, in a caravan of seven or so wagons. Arriving at Liepāja, they bought passage to Germany. Their final destination was a refugee camp in Lehrte, in Lower Saxony, in a "dilapidated gray barracks" behind barbed wire and under guard, with nothing to do and barely enough to eat. After three months, Agate's uncle, a doctor, then her father and a second uncle, both Lutheran ministers, were given work assignments at the Lobethal Institution for the Mentally Defective, a Lutheran-affiliated institution.[54]

Mirdza Labrencis caught the last train from Priekulė, Latvia, to Liepāja. She had worked under German supervision in the local post office and committed no war crimes, but as one who had collaborated with the occupying Germans she expected to be denounced and punished on the return of the Soviets. "When we arrived at the port town there were hundreds, maybe thousands, of people all in a state of forced transition. People, with wagons and animals, who had walked almost two hundred miles across Latvia with all that they could carry were at the dock waiting their turn for survival. . . . It was about one week's time before we received confirmation that our names were on a list for a ship due in the next day." That ship took her to Danzig, still under German control. From there, she and the other refugees traveled by train two hundred miles southwest to a camp filled with refugees: "Poles, Estonians, Lithuanians, German citizens—just ordinary working people who were now homeless and caught in the cogs of the war machine."[55]

3.

FROM THE CONCENTRATION
AND DEATH CAMPS

Relocated to Germany to Be Worked to Death

HEINRICH HIMMLER, Reichsführer of the SS, chief of the national police force, and Reich Commissar for the Strengthening of German Ethnic Stock, was charged with two incompatible tasks: killing every Jew and putting every able-bodied inhabitant of the Reich, including the Jews, to work. The contradiction was resolved, in most locations, though not everywhere, and not universally, by separating the Jews into two categories: those who would die now and those who would die later, those who would be gassed or shot and those who would be worked to death. In some areas, like Ukraine in 1941 and early 1942, the Jews were indiscriminately exterminated, including those with skills that might have been useful to the German war machine. Elsewhere, in the Baltic nations and in Poland, selections were made before the mass shootings or the transports to the extermination camps and the gas chambers. Children, women, the elderly, the infirm, and the frail were condemned to death, but those capable of work, always a minority, were spared—for the moment. They too would be murdered, but only after every ounce of productivity had been drained from their bodies.

The pendulum swung back and forth between death "now" and death "later." By 1942, the shooting and gassings had increased exponentially with the recognition that the first version of the "final solution," the expulsion of the Jews to the far reaches of the Soviet Union, would not be possible. "1942 was *the* year of mass Jewish death. If well over a million had perished the previous year, the death toll in this one rose to an estimated 2.7 million lives." And yet even during this period of intensified mass murder, Mark Levene has written, "there *still* remains the contradiction." Large numbers of Jews were neither shot nor gassed, but consigned to "a patchwork of slave camps, ghettos and factories [that] continued to practice 'annihilation through work'—or more accurately, perhaps, murder at the point where exhaustion or illness ensured that the worker was expendable."[1]

In December 1942, as losses on the eastern front mounted, Himmler warned SS officials that mortality in the camps "must absolutely become lower" so that more inmates could be made available for forced labor. His objective was the construction of an industrial empire in the east, with oversized factories, weapons plants, mines, quarries, and other enterprises worked by slave laborers and overseen by the SS.[2]

By mid-1943, however, as the Red Army pushed inexorably westward, it no longer made any sense to establish new industrial facilities or maintain old ones in areas that were in danger of being overrun by the Soviets. After a successful British bombing raid on August 17, 1944, on Peenemünde on the Baltic, a critical military testing facility for missiles, the decision was made to construct new armaments, U-boat, fighter jet, and rocket plants underground, in Germany, invisible to and protected from Allied bombers.

It was understood from the beginning that work in the underground plants would be done by slave laborers. "Satellite" camps, attached administratively to the major concentration camps, were constructed to house the Jews and other inmates who were transported into the Reich to be worked to death. Moving the camp inmates from Poland into Germany accomplished two objectives at once: it supplied the new plants with slave laborers, and it kept them out of the hands of the advancing Red Army.

The return of Jews to Germany was part of the Nazi endgame, though never acknowledged as such. As the possibility of defeat or stalemate or some form of negotiated truce became more of a likelihood, so too did the necessity for obliterating evidence of mass murder. No concentration camp inmates were to be left behind as testimony to Nazi brutality; no Jews would be allowed to outlive the Third Reich, seize arms against it, or take glory in its destruction. "If National Socialist Germany is going to be destroyed," Himmler was reported to have announced to his confidant and masseur, Felix Kersten, in March 1945, "then her enemies and the criminals in the concentration camps should not have the satisfaction of emerging from our ruin as triumphant conquerors. They shall share in the downfall. Those are the Führer's direct orders and I must see to it that they are carried out down to the last detail."[3]

As the Red Army moved westward, the Germans closed and dismantled their camps in the east one after the other, selecting the young and healthy for work assignments in Germany, and murdering the elderly, infirm, children, and most of the women. By mid-1943, the extermination camps in eastern Poland, Belzec, Sobibor, and Treblinka, where up to 1.7 million Jews had been murdered, had been shut down, the dead exhumed, corpses burned, gas chambers dismantled. In the summer of 1944, the camps in the Baltics were closed and the less than 10 percent of the 300,000 Jews who had survived the rampages of local militias, the organized SS death squads, and the ghettos were transported by train or on ships to Stutthof (Sztutowo), a camp outside Danzig, where they were sorted out once again, the able-bodied women left behind to work at nearby factories, the men relocated to satellite camps and underground munitions factories in Germany.

Jack Arnel and his family were among those transported in August 1944 from Kovno, Lithuania, in sealed boxcars to Stutthof. Allied bombing raids had destroyed track, bridges, and overpasses all along the route. Trains were rerouted, turned back, stalled while repairs were made. Without food, water, or toilets, inmates suffered and died inside padlocked cattle cars. At Stutthof, the Germans unsealed the boxcar doors and announced that the train had reached its final destination and that the women and children would be removed first, then the men and boys. As soon as the women were offloaded, the Germans and their Lithuanian helpers ran up and down the tracks, slamming shut and padlocking the doors. The train rolled off with the men locked inside, their wives and children gone.

The destination was Camp No. 1, a Dachau satellite camp. The passengers were offloaded and ordered to strip naked, their clothes and jewelry and belongings taken away. The next morning and every morning after that, they were marched off to what appeared to be a mountain of gravel, where they spent the day building the outer shell of an underground munitions factory. In the rear of the line of march were two empty wagons pulled by inmates. At the end of every shift, the corpses of those who had died were loaded into these wagons for the return trip to the barracks.[4]

That summer of 1944, some forty thousand Jews moved from Stutthof and from Auschwitz to Dachau satellite camps and put to work constructing underground aircraft factories. As the Soviets launched what they hoped would be their final attack in January 1945, the Germans removed fifty-six thousand more inmates from Auschwitz, forty thousand from Gross-Rosen, and fifty thousand from Stutthof. Some were loaded into sealed boxcars; most were marched out of camp on foot, watched over by SS guards whose instructions were to shoot stragglers, runaways, and those too ill to continue.[5]

Henry Aizenman was transported with his father, a skilled mechanic, from Auschwitz to the Braunschweig satellite camp near Hamburg, where the Büssing truck company had, in collaboration with the SS, constructed an underground heavy truck factory. Henry and his father worked in the "diesel bunker" producing cast-iron engines. Henry's task was to teeter-totter, as he called it, the engines back and forth from work station to work station, careful not to drop and damage them—the penalty for doing so was death. Every morning, he, his father, and the other inmates were marched half a mile or so from their barracks to the factory. The good people of Braunschweig looked the other way, except, Henry recalled a half century later, for one little old lady in a black overcoat, with a black hat, who one day threw a brown paper bag at the boy. He waited until his outhouse break—laborers were allowed one per shift—opened the bag, and found a piece of pound cake, more precious to him than gold. That evening he and his father cut the cake into tiny pieces that they traded for bread.

The Jewish inmates in the camp were forbidden to talk to the French POWs who worked underground with them but were housed and fed separately. One of the prisoners on occasion left behind a portion of his beer ration for Henry. "That may have saved my life." The beer was more nutritious than anything the Jewish inmates were given. Only the youngest, strongest, and most proficient at securing extra food survived. Henry Aizenman's father did not. He collapsed at work and was moved to a dormitory for the infirm, where he was given a lethal injection of air.[6]

Martin Aaron, from Czechoslovakia, who was interned at the labor camp at Gross-Rosen (Rogozhnica) was awakened in the middle of the night, ordered into the yard, and then marched out of the camp. He would spend the next four or five weeks marching west with the clothes he had worn at the labor camp on his back and nothing to eat other than what he could scrounge from the fields the line of march passed through. He survived on raw beets or radishes and an occasional piece of bread. Life was being drained out of him, "hanging in a hair," as he trudged forward. After he knew not how many days, those who had not fallen out of line or been shot trying to escape or frozen or starved to death or succumbed to the illnesses they carried with them were walked into the Dora-Mittelbau camp in the Harz Mountains near Nordhausen. Dora-Mittelbau was a Buchenwald satellite, where one of the first and largest of the underground factory complexes was being constructed.[7]

Because there appeared to be no shortage of concentration camp inmates, with Hungarian Jews now being transported en masse to Auschwitz, there was no need to provide those working in the armaments plants and underground factories and mines with sufficient food, shelter, clothing, and hygiene to keep them alive for long. It was more efficient to push them beyond human endurance, to soak out of them the last ounce of energy, to literally work them to death, then replace them with a new cadre of inmates.

In Dora-Mittelbau, the conditions under which the slave laborers lived and worked were such that one out of three perished within six months.

> Dora assaulted all the senses. The air in the sleeping tunnels was unbearable, a mix of sweat, urine, excrement, vomit, and rotting corpses. . . . There were no toilets . . . just open petrol drums that added to the stench. Prisoners gasped for breath, and they were also tormented by hunger and thirst. . . . Sleep was almost impossible inside the chambers, not least because of the deafening noise of machines, pickaxes, and explosions coming from other tunnels nearby, which reverberated through the prisoner quarters. Dora never fell silent, as inmates worked in two shifts around the clock, digging, moving machinery, and laying tracks through the maze of tunnels.[8]

"In late 1944," wrote Göran Rosenberg, whose father, David, worked in the underground Büssing truck factory, "between eight and ten corpses a day are stripped naked, relieved of their gold teeth, allocated numbers, and packed in paper bags" to await transport to their burial place. "In the meantime the corpses are stored in a hut, where the corpses often make the bags wet, so they tear easily when they're being loaded onto the truck. Eventually the bags are replaced by wooden boxes, each accommodating ten corpses."[9]

To the ever-present threat of death by starvation, disease, overwork, accidents, and exposure, there was added, in February and March 1945, a new, perhaps more deadly one. As the RAF and the American air force homed in on the underground factories, the bombs fell closer to their workplaces and barracks. Germans, and some of the Western European workers, were allowed to take cover in shelters; the Jews were not. For Henry Aizenman, the bombs that targeted the German armament factories were more welcome than feared. "We liked it even though some of us were killed."[10]

HEINRICH HIMMLER, recognizing that there was no way out, that the war was lost, the end weeks, if not days, away, attempted in late April 1945 to make a separate peace. To establish his bona fides as a civilized man with whom the Allies might negotiate and to protect the hostages he would need "as bargaining chips for the elusive deal with the Allies," he issued orders that the murder of the Jews be halted, the remaining camps closed, the survivors evacuated. But to where? The simple reality, which the now delusional Nazi leadership could not grasp, was that there was no safe place to warehouse the survivors until they could be released as hostages or, should a miracle occur and the war continue, be put back to work as slave laborers in newly constructed and protected secret weapon plants. "In late April 1945," Nikolaus Wachsmann writes, "as the last camps came into reach of Allied troops, some transports began to head for wholly imaginary sites" in the Alps or to the north, near the Baltic Sea, or perhaps even to Norway.[11]

The Jews who had survived the ghettos and concentration camps in Poland and the Baltics, the death marches into Germany, slave labor underground, and Allied bombardments were now hurled onto a vicious merry-go-round that robbed them of whatever life remained in their bodies. Starving, dressed in rags, their feet barely covered in bits of blanket bound by string, they were marched or conveyed in wagons or boxcars open to the elements—and Allied bombs—from camp to camp to camp, kept alive, but barely, just out of reach of the advancing Red Army in the east, the British, Americans, Canadians, and French in the west.

Henry Aizenman and David Rosenberg were transported from the Braunschweig-Büssing factories to Ravensbrück. No sooner had they arrived than they were moved again, a step ahead of the advancing Red Army, to Wöbbelin. Asked by an interviewer many years later what the surviving inmates did there, Aizenman answered simply, "We worked. Mostly we were dying."[12]

Jack Arnel and his father, who were interned at a Dachau satellite, in April 1945 were marched out and loaded into open boxcars. While their train was paused at a nearby siding, it was hit by Allied bombs. The Germans offloaded the prisoners, intending to reload them when the bombing ceased. Jack's father signaled to his fifteen-year-old son and the two escaped into the forest, away from the train and the guards, running until they dropped of exhaustion. The next morning, they awoke to the sight of German soldiers staring at them. They too were running away, but from the Americans. The Germans pointed the Arnels in the direction where they thought the Americans were encamped. After wandering in circles, lost in the forest for several days, Jack and his father arrived at a village and were nearly arrested by American soldiers who thought they were Germans. The Arnels protested, but in vain because they could not make themselves understood.

Finally, a jeep drove up with an officer who spoke to Jack in broken German, then shifted into Yiddish. The soldier led them to a house in the village and ordered the woman who lived there, whose husband had been killed on the eastern front, to open her closets. The Arnels were outfitted in civilian clothes, then put into an ambulance that took them to the St. Ottilien hospital, a former Benedictine monastery and German military hospital that had been liberated by a group of Lithuanian Jewish survivors, led by Dr. Zalman Grinberg, from Kovno.[13]

Grinberg had, like the Arnels, been evacuated by the Germans from Dachau, with fifteen hundred other survivors, and transported by truck to a railway depot. When the depot was bombed by American planes, the prisoners took flight. Some were shot, but eight hundred escaped into the forest. After days wandering from town to town, hiding from their former guards, begging for food or stealing it, and tending to their wounds, they arrived at the former monastery of St. Ottilien, which, with the agreement of the American military, Dr. Grinberg converted into a hospital/residence for the Dachau inmates who had escaped with him and those like the Arnels who would in the days to come seek refuge and medical assistance.[14]

Part Two

——— ◆—◆◆—◆ ———

"THE PLIGHT
OF THE JEWS . . .
IS STRIKINGLY
DIFFERENT"

· 4 ·

ALONE, ABANDONED, DETERMINED,
THE *SHE'ERIT HAPLETAH*
ORGANIZES

NEWS OF THE CONCENTRATION CAMPS exploded across American and British front pages in a series of articles that began with the Soviet liberation of Majdanek in July 1944 and continued through the liberation of Ohrdruf, Buchenwald, Bergen-Belsen, and Dachau. During the last weeks of the war and the first days of peace, Americans and British citizens could not pick up their newspapers, look at their weekly photo or news magazines, listen to the radio, or go to the movies without confronting first-person descriptions, photographs, and newsreels of German atrocities.

The impact of the written, spoken, and visual narratives that poured forth was formidable, with the focus on Nazi brutality. Lost in the torrent of accounts of torture and mass murder was the singularity of the genocidal assault on European Jews, on what we would later refer to as the Holocaust.

CBS radio commentator Edward R. Murrow, who had moved east into Germany with General Patton and the Third Army, toured Buchenwald on April 12, the day after it was liberated. Three days later, he described what he had witnessed there on his Sunday afternoon broadcast. "There surged around me an evil-smelling stink, men and boys reached out to touch me. They were in rags and the remnants of uniforms. Death already had marked many of them, but they were smiling with their eyes. . . . I pray you to believe what I have said about Buchenwald. I reported what I saw and heard, but only part of it. For most of it, I have no words. If I have offended you by this rather mild account of Buchenwald, I'm not in the least sorry." In his searing commentary and his interviews with Buchenwald survivors, Murrow identified Englishmen, Frenchmen, Czechoslovakians, German Communists, "professors from Poland, doctors from Vienna, men from all of Europe. Men from the countries that made America." There was no mention of Jews.[1]

Dachau and its satellite camps were liberated on April 29. *Time* magazine published its first-person report on Monday, May 7. "The main entry road runs past several largish buildings. These had been cleared; and now we began to meet the liberated. Several hundred Russians, French, Yugoslavs, Italians and Poles were here, frantically hysterically happy. . . . Here were the men of all nations whom Hitler's agents had picked out as the prime opponents of Nazism; here were the very earliest Hitler haters. Here were German social democrats, Spanish survivors of the Spanish Civil War, a correspondent for the *Paris-Soir*, who cried so hard I could not get his name." Though some twenty-two thousand of the sixty-eight thousand inmates in the main and satellite camps were Jewish, there was no mention of them in the *Time* story. The focus was on the perpetrators of the atrocities and the courage of the political prisoners who had survived.[2]

In late April, the U.S. Office of War Information released footage of the camps taken by the Signal Corps and commercial newsreel companies. Day after day, theaters across the country screened the newsreels— and the American public watched in disbelief. "Don't turn away," the offscreen narrator of "Nazi Murder Mills," produced by Universal, warned theater audiences as the camera panned inside an extermination oven at Buchenwald. "Look. Burned alive. Horror. Unbelievable, but true." The victims identified in the newsreel included captured Yanks,

Poles, Greeks, Russians, and "non-Germans." There was no mention of Jews.[3]

"In the first flush of victory and the chaotic conditions that followed," Israeli historian Zeev W. Mankowitz has observed, the Jewish "concentration camp survivors were, by and large, lost from sight." Too few had survived to make much of an impression in the whirlwind of victory. Six million Jews had disappeared from the face of the earth, but they had been murdered outside of Germany, half of them in the extermination camps in Poland, the other half in the ghettos or in shooting operations in Poland, Ukraine, the Soviet Union, and the Baltic nations. Few had lived long enough to be transported into Germany in the last months of the war to be worked to death. Large numbers had died in transit or in the underground factories and work camps where they were imprisoned on arrival. Those who survived all this were, at the moment of their liberation, too ill to speak, to interact with the soldiers, to be interviewed by reporters.[4]

TYPHUS RAGED THROUGH the concentration camps. During the first two months following liberation, 13,944 of the Bergen-Belsen survivors died. To contain the epidemic, the British evacuated 1,000 inmates a day by ambulance from the typhus-infested wooden huts to the comparatively luxurious German tank training center a mile away. By mid-May, the evacuation was complete, and on May 21, the last wooden hut was burned to the ground.[5]

To represent their interests with their British liberators, the Jewish survivors at Bergen-Belsen elected a committee, which was subsequently enlarged to represent the displaced persons in other camps in the British zone. The Bergen-Belsen committee and the enlarged Central Committee of Liberated Jews in the British zone were both chaired by Yossel (Josef) Rosensaft, the son of an esteemed Hasidic family from Będzin, Poland, who had escaped from Auschwitz, been recaptured, sent to Birkenau, then Auschwitz, Dora-Mittelbau, and Bergen-Belsen.

British soldiers burn concentration camp barracks,
Bergen–Belsen, Germany, May 1945.

The British intended to repurpose the tank training center to which
the survivors had been evacuated as a medical center and transfer them
to other camps. "After the first group of some 1,000 DPs had been
taken [to a camp near the Dutch border]," Yossel Rosensaft, according to
his son, "went to inspect the new accommodations and discovered that
they were significantly inferior. He then demanded that the Jewish DPs
be allowed to return to Belsen. When the British refused, my father simply told the DPs to return 'home,' as it were to Belsen, which many of
them did, and he prevented a second transport from leaving Belsen." The
British abandoned their plan to disperse the 10,000 Belsen survivors.[6]

As the Jewish survivors were removed from the concentration and
labor camps and transported to assembly centers, they were divided by
nationality. The Polish Jews were moved into facilities with non-Jewish
Poles, the Lithuanian Jews with non-Jewish Lithuanians, sometimes

*An aid worker helps a Jewish woman move her belongings
into a DP assembly center in the Kassel area.*

with those whose families had stolen from them, tortured them, or
served over them as kapos or guards in the various camps. Because the
Jewish survivors were in a minority, because they were weaker, sicker,
malnourished, and likely to be suffering with typhus or tuberculosis,
they found it difficult, sometimes impossible, to make their needs known.

At Buchenwald, as Rabbi Robert Marcus reported to the World
Jewish Congress headquarters in New York on May 12, the situation
was intolerable. "The Polish Jews must use the medium of the Polish
National Committee of the Camp to represent them. There has been a
universal complaint that the Poles on the National Committees were
formerly executioners for the SS, are anti-Semitic, and discriminate

against the Jews in so far as rations and clothes and general treatment are concerned. The Jews demand a direct representation in order to safeguard their rights."[7]

At Wildflecken, a camp designated for Polish nationals, Jewish DPs who had survived the war with false papers claiming they were Christian continued the subterfuge to protect themselves from discrimination.[8]

At Dachau, Chaplain David Eichhorn requested permission of the Inmates' International Committee to hold services in the main square of the compound on Saturday, May 5, the first Sabbath after liberation. Arriving at the camp on Saturday morning, the chaplain discovered "to my amazement [that] no preparation of any kind had been made. I . . . asked for an explanation [and was] informed that the service would not be held in the main square," but had been moved to the laundry room. "The Polish non-Jewish inmates had threatened that, if a Jewish service were held in the square, they would break it up by force." When Hollywood producer, now Lieutenant Colonel George Stevens, who had been assigned by the Army Signal Corps to Dachau, learned that the service had been relocated—and why—he grabbed Eichhorn and marched with him into camp headquarters, where "with loudness of voice and much banging of the table," he demanded that the service be rescheduled and held in the main square. The commanding officer agreed.[9]

The following morning, Sunday, May 6, at 10 a.m., Rabbi Eichhorn, "under the protection of an American military 'guard of honor,'" led a brief Torah service in the main square. Stevens and the Army Signal Corps filmed it. Eichhorn, razor-thin, mustached, balding, with thick eyeglasses, in military uniform with a worn prayer shawl around his neck and a yarmulke covering his head, delivered the Hebrew prayers in full, vibrant voice, then, in English, addressed the survivors in the square.

Today I come to you in a dual capacity—as a soldier in the American Army and as a representative of the Jewish community of America. . . . We know your tragedy. We know your sorrows. . . . What message of comfort and strength can I bring to you from your fellow-Jews? What can I say that will compare in depth or in intensity to that which you have suffered and overcome? . . . Words will not bring the dead back to life nor right the wrongs of the past ten years. . . . We have seen with our own eyes and we have heard with our own ears and we shall not forget. As long as there are Jews in the world, "Dachau" will be a term of horror and shame. . . . You are not and you will not be forgotten men, my brothers.[10]

But they were forgotten or, at least, ignored. Neither the American nor the British military nor UNRRA acknowledged that their suffering and loss had been unique and that they required, as such, special assistance, enhanced rations, medical care, and Yiddish-speaking advisers. They were instead treated like other displaced persons, sorted out by nationality and dispatched to assembly centers with non-Jews from their homelands. Requests made by Jewish voluntary agencies to visit the camps and provide relief to the Jewish survivors were turned down. "The Army didn't want to be bothered with refugee problems," recalled Eli Rock, who been an ambulance driver for the American Field Service, and after the war accepted a position with the Joint Distribution Committee (the Joint, or JDC), the largest and best-endowed and best-administered of the Jewish aid groups. The GIs had "fought a tough war. They had fought well and in the absence of . . . others to play a role . . . there they were with this refugee problem and these people were difficult, they were demanding . . . and these army guys were not social workers. Maybe some of them were anti-Semitic."[11]

"On May 8," Hadassah Rosensaft recalled in her memoir, "the war in Europe ended. I have often been asked how we felt on that day. . . . Of course, we were glad to hear the news of the Allied victory, but we in

Belsen did not celebrate on that day. For years, I have seen a film on television showing the world's reaction to the end of the war. In Times Square in New York, in the streets of London and Paris, people were dancing, singing, crying, embracing each other. They were filled with joy that their dear ones would soon come home. Whenever I see that film, I cry. We in Belsen did not dance on that day. We had nothing to be hopeful for. Nobody was waiting for us anywhere. We were alone and abandoned."[12]

The survivors had expected that when the world outside learned the full extent of German atrocities and Jewish suffering, civilized people everywhere—and Jews in the diaspora in particular—would open their hearts and shower them not only with sympathy, but with tangible assistance: cake, food, clothing, bandages, books, soap, perfume, shoes, hairbrushes, everything they had been without for the past four or five years. Nothing of the sort happened. "We urgently needed more doctors and nurses," Hadassah Rosensaft recalled. "We were hoping that some Jewish doctors in the United States would close their private practices for a little while and come to help us, if only for a month. To our great disappointment, none came. I still can't understand why."[13]

The Joint Distribution Committee, which had since 1914 raised and spent millions of dollars to provide food and material relief for impoverished, suffering Jews in Europe and the Middle East, was nowhere to be seen. The fault was not the Joint's. It was the military's, which was letting only essential personnel into Germany. Voluntary agencies that might have helped with the displaced Jews were kept out of the country for fear they might get in the Army's way.

It was not until June 26, eleven weeks after Buchenwald had been liberated, that Chaplain Robert Marcus, who had worked at the American Jewish Congress in New York before joining the Army, unburdened himself in a letter to Rabbi Stephen Wise, the best-known, most universally respected, and, because of his connections to the Jewish voter base and the Democratic Party, most influential rabbi in America. Apologizing for his harsh, "violent" tone, and insisting that his criticism was not "personal," Marcus lashed out not only at the Joint, but at the larger American Jewish community and leaders like Rabbi Wise. Day after day, Marcus explained, he and the other chaplains had had to make excuses, plead for more time, explain to the survivors that the American Jewish community cared for the survivors and was on its way to assist them.

In the absence of outside assistance, the chaplains had had to beg, borrow, cadge, trade on the open and black markets, and even steal food, clothing, medicine, and supplies for the survivors. "You might as well know that ninety-five percent of the things that I have done personally have been carried out despite restrictions, despite military regulations, despite recognized channels of communication. I could have been court martialed at least fifty times for some of them, (and probably will) but dammit, how could one stand idly by and see his brothers suffer when in a position to be of some assistance, even though subterfuge was necessary."

"Where are the results of all the political effort of organized Jewry in behalf of Jewish survivors?" Marcus asked Wise.

Why was not the ground work laid for an organized plan to meet the needs of our coreligionists when they would be liberated from the Nazi terror? Who is responsible for the chaos, the lack of coordination that exists in handling the Jewish situation in Germany—did our leaders plan on the basis of the fact that no Jews would be alive? Why was no understanding reached with UNRRA so that Jewish interests would be protected and that liberated Jews would not be placed in the same category as those who came willingly to work for the Germans? Do our leaders know how many Jews we have here; how many are on the road; how many are dying in the hospitals; how many are in small villages out of contact with anyone and not knowing what to do? Why have there been no centers set up for stateless Jews so that they would not have to live with Polish civilian workers

who in many instances murdered their loved ones—centers
where we could concentrate our people, look after them, send
them back to their countries or to America? . . . Where is the
Joint with its "trained" personnel, its millions of tons of clothes,
its promises and its diplomacy?[14]

The harshest, most intemperate, and most effective critic of the Joint
was Rabbi Abraham J. Klausner, assigned to the 116th Evacuation
Hospital stationed at Dachau. The survivors had in the days after liberation lived on hope, Klausner wrote a friend on August 1, 1945, that
"the Jews of America would come! The peoples of the world would
come! Three months have passed. They hope no longer. They did not
come. No! No one came, only Klausner."[15]

The chaplains and Jewish officers and enlisted men, tired of waiting
for the voluntary agencies to do their job, contacted friends, family, and
their congregations in the United States. They took photos, wrote letters, prepared first-person reports and articles for local and national
English and Yiddish newspapers and magazines, contacted their representatives in Congress.

Irving Heymont wrote his wife, Joan, from the Landsberg displaced
persons camp on November 5, 1945, with a list of items that "people and
organizations could ship here" through regular Army mail or to
UNRRA Team 311 in Germany or to the Jewish chaplains.

The religious group here need phylacteries, and prayer books.
In fact all books in Yiddish are in great need. They also need
elementary English books. The English classes now operate
without any books at all. The camp also needs large amounts of
ordinary needles and sewing machine needles and thimbles and
sewing machine oil. The women are in great need of bras-
sieres and sanitary belts. There is great need of warm gloves of
every description. There is also a shortage of women's shoes,

particularly of the winter type. . . . The other item of clothing giving us the most difficulty is raincoats. We could use plenty of them.[16]

Chaplain Eugene Lipman, a Reform rabbi in his middle twenties, wrote daily letters to his wife, who "distributed them here and there, wherever necessary as I wrote them," he recalled in a later oral history. "There were between ninety and one hundred Jewish chaplains in the European theater at that point . . . deeply involved with displaced persons. . . . We all wrote and American Jewry got information that way."[17]

Klausner went a step further and prepared what he called "A Detailed Report on the Liberated Jew as He Now Suffers His Period of Liberation Under the Discipline of the Armed Forces of the United States," which he mailed to the leaders of every prominent Jewish organization in the United States. The report was overwrought, vitriolic, melodramatic—but the circumstances, he believed, called for nothing less.

> At best, each of the camps are sub-standard. At Türkheim, 450 Jews continue to live in the double barbed-wire enclosure. . . . The camp is literally a cesspool. By any standards, the sight would be condemned. At Buchberg, 1000 Jews live in a once active powder factory. Built in barracks style, the dilapidated structures are overcrowded with individuals. Such items as soap, toothbrushes, linen, laundry facilities, bedding, food, clothing are out of the question. . . . The greater percentage of the liberated are still imprisoned in the striped uniform forced upon them by the oppressor.[18]

"I have travelled the entire area (Bavaria)," Klausner wrote to Rabbi Philip Bernstein, who as national director of the Committee on Army and Navy Religious Activities of the National Jewish Welfare Board, was in charge of supervising the Jewish military chaplains.

> I have visited with each of the camps . . . spoken with their leaders, observed their mode of life and I turned aside in the best situation and silently cried. . . . There seems to be no policy, no responsibility, no plans for these . . . stateless Jews. . . . Twelve hours a day I tell my lies. "They will come," I say. "When will they come?" they ask me. UNRRA, JDC, Red Cross—can it be that they are not aware of the problem? It is impossible. . . . Of what use is all my complaining; I cannot stop their tears. America was their hope and all America has given them is a new camp with guards in Khaki. Freedom, hell no! They are behind walls without hope. Can not the leaders of our people cry out demanding a new day for these who have hated the dawn of each day? There are so few left. Forgive my incoherence, calmness is not with me.[19]

As soon as the dead were buried and the Kaddish said, as soon as they were able to communicate—and had found someone who appeared to be in authority who spoke their languages—the survivors made known their primary, overriding concern. They were desperate to discover the fate of their loved ones.

Years before, they had been ripped from their homes, rounded up, and force-marched to killing fields or into the ghettos. When the ghettos were closed, in Warsaw, Łódź, Kraków, Białystok, Lwów, Lublin, Minsk, in Kovno and Riga and Vilna, in Budapest and elsewhere, those who had survived the starvation rations, the beatings, the epidemic disease, the mindless torture and brutality had been herded into sealed boxcars, bound for work or death camps. At each stop on the way to their final destinations, they had suffered the dreaded but inevitable "selections," watching, helpless to intervene, as their children, or elderly parents, or spouses, or siblings, or fiancées, schoolmates, friends, and

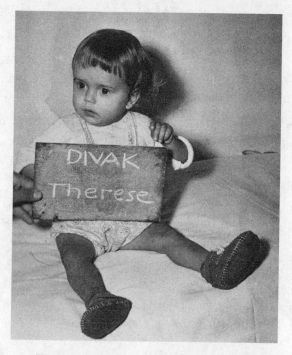

*Therese Divak in the Kloster Indersdorf displaced
children's home, where children hidden with non-Jewish
families during the war were housed after liberation. This
photograph was published in newspapers, including Yiddish
papers in the United States, in the hope that surviving
family members would see it.*

neighbors were pushed in one direction, while they, the living, were
directed in the other.

They had borne witness to the murder of loved ones, but they knew
that there had been survivors: runaways from the ghettos, escapees from
the transports and the camps, children who had been placed with
Christian neighbors, young men and women who had joined the partisans, families that had crossed into the Soviet Union, a few who had
miraculously survived the work camps they had been sent to. Where
were they? Who, they had to know, was among the living? Who had
perished?

In the first days and weeks after liberation, Chaplain Schacter at

Buchenwald began to "compile lists of survivors, which he sent off to
the chief of the Jewish rabbis [chaplains], for distribution elsewhere. . . .
People came, they wanted to write letters," he recalled. "They wanted to
let their loved ones around the world know that they are alive. Those
who remembered addresses were very fortunate. . . . We got paper, we
got envelopes and so on. And then what I did—we had no civilian
postal service—I took all their letters and simply placed them into outer
envelopes which I addressed . . . and these letters went out APO,
through the Army Postal Service."

At Stuttgart, Chaplain Eskin did the same and mailed telegrams
and letters to the American relatives of survivors who were fortunate to
have any.

Chaplain Klausner compiled a census of living Jews in Bavaria, several volumes of which were published under the title *She'erit Hapletah*
and distributed to every camp in Germany and Austria.[20]

THE LEADER OF the Jewish survivors in the American zone was thirty-
three-year-old Dr. Zalman Grinberg, a compact man with dark hair
and a trim mustache who had established a survivors' hospital at St.
Ottilien, the former monastery. On May 27, Grinberg, who was from
Kovno, organized a Liberation Concert by the surviving musicians
from the Kovno Ghetto orchestra.* He invited the survivors in the Munich area (some eight hundred attended) along with military personnel
and journalists to St. Ottilien for the event.

"Onto the stage men and women carried fiddles, horns, bass viols,"
recalled Robert Hilliard, a Jewish GI from Brooklyn who edited an
Army newspaper and had received permission to attend and report on
the concert. "Through the years in the camps, wood, string, metal parts
of instruments had been smuggled, cared for and put together to create
music, a link with what they remembered as a rational civilization. In

---

* The musicians had survived because the Kovno Jewish Council had appointed them as policemen.

some camps the Germans had provided instruments to designated groups of musicians. . . . The musicians played Mahler, Mendelssohn and others whose music had been forbidden for years. A concert of life and a concert of death."[21]

When the music was over and silence returned to the hall, Dr. Grinberg walked onto the stage. He apologized for speaking in German but acknowledged that it had become the "common tongue" of the survivors, the language most of them understood. He wanted to speak for the "millions" who had been exterminated, for the few who had survived, and to the wider world that had looked away—and continued to do so. Why, he asked, as did every survivor, had they been spared? "What is the logic of fate to let us . . . live?" There could be only one answer. The survivors had "to act as delegates of millions of victims to tell all mankind, to proclaim all over the world how cruel people may become . . . what a triumphant record of crime and murder has been achieved by the nation of Hegel and Kant, Schiller and Goethe, Beethoven and Schopenhauer." He proceeded to tell the story of the "stations of torture" he had experienced and endured, hoping that in doing so he might capture the imagination of those who had until now refused to listen, or, he feared, like the Jewish community in the United States, had listened but refused to act.

We have met here today to celebrate our liberation; but at the same time it is a day of mourning for us. . . . Hitler has lost every battle on every front except the battle against defenseless and unarmed men, women, and children. He won the war against the Jews of Europe. He carried out this war with the help of the German nation. . . . We are free now, but we do not know how, or with what, to begin our free yet unfortunate lives. It seems to us that for the present mankind does not understand what we have gone through and experienced during this period. And it seems to us that we shall not be understood in the future.[22]

On May 31, two days after the Liberation Concert, Dr. Grinberg and two survivors, one from Landsberg, the other from Munich, wrote the World Jewish Congress to ask for moral support and material assistance. "We, the surviving Jews of Europe, appeal to you as the central agency of the Jewish people. Four weeks have now passed since our liberation and no single representative of any Jewish organization has come to speak with us concerning what happened to us in the most horrible persecution that has ever transpired, to give us comfort, to alleviate our need or to bring us aid. We have had to help ourselves with our own poor strength. This has been our first great disappointment since our liberation and it is a fact that we cannot understand."[23]

The fear of the survivors, in those first weeks and months after liberation, was that the American and British military were going to force them to return to the nations and the peoples who had murdered their families. The official American policy, which the military officers on the ground were directed to enforce, was, as Rabbi Schacter was informed by a colonel at headquarters, to send all the DPs back "to the countries of their origins, the Hungarians would go back to Hungary, Poles, to Poland, Russians to Russia, where they came from . . . let them go back."

Schacter argued with the colonel late into the night "to make him understand that Jews can't go back. . . . He said to me, I remember quite vividly he says, 'I don't understand this, why isn't this in the book?'" He had no special orders concerning the Jews. As far as the Army was concerned, they were DPs and, like all the other DPs, were going to be repatriated.[24]

Rabbi Klausner had the same experience. When a group of Jewish DPs from a camp "on the outskirts of Munich" were told "to be ready for movement," they asked Klausner for help. Though he had no authority to do so, he told them to resist evacuation. The commanding officer in the district, on receiving the request that the Jews be allowed to remain where they were, "exploded, 'There are no Jews in the camp!'" According to the Army records, which listed DPs only by nationality, this was true. The order to repatriate the Jews had, Klausner learned, come directly from General Patton, who was in command of the Third Army and "doesn't want DPs in his area if he can help it."[25]

To block efforts to repatriate them and, as importantly, to pressure the military authorities into establishing Jewish camps for the Jewish DPs rather than forcing them to live with non-Jews from their home countries, the survivors in the American zone, like those in the British, organized committees to represent their interests. On July 1, 1945, forty-one delegates from camps in Bavaria met at a former Hitler Youth camp that had been converted to the Feldafing DP camp and together "set about creating an elected body that would serve as the official representative" of the Jewish survivors in Bavaria.[26]

On July 25, 1945, a more extensive grouping of delegates from more than forty camps representing some forty thousand Jewish DPs gathered at St. Ottilien. The conference convened at 7 p.m. and continued until 8 a.m. the next morning "in the hospital theater which had been decorated with Zionist flags. . . . The delegates occupied the front rows while patients from the hospital, anxious to hear the speakers, jammed every available inch in the room. They sat on the window sills and literally hung from the walls and ceilings, intent on following the proceedings." Each of the delegates reported on conditions in his camp.

"The substance of most of the reports," Chaplain Robert Marcus reported, "did not present a pretty picture."

> It was a story of starvation diets, callous American officers who disregarded military directives concerning treatment of stateless people and downright anti-Semitism; of bad food, tattered lager [camp] clothes and overcrowded sleeping quarters; . . . of pressure to return to lands they wish to forget; of sick Jews being forcibly taken from hospitals to displaced persons camps for people of their country of origin; of American Junior officers who carry on in a dictatorial manner, kick Hungarian Jews around [the Hungarians had fought the war on the side of

the Nazis], coddle Fascist Poles and treat the other DPs as though they were dumb beasts; of barbed wire enclosures and armed guards and tanks around camps which made one feel like a hounded criminal; of insufficient medical supplies and personnel.

The delegates did more than complain, however. "These were people," Marcus wrote, "who were alive because they had willed it so, because though enslaved by the Nazis, they had remained spiritually, innately free. They spoke of their hopes for the future. There was only one, just one salvation for them, Palestine. Never again would they return to the countries of their birth where Jews were still being destroyed, to cities which awakened memories of parents and children murdered. Only Palestine could heal their wounds though the scars and some of the pain would remain for always."[27]

"We have no intentions whatever to remain in Germany," declared Mr. Pinkusewitz, who represented survivors in the Frankfurt district. "All other nations are removing their sons from Germany, giving them a home in their own fatherland. Whither are we to go? The countries we came from do not spell home to us. There our dearest ones were butchered. . . . Not until we come to Eretz Israel will our life have any meaning."[28]

But how were they to get from their camps in Germany halfway across the world to Palestine? These were not stupid men, nor were they easily deluded by false promises. They were well aware that the British had no intention of allowing significant numbers of European Jews to emigrate to Palestine. "The prospects regarding Palestine are for the present limited," Dr. Nabriski from the Landsberg camp reminded his fellow delegates. "The effort aiming to make possible a large emigration to Palestine must be deepened and broadened. At the same time, however, we must do everything possible to improve our lot here on the spot." They had no choice but to turn their minds from Palestine for the present and prepare for the coming winter in their displaced persons camps in Germany.[29]

Their priorities were to establish Jewish-only camps, to set up educational and vocational programs within them, to establish a registry of survivors, and to organize the collection of "testimonies and evidence which would help bring Nazi criminals to trial."[30]

THE ZIONISTS WERE the best-organized, the most vocal, and the primary leadership cadre in the camps. Zionism was for the survivors not a utopian dream, but a practical necessity. To prepare for their eventual relocation to Palestine, however long that might take, they established ties with the Yishuv, the Jewish community in Palestine; the Jewish Agency, the governing authority there; the Jewish Brigade veterans who had fought alongside the British during the war and remained in Europe; and the Mossad l'Aliyah Bet, a special branch of the Haganah, the Jewish Agency's military arm, whose principal task was organizing the illegal immigration to Palestine, or Aliyah Bet.*

For a small minority of the displaced persons, delay in making aliyah was not an option. They had suffered enough in Europe and would remain not one day longer. Those survivors who were young enough, strong enough, and healthy enough for the journey smuggled themselves across borders, into Austria or Switzerland, then Italy, where there were ships ready to take them to Palestine. In Italy, the Mossad provided them with falsified documents and infiltrated them into UNRRA facilities, hotels, and seaside resorts. "Houses and villas were purchased in the names of Italian Jews who volunteered to help the Zionists, and these houses served as centers of operations, residences, and radio stations for maintaining contact with ships and with headquarters in Palestine."[31]

From June to mid-August 1945, some fifteen thousand Jews entered

---

* In response to the British White Paper of 1939, which severely restricted legal immigration, Mossad l'Aliyah Bet had begun organizing illegal immigration by sea from Europe to Palestine. Inactive during the war, it had resumed doing so thereafter. Aliyah Bet, or Immigration B, referred to illegal immigration to Palestine, in contrast to Aliyah Alef, Immigration A, which was legal.

Italy, six to seven thousand of them displaced persons from camps in Germany and Austria, the rest Romanian, Polish, and Hungarian Jews who had spent the war with the partisans or in hiding. The British did all they could to stop the movement into Italy and from there to Palestine, but they were as yet too disorganized to accomplish their purpose.[32]

A SECOND GROUP of Jewish survivors also left Germany in the weeks and months following the liberation, not for Palestine, but for their former homes to look for surviving loved ones and to let them know that they too had survived. Singly, but more often in groups, they set out on foot, grabbing rides when they could in the back of military or civilian wagons or trucks or trains. The journey home was never in a straight line. Roads were closed, tracks damaged, bombed-out bridges not yet repaired, border crossings tightly guarded by Army patrols that had been posted to prevent enemy soldiers, officers, and Nazi officials from escaping from Germany.

The Soviet-dominated Polish Committee of National Liberation and its successor, the Polish Provisional Government, welcomed the returning Polish Jews. In November 1944, a Central Committee of Jews in Poland had been organized. As the Germans retreated and Jews trickled out into the open from their hiding places or from the partisan squads they had fought with, local Jewish committees and community centers were established in liberated cities and towns. Among their primary tasks was to account for the living and to connect them to one another. "Registration in the local Jewish committees went on continually, from day to day, week to week, month to month."[33]

The first stops for the returning Jews were the community centers. If they were lucky, there was someone there who knew of someone who might know someone or had traveled home with someone who had seen or heard rumors that a sister, an aunt, a neighbor was still alive. Sometimes there was a note—with an address—filed away or stuck on a wall of notes. For most survivors, however, there was only silence: no notes, no rumors, no communications, no signs of the living.

How many survivors made the trip back from Germany to Poland is unknown. Most of the evidence we have is anecdotal, though there is some hard data, assembled by the local committees, compiled by the Central Committee of Jews in Poland, and preserved in the archives of the Jewish Historical Institute in Warsaw. The most reliable data is from Łódź, where in 1945 some 38,171 Polish Jews were registered by the local Jewish committee, 18,118, almost 48 percent of them, after being liberated from the camps.[34]

Henry Goteiner had turned down an offer by American soldiers to put him on a truck and take him from the Soviet zone where he was liberated to a displaced persons camp in the American zone. "I wanted to know exactly what happened to my family. I'll go home to Poland, take a look if anyone survived." Arriving in Łódź, he found his way to the community center and central registry where notices were pasted on the walls. "I found a cousin of mine and his sister, another cousin of mine. . . . They were in Feldafing. . . . But I see the name also of my [half] brother, the youngest, that he is in Łódź." Henry got the address, which was the wurst factory where the family had once gone to buy its salamis. "I come to the yard—I walk into the yard and I go in and I see my brother."

Henry got a job with his half brother making and selling salami, bologna, and other "wursts" until one afternoon, two or three months after his return, he heard machine guns firing in the streets. Members of the AK, or Armia Krajowa,* who "were against Russians and against Jews," were shooting at Jews in the street. Goteiner, with a handful of Jewish friends, left at once. "I have no place here," he told his half brother. "I am leaving back to Germany." Months later, his brother appeared in the displaced persons camp where Henry was now living. "I

---

* The AK, the Polish Home Army loyal to the London Poles, had been officially disbanded in July 1945, but elements had reconstituted themselves in armed opposition to the new provisional government, the Soviets, and their putative Jewish comrades.

got a letter in the mail to leave within twenty-four hours." The Poles wanted him out so they could take over his factory.[35]

Bluma Doman had been liberated from Weisswasser, a satellite of Gross-Rosen, when at roll call in the spring of 1945 the Germans announced that they were leaving the camp. "The Germans said you can go home to your family, but I said to myself, 'Where is my family?' . . . I remember my father says to all of us, who's going to survive this war comes back to Ozorków [Poland, about seventeen miles from Łódź] and waits for each other. So me, I went home." She traveled with a group of survivors. Most of the journey was by foot; occasionally they were able to board a train, but because the tracks had been destroyed during the war and not yet repaired, trains never went very far before the passengers had to get off. "We stopped in Łódź," where they remained for a few days to recuperate, then on to Ozorków. "There were ten Jews," and they remained together and looked for friends and family. "I walked up to the place where we lived and there opens [the door] a big Polish lady. I was so heartbroken I fell down completely the steps." She remained in Ozorków for five days, searching for family members. "Nobody shows up from my family. Everybody's crying." With five of her fellow travelers, she began the long walk back to Germany and the American zone of occupation. Four of the group of survivors she had traveled with stayed behind in the hope that they might find someone still living.[36]

Masza Rosenroth and her sister were liberated from another Gross-Rosen satellite camp and relocated to a DP camp in Munich. Masza, who was five foot five inches tall, weighed no more than ninety pounds; her sister was so frail she could not walk without difficulty. Still, as soon as they were able, they set out in search of living family members. Their brother, Leo, they knew, had escaped across the border into the Soviet Union. When he refused to declare himself a Soviet citizen, he had been deported to Siberia, which according to Masza saved his life.

The sisters made their way to Łódź, where they registered at the Jewish community center and sent letters to Leo in Siberia. One of their letters, miraculously, reached him, but Masza, not knowing this and incapable of remaining any longer in Poland, which for her was little more than a cemetery, crossed the border with a group of twenty young survivors to make her way back to Germany and the displaced persons camps. Her sister remained in Łódź, hoping that Leo, who had been seventeen when he left for the Soviet Union, might return. Months later, in December 1945, Leo arrived in Łódź. Together with his sister, they set out to find Masza and reunite what was left of their family.[37]

THE HARRISON REPORT

THE ORGANIZED AMERICAN JEWISH community was not oblivious to the suffering of the survivors, but powerless to do anything about it. The leadership of the World Jewish Congress (WJC) did what it did best: it studied the situation, reported on its findings, and pleaded with those in power to take action. Zorach Warhaftig, a rabbi from Byelorussia (Belarus) and Zionist leader who had relocated to New York City in 1942, was commissioned by the American Jewish Congress and the WJC in the summer of 1944 to study and comment on UNRRA plans and policies for the displaced. He argued that special provisions would have to be made for the Jewish survivors.

> The plight of the Jews in Axis and occupied territories is strikingly different from that of their Gentile co-nationals in the degree of their suffering. . . . The surviving Jews, undermined in health, despoiled of practically all material goods, surrounded by a population indoctrinated for years with zoological hatred, will have to wage a hard fight for mere existence, for their rescue from the effects of the Nazi war. . . . The extraordinary situation

of the Jewish population in Nazi Europe created by the Nazis' extermination policy can be redressed only by equally extraordinary means and ways.[1]

In a memorandum prepared for the second session of the UNRRA General Council, Rabbi Stephen Wise and Nahum Goldmann of the WJC, while acknowledging that "the principle of non-discrimination (for reasons of race, religion or political belief) in the distribution of relief is one of the foundations of the policy stated by UNRRA," concluded that if UNRRA's ultimate objective was to provide equal opportunities for recovery for all victims of Nazism, then the Jews, the most discriminated against and the only group "singled out for extermination . . . should be given equitable priorities in the distribution of food, medical aid and shelter, as well as in the field of return, repatriation, and resettlement of the displaced." And how did Wise and Goldmann suggest that UNRRA administer such "equitable priorities," a perfect contradiction in terms? They proposed that the nondiscrimination policy remain in force, but that the director general, former New York governor Herbert H. Lehman, not coincidentally a New York Jew, be provided with "strengthened . . . powers of supervision . . . in the field," that Jewish representatives be appointed as UNRRA "observers," and that Jewish social workers be added to the UNRRA field staff.[2]

No action was taken on any of these recommendations. UNRRA was not going to discriminate for or against the Jewish survivors. They would be treated like every other group displaced by war.

The WJC leadership continued to implore the American military, as well as UNRRA, to make special provision for the Jewish survivors. In November 1944, Dr. Arieh Tartakower, a member of the Executive Committee, wrote Major General John H. Hilldring, chief of the Army's Civil Affairs Division, to request that the Jewish survivors not be "placed in the same camps with Nazis or with other enemy nationals, at whose hands, only yesterday, they suffered most cruelly. It is certainly unnecessary to stress the unwelcome aspects of such a possibility."[3]

Tartakower's request was denied. The U.S. Army, like UNRRA, refused to afford the Jewish survivors any special treatment. Paragraph 710 of the *Handbook for Military Government in Germany Prior to Defeat or Surrender*, published and distributed to officers in the field in December 1944, stated explicitly that the military was to "locate, care for, and control United Nations displaced persons within the areas for which they are responsible." Displaced persons were to be segregated and housed by nationality. They were to be treated equally, given the same rations and clothing, and, as soon as humanly possible, repatriated to the countries they had lived in before the war.[4]

As the Allies entered German territory, American Jewish leaders, still unaware of exactly how many Jews had survived, but concerned that those who had would be ignored in the chaos of liberation, petitioned the military to appoint special "liaison" officers for the Jewish survivors. Liaison officers appointed by the Danish, French, Dutch, Italian, and every Allied government, including the Polish government-in-exile in London, were already in place in the camps, assisting the displaced persons and facilitating their repatriation. What the Jewish leaders requested was that Jewish survivors, though they were not recognized as citizens of a particular "nation," receive the same type of assistance.

In May 1945, Louis Lipsky, chairman of the Executive Committee of the American Jewish Conference,* asked Congressman Emanuel Celler of Brooklyn to organize a meeting between Jewish congressmen and representatives of UNRRA and the State and War Departments, to discuss the appointment of Jewish liaison officers. At the meeting, it was agreed that Celler should write General Eisenhower to recommend the immediate appointment of "special Jewish liaison officers."[5]

Eisenhower answered Celler and the Jewish congressmen by assur-

---

* The American Jewish Conference, not to be confused with the American Jewish Committee or the American Jewish Congress, had been organized in 1943 to bring together in one organization representatives of the major Zionist and non-Zionist groups. Its Zionist program led to the withdrawal of the American Jewish Committee in mid-1943.

ing them that the military was well aware of the "condition of Jewish survivors" and "steps [were] being taken to give best possible care." He did not approve or deny the request for liaison officers, but deftly passed the buck. UNRRA, he declared, was "making arrangement with voluntary welfare agencies to handle specific welfare problems" and it was the "policy of this headquarters that all voluntary organizations working in Germany shall be coordinated by UNRRA." In other words, if Jewish liaison officers were to be sent into Germany, they would have to be approved by and under UNRRA supervision.[6]

Lipsky followed up by drafting a letter for Thomas M. Cooley II, UNRRA's deputy director, Displaced Persons Division, to formally request that Jewish liaison personnel be appointed to work with the Jewish DPs.

> Reports reaching us from abroad reveal that the thousands of liberated Jews found in concentration and labor camps and other areas in Germany are utterly helpless in finding their way to Allied military or intergovernmental agencies for immediate relief. Their condition is particularly aggravated by the fact that their detention and ill-treatment has been extremely harsh and prolonged and that, as a result they are physically and mentally unable to start by themselves on the road to recovery. They are furthermore handicapped by language difficulties. . . . To help these people in their plight, they must be treated by persons who speak their language and who have a knowledge of their traditional and religious backgrounds. We, the undersigned,* therefore request UNRRA that, in giving aid to these liberated Jews, it should appoint Jewish liaison personnel in the European areas for the purpose of interpretation, advice and consultation on the specific needs of their beneficiaries.

---

* Lipsky's letter was signed by the leaders of the World Jewish Congress, the American Jewish Conference, and the Board of Deputies of British Jews.

Three days later, having in the meantime "received additional disturbing reports that the condition of [the Jewish survivors] had not improved but is rapidly deteriorating," Lipsky wrote Cooley a second letter. "We had hoped that after liberation the remnants of decimated European Jewry would receive immediate aid from Allied sources to restore their health and to avoid unnecessary additional loss of life. We realize that the road to rehabilitation is beset with many difficulties, but we submit that existing obstacles can be removed if a relief and rehabilitation program for the surviving Jews in Germany is organized without delay and if special Jewish liaison personnel is appointed to assist in this program."[7]

Still awaiting a response to their petitions, Congressman Celler met with UNRRA director general Herbert Lehman, a powerhouse, as was Cellar, in New York's Jewish and Democratic Party circles. Whatever Lehman may have wanted to do in regard to the Jewish DPs, he insisted that his hands were tied. "UNRRA is not entirely independent and is working under and in agreement with the military authorities." Like the military, UNRRA was bound by nondiscrimination directives. It was willing to and had hired "a number of Jewish social workers . . . for its relief teams," but it could "hardly appoint Jewish liaison officers who would then represent religious and political groups."[8]

On July 5, 1945, two months after liberation, still with no response to their requests and having been bounced back and forth between military and UNRRA officials, Meir Grossman and Louis Lipsky of the American Jewish Conference raised the issue of the liaison officers again, this time in memoranda to the War Department and to Lehman. Countering the claim that it would be inappropriate to grant the Jewish survivors assistance that would not be made available to other "religious and political groups," Lipsky argued again that "the position of the Jews of Germany is of a specific, complex nature and requires specialized, individual attention." If UNRRA was not prepared to ask the military to appoint Jewish "liaison officers" to serve in the same capacity as the ones from the Allied nations, might it not "mobilize from its own personnel a special welfare division . . . and appoint a number of Jewish officers to this division. . . . It is needless to say that the position of the Jews in Germany is of a specific, complex nature and requires specialized, individual attention."[9]

This proposal, like all the others, was rejected. General Eisenhower, for the American military, and Herbert Lehman, for UNRRA, had made it clear that they would take no special steps to alleviate the problems faced by the Jewish survivors.

LONDON, MAY TO AUGUST 1945

Simultaneously with and in coordination with the Americans, the leaders of the organized Jewish community in Britain requested that "His Majesty's Government . . . should authorize the establishment of special Jewish representation on the Allied Control Council for Germany,"* and that Jewish voluntary organizations be authorized to send volunteers to the camps that housed Jewish survivors. The Marquess of Reading, director of the Board of Deputies of British Jews, representing not only the Jewish Agency, which the British recognized as the official representative of the Jews in Palestine, but a number of other Jewish organizations, insisted that it did not seek "any preferential treatment for . . . Jews, but merely to ensure that they shall not be allowed to remain under their present disabilities."[10]

Lord Reading's memorandum was discussed at the Foreign Office, then handed off to the War Office. It was answered on July 26 by Lieutenant General Ronald Weeks, Field Marshal Bernard Montgomery's deputy military governor in the British zone of occupation. The British military, Weeks declared, opposed any differential or preferential

---

* The Allied Control Council, which consisted of the chief military commanders of the four zones of occupation in Germany, was established on June 5, 1945, as successor to SHAEF (Supreme Headquarters Allied Expeditionary Force).

treatment for Jewish DPs. "The policy should continue to be to emphasize a Jew's political nationality rather than his race and religious persuasion." Preferential treatment of Jews would be "unfair to the many
non-Jews who have suffered on account of their clandestine and other
activities in the Allied cause." It might even "give rise to persecution at
a later date." The Jews had indeed suffered, but "there have been many
other sufferers." The British occupying authorities had no intention of
providing the Jewish survivors with separate residences or special assistance. They had notified UNRRA, by memorandum, that regulations
"precluded [them] from dealing with Allied Jews as though they formed
a category separate from other persons whose nationality they share."
This policy applied to ex-enemy Jews as well. German Jews were to be
treated not as Nazi victims, but as Germans.[11]

In early August, three months after the first request for Jewish liaison officers had been made, several of the American Jewish military
chaplains, including Robert Marcus, traveled to London to meet with
Rabbi Stephen Wise to ask him to intervene. On August 3, Wise dictated a personal cable to General Eisenhower, the supreme commander
of the Allied Expeditionary Force. "There is urgent necessity to assign
liaison officer to headquarters . . . for purpose of coordinating activity
of Jewish Displaced Persons. . . . Immediate action advisable in order to
avoid suffering next winter and remedy deplorable conditions in some
camps as reported by daily press."[12]

A week later, Eisenhower answered Wise directly. "This Headquarters does not agree that the assignment here of a Liaison Officer for
Jewish displaced persons would materially assist such persons and
regrets that it cannot accept the proposal. Liaison Officers attached
to this Headquarters are selected on nationality basis and it is considered undesirable on many grounds to have one specially designated
for Jews."[13]

WASHINGTON, APRIL TO JUNE 1945

Help for the Jewish DPs would in the end come from Secretary of the Treasury Henry Morgenthau Jr., the only Jewish member of President Truman's cabinet.

Morgenthau was, in historian Henry Feingold's words, "a marginal Jew." He did not observe the Jewish holidays, did not go to temple, and had no significant attachment to any of the major Jewish organizations. During the war, he had been an active if wary adviser to Roosevelt on European Jewish refugees, and, after mid-1943, a fierce and outspoken opponent of what he believed was the State Department's criminal obstruction of efforts to rescue European Jews. It was on Morgenthau's pleading, and as a counterweight to the State Department, that Roosevelt had in January 1944 established the War Refugee Board, which reported to the president but was staffed with Morgenthau deputies.

Within the Roosevelt administration, Morgenthau had taken the harshest line on postwar Germany, which he argued should be stripped of its industrial capacity, partitioned, demilitarized, and made to pay significant reparations. All Nazi institutions should be disbanded, laws repealed, property confiscated, and war criminals punished. The Morgenthau Plan, though later abandoned as too punitive, was considered by Roosevelt, who incorporated some of its provisions into postwar planning documents and the proposals presented to Churchill and Stalin at Yalta.

Morgenthau had been briefed on the condition of the Jewish survivors in Germany by his former deputies, whom he had placed at the War Refugee Board, and by his friend Meyer Weisgal, who served as personal representative in the United States for Chaim Weizmann, president of the World Zionist Organization.

On May 23, unsolicited, the treasury secretary brought to President Truman's attention the "great problem of the resettlement of hundreds of thousands of displaced persons who are unable or unwilling to return to their homelands." He recommended that the president establish "a Cabinet Committee to deal specifically with the problems of the permanently displaced and non-repatriable groups in Europe." Though he did not mention Jews in his memo, it was clear whom he had in mind.[14]

When Truman turned down his request, Morgenthau drafted another "Memorandum for the president" recommending that he send a special mission to Europe to investigate the problems confronting Jewish displaced persons. "From various sources, information has reached me that the situation of the displaced peoples of Europe, and particularly of the approximately one million surviving Jews, is very serious. It has been pointed out that the position of the Jews is more difficult than that of any other element in the European community, that these Jews continue to be victims in many countries of racial hate engendered and intensified by the Nazis."[15]

Fearful that Truman, with whom he had never been close, would reject this recommendation also, Morgenthau sent his memorandum to Under Secretary of State Joseph Grew and suggested that the State Department sponsor the special mission to Europe.

Grew agreed with Morgenthau not only that the State Department should sponsor such a mission, but that the best person to head it up was Dean Earl Harrison of the University of Pennsylvania Law School. Harrison, a large man with "broad shoulders, curly blond hair, clear blue eyes, a firm jaw and a big smile," had been raised a Presbyterian, now attended a Society of Friends meeting, was a Republican, and had since 1940 served the government in a variety of positions. He had maintained a low profile and kept his name and office out of the papers. It was expected he would do the same in Europe.[16]

Before formally approving the mission, Grew cabled Robert Murphy, General Eisenhower's political adviser in Europe, to get the general's approval. "I feel that this is a matter which should have our wholehearted support and I should be grateful if you would take it up immediately with a view to securing permission to the survey." Murphy cabled back Eisenhower's endorsement.[17]

After Eisenhower had endorsed the project, Grew informed President Truman on June 21 that the State Department was sending Dean Harrison to Europe to investigate the condition of the DPs and asked the president to cosponsor the mission, which he agreed to do.[18]

While the Harrison mission was not an official Treasury matter, Morgenthau and his deputy, John Pehle, the former director of the War Refugee Board, intended to oversee it. On June 12, Pehle met with Harrison, "explained the interest of the Secretary of the Treasury in the matter and informed Mr. Harrison . . . of the pressure which had been received from various groups, particularly the political Zionists, for an investigation of this kind to be made. Mr. Pehle made it clear that Secretary Morgenthau was primarily concerned with the problem of the needs of these displaced people while the Zionist groups are primarily interested in obtaining information concerning the desire of these people to emigrate from Europe."[19]

Pehle's claim that his and Morgenthau's interests were not those of the "political Zionists" was only partially true. Meyer Weisgal, Morgenthau's Zionist friend, at a meeting set up by Morgenthau, explained to Harrison that the Jewish DPs did not "wish to return to the lands which they originally inhabited. It is not merely a question of their unwillingness to return because of the difficult conditions that may face them but a state of mind which would keep any man from going back to the city where he knew his mother or brother was killed before his eyes. Any attempt forcibly to return these Jews to scenes of perpetual terror will be as inhuman as the acts of these responsible for the decimation of millions of Jews." The only "home" for the "homeless" displaced Jews was Palestine, "a land which they can call their own and where they are welcome and within which they can develop themselves on a permanent, free, secure basis."[20]

Because Harrison was a neophyte when it came to Jews and Judaism and spoke no Yiddish, Weisgal suggested that he be accompanied on his visit by "an associate . . . thoroughly steeped in Jewish situation." After consulting with the leaders of the Jewish Agency and the American Jewish Conference, Weisgal recommended and Grew agreed that the best man for the job was Dr. Joseph Schwartz of the Joint Distribution Committee.[21]

DEAN EARL HARRISON was entering a diplomatic, political, and geopolitical minefield. His mandate was to investigate the conditions of the Last Million, "particularly the Jews," and "determine in general the views of the refugees with respect to their future destinations." From the moment he accepted the assignment, he had to have known that while some of the displaced persons with American relatives would choose to emigrate to the United States, the majority, as Weisgal had briefed him, would indicate Palestine as their preference. If and when Harrison carried this news back to Washington, it would put President Truman, the man who had endorsed his mission, in a difficult, if not impossible, position.[22]

Truman was not going to ask Congress to amend or rewrite the restrictive 1924 quota laws to allow Jewish displaced persons into the United States. He feared—and rightly—that to do so might very well lead to more restrictive legislation.

There was a simpler solution to the Jewish DP problem: let them emigrate to Palestine. The president naïvely believed that he would be able to persuade the British government, which had in 1922 been given the mandate for Palestine by the League of Nations, to open the territory to Jewish immigrants. The State Department, which was in full accord with the British refusal to increase immigration to Palestine, took it upon itself to dissuade the new president from pursuing this policy.

Just six days after Truman had taken the oath of office, then secretary of state Edward Stettinius Jr. had warned him that it was "very likely that efforts will be made by some of the Zionist leaders to obtain from you at an early date some commitments in favor of the Zionist program which is pressing for unlimited immigration into Palestine and the establishment there of a Jewish state. As you are aware, the Government and people of the United States have every sympathy for the persecuted Jews of Europe and are doing all in their power to relieve their suffering. The question of Palestine is, however, a highly complex one and involves questions which go far beyond the plight of the Jews of Europe. . . . We feel that this whole subject is one that should be handled with the greatest care and with a view to the long-range interests of this country." In other words, Truman should rely on the State Department to tell him what to do and when to do it.[23]

On May 1, 1945, Under Secretary of State Joseph Grew followed up on Stettinius's early warning by informing the new president that "although President Roosevelt at times gave expression to views sympathetic to certain Zionist aims," he had "promised" King Ibn Saud of Saudi Arabia when he met with him after Yalta "that as regards Palestine he would make no move hostile to the Arab people and would not assist the Jews as against the Arabs." Grew was twisting the content and tone of the communiqué to serve his and the State Department's purposes. What Roosevelt had promised was that he would take no action "without full consultation with both the Arabs and Jews."[24]

Despite or perhaps in direct defiance of the State Department's warning, Truman had in his first days in office welcomed Rabbi Stephen Wise, dean of American Zionists, to the White House "to talk to me about the Jewish victims of Nazi persecution and the serious problem of the resettlement of the refugees, which led naturally to a discussion of a proposed Jewish state and homeland in Palestine." While Truman promised nothing substantive, he explained to Wise that he too cared about and planned to do something to help "these unfortunate victims of persecution to find a home." He was already "skeptical," he wrote in his memoirs, though we don't know whether he confided this to Rabbi Wise, "about some of the views and attitudes assumed by the 'striped-pants boys' in the State Department. It seemed to me that they didn't care enough about what happened to the thousands of displaced persons."[25]

State Department fears that the new president, out of some sort of softhearted humanitarianism or bowing to political pressure from Jewish lobbyists, would pressure Britain to open the gates of Palestine were exacerbated when on July 24, 1945, at the Potsdam Conference, the president, though Palestine was not on the agenda, informed British prime minister Winston Churchill by letter that there was

> great interest in America in the Palestine problem. The drastic restrictions imposed on Jewish immigration by the British White Paper of May 1939 [which limited immigration certificates to seventy-five thousand for the next five years] continue to provoke passionate protest from Americans most interested in Palestine and in the Jewish problem. They fervently urge the lifting of these restrictions which deny to Jews, who have been so cruelly uprooted by ruthless Nazi persecution, entrance into the land which represents for so many of them their only hope of survival. Knowing your deep and sympathetic interest in Jewish settlement in Palestine, I venture to express to you the hope that the British Government may find it possible without delay to take steps to lift the restrictions. . . . I hope, therefore, that you can arrange at your early convenience to let me have your ideas on the settlement of the Palestine problem, so that we can at a later but not too distant date discuss the problem in concrete terms.[26]

Churchill never got a chance to respond. The day after Truman's letter was sent, the results of the recent general election were announced and Churchill was unceremoniously deposed. His successor as prime minister, Clement Attlee, in answering Truman's note a week later, did not dismiss his recommendation, but neither did he endorse it. "You will I am sure understand that I cannot give you any statement on policy until we have had time to consider the matter, and this is simply to inform you that we will give early and careful consideration to your memorandum."[27]

Truman did not let the matter drop. On his return to Washington from Potsdam, asked at a press conference about "the American view on Palestine," he declared that "we want to let as many of the Jews into Palestine as it is possible to let into that country. Then the matter will have to be worked out diplomatically with the British and the Arabs, so that if a state can be set up there they may be able to set it up on a peaceful basis. I have no desire to send 500,000 American soldiers there to make peace in Palestine."[28]

Truman's proposal to open Palestine to the immigration of the Jewish displaced persons, then decide its future as an independent state, satisfied no one. His outright refusal to send military personnel to Palestine to keep the peace did not sit well with the British. The Zionists were, for their part, disturbed that the president had mentioned the British and the Arabs, but not the Jewish community, as among those who would decide the future of Palestine, and that he appeared to accept the British claim that enhanced Jewish immigration would lead to warfare and bloodshed so widespread it would require a half million American soldiers to restore the peace.

Truman understood from the very beginning and was continually reminded by the State Department and the British that while the plight of the Jewish DPs was desperate, their suffering unimaginable, when it came to formulating Middle East policy, other considerations would have to be taken into account. The Near East and its oil, the State Department warned, were coveted by the Soviets. It was therefore in the national interest to prop up British authority in the region, if only to keep the Soviets at bay. If this meant the sacrifice of the Jewish dreams of a "homeland" in Palestine, so be it. Truman's objective, if that is not too strong a word for his evolving inclinations, was to separate out the issue of the displaced Jews and of the future of Palestine. The question of the Jewish DPs might, he hoped, be solved in the short term; that of Palestine would require lengthy consultation and negotiations with the British, the Arab nations, the Jewish Agency, American Zionists, and perhaps even the United Nations.

GERMANY, JULY 1945

On June 28, at 8 a.m., Dean Earl Harrison, armed with instructions from the State Department and a letter endorsing his mission from the president, departed New York City for London, where he spent three days, followed by three days in Paris and five more at SHAEF headquarters in Frankfurt, studying the relevant documents and interviewing government, military, and UNRRA staff and officials. To cover more ground, he and Joseph Schwartz, his co-investigator, divided responsibilities, Schwartz writing his own memoranda, large portions of which would be incorporated, sometimes nearly verbatim, into Harrison's report to the president.

Any expectations that theirs would be a whirlwind pro forma tour, orchestrated and circumscribed by the military, were quickly dashed. Harrison and Schwartz discarded the itinerary the Army provided them and wrote a new one. They met with Chaim Weizmann in London and Rabbi Klausner in Germany, interviewed UNRRA officers, consulted with Jewish chaplains, GIs, survivors, and members of the Jewish Brigade. Most significantly, they visited dozens of camps in the British and American zones of occupation and interviewed the displaced persons.

Harrison had been thoroughly briefed in Washington, London, Paris, and by Army officials in Germany, but he was overwhelmed by what he encountered in the dilapidated, filthy, indecently overcrowded former German army barracks converted into DP camps where he spent hour after hour listening to the horrifying narratives of survivors, many still in their ragged striped concentration camp uniforms. Their situation was desperate and would, unless drastic changes were quickly made, become even more so as the cold weather approached.

On July 23, Harrison visited the Bergen-Belsen displaced persons camp in the British zone, where he interviewed Yossel Rosensaft, who he noted, though "only 33—looks older."

Rosensaft spoke plainly. His desires were simply stated:

1. Peace & quiet—live out remaining years.
2. Can't go back; anti-S[emitism], parents killed—Land soaked with Jewish blood.
3. People outside E[urope] too quiet about what has happened—nobody seems concerned.

"Don't leave us in this bloody region," he implored. "Make effort to have doors of P[alestine] and other countries open so can find homes and be with relatives."

"Seldom have I been so depressed," Harrison wrote in his diary the day after his visit.

> I thought the lowest point had been reached at Munich. . . . But today at Belsen. Only seven hours spent there but it seemed like a life-time. And to think that I was told, quite officially, there was no need of my visiting Belsen because it had been burned down and no people were here. And then to come here and find a mere matter of 14,000 displaced people including 7200 Jews still confined here. Ah yes the Building #1 with its fiendish gas chambers and crematoria had been destroyed but the rest is bad enough. One loft, about 80 by 20, housing 85 people.[29]

On July 28, having completed his visits and interviews, Harrison cabled his preliminary findings to Under Secretary of State Grew and Fred Vinson, who had replaced Morgenthau as secretary of the treasury. He had, he informed them, "found complete confirmation of disturbing reports concerning Jews in SHAEF Zone of Germany." Vinson, disturbed by what Harrison had reported, sent a copy of Harrison's cable to the War Department, which forwarded it to General Eisenhower at SHAEF.[30]

Harrison completed the writing of his final report at the American embassy in London. On August 3, he sent it in two separate telegrams to the State Department in Washington. Somehow, either because the British intercepted the cables—as they had been doing since Joseph Kennedy's tenure as ambassador in 1938–40—or because the State Department leaked them, Harrison's report was read and debated in London before it reached President Truman in Washington.

WASHINGTON, AUGUST 1945

In office for only four months, Harry S. Truman was entering what he and everyone else expected to be the most critical moment in his presidency. On August 24, as he was editing, rewriting, adding to, and subtracting from the twenty-one-point domestic program he would soon deliver to Congress, he met with Earl Harrison at the White House and received his report. Given the other items on his agenda, it would have been understandable had he forwarded the report to an adviser or to the State Department for review. Instead, he read it in its entirety. It was, he recalled in his memoirs, "a moving document. The misery it depicted could not be allowed to continue."[31]

Harrison was a law professor, not a professional diplomat or politician. The strength of his presentation lay in his blunt, problem-solving, often impolitic approach. He not only addressed "the condition and needs" of the displaced persons, "with particular reference to the Jewish refugees," but offered practical and doable recommendations. This had to have appealed to Truman, who took great stock in a person's capacity for talking straight and getting things done. Had Harrison been merely another Cassandra crying in the wilderness, his findings might have been more easily dismissed.

Harrison's narrative of Jewish displacement and suffering was identical to that of the World Jewish Congress, the American Jewish Conference, Rabbi Wise, the chaplains in Germany, and Congressman Celler and his colleagues. So too his conclusions.

The circumstances under which Europe's Jews had suffered and died during the war dictated that they receive special treatment while in the camps and the opportunity to emigrate to Palestine. In the chaos of liberation, the British and American armies, the press, the American State Department, and the British Foreign Office had paid scant attention to their singular suffering and needs. They had been treated as just another group of displaced persons. No distinction had been made between those who had been deported to Germany as laborers "and those who suffered the torture of concentration camps," Joseph Schwartz had observed in a memorandum, large sections of which Harrison incorporated into his report to the president.

> The general tendency in the camps is to treat everybody on the same level. This results in a situation where people who had suffered all the hardships of concentration camps for many years and who had developed illnesses of all kinds were receiving the same kind of food as healthy people who had worked and who had been paid for their work and well fed by their employers. When we asked whether some special treatment could not be given to these concentration camp cases, we were told that Jews could not be considered as a privileged group and treated on a different basis than the rest of the camp population.[32]

The report that Harrison presented to the president was blunt and to the point:

> Generally speaking, three months after V-E Day and even longer after the liberation of individual groups, many Jewish displaced persons and other possibly non-repatriables are living under guard behind barbed-wire fences, in camps of several descriptions (built by the Germans for slave-laborers and Jews) including some of the most notorious of the concentration camps, amidst crowded, frequently unsanitary and generally grim conditions, in complete idleness, with no opportunity, except surreptitiously, to communicate with the outside world, waiting, hoping for some word of encouragement and action on their behalf.
>
> The first and plainest need of these people is a recognition of their actual status and by this I mean their status as Jews. Most of them have spent years in the worst of the concentration camps. In many cases, although the full extent is not yet known, they are the sole survivors of their families and many have been through the agony of witnessing the destruction of their loved ones. Understandably, therefore, their present condition, physical and mental, is far worse than that of other groups. . . . While admittedly it is not normally desirable to set aside particular racial or religious groups from their nationality categories, the plain truth is that this was done for so long by the Nazis that a group has been created which has special needs. Jews as Jews (not as members of their nationality groups) have been more severely victimized than the non-Jewish members of the same or other nationalities.[33]

It was incomprehensible to Harrison that the military was not doing more for the displaced persons in general, and the Jews in particular. It might not be possible to get them out of Germany—and the camps—

immediately, but it was possible to improve the conditions under which they were now living.

> It is difficult to understand why so many displaced persons, particularly those who have so long been persecuted and whose repatriation or resettlement is likely to be delayed, should be compelled to live in crude, over-crowded camps while the German people, in rural areas, continue undisturbed in their homes. As matters now stand, we appear to be treating the Jews as the Nazis treated them except that we do not exterminate them. They are in concentration camps in large numbers under our military guard instead of S.S. troops. One is left to wonder whether the German people, seeing this, are not supposing that we are following or at least condoning Nazi policy.[34]

While Harrison recommended, in the strongest terms possible, that the army of occupation do more to make life bearable for the displaced persons, better living conditions, more food, and decent clothing were palliatives.

> The main solution, in many ways the only real solution, of the problem lies in the quick evacuation of all non-repatriable Jews in Germany and Austria, who wish it, to Palestine. . . . It is inhuman to ask people to continue to live for any length of time under their present conditions. The evacuation of the Jews of Germany and Austria to Palestine will solve the problem of the individuals involved and will also remove a problem from the military authorities who have had to deal with it.[35]

Harrison had been asked to report back not only on the conditions under which the DPs were living and their needs, but also on their views "as to their future destinations." Everywhere he went, he got the same answers. "With respect to possible places of resettlement for those who may be stateless or who do not wish to return to their homes, Palestine is definitely and pre-eminently the first choice." Some of those who expressed a desire to emigrate to Palestine did so "because they realize that their opportunity to be admitted into the United States or into other countries in the Western hemisphere is limited, if not impossible." But many more had been converted to the Zionist belief that only in "Palestine will they be welcomed and find peace and quiet and be given an opportunity to live and work."[36]

Recommending that the Jewish DPs be allowed to emigrate to Palestine—and that the U.S. government "express its interest in and support of" this proposal—would, Harrison knew, bring him into direct opposition with the British government, which was opposed to any additional Jewish immigration, and the State Department, which backed the British in this regard. Still, instead of detouring around the problem, Harrison, pushed perhaps by his consultant and partner, Joseph Schwartz of the Joint, confronted it directly.

"The issue of Palestine must be faced." The British had, in approving the White Paper of 1939 that severely restricted Jewish immigration, responded to Arab fears that millions of Jews would emigrate to Palestine. The murder of six million European Jews should have alleviated such fears. "Now that such large numbers are no longer involved and if there is any genuine sympathy for what these survivors have endured, some reasonable extension or modification of the British White Paper of 1939 ought to be possible without too serious repercussions."

The British had allocated a limited number of certificates for European Jews wishing to settle in Palestine. Those certificates, Harrison had learned, would be "practically exhausted by the end of the current month [August 1945]. What is the future to be? To anyone who has visited the concentration camps and who has talked with the despairing survivors, it is nothing short of calamitous to contemplate that the gates of Palestine should be soon closed."

"The civilized world," Harrison concluded in the final sentence of his report, "owes it to this handful of survivors to provide them with a home where they can again settle down and begin to live as human beings."[37]

LONDON, AUGUST 1945

Warned in advance, the British Foreign Office had wasted no time preparing its response to Harrison's findings and recommendations. On August 24, the day Harrison met with Truman, Sir George Rendel of the Foreign Office cabled William Strang, the political adviser to Field Marshal Bernard Montgomery, the commander in chief of British forces in Germany.

Because Harrison's report "will reach high quarters in the United States Administration and probably Congress . . . we are . . . concerned to see how far his criticisms are justified and whether there is anything we ought to do by way of remedy." Rendel, for the most part, dismissed Harrison's recommendations and affirmed British policy regarding the Jewish DPs.

> We do not of course admit that Jews constitute a separate nationality, and are all against any attempt to label people as definitely and irrevocably 'non-repatriable' at this stage. . . . We are strongly opposed to the idea, sedulously fostered by many Jewish organizations, that Jewry enjoys a supra-national status, and it would indeed be disastrous for the Jews themselves if they were accorded special treatment on this basis in comparison with the people of the country where they live. . . . The policy of Ministers is to regard all displaced persons and refugees for the present as ultimately repatriable.

There would be problems in defending such a policy, Rendel admitted, but they could be addressed. "We must forestall criticism (which is already appearing) that we are disinterested in these people and that nothing is done for them." Such criticism, especially that coming from Jewish organizations in the United States and the United Kingdom, had to be aggressively countered or it would fester and grow. "We are, as you know, under constant pressure from Jewish organizations and others critical of the way in which displaced persons are being handled—there have been articles in the press on this subject and we may expect Parliamentary questions—and it is to our interest and that of the War Office to forestall criticisms and, where they can be at all substantiated, to do what we can to remedy them."[38]

Sir George was not being rash in taking preemptive actions against the Harrison Report and the recommendations he feared were going to be endorsed by President Truman. On August 31, 1945, James Byrnes, appointed as secretary of state the month before, in London for the Foreign Ministers Conference, hand-delivered to Prime Minister Attlee a copy of the Harrison Report and a personal letter from the president.

"Instructions were given to Mr. Harrison to inquire particularly into the problems and needs of the Jewish refugees among the displaced persons," Truman had written Attlee, who already knew as much. "I should like to call your attention to the conclusions and recommendations . . . especially the references to Palestine."

The new president then proceeded to instruct the new prime minister on the contours of the problem at hand—and the solution to it.

No other single matter is so important for those who have known the horrors of concentration camps for over a decade as is the future of immigration possibilities into Palestine. The number of such persons who wish immigration to Palestine or who would qualify for admission there is, unfortunately, no longer as large as it was before the Nazis began their extermination program. As I said to you in Potsdam, the American people, as a whole, firmly believe that immigration into Palestine should not

be closed and that a reasonable number of Europe's persecuted
Jews should, in accordance with their wishes, be permitted to
resettle there. . . . No claim is more meritorious than that of the
groups who for so many years have known persecution and enslavement. The main solution appears to lie in the quick evacuation of as many as possible of the non-repatriable Jews, who wish
it, to Palestine. If it is to be effective, such action should not be
long delayed.[39]

Attlee and Ernest Bevin, the burly, pugnacious, blatantly undiplo-
matic former dockworker and trade union leader, who was now foreign
secretary, were taken aback by Truman's audacity in suggesting a change
of policy for Palestine, whose past history and present complexities,
they believed, neither he nor any other American could hope to understand. Attlee, known for his considerable restraint, kept his counsel and
asked for time to consider Truman's request. He did however notify the
president that he had "learned with concern of a conversation which
Mr. Byrnes had today with the Foreign Secretary [Bevin] in which he
told him that you are preparing to issue a statement about Palestine this
evening and to include in this statement Mr. Harrison's report." Attlee
asked Truman to refrain from making the Harrison Report or his approval of its recommendations public. "Such action could not fail to do
grievous harm to relations between our two countries." Truman agreed
to postpone publication of the report.[40]

On September 16, Prime Minister Attlee responded to Truman's
letter at greater length. Echoing the rejoinder of the Foreign Office, in
near-identical language, he rejected Harrison's recommendation, which
Truman had endorsed, that the Jews deserved special treatment because
their suffering had been of a different nature than that of other victims
of Nazi persecution.

The British military government, Attlee asserted, had and would
continue to

avoid treating [the Jewish DPs] on a racial basis. . . . One must remember that within these camps were people from almost every race in Europe and there appears to have been very little difference in the amount of torture and treatment they had to undergo. Now, if our officers had placed the Jews in a special racial category at the head of the queue, my strong view is that the effect of this would have been disastrous for the Jews and therefore their attempt to treat them alike was a right one. . . . In case of Palestine, we have the Arabs to consider as well as the Jews and there have been solemn undertakings, I understand, given by your predecessor, yourself and by Mr. Churchill that, before we come to a final decision and operate it, there would be consultation with the Arabs. It would be very unwise to break these solemn pledges and so set aflame the whole Middle East. . . . Therefore, while sympathising with the views of Mr. Harrison and weighing them very carefully, we believe that the suggestion which he has made raises very far-reaching implications, which would have to be most carefully balanced against the considerations which I have set out above.[41]

Truman promised to "take no further action" until Secretary Byrnes had returned from London, but made it clear that he did not intend to abandon the issue. "I am aware of the complications of the problem from your point of view. It also makes difficulties for us. It is hoped that we can work out a successful program that will provide for them some measure of relief at an early date."[42]

For the Zionists in the United States and Palestine, the chaplains in Germany, and the displaced persons in the camps, the news or rather the lack of news out of Washington and London was disturbing. On September 18, Nahum Goldmann, who was in charge of the Jewish Agency's political office in Washington, forwarded the latest "information on the political situation" to David Ben-Gurion, chairman of the

Jewish Agency and the acknowledged leader of the Jewish community in Palestine.

> It becomes clear to me that . . . we have the help of the [Truman] administration on the issue of immigration but very little help, if help at all, on the major issue of the Jewish State. Zionism has been preached and propagandized in this country for many many years, especially in war time primarily, as a philanthropic and humanitarian cause. "Save refugees" was and is the main slogan. . . . We can get everybody, even the non- and anti-Zionist, to help us on immigration; when it comes to the issue of the state most have doubts and are not eager and not too convinced.[43]

Goldmann and Chaim Weizmann, among others, believed it highly likely that the Americans would succeed in persuading the British to accept more Jewish immigrants. Ben-Gurion disagreed. Instead of "bargaining for a certain quota of immigrants" or "begging for mercy," the Jewish Agency and Zionists everywhere, he argued, should continue to demand "that every Jew has the right to immigrate to Palestine."[44]

GERMANY, AUGUST 1945

American military leaders, like British government officials, had advance knowledge of Harrison's findings and recommendations and took preemptive action to lessen their impact. On August 3, General George Marshall, Army chief of staff in Washington, who had seen an advance copy, cabled Eisenhower at his headquarters with the request that he either verify or deny the substance of Harrison's criticisms of the American military's treatment of the Jewish DPs. A week later,

Secretary of War Henry Stimson cabled Eisenhower to voice similar concerns. "I want to emphasize the importance we attach to this problem and request that everything possible be done to improve present situation."[45]

Eisenhower, who was vacationing with General Mark Clark on the French Riviera, flew to Frankfurt to prepare his response to Harrison's report. Already a politician of the highest order, he fully understood the long-term and short-term effects of the report and attempted to dilute its impact in advance of its publication. After long opposing Jewish "liaison" officers, he was now willing, he wrote Secretary of War Stimson on August 10, to "designate a Jewish chaplain to be special advisor on affairs dealing with displaced Jewish persons." Twelve days later, he issued directives to "the commanding generals, western military and eastern military districts" that, from this moment on, all Jews who did not wish repatriation were to "be treated as stateless and non-repatriable" with no questions asked, no pressure applied to return to their former homelands, and that they were to "be segregated as rapidly as possible into special assembly centers," provided with "a high standard of accommodation," and given "priority of treatment over the German population." On August 24, he appointed Judah Nadich, a senior military chaplain, as "Consultant"* on Jewish Activities to the theater commander.[46]

Nadich's first task was to visit the displaced persons camps that housed Jewish survivors. On arrival, he informed the officers in charge that he had been appointed by Eisenhower and reported directly to Walter Bedell Smith, Eisenhower's chief of staff. Doors that might otherwise have been closed were quickly opened.

Nadich concluded that the criticisms Harrison had leveled were, though a bit exaggerated, for the most part accurate, as he would later report to Smith and Eisenhower.

---

* He saved face by appointing Nadich as a "consultant," not a "liaison," as the chaplains and the American congressman had requested. The terms notwithstanding, the "consultant" would do precisely what had been requested of the "liaison."

> In general the centers are overcrowded. . . . The thin walls
> make heating impossible. The roofs leak with every rain. . . . The
> food situation has improved somewhat, but much more remains
> to be done. . . . An almost general need is that of clothing, par-
> ticularly shoes, warm underwear and overcoats. . . . As regards
> furniture the greatest need is for more beds, mattresses, blankets
> and bedding . . . Fuel for the winter is another great problem.

Nadich recommended that additional buildings, even small villages, be requisitioned from the Germans and used to shelter the Jewish DPs; that food, clothing, medical and dental supplies, tools and materials for work programs, cleaning materials, and clothing of all kinds be made available; that the armed guards stationed at some of the camps be removed; that the Joint Distribution Committee be given "greater facilities" in the occupied zone to dispense relief; and that some sort of communication network be set up so that the displaced persons could locate and communicate with "relatives in other camps and in other countries."[47]

On August 31, General Eisenhower received the letter from the president that Chief of Staff Marshall and Secretary of War Stimson had warned him was forthcoming. "I have received and considered the report of Mr. Earl Harrison," Truman wrote Eisenhower.

> While Mr. Harrison makes due allowance for the fact that
> during the early days of liberation the huge task of mass repatri-
> ation required main attention, he reports conditions which now
> exist and which require prompt remedy. . . . I know you will
> agree with me that we have a particular responsibility towards
> these victims of persecution and tyranny who are in our zone. . . .
> I hope you will report to me as soon as possible the steps you
> have been able to take to clean up the conditions mentioned in
> the report. I am communicating directly with the British Gov-
> ernment in an effort to have the doors of Palestine opened to
> such of these displaced persons as wish to go there.[48]

Eisenhower responded that he was taking personal charge of recti-
fying the situation. "I am today starting a personal tour of inspection of
Jewish Displaced Persons installations. General officers of my staff have
also been so engaged for several days. It is possible, as you say, that some
of my subordinates in the field are not carrying out my policies, and any
instances found will be promptly corrected." He promised to give Truman "a detailed report after we complete our current inspections. . . . In
the meantime you can be sure that in the UNITED STATES Zone in
GERMANY no possible effort is being spared to give these people
every consideration toward better living conditions, better morale and a
visible goal."[49]

On September 15, General George Patton noted in his diary that he
had been "notified that General Eisenhower would arrive . . . near Munich at 0930 this morning, having flown from the Riviera. . . . I later
found out that the purpose of his visit was to inspect the DP camps,
particularly at least one occupied by Jews, to determine the condition of
these Jews in order that he may write a letter to Mr. Truman."

> One of the chief complaints is that the DPs are kept in camps
> under guard. Of course, Harrison is ignorant of the fact that if
> they were not kept under guard they would not stay in the camps,
> would spread over the country like locusts, and would eventually
> have to be rounded up after quite a few of them had been shot
> and quite a few Germans murdered and pillaged. . . . Evidently
> the virus started by Morgenthau and Baruch of a Semitic re-
> venge against all Germans is still working. Harrison and his as-
> sociates indicate that they feel German civilians should be
> removed from houses for the purpose of housing Displaced Per-
> sons. . . . Harrison and his ilk believe that the Displaced Person
> is a human being, which he is not, and this applies particularly to
> the Jews who are lower than animals. . . . I do not see why Jews
> should be treated any better or any worse than Catholics, Protes-
> tants, Mohammedans, or Mormons. However, it seems apparent

that we will have to do this, and I am going to do it as painlessly
as possible by taking a certain group of buildings in several cities
and placing the Jews . . . in sort of improved ghettos.[50]

Patton accompanied Eisenhower on his tour of the displaced persons
camps. Their first stop was a Baltic camp in Munich. "The Baltic people," Patton noted in his diary, "are the best of the Displaced Persons
and the camp was extremely clean in all respects." From the Baltic
camp, Eisenhower and his entourage were driven to Feldafing, now a
Jewish camp. The facility, Patton wrote, "had been a German hospital.
The buildings were therefore in a good state of repair when the Jews
arrived but were in a bad state of repair when we arrived, because these
Jewish DP's, or at least a majority of them, have no sense of human re-
lationships. They decline, where practicable, to use latrines, preferring
to relieve themselves on the floor."[51]

Eisenhower's reactions, as noted in his wartime memoir, *Crusade in
Europe,* were quite different. "The Jews were in the most deplorable
condition. For years they had been beaten, starved, and tortured. Even
food, clothes, and decent treatment could not immediately enable them
to shake off their hopelessness and apathy. They huddled together—
they seemingly derived a feeling of safety out of crowding together in a
single room—and there passively awaited whatever might befall." He
contrasted their condition and their camps with those of the Balts,
whom the American military also "classified as stateless; they had fled
because of a record of opposition to the seizure of their countries and
could not return. They were relatively healthy, strong, and quite ready
to work to improve their buildings and surroundings."[52]

General Eisenhower brought a camera crew that filmed him and his
entourage, Patton included, as they greeted passersby, hobnobbed with
civilians and Army officers, and walked through what looked from the
outside like a very pleasant German town. "We all made this inspection
together," recalled Eli Rock of the JDC, who accompanied Eisenhower,
"and we went through the camp and it was obviously overcrowded and

*General Dwight Eisenhower leaves the synagogue he visited on his
second tour of Jewish displaced persons camps in the fall of 1946.*

that was when . . . Eisenhower said to Patton, as we looked at the overcrowded rooms, 'George, if Harry could see this he would sure blow
his top.'"[53]

In what appeared to be a genuine and much-appreciated gesture of
solidarity, Eisenhower and his entourage attended Yom Kippur services.
"We entered the synagogue," Patton later wrote in his diary, "which was
packed with the greatest stinking bunch of humanity I have ever
seen. . . . The smell was so terrible that I almost fainted and actually
about three hours later lost my lunch as the result of remembering it."
Eisenhower, untroubled, it appeared, by the overcrowding or the smells
that so distressed Patton, spoke directly to the crowd through interpreters, promising that the Army would do all it could to make their lives
more comfortable.

The generals concluded their day by taking "a fishing trip on the
lake which," Patton recalled, "while not successful, at least removed

from our minds the nauseous odors and aspects of the camps we had inspected. We then took as long and as hot a bath as we could stand to remove from our persons the germs which must have accumulated during the day."

On leaving Feldafing, Eisenhower, according to Patton, "directed that sufficient Germans be evicted from houses contiguous to the concentration camps [Patton insisted on calling the DP camps with Jewish survivors "concentration camps"] so that the density per capita of DPs and Germans should be approximately the same." He ordered, as well, "that the American guards be removed from the camp except for a standby guard in case of a riot, and that guards composed of unarmed inmates take over the police of the camp proper."[54]

Conditions at Feldafing changed overnight. "As direct result [of] this visit several homes and a hospital will be requisitioned for DPs," a representative of the Joint, probably Eli Rock, cabled New York headquarters. "Military guards will be removed and substituted by DP guards. We [are] hopeful these developments will set pattern [for] other camps." In a later oral history, Rock recalled that the Army had been suddenly galvanized by Eisenhower's personal intervention. The overcrowding was relieved, food flowed in.[55]

The day after his trip to Feldafing, Eisenhower wrote Truman, outlining the steps he had taken to alleviate the deficiencies he had observed, while at the same time downplaying, denying responsibility, and shifting blame for them. He had "personally visited five camps, two of which were exclusively Jewish and a third largely so. . . . In one camp, which was Jewish, I found conditions less than satisfactory, but found also that the camp and local authorities were taking over additional houses in the immediate vicinity, throwing the Germans out of these houses in order to provide more and better accommodations for the displaced persons. . . . I found no instances of displaced persons still living in the old 'horror' camps." In a rather shameless attempt to explain away the horrific conditions Harrison had revealed, Eisenhower, as had Patton, blamed the sanitary problems on a "considerable minority" who had exhibited "a distinct lack of cooperation. . . . The most simple of sanitary regulations were constantly violated to a degree that in some instances could be termed nothing less than revolting, although this has much improved." He was referring to the toilets and latrines, which were permanently clogged and overflowing not because, as the Army complained and would continue to complain, the displaced persons refused to use toilet paper or didn't know that they were supposed to or enjoyed filthy, dangerously unsanitary bathrooms, but because there was a consistent shortage of toilet paper, cleaning supplies, disinfectants, brushes, and brooms. Eisenhower admitted that there had been "undeniable instances of inefficiency" in providing shelter, better food, and necessary supplies for the Jewish DPs, but he was "confident that if you compare conditions now with what they were three months ago, you would realize that your Army here has done an admirable and almost unbelievable job in this respect."

Eisenhower agreed with Harrison that "with respect to the Jews . . . most want to go to Palestine. I note in your letter that you have already instituted action in the hope of making this possible." Any decision in that regard, he admitted, was "distinctly outside any military responsibility or authority. . . . However, the matter draws practical importance for us out of the possibility that caring for displaced persons may be a long-time job."[56]

Eisenhower had succinctly alluded to the central problem that would haunt Truman and the U.S. government for the next three years, if not longer. There was no place on earth, other than the Jewish communities in Palestine, where the Jews were welcome. But as long as the British restricted immigration, the Jewish displaced persons would be condemned to remain in camps in Germany overseen by the military, supported by the American taxpayer.

LONDON, OCTOBER 1945

On September 22, the *New York Times* reported that President Truman had asked the British to immediately grant 100,000 certificates to Jewish DPs for immigration to Palestine. While the DPs, the Jewish chaplains, and those in the United States who were monitoring the situation applauded the president for implementing many of the recommendations of the Harrison Report, the British Foreign Office was near apoplectic that Truman had accepted and was acting on Harrison's "contention . . . that Jewish displaced persons (including persecuted German Jews) should be regarded as non-repatriable and segregated on a racial basis forthwith pending their removal to Palestine or to some other destination outside Europe. . . . To accept this policy," the Foreign Office cabled the embassy in Washington, "is to imply in effect that there is no future in Europe for persons of Jewish race. This is surely a counsel of despair which it would be quite wrong to admit at a time when conditions throughout Europe are still chaotic. . . . Indeed it would go far by implication to admit that Nazis were right in holding that there was no place for Jews in Europe."

"Our task," the Foreign Office declared, is "to create conditions in which they will themselves feel it natural and right to go home rather than to admit at this stage that such conditions are impossible to create. Nor must it be forgotten that the Jews are not the only persecuted group and that groups of German Christians have suffered almost as badly."[57]

The British tried desperately to disentangle the future of the displaced persons from that of Palestine, which Harrison and Truman had bound together. For the British, the only practical solution to the Jewish DP problem was repatriation. For the Americans, the only solution was emigration to Palestine.

On October 3, 1945, the British ambassador to the United States, the Earl of Halifax, reported from Washington that

the tempo of agitation over Palestine is rising here. Zionist organizations with familiar technique are inspiring a stream of post-
cards, letters and resolution of protest at the failure of His
Majesty's Government either to open Palestine to unlimited
Jewish immigration or at least to admit 100,000 Jews from Europe immediately. While there is much talk of broken pledges
the principal emphasis is being laid on the humanitarian aspect. . . . The Zionists are of course taking advantage of the fact
that the elections of 1946 are approaching and that both parties
are anxious to capture the Jewish vote particularly in the key
state of New York.[58]

A week later, Halifax notified London that he "was worried about
the agitation here over Palestine and thought that he would have to try
and do something to calm things down. He hoped to steady the president. He added that it was of course the New York City [mayoral] election that was partly responsible."[59]

The British were frightened that Truman would attempt to outflank
the Republicans, who were trying to steal the traditionally Democratic
Jewish vote in New York City by taking a tougher line on Palestine.
Senator Robert A. Taft had already tried to link negotiations for a loan
to Britain with the Palestine problem.

Prime Minister Attlee and Foreign Secretary Bevin opposed increased Jewish immigration, such as the Americans were pushing for,
because they feared it would result in a three-way civil war between
Arabs, Jews, and British military forces, a civil war that the already
stretched-to-the-limit British were ill-prepared to prevent. The British
worried as well that the Soviets were poised to capitalize on troubles in
the Middle East and enter "into Africa in some form. It is impossible to
foresee which way things are going to turn."

In a lengthy coded cable to British ambassadors in Washington,
Jedda, and Baghdad, Foreign Secretary Bevin insisted that while the
new Labour government required time and careful negotiations with

the Arab nations before any changes could be made in immigration policy, the Americans were, regrettably and unconscionably, forcing them to hasty action for the crassest of political reasons.

> I feel that the United States have been thoroughly dishonest in handling this problem. To play on racial feeling for the purposes of winning an election is to make a farce of their insistence on free elections in other countries. On the other hand the Jews have suffered terribly and this throws up a number of problems which President Truman and others in America have exploited for their own purposes. Should we accept the view that all the Jews or the bulk of them must leave Germany? I do not accept that view. They have gone through, it is true, the most terrible massacre and persecution, but on the other hand they have got through it and a number have survived. . . . I am not satisfied with Earl Harrison's report which looks to me like a device to put pressure on England. I should be very sorry to have to say these things in the House of Commons but I cannot go on submitting to intimidation.[60]

Bevin now believed that the best way to mute American criticism was to make the United States jointly responsible with the UK for the future of the Middle East. Perhaps when the Americans came to appreciate the difficulties posed by extended Jewish immigration into Palestine they would cease their agitation, take into account Arab concerns, and move away from their one-sided support for the Zionists.

Ambassador Halifax was delegated to propose to Secretary of State James Byrnes that their two nations convene a joint Anglo-American Committee of Inquiry "(i) To examine the position of the Jews in British and American occupied Europe as it exists today; (ii) To make an estimate of the number of such Jews whom it may prove impossible to resettle in the country from which they originated; (iii) To examine the possibility of relieving the position in Europe by immigration into other countries outside Europe; and (iv) To consider other available means of meeting the needs of the immediate situation. . . . The question of Jewish immigration into Palestine, among other countries, would fall to be considered . . . under the third" item.[61]

Halifax, in presenting the proposal to Byrnes, subtly chastised him and his government for venturing into territory about which it was entirely ignorant. The American "approach to the problem"—that the British immediately issue one hundred thousand certificates for immigration to Palestine—was not only "most embarrassing," but was "embittering relations between the two countries at a moment when we ought to be getting closer together in our common interests. . . . His Majesty's Government cannot accept the view that all the Jews or the bulk of them must necessarily leave Germany, and still less Europe. That would be to accept Hitler's thesis." Some Jewish DPs, Halifax admitted, had expressed a preference for immigration to Palestine, but their wishes had to be balanced against those of the Arabs who opposed any additional immigration. The important questions that Halifax and Foreign Secretary Bevin hoped the Anglo-American Committee would seek to answer were: how many Jews could be absorbed in Palestine, and was it possible to secure Arab consent to their immigration?[62]

Byrnes was not averse to the idea of an Anglo-American committee, but, as he told Lord Halifax, he worried about the political optics, particularly the fact that the "terms of reference," the issues the committee would be charged with investigating, "as set out do not even mention Palestine." Bevin, by omitting any reference to Palestine, was attempting "to divert the mind of the commission from the Palestine question to finding places [for the Jews] in other countries." Byrnes demanded that the "terms of reference" be amended to include an investigation of the issue of Jewish immigration to Palestine.

Ambassador Halifax agreed that "it might be possible . . . to have a more specific reference to Palestine," just so long as Bevin wasn't put "into a position of accepting a Hitler thesis that there is no room for Jews in Europe."

On November 13, a week after the New York City elections, which the Democrats won handily, President Truman announced that he had agreed to the British proposal for a joint Anglo-American Committee of Inquiry on Palestine. The negative response was immediate and sustained. Secretary Byrnes had earlier warned Halifax that "the Jews are going to say this is just another trick and nothing will be done." This is precisely what occurred.[63]

"The agreement for a joint inquiry," Herbert Matthews wrote in a front-page *New York Times* story, "was construed as a British rejection of [Truman's] plea for the immediate issuance of 100,000 Palestine entry permits. It was attacked" not only by Emanuel Cellar and Jewish activists, but by Democratic senator Kenneth McKellar of Tennessee, who characterized it as "a death sentence to European Jewry."

The outcry against Truman's decision to work with the British was exacerbated when Foreign Secretary Bevin, after briefing the House of Commons on the formation of the Anglo-American Committee of Inquiry, held an informal press conference and made what appeared to be blatantly insensitive, if not antisemitic, remarks. "I am very anxious that Jews shall not in Europe overemphasize their racial position. The keynote of the statement I made in the House is that I want the suppression of racial warfare, and therefore if the Jews, with all their sufferings, want to get too much at the head of the queue you have the danger of another anti-Semitic reaction through it all." Jewish organizations everywhere assailed Bevin's remarks and used the occasion to renew their criticism of President Truman for entering into a partnership with the British to solve the Palestine problem.[64]

"Bevin's declaration . . . generated a tremendous stir" in the Jewish DP camps in Germany, as the Yiddish paper *Undzer Veg* reported. "There was a great sense of disappointment." Any hope that the British Labour government might repeal the White Paper and open Palestine to DP immigration had now been quashed. Spontaneous anti-British demonstrations broke out at Landsberg, Föhrenwald, and Feldafing.[65]

President Truman, in part to counteract that impression that he was insensitive to the plight of the displaced persons and had capitulated to the British, announced on December 22 that he was, by executive order, taking a series of steps that would make it easier for displaced persons to apply for U.S. visas, including the establishment "with the utmost dispatch [of] consular facilities at or near displaced person and refugee assembly center areas in the American zones of occupation."

Truman's directive, though presented with great fanfare, was a charade, a grand public relations gesture, as the Last Million, the voluntary organizations, Congress, and the British officials understood at a glance. The president did not propose any increase in the meager quotas assigned to the Eastern European nations (6,524 from Poland, 386 from Lithuania, 236 from Latvia, and 116 from Estonia), nor did he recommend that the quotas "unused" during the war be made available to the DPs. There were upward of a million displaced persons in Europe; the 1924 quota system, which Truman declared would remain in place, allocated 3,900 visas a month, on a first-come, first-served basis, to all applicants, including displaced persons, from Central and Eastern Europe and the Balkans.

In the end, 22,951 visas would be issued as a result of Truman's directive. Of these, 15,478 would go to Jewish DPs in Germany, in large part because the German quota of 25,957 dwarfed all the others and because the Jewish voluntary agencies in Germany were better positioned than the Catholic or Protestant ones to provide the displaced Jews with the documentation required to get their visas. Catholic DPs received 3,424 visas, under the directive; Protestants 2,968. The fact that Jews far outnumbered Catholics and Protestants would be cited time and again during future debates as proof positive that any attempt to bring displaced persons into the United States would result in the nation being flooded with Eastern European Jews.[66]

Part Three

THE LAST MILLION
IN GERMANY

6.

THE U.S., THE UK, THE USSR, AND UNRRA

"Sharp Differences of Opinion"

B Y EARLY AUGUST 1945, two months after liberation, the Last Million had settled into their camps, been assigned living quarters, met their new neighbors, elected committees to represent their interests. They were safe, sheltered, adequately fed, and, with few exceptions, housed with other displaced persons from their homelands who spoke the same languages, worshipped the same gods. Their chief concern—and this was common to them all, Poles, Balts, Jews, Ukrainians—was that they did not know how long they would be allowed to remain in the camps.

The Soviets and the Eastern bloc nations, devastated by war, demanded that the camps be closed at once and the Last Million, with the exception of the Jews, be sent home to rebuild their war-torn nations. The Americans and the British did not disagree that the camps would have to be closed eventually, but they were not prepared to shut them at present and forcibly evict and repatriate the displaced persons within them.

The forty-four nations that had signed the resolutions establishing UNRRA in November 1943 had agreed to work together in the establishment and operation of a temporary emergency international agency in the hope and expectation that doing so would forestall the chaos, dislocation, mass hunger, economic devastation, political upheavals, and massive, revolutionary regime changes that had followed in the wake of the First World War. The Soviet Union had agreed to join UNRRA in large part because the organization's founding resolutions circumscribed its authority to the extent that it would not compromise the sovereignty and territorial integrity of participating nations.

As Dean Acheson would later put it, the Soviets demanded that "nothing might be done within any given country without that country's consent and except through its agencies." This principle was codified in Resolution 1, Part 1, which specified that UNRRA could not operate in any "geographical territory" without the consent of the civilian or military government that exercised administrative authority in that territory, and in Resolution 57, which directed that UNRRA could only "carry out operations in enemy or ex-enemy areas for the care and repatriation or return of displaced persons . . . in agreement with the government of the country of which they are nationals."[1]

BELGRADE, YUGOSLAVIA, AND LONDON, MAY TO AUGUST 1945

The first nation to invoke UNRRA Resolution 57 was Yugoslavia. In early May 1945, the government of Marshal Tito declared that absent its approval, which had not been given, UNRRA should desist at once from housing, feeding, and maintaining Yugoslav citizens in displaced persons camps, thereby delaying their return to their homelands. One and a half to two million Yugoslavs had been killed during the war, 24 percent of the orchards, 38 percent of vineyards, 60 percent of livestock, and more than 77 percent of rail locomotives and rolling stock destroyed. With the war now at an end, all able-bodied Yugoslavs were needed at home to rebuild the nation. Thousands of forced laborers who had worked in Germany during the war had already returned. But there remained thousands more Yugoslavs in Austria and Italy.[2]

Among them were many who had taken up arms against Tito and his partisans during the civil war that had accompanied the war against the Nazis. Tito was determined to put back together the nation that had been invaded, conquered, and dismembered during the recent war. He was also committed to eliminating all opposition to his rule. The idea that quislings and war criminals who had attempted to topple his regime should be supported by UNRRA was intolerable.

In declaring that UNRRA had no authority to assist Yugoslav citizens without the approval of his government, Tito was not only challenging UNRRA's authority but its very raison d'être. If UNRRA capitulated, Poland and other Eastern European nations might also forbid UNRRA assistance to their citizens. UNRRA would thereby, as the British Foreign Office concluded, be prohibited from taking "care of very large numbers of people in Germany or elsewhere for whose relief no other provision exists."[3]

Director General Lehman took the Yugoslav demand very seriously. If UNRRA continued, despite Tito's objections, to assist Yugoslav citizens, it might "lead not only to violent conflict between Jugoslav authorities and UNRRA with most adverse effect," but also to a "serious split" in the UNRRA General Council. After consulting with the American and British embassies in Belgrade, Lehman determined that the Yugoslav DPs should not be housed in UNRRA camps, but "held provisionally" in camps administered by the Allied military authorities, until an agreement had been reached on the issues Tito had raised.[4]

Barely two months after the war in Europe had come to an end, the future of UNRRA was at risk, and with it, the fate of the Last Million. On July 10, a memorandum from Clair Wilcox, director of the Office of International Trade Policy, to Assistant Secretary of State Will Clayton emphasized the critical importance of resolving the Yugoslav issue before the London UNRRA General Council meeting. "The central question is whether a member government of UNRRA may deny UNRRA assistance to those of its displaced nationals whom it regards as undesirable or possibly disloyal citizens." The Soviets and the Yugoslavs had answered this question in the affirmative. The Americans and British, though agreed that UNRRA assistance should be denied to war criminals, were not prepared to give the Yugoslavs or the Soviets carte blanche to decide who among the displaced persons was eligible and who ineligible for assistance.[5]

UNRRA, the Americans and British insisted, had been founded on and was committed to "the fundamental principle . . . that there is to be no discrimination" in providing relief to war victims "on grounds of race, religion or political belief." If UNRRA allowed member states to decide who would and would not receive such relief, it would in effect be condoning discrimination not only against collaborators, but also against those whose only crime was that they were "not in sympathy" with the governments in place in the countries from which they had been displaced. Refugees in need deserved support. To use "the withdrawal of relief as a lever" to compel the DPs to return was, the British Foreign Office declared, "repugnant to Anglo-Saxon views." The Americans took the same position on UNRRA's obligation to assist all DPs who refused repatriation. In a memorandum for Foreign Minister Molotov, Secretary of State Byrnes declared forcefully that "no other course of action would be acceptable to public opinion in my country."[6]

Sir George Rendel, the chief British delegate to UNRRA, met privately with the Soviet delegates in an attempt to hammer out a compromise in advance of the London General Council meeting. The British, Rendel insisted, did not disagree with the Soviet position that the displaced persons should be repatriated. "The policy of His Majesty's Government was to get the maximum number of people back to their own countries, but it would be to everyone's ultimate advantage that they should go willingly and not be sent back by force."[7]

A compromise was eventually arrived at. The USSR reluctantly agreed that UNRRA could continue to assist displaced persons without the approval of the countries they had come from, but only until mid-February 1946, at which time the issue would be taken up at the next UNRRA General Council meeting.

The USSR, which had submitted a request to UNRRA for $700 million in assistance for Byelorussia and Ukraine, had no real choice but to agree to this compromise. To refuse to do so would have jeopardized its chances of receiving the material assistance required for rebuilding industry, agriculture, and infrastructure.[8]

The most critical item of discussion at the second UNRRA General Council that August was the funding of its rehabilitation and relief budget. The first allocations, which totaled $1.883 billion, $1.35 billion of which came from the United States, had by August 1945 been spent. Director General Herbert Lehman asked the delegates from nations that had not suffered invasion to request of their governments a second allocation, equal to 1 percent of 1943 national income, which for the Americans would come to another $1.35 billion.

In November 1945, President Truman formally requested this amount from Congress. The House passed the measure by a large vote. To get the bill through the Senate, Truman had to assure critics in Congress that there would be no further requests for financial assistance, fight off Republican attempts to reallocate the money from UNRRA to the American Red Cross, and block a hostile amendment, clearly directed at the USSR, that would have barred assistance to any nation that restricted access to American journalists. After a rather strenuous debate with widespread criticism of UNRRA management and questions about whether U.S. dollars should go to Communist-dominated nations, the Senate agreed to the UNRRA appropriation.[9]

GERMANY, APRIL TO DECEMBER 1945

While every group of displaced persons worried about being forcibly ejected from the camps and returned to their former homelands, those who had fled Estonia, Latvia, Lithuania, and western Ukraine had the most to fear. The Soviets, having annexed their homelands, regarded them as Soviet citizens, and as such, subject to immediate repatriation, as agreed to at Yalta. The Americans and British, having never recognized the annexations, rejected the Soviet claims.

American military commanders, knowing that Baltic exiles would be forcibly repatriated if left behind in the Soviet zone, sought permission to move them into the American zones of occupation. On May 21, 1945, SHAEF issued a directive, signed by General Eisenhower, that Estonians, Latvians, and Lithuanians "should not be treated as Soviet citizens nor repatriated to the Soviet Union unless they affirmatively claim Soviet citizenship." Because such actions were bound to anger the Soviets, military personnel in the field were directed not to give "this information [about American policy decisions] to Soviet representatives. If any questions be raised by Soviet representatives concerning this interpretation of the CRIMEAN [Yalta] agreement, it should be suggested that they raise the questions on governmental level."[10]

When these "questions" were formally raised by Foreign Minister Molotov at the Council of Foreign Ministers meetings in London in September 1945, Secretary of State Byrnes patiently explained that "the United States wanted to do what was right about the matter, but under United States law it was difficult to say that a man was a citizen when there was no cession of territory ratified by the United States Government." Ernest Bevin had made the same point earlier in the negotiations. He also did not wish, he apologized to Molotov, "to cause difficulty," but it would be contrary to "Britain's oldest traditions and laws" to ratify changes in citizenship that had been induced by changes in frontiers and not confirmed by a "general peace treaty."[11]

The Baltic refugees might not be Soviet citizens, but neither were they citizens of one of the nations that had taken up arms against the Nazis. On these grounds alone, they should not have been eligible for UNRRA assistance, which, according to the founding resolutions, was to be extended only to citizens of member states of the United Nations.* Why then were Estonian, Latvian, and Lithuanian refugees in Germany recognized as "displaced persons" and afforded UNRRA protection and assistance? Because the American and British governments did not know what else to do with them. Washington and London were not going to direct their occupation forces to send them home, and because they did not recognize the Soviet annexation of the Baltic nations, they were not obligated by the Yalta agreements to do so. But neither could the occupying authorities in Germany leave the refugees alone to fend for themselves in a nation devastated by war. There was no alternative to allowing them to enter and remain in the displaced persons camps.

In the chaos of liberation, with millions of homeless foreigners roaming the streets looking for food and shelter and impeding military transports, the American and British military opened the assembly centers to almost anyone who showed up. Tens of thousands who should have been excluded were allowed inside. Those who did not belong— the quislings, war criminals, and collaborators, German civilians and deserters, and the *Volksdeutsche*—would, it was expected, be sorted out later and sent on their way.

Pranas Puronas, Rita Gabis's Lithuanian grandfather, who with his children and an older sister presented himself at Camp C in Ingolstadt on May 12, 1945, was one of those let inside, though he should not have been. "At the DP camp," according to his granddaughter's account, "he claimed that, during different time frames, he had been a merchant in Lithuania, in flight school and . . . a farmer." He had no trouble hiding

---

* Only in July 1946, fourteen months after liberation, was this anomaly remedied when without explanation, European Region Order 40A redefined "United Nations Nationals" to include "former residents of Estonia, Latvia, and Lithuania." (George Woodbridge, *UNRRA: The History of the United Nations Relief and Rehabilitation Administration*, vol. 3 [New York: Columbia University Press, 1950], 398–99.)

the fact that he had also been chief of the security police under the Gestapo in his hometown, Švenčionys, Lithuania; had worked with the SS there and elsewhere; and had been an active participant in several war crimes, including the "Shooters' Banquet" at Poligon where eight thousand Jews were murdered.[12]

"Our brief from the UN was to house, feed and care for the homeless peoples sent to us by the Army," recalled Mrs. H. Heath, the wife of the British director and welfare officer at a displaced persons camp at Hanau, a small town eighteen miles from Frankfurt.

> It was not for us to enquire into their ethnic or political backgrounds. There is no doubt that within the ten thousand or so people we sheltered there were some who were collaborators. . . . When in late 1945, early 1946 we had the great influx of Baltic peoples into the camps we did not realize what a potentially dangerous political minefield we were taking aboard. To us they were homeless refugees who did not want to return home while their homes were under Russian occupation. Only much later did their complicated history reveal itself. To us they were charming peoples to whom we could easily relate . . . but, it is now known that many of them welcomed the German invasion of their countries as freeing them from the odious Russian Yoke—particularly perhaps the Lithuanians and many of them actively aided the Germans, many more simply turned a blind eye to, for instance, the wholesale massacre of the Jews.[13]

All summer long and into the fall of 1945, Soviet repatriation officers, usually with NKVD connections, appeared at the camps to demand of their American and British counterparts and UNRRA officials that "Soviet citizens" be turned over for repatriation. On August 5, 1945, Mrs. Heath noted in her diary the arrival of a Russian major named Orloff.

Said he. "What do they feel about going home?" P. [the camp director] said he never asked them: it was not his business—it was his business to care for people in his camp and not to indulge in politics at all—all he knew was that the influx of Balts coincided with the taking over of new Kenigsberg [the East Prussian city of Königsberg] by Russia and therefore he presumed they had come because they didn't wish to return. The [Soviet officer] interrupted by saying, "you can't run a camp and not be political!" He was most grim throughout. . . . [The camp director] stated that the Americans and English regarded the Balts as having a right to choose but this was not Russia's view.

Major Orloff was then escorted into the room where the displaced persons were assembled. "He asked what nationality they were—the Estonian Chief said 'Estonian.' Then said the major, 'there is no such place as Estonia. It is the USSR so what nationality are you?' Said the Estonian 'I am a free man—I always have been and I hope I always shall be.' The major said he had the right to force people back to their country."

P said he knew an Estonian living in Estonia was Russian—he was not sure whether an Estonian living out of Russia could be forced back. The Major said it had been agreed at Berlin—which of course P has had no news of yet. P said when the U.S. Army or SHAEF tell him to ship Balts back he will do so without question but his orders for transport come from the army. The major said he considered the Balts had indulged in anti-Soviet propaganda. P said "not in this camp and if I found any man doing so he'd go out on his neck."[14]

The Soviet repatriation officers had one task, and one task only: to return to the USSR as many able-bodied men and women as possible to join in the task of rebuilding a war-torn nation. The Soviet nation had lost too many soldiers and citizens in the recent war to be able to afford even the smallest manpower drain westward and into the displaced persons camps. The Baltic DPs, for their part, wanted nothing to do with the Soviets, who had usurped their country. In several locations, they refused to meet with Soviet repatriation officers; in a few they attempted to forcibly remove them from the premises.

No matter what assurances the repatriation officers might give them, they knew what awaited them across the border. They were not going to be allowed to return directly to their homes and families. They would, on the contrary, have to endure weeks, if not months, of investigation by NKVD agents in "filtration camps." Those who had fought with the German military against the Red Army and those who had served as auxiliary policemen under Nazi command could expect minimum sentences of six years at hard labor. Others whose collaboration had been on the civilian rather than the military side could expect, on crossing into what was now Soviet territory, to be deported to work camps: the Ukrainians to coal mines, timbering industries, or construction sites far from home; the Estonians, Latvians, and Lithuanians to sites closer to home, repairing ports, piers, and naval facilities.*[15]

AMONG THE ALMOST two hundred thousand Baltic nationals[†] who ended the war on German soil were tens of thousands of POWs who had been captured in German uniform. The Americans and British did not know what to do with them. German and other enemy POWs would eventually be freed and returned to their homes and families. But the Baltic POWs refused to return home.

The diplomats who had represented Estonia and Latvia prior to the

* Because the Soviets believed that collaborators could be reeducated and rehabilitated, the majority of the Baltic collaborators would be released from their labor details by the end of 1946.
† This figure is from December 31, 1946. Since few Baltic DPs entered or left Germany from May 1945 to December 31, 1946, it can be considered accurate, if on the low side. ("Estimate: Baltic Displaced Persons in Germany," RG 59, b3, NACP.)

Soviet takeover and were still accredited to Washington, London, and a few other capitals insisted that the Baltic POWs be released from the camps in which they were incarcerated with German POWs and allowed to join their families in the displaced persons camps. Minister Alfred Bilmanis of Latvia patiently explained in a rather detailed letter to Secretary of State Byrnes that the Latvians who had joined Waffen-SS units had done so because they had been forced to, and only after the Germans had assured them that they would not be sent abroad to fight the Red Army but kept at home "as police forces and . . . their duties would be to maintain order in their own country." "Most of those who enlisted, even though on paper they might appear as volunteers, did so as a lesser evil. If a man refused to join the armed forces he was either sent to forced labor or to a concentration camp."[16]

Minister Bilmanis's request that the Latvian POWs be released from military custody was forwarded to the State-War-Navy Coordinating Committee (SWNCC),* which coordinated discussion of occupation issues that involved both military and political considerations. The State Department representative on the coordinating committee was opposed to transferring the Baltic POWs to the displaced persons camps. Despite the minister's arguments to the contrary, the State Department believed that it was "possible that many of these persons may have actually volunteered for service in the German armed forces and have been thoroughly indoctrinated in the ideology of National Socialism." Fully cognizant of the strain placed on the military, which had to staff and guard the POW camps, the State Department conceded that if "the military authorities in Germany, after careful investigation, consider that any individuals or small groups of persons of Latvian citizenship among German prisoners of war have been forced to serve with the German armed forces, they should be released from prisoner of war camps and segregated with other Latvian citizens in displaced persons camps."[17]

---

* SWNCC, later reorganized as the State–Army–Navy–Air Force Coordinating Committee (SANACC), had been created in December 1944.

The British Foreign Office was also opposed to the release of the Baltic POWs into the DP population.

> We regret that we cannot recommend favourable treatment for Latvians (or other Baltic nationals) captured in German uniform and now held as prisoners of war. It is impossible to distinguish between those who enlisted voluntarily and those who joined up under duress. The War Office say that the only concession which can be made is that of segregation from the Germans [but] any relaxation of security . . . is most undesirable in view of the fact that they are unscreened and in many cases have fought voluntarily against the Soviet Union.[18]

For the time being, at least, the Baltic soldiers and officers captured in uniform and interned as POWs would be denied status as displaced persons. Those, however, who had had the foresight to strip off their uniforms, destroy their army papers, and evade capture and imprisonment as POWs had no difficulty gaining entrance to the camps.

Andrejs Eglitis had served in the Latvian Luftwaffe squadron, but in January 1945 had left the unit, buried his uniform, stowed away on a barge to Danzig, and made his way to a farming community southwest of Berlin where he had spent the last months of the war. Soon after the German surrender, he learned that the Americans had organized a refugee assembly center about ten miles from the farm where he was working. Eglitis put on his best suit of clothes and walked to the center. "Original registration was done the first day of our arrival, identifying us by name and rationality. . . . I kept my 'soldier book' in my sock. This document I had to hide. If the Americans had found this paper identifying me as a German Luftwaffe member, I would have been put in a prisoner-of-war camp."

Once in the DP camp, he recalled, "a procedure was established to obtain papers. Two witnesses were needed to identify a person." Eglitis had no shortage of individuals who would vouch for him, including his friend Johan, a Latvian who had also served in a German military unit. Having secured signatures from his two witnesses, Eglitis presented them to the UNRRA officials, who approved his papers. "After I received my official ID papers, I felt I was an official person again, walking on the earth as a recognized citizen. Finally, I could get rid of my 'soldier book' identifying me as a German Luftwaffe member."[19]

THE SITUATION OF UKRAINIANS who had lived within the boundaries of Poland before the war was similar to that of the Baltic nationals. The Soviets, having annexed their lands, claimed them as citizens; the British and Americans, not having recognized the Soviet annexation, did not. For those who had lived east of the Curzon Line and had been Soviet citizens prior to 1939, there was no such ambiguity. They were, the Americans, British, and Soviets agreed, citizens of the USSR, and as such, subject to immediate, if necessary, involuntary repatriation.

The Ukrainians had arrived in Germany in two separate migratory waves: two million or so had been deported as forced laborers during the war; a much smaller number, including some collaborators, members of the Galician Waffen-SS units, and the ultranationalist Ukrainian Insurgent Army (UPA) partisans, had arrived in the last year of the war and thereafter. Most of the forced laborers returned home as soon as they were able. Two hundred thousand, however, including large numbers who had arrived in the second wave of migration, sought refuge in the displaced persons camps.[20]

Julia Bresinuk, a forced laborer who had been deported from her family's farm in Ukraine in the summer of 1943, had worked as a lathe operator in a German factory and lived in a nearby barracks for two years. With the war over, her first impulse, shared by most of the girls with whom she had worked, was to return home to her family farm. They were dissuaded from doing so by a former college professor they met in the village square where the Ukrainian exiles gathered after the war.

"Don't go home," the professor warned the younger Ukrainians.

"I had not seen my family in two years! What the hell was he talking about! 'Why not.'"

"It would be different if Germany had won the war," he argued. "Then the Ukraine would be a free, independent country again." He was wrong on this but that did not stop him.

"I've got a wife and two children in the Ukraine, but I'm not going back, I'm not risking dying in a Communist jail. Maybe I can send for my family later or go back when things get better. We could all wind up in jail back there."

"Why would I go to jail?" Julia asked. "I didn't do anything wrong."

"You helped build airplanes for the Germans," the professor answered, "and those planes dropped bombs on Russia. We could all be considered enemies. Ukrainians were never really part of Russia anyway, we were like slaves to the Russians. . . . You can do what you want, but I'm not going back."

Julia, her boyfriend, the professor, and their Ukrainian friends refused repatriation and, two months after the war had ended, worried that the section of Germany they were living in might soon be handed over to the Soviets, set off toward the American zone of occupation. "There were ten of us, each person had a bundle of clothes. Some of the men had bicycles and knapsacks; the women rode double. The men had stolen food from the people they had worked for. . . . We didn't really consider it stealing. We had all been treated like second class citizens by the Germans, and harassed by the police and Hitler youth. Whatever we took, we felt we deserved."

They rode bicycles until the bikes broke down, then walked. "We traveled for about a week, sleeping in fields, once in a ditch, and one night in an abandoned building that appeared to have been a small barracks. We followed the road the Americans had taken, there were railroad tracks next to it, and we tried to keep the tracks in sight. . . . We reached a big freight yard, but we didn't know where we were. The professor figured we had traveled over a hundred miles." They climbed "onto the emptiest boxcar of the westbound train. . . . After about three

Polish DPs on top of a train in an assembly center in
July 1945, awaiting assignment to a DP camp.

days, the slow train reached a refugee camp in Füssen, Germany. We
were half starved."

Scenes like this played out all through Germany and Austria, wherever Ukrainians gathered, in public squares after liberation, then in the
displaced persons camps, as men like the "professor," anti-Soviet and
anti-Communist, convinced younger, less well educated Poles and
Ukrainians to resist repatriation and seek admission to the displaced
persons camps.[21]

7.

INSIDE THE DP CAMPS

Marooned in Germany

B Y THE AUTUMN OF 1945, the task of sorting out the Last Million and moving them into more or less ethnically homogeneous camps had been completed. So too the preparation of the camps for winter weather. Responsibility for day-to-day administration had been turned over by the American and British military to UNRRA in October 1945, though the formal agreements would not be signed by the British until November 27 and the United States on February 19, 1946.[1]

With the assistance of the occupying military, UNRRA, and the voluntary relief agencies, the Last Million transformed their temporary shelters into near-permanent, self-sufficient island communities. After the pain and insecurities they had endured during the war, they were delighted to have roofs over their heads; living quarters that were overcrowded, but adequate; nurses and doctors to care for them; and the security that came with knowing that hostilities had ceased, that they need no longer fear marauding soldiers or aerial bombardments.

They had been dispersed to over a thousand camps, most of them in the American zones of Germany, a smaller number in the American zones in Austria and Italy. Dozens more camps had been set up in the British zones and several in the French. Not surprisingly, there were no camps in the Soviet zone. The USSR had soon after the German surrender notified UNRRA that it was not going to request its assistance in caring for the displaced persons in its zones of occupation. Soviet citizens would be sent home; DPs who required assistance were transported in Allied trucks across the zonal borders into the British and American sectors.

To demonstrate to the displaced persons that they did not intend to treat them as a subject population, American and British military officers held elections for camp committees in the fall of 1945. At Landsberg, a Jewish camp in the American zone, Major Irving Heymont conducted the elections "American style," as he wrote his wife, with speeches, handbills, posters, rallies, and printed ballots with space for write-ins. "One party hired a truck, decorated it with placards and people singing and shouting . . . and ran it all around the camp." Two weeks later, after the elections had been concluded, he wrote his wife again to tell her that he believed they had "served many good purposes. . . . For one, the army is very much afraid of being accused, as it has been, of not treating the people in a democratic manner. They have been accused of running the camp in a dictatorial manner and not allowing the people any voice. They have been accused of arbitrarily picking leaders and dealing exclusively with them. For that reason the army insists on having elections."[2]

As UNRRA took over the day-to-day administration of the camps, it continued the practice of permitting camp residents to elect their leaders—and for much the same reasons. Free elections, it contended, offered the Last Million who had lived "for years under Nazi totalitarianism . . . a chance to practice the fundamentals of democracy."[3]

Elected committees and camp residents appointed by them were put in charge of a wide variety of critical tasks: maintaining and repairing barracks, streets, and housing blocks; supervising the labor office and the post office; managing the admission of newly arrived displaced

A boxing match in the Neu Freimann DP camp, 1948.

persons and assigning them living quarters; policing camp interiors and perimeters and guarding the gates against intruders; overseeing communal kitchens; distributing food packages, clothing, and supplies from UNRRA, the military, the Red Cross, and other voluntary relief agencies; organizing sports clubs and intracamp and intercamp competitions (soccer in all the camps; volleyball, basketball, gymnastics, and track and field in the Baltic; boxing in the Jewish); planning and holding cultural events, dances, concerts, and patriotic and holiday celebrations and pageants; staffing libraries and reading rooms; setting up and supervising kindergarten, elementary, high school, and scouting programs for the young and vocational training centers for adults; running clinics, sickrooms, and hospital facilities.

Electing DPs to leadership positions in the camps was a double-edged sword for the military and UNRRA. In the short term, it made administering the camps possible. In the long term, however, the elections exacerbated political tensions in the camps and between the DPs and UNRRA and the DPs and the occupying military authorities.

Parties were formed, reflecting divisions over possible futures for the "nations" confined in the camps. In the Polish camps, the question of whether or not to return to a Poland under Soviet domination or to create an autonomous Polish nation in exile loomed large; in the Jewish camps, the initial divisions were between Zionists and Bundists,* then between factions aligned with the political parties in the Yishuv. In the Baltic camps, parties fought for the power and patronage that came with elected office; in the Ukrainian camps, where political tensions were most intense, the focus was on the structure and ethnic composition of a future Ukrainian nation.

THOUGH THE LAST MILLION lived in island communities, separated by wire fences from German civilians, they interacted with them on an almost daily basis. In all but the Jewish camps, a sizable number of displaced persons worked outside the camps. The Jewish DPs refused to work for or with Germans, or in fact to do anything that might contribute to German society or the German economy. They were nonetheless connected to the civilian population, as were the other national groupings, through the black market.

While DP rations were sufficient to keep body and soul together and larger than those given Germans, the camp diet was overloaded with bread, potatoes, bean soup, tinned meat, and turnips, and lacking in fresh vegetables and fruits, meats, eggs, milk, and butter. Packages from the Red Cross, CARE, and the voluntary agencies provided some foodstuffs, including cheese, sardines, Spam, dried milk, shortening, and occasionally chocolate, but the only place to secure fresh vegetables and meats was on the black market.

The Last Million were, of course, not alone in suffering from food

---

* The Bund was a secular Jewish political organization based in Poland and Latvia, which used Yiddish to appeal to and organize a working-class Jewish base. The party was ideologically socialist, but not Communist, and a strong advocate of trade unions. It sponsored cultural activities, was devoted to a secular Jewish education, had its own press, and supported a number of protest activities, some illegal. The Bund was also anti-Zionist.

shortages. Europe was starving in the immediate postwar years, with minimal rations allocated to civilians. The brutally cold winter of 1946–47 made everything worse. The Germans supplemented their rations with vegetables from their gardens or from nearby relatives' farms. They bartered for food with their neighbors and shopkeepers.[4]

There were open-air markets in every town and city square, in railway stations, and in some of the camps. Because the German reichsmarks were nearly worthless, certainly to the Americans, Lucky Strikes, Chesterfields, Camels, and Philip Morris cigarettes "became the universally accepted coin of the realm, the standard unit of exchange." American GIs and civilians like Lucy Dawidowicz, who worked for the JDC, were given allotments of a carton a week, but secured more from home to barter on the black market. "Cigarettes," Dawidowicz wrote in her memoir, "could buy you anything on the black market from a loaf of coarse black bread to a Persian rug. One of my colleagues bought a prewar German portable typewriter in good condition for five cartons; another bought a German radio for five cartons. With enough cigarettes you could acquire a fine leather suitcase or a stolen original artwork."[5]

The displaced persons functioned most often as middlemen in black market enterprises, trading cigarettes or soap—Palmolive was preferred—or chewing gum or other goods they got from the soldiers or from the camp warehouses and kitchens for food or clothing for their own use, or for currency, whiskey, cameras, perfumes, nylons, or other items, which they traded back to the GIs. UNRRA officials tried, without much success, to make sure that every item that came into the camp was consumed there. They guarded the camp gates and perimeters and staged frequent raids. But supplies disappeared from trucks and warehouses, only to be magically transmuted into coveted items, like the livestock that were butchered and distributed inside the camps: pork for the Poles, beef for the Jews.

"There is no doubt that black marketing is going on among the

DPs," Irving Heymont wrote his wife, Joan, on November 8, 1945. The Army and UNRRA were paying DPs to work in the camp by giving them items from Red Cross packages. These items were being traded on the black market, in addition to the cigarettes.

While most of the trading was small-scale and for food items, there were in every camp larger operators who had made the black market their full-time occupation. Their goal, according to Heymont, was "to accumulate either American currency or items like watches and jewelry. These people are out to build some form of tangible and highly portable wealth good anywhere. They want to build up a stake to start them off in their new life when they eventually get to some permanent place. They will pay exorbitant prices in marks for watches or jewelry or American dollars. They do this because they know that a watch or a diamond are easy to carry and can be converted into money anywhere."[6]

While every group of displaced persons participated in the black market, the Jews, and to a lesser extent the Poles, were harassed most often. The GIs and the Germans, without whom there would have been no black market at all, were seldom held accountable. Engaging in the oldest of slanders, German civilians accused the Poles of inbred criminality and the Jews of being scheming, thieving, unscrupulous scoundrels. They were both blamed for corrupting German civilians and despoiling their economy.[7]

In 1949, Theodor Adorno, with other members of the reconstituted Frankfurt Institute for Social Research, undertook a mammoth empirical study in which German citizens were questioned about their attitudes toward the displaced persons, the Jews in particular. "It is hardly saying too much that, throughout, [the DPs] function as scapegoats and are used to justify retrospectively what was done to the Jews, or at least as an appeal to extenuating circumstances. . . . The archaic hatred against the foreign per se merges here with the anti-Semitic stereotype and Sadism against those who have nothing." Some of the German farmers who were interviewed went so far as to blame the behavior of the Jewish DPs for German antisemitism. "Now we've got hatred for Jews, it didn't exist at all earlier!"[8]

THE LAST MILLION occupied a peculiar place and time—and they understood this. Theirs were among the first refugee camps of the twentieth century, the precursors for those to follow. Never before had so many civilian victims of war been gathered up as they had been, given food and shelter, sorted by nationality, and, when they refused to return home, allowed to remain in the camps that had been designed as staging centers for their repatriation. Though the Last Million were effectively "stateless," they governed themselves as if they were outposts of nation-states soon to be reborn. The Estonians, Latvians, Lithuanians, and Poles struggled to keep alive, in exile, the aspirations of their people for independent nation-states. The Ukrainians, in the camps as they could not in their homeland, sustained and openly displayed nationalist dreams of an ethnically homogeneous, independent Ukraine. The Jews pursued the Zionist project of creating a Jewish homeland in Palestine.

The central committees, as elected representatives of these nations-in-exile, functioned as symbolic national governments. Their main focus was on promoting a cultural nationalism that would hold their "people" together until such time as they could return to the "nations" that had been taken from them or, in the case of the Jews, were yet to be born. The committees maintained communications between the camps. Theater and music groups traveled from one camp to another. Intercamp sporting competitions in soccer, track and field, and boxing were organized. The Jewish camps held dozens of such competitions, including a zonal chess tournament and boxing championships. On the evening of January 29, 1947, some two thousand people from the Jewish camps attended the finals of the boxing championships in Munich. At this particular event, experience won out over youth, three of seven bouts ended in knockouts, and the Landsberg team did particularly well.[9]

Lithuanian kindergarteners in traditional dress for a national celebration.

Camp leaders oversaw the construction and presentation of patriotic displays and performances to commemorate the "nations" they were a part of. Local committee leaders and regional and zonal central committees sponsored history and language training for the young, as well as national theaters and choirs, orchestras, chamber music groups, and bands. Camp residents kept alive folkloric and handicraft traditions; wrote, edited, published, and circulated native-language newspapers, periodicals, and literary journals; and observed national holidays and independence days in folk costumes with parades, speeches, and musical events.

The Poles celebrated May 3, the day on which the Polish constitution had been adopted in 1719, and November 11, the day on which an independent Poland had been reborn in 1918. The Latvians' national holiday was "Proclamation Day" on November 18, the anniversary of the 1918 "Proclamation of Independence." The Jewish DPs, with neither homeland nor independence day, celebrated April 15 in the

British zone, the date when Bergen-Belsen was liberated. In the American zone, the Central Committee celebrated 14 Iyar on the Hebrew calendar, the date of the Second Passover, when those who had been unable to attend the seder were permitted to observe the holiday belatedly. The Jewish days of liberation were also marked as days of mourning for the dead.[10]

Anticipating that their nations-in-exile were the precursors of future independent nation-states, the central committees established historical commissions and assembled archival collections to document this transitional period in their national histories. Such archives, they hoped, would provide the vital link establishing a sense of continuity between their nations' past and future.[11]

THE BALTIC CAMPS

The camps that housed the Baltic displaced persons were, it was universally agreed by the military, UNRRA officers, voluntary agency staffers, and visiting journalists, cleaner, more hospitable to outsiders, and better organized than any of the others. There was no mystery as to why. Most of the Baltic DPs had left home voluntarily with their extended families, their health, and some of their belongings intact.

"The Lithuanians, Latvians and Estonians are by far the richest and most cultured," the British director of the DP camp at Hanau recorded in his diary in late July. "A very high percentage are intellectuals and some have high Government positions. They have brought mountains of baggage, furniture, motor cars and 84 horses. The feeding of these horses has been a problem but we have now arranged to hire some German farmers for payment and the army will feed the others."[12]

Settled in the camps, the Baltic refugees attempted—and to some degree succeeded—in replicating structures of daily life from their homelands. Mothers remained at home and cooked and cleaned. Fathers went off to work at jobs in the camp or outside. The children attended school. Young adults took classes in German universities or in the so-called Baltic University, taught in their own languages by professors and scholars from their homelands. On weekends and holidays, the children played sports or enjoyed the outdoors; families visited with one another and, on Sundays, attended church. There was a stability in the Baltic camps that was sorely missing elsewhere. Camp populations were stable, with no movement in of new refugees, as in the Jewish camps, and no movement out or pressure or debate over repatriation, as in the Polish.[13]

Eileen Egan of Catholic Relief Services, who visited several different camps, was most impressed by the Baltic. "Under the flags of Estonia, Latvia and Lithuania, nationals of the three countries' elected camp officials welcomed us with grave courtesy. We felt at home with them. They spoke smooth English. . . . More than a thousand Baltic exiles were proving that their little countries were advanced in democracy, in culture, more advanced in literacy than perhaps our own country."[14]

Kathryn (Kate) Hulme, UNRRA assistant director at Wildflecken, the largest of the Polish camps, had graduated from Berkeley, lived in Paris as an expatriate writer before the war, then worked as a welder in a California shipyard during the war. She arrived in Germany with the first contingents of UNRRA workers in July of 1945. In 1953, she published *The Wild Place*, a memoir about her work in Germany from 1945 to 1950. In 1956, she wrote the bestselling *The Nun's Story* about the Belgian nun who was, according to her *New York Times* obituary, "her companion and business partner for several years."

Though Hulme spent most of her time at Wildflecken, she visited several nearby camps for Baltic DPs on a regular basis and was struck by the difference between the Polish and the Baltic camps. While the Polish camps were marked by chaos, with new residents arriving and old ones leaving, with infighting over jobs and assignments, at the Baltic camps, the "camp organization . . . ran like well-oiled machinery with the same workers continuously in the same jobs, and theaters, choirs, schools and churches developed to a degree that made these camps seem like self-governing townships, each with an elected camp leader who functioned like the mayor of any small town."

Conflict between the residents and UNRRA officials was minimal. "The UNRRA people press buttons and get things done without threat or cajolery or the persuasion of an extra pack of cigarettes to meet a directive's deadline. The [Baltic] camps were the show places to which visitors were taken."[15]

The residents openly acknowledged their gratitude for the assistance they were receiving. As the *Lithuanian Bulletin,* a publication of the Lithuanian National Council in the United States, reported enthusiastically in November 1945:

> Lithuanian refugees realize fully the difficulties facing UNRRA, and they state that UNRRA has done and is doing all that is possible to provide better and more spacious quarters, and decent living and cultural standards. . . . The solicitous hand of the Military and UNRRA is seen everywhere and in everything—in material provisions for the refugees, in educational and recreational facilities, in providing medical assistance in cooperation with the Lithuanian Red Cross and Lithuanian Committees. . . . UNRRA encourages the establishment of primary, secondary, trade and professional schools. Professors and university students were allowed to meet and to establish their academic centers. A small number of Lithuanians, mainly doctors, nurses and social workers, are employed by UNRRA. . . . There is a Lithuanian Priests' (Roman Catholic) Seminary in operation, and a University is being planned. . . . Periodicals and almanacs are printed. Boy and girl scout movements are again rapidly reappearing among the Lithuanian youth. . . . Typewritten and mimeographed newspapers are printed in a great many centers. . . . Concerts and plays are regularly staged in the camps.[16]

The British and the Americans encouraged self-rule and cultural activities in the DP camps, while recognizing the inherent danger of overt expressions of cultural nationalism. In a lengthy memorandum, Thomas Brimelow of the Foreign Office directed its officers in Germany to erect and maintain an unbreachable boundary between educational and political activities in the camps.

> As regards the request . . . that university courses be organized by the Latvian Professors and Lecturers in the British zone for the Latvian students there, we think on balance it is desirable to grant this request provided you are able to exercise an adequate degree of control over the courses in order to ensure that they are purely academic and not political. We should not like the idea of leaving large numbers of teachers and students in idleness. On the other hand, we do not want them to build up a political group. Everything will therefore depend on the control which you are able to exercise.

The Latvians had requested permission to publish their own newspapers; the Lithuanians wanted to set up a "broadcasting service." The Foreign Office denied both requests. "We should see no objection, however, to the issue of Latvian translations of factual British news reports provided they are not accompanied by any comment." The same held true for Boy Scout and Girl Guides formations in the camps. They would be permitted in the camps, but only if "supervised by the British. . . . In general, we wish to discourage any form of political activity. . . . We do not want the Balts in our zone to be allowed to become a political entity, but they should be looked after, educated and trained for useful employment where it can be obtained for them."[17]

The American and British occupation authorities—and UNRRA— were engaging in a fool's errand in trying to erect and police the boundary between the cultural and the political. For nations-in-exile, be they Ukrainian, Latvian, Estonian, Lithuanian, or Polish, the cultural *was* the political. Performing national plays and dances; preserving languages and literatures; studying folklore and history; learning and singing songs; and wearing national costumes were expressions of cultural nationalism that were designed to sustain the "nation" in exile, until such time as the Soviet usurpers could be dislodged.

The children who grew up in the camps remembered them rather fondly. The journey from home had been marked by terror, hunger, sleepless nights, endless treks on foot. But once they arrived in the camps, everything changed, almost overnight. While their parents may have been tormented by the loss of their homelands, their property, their fortunes, and beset, no matter how often the Allies reassured them, by near-constant fears of the threat of forcible repatriation and punishment for real or perceived collaboration, the children enjoyed their friends, hikes in the fields, soccer and volleyball games, and abundant food—warm porridge in the morning, snacks in the afternoon, ice cream on special occasions.[18]

The overall mood in the Baltic camps was one of optimism. The displaced persons missed their homes, their family members left behind, and their nation-states, but their longing was tempered by the expectation that they would soon be able to return home, dig up the valuables they had buried in the backyard, and begin life again. They would devote their time in exile to preparing for a seamless return: to educating the young, keeping their culture and customs alive, and demonstrating to the western Allies that that they were civilized peoples who deserved whatever diplomatic or military assistance might be necessary to liberate their nations from the Soviets.

Ferdinand Kool, who had fled Estonia in September 1944, entered the Augsburg-Hochfeld DP camp with his wife and daughter in the summer of 1945 and remained there for five years. He would, on emigrating to the United States, create an impressive though unwieldy archive that was later merged with the archives of the Estonian National Council in the United States. In *DP Chronicle*, his massive annotated memoir and history, he recalled that "the time between the Spring of

*A Polish family
registers at the DP
assembly center,
May 1945.*

1945 and the end of the year, when life in the refugee camps was being organized, can justifiably be called the most hopeful and positive DP period. . . . It seemed impossible that the democratic West would allow permanent enslavement of the people in the Baltic States or in any other part of Europe." The occupation of their homelands by the Soviets, then the Germans, then the Soviets again, was not permanent, but a caesura, a pause, a brief interval.[19]

THE POLISH CAMPS

UNRRA and military officials focused much of their attention and re-sources on the non-Jewish Polish camps, where the largest portion of the Last Million resided, and from which they hoped and expected they would soon repatriate hundreds of thousands of DPs.

There was no possibility, UNRRA knew, of persuading any of the

Baltic, Ukrainian, or Jewish DPs to accept repatriation. The non-Jewish Poles were different. Large numbers had, at the moment of liberation, appeared more than ready to return to their homes. The Poles in the DP camps Quaker relief worker Margaret McNeill worked in were, she recalled, during "that hot summer of 1945, impatiently clamouring, 'When do we go back to Poland?'" Grigor McClelland, a volunteer for the Quaker Friends Ambulance Unit in Germany, observed as well that "most of the Poles here want to go back to their own country." The British chargé in Washington in a memo for the American secretary of state estimated in late August that "no less than 378,000 of approximately 500,000 Poles at present held in displaced persons camps in the British zone are willing to go home now. This number is far greater than was expected at this early stage."[20]

Their repatriation had been delayed when the Soviets demanded, and the British and Americans agreed, that Soviet POWs, soldiers, and civilians would be granted priority in repatriation. Only in August 1945, after the bulk of the Soviets had been returned home, was it even feasible to begin planning for the repatriation of the Poles. The provisional government in Warsaw, newly recognized by the Americans and British, was consulted, timetables were set, trains and trucks and ships requisitioned, transfer stations and routes designated. Some thought was given to marching the Poles by foot through Czechoslovakia, but that was rejected by President Bolesław Bierut of the provisional government, who "was apprehensive that physical condition of group would not permit their coming via foot-march." As late as mid-September, Under Secretary of State Dean Acheson pushed the American military to "proceed as rapidly as possible in order [that the] maximum number [of Polish DPs] be returned prior to beginning winter season." Arrangements had been secured with the Soviets, who would not offer their own trucks and trains to repatriate Poles, but would not block the British and Americans from using theirs.[21]

In October, 117,494 non-Jewish Polish DPs returned home from Germany; in November, another 106,400. By December, as bad weather

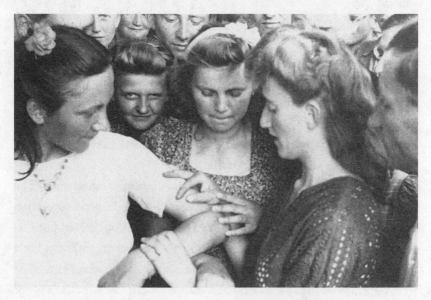

Polish girls who had been deported to Germany and forced to serve as workers, now liberated, gather in an assembly center. They are looking at a Nazi tattoo on one girl's arm.

made passage over most routes dangerous, if not impossible, the number of returnees decreased to 43,221; by January, repatriation had ceased entirely.[22]

By the time spring arrived and travel from Germany into Poland was again possible, a notable shift in attitudes toward repatriation was evident in the camps. A considerable number of the more than four hundred thousand to half a million Polish DPs who had spent the fall and winter of 1945–46 in the DP camps were now undecided about whether to return home or remain, for the time being at least, on German soil. There were myriad reasons to refuse or delay repatriation. The Poland the forced laborers had left when they were deported to Germany five to six years earlier no longer existed. Cities had been devastated, farms abandoned, infrastructure destroyed, 69,000 square miles in the east, including the cities of Lwów and Vilna, had been incorporated into the Soviet Union.[23]

Tough decisions had to be made, with very little concrete information. After years in Germany, and perhaps having learned enough of the language to get along, some Polish DPs had come to the conclusion that they had a better chance of feeding themselves and their families there than in Poland. Others delayed repatriation because they had been encouraged to believe that if they held out long enough, they would be invited to emigrate to lands of opportunity outside Europe: to the United States or Canada or Australia.

Political conditions in Poland remained fluid but unsettling. The pro-Soviet government had not yet stifled dissent, outlawed opposition parties, seized property, or collectivized the agricultural sector, but neither had it held promised free elections or withdrawn its military. For a minority of the Polish population, in the camps and at home, the Soviets were regarded as the heroes who had rescued them from the Nazis. For many more, however, they were brutes who had no intention of restoring independence, but on the contrary were preparing to incorporate Poland into a greater Russia or Soviet Union. Underground armed opposition to the provisional government and the occupying Soviet forces appeared to be strengthening. "The situation in Poland from 1945 to 1947," according to historian Halik Kochanski, "was close to a civil war."[24]

Given these uncertainties, it was no wonder that large numbers of Polish displaced persons who had lived in Germany for up to five years hesitated before returning home, frightened that there was no future for them there. There were countless historical precedents for the refusal of displaced Poles to go home again. Through the long nineteenth century, Poles in exile had, as Anna D. Jaroszyńska-Kirchmann argues in *The Exile Mission*, "struggled against the attempts of foreign administrations to make them forget who they were and to transform them into Germans or Russians. Poles consciously resisted the politics of denationalization and took special care to preserve and to develop Polish national culture, language, traditions, and history."[25]

The notion that the displaced persons could better serve their "nation" by remaining in exile than by returning home was promoted by the organized anti-repatriation campaign inspired, directed, and funded by the anti-Communist government-in-exile in London, which, though no longer recognized by the Americans, the British, or the Soviets, continued to exercise considerable moral authority in the camps. The argument advanced by the London Poles and their supporters was simple but effective: patriotic, freedom-loving Poles should not consider returning to their native land so long as it was dominated by the Soviets and their puppets. To do so would be to accept, to legitimize Soviet rule. Better to remain in exile soliciting international support and preparing for the overthrow of the usurpers.

Questions about repatriation dominated the election campaigns for leadership positions in the Polish camps. At Wildflecken, in northern Bavaria, where the Americans had converted a former military base into a huge camp with more than fifteen thousand Polish DPs, elections for a municipal council were "fractured along ideological lines drawn in large part around the issue of repatriation," historian Adam Seipp has written. "Camp politics revolved around a small leadership cohort with strong ideological ties to the London-based government-in-exile."[26]

"Most of the officer and property-owning class," Marvin Klemme, an UNRRA officer, later wrote of the Polish camps, "were afraid to go home because they believed that they would be wiped out, either by the Russians or by the Communists of their own country." They "used their influence to keep the workers from going back. This attitude produced considerable friction not only among the Polish groups but between the Polish leaders and British and American military government officials" charged with repatriating the DPs.[27]

In Bavaria, in the American zone, where Francesca Wilson, an UNRRA welfare officer, was stationed, anti-Communist Polish officers released from POW camps "volunteered for DP work, and became camp commandants and teachers of Polish children. . . . At one time, a number of Polish officers toured the camps, warning their people against return to a 'communist-controlled' Poland. The American authorities, longing to be rid of the DP nuisance, sent directives to camp commandants forbidding anti-Soviet propaganda, and many tried honestly to combat it, but the air was thick with it and it was not easy."[28]

The Polish provisional government in Warsaw attempted to counter the anti-repatriation propaganda with generous inducements to return home. A special office was established to provide assistance and land or jobs in industry and coal mining to displaced persons who volunteered to settle in the territories taken from Germany.

The members of the provisional government understood, as did their Soviet sponsors, that to win the support of a population, including the hundreds of thousands of displaced persons still in Germany and Austria, they had to establish some semblance of independence. To showcase their nationalist credentials, the Warsaw government implemented "a forceful campaign to transform Poland into an ethnically homogenous nation-state 'freed' from the 'burden' of large Ukrainian, German, Byelorussian and Lithuanian 'national minorities.'" To demonstrate that it was sensitive to the needs of the peasants and small landowners, it redistributed, but did not collectivize, large landholdings. "Large factories, mines, banks and trade enterprises were taken into state ownership, but smaller businesses were allowed to remain in private hands and Poland's strong cooperative movement was allowed to continue expanding."

Democracy was not in bloom in Poland, but it had not been prior to the war, either. The provisional government clamped down on outright political opposition to its rule and delayed the promised free elections, but it did not outlaw either of the two major non-Communist parties, the Polish Socialist Party and the Polish Peasant Party. And not only did it not move against the Catholic Church, it encouraged the church to extend its influence into the new territories taken from Germany. The onslaught of Stalinization that would transform the country had not yet occurred.[29]

American volunteers, military officers, and UNRRA staff in Germany could not quite understand the reluctance of the non-Jewish Poles to go home again. "There was little reason why most of the peasants and industrial workers shouldn't return," Marvin Klemme recalled in his

1949 memoir. "They had no property that anyone wanted and they were generally not on record as being opposed to Communism. They were the kind of people that the country wanted and needed, regardless of the type of government that might be in power. Probably the majority of these common people preferred to return home but were discouraged in different ways from doing so. . . . It wasn't the fear of political reprisals that kept most peasants and workers from returning to Poland, but rather it was the fear of conditions that they would find when they got there. Most of them were afraid that they would not be returned to their former homes," but would be asked or required to resettle in the new Polish lands that had been taken from Germany.[30]

At Wildflecken, Kate Hulme and the UNRRA staff posted the map of the new Poland—with territory taken from Germany highlighted. Ignatz, from a small village that had been part of the territory ceded to the Soviet Union, "gazed respectfully at the map of the new Poland which had been sent to encourage the homebound movements. . . . He ran his finger down the eastern frontier. . . . He brushed his fingers over the land east of Warsaw . . . the territory ceded to Russia. . . . 'Heimat' he said softly. 'My homeland.'"

Hulme interjected, pointing to the land in the west annexed from Germany. "'Just look what Poland got in exchange.' I showed him the thousands of square miles enclosed in Poland's new western addition." Ignatz was unmoved. Hulme asked a woman she called the "countess" to translate for her. "The two of them talked back and forth with a curious old smile on their faces as if they were humoring me. Then Ignatz bowed and put his finger again on the small village inside the USSR. . . . He begs your pardon for disagreeing with you," he told Hulme through a translator, "but he would never set foot on Polish soil as long as his natal village is on the Russian side of the new line."[31]

The non-Jewish Polish displaced persons were never quite able, as the Balts were, to establish stable living conditions for themselves in Germany. Instead, they were moved from camp to camp. UNRRA and the military insisted that this was done to relieve overcrowding. Camp residents believed that it was part of an orchestrated attempt to force them to accept repatriation. "We were loaded onto various transports and dispersed throughout Germany. First, we were taken to one camp, then to another, and another," Tadeusz Piotrowski recalled in his memoir, "until, by the end of 1945, we had been shuffled around like checkers through about twenty different residences. Sometimes we would be told to board a truck which would take us a hundred kilometers in one direction only to turn around and bring us right back to the spot from which we started out."[32]

The Polish displaced persons, and their advocates in the United States, complained that they were discriminated against in ways that the other DPs were not. Military authorities criticized their lawlessness, their activities on the black market, their open thievery from local farms, their drunkenness. Camp residents, for their part, charged the military guards and UNRRA officers with being too intrusive, too dismissive, too prejudiced against Poles, and too accommodating to the Jewish DPs, who were given the best facilities and enhanced rations.

Part of the difficulty the Poles faced in managing their camps was due to the demographics of the DP population. While there were in the Baltic camps an inordinately large number of professors, lawyers, doctors, judges and government officials, intellectuals, writers, and artists, they were relatively few in the Polish camps, or, for that matter, in Poland itself. The Germans had deliberately and successfully decimated the Polish elites as part of their campaign against Polish nationalism.

Only 6 percent of the Polish men and 7 percent of the women in the camps were professionals. The absence of intellectual, political, and cultural elites was partially compensated for by the relatively large number of Polish clergy and the considerable role they played in the religious, social, and cultural life of the camps. "Priests were invited to honorary committees, led invocations and prayers, gave speeches, and celebrated solemn masses." They performed marriages, of which there were many among the population, and officiated at baptisms. "Polish priests also organized schools and taught religion to Polish children, prepared them for sacraments, and provided religious instruction and activities, such as scouting." They oversaw, as well, a "religious press [that] included at least eight different newspaper titles aimed at general readers as well as children and military personnel." They also did their best to persuade the Polish DPs to refuse repatriation to a godless, Communist-dominated nation.[33]

THE UKRAINIAN CAMPS

The Ukrainian displaced persons included Ukrainian-speakers who had been citizens of the USSR prior to the war and those who had lived in that part of Poland annexed by the Soviets in 1939. The distinction was an important one in the weeks and months after liberation. Albert Hutler, who directed the Army's Displaced Persons Office in Mannheim, was willing to shelter Ukrainians who had been Polish citizens before the war, but was compelled by the Yalta agreements to deliver to Soviet repatriation officers those who had prior to 1939 been Soviet citizens. The difficulty he had was distinguishing one group from the other. Further difficulties were caused by the Russian DPs who lived among the Ukrainians and, to avoid repatriation, claimed that they too had been Polish citizens.

"A steady influx of Ukrainians . . . has become the most serious problem in the Mannheim area," Hutler wrote in his diary on August 29, 1945. A week later, he noted that

> a committee representing approximately 3000 Ukrainians in the Mannheim area [had] visited and stated that their people were strongly opposed to any move to repatriate them under the Soviet Union. At the same time Russian liaison officers are making every effort to find Soviet citizens still left in the area and in many cases uncover Ukrainians of Russian origin. According to

Seventh Army directives all Soviet citizens must be repatriated. Some final clarification must be made of the status of persons who claim to be Ukrainians and who do not want to return to their homelands.

On 6 Sept 45 we expect to move the first organized convoy of Russian Ukrainians from Mannheim camp to [the Soviet camp in] Stuttgart. It is expected that hundreds of these Russian Ukrainians will desert the camp in order to avoid being sent to Stuttgart. This has been the practice in the past and it is expected that only about a third of the original number of 650 will be on hand for the move on 6 Sept.

When the day arrived for the transfer, only 250 of the 650 Ukrainians were still in the camp, and they refused to be moved. The result was "near-rioting and considerable violence between security troops and DPs. . . . The matter has been the subject of many reports and higher headquarters has now taken cognizance of the fact that it is practically impossible to repatriate these people without bloodshed."[34]

On September 4, General Eisenhower issued new directives to military commanders in Germany. "Because of the grave danger of injury and loss of life to U.S. troops if used for forcible collection or repatriation of Soviet citizens, this Headquarters has directed the suspension of the use of troops for such purposes. . . . We have already encountered active resistance by deportees who also commit suicide frequently when faced with forcible deportation. The circumstances are such that a wave of unfavorable public opinion is to be expected if U.S. troops carry out forcible repatriation of unwilling Soviet citizens since injuries and loss of life on both sides are inevitable."[35]

Though refusing to formally recognize the Ukrainians as a distinct national grouping, the American and British military and UNRRA moved them into their own camps, if only to forestall the political violence that was likely to erupt when Ukrainians were housed with

Poles. Like other displaced persons, the Ukrainian DPs elected committees to administer day-to-day activities, arrange cultural events, organize schools, publish newspapers, and establish communications with Ukrainians in other camps, elsewhere in exile, and with American and Canadian relief organizations.

As was the case for the Jewish DPs for whom national independence was also aspirational, the collection and confinement of Ukrainians from different nations, with different histories, fostered a new and renewed awareness of nationalism. So did the experience of being governed by Ukrainians and engaging in endless debate about a Ukrainian future.

The "political refugees," those who had not been forced laborers but had left Ukraine on their own as the Red Army approached, became camp leaders. They were more educated, more likely to have been professionals before the war, more politically informed than the forced laborers or former prisoners of war, and uniformly anti-Soviet and anti-Polish. They were not, however, of one mind on how or by whom a future Ukrainian state should be governed.

Nowhere were the political battles more divisive, more brutal than in the Ukrainian camps. Ukrainian nationalists had been fighting among themselves for decades and brought their disagreements into the camps with them. The divisions were geographical: between the eastern Ukrainians who had been Soviet citizens and the western who had been citizens of Poland. But they were also political. Would the Ukrainian state be a democratic one or would it model itself on some variant of Italian Fascism or German National Socialism? Which faction among the nationalist groupings would lead the way forward and take control of the new state? Should the Ukrainians fight against Communism separately or in federation with other suppressed nations?[36]

The political factions fought for supremacy within the camps, for it was there that they believed a new Ukrainian nationalism would be constructed and the future leadership of the new state determined.

They engaged in debate, recrimination, violence; there were reports of political assassinations. Organizers traveled from camp to camp to spread their message, disseminate literature, and rouse the DPs to action. For the first year or so, there was, as in the Jewish camps, a tenuous unity among the various political factions. It didn't last long. By the fall of 1946, representatives of Stepan Bandera's OUN-B declared that "since they were the only political force continuing armed struggle in Ukraine, they were entitled to a monopoly of political power." Political disputes roiled through the camps, affecting not just elections to camp committees but everyday life for those who professed to be apolitical. The periods preceding and following elections were the most chaotic. "Fights broke out on numerous occasions. Some candidates resorted to smear campaigns, and voter intimidation occurred in many places. The Churches were drawn into this conflict, and the divisions within the camps threatened to destroy the unity that had existed previously."[37]

Tensions were exacerbated by reports that Soviet spies had infiltrated the camps, and were further inflamed when in the fall of 1947, Ukrainian Insurgent Army (UPA) partisans withdrawing, temporarily, they hoped, from their underground war against the Soviets crossed into Germany and took up residence in the DP camps.[38]

Desmond, a Quaker colleague of Margaret McNeill's, tried, without much success, to understand the dynamics and divisions in the Ukrainian camps. "The more I see of them, the more confused I get. The people in the camp are so decent and hardworking, you know, but their leaders seem very difficult men. I don't know if by temperament they're quarrelsome, but the Ukrainians in this area seem split from top to bottom in different feuds."[39]

Because the Soviets anticipated that the UNRRA camps that housed Eastern Europeans who refused repatriation would, absent special vigilance, become centers of anti-Soviet propaganda, agitation, and organization, they had at Yalta written into the secret agreements on repatriation a declaration that "hostile propaganda directed against the contracting parties or against any of the United Nations will not be permitted." Similar prohibitions were written into the founding UNRRA resolutions.[40]

The American and British military authorities tried to abide by these agreements. They did not dispute Soviet complaints that the displaced persons camps, the Ukrainian in particular, were riven with anti-Soviet activists. They recognized as well, as did UNRRA officials, that, as the Soviets charged, many of the most vociferous, most committed anti-Communists had collaborated with the Nazis during the recent war.

Regrettably, the only way to control anti-Communist propaganda in the camps was to restrict self-government and free expression. The Americans, loath to be considered "occupiers," were more reluctant than the British, with their long history of colonial "occupations," to do so, but they believed themselves compelled by the Yalta agreements, and joined with the British in censoring camp publications, restricting visits by suspected outside agitators, and prohibiting cultural or educational activities that threated to morph into political statements or actions.

JEWISH SURVIVORS IN POLAND, GERMANY, AND AUSTRIA

For the Jewish survivors among the Last Million, everything and nothing had changed in the wake of the Harrison Report and Eisenhower's visit to Feldafing. They had been segregated from the other displaced persons in their own camps; the military was providing enhanced food rations; their elected leaders administered the camps on a day-to-day basis; Jewish policemen stood guard; Jewish courts and Jewish judges heard and adjudicated disputes between camp residents; honor courts tried Jewish kapos and collaborators accused of assisting the Nazis in the torture and murder of Jews. But they remained in Germany with, as yet, no place on earth willing to accept them and Palestine closed to their emigration.

The largest of the camps designated for the Jewish survivors were Bergen-Belsen in the British zone of occupation and, in the American zone, Feldafing and Landsberg in Bavaria; Zeilsheim, a former camp for Russian forced laborers near Frankfurt; and Föhrenwald, a former IG Farben workers' planned community twenty-five kilometers from Munich.

Most of the Jewish camps were enclosed within mesh-wire fences that symbolically marked them as separate Jewish communities, in but not of Germany. Behind each of those fences, as Angelica Königseder and Juliane Wetzel have written of Föhrenwald, home to fifty-three hundred Jewish displaced persons, lay "a virtual Eastern European Jewish shtetl . . . with its own administration, political parties, police, law courts, religious institutions, synagogues, a *mikvah* [ritual bath], kosher food, health care system, newspapers, vocational training facilities, schools, kindergartens, theater groups, orchestras, sports clubs, and so forth."[41]

Belsen, as the Jewish residents referred to it, or Hohne, as the British called it, was the largest camp in the British zone and in all of Germany, a self-contained, self-administered Jewish village. Yossel Rosensaft, the chair of the governing committee, described it as "the last shtetl in Europe." Its official language was Yiddish, and Zionist politics quickly "became the order of the day." Befitting its huge size, with between twelve thousand and fifteen thousand residents, Belsen had its own hospital, multiple kindergartens, schools, newspapers, periodicals, a literary journal and a publishing house, two different theater groups, an orchestra, and sporting clubs that fielded soccer, table tennis, tennis, handball, and boxing competitions within the camp and with other camps.[42]

Though the survivors were, for the first time since the Nazi invasion, able to act and behave as free men and women, somewhat in control over their lives and community, they were marooned in Germany, the land of their murderers, while the Allies, who had won the war, debated their future. With the exception of the Bundists, who remained a minority, though in some camps an outspoken one, the survivors were united in the conviction that they could not remain in Europe.

Other displaced persons might dream of a return to their homelands. The Latvians, Estonians, Lithuanians, and Ukrainians longed for the day when, with the help of the U.S. Army, their nations would be liberated from the Soviet usurpers. The Poles hoped for a triumphant return to a Poland with its prewar boundaries restored, its economy recovered, and the Soviets and their puppets removed from power. For the masses of Jewish survivors, however, there were no conditions under which they could even contemplate repatriation. Europe was a dead zone, their former cities, towns, villages, and neighborhoods populated by men, women, and young people who had participated in the murder of their families and loved ones, stolen their property, burned their synagogues, despoiled their homes, and now wished them dead and gone forever.

"For the Jewish DPs," observed Koppel Pinson, who as JDC education director visited the camps from October 1945 through September 1946, "the war had not ended, nor has liberation in the true sense really come as yet. Their problems still unsolved, their future not in their own hands, they still consider themselves at war with the world and the world with them."[43]

In late October 1945, Susan Pettiss, who worked at the principal assembly center for displaced persons in Munich, plaintively wrote her aunt Katie about "the Jewish Problem,"

> the most complicated, the most evident one that faces this continent; and really, the world. . . . The suffering of the Jews has been beyond any stretch of the imagination. Millions killed in brutal, inhuman ways. Millions of children done away with. We find no Jewish babies—no children under twelve or thirteen. The suffering endured in the concentration camps, the

continuous shifting and mixing of the people, which separated families to such an extent that it is almost a hopeless task to unite them. The whole ethnic group is left without any property, any country, almost without hope. The TB rate is terrific.

     After their liberation they were left stunned. They went into DP Camps that were overcrowded, run as best they could under the strain of the times. At first there was an attempt to make no difference in nationalities or different ethnic groups for fear of discrimination. That didn't work. The Jews demanded to be segregated. They have been terribly difficult to help. They have been demanding, arrogant, have played upon their concentration camp experience to obtain ends. I saw rooms in our camp after they left—filthy dirty, furniture broken, such a mess as no other group ever left. They are divided into factions among themselves. One of our camps has to have six synagogues to keep the peace. They refuse to do any work, have had to be forced by gun to go out and cut wood to heat their own camps. American soldiers have developed bitter attitudes in many cases. I am still sympathetic, believe that only with great tolerance and patience can the problem even come near a solution. . . . It will take a long time for them to heal, to gain self-respect to believe in anything.[44]

There was a bit of condescension here, as there was in most of the observers' reports about the Jewish camps, but there was no other way of understanding, of coming to grips with the situation than by comparing the Jews to children, nasty, rude, spoiled children.

Francesca Wilson, one of the first UNRRA workers to arrive in Germany, was struck by the unbridgeable gulf that separated the Jews from other camp survivors. The Jews were "uprooted and bewildered. They belonged to fifteen different nations, but their persecution had led them to doubt whether any country in Europe wanted them anymore. Though the Germans had led the attack on them, they had often found no protection from their own [non-Jewish] compatriots, who had either handed them over to torture and death or taken no steps to save them."[45]

The Jewish camps were haunted by the dead and by the absence of old and young. "The dominant age level is in the 30s with few children and very few aged," reported Judah Nadich, the U.S. Army's special consultant on Jewish affairs, in the fall of 1945. "The elderly and the children because they could not work had been of no use to the Germans and the first to be killed. The absence of children among the survivors was striking—and heartbreaking." In one of the smaller camps in the town of Weiden, in Bavaria, where there were very few children, the absence of old people was even more striking. Only 3 of the 944 registered Jewish displaced persons were over sixty, only 22 between forty-five and fifty-nine. The survivors were, almost without exception, between sixteen and forty-four years of age.[46]

This would change—and rapidly—with the influx of tens of thousands of Polish Jews who had returned to their towns and cities after liberation to look for loved ones or who had spent the war in hiding, or with the partisans in the forests, or in the Red Army or at hard labor in the desolate northern and eastern interior of the USSR. The arrival of the Polish Jews would bring hope—and turmoil—to the camps, hope that there might indeed be a future for the Jewish people, turmoil due to the intense overcrowding and the need for new services: shelters, schools, hospitals, communal kitchens for the newcomers. But that was as yet in the future.

By the fall of 1945, the sense of being cut off from the world in general and the Jewish diaspora in particular had begun to dissipate with the arrival of relief workers from voluntary agencies and packages from overseas. The military, which had earlier prohibited visitors, welcomed them—and they came: from the Joint Distribution Committee, the Hebrew Sheltering and Immigrant Aid Society (HIAS), ORT (originally founded in 1880 as a Russian Jewish organization to promote Jewish education in the trades and agriculture), the World Jewish Congress, and in the British zone, the Jewish Relief Unit. The visitors brought with them news, encouragement, and, more vitally, supplies, food, books, and educational materials.

The JDC's delay in staffing up, locating jeeps, getting entrance permits from the military and UNRRA, and making its presence known, a delay that appeared to the survivors and the chaplains to have been near criminal, had come to an end in August 1945 in the American zone, a bit later in the British. Once in operation, the JDC was both a morale booster and a literal lifesaver. Dozens of doctors, nurses, and soldiers who had stayed behind in Germany after the war and social workers, childcare specialists, secretaries, and teachers arrived in the camps or at headquarters in Munich. Among them was Lucy Dawidowicz.

"Signing up for the JDC for work in Germany was almost like enlisting in the army," she recalled in her memoir.

> To enter Germany I needed, and received, military clearance and a military permit issued by the Joint Chiefs of Staff for the American zone of occupation. . . . Being, as it were, a subordinate of the U.S. Army, I was required to outfit myself with an olive-drab wardrobe of a U.S. Army officer. We wore blue-and-white chevrons, with the letters AJDC, on our uniforms. My rank was equivalent to that of army major and I was entitled to its privileges and priorities.
>
> The JDC provided food, clothing, and medical care, and a host of other services. It shipped staggering amounts of relief supplies to Europe—nearly 30,000 tons in 1946 and over 40,000 in 1947. Most of the tonnage was high-energy foods to supplement the local diet: canned fish and meat, butter, fats, sugar. The balance consisted of clothing and shoes, blankets, medicines, surgical equipment, even textbooks and educational materials for the over 10,000 children in schools which the survivors established in the camps. . . . JDC also provided for the cultural and religious needs of the DPs—provision of *shehitah* [kosher

butchering], kosher canteens, facilities for religious services, prayer books, religious texts, special foods for Jewish festivals, newspapers, and libraries.

Dawidowicz's assignment was "getting supplies for the educational and cultural institutions which the Jewish DPs had themselves created." She secured paper for textbooks, bulletins, Purim Megillot, a Haggadah for Passover, Yiddish matrices for linotype machines to print newspapers. She quickly learned how to barter American cigarettes and chocolate bars and whatever currency she could locate for the supplies she required.[47]

JDC staff, with their official-looking uniforms and, here and there, the ability to speak and understand Yiddish, provided direct evidence to wary, suspicious survivors that the world Jewish community recognized their plight and would do what it could to alleviate their suffering.

By the early fall of 1945, representatives of the Jewish community of Palestine had also established a presence in the camps. In late October 1945, David Ben-Gurion, the chairman of the Jewish Agency for Palestine, instantly recognizable by his small stature and very large head, visited Landsberg. He had come to Germany to see for himself where and how the survivors were living, to find out how many of them were willing and prepared to come to Palestine, to assure them that they were not forgotten, that the Jews of Palestine and elsewhere were committed to freeing them from their camps and from the horrors they had so recently endured. "To the people of the camp," Major Irving Heymont wrote his wife, Joan, on October 22, "he is God. His visit caused more excitement than if Pres. Truman were to visit the 5th Infantry."[48]

Ben-Gurion's visit was welcomed by the American military government, which provided him with full logistical support. In Frankfurt, he met with General Walter Bedell Smith, Eisenhower's chief of staff. Both men agreed that the displaced persons would have to remain in

David Ben-Gurion, chairman of the Jewish Agency Executive,
delivers a speech at a public forum during an official visit to
the Zeilsheim displaced persons camp, 1946.

the camps through the winter—and possibly longer. That being the case, they needed assistance in setting up recreation and education programs. Bedell Smith promised that the military would provide that assistance.

At the end of his almost two-week tour of the camps, Ben-Gurion returned to Frankfurt for a meeting with General Eisenhower. The rumpled, undersized but burly, fuzzy-haired future prime minister of Israel and the stately, thin, nearly bald future president of the United States recognized at once that their goals were complementary: both wanted the Jewish DPs removed from the camps as soon as possible. "Gen. Eisenhower," according to Ben-Gurion's notes on his visit, "asked when the people would be able to go to Palestine." Ben-Gurion explained to him, as he had to the residents of the camps, that he did not know, but that there might be a considerable delay. "Gen. Eisenhower assured him that they would do all they could for the DPs as long as they remained in Germany, would treat them with understanding of their problems and would give them all possible facilities for agricultural and other training. . . . Mr. Ben-Gurion was impressed by his humane approach and felt that he understood the problem."⁴⁹

The camps were a way station, a transition point for the survivors who dreamed of the day they could leave Germany and Europe for a new life in a new world, hopefully in a Jewish homeland in Palestine. This resting place was also an incubator of sorts, an enclosed, secure environment in which the *She'erit Hapletah*, the Surviving Remnant, could rescue and revive their culture, their religion, their language, their very being as a people, a decimated people, but a people still, and assume the collective responsibility for trying and punishing members of their community who had committed crimes against the people.

The American military had in the aftermath of the Harrison Report allowed the displaced persons to set up their own courts to try a variety of minor offenses, including corruption, slander, insult, black market activities, and theft. The elected judges in some of the courts also accepted cases brought by residents who accused fellows Jews of having collaborated with the Nazis in the ghettos and the concentration and death camps.

In Landsberg, as Margarete Myers Feinstein has written, the Jewish court "convicted Maier Rubin of stealing from, denouncing, and beating fellow Jews in a labor camp. He was sentenced to four months in the Landsberg camp jail and lifelong banishment from the Jewish community. . . . In a spring 1946 case, an accused kapo was convicted of collaborating with the Germans and maltreating Jewish inmates. Sentenced to two years' imprisonment, the kapo, in a rare move, was reportedly handed over to German authorities, who enforced the sentence."⁵⁰

The accusations and court actions taken against suspected kapos and Judenrat, or Jewish Council, members who had collaborated with the Nazis were so widespread and varied that in February 1946, the Central Committee of Liberated Jews in the American zone organized a Judicial Division and, in June, an appeals court and a central Court of Honor in Munich.

The court system, like everything else in the DP camps, was sui generis. It lacked formal procedures, could not refer to written or common laws or precedent in handing down its verdicts, was confined to trying crimes committed by Jews against Jews, and might at any moment be abolished by the American military. Acting on behalf of the collective Jewish community, the Honor Courts in the DP camps punished those found guilty by publicly reprimanding or censuring them, denying them preferential housing, and, in the most extreme cases, banishing them from membership in the Jewish community. If found guilty of acting in such a way as to cause death to other Jews, the defendants were transferred to military courts for final decision—and punishment.[51]

The Jewish survivors could not escape their recent past, but had nonetheless to find a way to come to terms with it. They did so not only by punishing those among them who had participated in the atrocities, but by compiling an historical record, an archive of their lives before and during the Nazi regime. The central committees in both the American and British zones established historical commissions to take eyewitness testimonies and collect documents. The DP historical commissions were, in structure and purpose, similar to the Central Jewish Historical Commission (CJHC) that Jewish survivors had established in Lublin and later relocated to Łódź.

The CJHC had deployed a small army of paid workers and volunteers in five district and twenty-one local commissions to distribute questionnaires and collect diaries, letters, poems, songs, photographs, even jokes and riddles. Though its central focus was on the Jewish survivors, the CJHC had also located and archived troves of German civil, military, and concentration camp documents and several thousand photographs and reels of film footage left behind when the Germans retreated from Poland in the spring of 1945. It had been instrumental as well in exhuming and preserving the boxes of documents that had been collected by Jews in the Warsaw Ghetto under the supervision of historian Emanuel Ringelblum and buried in the rubble to protect them from the Nazis.

In one of the boxes was a message from nineteen-year-old David Graber, who had worked with Ringelblum. "What we were unable to cry and shriek out to the world we buried in the ground. . . . I would love to see the moment in which the great treasure will be dug up and scream the truth at the world. So the world may know all. . . . May the treasure fall into good hands, may it last into better times, may it alarm and alert the world to what happened . . . in the twentieth century. . . . We may now die in peace. We fulfilled our mission. May history attest for us."[52]

The CJHC would eventually be closed down by the Polish provisional government, but the testimonies and documents and studies it had collected, including those from the buried Ringelblum Warsaw Ghetto archive, would be preserved and transferred to a newly organized Jewish Historical Institute in Warsaw. Several of CJHC's founders and principal activists left Poland and relocated to displaced persons camps where they carried on the work they had begun.[53]

In November 1945, the Central Historical Commission in Munich, modeled on its Polish predecessor and assisted by some of its founders, was organized by a group of displaced persons in Germany. "It was the sacred duty of the survivors," the organizers declared, "to save whatever could be dredged up from the past for the sake of the future. Each of them was, without exception, a font of knowledge about the past that could be critical in preparing the foundation of the historical edifice yet to be erected."[54]

The JDC arranged for historian Philip Friedman, who had been instrumental in setting up the CJHC in Poland, to come to Munich to assist in the founding of the displaced persons' commission. Survivors were recruited, cajoled, and shamed into testifying orally or in writing on their experiences. "Do not forget that every document, picture, song, legend is the only gravestone which we can place on the unknown graves of our murdered parents. . . . The Jews themselves must document this bloody epoch."[55]

The response was impressive. The myth of the silent survivor was just that. The displaced persons in the camps were hungry to tell their stories to whomever would listen. "The DP," Koppel Pinson of the JDC would observe,

> is preoccupied almost to the point of morbidity with his past. His historical interest has become enormously heightened and intensified. He is always ready to recount in minutest detail the events of his past or the past of his relatives. . . . With this preoccupation with their immediate past has come a heightened historical sense that is responsible for the almost passionate devotion of the DP's to the collection of historical and material data on ghetto and *kotzet* [concentration camp] life and death. Every DP is a private document center and every DP camp has an historical commission.[56]

The survivors in the camps, Lucy Dawidowicz recalled,

> had a compulsion to talk. Telling their story helped them to expiate the guilt feelings that tormented them. They wanted to talk about their losses—of parents who perished, sisters and brothers who vanished, even of their own children who were murdered. . . . In telling their stories, the survivors liked best of all to talk about their former lives, to describe the houses they lived in, the family businesses, their schooling, their place in the community. By defining themselves in their previous existence, they were confirming their identity as individuals entitled to a place in an ordered society. . . . When they talked about the terrible deeds the Germans had done, how the Germans, assisted

by Lithuanians, separated husbands from wives and children from parents, abused them, murdered their families, they wept. Crying came easily to them. But they wanted more than pity. They wanted the Germans punished for their crimes. . . . The survivors told their stories to each other, to listeners like me, and in court. But they wanted also to record their experiences, to present them for history and posterity.

And they did so "under the guidance of the Central Historical Commission."[57]

Historical commissions were also founded in Austria to gather testimonies and documents from the displaced Jews there. As had been the case in Munich, a former member of the CJHC who on fleeing Poland had taken up residence in a camp near Linz was instrumental in setting up the organization, but the principal activist behind the Jewish Historical Documentation Center in Austria was Simon Wiesenthal, a survivor of several camps who had moved with other DPs into the Bindermichl neighborhood in southern Linz.

As it became clear that few, if any, Austrians were going to be punished for their crimes against the Jews, the Jewish Historical Documentation Center focused its attention on taking testimony that could be used in courts of law against suspected war criminals already under arrest and the many more who were hiding in plain sight. The center created a card-indexing system that matched war criminals at particular work and death camps with witnesses from those camps who could testify against them. Concentration and death camp survivors were solicited to submit testimonies identifying guards and the crimes they had committed.

When word reached Simon Wiesenthal of the name of a suspected war criminal, he appealed directly to the displaced persons in the camps, with posters and news articles, pleading with them to come forward. "Attention, former concentration camp inmates of KZ Mauthausen! All persons who know something about the behavior and deeds of Josef

Giett, picture below, born December 12, 1906, . . . guard in Mauthausen between September 1, 1944, and March 30, 1945, are requested to report to the Jewish Historical Document, Linz, Goethestrasse 63, in writing or orally."[58]

The historical commissions in Austria had a prosecutorial bent. Those in Germany, as in Poland, were also interested in taking testimonies that might prove useful in the identification and prosecution of war criminals, but their primary goal was to preserve a record of the crime and its victims, an archive of life before and under the Nazis that might serve as the foundational building block in the writing of histories of Eastern Europe, the war, and the Jewish people.

The displaced persons who founded the Central Historical Commission in Munich intended from the outset that their materials would one day be transferred to the Jewish homeland. In the fall of 1948, they met in Munich with the Israeli officials tasked with building Yad Vashem, the government-sponsored Holocaust memorial in Jerusalem, and arranged for the transfer of their archives. Beginning in November 1948 and continuing through the following spring, the archival collections they had assembled, tens of thousands of testimonies, Nazi documents and publications, and cultural artifacts, were packed into boxes and "sent via Marseille through the Immigration Department of the Jewish Agency." The smaller but still significant archives collected by the historical commissions in the British zone were later divided and transported to several American and Israeli institutions.[59]

8.

"THE WAR DEPARTMENT
IS VERY ANXIOUS"

*DPs, Expellees, POWs, and the
Overburdened Armies of Occupation*

THE TASK OF MANAGING postwar refugee problems had been divided between UNRRA, which was charged with facilitating the repatriation of the displaced persons, and the Intergovernmental Committee on Refugees (IGCR), which was responsible for resettling those who were "stateless" and could therefore not be repatriated.

Since 1938, when it had been organized by President Roosevelt to provide a lifeline to get Jews out of Germany, the IGCR had demonstrated a consummate inability to accomplish much of anything. In the postwar period, pressured by the UK, which feared that an active resettlement program would energize Jewish displaced persons to demand immigration to Palestine, the IGCR stalled and stonewalled, then in early November 1945 committed institutional suicide by declaring that it would henceforth confine "resettlement activities to those persons who are definitely stateless, presumably German and Austrian refugees denationalized by the Nazi regime. . . . The result of this policy," Secretary of State Byrnes wrote John Winant, the American ambassador to the UK, was that there was now no international organization committed to assisting the Last Million in resettling outside of Germany.[1]

The withdrawal of the IGCR from resettlement activities meant that those among the Last Million who refused repatriation would have to remain, indefinitely it appeared, in the camps, costing the American taxpayer more than a billion dollars a year (Americans paid 72 percent of the UNRRA budget, the British 17 percent) and committing the military to a mission without end that drained it of manpower and resources.[2]

On November 29, 1945, following the IGCR announcement that it would not assist in the resettlement of the Last Million, Secretary of War Robert Patterson complained to Secretary of State Byrnes "about the lack of planning or activity" by the State Department for the future resettlement of those who refused repatriation. "In view of the critical food, fuel, and housing shortage in Germany and Austria, as well as the tremendous problems being created by mass influx of Germans from Eastern Europe [the so-called *Volksdeutsche*], the War Department is very anxious that plans be made for temporary or permanent resettlement outside of Germany and Austria of the maximum number of stateless and non-repatriable persons."[3]

GERMANY, FALL AND WINTER 1945–46

The burden on the American army of occupation in Germany was insupportable. Its responsibilities included not only providing for the Last Million, but feeding, sheltering, and policing the German civilian population and overseeing the rebuilding of infrastructure. The Allied military had expected on entering German territory to see damage equivalent to that suffered by the British during the Blitz, but "in absolute terms the damage to living spaces in Germany was nearly eighteen times as bad as it was in Britain." The cities were hit the worst. "Berlin lost up to 50 per cent of its habitable premises, Hanover 51.6 per cent, Hamburg 53.3 per cent . . . Cologne, 70 per cent."[4]

Large parts of the nation were virtually uninhabitable; there were shortages of food, clothing, and other necessities. Millions of destitute and homeless German civilians, POWs, and displaced persons were competing for scarce resources. Into this devastated country there arrived, in the second half of 1945, millions more shattered, starving old people, women, and children, the *Volksdeutsche* expelled from East Prussia, Poland, Czechoslovakia, Hungary, and elsewhere in Eastern Europe.

The ethnic German populations in each of these nations had played significant roles in providing assistance, if not leadership, to the Nazis during the war. They had welcomed the invading German military and during the occupation been rewarded with positions of power, privilege, and responsibility, and with land and assets seized from native non-Aryan populations. They had actively betrayed the nations in which they and, in many cases their forebears, had lived for generations.

At the moment of liberation from German rule—and in the months thereafter—the peoples and governments of Eastern Europe took their revenge; they imprisoned, conscripted for slave labor, dispossessed, and sent into exile millions of ethnic Germans. Nearly three million were expelled from Czechoslovakia. Some five million would voluntarily depart or be expelled from Poland, the largest segment from those formerly German regions—Silesia, East Prussia, eastern Pomerania, eastern Brandenburg—that had been ceded by the Allies to Poland. From Hungary 150,000 would be expelled, 110,000 from Romania, 210,000 from Yugoslavia. Hundreds of thousands more had, anticipating deportation or worse, abandoned their homes and families in the last months of the war and retreated into Germany with the German armies.[5]

At Potsdam, the United States, the Soviet Union, and Great Britain had authorized this massive and unprecedented ethnic cleansing operation, with little debate and no dissension. "The three Governments . . . recognize that the transfer to Germany of German populations . . . remaining in Poland, Czechoslovakia and Hungary, will have to be undertaken. They agree that any transfers that take place should be effected in an orderly and humane manner."[6]

Instead the expellees, as they were known, were boarded onto trucks or marched to the nearest rail station, crammed into boxcars without sufficient food or water, and transported into Germany. Thousands would die along the way; those who survived arrived near starvation, dehydrated, more dead than alive. Like the DPs before them, the expellees, those already in the country and those about to arrive, were rounded up and transported to temporary transit camps where German relief organizations tried to feed and shelter them. British and American military authorities, worried about the concentrations of homeless *Volksdeutsche* in the bombed-out cities, moved as many as they could to camps in rural areas where they had already established camps for the displaced persons.

The expellee population, unemployed and homeless like the DPs, competed with them for food, clothing, building supplies, and everything else. The local German population had little love for the expellees, but even less sympathy for the displaced persons who remained in their midst—and whom they were forced to feed. Why, with millions of homeless, unemployed *Volksdeutsche* among them, did German civilians, they asked, have to give precedence in food, housing, employment, and every other necessity to the refugees? Why were displaced persons' rations greater than those for locals or expellees? Why had former military facilities that should have been utilized for economic development or housing or shelter for homeless German civilians and expellees been reserved instead for the DPs? The occupying authorities who had responsibility for all three groups—the civilian population, the displaced persons, and the expellees—had to answer such complaints on an almost daily basis.[7]

Kate Hulme, as assistant director at the Wildflecken camp, was responsible for securing food, sanitary supplies, building materials, and other necessities for the thousands of Poles at her camp. She paid no attention to the expellees nearby, until she was visited on October 3, as she noted in her diary, by an American lieutenant who "accused Hulme of allowing 'her' Poles to steal from local farmers with abandon."

Hulme fumed. "Every German who loses a sheep runs to MG [military government] and complains of Poles, Poles, Poles. . . . The poor Pole in rags with wild blue eyes looks evil besides the bowing paragon of a German."

The lieutenant was as angry at Hulme as she was at him. He accused her of being so focused on the plight of the displaced Poles that she had become impervious to the suffering of the expellees. She fought back, but was "haunted by the story of the typhus-ridden German refugees being kicked across borders back into their own land, which is mainly occupied by DPs who do not wish to return to their own country."[8]

ADDING TO THE AMERICAN and British military's burden was responsibility for feeding, sheltering, and policing the large number of POWs still under armed twenty-four-hour-a-day guard. German POWs were gradually being released into the general population, but the Baltic and Yugoslav Ustaša* POWs who had fought with, not against, the Germans remained imprisoned, in large part because neither the Americans nor the British knew what else to do with them. They could not be held indefinitely, but neither would they agree, if freed, to return home. Releasing them from the POW camps, only to dump them into the German population to compete with German POWs, civilians, and *Volksdeutsche* expellees for scarce food, shelter, and work, was unthinkable. The only viable option was to relocate them to displaced persons camps where UNRRA would share the burden of feeding and sheltering them.

The Baltic diplomats still accredited to the United States and the United Kingdom had recommended this in October 1945, but the State

---

* The Ustaša was a Catholic Croatian fascist party that was responsible for the violent murder of hundreds of thousands of Serbs and Jews. When the Germans invaded Yugoslavia in April 1941, they created a Croatian satellite state, run by the Ustaša and its leader, Ante Pavelić.

Department and the Foreign Office had rejected their proposal. In early December, Sir Brian Robertson of the military government in the British zone of Germany made the same request, not out of any special concern for the well-being of the Baltic POWs, but because the British army needed to be relieved of the burden of guarding them. Robertson inquired of General Frederick Morgan, the chief of UNRRA operations in Germany, whether the "ex-prisoners of war . . . who either could not or would not return to their home countries" might be admitted to the UNRRA camps. He was told that UNRRA policy was that "ex-prisoners of war are not the concern of UNRRA, and . . . therefore, can not be admitted into our camps."[9]

The British command in Germany turned to the Foreign Office for support. "These Balts are held as Prisoners of War . . . under direct British administration and guarding. This involves a commitment in British manpower which we cannot afford. . . . These men are well disciplined and have been most cooperative. The families of many of them are in DP camps. We therefore propose they should be discharged and held in DP camps where they will be under adequate control . . . without waste of British manpower and funds. This will not prejudice any decisions that may eventually be made as to their future disposal. Before discharge they would be carefully screened" and those with German citizenship released into the general population.[10]

The Foreign Office turned down the military's request. "I am afraid there would be serious political objections to the action contemplated," Douglas MacKillop, head of the Refugee Department, wrote military command in Germany. "Balts who, while not of German origin, actually fought in the Wehrmacht . . . are ex-enemies, the question of whose disposal is complicated by the fact that it would be incompatible with our general policy to send them home against their wish. Nevertheless we see no reason why they should be treated as displaced persons and as such get better treatment than the ordinary German population."[11]

In the end, the military got its way. With limited resources to allocate to their occupation forces in Germany, the British government had no alternative other than to move the ex-Baltic soldiers out of the POW camps. Because UNRRA had refused to accept them in its displaced persons camps, they were transferred to British-administered facilities. The numbers involved were significant: 11,701 Latvians, 1,933 Lithuanians, and 2,850 Estonians. The POWs were supposed to be screened before their status was changed to displaced persons. The Foreign Office in London cabled military command in Berlin and Lübbecke on February 2, 1946, to exercise caution in doing so. "We cannot regard Baltic nationals as war criminals or traitors when the only charge against them is that they fought against Soviet armed forces; but we have no wish to withhold them from justice if they are war criminals in the accepted sense. You should therefore ascertain in each case on the production of satisfactory *prima facie* evidence that the person concerned has been guilty of a war crime in the ordinary sense and in doubtful cases you should refer to this office for instructions."[12]

The Foreign Office provided the military with no additional resources, no detailed instructions, no experienced investigators, and no specialized staff with the historical background and language skills necessary to carry out the screening. Forty years later, Home Secretary Douglas Hurd initiated a special war crimes inquiry into "allegations that persons who are now British citizens or resident in the United Kingdom committed war crimes during the Second World War." In the course of the inquiry, evidence was sought to determine whether the Baltic POWs who had been "given full DP status" in January 1946 had been "screened for war criminals." Though it was "assumed" that such screening had taken place, the inquiry determined that this was "not clear from the papers available."[13]

The American debate over the future of the POWs captured in German uniforms mirrored the British one. The State Department objected at first to releasing the POWs, but by the spring of 1946, not knowing what else to do with them, agreed to do so. On March 9, 1946, the Joint Chiefs directed military officials in Germany that "all Baltic and Polish nationals captured while serving in the Wehrmacht should be released from Prisoner of War status and given the status of Displaced Persons, except for those against whom there is satisfactory evidence that they are war criminals." As was the case with the British, the military screeners were not given sufficient resources or instructions, nor did they have the language skills or historical knowledge to identify suspected war criminals among the POW population. They routinely released, almost without exception, the Baltic POWs they had been holding.[14]

The plan to move the former prisoners in American custody from POW to DP camps was delayed when UNRRA officials at headquarters instructed local camp directors to "resist all attempts by the military to declare eligible for UNRRA care any Wehrmacht Balt, Pole, or whatever." If, however, the military insisted "over your strongest objections" that ex-POWs be "given UNRRA care you will request and receive from the military a written certificate that 1. the released POW is a United Nations Displaced Person. 2. He is not a war criminal, traitor, or collaborator." Only POWs with such certificates would be admitted to UNRRA camps. We do not know whether UNRRA followed through on these demands, and, if they did, whether the military screened the POWs before providing them with the required "certificates."[15]

WITH DEMOBILIZATION fast-moving and inexorable, there were fewer and fewer British or American soldiers and officers to fulfill the multiple tasks assigned the occupying armies. With a shortsighted naïveté that in retrospect appears rather frightening, British and American military commanders and the civilian governments they reported to, rather than delaying or canceling redeployments, enlisted former POWs and displaced persons to replace the departing soldiers.

Polish army veterans who had been interned in Germany as POWs or fought alongside the British were hired at minimal wages to provide security for displaced persons, expellee and German POW camps, the prisons where German war criminals were being held, American military installations, warehouses, offices, and airports, and the towns, villages, and cities adjacent to these sites.

In the British zone, where the majority of the Polish displaced persons were domiciled in the Emsland region, military authorities handed over police powers and administrative authority to veterans of the 1st Polish Armoured Division.* The Polish veterans presided over the creation of an orderly series of Polish enclaves, but they also intervened in internal political affairs by spreading "propaganda amongst their politically naïve countrymen against the government in Warsaw and against repatriation in general. . . . General Rudnicki, commander of troops stationed in Emsland, was purported to have said: 'We shall return to Poland—but only with arms in hand.' Many of the Displaced Persons had no such desire to find themselves between two fronts and in such a war."[16]

The American army had also in the winter of 1945–46 begun to recruit Polish veterans and displaced persons to replace demobilized soldiers. The State Department, which had not been consulted, objected strongly. "It has come to my attention," Secretary of State Byrnes wrote Secretary of War Patterson on January 7, 1946,

> that the United States military authorities in Germany . . . inaugurated some time ago a system of employment of Polish displaced personnel organized as Polish guard units. I understand that these men wear dyed American uniforms, are issued arms and ammunition on a rationed basis and receive pay according to the Polish Army pay schedule. I further understand that there are at present 37,500 Polish nationals employed by our forces in these guard units and that, since this experiment has proved satisfactory, the theater commander plans to employ 13,750 additional Polish nationals for this service. I realize, of course that

---

* The 1st Polish Armoured Division had, as part of the Allied expeditionary forces, fought its way through France and into Germany with the First Canadian Army, and then taken part in the occupation of Germany.

because of redeployment United States theater commanders are
facing a manpower shortage in Germany and can understand,
therefore, their desire to utilize groups of this kind to assist them
in their work. I feel, however, that I must point out that the use
of these Polish nationals as para-military units in the American
occupation zone in Germany may have serious political repercussions. The Polish Government has on several occasions indicated that it desires to have all Poles in the west return to their
native land as soon as possible. . . . It is possible, therefore, that
because we are feeding, clothing, housing and employing large
numbers of Poles for guard duty, the Polish Government may
allege that by utilizing this group in this manner we are encouraging them to remain in our zone instead of returning to
Poland.[17]

State Department opposition resulted in a short-term suspension of
the program. When General Joseph T. McNarney and the secretary of
war protested, however, that, given the pace of demobilization, the
American army had no choice but to enlist displaced persons to replace
departing American soldiers, the State Department, though still in opposition, did not press the issue.[18]

By early 1946, the U.S. Army had organized thousands of Polish
and a smaller number of Yugoslav veterans and displaced persons into
paramilitary formations and provided them with uniforms, enhanced
rations, decent wages, and "the privilege of buying cigarettes, chocolate
and other luxuries at American post exchanges." There was nothing, in
principle, wrong with paying displaced persons to perform specific and
necessary tasks, but by putting ex-military men who opposed repatriation in positions of authority in the Polish DP camps, the occupation
forces were undermining their primary mission, which was to facilitate
and hasten the return of camp residents to Poland.[19]

The Polish ex-military officers, some of whom had belonged to
nationalist partisan units like the Holy Cross Brigade, were fiercely

anti-Communist, anti-Soviet, and anti-repatriation. Their distrust, indeed hatred, of the Soviets had been reinforced by news of the massacre at Katyn, where Soviets murdered thousands of Polish army officers, then, when the bodies were discovered, blamed the atrocities on the Germans. As General Władysław Anders, the commander of the Polish army, which had been organized in the Soviet Union but fought with the British, wrote Field Marshal Harold Alexander in August 1945, the Polish soldiers who ended the war outside Poland would not consider repatriation until their nation had been liberated from Soviet tyranny. They would discourage their countrymen as well from returning to a "Poland [that] was even more enslaved than under the Germans."[20]

The Soviets, the Polish provisional government, and the Yugoslav government of Marshal Tito protested strenuously against the American and British recruitment of their sworn enemies. The U.S. Army practice of "recruiting, equipping and arming disaffected Poles and Yugoslavs to replace the too hastily redeployed American troops," Raymond Daniell of the *New York Times* reported in a front-page story on February 4, 1946, "is arousing suspicion in Russia, Poland and Yugoslavia, fostering the German hope of a future rift between Russia and her western Allies and defeating our effort to induce displaced persons to go home. . . . These armies of mercenaries are dominated by anti-Semitic and anti-Soviet sympathizers. . . . This concentration is regarded in Polish, Russian and Yugoslav eyes as the nucleus of a counter-revolutionary force in central Europe." The British and American governments had supported counterrevolutionary military forces in their attempt to overthrow the Soviet government after the Great War. Were they contemplating doing so again?[21]

The program of enlisting DPs to replace demobilized American soldiers was extended to Estonian and Latvian war veterans. Andrejs Eglitis, who had flown for a Latvian unit attached to the Luftwaffe, then, after the war, disguised his military background and been admitted to a displaced persons camp, was among the veterans who applied to the program.

"Several hundred signed up from our camp. Myself included, and I'm sure many others from other camps. Several Latvian platoons were formed. . . . American trucks with white stars arrived" to transport the recruits to their assigned locations and duties. "We spent our time in Germany in the U.S. Army rather pleasantly." Five thousand Estonian veterans were also enlisted in guard companies. We do not know how many of the Latvians and Estonians in the program had previously, like Eglitis, fought alongside the Germans.[22]

"U.S. BEGINS PURGE IN GERMAN CAMPS. WILL WEED OUT NAZIS, FASCIST SYMPATHIZERS AND CRIMINALS AMONG DISPLACED PERSONS," *THE NEW YORK TIMES*, MARCH 10, 1946

WASHINGTON, JANUARY TO MARCH 1946

It was common knowledge, certainly among military authorities, that the UNRRA camps housed Nazi collaborators, war criminals, and Estonians, Latvians, Lithuanians, and Ukrainians who had fought alongside the Germans on the eastern front. On October 19, 1945, in an article datelined "Frankfort on the Main," and headlined "Displaced Balts Studied by Allies; Many Under Army's Care Are Pro-German Fascists Who Spread Propaganda," Drew Middleton of the *New York Times* reported that "a reliable source" in military headquarters had informed him that "at least one-third and probably more of the Balts are former members of the Saulis, a Baltic Fascist organization, and the Latvian, Lithuanian and Estonian Legions raised to fight the Russians by the Germans. Almost all of them prefer our enemy, Germany, to our ally, Russia."[1]

The *New York Post* reported the same story on October 26, apparently from the same source. "Allied Military Government officials . . . estimate that 10 to 30 per cent of the inmates should be classified outright Fascists, or at least unreconstructed admirers of German ways."[2]

There was no response from the government to either of the stories and no significant public outcry at the news that the UNRRA camps in the American zone of Germany were housing Nazi collaborators.

Two months later, on December 31, 1945, perhaps the slowest news day of the year, the *New York Times, Baltimore Sun, Washington Post, Christian Science Monitor,* and other newspapers, again acting on a source at military headquarters in Frankfurt, reported "that a large percentage of Baltic nationals enjoying United Nations refuge in at least two displaced-persons' camps had been found to be Nazi sympathizers. . . . An official spokesman of the United States Army said, however, that the United Nations were still pledged to feed the Balts and Poles who do not want to go home even though they had been found to be pro-Nazi." The story had a Frankfurt dateline, suggesting that officers at headquarters had given it to reporters there.[3]

Again, there was no public response to the story, no denials or confirmations from Washington. The War Department, however, in a "Secret" cable to Frankfurt headquarters, acknowledged the accuracy of the reporting by directing military officials in Germany to begin "careful and individual" screening of all displaced persons and discharge from the camps "those who support or have supported Nazi or Fascist doctrines or have collaborated with the enemy such collaboration to be determined on the basis of convincing evidence." Screening was also ordered to identify and discharge German nationals, Baltic Germans, and *Volksdeutsche* who had snuck into the camps with false papers.[4]

On February 18, the *Washington Post*, the *Los Angeles Examiner,* and other Hearst papers reported that "Pro-Nazi Balts Will Be Sent Home by U.S. . . . Nationals of Baltic countries who willingly served the Nazis and now are enjoying preferential treatment in displaced persons camps will be returned to their homelands, by force if necessary. Information disclosed that a great proportion of the Baltic residents showed pro-Nazi leanings."[5]

The Hearst papers had gotten the story wrong. The Army, General McNarney, commander in chief of the American forces in Germany, declared, had decided to forcibly eject Nazi sympathizers and collaborators from the camps, but not to send them home. The *New York Herald Tribune* felt obligated, in reporting McNarney's correction, to question the Army's decision. "It seems unwise to locate them in Germany, where they might seek trouble between the western Allies and Russia, but that looms as the only recourse unless some other country welcomes them."[6]

The British Foreign Office, fearful that the Americans, despite General McNarney's denial, might unilaterally begin deporting anti-Soviet Nazi collaborators to Estonia, Latvia, and Lithuania, putting pressure on them to do the same, contacted General Lucius Clay, McNarney's deputy, for clarification. General Clay assured the Foreign Office that "policy as regards repatriation of Balts remains unchanged and is the same as that of the British authorities. What the United States authorities are doing is to screen their Balt displaced persons with the object of denying to certain classes of them the preferential treatment given to displaced persons. Those who will no longer be eligible for such treatment are broadly speaking those who came voluntarily to Germany.* These will receive treatment similar to that of the German population. There is no question of their forced repatriation."[7]

On March 10, 1946, Sydney Gruson of the *New York Times* reported from Frankfurt that the "United States Military Government officials have begun a vast sifting operation in the United States zone of Germany to break the back of the displaced persons problem and relieve the United Nations of the burden of caring for thousands of collaborationists, Nazis and Fascists believed to be living in refugee camps. . . . Those proved to have entered voluntarily to aid the Nazis will be cut off from

* Clay was clearly misspeaking or had been poorly briefed. Almost all of the Baltic displaced persons had come "voluntarily"; only the smallest minority had been deported as forced laborers.

198 THE LAST MILLION

help . . . and turned loose to fend for themselves among the Germans. War criminals or those wanted for civil crimes in their native countries will be returned, but the number falling into these categories is not expected to be large."

Buried in the second column of the story was a hint that a more significant shift in U.S. policy was under consideration. The military government in Germany had affirmed, according to Gruson, that it was not going to "return any one deserving of United Nations help to his native land against his will. But United States officials are trying to persuade as many as possible to go home. By the end of 1946 they expect to have on their hands no one except 'non-repatriables' by virtue of their opposition to the present Governments of their native countries. These 'non-repatriables' are expected to be mostly Balts and Poles, and if no other arrangements are made for them they will simply enter the German community at the end of the year."[8]

Almost casually, the American military was testing the waters for the bombshell that would be exploded later that week when Secretary of State Byrnes would announce that the American government had decided to close the displaced persons camps in Germany.

WASHINGTON, MARCH TO MAY 1946

For the military in Germany and the War Department in Washington, the burden of policing and supplying the DP camps had become untenable. No one disputed the need for an occupation force in Germany, but why were Americans providing support for displaced persons who had not only not fought against the Nazis but might have collaborated with them? Why was so much of the burden being borne by the American military? The present situation was bad; the future might be worse.

What military officials feared, and rightly so, was that with the dissolution of UNRRA, which had been organized as a temporary and not a permanent international agency, the occupying armies would be left with sole responsibility for administering the DP camps. The morale, well-being, and sense of mission of the peacetime Army in Germany was already endangered by the prolonged and seemingly endless occupation. "Military government had entered what Dwight D. Eisenhower termed its 'static phase.' No longer staging grounds for imminent departure, assembly centers [i.e., DP camps] solidified into semipermanent settlements."[9]

All through January and February 1946, the newspapers were filled with stories about GIs "rioting" in Germany, while their wives in America lobbied their elected officials to bring them home. The White House and War Department were in agreement that the GIs and their officers on occupation duty in Germany would either have to be sent home or to a more appropriate military assignment. Unfortunately, this was not possible as long as hundreds of camps with nearly a million displaced persons were entrusted to their care.[10]

The Last Million refused still, more than six months after VE Day, to return home. The only way to force them to do so, the military had concluded, was to close the camps.

On February 8, 1946, General John Hilldring, head of the Civil Affairs Division of USFET (United States Forces European Theater) in Frankfurt, submitted to Washington the Army's plan to close the camps in the American zone on June 1, 1946, to all but the Jewish DPs. The plan was simplicity itself: three months' notice would be given before the camps were closed; those who agreed to return home would be provided free transportation; those who refused would be allowed to "remain in the U.S. Zone of Germany, but it will be necessary for them to work, live, and take their place in Germany among the German people"; those who "belong in the persecuted categories [i.e., the Jews] and all unaccompanied orphan children . . . will continue to be afforded the care and treatment now received until plans can be made for their resettlement in suitable new homes." Secretary of War Patterson forwarded the plan to Secretary of State Byrnes, who approved it.[11]

The British Foreign Office, notified of the American decision, expressed its displeasure that it had not been consulted before the policy was arrived at. It requested that any announcement of the closing plan be delayed until bilateral discussions could be held "in London in the endeavor to reach a co-ordinated policy."

"There are so many disquieting implications that a decision . . . cannot be reached without further examination." Where would those DPs who remained in Germany be housed? How might releasing thousands of DPs into the German population affect the expellees who were still returning to Germany and needed shelter? Was there a "risk of further uncontrolled mass movements if the camps were liquidated?" Would that not result in increased crime and chaos?[12]

Secretary of State Byrnes dismissed the British request for bilateral discussion, but agreed to push back the date on which the camps would be closed. On March 15, he publicly announced that the State and War Departments were considering closing the "displaced persons' camps in the American zones in Germany and Austria, between August 1 and Sept. 1, because the camps could not be maintained indefinitely and some time must be selected for closing them." None of the displaced persons, he emphasized, would be forcibly repatriated. Those who did not want to return home could remain in the "American zones after the camps have been closed." While he did not specifically mention the Jewish DPs, he declared that "if and when the camps were closed . . . centers for persecuted persons would not be affected and they would continue to be cared for." Everyone else would be evicted. Though the closing was months away, Byrnes declared that he was making his announcement now so that the fourth UNRRA General Council, in session in Atlantic City, New Jersey, "could consider what it might want to do about taking care of the displaced persons. He assumed that UNRRA or some other international organization might take over the work."[13]

Byrnes's announcement caught UNRRA officials and the voluntary agencies that were working in the camps by surprise. Though it was widely known that the American military was overstretched and overburdened, few expected that the United States was prepared to withdraw from the responsibilities it had assumed on behalf of the Last Million. "I was stunned by an almost unthinkable reality," recalled Eileen Egan of War Relief Services, the principal American Catholic agency in Europe. "I could envision the effect of stripped, defenseless strangers, chiefly Poles, on communities where German civilians and expelled people were already scrounging for life itself." Egan, who was an observer at the UNRRA General Council meeting, approached Sir George Rendel, the British delegate, to get his advice on what could be done to reverse the plan to close the camps in the American zone. Rendel advised her that the decision had been made in secret at the highest government levels, and only at the highest levels "could such an order be postponed or rescinded."[14]

Monsignor Patrick A. O'Boyle, Egan's superior and director of War Relief Services, contacted Cardinal Spellman, who arranged a private meeting for O'Boyle with Secretary of State Byrnes. O'Boyle pleaded with Byrnes not to close the camps. To do so, he argued, was equivalent to sentencing "many people to death." Byrnes dismissed O'Boyle's pleadings with a particularly egregious analogy. "Totally misreading the situation, he cited his own experience as a circuit judge in South Carolina, where he would often see men loafing on the courthouse steps. He compared these men to the displaced persons in Germany."

O'Boyle departed, outraged at Byrnes's insensitivity. He prepared a memorandum outlining the reasons why the camps should not be closed, sent copies to Byrnes and to the American bishops, and arranged for Cardinal Stritch, chairman of the National Catholic Welfare Conference (NCWC) and archbishop of Chicago, to deliver a copy of the memorandum to President Truman. Should Byrnes not rescind the order to close the camps by March 31, Cardinal Stritch was directed to send copies of the memorandum to Senators Mead, Vandenberg, and Lucas.*[15]

The issue of the displaced persons was, O'Boyle argued in the memorandum, "a humane problem and as such is of concern to all who fought in and supported World War II. . . . Since 80% of these Displaced Persons are of the Catholic faith,† it is of double concern and of immediate importance to the Catholic people of the United States." Closing the camps would

> result in unwarranted suffering and injustice: a) It would be a deliberate injustice to turn loose on the famine economy of Germany hundreds of thousands of helpless men, women and children without any provision for their welfare. . . . b) In effect, it would result in the denial of the Right of Asylum to innocent refugees and the denial of freedom of choice to them . . . since such a policy would undoubtedly force repatriation out of abject despair. c) It would make for unjustifiable discrimination between racial groups of Displaced Persons that would call forth bitter recriminations from many quarters. There is no sound basis for dividing the Displaced into persecuted [the Jews] and non-persecuted persons [the non-Jewish DPs]. All are in equal need and in equal helplessness and insecurity.[16]

O'Boyle, Stritch, Spellman, and the Catholic hierarchy did not deny that the Jews had suffered during the war, but they refused to recognize that their suffering was substantially different from that experienced by other groups of displaced persons. Tens of thousands of Jews were, as a result of the war, displaced, homeless, and stateless, but so too were hundreds of thousands of Catholics whose countries had been taken

---

* Senator James Michael Mead, Democrat of New York, was running for governor against Thomas Dewey in November and would require Catholic support to win; Senator Arthur Vandenberg of Michigan was the recognized leader of the Republican Party in foreign policy matters; Senator Scott Lucas of Illinois was the Democratic Party whip and would in 1948 become majority leader.
† This was an exaggeration. Eighty percent of the DPs were Christians; 60 to 70 percent were Catholics.

over by Communist governments. In his letter to the American arch-bishops enlisting their support in the campaign to keep the camps open, Cardinal Stritch focused their attention on the favoritism being shown the Jews by Washington. "The Jews in the American zone of Germany have their own Displaced Persons Camps which are supported by our War Department and by UNRRA. The statement of our Department of State clearly says that closing the Jewish Camps is not under consid-eration. . . . The excuse given is that the Jews are considered in the special category of persecuted people."

Stritch warned that while it was important to put pressure on Wash-ington to keep the camps open, it had to be recognized that they could not "be kept open for an indefinite period." They would eventually have to be shuttered, and when that occurred, places would have to be found to resettle the Catholic displaced persons now in Germany. "The Jewish people of the United States have raised a large sum of money and they are ready to stand any expense in resettling the Jews who are in the special Camps in our zone in Germany." The Catholics had to fol-low suit.[17]

The bishops responded positively to Stritch's special delivery letter. "I have always felt that we have not pressed our government to do at least 10% as much for the persecuted Catholics as it has done for the Jews under, of course, persistent pressure," John Noll, the bishop of Fort Wayne, wrote Cardinal Stritch. While "Catholics in the Ukraine, in Poland generally, in Hungary and in other countries have been treated shamefully by Russia . . . the [American] government has not opened its mouth because we have never asked it to."[18]

The campaign against closing the camps proceeded on several levels. A meeting with President Truman was arranged for leaders of the Na-tional Catholic Welfare Conference, who brought along representatives of the Protestant Federal Council of Churches of Christ in America, the American Federation of Labor (AFL), and the Congress of Indus-trial Organizations (CIO). No one from any of the Jewish organizations was invited. The White House and key Democratic congressmen and senators were reminded that the Polish Catholic vote was vital in Chicago and other immigrant cities and that Catholics remained a large and influential segment of organized labor, a pillar of support for the Democrats.[19]

On April 12, Secretary of State Byrnes, who remained in favor of closing the camps, notified Truman about the religious and labor organizations that were campaigning to keep them open. "These groups appear to recognize that the camps cannot be maintained indefinitely, but they are alarmed by a plan to close them on any given date. Criticism has also been expressed," Byrnes warned Truman, "particularly in Catholic quarters, of the exception of 'persecuted groups' from the plan to close the camps. The Catholic spokesmen argue that if this is intended to include only Jews or primarily Jews, it is unfair because, they allege, Catholic displaced persons would also be subjected to persecution if they were to return to Yugoslavia or the Baltic states. No answer is likely fully to satisfy this criticism."[20]

The pressure was too much for Truman to withstand. Though his secretaries of war and state, together with the military authorities in Germany and Austria, held fast to their position that the camps should be closed, Truman, after initially signaling his agreement, backed down. On April 22, Secretary Byrnes announced that "it was decided [the passive voice here allowed Truman to evade full responsibility for the decision] to defer closing the camps for DPs in the American zone in Germany." The president agreed "with the position of the Army that these camps could not be maintained indefinitely," but he had chosen to keep them open at least until September, when the UN would reconvene to take up discussion of a successor organization to replace UNRRA. Three days later, in a personal letter to "My dear Cardinal Stritch," Truman confirmed that the camps would not be closed and apologized for not writing sooner.[21]

The decision to keep the camps open pushed the military back into an impossible situation. A month after Truman's decision was reached, on May 27, 1946, Howard Petersen, assistant secretary of war, urged

Secretary of War Patterson to raise again with Truman, "at the earliest opportunity," the question of closing the camps. The burden of $6 million a month in expenditures and eight thousand soldiers on active duty in the camps was simply too much. Patterson wrote Secretary of State Byrnes to request that Truman be asked to reconsider the decision to keep the camps open. Byrnes reported back that he had no intention of reopening the discussion. Truman had reversed himself once—and would not do so again. Patterson agreed that it was futile to approach the president. The camps would remain open.[22]

LONDON, SPRING TO SUMMER 1946

British military officials charged with caring for the Last Million were just as frustrated as the Americans by their government's refusal not to close the camps in their zones of occupation. Negotiations were under way to replace UNRRA with a new international refugee organization, but unless some dramatic change in policy was made, that organization would be faced with the same intractable problems. The Baltic and Ukrainian displaced persons were never going to accept repatriation; there remained a hard core of hundreds of thousands of Poles who appeared willing to stay in the camps indefinitely; and there was nowhere for the Jews but Palestine, which the British intended to keep closed to additional immigration.

In a July 4, 1946, internal "minute," Douglas MacKillop, head of the Refugee Department of the Foreign Office, argued rather strenuously, as had his American counterparts, that the camps should be closed and the DPs in them forced to return home or sink or swim in Germany.

> The duty of UNRRA and of the Allied military authorities was to locate the slave-workers, etc., forcibly expatriated by the Germans and to return them to their homes. It was obvious good

sense to concentrate such people in convenient centres for repatriation and to give them, pending their repatriation, a sufficient
dietary, that is to say a dietary superior to that of the population
generally, to remedy their undernourishment and to render them
fit to travel. But this was only as a preliminary to repatriation;
and now we have the indefensible anomaly that people who have no
intention of being repatriated are still being kept in centres and are
still being fed.

Moreover, UNRRA are spending $50 million in their dis-
placed persons administration in Germany alone this year; this
does not include food for displaced persons or any transportation
costs. The British people pay 17% of this. . . . There are few
genuine displaced persons in Germany and Austria now that repatriation is drying up, except the Jews. . . . There is nothing
complex about what should be done with non-repatriable displaced persons; they should be regarded and treated as ordinary
aliens living in Germany and Austria. . . . Non-repatriable displaced persons are simply refugees, and the practice of civilized
governments (and we govern part of Germany) has always been
to grant asylum but not assistance to them. Karl Marx enjoyed
asylum here, but neither the British nor any other government
paid him a pension or bought him a farm in Brazil. I except
Jewish displaced persons from these conclusions for the simple
but compelling reasons that the question of European Jewry is a
separate one.[23]

Despite these arguments, nothing was done to close the camps,
not that spring or summer or for years to come. Truman declined to
close them for overtly political reasons: he dared not arouse the ire of
the Catholic clergy or Polish ethnic associations. The British Labour
Party refused to close them because it feared that if hundreds of thousands of nonrepatriable Eastern Europeans were released into German
society, chaos would reign. The British Foreign Office feared, as well,

that closing the camps for non-Jewish displaced persons would raise questions about closing the Jewish ones—and that would inevitably put unwanted pressure on the British to allow them to emigrate to Palestine. Better to keep the camps open and operating.

GERMANY, MARCH TO MAY 1946

The military's only remaining option was to attempt to reduce the number of displaced persons in the camps by rigorously screening and removing those who did not belong: Baltic Germans who had become German citizens, *Volksdeutsche*, Nazi collaborators, and war criminals. Five days after Byrnes's announcement that the camps would remain open, the Adjutant General's office in Washington cabled Generals McNarney in Germany and Clark in Austria: "Indefinite postponement of closing DP camps necessitates screening of DP's remaining in centers be intensified rather than discontinued, and that those found ineligible for UN treatment be promptly discharged from assembly centers or placed under arrest or forcibly repatriated in accordance with existing directives."[24]

The British occupation authorities followed the American lead and expanded the screening of camp residents in their zones of occupation. If they had not done so, the Foreign Office feared, "other Governments concerned might allege that, by implication, we are harbouring as Displaced Persons, collaborators who should be forcibly repatriated." Still, the War Office made it very clear to the Foreign Office, which had ordered the screening, that "it may be extremely difficult to differentiate between those Displaced Persons who have assisted the enemy voluntarily, and those who have done so through *force majeure* [i.e., unforeseeable circumstances]."[25]

Screening questionnaires were distributed to the Last Million. They were asked for date of birth, nationality, citizenship, profession, vocation, and past employment, whether they had belonged to any political or military organizations, why and when they had left their homelands, why and when they had arrived in Germany, and whether they had come voluntarily or in an organized group.

The displaced persons worked together, prepped one another, and came up with stock, safe answers to each of the questions. "Before filling out the questionnaire," Ferdinand Kool would recall later, "all questions were weighed carefully with the National Committees and with acquaintances." When the questionnaires were completed and submitted, the displaced persons were called, in alphabetical order, before a tribunal of two military officers and an UNRRA observer, and asked to clarify or expand their answers.

"During the screenings," Kool recalled, "some quite comical dialogues appeared, like the following":

> "Are you learning English?"
> "No."
> "Why not?"
> "This language is not necessary."
> "How so?"
> "If the West wins, we will be able to return home and will
> have no need of English. If the Russians win, then we have to
> learn to speak Russian, but we already had to learn Russian."[26]

The screening process was slow and ineffectual. "In general there is no question but that under present conditions, given present facilities and personnel, it will be absolutely impossible for the Military Authorities to conduct a screening program which may be considered effective by even the most minimum standards," the UNRRA Central Committee reported to member nations on June 1, 1946. "The redeployment of skilled intelligence and counter-intelligence personnel in the British and American Armies has meant that the problem of screening has had to be assigned to inexperienced officers and enlisted men." The screeners were, with few exceptions, untrained, unprepared, and "completely uninterested in their assignment." Not able to read or speak the same languages as the DPs, they had to rely on interpreters, who were biased, usually on the side of the displaced persons. "The detection of collaborators in itself is not an easy process. Experience to date shows conclusively that the mere use of a questionnaire is wholly inadequate and that this must be followed up by intense investigations into the individual's background and extensive interrogations. Meanwhile it must be recognized that the collaborator will conveniently divest himself of any incriminating documents or other evidence."[27]

In August 1946, shortly after replacing Herbert Lehman as UNRRA director general, former congressman and New York City mayor Fiorello La Guardia convened a conference with high-ranking military officers to discuss screening and other matters of common concern. "Most respectfully," he requested that the British and American military "assign experienced and trained persons to the task of screening. By that I mean persons who have had experience in investigations, or in law, or in the enforcement of law." It was necessary, as well, that "a time limit" be set "beyond which the screening will not continue. Surely this cannot be kept up indefinitely. If screening has lagged and has been inefficient, the proper thing to do is to improve that service. It should be continued, but expeditiously and thoroughly, with a view to the termination of that work."

The military officers defended themselves by intimating, without much subtlety, that La Guardia, new to his position, didn't know what he was talking about. "In as much as the Director General apparently was dissatisfied with screening processes," Colonel Mickelson of the U.S. Army responded, rather facetiously, "I think we should tell him what we have done. . . . In March, we started our own program. We made a test screening to find out whether" the questionnaires were effective in identifying those who did not belong in the camps. "We screened some eighteen to twenty thousand people in and found it was no good. The DP's are clever; they have lived by their wits for many years, and to detect something that they don't want you to know, is very difficult." At the end of May 1946, the Army suspended screening to rewrite its questionnaire and retrain its personnel.

"Since that time," Mickelson triumphantly declared, "I am happy to inform you (this is not for publication) that we have screened 107,677 persons. Imagine what that means! 8,520 or 7.9% were found to be ineligible for UNRRA support, 35/40% were *Volksdeutsche.* 35% were eliminated because they had made false statements of some sort. 10% were found to be ex-enemy civilians. . . . Another 10% were found to be ex-enemy soldiers of one sort or another, and 5% were suspected of subversive or underground activities."[28]

Deconstructing these figures, we discover that the screening process Mickelson was so proud of had discharged 8,520 out of 107,566 DPs from the camps for a variety of reasons, but none, according to his own statement, because they had committed war crimes or collaborated with the Nazis.

The process the Army had set up, based on questionnaires, was never going to root out the collaborators and war criminals who had lied their way into the camps. Had the military authorities in Germany—or their commanders in Washington and London—been fully committed to rigorous and effective screening, they would have found a way to cooperate with Soviet, Polish, and Yugoslav government and army officers, who had the means of identifying the war criminals in the camps. The Allies had documentary evidence on German civilians, soldiers, and officers who had committed war crimes, but only the Soviet bloc had documents, many of them captured from the Germans, that might have established whether displaced persons now in the camps had volunteered for service in the German military or police forces or committed war crimes or cooperated with the Nazi occupying authorities in their homelands.

The Soviets had offered to share whatever evidence they had with the western Allies, but only if they were permitted to undertake or participate in the screening process. They had insisted that officials from the nations the DPs had come from, not those where they were currently living, were the only ones capable of effectively rooting out suspected collaborators and war criminals. Only their co-nationals spoke the DPs' languages, knew what questions to ask about family, work, and military service, and had the corroborating sources to sort out truth from lies.

The British and Americans, fearing that the Soviets wanted to take over the screening because they were intent on punishing not just those guilty of high-level collaboration, but also citizens whose only crime was opposition to the postwar Soviet-backed regimes, refused to allow them access to the camps or any role in the screening process. Rejecting Soviet offers to participate in the investigation process protected innocent displaced persons whose only crime was speaking out or quietly opposing the Soviets or the governments they backed. But it also had the effect of protecting thousands of collaborators and war criminals from discovery, trial, or, should they be found guilty, punishment.

There was another source that the military ignored in its screening, and that was the Jewish displaced persons themselves. There were among them numerous witnesses to atrocities committed in their hometowns and in the concentration, labor, and death camps. Had the Army attempted to utilize this source of evidence, it might have been able to apprehend some of the war criminals and collaborators hiding in plain sight in the camps. But the military had no intention of involving civilians, displaced persons in particular, in its screening.

10.

THE ANGLO-AMERICAN COMMITTEE
OF INQUIRY ISSUES ITS REPORT

*The British Reject Another Recommendation
for One Hundred Thousand Certificates
for Immigration to Palestine*

W HILE THE DEBATE OVER closing the camps continued in London and Washington, the Anglo-American Committee of Inquiry on Palestine, which President Truman had agreed to in November 1945, launched its investigation.

Its mandate was imposing in the extreme:

1. To examine political, economic and social conditions in Palestine as they bear upon the problem of Jewish immigration and settlement therein and the well-being of the peoples now living within. 2. To examine the position of the Jews in those countries in Europe where they have been the victims of Nazi and Fascist persecution, and the practical measures taken . . . to enable them to live free from discrimination and oppression and to make estimates of those who wish or will be impelled by their conditions to migrate to Palestine or other countries outside Europe. 3. To hear the views of competent witnesses and to consult

representative Arabs and Jews on the problem of Palestine. 4. To make such other recommendations as may be necessary to meet the immediate needs of the Jewish displaced persons in Europe by taking remedial action in the European countries so that the Jews might remain there or by the provision of facilities for emigration to and resettlement in countries outside Europe.[1]

As committee member James McDonald wrote entertainer and Jewish activist Eddie Cantor, the "job" the committee members had been entrusted with was so multilayered, so dense, "so difficult that the chances of success must be rated considerably less than even."[2]

Bartley Crum, another committee member, on arriving in Washington, had been taken aside by Loy Henderson, head of the State Department's Office of Near Eastern and African Affairs, who briefed him on the impact committee decisions would have not just on Jews and Arabs, but on the larger Western world. "There is one fact facing both the United States and Great Britain, Mr. Crum. That is the Soviet Union. It would be wise to bear that in mind when you consider the Palestine problem."

Crum would later be given the same warnings by a representative of the British Foreign Office. "British policy," he was told, rather sternly and more than once, "was based on the protection of British interests against Russia . . . [and] it should be in our interests to fall in with that policy."* The implications were obvious. No matter what the moral or humanitarian case for permitting Jewish displaced persons to immigrate to Palestine, if such immigration pushed the Arabs out of the British sphere of influence and into the Russian, it would cause the free world unimaginable harm. To safeguard the Middle East and its oil from the Soviets, it was necessary that the British and the Americans maintain a friendly relationship with the Arabs, even if that meant denying the Jewish displaced persons access to Palestine.[3]

---

* Henderson would, in a later oral history interview, deny having said such a thing, but he did not deny that he and the British believed the future of Palestine had to be considered within the context of threatened Soviet expansion into the Middle East.

The committee's first public sessions were held in Washington from January 7 through January 17, 1946. The focus, perhaps because it was Washington, was on Truman's request that one hundred thousand European Jews be given certificates to immigrate to Palestine. Jewish leaders and Earl Harrison, Dr. Reinhold Niebuhr, and Albert Einstein urged that Truman's recommendation be implemented at once. Arab leaders argued that increased Jewish immigration to Palestine would be, as Dr. Philip Hitti, the Lebanese-born professor of Semitic literature at Princeton, put it, "an imposition on the Arabs of an alien way of life which they resented and to which they would never submit. . . . 'Jewish immigration seems to us an attenuated form of conquest.'"[4]

The testimony in London followed the same pattern as in New York, but with more anti-Zionist witnesses, including British government officials who focused attention on the already unstable environment in Palestine. The Jewish underground, or Jewish Resistance Movement, which included the Haganah, the Palmach, its elite striking force, and two smaller but more violent dissident militias, the Irgun* and the Lehi, or Stern Gang,[†] had carried out numerous, sometimes murderous acts of what the British referred to as "terrorism," the Jews "resistance." Police stations and headquarters, government buildings, railway lines, military trucks and installations had been bombed; British officials, policemen, and soldiers murdered. The British had met each incident with more violence, leading to a spiral of bombings, incarcerations, and death. It would, the British implied, be foolhardy to introduce a new irritant into this already violent region by adding one hundred thousand Jews, thereby fomenting Arab violence, at a moment when the British were already overwhelmed with defending themselves against the Jewish underground.

From London, the Anglo-American Committee traveled to Europe,

---

* The armed wing of the Jewish underground organization connected to the right-wing, nationalist Revisionist Movement of Vladimir Jabotinsky, led by Menachem Begin.
† Lehi, the Zionist paramilitary organization, was often referred to as the Stern Gang, after Avraham Stern, its founder. It had once been part of Irgun but had separated from it.

where it split up into subcommittees to take testimony from military officials, government representatives, religious leaders, and displaced persons in Paris, Berlin, Łódź, Warsaw, Italy, and Vienna.

Bartley Crum with Sir Frederick Leggett, a British delegate, visited DP camps in Germany and Austria to "see for ourselves the condition of the displaced persons—those for whom President Truman had asked the chance to go to Palestine." At their first stop in Frankfurt, they were provided the results of an extensive UNRRA survey of the Jewish DPs' "desired place of residence." Of the 19,311 DPs queried, 18,702 had indicated Palestine. Crum and Leggett, in subsequent visits to the camps and interviews with the Jewish DPs, were able to confirm that the results of the UNRRA survey were accurate and that the vast majority of the Jewish DPs, as Dr. Grinberg, chairman of the Central Committee of Liberated Jews, told them in Munich, were determined to emigrate to Palestine.[5]

On February 28, the full committee, having completed its visits and interviews in Europe, flew to Cairo for a week, then took the train to Palestine, where it took statements from and interviewed witnesses for another three weeks. Subcommittees traveled to Damascus, Baghdad, and Amman to meet with Arab spokesmen.

The committee concluded its hearings in Jerusalem. In his testimony, which lasted four and a half hours, Chaim Weizmann emphasized that there was no future for Jews in Europe. "My brain reels when I think of the 6,000,000 Jews who were killed off in such a short time. . . . We are an ancient people. We have contributed to the world. We have suffered. We have a right to live—a right to survive under normal conditions."[6]

David Ben-Gurion opened his testimony by declaring that he and the Jewish Agency had spent long hours debating whether to cooperate. "It was said that the appointment of the Commission was practically a means of putting off the request of the president of the United States for an immediate admission of 100,000 refugees from Germany." In the end, it was decided that Ben-Gurion should testify because, while the committee had heard much from Jews from abroad, it needed to hear from someone who lived in Palestine. Unlike other Jewish spokesmen, in Washington, London, Europe, and Palestine, Ben-Gurion did not focus on the plight of the European Jews or the need to remove the survivors from Germany, but rather on the love of the Jewish people for the "Land of Israel." Six hundred thousand Jews lived there now and intended to remain, Ben-Gurion declared, whatever the Anglo-American Committee decided or the British decreed.

Committee members tried to get Ben-Gurion to comment on the Haganah and on Jewish violence against the British, but he refused to do so. Instead he affirmed, as Weizmann had, that he was against violence and that the Jewish Agency had no relationship to the Haganah or any other armed or paramilitary Jewish group. In the light of abundant evidence to the contrary, his testimony satisfied no one.[7]

As its three-month investigation came to a close, the committee heard from Albert Hourani, a British historian born in Manchester of Christian Lebanese parents, who had since the end of the war been working with the Arab Office in Jerusalem, the unofficial Palestinian foreign ministry. What the Arab Palestinians wanted, Hourani declared, was what the Western nations had fought for, particularly the United States, for two hundred years: their own government.

Point by point, Hourani dissected the three "intermediate solutions" to the Palestine problem that were under consideration by the committee: partition, a binational state, and the immediate admission of the hundred thousand Jewish survivors with decisions about a political settlement put off until a more propitious moment. The problem with all of them, including partition and a binational state, Hourani insisted, was that the Zionists would never be satisfied with them, but would continue to push for a larger and larger Jewish state. As for the proposal that one hundred thousand Jewish displaced persons be allowed to immigrate to Palestine, the Arabs could not even consider such a possibility until they were "given responsibility for their own national affairs. . . . The Arabs do not understand by what right Great Britain and the

United States demand of them that they should bear the main burden of solving the problem of refugees. The guilt for creating that problem does not rest upon the shoulders of the Arabs, but on those of Europe. The Arabs have already been compelled to bear more than their fair share of solving the Jewish problem."

The question of whether or not to remove one or a hundred thousand Jews from Europe and allow them to immigrate to Palestine had to be "seen in its general political framework. It must always be remembered that what the Zionists are aiming at is not to solve the refugee problem for its own sake, but to secure political domination in Palestine, and that their demand for immigration is only a step towards dominating Palestine."[8]

Following its exhaustive three-month tour of three continents, the committee flew to Lausanne, Switzerland, to write its report. The Americans declared that the issue of the hundred thousand certificates for immigration to Palestine was nonnegotiable; the British, that Palestine remain under their government's control for the time being.[9]

After a monthlong debate, the committee issued its report, with ten recommendations. It approved the issuance of the hundred thousand certificates for immigration to Palestine that President Truman had demanded and rejected the proposal for a Jewish homeland, which the British had opposed. In accordance with British wishes, it formally deplored the violence in Palestine, suggested that the Jewish Agency could, if it wished, control "the organization or use of illegal armies," and urged cooperation between the agency and the British authorities in reducing hostilities.[10]

The report pleased no one, certainly not the Zionists, who were denied a "Jewish homeland," or the Arabs, who were opposed to increased Jewish immigration. Foreign Secretary Bevin was particularly disturbed. When he promised the committee members that he would accept their recommendations should they be unanimous, he had counted on the British members, whom he had appointed, to reject any call for the immediate issuance of one hundred thousand certificates of immigration to Palestine. What Bevin hadn't taken into consideration, having himself never toured the concentration camps or the displaced persons camps or the abandoned, devastated ghettos, was the impact firsthand visits and reports on conditions there would have on committee members, American and British. "They had smelled the unique and unforgettable smell of huddled, homeless humanity," committee member Richard Crossman would later write. "They had seen and heard for themselves what it means to be the isolated survivor of a family deported to a German concentration camp or slave labor. . . . They knew that they were not wanted by the Western democracies. . . . They knew that far away in Palestine there was a national home willing and eager to receive them and to give them a chance of rebuilding their lives, not as aliens in a foreign state but as Hebrews in their own country. . . . Judged by sober realities, their only hope of an early release was Palestine."[11]

WASHINGTON AND LONDON, APRIL TO JULY 1946

As soon as the report was completed, Judge Joseph Hutcheson, the chair of the American delegation, flew to Washington to present it to President Truman; Sir John Singleton, his British counterpart, left for London to deliver it to Foreign Secretary Bevin.

The British put off making any formal response and tried to persuade Truman to do so as well. The president refused. Instead, he announced triumphantly on April 30 that he was "very happy that the request which I made for the immediate admission of 100,000 Jews into Palestine has been unanimously endorsed by the Anglo-American Committee of Inquiry. The transference of these unfortunate people should now be accomplished with the greatest dispatch."[12]

The following day, on May 1, Prime Minister Attlee, at the close of question hour in the House of Commons, obliquely answered Truman.

While the committee "report recommends that 100,000 certificates for the admission of Jews to Palestine should be awarded immediately," he declared, "the practical difficulties involved in the immediate reception and absorption of so large a number would obviously be very great. It is clear from the facts presented in the report regarding the illegal armies maintained in Palestine and their recent activities that it would not be possible for the Government of Palestine to admit so large a body of immigrants unless and until these formations have been disbanded and their arms surrendered." The committee, he emphasized, had not only "drawn attention to the failure of the Jewish Agency to cooperate in dealing with this evil [but had] expressed the view that the Agency should . . . take a positive part in the suppression of these activities."[13]

Attlee had made it clear that despite the recommendations of the Anglo-American Committee, the British government had no intention of permitting one hundred thousand or one thousand Jewish DPs to immigrate to Palestine, nor would it consider doing so until the Jewish Agency had "suppressed" the Haganah. This, the Jewish Agency would never do, as it considered the Haganah its only protection against Arab violence and the British military.

"If the Prime Minister meant what he said—and on this occasion, I am afraid that he said exactly what he meant," Ben-Gurion wrote to Zionist and Labour Party stalwart Harold Laski, "that nullifies the only, or at least the main, positive recommendation made by the Commission."[14]

General John Hilldring, who had resigned from the Army to take up the post of assistant secretary of state for occupied areas, was incensed, though not entirely surprised, by the British response. "As anticipated, the British are stalling on the Anglo-American Committee's recommendation for authorization of 100,000 immigration visas to Palestine," he wrote Under Secretary Dean Acheson, to whom had fallen by default the unofficial position as Middle East policy director. The U.S. government, Hilldring argued, could not permit the British to turn down its own committee's unanimous recommendation. "Our military and political interests in Germany and Austria require that we press for immediate implementation of the Committee's recommendation. I believe that unless we exercise unremitting pressure to this end, these interests will not receive adequate representation by our Government and there will be no effective counteraction to British tactics of stalling and confusing the entire issue." He suggested that Acheson request that the president make a public statement "stressing the urgent necessity . . . for issuance of 100,000 immigration visas" and offer to "assume primary responsibility for movement of all of the 100,000 from Europe to Palestine."[15]

Hilldring's urgency was shared by President Truman, who, for a variety of political, economic, military, and no doubt humanitarian reasons, was anxious to get the Jewish survivors out of Germany and the American camps. Unfortunately, as the State Department knew only too well—and Truman was beginning to learn—there were limits to the reach of American influence on British policy in the Middle East.

Acheson, fearful that the gulf—and the public demonstration of it—between the president and the prime minister was unnecessary and unproductive, proposed as a step forward that each government begin unilateral consultations with the Jews and with the Arabs on the report's recommendations, and then convene bilateral talks to hammer out an Anglo-American position on Palestine. Truman approved Acheson's proposal and forwarded it to Prime Minister Attlee.[16]

Attlee, for his part, thanked Truman "very much indeed for your message of yesterday about Palestine and for your kindness in consulting me" and agreed that consultations with the Jews and Arabs would be a good idea, but before that could take place, a study should be undertaken "by experts of our two Governments of the financial and military liabilities involved."[17]

The president, fearful that Attlee was attempting once again to delay any final decision on the hundred thousand certificates for immigration, requested "some indication of subjects which your govt thinks should form basis of these discussions." Attlee responded with a list of forty subjects that required study before bilateral negotiations could begin.[18]

Despite the British stalling tactics, Truman remained confident that he would in relatively short order convince Attlee and Bevin to accept the Anglo-American Committee's recommendation. David Niles, the president's chief assistant on Jewish affairs and Palestine, informed David Ben-Gurion that the War Department had already "expressed an official view that the transfer of the 100,000 to Palestine would not necessitate more than two months' time. The War Department wants to finish this job in the shortest possible time due to the problems which they face as long as the Jewish D.P.s remain predominantly in the American Zone of Occupation in Germany." The State Department, often a source of delay, certainly on implementing decisions like this one, offered no resistance. According to Niles, State understood "perfectly well that the president's interest in the 100,000 is very great and that they cannot overlook his desire in seeing this part of the report realized in the shortest period of time."[19]

Truman and Niles were mistaken. The British were not going to formally reject the proposal for the hundred thousand immigration certificates, but neither did they have any intention of implementing it. As Foreign Secretary Bevin declared rather forcefully, in a memorandum shared with the secretary of state, "Before any decision is taken as to whether the report should be put into force or not the British Govt must know what assistance they can count on obtaining from the U.S. Govt. . . . Before any decision could be taken to admit 100,000 additional immigrants as recommended in the report, the illegal Jewish armies must be suppressed and there must be a general disarmament throughout Palestine. Otherwise these armies would be swollen by recruits drawn from the new immigrants."[20]

The escalation of Arab-Jewish violence in mid-June and July 1946 and a series of brazen attacks by the Jewish underground forces against British officials in Palestine strengthened Attlee's and Bevin's determination not to yield to American demands. They were incensed that Truman was demanding that the British open the gates of Palestine to Jewish immigration, while refusing at the same time to spend money or send troops to keep the peace. While Attlee, as was his manner, proceeded cautiously, his foreign secretary, Ernest Bevin, could not.

"Regarding the agitation in the United States, and particularly New York, for 100,000 Jews to be put into Palestine," Bevin declared at the annual Labour Party conference in mid-June, he hoped "it will not be misunderstood in America if I say, with the purest of motives, that that was because they did not want too many of them in New York."[21]

Bevin was correct, of course. Truman was doing all he could to resettle the Jewish survivors in Palestine because he feared he could not get them visas for America. Unfortunately, in stating the obvious, Bevin had again put his foot squarely in his mouth. The response to his remarks was immediate, especially in New York City, where protests were organized, rallies held, voices raised, statements issued. The British foreign secretary was denounced, asked to resign, accused of being another Hitler.[22]

Lord Inverchapel, Halifax's successor as British ambassador to the United States, cabled Bevin in London:

> Your remarks at Bournemouth have caused the inevitable uproar here. They provided the major theme for last night's long scheduled meeting to protest against the Palestine delays, held at Madison Square Garden, New York, and attended by some 12,000 persons. . . . More serious, however, than this local ferment is the fact that your remarks are being widely interpreted here as an indication that His Majesty's Government have already made up their minds not (repeat not) to admit the 100,000 and never intended to carry out the Anglo-American Committee's recommendations. In view of the president's personal association with the 100,000 proposals, it is being argued in anti-Administration circles that you have made the president

look foolish. . . . Your criticism of New York has, of course, not only hit the nail on the head but driven it woundingly deep.[23]

TRUMAN HAD LOST HIS FIGHT, though he still didn't know it.

In mid-July, yet another Anglo-American committee, led by Herbert Morrison, British home secretary, and Henry Grady, a career American diplomat, was organized to reconcile the divergent American and British responses to the Anglo-American Committee's recommendations.

The Morrison-Grady committee, as it came to be known, devised a plan to divide Palestine into semi-autonomous Jewish and Arab cantons under British trusteeship and a British sector that included Jerusalem, Haifa port, and the Negev. It specified that no element of the plan, including the issuance of the hundred thousand certificates for the Jewish displaced persons, could be implemented until the plan, in its entirety, had been approved by both Jews and Arabs. That provision alone doomed the proposal. The Jews were not going to settle for a semi-autonomous sector under British trusteeship; the Arabs were not going to agree to any plan that included the immigration of Jewish DPs from Europe.[24]

On July 27, James McDonald, a member of the Anglo-American Committee, accompanied by Democratic senators Robert Wagner and James Mead of New York, met with Truman at the White House to voice their concerns and urge him not to accept the Morrison-Grady plan, which McDonald declared in a written memorandum for the president was "wholly inconsistent with the recommendations of the Anglo-American Committee" and nothing less than "a direct repudiation of the president's insistence that the admission of the 100,000 should not be made contingent upon agreement on long-term involved and controversial political policies." Truman interrupted McDonald several times during their meeting to admonish him for criticizing a plan that hadn't been officially released. "He didn't want this thing questioned," McDonald wrote his friend Eddie Cantor.[25]

On July 30, Senators Wagner and Robert Taft assailed the plan from the floor of the Senate. "Mr. Wagner called the plan 'a deceitful device to stifle the hopes of a long-suffering people.' Mr. Taft said that it was a 'cynical plan' that would mean the 'complete frustration of' Jews in Palestine and 'deep despair for the million and one-half surviving Jews in Europe.'" That same day, the president was visited by a group of New York congressmen who urged him to reject the proposal and "insist on the immediate admission of 100,000 Jews." The president was inattentive, annoyed, and dismissive. He had had his fill of complaints. "He ended the conference abruptly, the witnesses said, before the Representatives were ready to leave." Still, he had heard what they had to say.[26]

Under Secretary of State Acheson informed the British ambassador in Washington that Truman could not endorse the new plan because "he could not carry with him the support necessary to fulfill the proposals which he was called upon to make," among them that the United States not only provide "moral support" to the plan, but that the president ask Congress to admit fifty thousand displaced persons and allocate $50 million as a grant to Palestine and $250 million in loans for Middle Eastern area development projects. There was no way that Congress was going to approve such requests.[27]

The British were aghast at the president's precipitous rejection of a plan that he had barely had time to review. Lord Inverchapel cabled London:

> This deplorable display of weakness is, I fear, solely attributable to reasons of domestic politics which, it will be recalled, caused the Administration last year to use every artifice of persuasion to defer the announcement about the establishment of the Anglo-American Committee until after the New York elections. The director of the Near Eastern Division [Loy Hen-

derson], the official in the State Department responsible for handling the Palestine question, frankly admitted as much in talk with me this evening. But for the attitude of the Zionists, he declared, there was nothing in the joint recommendations which would not have been acceptable to the United States Government. Unfortunately, the Zionists had seen fit to condemn the recommendations root and branch.[28]

The British were further infuriated that while the Americans continued to demand that the British open the gates of Palestine, they refused to open their own or ask any other nation to do so. Six weeks earlier, at a June 15, 1946, news conference, when "asked whether the United States might not get along a little better with Britain in the matter [of the hundred thousand immigration certificates to Palestine] if we made some gesture toward letting some of them into this country," the president responded that he intended to abide by the nation's current immigration laws. "He had no intention of asking Congress for a modification of the immigration laws to permit admission of a larger number of Jews into this country."[29]

GERMANY: THE JEWISH DP CAMPS, MAY TO JULY 1946

The twists and turns in Anglo-American negotiations had a visceral effect on the Jewish displaced persons in Germany. They had been elated when in May 1946 word spread that the Anglo-American Committee of Inquiry had unanimously recommended the issuance of a hundred thousand certificates. Their prayers had been answered; they would soon be released from their German purgatory to enter their promised land. Then came the crashing realization that Prime Minister

Attlee and Foreign Secretary Bevin had no intention of issuing any new immigration certificates.

"By mid-1946," according to Zeev Mankowitz, "the remnants of European Jewry began to feel themselves trapped on German soil. What was supposed to have been a way station and staging ground for mass aliyah was beginning to look like a *cul-de-sac.*"[30]

Not every Jewish survivor dreamed of a new life in Palestine—there were anti-Zionist factions, parties, organizations in each of the camps—but the vast majority, somewhere in the vicinity of 90 percent as the UNRRA survey of early 1946 had demonstrated, whether or not they envisioned Palestine as their promised land, understood the need to establish a Jewish homeland there.

"For most DPs," as Atina Grossmann observed in *Jews, Germans, and Allies,* "Zionism was not a deeply held ideological or religious belief but rather, as various Israeli scholars have suggested, a 'catastrophic Zionism,' born of the conviction that there could be no viable future in a blood-soaked Europe. It was a 'functional' Zionism that provided a coherence to their lives and some sense of future possibility, both individual and collective."[31]

The British had affirmed that they would keep closed the gates to Palestine, but the Jewish DPs refused to abandon hope. They would beat against those gates, climb over and under, break through, organize, and immigrate illegally, if they could not do so legally. They would not give up until the British permitted them to proceed from their camps to their promised land.

II.

———

THE POLISH JEWS ESCAPE
INTO GERMANY
The British Hold Firm on Palestine

GERMANY, NOVEMBER 1945 TO 1946

The exodus was unexpected and inexorable. Thousands of Polish Jews who had spent the war in hiding or with the partisans or in the Soviet Union and thousands more who had at war's end returned to their villages, towns, and cities to search for family or relatives were by the winter of 1945–46 crossing back from Poland into the American zone of occupation in Germany, fleeing a murderous antisemitism for the safety of displaced persons camps.

The years of Nazi occupation had not lessened Polish antisemitism, but rather, in a frighteningly perverse way, had legitimized, hardened, regularized it. The murder of three million Polish Jews had opened up new social spaces and economic opportunities for non-Jews. Peasants, townspeople, small and large landowners and businessmen, local officials took what they could from the absent Jews: land, farms, apartments, homes, shops, factories, and whatever assets the departing Jews had not been able to hide or carry with them. With the war now over, their country devastated, and their own resources diminished, the

Poles had no intention of giving back to the Jews what they had taken from them.

To protect themselves, their families, and their newly acquired assets, the non-Jewish Poles informed the returning Jews that it would be best for all if they left. An unnamed Jewish military chaplain in Frankfurt, in a letter to his American family on January 19, 1946, recalled how "numerous Polish Jews have come into the office during recent weeks, all with similar stories: having returned home to Poland after the war, they received letters warning them to get out before three days if they wish to remain alive." Had the threats against the Jews been idle ones, the survivors might have stayed in place. But the violence that accompanied them was all too real.[1]

The Polish provisional government had welcomed the Jews, several of whom assumed positions with the central leadership. Unfortunately, outside the larger cities the provisional government had neither the popular support nor the influence nor the police power to protect them. The returning Jews were caught in the cross fire between pro- and anti-government forces. It was assumed, as it had been during the war and would be afterward, that there was an unbreakable affinity between Bolshevism and Judaism, that the Jews were proponents of the new pro-Soviet provisional government. "Jews and Communists were," Yehuda Bauer has written, "equated in right-wing propaganda in the well-worn Nazi manner. The Jew-hatred of many Poles, and especially among the peasantry, was now whipped up for antigovernment attacks."[2]

The pogroms, the beatings, the shootings in the street were not ordered or directed from above. The violence against the Jews was homegrown, endemic, and encouraged by popular support. It was not carried out in the middle of the night, but often in broad daylight, in public view. Local officials could not halt the violence even had they tried to, which they rarely did.

The flight from Poland required enormous sacrifices: journeys by foot of hundreds of miles; the liquidation of assets to pay smugglers and bribe bandits, police, army, and border guards; the never-ending fear that they would be jailed or returned to the hometowns they had fled. But the horrific reality is that tens of thousands of Polish Jews endured these hardships and smuggled themselves into Germany and the American zone of occupation because they felt safe nowhere else.

"Every day," Eli Rock of the JDC wrote on November 11, 1945, to Simon Rifkind, Jewish adviser to the military,

> at least a hundred people come into the Munich area from Poland, but at the present time there is not a single Jewish camp in the neighborhood which has place for them. While some of them do manage to slip into the existing camps, many of them are less successful and have no choice but to remain in Munich, either in the entirely unsatisfactory quarters of the Deutsches Museum transit center or simply on the streets or God knows where else. When it is recalled that a large percentage of these Polish emigres are acutely in need of medical care (of one recent group, 40% were found to be tubercular) and that most of them have desperate need for clothing and food, the crisis character of the present situation becomes evident. . . . Unquestionably this whole problem of space for the Polish infiltrees has reached an emergency stage and further delay of even a few days seems hardly possible to tolerate.[3]

By early December 1945, Chaplain Abraham Klausner estimated that some ten thousand of the twenty-five thousand Jewish DPs in Bavaria had recently "fled from Poland and have come to whatever sanctuary this area has to offer. At the present time the Polish Jews are arriving in large numbers and as difficult as it is we manage to share our misery with them."[4]

In Munich, at the Deutsches Museum, which served as the assembly center for arriving DPs, conditions were rapidly deteriorating. Susan

Pettiss, a social worker with UNRRA, noted in her diary that there were 1,500 people in a building with 1,000 beds and cooking facilities for 800. "On arriving back at the Museum I had found a group of 113 Jews had arrived after traveling for eight days, tired, cold and hungry. Every bed and room at the Museum was filled. . . . Finally arranged for disinfection, setting up cots in a hall, feeding with Kosher food. For the first time it was necessary to say we could take no more people. It was one of the most heart-rending things I ever had to do—on a cold, wet night."[5]

WASHINGTON, DECEMBER 1945
TO JANUARY 1946

Though UNRRA staffers in Germany like Susan Pettiss were charged with the day-to-day operations at the assembly center and camps, it was the American army of occupation that bore the burden of feeding, sheltering, and caring for the new arrivals from Poland.

On November 30, 1945, Major General John Hilldring warned Secretary of War Patterson in Washington of the "urgent and complicated problem resulting primarily from acute anti-Semitism in eastern Europe, mainly Poland. . . . The Jews of Europe sustained terrible persecution and enormous losses under German occupation (less than 10% of pre-war Polish Jewry survived) and the comparatively few remnants are even now not able to survive in many parts of eastern Europe. Realistically, there is only one haven in all Europe for these people and that is the United States Zone, Germany." Regrettably, Hilldring conceded, the military and UNRRA could care for only a finite number of additional displaced persons. Providing "a haven for religious and racial persecutees" fleeing Poland, while maintaining an "adequate standard of care" for those already in the American zone of occupation, would require enhanced funding, imports of goods and foods from the United

States, and "additional personnel, military or civilian," which would be difficult, if not impossible, to wring out of Congress.[6]

On December 19, Secretary of War Patterson wrote Dean Acheson at the State Department to ask for "a firm policy decision" on how to handle the influx of Polish Jews.[7]

The State Department, before responding to Patterson's request, cabled Ambassador Arthur Bliss Lane for his assessment of the situation. Lane replied that the "reports regarding persecution of the Jews and pogroms in Poland are greatly exaggerated. . . . I have personally investigated reports regarding alleged pogrom in Krakow last August and am convinced this was isolated demonstration of ill feeling which broke out because of irresponsible acts of some young hoodlums."[8]

Based on Ambassador Lane's review, the State Department concluded that while the "refugees . . . give reports of pogroms and persecution . . . so far no evidence has been uncovered supporting reports of physical persecution, nor does the appearance of the refugees even in regard to nourishment or clothing indicate that such has been the case." Therefore, and because "the number of persons who can be received and cared for in the United States zone in Germany is, according to the reports, already exceeded," the State Department recommended that the borders be closed to the entrance of further displaced persons.[9]

On January 13, the chief of staff of the War Department cabled military commanders in Germany that the State Department had ordered them to close the borders into the American zone of occupation in Germany "at such time as maximum absorptive capacity of U.S. Zone is reached." Because the "maximum absorptive capacity" in the American zone, which was estimated to be 16.5 million, had not yet been reached, the borders would, for the time being at least, remain open.[10]

LONDON, DECEMBER 1945
TO JANUARY 1946

While the occupying military in the American zone in Germany and the State Department in Washington debated whether and how long to keep zonal borders open, the British had no difficulty reaching a decision. The British commander in chief in Berlin had determined in early December that because the Polish Jews were "Polish citizens, they cannot be described as persons displaced by their homes by reason of the war, nor as refugees from persecution instigated by Germany or her allies. We are therefore refusing them food and accommodation in our sector of Berlin and onward transit into our zone."[11]

"The precise reason for the British order is uncertain," Gladwin Hill of the *New York Times* reported on December 9, 1945, in an article headlined "Polish Jews Face Hunger in Berlin." Still, Hill concluded, "there are some indications that the British, because of the Palestine problem, are reluctant to give special cognizance to this new and unexpected aggravation of it."[12]

The British military in Germany and the Foreign Office in London recognized that turning away the Jewish refugees from Poland would cause an uproar in the press and put them at odds with the Americans, but this did not deter them. Ian Henderson, a refugee specialist at the Foreign Office, when informed that the British military authorities had closed the border to Polish Jews, applauded the decision. "The influx of Polish Jews into Berlin is doubtless, as indicated by the Commander-in-Chief, a part of the present Zionist plan for embarrassing the military authorities in Germany and pushing the idea that Europe is unfit for Jews to live in and therefore that as many of them as possible should emigrate to Palestine."[13]

While Bevin and the Foreign Office insisted, as had American ambassador Lane, that the Jews in Poland were in no danger and that the movement of thousands into Germany was part of a vast Zionist conspiracy, the British ambassador, Victor Cavendish-Bentinck, disagreed. He wrote Bevin on December 19:

> The Poles appear to me to be as anti-Semitic as they were twenty-five years ago. All the Jews at present in Poland are anxious to leave and . . . in a few years' time Poland will be one of the countries in the world where there will be practically no persons of Jewish extraction. The Polish population are now determined to keep trade in their own hands. Although some 180,000 Polish Jews are expected to return from Russia, they will find it very hard to establish prosperous businesses such as Jews had there before the war. . . . I have no evidence at present of direct Zionist inspiration [for the] movement out of Poland, and I believe that the facts mentioned in this dispatch are a sufficient explanation of it. I regret to state that a number of reports have been received at this Embassy of murders of Jews throughout Poland, mainly in small towns and villages.[14]

Robin Hankey, the chargé d'affaires at the British embassy in Warsaw, in a separate dispatch to London, confirmed that the exodus of the Jews was not part of a Zionist conspiracy. "Most of the movement is spontaneous and is due to the fact that twenty-five million Poles dislike Jews. . . . If the Jews do not live now-a-days in very much physical danger (though there have been murders), this is definitely not an easy country for a Jew to earn a living in and I was told by the president of the Jewish Socialist Organization here yesterday that in the whole of Warsaw, there were only about ten Jewish shops. This I regard as a picturesque exaggeration but there certainly are extremely few."[15]

Despite evidence to the contrary, conspiracy stories continued to be employed by British officials who should have known better. In early

January, Lieutenant General Sir Frederick Morgan, formerly of the British army and now chief of UNRRA's displaced persons operations in Germany, declared in impromptu remarks after a January 2, 1946, press conference that the Polish Jews who were arriving in Berlin appeared well dressed, well fed, their "pockets bulging with money." They had not fled pogroms, but were instead infiltrating into the British zone of Germany as part of a Zionist conspiracy.

Morgan's comments were picked up by newspaper editors everywhere who knew a good story when they saw one. "The London *Star* headed its leader with the word STUPID. . . . The Manchester *Guardian* (January 4) termed Morgan's remarks 'childish nonsense' at best, 'and at worst too close an echo of Hitler's ravings.'" Eddie Cantor took out a paid advertisement in the *New York Times* in which he declared that he had "thought that Hitler was dead." The World Jewish Congress and every Jewish organization in Britain and the United States called for Morgan's resignation.[16]

Had Morgan not been the highest-ranking UNRRA official in Europe or a close associate of British foreign secretary Bevin, or a trusted, beloved member of the British military, his remarks would have had less force. But coming as they did from so prominent a British official, they had to be taken seriously. British UNRRA officials asked Morgan to resign, but he refused, claiming he was not and had never been an antisemite. Instead he boarded a ship for America to argue his case with Director General Lehman. Supported by a number of military men and some Jewish officials who vouched for him, Morgan succeeded in holding on to his position. His crime had been a lack of discretion, of saying aloud what so many in London and Washington expressed in private.

POLAND, EARLY 1946

The exodus of Polish Jews to safety in the American zone of occupation had just begun. Large numbers of those who had survived the war* had escaped the killing fields and gas chambers by crossing the border into the Soviet Union. Their exile lasted for years. Children were born, parents died, young men and women aged into adults in a foreign land, not knowing if they would ever return to the place of their birth. The war ended in May 1945, but Poland remained thousands of miles away, and the exiles, without papers or bribe money, remained in place, until on July 6, 1945, they were informed by the Soviet government that they were not only free to leave the USSR, but that transportation would be supplied for their journey back to Poland, as soon as the Soviets had completed the transfer of their own citizens.

Edith Milman was one of the 200,000 to 250,000 Polish Jews who with her extended family had spent the war in the Soviet Union. The Milmans had fled Kraków in advance of the German invasion and re-settled with thousands of other Polish Jews in Soviet-occupied Lwów. In the spring of 1940, after her father turned down the offer of a Soviet passport and citizenship, the family was visited by the secret police, told to pack their belongings, and deported to Sverdlovsk in the Urals, where they were moved into a small house in a camp compound and put to work. When, after the German invasion of the Soviet Union, Stalin offered the Poles—who were now his allies against the Germans—amnesty for their supposed crimes, Edith and her family were allowed to leave the compound and, with thousands of other Jews, traveled as far south and east as they could, desperate to escape the Russian winter. They ended up in Tajikistan in Central Asia, where they would make their home for the next five years.[17]

---

* Of the 380,000 Polish Jewish survivors (out of a prewar population of 3.25 million), 200,000 to 250,000 had spent the war in the Soviet Union.

Rachel Golant, the mother of Joseph Berger, the *New York Times* reporter, editor, and author of the memoir and family history *Displaced Persons*, escaped Poland during the German invasion in the fall of 1939. After several detours, she made her way with friends and her brother Simcha to Lwów, where they registered for work in the Soviet Union and were put on a freight train for the journey of sixteen hundred miles to "the foot of the Ural Mountains and the smokestacks of the industrial city of Lys'va." The workers' paradise they had hoped to find was anything but. There was never enough food to eat, spies were everywhere hunting down "Zionist traitors," the work was exhausting, the barrack rooms cold and overcrowded, thievery rampant. Her older brother, Simcha, who suffered from tuberculosis, was arrested for "speculation" and went into hiding to escape what he knew would be a death sentence should he be sent to jail. Simcha would not survive the war. Rachel also spent time in jail, but she was healthy enough to come out alive. In the spring of 1943, she was introduced by her younger brother, Yasha, to Marcus, a Polish Jew who had been drafted into a Soviet army work battalion and assigned to a factory that made shoes and boots for the Red Army. In December, Rachel and Marcus were married. They were able to make a life in Lys'va, in part because Marcus "earned enough for us to eat regularly."[18]

In the early spring of 1946, the Milmans, the Bergers, and tens of thousands of other Polish Jews boarded cattle cars and freight trains for the long journey home. The Bergers planned to resettle in the formerly German regions of Silesia, but when Marcus Berger, Joe's father, learned that there was no acceptable housing there, he moved the family to Warsaw, a short train ride from Otwock, his wife Rachel's birthplace and family home.

"I didn't have the courage to go to Otwock, but I finally made myself go," Rachel recalled. "The station was exactly the same. . . . What was different was that in the crowd of passengers I didn't see a single Jewish face. Otwock when I was a girl was full of Jews—Hasidim, socialist

Jews, plain Jews. . . . I walked around the station. I couldn't make myself go into the town."

In the station, she met by chance "the man who delivered milk among our neighbors when I lived in Otwock. . . . He didn't know what happened to my father and the children. He told me that many Jews starved to death. Anyone who survived was shot when they liquidated the ghetto or else they were taken to Treblinka. 'There's no use leaving the station because no one is here anymore.'" Rachel took the next train back to Warsaw.[19]

The Milmans returned from Tajikistan to their home in Kraków in the summer of 1946. They were greeted at the entrance to their former apartment building by the superintendent, who insisted that there was nothing for them there anymore, that the Germans had taken all the furniture. They walked around town, but found no one they had known. "The Jews were all gone."[20]

WASHINGTON, MARCH TO JULY 1946

On May 2, 1946, Under Secretary of State Acheson alerted Truman that the War Department had "urged the necessity of closing the borders immediately, at least as an interim measure, to prevent any large influx in the near future." Acheson advised Truman to reject the military's request. "It would be unfortunate, particularly in view of the humanitarian reputation achieved by our policy to date, for the issues to be blurred and good will to be dissipated by closing the borders at this time if it is not really essential. It must be borne in mind that the borders can be effectively closed only by using German border patrols." Acheson suggested as an alternative that a "few key Jewish leaders . . . should be invited to a confidential conference with the Acting Secretary of State and the Secretary of War to discuss only the border closing." At this conference, the Jewish leaders would be asked to do whatever they could to discourage the Polish Jewish exodus into Germany "by making known in Jewish circles in Central and Eastern Europe the complications which would result." The implication was that if the Jews themselves did not reduce the numbers attempting to enter the American zone, the military would have no alternative but to close the borders.[21]

The Jewish leaders agreed to cooperate with the government "to prevent a stampede into the American Zone, which would pose unmanageable difficulties for the military authorities." Rabbi Philip Bernstein, newly appointed as the Jewish adviser to General McNarney, Eisenhower's successor in Germany, was charged with conveying this message and warning to Jewish organizations in Europe.

Unfortunately, as Rabbi Bernstein reported back to New York, there appeared to be no way to stop, much less stabilize or decrease, the exodus.

> This is due not only to the greater ease of movement during the summer months, but also to the increasing violence of uncontrolled anti-Semitism in Poland and the desperate hope of early migration into Palestine. On the basis of personal conversations with many hundreds of recent Polish Jewish infiltrees, I can say that this infiltration is spontaneously motivated and that many of these people are literally fleeing for their lives.
>
> Closing the borders would be impractical because it would not work. These people, I repeat, are fleeing for their lives. Obstacles do not and will not deter them. If they will not be able to enter through proper channels, they will find other ways. . . . It may be said that the Army could keep them out by the use of force. It is my opinion that if these borders were to be closed, the United States Army would then be called upon to shoot down thousands of Jews or even worse because of the shortage of American personnel, it would call upon German guards to do this.[22]

KIELCE, POLAND, JULY 1946

Rabbi Bernstein's letter was written on June 28, 1946. A week later came news of the pogrom in Kielce.

A nine-year-old boy, the son of a shoemaker, had on July 4, 1946, appeared at the local police station to report that he had been kidnapped and held captive for two days in the cellar of a building where a few hundred Jews recently repatriated from the Soviet Union were living. While captive, he claimed to have witnessed the ritual murder of several Christian children. The police escorted the boy back to the building, where a crowd had already gathered. Soldiers and local policemen entered the building to search for Polish children and Jewish weapons. A shot was fired—no one knows by whom.

"Some 20 people," Baruch Dorfman, who was on the third floor, recalled, "locked themselves in a small room. But they started shooting at us through the door, and they wounded one person, who later died from the injuries. They broke in. These were soldiers in uniform and a few civilians. I was wounded then. They ordered us to go outside. They formed a double row. In the staircase there were already civilians and also women. Soldiers hit us with rifle butts. Civilians, men and women, also beat us. . . . We came down to the square. Others who were brought out with me were stabbed with bayonets and shot at." When it was over, some forty to forty-five Jews who had returned from the Soviet Union to make a home for themselves in Poland had been stoned to death, beaten to death, thrown from windows, shot, bayoneted.[23]

The number of Jews fleeing Poland increased dramatically as news of Kielce spread throughout the country.

*A woman mourns her husband at a public burial for
the victims of the Kielce pogrom, July 1946.*

WASHINGTON, JULY 1946

On July 22, at 11 a.m., in response to the accelerating exodus from Poland, Dean Acheson convened an emergency meeting with Secretary of
War Patterson, Assistant Secretary of State Hilldring, several high military officials, and the leaders of the major Jewish organizations. The
first item on the agenda was the reading of a report from General Mc-
Narney. The cost of providing food, clothing, and other expenses for
the Jewish displaced persons was approaching $2 million a month; the
camps were overcrowded; there was a shortage of "adequate facilities"
for new DPs; and the "preferential treatment of Jewish DP's [was] caus-
ing considerable difficulty in the handling of other DP's as well as of
the German population."

After reading McNarney's report, Acheson informed the Jewish
leaders that because of the "sharp increase in infiltration since the

previous meeting in May, the American Government has no choice but to close the border as of September 1." Though Acheson "maintained that there was no room for delay . . . he assured the Jewish delegates that no action would be taken without the authorization of Mr. Truman."[24]

It is quite possible that Acheson was giving the Jewish leaders advance warning so that they might organize against the decision to close the borders, which the military had requested (and he had tentatively approved). If this was indeed his intention, it had the desired effect. The World Jewish Congress, American Jewish Committee, Joint Distribution Committee, and American Jewish Conference, whose leaders Acheson had met with, organized and put into immediate operation an extensive lobbying campaign to persuade the president to keep zonal borders open to escaping Polish Jews.

On July 23, David Wahl of the American Jewish Conference reported on the progress made in the twenty-four hours since the conference at the State Department.

> A letter has already been received by the president from the Majority Leader of the House of Representatives, John McCormack. . . . Senator Mead has promised to call the President on the telephone to urge that the border be kept open indefinitely. Senator [Joseph F.] Guffey [Democrat from Pittsburgh] will take similar action with the president, if possible. Senator Wagner's office is also taking appropriate action with the president. . . . Arrangements have been made for Henry Wallace to speak with the President in the morning on the same subject. David Niles is seeing me at 11 a.m. tomorrow to discuss the situation with a possibility of his discussing it with the President. In all these cases, the presentation which is being made to the President is mainly on the humanitarian grounds but also on political grounds, pointing out that the blockading of the border to refugees escaping for their lives is no solution to the problem

of military government in the American occupation zone. It is, in fact, the seeds of a much more serious problem for the Truman administration than the mere inconvenience of feeding and housing several thousand people in addition to those already in the zone. It is reasonable to expect that, because of these activities, the border will stay open at least until December.[25]

On July 26, perhaps as a result of the pressure applied in the lobbying campaign, Secretaries Byrnes and Patterson notified the president that they had instructed General McNarney not to close the zonal borders with Poland and "not to . . . limit in any other way the number of persecutees to be admitted to DP centers and properly cared for in the U.S. zone."[26]

The choice of the term "persecutees" was intentional and highly significant. The secretaries of state and war were notifying the president that, henceforth, only those designated as "persecutees," i.e., Jews, would be permitted to cross into the American zones of occupation in Germany and Austria.* That an exception was being made for Jewish "persecutees" was not lost on representatives of the National Catholic Welfare Conference in Germany. Nor was the fact that the Army's newly promulgated policy mandated that recent Polish Jewish arrivals would be placed in the better camp facilities and, to make room for them, displaced persons from "less static groups who have a homeland to which they can return"—that is, non-Jewish Poles—would be transferred to facilities that had previously been "considered sub-standard."

Reverend Richard A. Flynn of the National Catholic Welfare Conference, in a three-and-a-half-page, single-spaced letter to General McNarney, claimed that the Army's new policy, which discriminated against non-Jewish Poles, was "as invalid and it is offensive and

* Since the Harrison Report, the "persecutee" label had been used to distinguish the Jews from other displaced persons. (On "persecutee" as a category of refugee, see Anna Holian, *Between National Socialism and Soviet Communism: Displaced Persons in Postwar Germany* [Ann Arbor: University of Michigan Press, 2015], 62–66.)

nauseating," and was "tainted with the odor of 'forced repatriation.'" The Army was attempting to force the Polish DPs to leave Germany by depriving them of livable shelter.

There should, Flynn argued, be no difference between the treatment of Jewish and non-Jewish DPs: no increased food rations or enhanced facilities or permission to infiltrate into the American zone granted to Jewish "persecutees," but denied to non-Jewish Polish DPs. The "indisputable and glaring fact," which the Army and UNRRA were now conveniently forgetting, but which Flynn felt obligated to remind them of, was "that the Nazi regime stamped all Poles, regardless of whether they were Jews, Catholics or protestants, as members of an inferior race, and, rated as such, they were all viciously and superabundantly subjected to the common law of life for such peoples under the Nazis, suffering."[27]

It took a full six weeks for General McNarney to respond to Reverend Flynn's letter. "I appreciate that to you housing for these unfortunate people is paramount. With the Army it is a matter of housing for Displaced Persons, persecutees, German nationals, refugees, prisoners of war, civilian internees, and even arrestees." As for Flynn's charges that the Jewish persecutees were receiving better treatment than other displaced persons, McNarney assured him "that distinctions are not made on the basis of religious creeds. The Jewish Displaced Persons and refugees do receive special treatment as a racial group," but only because, unlike the non-Jewish Poles, they were considered to be "completely stateless. The fact that they receive special treatment is well-known, I believe, by the public generally, and this treatment has received favorable endorsement in many cases from prominent non-Jews."[28]

POLAND AND GERMANY,
AUGUST TO OCTOBER 1946

The flight out of Poland fueled by the Kielce murders accelerated throughout the summer of 1946. "The Kielce pogrom," Rabbi Bernstein reported to General McNarney, who had sent him to Poland to investigate conditions there,

> gave new impetus to this feeling of desperate fear. Even Jews who had become hardened to the manifestation of Jew-baiting in Poland . . . were shaken and horrified by the events of 4 July 1946. The old hoax about Christian blood was used to start the flame. But the inflammable material was ready, apparently, in the enthusiastic cooperation of all elements in the community in these acts of brutal murder. . . . The police and local militia lent themselves to the pogrom. . . . The church authorities declined to intervene. . . . The Jews in Poland became panic stricken. If this could happen in Kielce, they asked, was Jewish life safe anywhere in Poland. . . . I found that most of the Jews in central Poland believe that their lives are unsafe and want to get out.[29]

The Polish government, recognizing that it was incapable of protecting the Jews, opened the borders to Czechoslovakia to those attempting to depart. The exodus was coordinated for the most part by Brichah* agents, funded and assisted by the Jewish Agency and the Joint Distribution Committee, who led the Polish Jews from Stettin (Szczecin), the

---

* Brichah (which means "flight and escape") had been organized by Jewish partisans in areas liberated by the Red Army. As the volume of Eastern European Jews who sought to emigrate to Palestine or elsewhere grew, Brichah became a popular, near mass movement, supported not only by Zionist activists and former soldiers from Palestine, but by members of the American military and American charitable organizations.

former Prussian port annexed by Poland in July 1945, to Berlin and along several routes from Poland into Czechoslovakia and Austria.

Even with support from Brichah, the escape was perilous. On their journey, by foot or horse-drawn wagon toward the Czech border, the fleeing Jews were, Rabbi Bernstein reported,

> beaten, robbed and some of them were killed. They were gathered in shelters near the border where they lay on the floors, no beds, no pillows to rest their heads on; and in some cases, no food, for everything was taken from them. Like criminals, they had to steal out at night. As one of them said to me, "Apparently we are criminals. Our crime is that we are Jews." I saw them crowded into trucks, fifty-eight by actual count in one truck, men, women and children,—the old, the infirm and the sick, the pregnant women and little babies, each allowed space only for such possessions as could be carried in a small bag or a briefcase and again on the way to the borders their last possessions were stolen from them. . . . The crowning indignity was their inability to be transported across the border by vehicle. They were dumped unceremoniously some distance east of the border and then had to walk with their possessions and children and ailments over the frontier to Czechoslovakia where they received more humane care.[30]

The Berger and Milman families were among those who fled Poland after Kielce. The Bergers had tried to make a life for themselves in Warsaw. "Marcus found a job as a shoemaker," Rachel later told her son Joseph,

> and we were promised a two-room apartment, something that would put an end to our vagabond life. . . . But we never took that apartment. One morning outside our barracks, a refugee was cooking powdered eggs . . . and there was a strong

explosion. Someone had placed a bomb in the stove the refugee had rigged together. The man was instantly killed and another person nearby was maimed. . . . A week after this incident, a radio broadcast told us of a savage pogrom in the Polish city of Kielce. . . . The next day we took every piece of clothing we did not immediately need and our pots and pans and sold them on the market.

Rachel, Marcus, her younger surviving brother, Yasha, and her infant son, Joey, departed for Stettin, where they paid a steep price to "a gang of smugglers" to stow them away in trucks—mother and child in one, brother and husband in another—and drive them into Berlin. The Bergers eventually found their way to the outskirts of the city, where, Rachel remembered, "the Americans had converted German army barracks into housing for displaced persons. This DP camp, with blocks of long, low wooden buildings arranged around a sandy field, would be our temporary home, we were told." Joey, his mother and father, and Uncle Yasha were

given our own room in Block 11, with a window that faced the camp's entrance. We had four olive-green American army cots, four olive-green blankets, four olive-green sheets, and four olive-green pillows. I began thinking of this room as my home. . . . Who knew how long our stay would be? When I opened the door to the long hall, I heard the voices of small children, all belonging to young mothers who had survived the war by fleeing to Russia. . . . The young men and women in the winter of 1946 and 1947 included the still-frail survivors of the concentration camps, those who had spent the war hiding in forests or basements, and the Poles like ourselves who had fled to Russia. It began to dawn on me that in our camp there were few middle-aged and elderly people and only a handful of children over five. Hitler had killed off those too old to work and all small children.[31]

The Milman family had also spent the war years in the Soviet Union, then attempted to start life anew in Breslau (Wrocław), which was now part of Poland. In late summer, not long after they had arrived, Edith's father took a train back to his family birthplace outside Kraków "to see what was going on there, to find anybody. Everybody was gone." His train was stopped in Kraków, where Polish hooligans pulled seven Jewish men off and killed them. This was not uncommon, according to Jan Gross. "Jews were particularly vulnerable to attack on trains in postwar Poland." Back in Breslau, Edith's father gathered the family together. "We are leaving this country forever and ever and ever. Enough is enough." The next day they joined the exodus, through Czechoslovakia to the safety of the American zone in Austria. Warned by Palestinian Jewish smugglers who helped them cross the borders, they kept silent during the trip, spoke no Polish, hid any documents they might have had that were in Polish, and claimed to be Greek Jews.[32]

The Jews escaping from Poland had no choice but to migrate, at whatever the cost, to the American zones of occupation; they were welcome nowhere else. Rabbi Bernstein, with General McNarney's informal assistance, had tried to persuade other European countries to accept some of them, but, as he reported to a gathering of Jewish leaders at New York City's Biltmore Hotel on October 1, "not a single government in Europe has been prepared to offer more than temporary shelter to these people."[33]

When on August 15 the Americans sought British help in persuading the Italians to take in twenty-five thousand Polish Jews who had crossed from Poland into Czechoslovakia and were now housed in overcrowded UNRRA camps in Austria, the Foreign Office denied the request. "To agree would be inconsistent with the policy of His Majesty's Government in endeavouring to stop this type of Jewish migration

*A displaced persons assembly center in Salzburg, where recent arrivals
from Poland, bound for DP camps in Germany, were housed.*

which almost invariably proved itself to be the precursor of illegal immigration into Palestine. The transfer of these Jews to Italy would
merely encourage further migration. . . . Italy is the country from which
it is most easy to smuggle illegal immigrants into Palestine."[34]

LONDON, JULY TO SEPTEMBER 1946

Despite the increased violence in Poland, the British sealed their zonal
borders against Polish Jews, insisting that their attempts to cross into
Germany were part of a Zionist conspiracy.

Simultaneously with closing their borders to the Polish Jews, the
British government opened them to *Volksdeutsche* expellees. As part of

what they called "Operation Swallow," they assigned special trains to move expelled ethnic Germans from Poland into the British zone of occupation. When the British deputy military governor in Berlin learned that Polish Jews were smuggling themselves into Germany on the Operation Swallow trains, he informed the Foreign Office in London. "We feel that you would wish to know of this fresh evidence that there is a powerful Jewish organisation working in Europe to effect the emigration of JEWS from this Continent." One of the trains arrived "at 1100 hours on 19 May filled mostly with Jewish Personnel. Out of the 2028 on board there were only 56 genuine Swallows. These Jews were well-fed and dressed and in actual fact, they were not expellees, but volunteers for the American zone. . . . We had the greatest difficulty controlling these people. Roughly 90% refused to be deloused and registered. . . . Only under a display of arms did the people attempt to obey orders."[35]

In early August, British military command in Berlin notified London that "a number of Jews from Eastern Europe have again been arriving by devious means into British Zone. . . . We have evidence that the movement is facilitated by individuals in the UNRRA organization and by Jewish Relief organizations." To prevent any further "infiltration" of Jews into the British zone of Germany, the military commander recommended that Operation Swallow be suspended.[36]

On September 5, Fiorello La Guardia, UNRRA director general, met with Prime Minister Attlee in London and appealed to him to admit the Polish Jews "to the British Zones in Germany and Austria [and accord them] the same comparatively favourable treatment as that accorded to ordinary 'displaced persons.'"

"The Prime Minister," according to the British record of the meeting, "said that he could not admit Mr. La Guardia's premises. Our evidence was that this was an artificial movement engineered largely with a view to forcing our hands over Palestine. Anything we did to facilitate it would merely encourage and increase it, and make the position more difficult for everyone concerned."[37]

The British Foreign Office warned Washington that the movement of Polish Jews into the British zone of occupation, assisted by the American army and the Joint, was part of a Soviet conspiracy "to embarrass His Majesty's Government in their exercise of the Palestine mandate and further to influence the Arab/Jewish problem, which is critical for the whole Middle East. . . . We have received more than one report that the Soviet authorities are training young Jews for subversive activity in Palestine and then facilitating their onward journey." The Foreign Office directed the British ambassador in Washington to "make it clear to the State Department that this United States encouragement and assistance to the present exodus of Jews from Eastern Europe only makes it more difficult to reach a settlement of the Palestine problem acceptable to the Jews." Sir George Rendel and Hector McNeill, the senior members of the UK delegation to the United Nations, made the same point in a meeting with General John Hilldring, recently appointed as assistant secretary of state for occupied areas. Unfortunately, as Rendel reported to London, "It was impossible to obtain any undertaking from General Hilldring that any really effective measures would be taken by American authorities to check flow."[38]

GERMANY, JULY TO DECEMBER 1946

The influx of the Polish Jews could not be stopped. The number of Jewish displaced persons receiving UNRRA assistance in Germany doubled between December 1945 and January 1946, from 14,000 to 27,194; by April 1946, UNRRA was assisting 41,366 Jews; by August, 104,398; by October, nearly 140,000. In just ten months, between December 1945 and October 1946, the proportion of Jews among the Last Million in Germany had increased from 2 percent to over 20 percent.[39]

The arrival of the Polish Jews transformed every aspect of daily life in the Jewish camps. The sound of children playing could be heard again; baby carriages were everywhere. "There had been literally no children under six when the Jews were liberated in 1945. By the end of 1946, such children accounted for 8.5 percent of the Jewish population, and another 12 percent were between the ages of six and seventeen."[40]

By 1946, the Jewish birth rate in occupied Germany was, according to historian Atina Grossmann, "estimated to be 'higher than that of any other country or any other population' in the world. . . . Jewish DPs were marrying and producing babies in record numbers." The younger Jews in the camps were rebuilding, birth by birth, a Jewish people, substituting new lives for those taken away. "For the DPs themselves—and for those who managed and observed them—the rash of marriages, pregnancies, and babies collectively represented a conscious affirmation of Jewish life as well as definitive material evidence of survival." It contributed to the sense that there was another chapter to the story, that the Jewish people would survive and build a future for themselves.[41]

The Polish Jewish arrivals were less traumatized, more hopeful, stronger, and healthier than the survivors. "They took over all the functions of the camps. They became its teachers, nurses, cooks, policemen, garbage collectors, shoemakers, etc." With the assistance of UNRRA and the Jewish voluntary agencies, new workshops and small industrial enterprises were organized to manufacture hand-crafted toys, shoes, clothing, utensils, religious accessories like menorahs, and other products. With help from emissaries from Palestine, new agricultural kibbutzim were organized.[42]

Among the "infiltrees" from Poland were thousands of "unaccompanied children," as UNRRA referred to them, orphans, runaways, members of kibbutzim who had traveled together with their leaders from Poland, children who had been hidden with non-Jewish families to protect them from the Nazis. They were placed in children's absorption centers and youth kibbutzim, some inside the camps but in separate quarters, others in self-standing communal farms. Here, it was hoped,

Members of the Kibbutz Nili hachshara, a Zionist collective on their way to work in the fields. The entrance arch to their DP camp reads "Welcome."

they would learn to trust adults again, realize that they were not alone, and recognize that they too had a future distinct from their pasts. With the assistance of teachers, tutors, lecturers, military advisers, nurses, doctors, and organizers, many dispatched by the Jewish Agency, kibbutzim members were prepared for what was hoped would be new and radically different lives in Palestine; some were trained for military service, others to work on the land; all received instruction in geography, history, mathematics, Zionism, Jewish history, and, the cornerstone of their education, Hebrew language and literature. UNRRA and the American military authorities, though troubled by the partisan Zionist indoctrination, supported the kibbutzim movement because it provided productive work and schooling for those who might otherwise have been consumed by idleness, illiteracy, and anger.[43]

WASHINGTON, JULY 1946
TO JANUARY 1947

The arrival in the American zone of 150,000 to 200,000 Polish Jews had, as the British had feared, pushed the Americans to renew with added urgency their request that 100,000 certificates for immigration to Palestine be issued to the Jewish DPs. The British, as had been their policy, did not explicitly reject the request, but insisted that they could not support increased immigration absent an end to Jewish violence in the region and a comprehensive plan for the future of Palestine that both Jews and Arabs could agree to. Truman, worn down by British intransigence and domestic lobbying, temporarily washed his hands of the matter and publicly handed off the issue to a newly established "Cabinet Committee on Palestine and Related Problems," chaired by the secretary of state, with the secretaries of war and treasury as members.

In an attempt to bring the Truman administration back into the conversation, the Jewish Agency Executive Committee at its August 1946 meeting in Paris reluctantly set aside its demand for a Jewish state that encompassed all of Palestine. It proposed instead "the establish-ment of a viable Jewish state in an adequate area of Palestine," "the immediate grant of 100,000 certificates," and a guarantee that the fu-ture Jewish state would have full control over immigration. The new Jewish state needed the Jewish DPs as much as they needed it. Without the European immigrants, it would be difficult, if not impossible, to sustain an independent Jewish entity in a region where Arabs outnum-bered Jews.[44]

Nahum Goldmann, the representative of the Jewish Agency in Washington, was delegated to present the new plan to the Americans. President Truman did not formally endorse the plan, but instead noti-fied the Attlee government that the United States believed that the "search for a solution to this difficult problem should continue" and hoped that the British would be open to discussing "certain suggestions which have been made to us and which, I understand, are also being made to you." The "suggestions" referred to so coyly were those put forward by the Jewish Agency Executive Committee.[45]

The White House subsequently released a new statement on Palestine, in which Truman publicly acknowledged for the first time "that the solution of the problem of Palestine will not in itself solve the broader problem of the hundreds of thousands of displaced persons in Europe." He had once believed that the British could be persuaded to accept all the displaced Jews for resettlement in Palestine, but he recognized now that this was not about to happen. He proposed as an alternative that at least some of the displaced Jews be resettled in the United States. "The President has been giving this problem his special attention and hopes that arrangements can be entered into which will make it possible for various countries, including the United States, to admit many of these persons as permanent residents. The President on his part is contemplating seeking the approval of Congress for special legislation authorizing the entry into the United States of a fixed number of these persons, including Jews."[46]

The reaction to Truman's declaration that he was "contemplating" asking for legislation to admit displaced persons to the United States was immediate. The *New York Times,* the *Washington Post,* and most major newspapers and American Jewish organizations endorsed his proposal. Republicans and southern Democrats opposed it. Senator Charles Andrews, Democrat from Florida, "said flatly that 'in my judgment the Immigration Committee will not be in favor of increasing the quotas.' . . . [Republican] Representative Noah M. Mason of Illinois, ranking minority member of the House Immigration Committee, took a similar position." Democratic House member John Rankin of Mississippi contended that there were already "too many so-called refugees pouring into this country bringing with them communism, atheism, anarchy and infidelity." His Texas colleague Ed Lee Gossett declared that he would not only "'vigorously oppose' any increase in immigration quotas," but that he "would try to cut quotas in half for ten years."[47]

Truman had nothing further to say on Palestine, the displaced persons, or the Jewish Agency plan for partition. His six weeks of silence was a cause of some concern to Democrats who were worried about the Jewish vote in the upcoming midterm elections. Finally, on October 4, Yom Kippur, the holiest holiday in the Jewish calendar, and one month before election day, the president issued a statement. "Substantial immigration into Palestine cannot await a solution to the Palestine problem . . . it should begin at once. . . . In the light of the terrible ordeal which the Jewish people of Europe endured during the recent war and the crisis now existing, I cannot believe that a program of immediate action along the lines suggested above could not be worked out with the cooperation of all people concerned."[48]

Prime Minister Attlee reacted immediately to Truman's Yom Kippur statement, warning him by letter that any attempt at modifying policy regarding Jewish immigration into Palestine before a comprehensive agreement had been reached would constitute "a breach of faith with the Arab Delegations. I ought therefore to leave you in no doubt that His Majesty's Government could not in any event allow the movement of 100,000 Jews into Palestine to begin . . . or commit themselves to any such change of policy. . . . Your suggestion that a decision might be taken on immigration without awaiting 'a solution to the Palestine problem' seems to overlook the fundamental fact that Jewish immigration is the crux of the Palestine problem."[49]

Truman conceded nothing. While Attlee and Bevin had tried to direct his attention to Arab sensibilities and the future of Palestine, the president remained focused on the plight of the Jewish displaced persons in Europe. The resettlement of the Jewish DPs was the president's "greatest concern," Dean Acheson told Eliahu Epstein, a Jewish Agency representative in Washington. Truman had made this clear in his letter to Attlee:

The failure to reach an agreement which permits their entry
to Palestine has had a most distressing effect upon the morale of
the European displaced Jews, who have seen nearly a year and a
half pass since their liberation with no decision as to their future. . . . I am sure that you will agree that it would be most
unfair to these unfortunate persons to let them enter upon still
another winter without any definite word as to what disposition
is to be made of them and specifically as to whether they are to
be allowed to proceed to Palestine, where so many of them wish
ardently to go. I felt that this government owed it to these people
to leave them in no doubt, at this particular season with all its
additional associations, as to its continuing interest in their
future and its desire that all possible steps should be taken to
alleviate their plight.[50]

The British would not yield. The problem with the Americans,
Thomas E. Bromley, first secretary at the British embassy and reigning
expert on the United States, declared in a November 1946 memorandum, was that they were soft-headed; easily swayed by sentimental, humanitarian arguments; not particularly well versed on Middle East
history; and not sufficiently frightened by Soviet ambitions and aggression. The State Department could be counted on to listen to (British)
reason, Bromley declared, but Truman, worried about the upcoming
midterm elections, could not.

Indulging in the oldest of antisemitic myths, Bromley explained that
the Zionist cause was promoted by the "press, much of which in the east
is Jewish owned or dependent on Jewish advertisements." Though U.S.
opinion with regard to Zionism was largely indifferent, there was "considerable, though often-ill-informed, sympathy for the Jews amongst
idealists such as school teachers, professors and social workers who
are responsible for much that is best in American life. . . . To them
are allied those into whom a sense of guilt has been instilled by the

anti-Semitism of their neighbors." The only bright spot in all of this was that a "rising tide of Russophobia" was beginning to push some liberals to "support Anglo-American co-operation in the areas most gravely threatened" by Soviet encroachment in the Middle East.[51]

LONDON, FEBRUARY 1947

On February 12, having tried and failed on several occasions to get Arab and Jewish representatives to agree on a plan for the future of Palestine, Foreign Secretary Bevin signaled that he had had enough, that all options for a peaceable settlement having been turned down, the British intended to give up their mandate and hand off the entire problem to the UN General Assembly.

Ben-Gurion, desperate to increase the population of Jews in Palestine and fearful of what the General Assembly might do, signaled that he was prepared to make major concessions in return for the British agreement to allow increased immigration. He advised Lord Chancellor Jowitt, a senior member of the British cabinet, that the Jewish Agency would abandon its partition plan and accept the status quo in Palestine and the continuation of the Mandate for five or ten years if, in return, the British lifted restrictions on purchasing land and agreed to admit one hundred thousand immigrants "within a year or two." Decisions on immigration would thereafter be made by the British high commissioner on the basis of "maximum economic absorptive capacity." Jowitt promised to bring this latest proposal to the cabinet.[52]

At the British cabinet meeting the next day, Lord Chancellor Jowitt introduced Ben-Gurion's proposal. Bevin responded that "such a policy was bound to excite the active hostility of the Arabs in Palestine." Ben-Gurion's compromise was dismissed out of hand. The cabinet then formally accepted Bevin's recommendation that the British government "refer the problem of Palestine to the General Assembly of the United Nations."[53]

For Dean Acheson and the American State Department, as well as the Jewish Agency, the British decision to abandon the Palestine mandate portended future disaster. If the British truly intended to lay "the whole matter before the General Assembly without recommendations" and maintain "as an interim policy the immigration policy at present in force, that is, 1500 a month," Acheson wrote Loy Henderson, "1947 is going to be a bad year in Palestine and the Middle East, with increasing violence and grave danger to our interests in that area."[54]

After trying unsuccessfully to reach the British ambassador in Washington, Acheson telephoned Sir John Balfour, second in command, to request that the British consider increasing the interim monthly immigration quota from fifteen hundred to three thousand before handing over their Palestine mandate to the UN. "This," Acheson told Balfour, "would be great help to us domestically." The American chargé in London responded that while "British officials sympathized deeply with Jews in DP camps . . . there is strong feeling in London that nothing should be done to tilt scales in favor of either side between now and UN decision." The immigration quota would remain at fifteen hundred a month.[55]

On February 21, 1947, George Marshall, who had succeeded James Byrnes as secretary of state, tried one last time. "Is it possible," he asked Foreign Secretary Bevin, almost plaintively,

> without bringing about any marked deterioration of the situation in Palestine, to increase appreciably the number of displaced European Jews who might be admitted into Palestine between the present and the final disposition of the problem by UN? Increase in number of displaced European Jews into Palestine during next few months would have beneficial effect among Jews in displaced persons centers in Europe and would meet with public approval in this country. . . . Since, however, Brit Govt bears

onerous responsibility for maintenance of order in Palestine we must leave this decision to your judgment.[56]

Marshall got his answer four days later, when Foreign Secretary Bevin, addressing the House of Commons, declared that he would not increase the rate of immigration from Europe to Palestine beyond fifteen hundred, which he had told the Arabs he would maintain. He then proceeded to lay the blame for the failure of a Palestine agreement on the Americans.

"I do not desire to create any ill feeling with the United States; in fact, I have done all I can to promote the best possible relations with them, as with other countries, but I should have been happier if they had had regard to the fact that we were the Mandatory Power, and that we were carrying the responsibility . . . and if they had only waited to ask us what we were doing. Then we could have informed them." The foreign secretary rambled on, criticizing President Truman for intervening in matters he had no knowledge of, and scuttling British solutions because they did not comport with his political needs at home. "In international affairs, I cannot settle things if my problem is made the subject of local elections. I hope I am not saying anything to cause bad feeling with the United States, but I feel so intensely about this."[57]

Once again, Bevin had spoken too frankly, revealing for all the world his and his government's contempt for the Americans and their president. British officials tried to explain away Bevin's criticisms by insisting that they had not been in his prepared text, but that he felt so intensely about the issue that he had inserted them into his remarks. It didn't much matter who said what or who blamed whom. After eighteen months of negotiations, pressure, memoranda, conferences, committees of inquiry and committees of experts, internal and bilateral discussions and debate, the British had slammed the door on President Truman's repeated formal and informal, public and private requests that one hundred thousand Jewish DPs be given certificates for immigration to Palestine.

The British decision to give up the Mandate for Palestine, which they had held since 1922, meant indefinite delay for the displaced persons who had hoped to immigrate to Palestine. Their fate, formerly in the hands of the Americans, the British, and the Soviets, was now, it appeared, going to be determined by the fifty-six member nations of the United Nations.

FIORELLO LA GUARDIA
TO THE RESCUE

The Campaign Against UNRRA

NEW YORK, MARCH 1946

In March 1946, Herbert Lehman had resigned as UNRRA director general. He was sixty-eight years old and no doubt exhausted from the stress, the travel, the fight for funding with Congress and the president. UNRRA had been conceived as a temporary agency to handle immediate postwar relief and rehabilitation. Lehman had presided over its birth; he chose not to preside over its imminent dissolution. Though he had cited ill health as the reason for his resignation in March, in May he let it be known that he would accept the nomination for senator from New York should it be offered to him.

Former mayor Fiorello La Guardia, his successor, in accepting appointment as UNRRA director general, understood that he would be responsible for closing down the camps and suspending assistance to the displaced persons. Before the camps were shuttered, he tried one last time to empty them by providing new incentives for the Last Million to return home. Recognizing that there was no possibility of repatriating the Baltic or Ukrainian DPs or the Jews, he concentrated his efforts on the more than four hundred thousand non-Jewish Poles who constituted the majority of the Last Million in Germany.

GERMANY, JUNE TO SEPTEMBER 1946

La Guardia was convinced, and not without reason, that the Poles who were refusing to go home again had been persuaded not to do so by the ex-military officers, property holders, professionals, clergymen, and London-affiliated liaison officers who remained in the camps and flooded them with a steady stream of anti-Soviet, anti-Communist, anti–provisional government propaganda. Something had to be done to diminish the volume and effectiveness of the anti-repatriation campaign.

The new UNRRA director general did not wish to limit free speech in the camps, or so he said, but neither was he going to permit anyone to actively oppose repatriation. Those who discouraged others from going home would be separated from the general population. "Displaced persons and refugees, whether elected or self-appointed leaders, who strive to influence adversely or prevent the repatriation of other displaced persons and refugees, shall be removed to other Assembly Centres where their efforts to prevent the repatriation of other displaced persons and refugees will be minimized."[1]

This was not going to be easily accomplished. By the time he took office, the camp leaders he wanted evicted had had a year to build support by distributing favors, dispensing food and supplies from outside charity organizations, allocating housing, admitting new members, appointing and overseeing security forces, and, in all too many instances, intimidating, threatening, and retaliating against pro-repatriation spokesmen or those who threatened their leadership prerogatives. They had succeeded in forging alliances with one another, with influential individuals in ethnic and religious support groups in the UK, United States, and Canada, and with American military officers in Germany who shared their anti-Communist sentiments.

Try as he might, La Guardia failed to secure the cooperation of the military in evicting the anti-repatriation leaders. His "ambitious plan of separation and segregation was never carried out," according to Ralph Price, chief of repatriation in the U.S. zone, "because of the opposition or lack of enthusiasm on the part of the military authorities. . . . The identification of this [anti-repatriation campaign] leadership was not difficult but their removal was practically impossible. The military authorities either lacked insight, lacked enthusiasm for repatriation, or accepted without discrimination, any leadership which maintained that it was 'anti-Soviet.'"[2]

Simultaneously with evicting, or attempting to evict, anti-repatriation advocates from the camps, La Guardia offered those who accepted repatriation a sizable reward for doing so. Convinced that large numbers were refusing to go home because they feared they would not be able to find work or feed their families, he designed what he called "Operation Carrot." Polish DPs who agreed to repatriation were promised new sets of clothing and a sixty-day food ration. On arriving in Poland, they could do whatever they wanted with their newfound bounty: eat the sixty-day food ration and wear their new clothing or sell part or all of it on the black market.

With the flair of the showman politician he had been and remained, Fiorello La Guardia, the tiny, roly-poly, effervescent, Yiddish-speaking, publicity-seeking, photogenic three-term Italian American Republican reform mayor of New York City, orchestrated his own multimedia spectacle to promote Operation Carrot.

"We set the scene on a night in September while Wildflecken was sleeping," Kate Hulme recalled.

We went forth with flashlights and paste pots and rolls of
billboard material which a special courier from higher levels had
delivered to us. When our DP's awakened next morning, they
found their camp city plastered with a magnificent 'Proclamation Addressed to All Poles in Germany' from the President of
the Minister's Council in Warsaw, promising friendly reception
to the brothers in exile, reconstruction jobs in all walks of life,
free transport . . . inside Poland and a two-month reserve of
food. . . . In the big general meeting place of the camp canteen,
we set up a permanent preview of the sixty-day food ration, which
amounted to some ninety-four pounds of food per person—
flour, dried peas, rolled oats, salt, evaporated milk, canned fish
and a small mountain of lard. . . . On another table longer and
stronger we set up what a family of four would receive, three
hundred and seventy-six pounds of food, and the mound of lard
in this display had enough mass to permit sculpture of the white
eagle of Poland on its front surface.[3]

To counter the anti-repatriation publicity that for more than a year
had portrayed postwar Poland as beset by civil strife, homelessness,
and starvation, La Guardia, in partnership with the Polish government
in Warsaw, produced and distributed pamphlets, posters, newspaper
articles, a leaflet entitled "What Every Returning Citizen Should
Know," and a film, unambiguously titled "The Road Home," all intended to paint the best possible picture of Poland's current and future
prospects.[4]

General Joseph McNarney, in an open letter to the four hundred
thousand non-Jewish Polish DPs in the American occupation zone,
urged them to take advantage of the sixty days' ration plan and return
home before winter set in and travel became difficult again. He "painted
a discouraging picture of their prospects of emigration to new homes
overseas and urged them to 're-examine the desirability of repatriation

to your homeland while there still are a few months of moderate weather ahead.'"[5]

The results of La Guardia's multipronged repatriation campaign were impressive, but not overwhelming. The number of displaced persons who returned to Poland from Germany had already begun to pick up with the return of good weather in the spring of 1946. It would remain constant, with a bump in October, through the rest of the year. By December 1946, the number of non-Jewish Poles receiving UNRRA aid had decreased to 272,712, from 553,000 the year before.[6]

UNITED STATES, OCTOBER TO DECEMBER 1946

La Guardia's success in increasing the rate of repatriation through Operation Carrot came with a heavy price. The uptick in repatriation—and the tactics used to secure it—generated a substantial backlash in the United States against La Guardia in particular, and UNRRA in general. The former congressman and mayor was a savvy politician, but not sufficiently attuned to the anti-Soviet, anti-Communist currents of opinion that were gaining strength in parts of the country outside his hometown of New York City. His repatriation campaign was quickly caught up in, then nearly derailed by, charges that, intentionally or not, by repatriating displaced persons to Communist-dominated nations, he and UNRRA were assisting Soviet attempts at world domination.

On October 11, 1946, as Operation Carrot took effect and thousands of displaced persons returned home to Poland, Charles Rozmarek, the president of the Polish American Congress (PAC), the nationalist and anti-Soviet organization formed in the spring of 1944, demanded a congressional investigation of UNRRA, which he had denounced after a two-week tour of DP camps in Germany as a "political tool of Moscow."[7]

In a report delivered to Secretary of State Byrnes and later published and widely distributed to Polish Americans throughout the United States, Rozmarek described UNRRA as "an instrument of coercion and a political weapon, employed by Soviet Russia to force repatriation on Displaced Persons to serve its own selfish purposes." UNRRA had, Rozmarek charged, in its efforts to push the Poles out of the DP camps and back to Soviet-dominated Poland, closed Polish schools; restricted the diet of DPs to a starvation-level 1,250 calories a day; suspended publication of "newspapers unsympathetic to communism"; punished "anti-communist editors" and mistreated journalists; "banned visits by Polish Red Cross officers from London . . . although communist agents come and go at will"; deprived Polish priests of "certificates permitting them to visit the Displaced Persons camps"; harassed DPs by constantly moving them from one camp to another and continually screening and rescreening them; denied "legal status" to Polish civic organizations; and refused to allow into the camps members of the Polish Underground, or so-called Home Army.[8]

The charges were baseless and UNRRA effectively rebutted them, though it did confirm that the military was exercising more control than previously over visitors and materials published in the camps. Still, the damage had been done. From this point forward, La Guardia and UNRRA officials would have to defend themselves against the accusation that repatriation, which they were promoting, was a Communist ploy to capture and imprison innocent DPs whose only wish was to live in freedom.[9]

Rozmarek's fact-finding trip to Germany had had as its objectives not only the derailment of Operation Carrot in Germany, but the election of anti-Communist Republicans in the United States. His dispatches from Europe and his demand on October 11, 1946, three weeks before the elections, that Congress investigate UNRRA, reinforced charges that the Democrats should be voted out of office because they were soft on Communism. In Chicago, a Polish American Congress stronghold, where Rozmarek's remarks were widely covered in the press, in particular in Colonel Robert McCormick's rabidly anti-Communist *Chicago Daily Tribune,* Republican challengers accused "Democratic congressmen from Chicago districts [of having] voted as a bloc for Russia and against the interests of Poland and other European minorities." In the end, four of the five Democratic congressmen targeted won reelection in their safe districts, but by substantially lower margins than two years earlier; the fifth, Congressman William Link, was defeated.[10]

The Catholic Church leadership joined the battle against UNRRA. In mid-November 1946, *America,* the Jesuit magazine, published an editorial calling for "a thoroughgoing investigation of UNRRA officials' activities." It cited a series of allegations made by a London weekly that had criticized UNRRA for its attempt "to secure repatriation by any means whatever, however ignoble, short of physical force." The *Tablet,* a London Catholic weekly, *America* reported, had appealed "to Cardinal Spellman and all the great Catholic electorate of New York City to inform themselves clearly about these policies of UNRRA, for which a New York figure, ex-Mayor La Guardia, must be held responsible."[11]

The protests intensified after the midterm elections as UNRRA bashing moved from the fringes of political discourse toward the center. One week after Charles Rozmarek recklessly charged before an audience of eight thousand in Chicago that UNRRA was "under communist domination [and was] being used as an instrument of political persecution and coercion," both the governor of Illinois and the mayor of Chicago attended a dinner in his honor. Republican governor Dwight Green, echoing Rozmarek, criticized Washington for hiding from the American people "the whole truth about postwar Europe [and] Soviet Russia's 'iron curtain' . . . behind which the Moscow empire hides its deeds of violence." Democratic mayor Edward Joseph Kelly "lauded Rozmarek as 'a great citizen.'"[12]

The assault against UNRRA was in some sense inevitable. The organization had been founded on the mutual understanding, promoted by President Roosevelt, that postwar reconstruction and relief was too enormous and too weighty a project to be left to any one nation. Large segments of the American public and its elected representatives, including Republicans and Eastern European immigrants, ethnics, and Catholics who usually voted Democratic, had followed Roosevelt's lead in 1943. Their commitment to internationalism was not to survive the war that had engendered it. With Roosevelt, UNRRA's founder and major advocate, gone, the war won, and the Soviets more enemy than ally, UNRRA lost whatever appeal it had once had. Why, congressmen began to ask, was the United States paying more than three-quarters of the UNRRA budget when it controlled only one of four votes in the Central Committee and only one of forty-four in the Council? It was well and fine that the UNRRA director general was an American, but why should he have to take his directions from foreigners? Neither the soft-spoken Herbert Lehman nor the outspoken Fiorello La Guardia nor the new president was up to the task of making the case that it was in the interest of the United States to work with other nations, including those in the Soviet bloc, to put back together again a world torn apart by war.

GERMANY, NOVEMBER TO DECEMBER 1946

The UNRRA General Council, officials at the U.S. zone headquarters in Heidelberg, and Director General La Guardia, instead of backing down in the face of criticism, extended their new repatriation campaign from Poles to Baltic nationals and Ukrainians and solicited the assistance of Soviet officials in persuading the DPs to go home again.

On November 11, 1946, a week after the midterm elections in the United States, UNRRA released "Administrative Order No. 199," which established guidelines and procedures for encouraging the repatriation of DPs to lands that had been annexed by the Soviet Union. As part of the new campaign for repatriation, La Guardia and UNRRA planned to distribute to the DPs in the camps "Soviet proclamations, literature, films and newspapers. . . . Some such material is now available for distribution and additional material has been promised by Soviet officials. Cultural activities will be utilized and turned toward the theme of repatriation, and every opportunity will be utilized by Repatriation Officers to assist the people in their re-evaluation of their life plans and in their serious consideration of taking advantage of repatriation opportunities now offered."[13]

These orders with explicit directives that UNRRA staff cooperate with the Soviets to promote repatriation, according to Ralph Price, "immediately produced a chain of organized negative reactions from the anti-repatriation leadership in Assembly Centers, military authorities, W.R.S. [the Catholic War Relief Services], N.C.W.S. [National Catholic Welfare Services], and a certain section of the press in the United States, especially the 'Chicago Tribune' and the 'New York Daily News.'"[14]

In early December, Francis X. Mayers, acting field director of Catholic War Relief Services in Heidelberg, delivered a blistering attack on UNRRA and Administrative Order No. 199 in a memorandum to John Whiting, UNRRA director in the American zone in Germany.

The displaced persons, Mayers maintained, had a right to remain in the UNRRA camps for as long as they so desired. UNRRA's mandate was to provide for their welfare, nothing more, nothing less. It had neither the moral nor the legal authority to promote repatriation by working with Soviet or Polish government officials or by inviting pro-repatriation spokesmen, literature, and films into the camps. Nor did it have the right to remove or punish camp leaders who opposed

repatriation or to restrict cultural activities or to censor publications or
to provide bribes of extra clothing and food rations to those who agreed
to repatriation. The National Catholic Welfare Conference "stands unalterably opposed to any program or 'drive,' or any policy deriving there-
from which tends to create in the minds of the Displaced Persons the
feeling or fear that enforced repatriation is taking place, about to take
place, or is being acquiesced in by UNRRA."

He protested as well against the special treatment UNRRA afforded
Jewish displaced persons. Why were the Jewish DPs the only ones who
were not being pressured to return home? "In all fairness and decency,
and in the name of Justice why can't we manifest the same spirit in favor
of other peoples who are just as much in need of consideration for resettlement at the present time?"[15]

The leaders of the Catholic voluntary organizations, the Polish
American Congress, and the Catholic hierarchy proposed that the DPs,
instead of being forcibly repatriated, should be resettled, preferably in
the United States. Charles Rozmarek, president, and Ignatius Nurkiewicz, vice president of PAC, concluded the October 1946 letter to
Secretary of State Byrnes in which they protested UNRRA policies by
recommending that "the United States . . . admit 150,000 Displaced
Persons to the United States proper and to Alaska." Congress had a
moral duty, the PAC proclaimed, to "amend the immigration laws" and
admit the Polish DPs because the U.S. government had been "responsible for the Yalta decisions which robbed the displaced persons of their
legal government and a free homeland."

The PAC officers did not suggest that the 1924 quota system, which
restricted the numbers of Eastern European immigrants, be abandoned
or substantially changed. That was politically impossible—and they
knew it. They proposed instead that non-Jewish Polish displaced persons be admitted under the unused quotas from the war years, that Polish war prisoners and forced laborers still in Germany be admitted
under the German quota, that Polish soldiers be accepted into the U.S.

Army "with the right to American citizenship," and that Alaska be opened to displaced persons. To strengthen their case, the PAC leaders emphasized that the Polish DPs were "thoroughly imbued with democratic ideals, are opposed to totalitarianism, and would make good law-abiding citizens."[16]

Part Four

————————— ◆ —————————

RESETTLEMENT

13.

THE DEATH OF UNRRA

The Birth of IRO

IN AUGUST 1945, the UNRRA General Council had resolved that it would in six months' time suspend assistance to DPs who refused repatriation and close the camps. In January 1946, at the expiration of that six months, with nearly a million displaced persons still under UNRRA care, the General Council voted to keep the camps open for another six months, until August.

It was left to the UN General Assembly meeting in London in January 1946 to determine what would happen to the Last Million when UNRRA was dissolved and the camps closed.

There were a limited number of options:

1. The American and British governments could take over the administration of the camps.
2. The camps could be closed and the displaced persons forced to go home or fend for themselves in Germany without UNRRA assistance.
3. The United Nations could establish a successor organization to replace UNRRA, maintain the camps, and resettle

those among the Last Million who continued to refuse repatriation.

The third option was the only viable one. Neither the British nor the Americans had the resources, the will, or the support at home to keep the camps open without UNRRA support. The Last Million were not going to change their minds and go home; nor, given massive unemployment, housing shortages, and the recent influx of millions of *Volksdeutsche*, was it likely that they were going to find work, shelter, and acceptance in German civil society. They would have to be removed from the camps and a new international agency organized to resettle them outside Germany.

ACT I: LONDON, JANUARY TO FEBRUARY 1946

In January 1946, at the UN General Assembly meeting in London, the British delegate, Philip Noel-Baker, took the first formal steps toward creating a new international refugee organization. Reiterating the principles enunciated in Washington in 1943 when UNRRA was founded, Noel-Baker declared that the problem posed by the displaced persons was an international one that required for its solution an international organization. He recommended that the United Nations replace UNRRA with a new agency "under the direct authority of the Assembly." Eleanor Roosevelt, the American delegate, expressed her nation's full agreement.[1]

The Yugoslav delegate, Aleš Bebler, speaking for the "countries of origin" from which the DPs had come, opposed the British proposal and the premise behind it. "The problem of displaced persons," he declared, "has ceased to be one of the important international questions by the very fact that owing to the capitulation of Germany the basic reasons which prevented the return of these persons to their countries has disappeared. . . . It is in the interest of good relations among the Members of the United Nations Organization that these persons return to their countries as soon as possible." Those who were not suspected of being war criminals or traitors should be given four months to return home, after which all "assistance at the expense of international organizations or of their state of origin" would be withdrawn. Those who were suspected of being war criminals or traitors should be identified, forcibly repatriated, and "brought to justice."[2]

It was, Bebler declared four days later, highly questionable, if not brutally absurd, for the United States, the UK, and the nations of Western Europe, the British Commonwealth, and South America, none of which had suffered as the Eastern Europeans had at the hands of Nazis and their collaborators, to now ask them to contribute to the ongoing support and/or possible resettlement of collaborators, quislings, and war criminals who were posing as displaced persons.

> Has it ever been known in the history of international relations that a Government contributed to the cost of maintaining its political enemies who have fled abroad or . . . emigrants who have in fact committed crimes against the people? No, nothing of the sort has ever been known. . . . We must not, if we wish to maintain good relations among nations, allow ourselves to be induced to give those who collaborated with the aggressor and committed crimes in his service general absolution by conferring on them the legal status of refugees and even providing material help for them.

The British and the Americans had "willy nilly" sent back to France, Belgium, England, and Holland citizens of those countries accused of having been war criminals or traitors. "There was no special formality followed in the case of Marshal Petain or M. Laval. Why create difficulties for other countries? Why discriminate?" Why should the

Yugoslavs, Poles, and Czechs not be given the same rights to bring to justice their former citizens?[3]

As the debate proceeded, delegates from the countries of origin—Poland, Yugoslavia, and the USSR—demanded that their representatives be allowed into the camps to counsel their countrymen; that a census of displaced persons be taken to facilitate the identification of traitors and war criminals; that censorship protocols be written and enforced to prevent the dissemination of anti-Soviet, anti-Communist propaganda that might, by disparaging the postwar governments or exaggerating hardships at home, discourage repatriation.[4]

The American and British delegates and their allies turned aside each of these proposals. They were particularly outspoken in their opposition to the censorship regime that the Soviet bloc nations called for.* As long as they resided in the camps, Mrs. Roosevelt declared, the displaced persons should have the right to read whatever they pleased; there should be no restrictions placed on newspapers, journals, pamphlets, films, radio broadcasts, no censorship of the letters they received. To bolster her arguments, Mrs. Roosevelt cited the example of the American government, which did not restrict the rights of Puerto Ricans who advocated independence from the United States. "I think that we can stand up under having them free to get whatever information comes their way and make up their own minds. They are free human beings."[5]

Andrey Vyshinsky, the Soviet deputy minister of foreign affairs and, according to Eleanor Roosevelt, "one of the Russians' great legal minds, a skilled debater, a man with ability to use the weapons of wit and ridicule," took direct aim at Mrs. Roosevelt and the British and American delegates who "propounded the thesis of unrestricted freedom." Such "unrestricted freedom," he declared, does not exist in any country. No nation had ever provided its citizens with "unrestricted

---

* The American and British governments would not, however, object to La Guardia's attempts later in the year to censor anti-repatriation literature in the camps.

freedom" to commit treason, which was precisely what the dissidents in the camps were engaging in—and what the Soviet and Yugoslav representatives sought to curtail. Mrs. Roosevelt was trading in abstractions, but he, Vyshinsky, was concerned with the real world, where

> there are camps, in which thousands and sometimes tens of thousands of men are gathered together, and the minds and souls of these men are being influenced day by day, a systematic agitation is being carried on to set them against their native land, their native country. Yugoslav fugitives are being subject to agitation to set them against Tito and the Yugoslav Republic. Polish refugees and emigres are being set against the present Polish Government. . . . Our concern is not to permit such malicious and criminal propaganda. It is nothing short of the perpetration of a crime, because it is incitement to crime . . . an appeal to commit treason . . . an incitement to engage in hostile activities.

For Vyshinsky and the Eastern European delegates, the war was not over; the fascists had not been eliminated but were regrouping: in London, where the anti-Soviet, anti-Communist government-in-exile plotted the overthrow of the Warsaw government; in Poland, where the underground armed resistance engaged in guerrilla warfare; in the Baltic states, where the "forest brothers" were organizing armed resistance; and in the displaced persons camps, where the Americans and the British were conveniently looking the other way as fascist collaborators spewed their anti-Communist, counterrevolutionary poison. The Americans and the British urged the Soviets and their allies to be tolerant, to allow for the expression of oppositional viewpoints in the camps. But such tolerance had contributed to the rise of Hitler, Nazism, and fascism in the past and would do so again if not curtailed.

"We do not want such tolerance," Vyshinsky declared. "We are apprehensive of such tolerance. We decline such tolerance. It is costing us very much in blood and lives. 1,700 of our towns have been destroyed;

tens of thousands of our villages have been destroyed and laid in ashes; millions of our people have perished; whole areas of our country are now a wilderness. . . . We no longer want to show such tolerance, which leads to the growth of Hitlerism, as it already did once before."[6]

The Czech delegate underscored Vyshinsky's cautions. Most of the General Assembly delegates, he noted, came from nations that had not been occupied by the Nazis, nations whose citizens had not been slaughtered, whose lands and industry and infrastructure had not been devastated. As a result, they could not understand the fears of the Eastern Europeans. "I think we in Europe have a right to look at things our own way. We have suffered much more than many delegates in this room can imagine. There are delegates in this room who had spent some time in concentration camps, and if they are seemingly less humanitarian, it only means that they are more on the guard against any possibility of the return of anything even remotely resembling fascism or nazism."[7]

What came out clearly in the London General Assembly sessions in early 1946 was that whatever spirit of comity, of alliance, that had been present in 1943 when the UNRRA agreement was signed in Washington had disappeared, perhaps forever. The debate between East and West over the mission and structure of the new international organization that was to replace UNRRA was fierce, but purposeless. Both sides knew that the Western delegates had the votes to defeat amendments offered by the Soviets and the Eastern bloc nations. The American-drafted resolution that was finally approved contained no provision for providing access to the camps to representatives of the Eastern bloc nations, no mechanisms for identifying and forcibly repatriating war criminals and high-level collaborators, no prohibition against hostile propaganda.

Despite its proposals having been defeated rather decisively one after another, the Soviet bloc voted to approve the final agreement. The Soviets were not yet prepared to walk away, either because they hoped that they would succeed in the next round of deliberations where they had

failed in London, or because for propaganda purposes they intended to
continue to argue that the British and Americans were protecting fascist
war criminals by providing them refuge in DP camps.

George Kennan, in his "Long Telegram" sent from Moscow on February 22, eight days after the General Assembly plenary meetings in
London had adjourned, described what he believed to be the Soviet
strategy moving forward:

> Russians will participate officially in international organiza-
> tions where they see opportunity of extending Soviet power or of
> inhibiting or diluting power of others. Moscow sees in UNO
> [the United Nations Organization] not the mechanism for a per-
> manent and stable world society founded on mutual interest and
> aims of all nations, but an arena in which aims just mentioned
> can be favorably pursued. As long as UNO is considered here [in
> Moscow] to serve this purpose, Soviets will remain with it. But
> if at any time they come to conclusion that it is serving to embar-
> rass or frustrate their aims for power expansion and if they see
> better prospects for pursuit of these aims along other lines, they
> will not hesitate to abandon UNO.

The Soviet "attitude" to the UN and other international organizations "will remain essentially pragmatic and tactical." It was incumbent
on the United States to recognize this and act accordingly.[8]

ACT II: LONDON, APRIL TO JUNE 1946

The deliberations at the General Assembly meetings in London in early
1946 had been but the first act in the three-act production that resumed
in London on April 8 at the convening of a Special Committee on Refugees and Displaced Persons charged with drafting a constitution and

financial plan for the international refugee organization that would replace UNRRA.

The Americans were determined that the new organization should succeed where UNRRA had failed and remove the Last Million from Germany. To maximize the number of displaced persons who could be resettled by the new organization, the Americans and their allies reconfigured the definition of those eligible for international assistance. UNRRA, at its founding in 1943 and thereafter, had provided assistance only to those it determined to be "displaced persons." At the UN Special Committee meeting in London, the list of those eligible for IRO assistance was expanded to include "*bona fide* refugees," with "refugee" newly defined as "a person, other than a displaced person . . . who is outside of his country of nationality or former habitual residence, and who, as a result of events subsequent to the outbreak of the second world war, is unable or unwilling to avail himself of the protection of the Government of his country of nationality or former nationality."[9]

As Andrew Paul Janco has written, adding the word "unwilling" to the definition constituted a veritable "revolution in refugee status," as it gave individuals the right to declare themselves "stateless" by renouncing their former citizenship. Prior to this, international law had recognized as "stateless" only those like the Spanish Republicans and European Jews whose citizenship had been taken from them.[10]

The Soviets and Yugoslavs objected strenuously to this new definition. Individuals could not unilaterally declare themselves stateless, they argued, so long as there were functioning governments willing to afford them protection. Their position was consistent with prewar definitions of "refugees" and "statelessness," but it didn't much matter. The new definition was approved by the Special Committee by a vote of eleven to six, with three abstentions.

To further enlarge the pool of displaced persons who would be eligible for resettlement assistance, the IRO guidelines formulated at the London Special Committee meetings made no distinctions between those who had been persecuted "for reasons of race, religion, [or] nationality" and those who had not yet been persecuted but feared that they might be for their "political opinions" should they be repatriated. Prospective, presumptive persecution of Eastern European DPs as political dissidents was conflated with actual, documented persecution of those who had suffered at the hands of the Nazis for political or religious reasons or because they were Jews.[11]

A new narrative of Communist horrors was in the process of being constructed. In this narrative, Soviet gulags and labor camps were equated with Nazi concentration and death camps, deportations to Siberia with Nazi death marches, the NKVD with the Gestapo, Stalin with Hitler. The lived experience of the Jewish displaced persons and others tortured and murdered by the Nazis was equated with the fears of Baltic nationals, Poles, Ukrainians, and Yugoslavs that they might suffer persecution as political dissidents should they return home.

The Soviets regarded the British and American decision to establish an international organization charged with resettling displaced persons and refugees who had not suffered Nazi persecution as a hostile act directed against them and the other "countries of origin." The Americans and British were, the Soviets believed, intent on using the IRO as a Cold War weapon. The resettlement of the Last Million outside their former homelands would, at one and the same time, deprive Eastern European governments of the labor power required to rebuild their nations; protect pro-Nazi, anti-Communist war criminals and quislings from prosecution; and assemble and sustain a potential army of anti-Communist, anti-Soviet propagandists to spread their gospel of hate and lies wherever they might be resettled.

On most issues concerning the formation of the International Refugee Organization and the enlargement of the pool of displaced persons eligible for assistance, the Americans and the British voted together. Only on questions having to do with the future of the Jewish DPs did they part ways. The Americans, with the support of the Soviet bloc,

proposed that German and Austrian Jews be included within the definition of refugees eligible for IRO assistance in resettlement. The British,
fearful that this would increase the number of Jewish displaced persons—
and the pressure on them to open Palestine to Jewish immigration—not
only voted against this proposal but demanded that their written objections be included as an annex to the Special Committee's final report.
Austrian and German Jews, they contended, having never left their
homelands, could not be considered refugees.

> If the door is once opened to the new International Refugee
> Organization acting as a relief agency in regard to persons inside
> their own countries, it will be exceedingly difficult to draw the
> line between the tasks which it should and should not under-
> take. . . . Terribly as the Jewish people have suffered at the hands
> of their Nazi oppressors, it is generally recognized that they were
> by no means the only victims of Nazi persecution. Very large
> numbers of Christians of various denominations and of persons
> holding political opinions unwelcome to the Nazi regime suf-
> fered persecution no less acute, though perhaps on a smaller
> scale. . . . As His Majesty's Government have frequently empha-
> sized, while they feel the utmost sympathy for the suffering of
> the Jewish race, they hold strongly that, whatever may have been
> the policy of the Nazis, no distinction should be made by the
> United Nations between the various racial, religious or other mi-
> norities existing in any country.

Any provision designating Jews as a separate class of displaced
persons or refugees "might well involve the new International Refugee
Organization in schemes of Jewish immigration into Palestine, a matter
which is being separately dealt with by bodies specially concerned with
that problem."[12]

The Jewish Agency for Palestine and American and European

Jewish organizations had, at the onset of the Special Committee's deliberations on a constitution for the IRO, submitted memoranda countering
the British arguments and urging the delegates to focus their attention
on the unique suffering and circumstances of the Jewish survivors.

"The Jewish Refugees and Jewish Displaced Persons have a tragic
distinction," the American Jewish Committee declared in its memorandum.

> They are the remnants of a people singled out as the foremost
> victims of fascism and subjected to the heaviest sacrifices. Six
> million Jews perished at the hands of fascist torturers. In dealing
> with the problems of the Jewish Refugees and Displaced Persons
> their status as genuine victims of fascist oppression must con-
> stantly be taken into account. . . . They should not be given the
> same treatment as DP's who cooperated with the Nazis, tortured
> and murdered their Jewish compatriots, and even voluntarily
> fought against the United Nations as members of the Wehr-
> macht and Waffen SS.

The American Jewish Committee, as a non-Zionist organization,*
did not call on the British to open the gates of Palestine. It was concerned instead with the absence of options for Jewish survivors who
either could not or preferred not to immigrate to Palestine. "Present
legislation and restrictive practices in the [British] Dominions present
obstacles to the admission of large numbers of immigrants. In the
United States, existing quota laws discriminate against immigration
from the countries of Southern and Eastern Europe, the very countries
from which come the groups of Jewish refugees whose need for immigration is greatest. Latin American constitutions pledge their respective

---

* Founded in 1906, the AJC was supportive of Jewish settlement in Palestine but did not believe it the duty
or destiny of all Jews to relocate there.

governments to facilitate European immigration; unfortunately, this legislation is belied by restrictive practices." It was imperative that the Special Committee, in designing a new International Refugee Organization, "secure the liberalization of the naturalization laws and procedures of the various states" and demand that "non-discrimination between racial, religious and ethnic groups should be the basic principle of immigration policy."[13]

The Special Committee paid no attention to the memoranda or recommendations submitted by the Jewish organizations or the Jewish Agency. Very much like its predecessor, UNRRA, IRO's mandate was to treat all displaced persons as if they were cut from the same cloth. What mattered was that they were now "displaced." How that came to be, whether they attained that status by leaving their nations voluntarily, like the Baltic nationals, or were deported to Germany, like the Poles, or sent there to be worked to death, like the Jews, was immaterial.

ACT III: LAKE SUCCESS, OCTOBER TO DECEMBER 1946

In October 1946, the Special Committee submitted to the UN General Assembly the IRO draft constitution and financial plan it had drafted.

Though the end result was predetermined—the Americans and British had the votes to pass whatever they wanted—the Soviets and their allies arrived for the UN General Assembly meeting in Lake Success, New York, armed for rhetorical battle. In part because the Americans had enlisted Eleanor Roosevelt as their spokesperson, the otherwise obfuscatory, deadly boring debate over semantics and regurgitated amendments, sprinkled with an occasional theatrical demonstration, managed to solicit no small amount of press attention.

On November 8, as reported the next day in the *New York Times*,

Mrs. Roosevelt, employing the language of human rights, objected to Vyshinsky's demand that the displaced persons be repatriated. Every displaced person, she declared, was entitled to the freedom to decide whether to return home or accept resettlement elsewhere. The refugees who were refusing repatriation were doing so because of "post-war political changes in some states. These changes cause many refugees to 'choose miserable life in camps in preference to the risks of repatriation.'

"I gather that Mr. Vyshinsky felt that any [displaced persons] who did not wish to return to their homelands must of necessity be Fascist," Mrs. Roosevelt added. "I talked to a great many of these people who did not strike me as Fascist." The *New York Times,* which reported this exchange, added parenthetically that "Mrs. Roosevelt visited camps near Frankfort on the Main, where most of the refugees were from Estonia, Latvia and Lithuania."[14]

Mrs. Roosevelt's response to Vyshinsky was widely applauded in the press and in the chamber by all but a handful of Eastern European delegates. It was received rather differently by Abraham Duker,* a former American researcher at the Nuremberg trials, who declared, tongue-in-cheek, in the English-language supplement of the Yiddish newspaper *Der Tog,* that neither Roosevelt nor Vyshinsky "[should be] 'the winnah' in the round of debate . . . before the United Nations General Assembly at Lake Success."

Though Duker conceded that there were some refugees who refused to go home for legitimate reasons, many more rejected repatriation because, as Vyshinsky had charged and Duker had agreed with based on his research at Nuremberg, "they know that they will be recognized for what they really are: Hitler collaborationists, murderers and pogromists, who joined the Nazis and betrayed their own countries. Such people should not be permitted to masquerade as legitimate political refugees. True, their life is in danger, but we'd have one hell of a world, if it were not. . . . Why such people should not be delivered back to justice, be it

---

* In these articles, Duker wrote under the pseudonym Ben Asher.

Soviet or Polish, is one of the mysteries of U.S.-British policy. It is here that Vyshinsky scored a telling blow."

As for Mrs. Roosevelt's claim that the Baltic refugees did not strike her as fascists, "with all due respect to Mrs. Roosevelt, we are convinced that Jewish DP's would do a better job in helping to separate the chaff from the grain." They would have no trouble identifying those among the displaced persons who were not only fascists, but war criminals.[15]

As in earlier General Assembly debates, there were scant references during this one to the Jewish displaced persons, now numbering between 200,000 and 250,000 and comprising nearly 25 percent of the DP population. The Yugoslav delegate, in an attempt to draw attention to the special circumstances of Jewish displaced persons and highlight the stark differences between their "valid objections" to repatriation and those proffered by the non-Jewish Balts, Yugoslavs, Poles, and Ukrainians, introduced an amendment identifying European Jews as an exceptional category of persons that should automatically be exempted from repatriation and given assistance in resettlement. Dr. Medved of the Ukrainian delegation supported the amendment on the grounds "that European Jews deserved exceptional consideration."

In rapid succession, delegates from the Union of South Africa, Canada, the Netherlands, the United States, the United Kingdom, Belgium, and Australia objected to any amendment that singled out Jews as a special category for whom "repatriation" was not possible. Mrs. Roosevelt declared that her country could not support the amendment, that all displaced persons who had "expressed valid objections" to returning to their countries should be given assistance in resettlement. There was no need to pass any resolution that singled out the European Jews. The Yugoslav proposal was defeated by a vote of 22 to 7.[16]

On December 15, 1946, the General Assembly, in plenary session, met for final debate and to vote on a draft constitution and preliminary budget for the IRO. The first speaker called to the podium was Mrs. Roosevelt, who declared unequivocally that it was in the interest of every nation represented in the General Assembly to find a solution to the displaced persons problem. "As long as a million persons remain with refugee status, they delay the restoration of peace and order in the world." The choice before the delegates was to condemn the Last Million to idleness in the camps or resettle them "somewhere so that the world may profit from their work." She urged "all nations here represented to sign and support the constitution in their own interests and in the interest of over a million people who have suffered long enough."[17]

Mrs. Roosevelt was followed to the podium by Andrei A. Gromyko, permanent representative of the Soviet Union to the United Nations. Gromyko's closing speech, though spoken in a calm, almost academic tone, took twice as long to deliver as Mrs. Roosevelt's. He did not disagree that the problem presented by the Last Million was a serious one, but insisted that the solution was not to be found in creating a new international organization whose mandate was to resettle the displaced persons in new homelands.

> In the first place, resettlement measures create conditions which enable war criminals, quislings and other traitors to escape punishment. In the second place, even from the purely humanitarian point of view, we cannot approve of those who advocate the resettlement of these persons in other countries thus turning them from refugees into emigrants, condemned to a joyless existence, far from the native countries and subjected to all manner of discrimination. It appears that those who speak in favour of resettlement and those who express the desire to accept such emigrants wish to take this opportunity of obtaining cheap labour.[18]

Late that evening, after the delegates from other nations had had their say and a final round of Soviet bloc amendments was presented and rejected, the IRO constitution was approved by a vote of 30 to 5, with 18 abstentions. Byelorussia, Poland, Ukraine, the USSR, and Yugoslavia voted no; Czechoslovakia joined a number of South American nations, India, Sweden, and the Arab nations in abstaining.

The British and the Americans had achieved all they had sought at the United Nations. Though the "main mass of displaced persons," Dr. Medved of the Ukrainian Soviet Socialist Republic noted in his final remarks at Lake Success, were citizens of the Eastern European nations, the United States, Great Britain, and France, "which have armies of occupation in territories where there are camps for refugees and displaced persons . . . have now become the absolute masters and arbiters of the fate of the refugees and displaced persons." Despite the opposition of every one of the countries of origin, the Americans and the British had, under cover of the United Nations, constructed a new International Refugee Organization dedicated not to repatriating the Last Million to their former homelands, as UNRRA had been, but to resettling them elsewhere.[19]

THE DEBATE OVER the founding of the International Refugee Organization and the Last Million's future had, in the year since it had begun in London, become increasingly hostile. "Negotiating with the Russians," James Reston would later write, reflecting the views of the State Department and White House, had been "like playing tennis on a court without lines or umpire." In private, the Soviets were affable, conciliatory. In public, they were angry, tenacious, and snarling. They had entered into

> postwar negotiations with their allies, not in a mood of compromise, but on the assumption that the experience of the war had changed nothing; that this was the same old United States and Britain which had opposed their revolution at the end of the first world war and sent expeditionary forces into the new Soviet Union to bring them down; that we were really out to encircle

them. . . . They appeared from the end of the war to accept the melancholy assumption that we were really out to create an anti-Soviet bloc for the purpose of destroying them; they seem to have based their diplomacy on that premise.

Reston understood full well the roots of the Soviet reluctance to negotiate in good faith, though he considered it to be wrongheaded and ill-advised, "one of the great diplomatic blunders of our time." Still, he admitted, it was "not difficult to see how the blunder was made."

We did intervene in their affairs after the first world war; we did send our troops into their country; we did try to bring them down; we did outlaw them and ridicule them and refuse to recognize them for a generation; and the men we ridiculed and vilified for nearly twenty years (this rabble from the gutters and ghettos of Eastern Europe, Churchill called them), these men who lived like hunted animals in their formative years and were forced to govern against a hostile world after they took power—these men (who had naturally developed a conspiratorial mentality in the process) were precisely the same men who were now negotiating for Russia in the settlement of a second world war (which they did so much to win).[20]

THE IRO CONSTITUTION, approved on December 15, 1946, would not "come into force" until fifteen member nations whose contributions totaled at least 75 percent of the first year's operational budget had "become parties to it." Until that time, a "preparatory commission," the PCIRO,* would, as the name implied, prepare for the transition and transfer of powers and responsibilities from UNRRA to IRO. It would

---

* For the next fourteen months, PCIRO would oversee the activities that would be formally taken over by IRO in August 1948. For clarity's sake I shall refer to both organizations as IRO.

take almost two years, until the fall of 1948, when Denmark ratified the constitution, for the IRO to become fully operational.

More than half of the signatories to the UNRRA agreement in 1943 declined to join the IRO, including a majority of the South American nations, as well as India, Panama, South Africa, Ethiopia, Greece, Egypt, Iraq, Iran, and the countries of origin of the displaced persons: Czechoslovakia, Poland, the USSR, and Yugoslavia.*

IRO would never be a truly international organization, as UNRRA had been, but was rather a creature of the Americans and British, funded by, staffed by, and beholden to them. While it would pay lip service to the desirability of repatriating the displaced persons, its raison d'être was to resettle them in nations other than their former homelands.

---

* For the IRO start date and lists of nations eligible for and joining IRO, see Louise W. Holborn, *The International Refugee Organization: A Specialized Agency of the United Nations: Its History and Work, 1946–1952* (London: Oxford University Press, 1956), 583, 590; for a list of UNRRA states, see Woodbridge, *UNRRA,* 3:29–32.

14.

"SEND THEM HERE," *LIFE* MAGAZINE, SEPTEMBER 23, 1946

Round One in the Campaign for a Displaced Persons Bill

I N SEPTEMBER 1946, in a major policy speech in Stuttgart, Secretary of State Byrnes announced what sounded very much like the imminent end of the occupation and, with it, the displaced persons camps. It was, he declared, "the view of the American Government that the German people throughout Germany, under proper safeguards, should now be given the primary responsibility for the running of their own affairs." For the Jewish DPs the announcement evoked the worst of all nightmares: that the Germans would take over the administration, supply, and policing of the camps, or that the camps would be shuttered and their residents, Jews included, forced to make their own way in the nation and among the people that had nearly succeeded in exterminating them.[1]

Byrnes's announcement and the continued refusal of the British to open Palestine to the immigration of the Jewish DPs made it more imperative than ever that America's Jewish community initiate efforts to resettle the survivors in the United States.

NEW YORK CITY, OCTOBER
1946 TO JULY 1947

In the year and a half since liberation, the American Jewish organizations had raised significant sums of money for the relief of the survivors; argued that because of the unique suffering they had endured, they required additional assistance, extra rations, the right to govern themselves, and their own camps; and lobbied the Truman administration to keep the German borders open to the Polish Jews and to pressure the British to allow Jewish immigration to Palestine. What they had not done was to campaign for any change in American laws that would have authorized the immigration of sizable numbers of displaced persons, Jews and Christians.

Haunted by fears of an antisemitic backlash, the leaders of the American Jewish community feared that any attempt at revising American immigration policy might very well result in a decrease, not an increase, in the number of Eastern European and Jewish immigrants allowed into the country. A Gallup poll taken in December 1945 had asked interviewees whether they favored increasing, reducing, or maintaining the number of Europeans admitted to the United States. Five percent had answered that they would favor allowing more immigrants; 32 percent would maintain the current levels; 37 percent would reduce them. Another Gallup poll, this one taken in August 1946, asked a sample of Americans whether they agreed or disagreed with President Truman's plans to ask Congress to "allow more Jewish and other European refugees to come to the United States to live than are allowed under the law now. . . . Only 16 percent of the respondents answered affirmatively; 72 percent disapproved; 12 percent had no opinion."[2]

While the Jewish organizations stayed largely silent, Catholic and Protestant organizations, the editors of *Life* magazine, the pope, and even President Truman were by the second half of 1946 beginning to speak out in favor of special legislation authorizing the entrance of Eastern Europe's displaced persons.

The Vatican had already called on the nations of the world, including the United States, to open their doors to the displaced, a call echoed in editorials in *Commonweal,* the highly influential lay-edited Catholic periodical, and the Jesuit journal, *America.*[3]

The Federal Council of Churches, representing Protestant churches, had also declared that the United States had a moral responsibility "by reason of its democratic heritage and present resources, to receive a generous share of the remaining displaced persons."[4]

Life magazine, with a net paid circulation of five million a week, made the same demand in a strongly worded editorial, "Send Them Here! Europe's Refugees Need a Place to Go and America Needs to Set a World Example," published on September 23, 1946. "The most shocking fact about the plight of these displaced persons is not that they are interned. It is the fact that the U.S. government and people have the means to open the door for many of them but have not done so. Instead we are getting used to the idea of concentration camps."[5]

The American Jewish organizations lingered on the sidelines until, three days after President Truman's Yom Kippur statement, Judge Joseph M. Proskauer, president of the American Jewish Committee, announced that the "Administrative Committee [had] decided that the AJC should undertake to devote its utmost efforts to the promotion of a liberalized policy of immigration into this country."[6]

Emanuel Celler, congressman from Brooklyn, and an AJC member, responded to Proskauer's letter by informing him that, depending on the results of the upcoming midterms, he intended, either as "ranking member on the Democratic side or Chairman of the House Judiciary" committee, to "offer bills to provide for the immediate admission into the United States of at least 100,000 DPs, of which a goodly portion probably will be Jews." He cautioned Proskauer that other bills were going to be introduced to cut "present immigration quotas in half. . . . We shall need all the strength we can possibly muster" to defeat these "restrictive measures" and pass new immigration legislation.[7]

Proskauer and the AJC, in partnership with Lessing Rosenwald and the anti-Zionist American Council for Judaism (ACJ),* organized the Citizens Committee on Displaced Persons (CCDP), a coalition of Jewish, Catholic, and Protestant agencies and associations. Rather than advocate for the admission of Jewish DPs only, which both men believed would be suicidal, the nonsectarian Citizens Committee would campaign for the admission of four hundred thousand displaced persons of all faiths. Since Jews made up 20 to 25 percent of the overall DP population, it was anticipated that one hundred thousand of the four hundred thousand admitted under the bill would be Jews.

There was a dangerous downside to this strategy. It had become common knowledge by late 1946 that resident in the displaced persons camps in Germany were thousands of Nazi collaborators and sympathizers, some of whom had played an active role in the slaughter of Jews in their homelands. The newspapers had reported as much; the military and UNRRA had acknowledged their presence; so too the chaplains and the representatives of the Jewish organizations in Europe and in the camps. By campaigning for the admission of four hundred thousand DPs, more than three-quarters of whom would be non-Jews, the American Jewish Committee, the American Council for Judaism, and their supporters would be facilitating the entry of significant numbers of Nazis and antisemites. This was, regrettably, the price that the Proskauer, Rosenwald, and their organizations believed would have to be paid to get the Jewish DPs out of Europe and into the United States.

The Jewish organizations having founded and funded the nonsectarian Citizens Committee retreated into the background. At its November 5, 1946, luncheon meeting, the AJC Immigration Sub-Committee recommended that the Citizens Committee "executive and

---

* The ACJ, founded and funded by Rosenwald in 1942, regarded Judaism as a religion, nothing more, nothing less. It was fiercely anti-Zionist, anti-nationalist, and opposed to the creation of a Jewish state.

advisory board should be primarily a non-Jewish Board and should have representatives of industry, labor, veterans, women's groups, educators, etc., all of whom would be well-known public figures."[8]

Judge Simon Rifkind warned the representatives of the almost one hundred Jewish organizations that belonged to the American Jewish Conference that "passage of legislation will be rendered impossible if it is believed that the sole effect would be importation of thousands of Jews." As a result of Rifkind's warning, several Jewish organizations withdrew support from the Federation of Polish Jews, which had demanded the immediate admission of one hundred thousand Jews to the United States.[9]

While the campaign for a new law authorizing the admission of four hundred thousand displaced persons was funded, organized, staffed, and administered by Jewish organizations, it was framed as an "American," not a Jewish, effort. To head up the Citizens Committee on Displaced Persons, the AJC approached Earl Harrison, who accepted the assignment, while making "it plain that his commitments are such that he could give only a limited amount of time to the project." That was fine with Proskauer and Rosenwald, who were recruiting him to act as the "face" of the campaign, not its guiding force.[10]

Irving Engel, the chair of the AJC's Immigration Committee, the operational center for the campaign, met with several Catholic officials, including Bishop James Francis Aloysius McIntyre, associate bishop of New York, who ran day-to-day operations of the New York archdiocese for Cardinal Spellman, to solicit their support and participation in the new organization. Given the church's declared interest in the displaced persons, Engel had hoped that Cardinal Spellman would attend the Citizens Committee's first organizational meeting. He did not, but delegated Archbishop McIntyre to represent him. Monsignor Edward E. Swanstrom, the assistant executive director of the National Catholic Welfare Conference, also attended and recommended to his superiors at NCWC "that we should lend wholehearted support and cooperation to the work of this Committee as its aims are in line with the pronouncements of the

Holy Father. If we expect other countries to accept these people, America must show the way." Swanstrom recommended as well that "our people should be advised to participate" in the local Citizens Committees that were going to be organized around the country.[11]

The ACJ and AJC congratulated themselves on the number of distinguished Christians they had recruited for the new organization. Participants at the first organizational meeting on December 20, 1946, chaired by Earl Harrison, included not only Catholic clergymen, but representatives from the Episcopalians, Quakers, and the Federal Council of Churches. Also in attendance were Major General William J. Donovan, who had served as director of the Office of Strategic Services during the war, Dr. Alvin Johnson of the New School, Charles P. Taft (Senator Robert Taft's brother), Walter White of the NAACP, Philip Randolph of the Brotherhood of Sleeping Car Porters, businessman Marshall Field, former postmaster general James Farley, and Justice Owen Roberts of the Supreme Court. Eleanor Roosevelt, Fiorello La Guardia, William Green, head of the American Federation of Labor, and Edward Stettinius, the retired secretary of state, would later join as vice chairmen. The only Jews on the board were Herbert Lehman, Rabbi Louis Finkelstein of the Jewish Theological Seminary, and two of the four labor representatives, David Dubinsky of the International Ladies' Garment Workers' Union and Jacob Potofsky of the Amalgamated Clothing Workers.

While delighted with the number of Christians on its board, the AJC worried that the CCDP was still too visibly Jewish. In a December 20, 1946, memorandum, AJC chapter members were encouraged to nominate citizens in their communities for membership in local Citizens Committees, but to focus on individuals who were, in descending order of importance:

(a) Christians mainly—since the majority of Displaced Persons are Christian and if this fact is made clear, a more effective political action program will result.

(b) Business and professional people influential in the community and, if possible in the state.

(c) Labor leaders, with a substantial local or state following.

(d) Churchmen, editors and educators.

(e) Leaders in welfare work or philanthropic activity.

(f) Leaders in local Jewish communal activities.[12]

WASHINGTON, NOVEMBER 1946 TO JUNE 1947

The Jewish organizations and the Citizens Committee had a difficult task in front of them, made more difficult by the Republican landslide in the 1946 midterm elections. The problem was not just that the Republicans had taken control of Washington, but the way in which they had done so. The first national elections since the German and Japanese surrenders should have been a moment of triumph, of national exhilaration: the soldiers were home, the economy was booming, production was up, unemployment down. But instead of reveling in victory and the return of peace and prosperity, the electorate was growing anxious about the future. In the months leading up to the 1946 midterms, anti–New Deal, anti-Truman politicians of both parties and sensation- and ratings-seeking newspapermen like Drew Pearson, Walter Winchell, and Westbrook Pegler, in print and on the radio, frightened voters by linking together into Cold War conspiracy-narrative reports of Soviet espionage in Canada, Red Army troop movements in Iraq, subversion in Eastern Europe, political intimidation in Western Europe, labor militancy, strikes, and meat shortages at home, and a Democratic president and Congress who appeared unwilling or unable to face down the Soviets.

The strategy of stoking American fears about labor agitation, strikes, and Communists, abroad and at home, paid off for the Republicans. For the first time in eighteen years, they carried both houses of

Congress—and by substantial margins, 246 to 188 in the House, 51 to 45 in the Senate. Richard Nixon in California and Joseph McCarthy were but two of the Republicans who defeated incumbents in the West and Midwest. In New York, Thomas Dewey, the Republican governor and 1944 and possible 1948 presidential nominee, was reelected with a greater margin than the voters had given any Democratic governor, including Franklin Delano Roosevelt.

The Grand Old Party was in control now. Arthur Vandenberg would oversee foreign affairs, with Senator Taft directing domestic policy and chairing the Republican Senate Steering Committee.

One of Taft's first initiatives was to appoint Senator Chapman Revercomb to a one-man subcommittee of the Republican Senate Steering Committee charged with investigating the admission of displaced persons. Revercomb's appointment was a clear signal that the Republican Party under Taft was not going to be sympathetic to writing new legislation to admit displaced persons to the United States.[13]

There was probably no senator in the nation as opposed to immigration reform as Revercomb from West Virginia. An old-fashioned southern gentleman, an archconservative, a devout Baptist, a lawyer, and a stickler for proper procedures, of which he had an encyclopedic knowledge, "Chappie," as his colleagues referred to him (as if he were a cuddly pet, rather than a crafty senator), considered it his near-sacred duty to preserve the discriminatory quota system established in 1924 and keep Eastern European Catholics and Jews from immigrating to the United States.

On December 30, 1946, a little more than a month after Taft had assigned him the task, the senator from West Virginia presented his "Report . . . on the Possible Admission of Displaced Persons to the United States." Revercomb had not visited Europe or interviewed military or UNRRA officials in charge of the DP program. His "conclusions" could have been written before his investigation was launched. "Many of those who seek entrance into this country," he declared, without providing any evidence, have little concept of our form of government. Many of them come from lands where communism has had its first growth and dominates the political thought and philosophy of the people. Certainly it would be a tragic blunder to bring into our midst those imbued with a communistic line of thought when one of the most important tasks of this government today is to combat and eradicate communism from this country. The point of whether these displaced persons who are undesired in their own country, and who for some reason have made themselves undesirable, or who from their own choice are not willing to attempt to get along with their own governments, should be brought into this country to dwell among our people, is worthy of study.[14]

The implication was that Eastern Europeans from homelands that were now under Soviet control were prima facie potential subversives, probably "communistic" in their thinking, and therefore a threat to the future of the republic. With the tacit approval of Senator Taft and the Republican Party, the senator from West Virginia was repurposing the anti-Communist narrative his party had employed in its successful midterm campaign to argue against the admission of displaced persons.

Revercomb had set the agenda for future debate. Advocates for the admission of Jewish DPs would from this point forward have to counter the unsubstantiated yet powerful charge that large numbers of them were Communists and/or pro-Soviet.

In the immediate postwar environment, no one in the Senate was going to use the kind of antisemitic language that might have been commonplace and acceptable before Hitler had murdered the six million. Instead, Revercomb, in arguing against the admission of displaced persons from "lands where communism has had its first growth and dominates the political thought and philosophy of the people," employed what amounted to a new coded antisemitism. The only displaced persons who had entered the displaced camps from "lands where communism . . . dominates" were the Polish Jews. The Baltic nationals, western Ukrainians, and non-Jewish Poles had left their homelands during the war and before the Soviet invasions and annexations.[15]

Isaiah M. Minkoff, executive director of the National Community Relations Advisory Council (NCRAC), formed in 1944 to protect Jewish communities from antisemitism, noted in an article for the 1946–47 *American Jewish Year Book* that there was

> much evidence that the anti-Semites were . . . seeking for and experimenting with new avenues of attack, exploring the possibilities of exploiting new issues, now that peace had deprived them of their war-time pretexts. Thus, one of their major devices was the use of propaganda based on the false identification of Jews with Communism. Despite the utter absurdity of the charge, the anti-Jewish press and bigot organizations persistently hurled the accusation of Communism against a Jewish community mobilized almost unanimously against all totalitarianisms. More than seventy-five anti-Semitic organizations were found peddling these falsehoods. New publications came into existence with the "Jew-Communist" line as their principal commodity.[16]

The organized Jewish community and the Citizens Committee could not argue that Jewish displaced persons were neither Communists nor Communist sympathizers when the fact was that a minority were or had been and larger numbers still were grateful to the Soviets for harboring them during the war and/or liberating them from the Germans. Instead of confronting the issue head-on and admitting that while some Jews might have been Communists, they constituted but a tiny percentage of the DP population, the American Jewish leaders ignored the charge and encouraged advocates for the admission of DPs to the United States to do so as well. The less said about the Jewish DPs, the easier it would be to pass DP legislation.

William S. Bernard, the secretary and operational leader of the

Citizens Committee, presenting the case for the admission of displaced persons in a February 1947 article in *Survey Graphic*, described them collectively as "among the first victims of totalitarianism and war. . . . They are, a large part of them, the men and women who first dared to oppose dictatorship—and fled their homes rather than submit to it. They are the men and woman who found religious and political freedom more precious than security." The only time Bernard mentioned Jews in his article was to point out that they comprised "about 20 percent" of the DP population. Identifying the groups that supported the admission of displaced persons, Bernard listed the "American Federation of Labor, the CIO, the Federal Council of Churches of Christ in America, the National Catholic Welfare Conference, the National Council of American Veteran Organizations," but neither the American Jewish Committee nor the American Council for Judaism.[17]

The introduction to the Citizens Committee's pamphlet *The Displaced Persons "What's What"* did not mention the Jewish DPs at all. "Since V-E-Day, more than 11,000,000 former slave laborers, prisoners of war and concentration camp inmates have been sent home. Some 850,000, still in camps, can never go home. . . . They are Poles, Latvians, Lithuanians, Estonians, Yugoslavs, Greeks, Ukrainians, Czechoslovaks. Brought into Germany as slave laborers and concentration camp inmates, they cannot return to their Soviet-dominated lands because of fear of political and religious persecution."[18]

This description of the Last Million was simply not true. Large numbers of displaced persons now in the camps, including almost all of the Estonians, Latvians, and Lithuanians, had not been brought into Germany as forced laborers and had never been concentration camp inmates. By attempting to eradicate the very different circumstances under which the Last Million had spent the war years and their paths into Germany at war's end, the Citizens Committee ignored not only the wartime suffering but the very existence of the 200,000 to 250,000 Jewish displaced persons.

THE ADVOCATES FOR the admission of displaced persons were agreed
that it would be fruitless, if not counterproductive, to recommend any
wholesale changes in the 1924 quota system that discriminated against
Eastern Europeans.* Instead, they proposed that Congress approve an
"emergency" displaced persons act that would, in the words of Aristide Zolberg, open "a side entrance" for the displaced persons now in
Europe.[19]

Beginning in early 1947, the Citizens Committee and the AJC
searched Washington for the most influential senator they could find to
sponsor their legislation. Their first choices were Senators Taft of Ohio
and Arthur Vandenberg or Homer Ferguson, both of Michigan. When
these senators declined their request, the CCDP organizers moved on
to the House of Representatives, where, again, they failed to interest
any prominent midwesterner or Republican member of the Judiciary
Committee. Finally in mid-March Representative William Stratton,
congressman at large from Illinois, agreed to sponsor their bill.

"Billy the Kid," as he was known, had served a term in Congress
from 1941 to 1943, run for and been elected Illinois state treasurer,
joined the military in 1945—after hostilities had concluded—then returned to the House in the Republican landslide of 1946. He was thirty-
two years old and totally unprepared to enter into rhetorical battle with
the bill's opponents. He had been chosen simply because no one else had
volunteered. Fortunately, the ranking Democrat on the Immigration
Subcommittee was Emanuel Celler of Brooklyn, who, unlike Stratton,
was well versed in immigration legislation, rhetorically combative, and

---

* While almost all of the near quarter million displaced Jews in the camps were Polish, Latvian, or
Lithuanian, the annual quota—for Jews and non-Jews alike—from these countries was 6,524 for Poland, 246
for Latvia, and 386 for Lithuania. (Leonard Dinnerstein, *America and the Survivors of the Holocaust* [New
York: Columbia University Press, 1982], 119.)

eager and prepared to take on those opposed to new immigration legislation.[20]

With their displaced persons bill written and a sponsor prepared to introduce it, the Citizens Committee paused while Congress debated American participation in and funding for the newly established International Refugee Organization. Senator Vandenberg, once an isolationist but now committed to a bipartisan foreign policy that recognized America's responsibility toward Europe, led the fight for IRO recognition and funding. Before he had had a chance to make his opening statement, he was interrupted by Chapman Revercomb of West Virginia, who "offered on behalf of myself and the Senator from Nevada," Democrat Patrick McCarran, an amendment stipulating that membership in the IRO would not obligate the United States to abrogate, modify, add to, or supersede current immigration laws.

Though Vandenberg insisted that the question on the floor was not immigration or admission of the DPs, Revercomb ignored him and proceeded to dominate the hearings with a one-man defense of current immigration restrictions. The nation had, he conceded, been built by immigrants, but of an entirely different nature than those who sought entrance from the DP camps.

> Over the last few decades there has been constant turmoil through the countries of Europe. . . . There is certainly no good sense in any program that imports a great segment of European agitation into the American hemisphere.
>
> We know the threat of subversive activities; we know that communism, with its vicious purposes and its hidden boring-in tactics, already has sent its Trojan horsemen into the United States.
>
> Let us proceed to maintain here our own form of government and not endanger it through the admission of persons who may bring to us, and carry among us, the contagion of political

disease; and let us not destroy the economic progress of our people here in a day of reconstruction.

Revercomb's amendment was approved by unanimous consent,
though as Senator Vandenberg had explained, it was entirely superflu-
ous. Authorizing participation in the IRO would have no effect on
American immigration laws.[21]

IN JUNE 1947, the Subcommittee on Immigration and Naturalization
of the House Committee on the Judiciary opened debate on the displaced persons bill sponsored by Congressman Stratton, which authorized the admission, on an emergency basis, of 100,000 displaced
persons a year, for the next four years. Two years and a month had
passed since liberation and the relocation of the Last Million to the DP
camps. Even for the Republican do-nothing (Truman's characteriza-
tion) 80th Congress, the lack of urgency displayed was remarkable.
"Congress, which gave prompt and pressing attention to surplus war
material and the dismantling of the mechanism of conflict, finally got
around this week to another kind of war surplus, the thousands of
homeless, suffering displaced persons in Europe," Samuel A. Tower of
the *New York Times* reported on June 8, 1947. "Leisurely, skeptically,
almost with indifference on the part of some members, a House Judiciary subcommittee opened hearings to admit some of the displaced
persons into this country."

Tower and other observers doubted that much would come of the
hearings. Even should the bill be reported out, which was rather unlikely given "the high hurdle of opposition in the subcommittee," it
would have to be approved by the full Judiciary Committee, then given
"the go-ahead for floor action by the Rules Committee." Should it reach
the floor of Congress, it would do so "at the same time Congress is
looking forward to the adjournment set for the latter part of July." The

timing guaranteed failure. There was little chance that the bill would come up for a vote before adjournment.[22]

The White House did not publicly endorse the Stratton bill, perhaps because it had been introduced by a Republican. Instead, Truman delegated his adviser David Niles to work behind the scenes with Stratton and the CCDP. Goldthwaite Dorr, a prominent New York lawyer and State Department consultant on immigration and the IRO, was assigned to assist Congressman Stratton.

Dorr's first task was to assemble a credible and powerful witness list for the public hearings. "It was obvious," he recalled in a later oral history, "that we had to put on people who were interested in these various types—like the Balts—put on people who knew about them, put on people who knew the Ukrainians, knew the Poles, and so forth. And it was obvious that there was going to be quite an influx of Jews and we didn't want to overemphasize it."[23]

Congressman Stratton opened debate on H.R. 2910 by emphasizing that his bill was a practical measure, not a humanitarian gesture. It would bring into the nation workers, skilled and unskilled, needed to "fill our manpower shortages." Among the DPs eligible for resettlement were some "77,000 farmers, 18,000 agricultural workers of other types, more than 20,000 construction workers, 22,000 domestics, 9,000 household workers, and 4,000 nurses. Experts in the Department of Labor tell us that there are shortages in those fields, and we can certainly strengthen our economic well-being by the immigrations of these skilled DP's."[24]

These points would be reiterated by witness after witness in the days to come. Even Rabbi Philip Bernstein, one of only three Jews called to testify (the others were Congressman Jacob Javits of New York and former governor and UNRRA director general Herbert Lehman), devoted much of his testimony to emphasizing what the displaced persons, as workers, had to offer America. "A great variety of labor skills is represented among these DP's. Artisans predominate, namely, carpenters, painters, textile workers, shoemakers, tailors. There is a fair-sized group of technicians specializing in auto mechanics, electricity, dentistry, et cetera. Nurses and doctors, because they were found necessary by the Nazis, survived in goodly numbers. Actually, the largest single group, about 15 percent, consists of tailors, male and female. This happens to be an industry in which the United States is actually short of skilled help at the present time."[25]

The Citizens Committee intended to present the displaced persons not as victims but as survivors, as assets not liabilities. The witnesses the CCDP called to testify emphasized the displaced persons' strength, resilience, fortitude, diligence, and workplace skills; there was scant mention of torment, torture, or abuse.

The bill's opponents focused as well not on the humanitarian issues, but on the potential effect on the nation and the economy, which they considered to be negative, of admitting hundreds of thousands of Eastern European refugees. Jeremiah J. Twomey, chairman of the Subcommittee on Immigration and Naturalization of the American Legion's National Americanism Commission, testified that because of the difficulties returning veterans were having in finding work and housing, the Legion was opposed to any revision in the nation's immigration laws. "While it is true that the appeal of those who would admit hundreds of thousands of immigrants touches the heart, such generosity can only be practiced at the expense of our own people, and particularly our World War II veterans."[26]

Advocates for the displaced persons claimed that they would strengthen the nation not only through their labor but through their commitment to freedom and their opposition to all forms of totalitarianism. Charles Rozmarek of the Polish American Congress testified on June 13, 1947, that the Polish displaced persons' "staunch opposition to all forms of totalitarianism aiming at the destruction of democracy, would make them the kind of citizens America needs right now when world communism directed from Moscow has set out to destroy us from within before an attempt will be made to destroy us from without."[27]

Republican Noah Mason from Illinois made the same point when he declared that "the great preponderance of these displaced persons are displaced persons because they object not only to communism but to the puppet governments that have been set up in their home countries, and they do not want to go back and submit themselves to that, and because of that fact, and because of their love of liberty, and because of their objection to that form of government, I say they are the kind that we need and want in our democratic government."[28]

By focusing attention on the anti-Communist credentials of the Eastern Europeans who refused to return to Communist-dominated homelands, the witnesses, perhaps unintentionally but effectively, drew a sharp contrast between them and the Polish Jewish DPs who had survived the war because they had been sheltered by the Soviets.

Ed Lee Gossett, the anti–New Deal and antisemitic* Democratic congressman from Texas, who had the year before introduced a bill to cut immigration quotas in half for a ten-year period, repeatedly pointed out that large numbers of displaced persons had entered the camps in Germany after the war and after having lived in Communist-dominated lands. "I have been told, although I cannot verify these facts, that at least a good many of those people were more or less induced to come into our camps with the idea of being troublemakers, some out of Russia, Lithuania, Czechoslovakia, and Poland. Some arrived as recently as last year. They were professional revolutionaries, as it were."

After Secretary of State Marshall, perhaps the most respected man in Washington as a result of his wartime and postwar service, had testified, Gossett questioned him about the dangers inherent in admitting DPs who had resided in Communist-dominated nations:

Mr. GOSSETT. . . . We do know that thousands upon thousands, and perhaps 200,000, of those persons now in our DP

---

* The "finding aid" for the Gossett Papers at Baylor University states that "anti-Semitic sentiment pervades the topics of immigration, Communism, Palestine, and race relations."

camps, have come out of Russian-occupied areas since the shooting stopped. Now, it seems reasonable to me—and if it is not
reasonable, I would like for you to point out to me why it is not—
that Russia is not going to permit people to leave her zone unless
she wants to get rid of them or unless she has some reasons for
sending them to our zone. They have been letting those people
leave by the thousands. . . . Now is it not reasonable to assume
that if the Russians are permitting this great migration of persons from their zones into our camps, they are not doing it for
our benefit? . . .

Secretary MARSHALL. There are a good many assumptions you are making there that are a matter of debate.

Mr. GOSSETT. I grant you they are assumptions. . . . Now,
General, in kindness to yourself—and I am one of your greatest
admirers, sir, if you want to know it. I am not trying to embarrass
you any at all. . . . Now, I have the feeling and I grant you here
again, it is merely based on what people have told me—I have not
been there—that there are a lot of folks in those camps who would
be detrimental to us, who are hostile to America and the American way of life, and there are possibly a good many there who have
subversive intentions in seeking entry into this country.[29]

AS THE HOUSE hearings wound on and the summer recess approached,
Senator Homer Ferguson of Michigan, with six other Republican and
two Democrat senators, introduced a displaced persons bill in the upper
chamber. To make their bill more palatable to anti-immigration senators, sponsors of the Ferguson bill did not specify how many DPs would
be admitted, but left the number to be determined at a later date. To
remove any suggestion that their bill would favor Jews, who were more
likely than the other DP groups to have relatives in the United States,
the bill did not, as the Stratton bill had, grant priority to DPs with

relatives in the United States, but instead gave priority to "persons possessed of special trades, skills, professions, or aptitudes as will best meet the economic needs of the United States and contribute to its cultural, religious, economic, or industrial welfare and prosperity." This provision, AJC organizers feared, might well be applied to favor non-Jews over Jews.[30]

Five days after Senator Ferguson introduced his bill, President Truman, on July 7, 1947, still without endorsing either the House or Senate versions, delivered a message to Congress on the need for displaced persons legislation. "It is unthinkable," he declared, that the displaced persons "should be left indefinitely in camps in Europe. We cannot turn them out in Germany into the community of the very people who persecuted them. Moreover, the German economy, so devastated by war and so badly overcrowded with the return of people of German origin from neighboring countries, is approaching an economic suffocation which in itself is one of our major problems. Turning these displaced persons into such chaos would be disastrous for them and would seriously aggravate our problems there."

Truman reminded Congress that it was not being asked to approve a "proposal for a general revision of our immigration policy [or] to waive or lower our present prescribed standards for testing the fitness for admission of every immigrant, including these displaced persons."

> Those permitted to enter would still have to meet the admission requirements of our existing immigration laws. These laws provide adequate guarantees against the entry of those who are criminals or subversives, those likely to become public charges, and those who are otherwise undesirable. . . . We are dealing with a human problem, a world tragedy. Let us remember that these are fellow human beings now living under conditions which frustrate hope. . . . Let us join in giving them a chance at decent and self-supporting lives.[31]

On July 18, 1947, according to ultimate insider Drew Pearson, the president summoned the congressional leadership to his office and implored them to do something about the stalled displaced persons bills.

> The Congressional chiefs had claimed that the American people had to be "educated and adjusted" to receiving the foreign homeless; but Mr. Truman rejected this, declaring that all but a few American citizens were ready to welcome the D.P.'s to our shores. The 400,000 persons, he contended, could easily be assimilated in our economy, and he maintained it was chiefly an American responsibility to give them refuge. To this ex-Speaker Sam Rayburn of Texas replied that southern Democrats in the House would vote almost en bloc against the displaced persons. Senators Vandenberg of Michigan and Barkley of Kentucky also expressed doubts that the bill would "have a chance" in the Senate—though they agreed it stood a better chance there than in the House. Truman finally gave in but only on the promise that the D.P. issue would have a top legislative priority at the next session of Congress.[32]

That same day, the Stratton subcommittee heard its last witness, the Honorable Tom C. Clark, attorney general. In questioning the attorney general, who supported the Stratton bill, Ed Lee Gossett asked whether "at least a substantial part of those persons are Communists, who have been purposely permitted to come out of Russia and enter DP camps for the purpose of infiltrating this country?"

Congressman Celler, who had been sparring with Gossett throughout the hearings, interrupted:

> Mr. CELLER . . . I must challenge the statement of my good friend from Texas who always places in juxtaposition the obnoxious use of communism with the use of the word Jews.
> Mr. GOSSETT. No, I do not.

Mr. CELLER. The gentleman does without question and has been all through the hearings, giving the impression that the Jews are as a rule Communists and nothing else, and I challenge that statement.

Mr. GOSSETT. Most Jews are not Communists, but I had reference to the Polish Jews, those that came out of Russia. I know most Jews are democrats.[33]

The debate had been going in circles for some time, with increasing rancor, until Attorney General Clark, who had claimed he had an early cabinet meeting to attend, excused himself. With this, the hearings came to an end. The House adjourned for its summer recess without the Immigration Subcommittee having taken a vote on the Stratton bill. The Senate also adjourned without taking any action on Senator Ferguson's bill.

15.

FACT-FINDING IN EUROPE

Round Two in the Campaign for a Displaced Persons Act

WHILE NO LEGISLATION WAS voted out of subcommittee during the first session of the 80th Congress, the Jewish organizations and the Citizens Committee had succeeded in placing the future of the displaced persons on the national agenda and shifted public opinion in their favor, as evidenced by letters to editors and congressmen, newspaper editorials, and endorsements from major labor unions and dozens of religious, women's, social, civic, educational, and ethnic organizations. Still, as Irving Engel observed in an August 25, 1947, letter to his colleagues, it was by no means "a foregone conclusion that emergency legislation" would be passed in the second session. "Both in the country and in Congress there is stubborn opposition reflecting distrust of foreigners in general and, to a shocking extent, of Jews in particular. It is to be feared that, if the legislation cannot be sidetracked entirely, an attempt may be made so to shape its terms as to reduce the number of Jewish DP's who could benefit by it."[1]

WASHINGTON, JULY TO OCTOBER 1947

The major obstacle was Senator Chapman Revercomb of West Virginia. In the final days of the first session, he had introduced a resolution authorizing a Judiciary Committee subcommittee "to make a full and complete investigation of our entire immigration system including . . . the situation with respect to displaced persons in Europe and all aspects of the displaced-persons problem; and . . . the effect upon this country of any change in the immigration laws." Revercomb's resolution specified no end date for the completion of the investigation and recommended that the subcommittee be composed of two members: Revercomb and Democratic senator Pat McCarran of Nevada, who was as opposed to any change in the immigration laws as he was.[2]

"Extremely important defeat Senate Resolution 137 which authorizes seven months investigation of immigration practices and displaced persons," Citizens Committee lobbyists in Washington telegraphed John Slawson of the American Jewish Committee in New York. "We believe sole intention is to sidetrack legislation for displaced persons. . . . Urge you and your local branches wire Senate leaders Vandenberg, Taft, Barkley, White, and your own senators."[3]

The full Judiciary Committee amended the resolution to enlarge the subcommittee from two to five members and required it to report back by the start of the second session, in January 1948. But the damage had been done. Revercomb's report to the Senate Judiciary Committee would set the agenda for debate in the second session.

On July 31, Goldthwaite Dorr, the State Department consultant on the IRO and all matters concerning the displaced persons, wrote to warn William Hallam Tuck, the director general of the IRO, that Revercomb and his committee would be touring Europe that fall. "They will make an examination of the D.P. camps in Germany and Austria, and it is vitally important to my mind that both the Army and the State Department, as well as the I.R.O., make adequate preparations to give

them a full picture of the facts and thus prevent the investigators of
the committee, who may be picked by Revercomb, from giving an adverse twist to the whole thing by emphasis on the adverse aspects of
D.P.'s and the D.P. problem."[4]

Dorr wrote separately to Lucius Clay, now military governor in Germany, to bring him up to date on what was going on in Washington and
prepare him for the Revercomb visit.

> I have been devoting pretty much of my time for the last four
> months to trying to get some action over here in Congress which
> would help get the DP problem off your hands [and] get things
> loosened up here so that some of the displaced persons could
> come to the United States. . . . Action at the next session of the
> Congress is going to depend very largely on the results of the
> observations of members who will be in Germany between now
> and then. As you know, there are many such visits in contempla-
> tion . . . and among them is likely to be a full-scale examination
> of the displaced persons problem by a committee of the Senate
> [the Revercomb subcommittee] and very possibly also by one of
> the House. It is highly important that they get a full and fair
> view of the displaced persons work.[5]

GERMANY, SEPTEMBER TO OCTOBER 1947

The Revercomb subcommittee was, as Dorr had warned General Clay,
only one of several influential committees planning a fact-finding trip
to Europe and the DP camps that fall.

When the White House got word that an American Legion contingent was planning a fall trip to Europe to commemorate General Patton's march along the "Road to Liberty" from the coast of France into
Belgium, immediate Past National Commander Paul H. Griffith was

summoned to a meeting with the president. Truman suggested to Griffith, who was to lead the delegation, that it add to its itinerary "an inspection of Displaced Person Camps in Germany." He then instructed his aide Harry Vaughan to ask General Lucius Clay to arrange the logistics.[6]

General Clay furnished the delegation with "special air transportation" to Frankfurt and invited them to sit in on his regular staff meeting and lunch with him and Robert Murphy, his State Department adviser. Following these meetings, the Legionnaires were escorted on a visit to six displaced persons camps in Berlin and Frankfurt, one of them Jewish.

The visit to Clay's headquarters and the camps proceeded as Truman had hoped it would. In the report that he submitted on his return to the United States and in his informal remarks to his colleagues, Griffith repeated many of the arguments that Truman had made in his July 8 message to Congress.

> These persons have been driven from their countries by persecution during the last war, or have fled from the tyranny of later established Communistic dictatorships. There are no homes to which they may return, and there is no hope of re-establishing them where they now are. Neither can they remain in the camps in which they are presently located forever, the objects of our nation's charity. They must be permitted to re-establish themselves in new lands in which they may pick up the broken fragments of their lives and to work out their own destiny. . . . The ability they have, the occupations they pursue are sorely needed in many parts of our land. There are no Communists among them.

In late June, Legion representatives testifying before Stratton's subcommittee had publicly opposed any bill that might alter the "racial composition" of the nation as enshrined in and protected by the 1924 immigration quotas. Griffith did not propose that the American

Legion abandon its steadfast support for the quotas. Instead, he and the Legion Subcommittee "recommended that the United States . . . permit the emergency immigration to this country [of displaced persons] in numbers proportionate only to America's fair share."[7]

To make these recommendations more palatable to those who feared a sudden influx of Jewish displaced persons, Griffith reported that surveys in the camps "indicated that 80 per cent would like to enter Palestine." The Legion Subcommittee on Immigration and Naturalization subsequently approved a special resolution endorsing the partition of Palestine and unrestricted immigration for "all displaced persons who desire to find haven" there. The intent was clear: the greater the number of Jews entering Palestine, the fewer would be left behind in Europe to apply for admission to the United States.[8]

The visit of a subcommittee of the House Committee on Foreign Affairs, chaired by Republican congressman James G. Fulton from Pennsylvania, overlapped with that of the American Legion delegation. The Fulton subcommittee met with military officers, visited DP camps, interviewed displaced persons, consulted with the IRO officers in charge of resettlement, and monitored the activities of the "selection teams" dispatched from several IRO member nations, but not the United States, to interview, evaluate, and recruit displaced persons for resettlement.

Though the IRO had banned religious discrimination in the selection of DPs for resettlement, the Fulton subcommittee found substantial evidence that Jewish DPs were being discriminated against. Examining the passenger lists of four ships of displaced persons bound for Brazil, Venezuela, and Canada, the congressmen identified hundreds of Roman Catholics, Greek Catholics, Orthodox, Protestants, Evangelical Lutherans, and Baptists, but not one Jew. "Only 22 percent of the displaced persons are Jewish. Yet to date," there had been no progress in resettling them in any of the IRO member nations. The result of such discrimination, the subcommittee reported, was that the present resettlement trend "does not contribute substantially to the solution of the Jewish facet of the displaced persons problem. . . . The opening up of Palestine to the resettlement of Jewish displaced persons would break the log jam. The United States, therefore, has a real stake in the effort to open Palestine to these Jewish displaced persons. . . . The subcommittee recommends that the United States representative at the United Nations should make it a prime element of the United States policy . . . to open Palestine's doors to the immigration of Jewish displaced persons."[9]

The last of the American delegations to visit the DP camps that fall was the Revercomb subcommittee. "I met Revercomb and his party in London for over an hour early this week," Tuck wrote Goldthwaite Dorr on November 7, "and tried to satisfy them insofar as possible. Revercomb seems to mirror the thought that IRO ought not to be responsible for DPs who were part of the 1946 influx from Eastern Europe. These are Jewish migrants to a large extent."[10]

While the Revercomb subcommittee's final report conceded that it could not "be categorically stated that migration of Jews from Eastern Europe into the American zones of occupation was planned and managed by the various Jewish agencies operating in America and in Europe," it maintained nonetheless that "such agencies have actively aided the movements after they started and have contributed money and effort in arranging transportation, food, and shelter for many thousands."[11]

Revercomb and his subcommittee interviewed several consular officials in Germany and Austria who, they reported, "expressed alarm because of the widespread use of false and fraudulent documents in support of applications for visas. . . . An estimated 40 percent of applications for visas filed by displaced persons in Germany and Austria which were being processed were found to be fraudulent or supported by fraudulent documents. . . . The practice was said to be on the increase." The implication was clear. There was a Jewish conspiracy at play here to game the system and flood the American zone of occupation with Polish Jews, then demand that they be transported to Palestine.[12]

The DP camps had not only been inundated with Polish Jews, as part of a Zionist conspiracy, they were also, Revercomb charged, hotbeds of Communist agitation. While the subcommittee had found no "overt activity" by Communists in the displaced persons camps,

> the view was expressed, however, [by whom we are not told] that a few Communists may be among the displaced persons, but that they are in a "dormant" state. . . . Activities would not begin until they reach America. The subcommittee was told that information gathered by the military authorities indicates that there are about 6,000 known Communists in the Stuttgart area. In one displaced persons camp it was estimated that perhaps 2 percent of the camp population was Communist.
>
> The possibility of Communists infiltrating the camps and eventually gaining entrance into the United States was discussed with consular officials. The opinion was expressed [again we are not told by whom] that the situation was "tailor-made" for effecting illegal entry on false documents because it is difficult to verify identifying data or check proof of nationality. Attention was called to one or two such cases where Communists had presented false documents but had been caught.[13]

That there was no "overt" activity in the camps was presented as proof positive that the Communists had gone underground, but would spring into action as soon as they left the displaced persons camps for the United States.

WASHINGTON, DECEMBER 1947
TO MARCH 1948

The key to forward progress on the displaced persons bill was Senator Robert Taft of Ohio. Without his support, and that of other midwestern and western Republicans, it would not be possible to report a bill out of the Judiciary Committee. In late September, the senator gave the sponsors a scare when, during a campaign visit in Oregon, he cast doubt on the wisdom of letting too many displaced persons into the United States.

> We have adopted long ago an immigration policy to prevent the complete flooding of this country by people who have not the background or the knowledge of American institutions. I have always felt that the tremendous influx of immigration from, say, 1900 to 1915 was greatly overdone and should have been much more limited. . . . As to the displaced persons problem, Congress I think is prepared to consider what the United States should do [toward] relieving a specific problem that presents tremendous international difficulty. . . . I have not absolutely opposed any admission of displaced persons, but I think it certainly should be carefully limited and very carefully screened.

Though the questioner had made no reference to the Jewish DPs, they were obviously on Taft's mind. "I think the disposition of the Palestine problem would take a large part of the edge off if we could support that plan." This had now become almost a mantra, repeated again and again, not only by Taft but by the American Legion delegation and the House subcommittee that had that fall visited Europe. The fewer the number of Jews eligible for immigration under a DP law, the easier it would be to pass that law.[14]

On October 29, Senator Taft, no doubt through the intervention of

his brother Charles, a founding Citizens Committee member, met at
the Yale Club with leaders from the American Jewish Committee and
the Citizens Committee. He would most likely vote for a displaced persons bill should it come to the floor, he told the group in confidence, but
he "would take no lead in pushing its passage." He volunteered to stay
in touch and provide advice "from time to time on how the various
Senators and Congressmen stand on displaced persons legislation." Beyond this, he would not venture.[15]

It was clear from the opening bell of the second session that the
major impediment to passing a displaced persons bill was the perception
that it was a "Jewish" initiative that would precipitate an invasion of
Eastern European Jews. On January 22, 1948, in a "Personal and Confidential: Strictly Not for Publication" memo on "legislation to admit
displaced persons to the United States," Monsignor Edward Swanstrom, executive director of War Relief Services, reported to Monsignor
Howard J. Carroll, the executive director of the National Catholic Welfare Conference, that his sources on Capitol Hill had informed him that
the Stratton bill "appears to have little chance of passing" for this very
reason.

> Information has reached us that this bill is unpopular because
> in its administration a disproportionate number of Jews would
> enter the United States under its provisions. . . . The biggest
> obstacle in Congress appears to be a feeling that if the legis-
> lation is passed the Christian groups of the United States are not
> prepared to take their full share of the people admitted under the
> bill. The line of reasoning that follows is that since only
> the Jewish group is adequately prepared to handle this problem,
> the vast majority of the people entering the United States
> will be of Jewish Faith. This opposition is not out in the open. . . .
> We are convinced, however, that this single factor looms
> large in the minds of a great number of the members of
> Congress.[16]

The Jews, it was argued, had, with guile, organization, and money, taken advantage of the first-come, first-served procedures written into the Truman directive of December 1946 and secured two-thirds of the visas, though Jews made up only 20 percent of the DP population. On the eve of Congress's reconvening for its second session in 1948, Cardinal Spellman forwarded to Archbishop John T. McNicholas, the chair of the National Catholic Welfare Conference, what he believed to be rather direct evidence of such Jewish chicanery. He had in his possession a "confidential letter received from Vienna which seems to require some consideration and action." An unnamed informant had claimed that at a recent dinner, "an Embassy official [had] mentioned how tired he was of sending Jews to the States. He said that they are about the only ones who have all their papers in order. He added: 'We don't particularly want to send them but we have no others to send.' . . . This Embassy man said that every time we have a new quota to fill, e.g., 42, the Jewish organization is Johnny-on-the-spot with 42 applicants, papers in order, affidavits signed and certified." Spellman's guess was that the Jews were getting advance information from the consulate or from Washington.[17]

The Catholic hierarchy favored the passage of a displaced persons bill but recognized that to get such a bill through Congress it would have to convince wary congressmen that the proposed legislation was not going to result in the immigration of a disproportionate number of Jewish DPs. To prevent that likelihood, the Catholic Church had to strike out on its own, organize its parishioners, and focus its attention and resources on getting Christian displaced persons into the country. "This is a Christian problem," Monsignor Swanstrom declared in a memo entitled "Suggestions on How We Can Meet the Questions Raised by Members of Congress." "Approximately 82% of the displaced persons are of Christian Faith. It is considered advisable to emphasize this fact."[18]

The Catholics were late to the game, but, once engaged, put together their own dynamic public relations campaign on behalf of the displaced persons, the vast majority of whom, they emphasized over and over again, were Christian. From the office of the National Catholic Resettlement Council (NCRC), which the War Relief Services had organized in 1945, there issued a steady stream of literature, encouragement, and exhortation. To help organize and educate parishioners, the national office distributed "Parish Resettlement Kits"; published a series of instructional booklets including "Suggestions on Finding Homes and Jobs for Displaced Persons," "Resettlement Facts You Should Know," and "Questions and Answers on the D.P. Problem"; and prepared radio speeches, sermons, and addresses.[19]

The Protestant churches, simultaneously, stepped up their organizational activities and public relations campaigns. On January 13, at its meeting in Atlanta, the Federal Council of Churches of Christ in America, the leading ecumenical organization of Protestant denominations, released "A Statement Calling for Immediate Congressional Action in Behalf of Displaced Persons."

> Eighty per cent of these unfortunate victims of the war are Christians. The largest part of them are in camps now under the supervision of the United States Military Government. We, as members of Protestant and Eastern Orthodox churches, are deeply interested in the fate of all Displaced Persons, but have a special concern for the moral, spiritual and physical welfare of these our fellow Christians. . . . Church World Service, our interdenominational cooperating organization for relief and rehabilitation, through its Committee on Displaced Persons, is ready to act.[20]

Despite the increased activity of the Christian groups, the nonsectarian Citizens Committee, funded and staffed by Jewish organizations, remained the major lobbying and publicity force behind the campaign for a displaced persons bill. By December 1947 it had placed advertisements in 118 papers, special illustrated features in 50, a comic strip in

862, and a special article on displaced children in 850 foreign-language papers. It had produced as well 40 radio spot announcements, 6,000 posters, 85,000 pamphlets, over 140,000 reprints of editorials and articles, and a "Parents Forum" radio script for 200 local stations.[21]

In March 1948, its campaign was augmented by the release of *The Search*, a feature-length MGM motion picture directed by Fred Zinnemann and starring an as yet unknown Montgomery Clift. *The Search* told the story of a displaced child who had forgotten his past and his language, but was rescued by a kindhearted GI, Clift, who tried, without success, to adopt the boy and bring him back to the United States. Fred Zinnemann, who was Jewish, had, with UNRRA encouragement, chosen a blond-haired, blue-eyed Czech boy to represent displaced European children. This made the film even more useful for the Citizens Committee, which not only publicized it, but arranged for special screenings for congressmen.[22]

The Citizens Committee, in its campaign for a DP bill, focused its attention on identifying and celebrating the DPs' love of freedom, their hatred of the Soviets, their refusal to be repatriated to homelands dominated by Soviets, and their fierce anti-Communism. This line of argument unsettled not a few supporters, including Henry M. Busch, a delegate from the Protestant Church Peace Union, who was troubled when, at a regional meeting in Cleveland, "the public relations counselor for the Citizens Committee on Displaced Persons" advised the participants that "in presenting this issue to the public [they should] play up the anti-communist angle for all it is worth." This was, for Busch, a dangerous line of reasoning. The Citizens Committee should not be fanning the flames of Cold War, anti-Communist hysteria.

Just to keep the records straight, I am anti-Communist on general philosophy, on political tactics, on ethical principles. . . . I do not like them and they don't like me. Nevertheless in these days of indiscriminate witch-hunting when there is a grave danger of confusing everything liberal with communism and when so many fakers and reactionaries are exploiting the anti-communist feeling which now exists I think it is shocking for any representative of a great national organization like ours to tell a large audience to exploit anti-communist feelings for all it is worth.[23]

George Hexter of the AJC in answering a similar complaint did not apologize for or deny that the Citizens Committee was exploiting anti-Communist fears. Instead, he defended the tactic. "One of the most persistent arguments used by the opposition to the Stratton bill was that it would open the doors of this country to communists. The Executive Committee of the Citizens Committee therefore decided that it would be advisable to stress the fact that the vast majority of DP's come from communist and communist-dominated countries, and that their refusal to return there was in itself evidence that they were not communists."[24]

16.

"THE BEST MIGRANT TYPES"

The Balts, Ukrainians, and Poles

GERMANY, JULY 1947 TO 1948

On July 1, 1947, the IRO* formally took over administration of the camps from UNRRA.

"During the summer of 1947, uncertainty hung as menacing over our heads as it hung over our DP's—a protracted period in which we seemed to have no more future than they," Kate Hulme remembered. "The blue life-preserver insignia of the successor IRO (International Refugee Organization) was painted over our headquarters, over camp gates and on the hoods of all our official vehicles. The scenery for the last act, the final phase, was set up swiftly as if something totally new were about to begin."[1]

The Americans and British were determined to end their formal occupation and establish a provisional government in their zones of Germany but they could not do so as long as hundreds of thousands of foreign displaced persons, including 200,000 to 250,000 Jews, remained within German borders, under international supervision. The Last

---

* In actuality, it was PCIRO that took over administration, though in practice there would no real difference between the administration of the camps by PCIRO and IRO.

Million had for more than two years been soaking up food, shelter, and other resources required to rebuild the German economy and integrate the millions of recently returned *Volksdeutsche* expellees. Their care and maintenance were costing American taxpayers millions of dollars at a moment when that money might be better spent on rebuilding Europe through the Marshall Plan, which the secretary of state had outlined in his Harvard commencement address on June 5, 1947. The DP camps also monopolized valuable real estate, including former military barracks and bases, which the Germans wanted to repurpose for economic development and the Americans for military bases.[2]

To facilitate the removal of as many displaced persons as possible as quickly as possible, the IRO had rewritten and broadened the eligibility requirements under which UNRRA had operated. The new requirements certified as eligible for assistance more than sixty thousand DPs, including former POWs whom UNRRA had excluded. "The constitution of the International Refugee Organization apparently will embrace political refugees other than victims of the Nazi regime," Major General Daniel Noce, chief of the Civil Affairs Division in Washington, assured the acting consul general of Estonia. "It appears, therefore, that most of the Baltic and other nationals who do not qualify under our definitions of displaced persons, may receive from [IRO] international recognition of their status and the attendant sense of protection and security they desperately need."[3]

The Baltic displaced persons who had since liberation worried that the Americans would forcibly repatriate them to their Soviet-annexed homelands could breathe easier now. "When the UNRRA was in charge," a Latvian DP from a German camp recalled, "there were special American officers constantly searching among the DPs 'for war criminals and former SS troops.' Once the IRO took over . . . the intimidation eased off."[4]

For the Ukrainian displaced persons the handover from UNRRA to IRO was especially significant. With the Soviets and their allies no longer in the picture—they were not member nations—IRO officials were able to work more closely with the Ukrainian committees that had been set up to run the camps. "Political changes at the international level made it possible for the IRO to stop denying that the Ukrainians were a separate national group. . . . Largely because of the continued lobbying by Ukrainians, gradually both refugees and diaspora community leaders were recognized as having a valuable role to play in the provision of welfare and the process of resettlement."[5]

In the fall of 1947, IRO began registering camp residents for assistance—and eventual resettlement—by having them fill out CM/1 (Care and Maintenance) questionnaires for themselves, their spouses, their children, and other family members with their names, dates of birth, town, province, and country of birth, nationality, religion, marriage status, places of residence for the past ten years, employment for the past ten years, education, languages, financial resources, relatives, and whether they had received prior assistance from UNRRA or any voluntary agencies.

When Estonian, Latvian, and Lithuanian camp leaders protested, fearful that the information gathered would be mined to evict residents who did not belong, retired major general John S. Wood, now working for the IRO, reassured them,

> in the most earnest manner, that the International Refugee Organization has no intention whatsoever of carrying on a political screening for the purposes of forcible repatriation or elimination from IRO care of any person who is entitled to its protection. . . . No one will be required to give information that he does not desire to furnish. . . . Unless accurate data can be obtained as to the numbers of persons involved and their desires insofar as resettlement is concerned, there can be no proper planning and no definite proposals can be made by the IRO to the nations concerned.[6]

The IRO constitution had established criteria for determining who among the Last Million was eligible for assistance and who was outside "the concern of the organization." The questionnaires were, despite the disclaimers, designed as tools to distinguish the former from the latter. Because the *Manual for Eligibility Officers* directed them not to question the information on the CM/1s, but to accept it as truthful, the DPs, as long as they were careful in filling out the questionnaires, had nothing to fear.

"The process of discovering whether an applicant is within the mandate is a cooperative venture between him and the Organisation," the eligibility officers were instructed. "It is a logical impossibility to prove a negative, and thus an applicant cannot be expected to prove that he *is not* a war criminal or that he did not voluntarily assist the enemy forces."

As for the requirement that the displaced persons provide documents to support the information on the CM/1s, the *Manual* declared that "if the applicant has no documents"—and most of them did not—"then he should make an attempt to obtain them; if he has done so or if it is impossible to do so, and if his story is otherwise credible, he should be given the benefit of the doubt. The amount and type of evidence required in any particular case must be determined by the Eligibility Officer concerned; a sufficiently plausible story may be adequate. . . . Not only the applicant's history but also the reason for absence of the documents should be plausible."[7]

There were no penalties prescribed for lying or presenting forged documents. "It is realised that many applicants, for IRO assistance, even *bona fide* refugees, are under various pressures to make false statements. . . . It often occurs that an applicant gives different information at different times. If he can show that one of his stories is true, then it should be used as a basis for judging the case. His statement must, however, be either consistent or the inconsistencies explained."[8]

The IRO constitution declared "war criminals, quisling and traitors" ineligible for assistance, but the guidelines given eligibility officers for identifying them made a mockery of the restrictions. "IRO is not equipped to conduct criminal investigation," eligibility officers were instructed.

"Any Eligibility Officer in the Field who has doubts concerning the criminal activity of an applicant should refer the case to the IRO Headquarters of the Zone . . . or to the authorities where he is residing, where the necessary checking and identifying can be done."

At headquarters, the suspected war criminal's name would be checked against lists compiled by the United Nations War Criminal Commission (UNWCC) in London or the Central Registry of War Criminals and Security Suspects (CROWCASS) in Berlin. The problem with these lists, as the IRO acknowledged, was that they were restricted to "mostly Germans (including Austrians)." Because the Soviets had declined to join the UNWCC, there were almost no Soviet, Baltic, Ukrainian, Polish, or Yugoslav names on the lists. The CROWCASS list, as of June 1948, included forty thousand Germans, but "only one Estonian, six Latvians, two Lithuanians, about 100 Poles, 24 Russians and five stateless persons. The last three categories presumably also include Byelorussians and Ukrainians." Four decades later, in a report commissioned by the British home secretary, Sir Thomas Hetherington and William Chalmers concluded that "reliance on such lists made the screening process a charade."[9]

While the IRO constitution specified that assistance should be denied to persons who had "assisted the enemy in persecuting civil populations [or had] voluntarily assisted the enemy" in waging war against the Allies, the IRO *Manual* instructed eligibility officers that "the word 'voluntarily,' i.e. the intentional element, is the crux of the matter." What that meant was that those who had joined the Baltic or Galician Waffen-SS divisions and waged war against the Allies could receive IRO assistance if they could establish that their enlistment had not been voluntary.[10]

Applicants initially denied IRO status as displaced persons or refugees could and did appeal to special review boards. As pressure groups—and elected officials—in the United States and Canada lobbied on behalf of the former "Baltic soldiers" and as labor recruiters from IRO member nations visited the camps in search of able-bodied DPs to alleviate labor shortages at home, the review boards adjusted their standards in the direction of "greater leniency in deciding eligibility. . . . Although the Constitution was not altered, it became apparent," according to Louise Holborn, author of the comprehensive history of the IRO, "that member governments were developing a wider conception of a *bona fide* refugee than that which had prevailed at the beginning. The Board therefore endeavoured to apply leniency to the widest extent possible."[11]

Osvalds Pabijans, who claimed that he had been involuntarily conscripted into the Latvian Waffen-SS Legion on September 11, 1944, but had no documents to prove this, told the review board that he had been a farmer until "the Russian advance caused him to flee from his farm and he arrived in Riga as a fugitive," was rounded up by the Germans, taken to a military barracks, then shipped to Danzig. The eligibility officers who first heard his story, in January 1948, found him ineligible for IRO assistance. Sixteen months later, the review board granted his appeal. "Petitioner's story is plausible and without discrepancy. On interview he has given the impression of sincerity, and it is accepted that his service in the Legion was not voluntary."[12]

Janis Paegle, a twenty-six-year-old Latvian mason who had served in the Wehrmacht, provided the review board with the postcard that he claimed had summoned him to "report for mobilization" in March 1943. Although he had joined the military before the date at which the IRO had determined that mandatory conscription had been instituted, the review board, on the basis of that "postcard," declared him eligible for assistance. "In view of the evidence produced by Petitioner, he is extended the benefit of the doubt as a genuine refugee who has expressed valid objections to repatriation."[13]

Gustaves Palaitis had originally told the eligibility officers that he had voluntarily left Lithuania, then under Soviet control, in March 1941. The Germans had resettled him in Poland, then permitted him to move to Germany, and, in August 1943, to return to Lithuania. He was not asked—and did not volunteer to the IRO eligibility officers—the reasons why the Germans had let him return. The only plausible explanation was that native speakers were needed to assist the occupying authorities. In July 1944, as the Red Army approached, Palaitis fled Lithuania again. The review board that heard his appeal did not ask whether he had assisted the Nazi war effort while working in Poland, Germany, or Lithuania. The only criterion they ruled on was whether he had or had not taken out German citizenship during his residence in Germany. He had not and was on this ground found eligible for IRO assistance.[14]

THE IRO HAD been founded to resettle outside of Germany those DPs who refused repatriation. In the course of doing so, it transfigured the Last Million from near-helpless problem children who required food, shelter, protection, and provisions to stout-hearted workers who would provide an instant solution to the labor shortages that stood in the way of postwar recovery. There were not enough laborers in Belgium, France, or the United Kingdom to mine the coal; run the railways; raise food; rebuild infrastructure, roads, and residences; restart industrial production; or staff hospitals, tuberculosis clinics, and rehabilitation centers.

The postwar labor shortage had been temporarily alleviated by the use of German POWs, 800,000 of whom still remained in the Soviet Union, 600,000 in France, 250,000 in Britain. The Allies had pledged to repatriate them by 1948, though according to *New York Times* reporter Michael Hoffman, the "countries in which the bulk of prisoners are held do not want to let them go because these men are working and by all accounts working hard and efficiently. If let go, there is no local manpower to replace them and the loss would be measured in crops unharvested and in coal undug."

The IRO now made the case that the displaced persons in the camps would solve labor shortages that had been temporarily alleviated with German POWs. According to the November 1947 UN Economic

Commission for Europe, the "total manpower deficit of the European countries is 1,130,000 workers" and the number of DPs "about 1,500,000 . . . of whom the IRO always has estimated roughly two-thirds will need permanent resettlement."[15]

Having certified the vast majority of the Last Million as eligible for assistance, the IRO turned itself into an employment agency to place them. Drawing on the information collected by UNRRA and from their own questionnaires, IRO staffers prepared tables of occupational and job skills data (6.3 percent of the DPs, 5.5 percent of men, and 7.8 percent of women, for example, were said to have clerical and sales skills), which they presented to the recruiters. They created new vocational training programs and maintained already established UNRRA programs to give DPs the skills the member nations required; assigned doctors and nurses to evaluate physical capacity for employment; offered language training, particularly in English; provided logistical support for the recruitment teams that visited the camps; and assisted the DPs in preparing documents and prepping for in-person interviews.[16]

Belgium, Great Britain, France, Canada, Australia, and a number of South American nations had already arranged to resettle some displaced persons, but not very many. Now, with the backing of the IRO, which agreed to pay for the transportation of the displaced persons, the member nations doubled their efforts.

Labor ministries or their counterparts consulted with local businesses, chambers of commerce, and industry and trade associations, compiled lists of jobs, skilled and unskilled, that needed to be filled, and sent recruiting missions to select displaced persons to fill them. Belgium needed miners; the UK, domestic workers, farmers, miners, and textile workers; Canada, lumberjacks, farmers, sugar beet workers, bricklayers, tile workers, agronomists, veterinarians, nurses, doctors, textile mill workers, and rural construction workers; Australia, forestry workers, typists, hospital domestics, waitresses, road workers, electricity workers, female domestic workers, and male common laborers; Argentina and Brazil, agricultural laborers; Chile, metallurgists, mechanics, chemists,

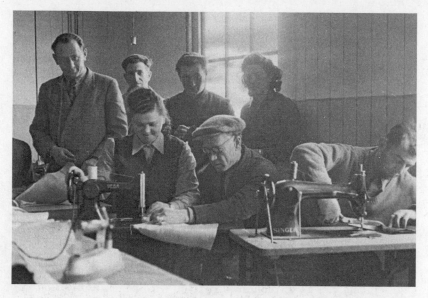

A sewing workshop at the Neu Freimann DP camp, where Jewish survivors were trained for jobs made available by IRO member nations.

printers, ceramic, textile, wood, glass, and leather workers; Peru, domestic servants, farmers, cattle raisers, machinists, carpenters, coal miners, and fishermen.[17]

In camps across Germany, displaced persons, male and female, anxiously scoured bulletin boards and consulted IRO staff and volunteers in search of positions they might apply for. "The scramble of the DP's to get out of Germany was at once heartbreaking and humorous," Kate Hulme recalled.

> The camp bulletin boards listing all the current avenues of escape made you think of some kind of macabre stock market that dealt in bodies instead of bonds. The DP's read the job offerings and rushed to qualify. When, for example, we posted the advance news that Canada would accept qualified tailors, everyone who had ever sewed on a pants' button was a master tailor. Our DP nurses with diplomas from Leningrad, Warsaw

and Kiev swore they had done a bit of tailoring before they studied nursing. Ace mechanics in our garages dropped their tools and lined up at our employment office to try to have the record on their work-tested card changed from mechanic to tailor.

And then, inevitably, came further news of more exact requirements that no one could meet—and notification that, instead of thousands, less than two hundred positions were on offer. The displaced persons who had planned and dreamed of landing these jobs—and being reset-tled, with or without their families—had to start all over. "Again and again, we picked up and dusted off the rejected ones."[18]

Each nation's recruiting delegation arrived in the camps with specific requirements, not all of them having to do with job skills or prior em-ployment experience. The British Ministry of Labour official who visited the camp Margaret McNeill worked at had been instructed to recruit only Latvians, Estonians, Lithuanians, and "Soviet" Ukrainians. There were in the camp a number of White Ruthenians.* The British recruiter "candidly admitted she had never heard of them before, and doubted if anyone in the Ministry had," but she was willing to lump them in with the Ukrainians. The immediate problem was that most of the Ukraini-ans in the camp had insisted that they were "Polish" to avoid mandatory repatriation as Soviet citizens. They now had to admit that they had told less than the full truth and reclaim their Ukrainian identities to be chosen by the British recruiters. The Poles who spoke Ukrainian also declared themselves Ukrainian to qualify for the British jobs.[19]

In the spring of 1948, the IRO established eighteen "Resettlement Processing Centers" where recruitment officers could set up shop and inspect and interview displaced persons preselected by IRO staff. "The arising of the Resettlement Center in spring of '48," Hulme later wrote, "sent waves of excitement through our vast sprawling area." Along

---

* Also known as White Russians, these were former residents of eastern Byelorussia.

"the long middle hallway" of the former Wehrmacht barracks that had been refitted as a resettlement center were "neat signs angling out from the repainted doors naming the mission within—CANADA, BELGIUM, UNITED KINGDOM, FRANCE, AUSTRALIA, SOUTH AMERICA. . . .

"From its first days . . . the Resettlement Center was as exciting as Grand Central Terminal, with an atmosphere totally opposite to the camps it resembled physically. Here every face had that going-away look and everybody was clad in his Sunday best." Here, the DPs would be interrogated, their papers checked, their bodies probed for tuberculosis or other diseases, their wartime activities questioned to make sure they were not fascists or, worse yet, Communists.[20]

It was a buyer's market. Recruiters competed with one another for strong and stout young men who were single or willing to leave their wives and children, their elderly parents, their comrades in the camps, and travel, sometimes a world away, to perform the most menial of tasks. "The whole proceedings smacked of the slave-market," Margaret McNeill would later write. "What was wanted was strong healthy labour. Volunteers who were underweight would not be considered, we were told, with unconscious irony. Brawn was required, not brain; and education was at a discount. . . . It was all so different from the mass emigration which the DPs and we ourselves had dreamed of."[21]

"The resettlers," Eileen Egan of Catholic Relief Services, who visited the camps in September 1947, later wrote, "were chosen by strength, by muscle, by the fact of being single, or of being willing to travel without the encumbrance of a family. 'Cattle market deals,' said welfare workers as truckloads of able-bodied males rolled out of the camps for Belgian mines and French farms."

The DP camp leaders, ably assisted by IRO officials, went out of their way to advertise their human wares for the recruiters. There was something disconcerting, at least to Egan, about the "glib advertising pitch" with which they addressed their visitors. The Baltic camp at Hanau was "obviously a showplace," organized and designed to impress recruiters with the residents' work ethic, good taste, good manners, dedication to democracy, English language skills, and facility with textile work, embroidery, and woodworking machinery. "These displaced persons were selling themselves. They saw themselves as being exhibited in the form of heaped-up woodwork and piles of embroidered cloth. But they sold themselves and their cause with dignity, without loss of face."[22]

BELGIUM, FRANCE, AND THE UNITED KINGDOM, 1947 TO 1948

Belgium was one of the first nations to take advantage of the cheap labor force offered up by the IRO. The Belgian mining industry recruited some twenty thousand displaced persons in 1947. They were offered two-year contracts, with wages equal to those of Belgian workers, and were allowed to bring their dependents with them after three months. A large number, particularly those with no prior experience, unable to keep up with the work, homesick for their families, and treated badly by supervisors who did not speak their language, returned to their former camps and their families within weeks of their arrival.

The Soviets protested to the State Department against the transfer of fifteen thousand Baltic displaced persons from the American zone of occupation to work in Belgian mines. Such labor schemes, the Soviets remonstrated, were all too reminiscent of Nazi forced labor programs. The State Department dismissed the protest with barely a shrug. "Balts are not deemed by the United States Government to be Soviet citizens; this transfer is a normal case of resettlement of displaced persons not subject to forcible repatriation." A month later, the British rejected similar Soviet objections to their plan to recruit "85,000 to 100,000 displaced persons . . . for work in the agricultural and in the textile and mining industries of Great Britain."[23]

France had met its labor shortages with German POWs, a significant portion of them "leased" from the Americans, until, in 1948, with most of the POWs having been or about to be repatriated, it had no choice but to recruit displaced persons. By June 1948, sixteen thousand were working in French agriculture and mines.

The postwar labor shortage was most pressing—and most frightening—in the UK, where in the eighteen months after VE Day almost one and a half million workers had withdrawn from the labor force: married women and the elderly who had because of the war worked past their retirement age; teenagers who had worked during the war but were now required to return to and stay in school; and entire families who having struggled through the war decided the time had come to seek more peaceful, prosperous pastures in Canada or Australia.

The labor shortage might have been alleviated had the British rapidly demobilized and brought home their soldiers, but the new Labour government refused to do so, fearing that any significant reduction in military strength might weaken its influence in the colonies and in Europe. The UK might also have met its labor shortages by enlisting West Indians and Asians from the Empire who had fought in the war and worked in munitions factories at home, but the government preferred not to expand the population of nonwhites. Why encourage racial outsiders to remain or immigrate to Britain when there were available hundreds of thousands of white Eastern Europeans without any claims on British citizenship?[24]

The first foreign laborers recruited for work in the UK were the Polish soldiers and officers who had fought under British command. At war's end, those who refused repatriation were relocated to the UK from POW and DP camps in Italy, Germany, North Africa, and the Middle East. In May 1946, the War Office formally disbanded the Polish military units and organized the soldiers and officers into what it called the Polish Resettlement Corps, moved them into special camps, provided them with vocational and language training, and attempted to place them in jobs where there were critical shortages. Those who preferred

not to work in Britain were given assistance in repatriating or emigrating to the Dominions.* The Polish soldiers did not make much of a dent
in the UK's labor shortage. There were not enough of them, and as
often as not, they were neither willing nor able to do the work the British needed done.[25]

In the spring of 1946, the British Labour government had begun to
look to the displaced persons camps in its zone of occupation for the
laborers it needed. In April 1946, the cabinet approved the ingeniously
named "Balt Cygnet"† program, under which a thousand single young
female Latvian, Lithuanian, and Estonian displaced persons were recruited to work in understaffed tuberculosis sanatoria. "Many of them,
(especially the younger ones)," a memorandum prepared for the Foreign
Labour Committee explained, "already speak English quite well. The
women are of good appearance; are scrupulously clean in their persons
and habits; have a natural dignity in their bearing."

While the name of the program brought to mind the image of young
swans swimming in a pond, the Baltic "swans" were recruited to do the
types of backbreaking labor that British women, with other options,
were reluctant to do: mopping floors on hands and knees, changing
linens, emptying bedpans, removing the trash, doing laundry, washing
dishes, serving and cleaning up after meals. The pay was meager, the
sanitaria located in remote regions, and there was, as in any tuberculosis
facility, the ever-present fear of contagion.[26]

The "swans" began arriving in Britain in October 1946. Newspaper
reporters extolled their intelligence, their language skills, their deport-
ment, character, good looks, and grooming; their supervisors gave them
high marks for discipline, the ability to work long hours and do the
most menial tasks without complaint. "Most of the women," Kanty
Cooper, who worked with displaced persons in the British zone, wrote

---

* The British Dominions in 1945—Canada, Australia, Ireland, Newfoundland, New Zealand, and South
Africa—were semi-autonomous political entities, part of the British Empire, swearing allegiance to the
crown, but with their own elected governments.
† A cygnet is a young swan.

in her autobiography, "would look more at home in the drawing room than in the kitchen, yet they were all prepared to act as scullery or ward maids for the first three months of their stay in England."

"You have to be realistic," one of them, "an aristocrat to her elegant finger tips," told Cooper. "I can't go back to my home. I can't live independently without money. I have no profession but I am strong, not afraid of work and, I hope, moderately intelligent. To clean a room or peel potatoes can't be hard to learn. I shall do whatever I am asked to do however dirty. I am lucky that I speak your language."[27]

The recruitment and insertion of the first thousand Baltic girls and women went so well and caused so little friction that the Labour government decided to recruit five thousand additional "swans," Balts as well as Ukrainians. To stimulate recruitment for jobs no British locals were willing to accept, in places far from friends, families, and those who spoke their language, potential "swans" were told that if they did their work well, they might be "promoted, if there are vacancies, to posts as Ward Orderly, Matron's Maid, Assistant Cook, etc." A few might even be plucked off the wards and sent away to be trained as nurses.[28]

Following and because of the success of the "Balt Cygnet" project, the Labour government designed a second, much larger program—again with a catchy name, "Westward Ho!"—under which it planned to recruit one hundred thousand Eastern European displaced persons, men as well as women, to work in mining, manufacturing, construction, domestic labor, and agriculture. Those selected for the program had to come unencumbered; they were not allowed to bring any dependents with them. Because "DP" carried vivid and negative connotations of sick, distressed, and depressed Eastern Europeans, the Foreign Office and Labour Ministry referred to the new recruits as EVWs, "European Volunteer Workers." The trade unions, worried about the importation of a hundred thousand foreign laborers, were assured that the EVWs would only work in jobs that British citizens did not want, at wages comparable to those paid union members. Should "redundancies" occur, the EVWs would be the first out.[29]

"The vast majority" of displaced persons recruited for work in the UK, declared Major Richard Rapier Stokes, a resolutely right-leaning Labour MP from Ipswich who supported the program, "are first-class people who, if let into this country, would be of great benefit to our stock, would help to raise the standard of living, and would be of immense use anywhere where there was a labour shortage." Such references to "our stock," shorthand for white and Protestant, would come up repeatedly in parliamentary debate, official economic surveys, Foreign Labour Committee discussions, Royal Commission on Population reports, even in Fabian Society pamphlets.[30]

Though the displaced persons recruited by the UK and other Western European nations were not by any stretch of the imagination subjected to the same conditions as Nazi forced and slave laborers, as the Soviets charged, neither were they, despite the nomenclature, "voluntary workers." They were not allowed to choose their place of employment. They were instead assigned by the Labour Ministry to specific jobs in specific workplaces under prescribed conditions with preset wages and prohibited from leaving those workplaces for others without the consent of the local Labour Ministry office. Those incapable or unwilling to do the job to which they were assigned were returned to Germany.[31]

The priority for both the Foreign Office, which was responsible for the oversight of the displaced persons camps in the British zone in Germany, and the Home Office and Labour Ministry, whose task it was to rebuild infrastructure, increase the food supply, and repair war-damaged vital industries in the UK, was to recruit and resettle as many healthy young workers as possible. The need was massive, but so too was the supply. When the population of Baltic men willing to accept the terms offered dried up, the recruiters turned to Ukrainians and then Poles, who were believed to be less cultured, less educated, and less assimilable than the Balts, but far more acceptable than Jewish displaced persons.

Almost no Jewish DPs, other than a small number of orphans and some displaced persons with relatives in the UK, were resettled as a result of these programs. According to IRO statistics, only 586 of the 86,346 displaced persons resettled in the United Kingdom were Jewish.*[32]

The British recruiters did not question the applicants about their activities during the recent war or set up a process to screen out suspected war criminals or collaborators. The operating assumption was that the military authorities, UNRRA, and the IRO had already done that. As a result, significant numbers of former Waffen-SS men with blood-type tattoos under their left armpits or scars from trying to remove them were able to enter the country. Britain needed strong bodies to work in its mines, fields, and factories. Whatever crimes they might have committed during the war, these former soldiers, the government believed, posed no civil or political danger as civilians.

The decision to import into Britain former SS men was, the government knew, not going to be popular among many segments of the population: the Jews, military men who had fought against the Germans, civilians who had suffered during the war and did so still, and those who believed that it was both morally and politically imperative that suspected Nazi collaborators be brought to justice.

In October 1947, a Polish doctor who worked in one of the London hostels that received arriving labor recruits from Germany discovered a number of the young Latvians had SS tattoos on their left arms and questioned them about their wartime activities. Monsieur Charles Zarine, the still accredited diplomat from the defunct prewar Latvian government, contacted Thomas Brimelow of the Foreign Office to complain about the discomfort the Polish doctor's questions had caused the Latvians. SS tattoos, Zarine explained to Brimelow, did not mean that the Latvians had been Waffen-SS members. The Germans, Zarine insisted,

---

* The statistics I use on the resettlement of the displaced persons are from Holborn, *The International Refugee Organization,* and Vernant, *The Refugee in the Post-War World.* There are often slight discrepancies between the two sets of figures.

contrary to all evidence to the contrary, had intended to give blood-type tattoos to all military men, but had been able to tattoo only their SS and the Baltic soldiers before halting the program. Because, "apart from the Baltic soldiers only the SS had these marks, unscrupulous propagandists have often used this to try to prove that the Latvian men have been members of the SS and therefore politically undesirable and unreliable. . . . It is certainly quite wrong to brand the Latvian men who have served in the Legion and who bear markings of their blood groups on their bodies as Nazis. . . . Therefore, Dear Mr. Brimelow, I should be very grateful indeed if steps could be taken to stop these examinations, which only cause unnecessary anguish."[33]

We do not know whether the officials in the Foreign Office who received Zarine's letter believed his absurd claim. One hopes they did not. It was common knowledge among the military, Allied government officials, UNRRA, and the IRO that the blood-type tattoos were intended as a badge of honor to distinguish members of the SS and the Waffen-SS from other German soldiers. The IRO *Manual for Eligibility Officers,* in fact, included a special appendix on "tattoo marks" as an aid to identifying SS veterans. "The Nazi Government," the *Manual* noted, had "instituted the system of tattooing" as a means of differentiating the "elite" from "normal personnel."

Still, the British Foreign Office accepted Zarine's explanation. The Labour government was intent on accelerating, not slowing down, the flow of healthy young Latvians and was not about to obstruct the pipeline because a few SS men had found their way into it. Brimelow at the Foreign Office contacted the Ministry of Labour, which assured him "that in future the MO [medical officer] will be asked to confine his attentions to the sick and NOT to meddle with blood groups."[34]

The following month, the Foreign Office was again confronted with questions about the wartime activities of "Westward Ho!" recruits, this time from a Dr. Franz Burger, a German Jew and naturalized British subject who had been hired to lecture newly arrived EVWs on "the British Way of Life and Government."

"In a chance conversation with a Latvian camp-resident, who attended most of all of my meetings," Burger wrote in a "special report" to his supervisor,

> I learned to my great surprise that he . . . was a member of the
> S.S. . . . He said there were many other men in the same position
> (i.e. former S.S. men) among the residents of the camp. If his
> statements are correct (and I cannot see any reason why he should
> have invented such a story) the position is that quite a number—
> perhaps many hundreds or even a few thousands—[of] former
> S.S. men enter this country as D.P.'s. . . . The prospect seems to
> give cause for grave concern. . . . From my own long experience
> as a prisoner of the S.S. I know what sworn enemies of every-
> thing British they are. . . . I do not know whether the authorities
> concerned with the recruitment and administration of E.V.W.'s
> are fully aware of the antecedents of these men and of the poten-
> tial danger their admission to this country may involve. I read a
> day or two ago that another 30,000 D.P.'s are to be brought over
> here as miners. . . . This plan will afford great scope for former
> S.S. members . . . if great care is not used in recruiting them. As
> far as S.S. members are concerned the tattoo I mentioned should
> facilitate a check on the Continent on applicants, and possibly
> on people who are already in this country.[35]

Dr. Burger's letter was passed up the chain of command to Andrew Rouse, assistant secretary of the Labour Ministry, who forwarded it to E. B. Boothby in the Foreign Office Refugee Department. Boothby reassured Rouse and everyone else in the Ministry of Labour that Burger's fears were unfounded and inconsequential. The blood-type tattoos, which on German arms signified membership in the SS, did not mean the same when found on Latvian arms. "The tattooings referred to by Dr. Burger are perfectly innocuous. . . . As all persons selected for 'Westward Ho' have been screened and re-screened by our security authorities as well as by U.N.R.R.A. and the Preparatory Commission of the International Refugee Organisation, I think, that there is little, if any, possibility of any person with an undesirable wartime record being brought to this country."[36]

When British miners who had fought in the recent war or lost friends or relatives on the front refused to work alongside Waffen-SS veterans, the National Coal Board recommended that they be kept out of the mines and any other jobs where they might have to remove their shirts.[37]

The "Westward Ho!" resettlement program accomplished several purposes at once. It removed from Germany more than 85,000 displaced persons, more than two-thirds of them men; 24,260 Estonians, Latvians, and Lithuanians; 34,544 Poles or Ukrainians; and another 8,128 former Ukrainian POWs. It alleviated critical labor shortages in agriculture, coal mining, domestic service, and textile mills. It also provided the Foreign Office and MI6, the UK's foreign intelligence service, with a rich source of potential assets.[38]

The British had through the 1920s and 1930s established networks of contacts in the Baltic republics and Ukraine that provided them with intelligence on the Soviet Union. In the postwar world, it was imperative that these contacts be strengthened and expanded. With the assistance of Charles Zarine, who, we saw earlier, remained accredited as a diplomat, though the Latvian government that had appointed him had long disappeared, MI6 operatives tracked down former Latvian, Estonian, and Ukrainian Waffen-SS members already in the UK and recruited them for a variety of clandestine missions. Some were reinserted into their former homelands to gather information or make trouble for the Soviets. None of these efforts, nor those of the American CIA, which had its own operations and participated in some with the British, yielded much. The agents recruited were frighteningly unreliable and Soviet intelligence was quite adept at discovering and "turning" them.[39]

The Soviets had, of course, always feared—and made those fears public—that the British and Americans were offering protection and resettlement to Baltic and Ukrainian refugees in DP camps because they intended to make use of them as a reserve army of anti-Soviet propagandists, provocateurs, and, should the opportunity present it, invading soldiers. Such fears, though dismissed by British and American diplomats as ridiculous, were not without foundation.

BRAZIL, ARGENTINA, CHILE, 1947–48

British and Western European policies for resettling DPs were replicated in South American nations, which, though suffering no manpower shortages due to the war, were committed to developing natural resources and expanding manufacturing, each of which required an influx of laborers, skilled and unskilled.

As early as June 1946, while the IRO was still in the planning stages, the government of Brazil had declared its intention to accept a sizable number of Europe's displaced persons. "We wish . . . to strengthen the European element in our ancestry. . . . Brazil wishes the newcomers to be able to integrate and assimilate themselves and to blend fully with a nation which is proud of her contribution to western civilization." Those accepted for resettlement would be put to work where it would best benefit the nation, for the most part in underpopulated rural areas and new industrial plants. "No immigrant" would be "allowed to settle or set up as a tradesman or accept other occupation in the urban centres of population." This proviso was intended to discourage the immigration of Jewish displaced persons and did so rather effectively. Almost thirty thousand displaced persons resettled in Brazil under the auspices of the IRO, two thousand of them Jews.[40]

The government of Argentina also accepted about thirty thousand displaced persons, most of them to work in agriculture. Though Argentina had no "formal restrictions against Jews as such, persistent reports," Sidney Liskofsky declared in the *American Jewish Year Book*, "indicated that the Argentine consuls in Europe were functioning on the basis of instructions from the central authorities in Argentina not to issue visas to Jews, either permanent or transit."[41]

Chile did not need large numbers of settlers for agricultural work. Its need was for skilled craftsmen and technicians, but only those who fit specific religious and ethnic requirements. According to Louise Holborn, "Preference was given to Balts and Ukrainians, and very few Jews were accepted."[42]

AUSTRALIA, 1946–48

Australia's entrance into the displaced persons sweepstakes was driven by the belief that the nation was frighteningly underpopulated and required massive infusions of new immigrants to compete economically in the postwar world and survive another war in Asia. The government's preference had always been "Britishers," but next to the British, there was no better source than a carefully curated selection of white European displaced persons.

As Australian soldiers were demobilized and returned home, Arthur Calwell, head of the newly established Department of Immigration, went off to Europe to negotiate an agreement with the IRO and arrange for the recruitment, selection, and importation of tens of thousands of displaced persons. "So many countries are now alive to the possibility of displaced persons as a source of manpower," Calwell cabled Prime Minister Ben Chifley from Europe on July 18, 1947, "that we must act quickly otherwise we will be left with their rejects. Many missions are already operating on behalf of other countries particularly from North and South America. Australia is so much further removed from Europe than these countries that we must tackle the task now if we are to successfully compete with them."[43]

There were regrettably not enough Baltic refugees to go around by the time Calwell arrived in Europe. Large numbers had already been recruited by the Europeans. But there were, according to "a memorandum from the head of the Australian Military Mission in Germany," cited by historian Jayne Persian, other "very good types" in the DP camps, among them Poles and Yugoslavs.[44]

On arrival in Australia, the displaced persons were put in transit camps. From there, they were dispersed—to the more remote regions where native-born Australians preferred not to work—and, no matter what their previous education and employment might have been, assigned to unskilled jobs in the railways, construction, mining, fruit picking, clearing land.

Under the terms of the contracts the displaced persons signed with the Australian government, they were obligated to remain for two years in the jobs for which they had been recruited. They were allowed to bring only three dependents with them. Those who were sent to work where there were no suitable accommodations were housed in single-sex government dormitories adjacent to their workplaces; their dependents were placed in separate reception centers, sometimes a considerable distance away.[45]

There were warning signs from the outset that among the Balts, Ukrainians, and Yugoslavs accepted for immigration there might be former Nazi collaborators, including men who had fought in German-organized and -commanded military units. The Commonwealth Investigation Service, the precursor of the Security Intelligence Organisation, after discovering a number of Baltic DPs with scars on their left armpits indicating that their SS tattoos had been surgically removed, reported its findings to the Immigration Department. No action was taken.

The organized Jewish community, led by the Jewish Council formed in 1942 to encourage Australia to admit Jewish refugees, undertook its own investigations. It sent undercover agents into the assembly centers where the displaced persons were gathered, and discovered among them significant numbers of former Nazis and Nazi collaborators.[46]

Again, no action was taken. The fact that some members of the Jewish Council were also members of the very powerful Australian

Communist Party and that the first and primary accounts of Nazi collaborators were published in left-leaning papers was enough to discredit the allegations. Only in April 1949, twenty months after the first displaced persons were selected for immigration, did the Australian government dispatch military intelligence officers, but only two of them, to Europe to screen potential immigrants. It would take another fourteen months, until June 1950, before "the Minister of Immigration approved the first statement of criteria for securing checking" of displaced persons who had applied for immigration. By that time tens of thousands had already been admitted.

Among them was Konrads Kalējs, a former company commander and first lieutenant in the Arājs Kommando, which had assisted the Nazi occupiers in identifying, locating, torturing, and murdering Jews in the Riga Ghetto and elsewhere. Kalējs had fled to Germany after the war and sought and gained admission to a British DP camp. In 1950, he applied for resettlement to Australia and told recruiters that he had spent the war as a farm laborer, though he had no papers to document this. They had all, he claimed, been destroyed in a fire in 1947. Though this story conflicted with the one he had told IRO investigators, to whom he had admitted that he had also served as a lieutenant in the Latvian army, he was accepted for immigration to Australia, and, on arrival, given the position of documentation clerk at one of the larger resettlement camps, where he was able to assist other Baltic DPs who might have been suspected of war crimes or collaboration. In 1958, Kalējs applied for and was granted a visa for the United States.[47]

Some 8,000 of the 182,159 displaced persons resettled in Australia were Jews. Pressure from the Australian Jewish community had resulted in a "humanitarian" program, approved by Arthur Calwell, minister of immigration, in August 1945. Under this program, two thousand survivors with family in Australia willing to sponsor them would be permitted to immigrate, but would "not receive priority with shipping and would have to travel on non-British ships, since British ones were reserved for returning Australians, the wives, families and fiancés of ex-servicemen, and for British migrants."[48]

The opposition to this "humanitarian" gesture was immediate. H. B. Gullett, a Liberal member of Parliament, voiced the usually unspoken views of many when he claimed during a parliamentary debate in December 1946 that Australia was "not compelled to accept the unwanted of the world at the dictate of the United Nations or anyone else. Neither should Australia be a dumping ground for people whom Europe itself, in the course of 2,000 years, has not been able to absorb."

To reassure the nation that the Jewish survivors would not be given special treatment or arrive in such numbers that they would overrun the nation, regulations were put in place limiting the number of Jews on any ship or plane to 25 percent of the total passengers, a restriction placed on no other group of immigrants. Only at the end of 1948 was an agreement reached that increased the number of Jews allowed on a ship or plane to 50 percent, in return for a pledge that no more than 3,000 Jewish DPs would immigrate in any one year.[49]

The restriction, formal and informal, on the resettlement of Jewish displaced persons worked well. There were no Jews among the first 1,800 DPs who sailed from Europe to Australia in the fall of 1947. Only 150 of the 50,000 accepted for resettlement by September 1949 were Jewish. In the end, Australia would resettle more displaced persons than any other nation, save the United States, but only 4.5 percent of the total would be Jewish.[50]

CANADA, 1946–48

While Canada was, like Australia, committed to substantially "enlarging the population of the country" after the war, it intended to do so, as Prime Minister William Lyon Mackenzie King declared on May 1,

1947, without making any "fundamental alteration in the character of our population." Displaced persons with close relatives would be allowed into the country, regardless of their work skills, training, or experience; those without such relations would be permitted to enter only if they could demonstrate proficiency or willingness to accept positions in specific skill or job categories.[51]

Recruiters armed with job descriptions were dispatched to the displaced persons camps in July 1947. Two thousand garment workers, 2,720 forestry workers, 400 laundry workers, and a bit more than 1,000 other tradesmen were approved for resettlement.[52]

As in Australia, the movement of displaced persons to Canada was delayed until the servicemen, their wives, and their children had been repatriated, but by 1948 it was in full swing. According to IRO figures, more than 120,000 DPs would eventually be resettled in Canada, including almost 47,000 Poles, more than 20,000 Balts, and almost 15,000 Ukrainians. Thousands of men and women were placed on farms, thousands more men in the forests, mines, and railways, and a smaller number in textile mills. A large number of girls and women, more than 11,000, were recruited as domestics.[53]

Unlike the other IRO nations, the Canadian government took special precautions to prevent Nazis and Wehrmacht and Waffen-SS veterans from getting exit visas for resettlement. Attached to each labor recruitment team were noncommissioned officers from the Royal Canadian Mounted Police (RCMP) tasked with screening recruits. RCMP officers studied the IRO CM/1 questionnaires the DPs had completed, interviewed the applicants, consulted military authorities and camp officials, and checked German military and civil records. They were on the lookout not only for Balts who had "voluntarily" served in the Waffen-SS or other military units, but for civilian collaborators who had assisted or worked for the Nazi occupiers. "We find it difficult to believe," a high-ranking RCMP officer explained, "that proposed immigrants who are disloyal to the country of their birth would in fact be any more loyal to the country of their adoption."[54]

Baltic DPs who had served in the German armed forces were automatically barred from immigration. "As a result," Howard Margolian has written, "a large percentage of the Balts whom IRO had approved for inclusion in bulk-labour movements were subsequently rejected by Canadian immigration teams." So too were hundreds of other displaced persons, including Polish army veterans who had been granted exit permits by the British. "The number of Canadian rejections of would-be immigrants who had been passed by British military intelligence sometimes reached 30 per cent of all applicants."

Only in mid-1948, under pressure from Baltic and Ukrainian ethnic associations, executives from companies that were short of laborers, and the IRO, whose mandate it was to empty the camps, did the Canadian government adjust its earlier policy and begin admitting former Waffen-SS members, but only those who could provide evidence that they had been conscripted "involuntarily." Even with tightened screening and the denial of visas to fifteen thousand displaced persons suspected of being collaborators or war criminals, upward of two thousand were able to gain entry.[55]

The Canadian record on admitting Jewish DPs was better than that of most other IRO nations. This was due in large part to the persistence, funding, and organization of the Jewish community.

In June 1947, in response to a petition by the Canadian Jewish Congress, immigration authorities, with the cooperation of the textile workers' union, agreed to recruit five hundred experienced tailors for work in the clothing industry, three hundred of them Jewish. The competition for these positions was so great that the Joint Distribution Committee had to install sewing machines to train, then test the displaced persons to determine who among them were truly eligible. In 1948, more than 7,000 Jewish displaced persons were admitted to the nation: 3,000 under the "Close Relatives Scheme," 2,439 under the "Garment Workers' Project," 655 under the "Fur Workers Project," and 1,000 or so forestry workers, agricultural laborers, and domestic servants.

Between April 1947 and the end of 1951, 15,555 Jews, or "Hebrews," as they were classified by the Canadians, entered the country out of a total of 157,687. This number included those who were resettled with the help of the IRO and those who were sponsored by family members.[56]

WASHINGTON, APRIL 1947

The Americans too faced a labor shortage, but of an entirely different sort than that of other nations.

On April 1, 1947, the law that had authorized the draft expired and Congress declined to renew it. The Army, which had been awash in recruits through 1946, would, it was expected, meet future requirements—estimated at thirty thousand a month—with volunteers. In January 1947, thirty-five thousand had volunteered for military service. The February total, however, was only twenty-two thousand, with the trend from there decidedly downward: twenty thousand for March, sixteen thousand for April, and an estimated twelve thousand for May.[57]

On May 28, 1947, Major General W. S. Paul, Army director of personnel and administration (P&A), proposed to the director of plans and operations (P&O) in a memorandum entitled "Enlistment of Foreign Nationals" that an efficient and effective way to at least partially alleviate the "personnel shortage [in the] next fiscal year" would be to recruit foreign nationals to serve "with the occupation forces in Germany." Army Intelligence, G-2, in Frankfurt, to which the proposal was forwarded, after reviewing it, concluded "that the possible advantages [did not] outweigh the disadvantages." Recruiting displaced persons would represent "a debilitating influence on our own manpower" and open the door to "unfriendly infiltration"; foreign nationals "could not be counted on to approach our occupational problems from an American point of view"; and the Polish Guard Corps, composed of displaced persons with military training, was already providing all the supplementary "foreign" manpower the military required.[58]

P&A in Washington dismissed the objections of Army Intelligence in Frankfurt and added a new rationale for the enlistment program.

> It appears that the United States at some future date will accept large numbers of Displaced Persons and in that event these persons will be diffused into the civilian economy. These people then might well have greater opportunities for joining any subversive societies, fomenting disorders and engaging in criminal or anti-American activities than would the smaller numbers of persons contemplated for entry in the United States Army under this plan. Those persons selected are to be highly screened, and their actions by virtue of the fact that they are to be members of the United States Army would be accounted for 24 hours of the day.

It was a bizarre rationale for a highly questionable program, akin to recruiting criminals for the Army to keep them under watch and out of trouble. If the displaced persons who were eligible for this program, namely Balts and Poles, were unreliable, why let them into the United States in the first place?[59]

P&A pushed forward with its plans. It intended to draw its first set of "foreign nationals" from the 25,000 Polish DPs working for the American occupation authorities "in quasi-military guard and service type organizations" and the "18,000 individuals from the Baltic nations similarly engaged in guard and service duty." These individuals had already received some instruction in the English language and "a modicum of American type military training." Most were "veterans of several European campaigns." Left unsaid was that the military experience the 18,000 Balts had acquired had been as members of Waffen-SS divisions, fighting under German command in German uniforms. None of this apparently caused Major General Paul and the other officers in P&A much concern. What mattered was that the displaced persons they intended to recruit were young, healthy, able, and "more than willing to enlist in the United States Army, especially if that enlistment carried with it ultimate naturalization in the continental United States."

The beauty of the P&A plan was that it could be implemented at once, without congressional approval or oversight. "The Department of the Army has sufficient legislative authority at the present time to enlist into the Regular Army a portion of these displaced and stateless persons." The plan was, Major General Paul declared, and Plans and Operations agreed, "both practical and feasible . . . 50,000 displaced and stateless persons from the United States zone in occupied Germany [would be screened and enlisted into the Regular Army] on a selective basis with a possible ultimate goal of up to 100,000 such persons." P&O, in reviewing the plans, concluded that the "enlistment of white non-enemy aliens does appear to be a source that could assist the U.S. Army in selecting its present recruiting deficits." Other available options for relieving the manpower shortage, including stimulating recruitment and retention by raising pay, reinstituting the draft, and relieving the Army of some of its current responsibilities, had been considered and rejected.[60]

On January 16, 1948, Army officials in Washington requested a study of how many, how healthy, and how loyal potential DP recruits might be. EUCOM, United States European Command, reported back on February 25, 1948, with a breakdown, by national grouping, of unmarried, physically fit men aged eighteen to thirty-four, ranked by political reliability. Estonian, Latvian, and Lithuanian displaced persons were found to be 100 percent reliable, Ukrainians and Yugoslavs only slightly less so at 90 percent, non-Jewish Poles at 80 percent. Jews were judged to be the least reliable; only about 50 percent were accorded a "politically acceptable" rating. No explanation was given as to how these "reliability" figures were arrived at. Looking at the figures, however, with 100 percent "politically acceptable" ratings for the Estonians, Latvians, and the Lithuanians and 50 percent for the Jewish displaced persons, we can only conclude that "reliable" meant reliably anti-Communist.[61]

While P&A and P&O were ready to begin implementation of the plan, the chief of staff and secretary of the army were unwilling to do so without congressional approval. Discussions were initiated with Senator Henry Cabot Lodge Jr., who, after returning to the Senate from military service in Europe in 1946, had introduced a "Bill to Create a United States Foreign Legion," not entirely dissimilar to what the Army was now considering.

Lodge's bill had been introduced three times and failed to gain traction each time, most recently on January 19, 1948, in large part because the State Department opposed it. As Charles Bohlen cautioned in a February 23, 1948, memo, "This measure marks a very definite departure from our previous policy in regard to recruitment for the U.S. Army and from the point of view of foreign policy is extremely undesirable. It in effect announces to the world that the U.S. cannot obtain the necessary manpower from among its own citizens for its own Service and has to recruit foreign mercenaries abroad. It is obvious what use Soviet propaganda will make of such a development." The Lodge bill was opposed as well by congressmen who agreed with the State Department that it was un-American to enlist foreigners in the U.S. Army—that was something the British and French might be comfortable with, but not Americans. The bill was also opposed by liberals and civil rights activists who accused Lodge of attempting, rather blatantly, to substitute foreign white soldiers for black Americans.

The senator did not give up. On June 30, 1950, he succeeded in getting through Congress the Lodge-Philbin Act, a vastly scaled down version of the plan that Army P&A had proposed three years earlier. The act permitted up to 2,500 aliens, no more, to enlist in the Army and, after five years of service, be guaranteed citizenship. The act, according to historian James Jay Carafano, "proved spectacularly unsuccessful overall. . . . For all of Europe, there were only six thousand applicants, of whom two-thirds were immediately rejected as unqualified by the Army. Of the 2,366 applications accepted during the first year, fewer than four hundred qualified for enlistment."[62]

17.

"SO DIFFICULT OF SOLUTION":
JEWISH DISPLACED PERSONS

Aliyah Bet and the Exodus 1947

I T IS NEAR IMPOSSIBLE to overemphasize the degree to which the IRO and the recruiting nations, in stressing utilitarian and political over humanitarian rationales for resettlement, paved the path the developed world would follow when confronted by similar refugee crises in the second half of the twentieth and the first quarter of the twenty-first centuries.

The IRO turned upside down what might have been—should have been—its primary mission. No nation was invited or encouraged to take in displaced persons because they had suffered during the past war; no moral imperative was placed on the victors to care for or assist the most innocent and tortured survivors. On the contrary, the IRO permitted its member states to select for resettlement only those who, they believed, would benefit their nations by working hard and effectively at jobs no one else wanted, were reasonably assimilable, and reliably anti-Communist. Unintentionally perhaps, it set in motion a harsh Darwinian resettlement calculus that victimized those who had suffered most and rewarded those among the displaced persons populations who had suffered least.

While young, healthy, unmarried non-Jewish Latvians, Estonians, Lithuanians, Ukrainians, and Poles were leaving the camps for work assignments and resettlement in IRO nations around the world, the Jewish displaced persons were left behind. There were two interrelated obstacles to their migration, according to Sidney Liskofsky's report on "Immigration Prospects" in the 1947–48 *American Jewish Year Book*. "One was the principle of 'selective' immigration, whereby preference was to be given to persons with particular occupations or skills . . . agriculture, mining, lumbering and certain others in which Jews were not adequately represented. The other important obstacle was the unofficial anti-Semitism which lingered in the immigration policies of many countries."[1]

Rae Kushner, grandmother of Jared Kushner, had at war's end escaped with her father, sister, future husband, and a few others from Poland into Czechoslovakia, Austria, Hungary, then Italy. "In Italy we sat in a Displaced Persons camp. It was like being in the ghetto again," she recalled in an oral history interview. "We were there for three and a half years. My oldest daughter, Linda, was born there. . . . We wanted to go to Africa, to Australia, to Israel. We would go anywhere where we could live in freedom but nobody wanted us. Nobody opened their doors to us. Nobody wanted to take us in."[2]

Though the IRO constitution forbade discrimination by religion, the recruiters who visited the camps to select DPs for immigration found their way around this. As investigators dispatched by the UN secretary-general to investigate IRO resettlement reported in June 1948, "without openly declaring that they are unwilling to accept Jewish immigrants, the various missions almost invariably turn down Jews who come before them. . . . The hard fact remains that unless governments can be prevailed upon to open their doors, Jewish immigration from the camps and areas outside the camps to countries other than Palestine will be a mere trickle."[3]

Deprived of the resettlement options other displaced persons enjoyed, the Jews could wait and hope to be to be awarded one of fifteen hundred certificates a month for immigration to Palestine that the British had made available to the Jewish Agency. (It would, at this rate, given the exceptionally high birth rate in the camps, take from fifteen to twenty years for them all to get these certificates—if, that is, the British continued to offer them.) They could wait and hope that the United States would pass legislation to admit them, though no one knew if or how long that might take. Or they could attempt to enter Palestine illegally.

Those who chose to do so would not have the support of the IRO, its member nations, its ships, or its multimillion-dollar budget. They would instead be assisted on their journey from the DP camps to European ports and hence to Palestine by a network of Jewish organizations and individuals. Included among them were Americans who raised and contributed large sums of money; Mossad, Palmach, and Jewish Agency officers and operatives from Palestine; Jewish Brigade members who had ended the war on Italian soil; and Zionist youth leaders, organizers, couriers, and counselors in the camps. Ships' crews were recruited; seaworthy vessels bought, refitted, and provisioned; and displaced persons trained, prepared, selected, outfitted, secreted out of the camps, loaded onto trucks and trains, and transported to port cities in Italy, France, Greece, Turkey, and the Balkans.

"Our work in the DP camps was well-organized and progressed smoothly," recalled Zev Birger, a Lithuanian Zionist and Dachau survivor who worked with the Mossad office in Frankfurt.

> It was a big network, and we, in Frankfurt, were only one of the centers. The minute we got word that a group was about to arrive, we prepared trains, and beverages and something to eat ready at the railway station. . . . The refugees who came to us needed papers that would secure their passage out of Germany as well as the journey beyond. . . . We got travel visas to South American countries for five hundred to one thousand

persons, and with these visas we went to the headquarters of the American forces in Frankfurt, in order to obtain the exit permits as well as the transfer permits for the journey through the French zone. We drew up lists of names with the help of telephone books. We then had these lists stamped at the headquarters and also asked for a stamped copy—supposedly for our own documents. But in fact we used the original and the copy and set up two different transports using the same list, one by train and one via trucks or other vehicles. This way we could quickly get twice the number of refugees out of the country.[4]

Preparation for the illegal migration began in the camps, most often in kibbutzim organized for this purpose. In the fall of 1947, Eileen Egan and a delegation from the National Council of Catholic Women visited Zeilsheim, a Jewish camp with well over three thousand inhabitants, twelve miles west of Frankfurt. They were escorted through the camp by a survivor of the Warsaw Ghetto. "His first wife had died in the ghetto massacre. A Polish family had hidden him. His second wife and small child were with him at Zeilsheim."

"Most people here wish for Israel," he told Egan and the others. "But I am too tired to be a pioneer." He directed Egan and her delegation across the road from the main camp to a kibbutz where

a hundred young D.P.s had segregated themselves into a collective, for both working and living. They were Spartan types, teenagers and people in their early twenties, who could not be bothered with the interruptions of visitors. One light-haired young man, short and muscular, took us on a quick tour of the settlement. . . . He led us . . . into a common dining room in a large shed. Young men and women, many of them parents of the small children who were playing in a garden, sat down at two long tables for the midday meal. They were dressed in work

shorts as though they had just come in from field work. This was
a kibbutz, a community ideologically and nationally committed.
It was one of close to three hundred such communities. . . . The
kibbutzim, gathered in tight knots of farmer and workers all over
D.P.-land, were the shock troops of the Aliyah Beth, ready to
organize illegal transports to Palestine on orders from their high
command. . . . "Next year in Jerusalem" had a literal meaning,
and they defied the Allied power that had helped liberate them
to make it come true.[5]

The Mossad l'Aliyah Bet played the principal role in the movement
of the Jewish DPs to Palestine, smuggling large groups into Italian port
cities where they were housed in private residences or in UNRRA or
IRO camps until their ships were ready to depart. Imre Rochlitz, a Hungarian Jew in Italy at war's end, worked for the Joint in Rome as a welfare
officer in charge of ten small refugee centers, each with about a hundred
displaced persons. On a regular basis, he would receive a message from
Mossad agents suggesting that he not visit a certain site the next day.
Though he was never told or asked why he should stay away, he knew
the reason was that the Mossad was going to transfer camp residents to
ships and, that same day, replace them with the exact number of displaced persons recently arrived in Rome. When Rochlitz visited the
site the next day or soon afterward, he was able to report to UNRRA,
as he was required to do, that there had been no change in the "count,"
that there remained in camp the same number of refugees that had
been there during his last visit.[6]

The American journalist I. F. Stone accompanied one of the ships
that departed from an Italian port in early 1946. "The people coming
aboard had been traveling all night from distant camps and cities, some
more than a hundred miles away." Each group was accompanied by "an
underground worker as an escort." One of them described for Stone the
last legs of their journey. The DPs, smuggled out of their camps, were
loaded onto the trucks.

Our three trucks turn into a courtyard. I follow in a small car. In the courtyard one sees nothing, hears nothing. But when I get out of my car I see a long line of people, like shadows along the wall. They stand in silence, their baggage already on their backs, their backs bowed. It is a few minutes past one in the morning, and at a signal from a man at the head of the line the people begin to climb on the trucks one by one, like soldiers on the eve of an invasion. I stand by the trucks and watch a group of women and children climb on the trucks, children without mothers, mothers without children. I look on and see *tayere yunge yiddishe ponimer* [dear young Jewish faces]. There are packs on their backs and a hot fire in their eyes. Some smile. Others cry with joy. Some hug and kiss each other and hold hands. Nobody says a word. I ask a small girl near me—it is a cold night, with rain and a chilling wind—"Are you cold?" She answers in a whisper, "How can I be cold on a night like this?"[7]

The British government did everything in its power to halt the illegal immigration. Officials at the highest levels pleaded with the U.S. State Department to stop American financing of the purchase and refitting of the ships. They demanded that the Turkish, Romanian, Yugoslav, Bulgarian, Greek, Soviet, French, and Italian governments monitor their ports and block the departure of ships bound for Palestine. They threatened UNRRA and IRO officials and the Joint, which they believed, rightly, were assisting the immigration or looking the other way.[8]

As the number of illegal immigrants increased steadily, the British, having failed to prevent the ships from sailing, stepped up patrols in the waters off Palestine, apprehended the ships, escorted them to port, offloaded and arrested the passengers, and delivered them to prison camps and detention centers, first in Palestine, then, after August 1946, to Cyprus, where camps had been constructed for ten thousand illegal immigrants. As the illegal immigrants kept coming, the British increased capacity in the Cyprus camps to twenty thousand, then thirty thousand.

Running out of room in Cyprus and unable to prevent the movement from camps in Germany across the border to French and Italian ports, British officials came up with a new strategy. On April 1, 1947, the British ambassador notified the Italian foreign minister that "the British government would in the future demand that Italy take back illegal immigrants who had set sail from Italian ports." A similar announcement was made to the French Foreign Ministry in mid-May. Instead of removing the illegal immigrants from their ships and detaining them in camps in Cyprus, the British were going to deport them back to where they had departed from in Italy and France.[9]

Of immediate concern to the British were the movements of the *President Warfield*, later to be named *Exodus 1947*, a retired Chesapeake Bay steamer, with a capacity of forty-five hundred illegal immigrants, by far the largest ship Mossad had ever used. On March 29, 1947, after several false starts and returns to port for repairs, the ship set sail from Baltimore for an Italian port, which it reached on April 25, 1947. Mossad's plan was to refit the *President Warfield* in Italy, then move it to a Yugoslav port, load it with displaced persons, and sail it to Palestine.

LAKE SUCCESS, APRIL–MAY 1947

The status quo in Palestine could not hold. The British had failed to stop or slow the illegal immigration of the displaced Jews. The situation on the ground in Palestine was also spiraling out of control, with the British military and police forces incapable of containing the escalating violence with existing forces and the Attlee government without the funds to add to them. The strategy of maximum pressure, pursued by

Lehi, Irgun, and, to a lesser extent, the Haganah, had helped to convince the British that it was time to depart.[10]

In early 1947, the British had formally surrendered their mandate and requested that the question of Palestine be placed on the agenda of the next regular session of the General Assembly. A Special Committee on Palestine (UNSCOP) had been appointed and given "the widest powers to ascertain and record facts, and to investigate all questions and issues relevant to the problem of Palestine."

Convening in New York in May 1947, one of UNSCOP's first and principal tasks was to determine whether and to what extent it should, in its consideration of the "issues relevant to the problem of Palestine," take into account the 200,000 to 250,000 Jewish displaced persons in Europe, their desire to immigrate to Palestine, and the Jewish Agency's claim that they should be permitted to do so.

Henry Cattan, a member of the Arab Higher Committee, declared in his testimony that UNSCOP had neither the obligation nor the right to consider the displaced persons in determining the future of Palestine. "Palestine, he told us," Jorge García-Granados, the UNSCOP delegate from Guatemala, recalled, "had no relation to the Jewish Displaced Persons now in Europe. That was the responsibility of all the nations, not of Palestine alone."

Rabbi Abba Hillel Silver, representing the Jewish Agency, disagreed and recommended that UNSCOP delegates "must visit not only Palestine . . . but must also visit the Displaced Persons camps of Europe. Allow the committee, he said, to see 'with their own eyes the appalling human tragedy which mankind is permitting to continue unabated two years after the close of a war in which the Jewish people was the greatest sufferer.'"

"It was against this background," García-Granados recalled, that the committee members debated whether "we should go to the Displaced Persons camps. We realized that if we agreed to go, it would be interpreted at once as a pro-Jewish move; if we decided against it, the Arabs would claim a victory. . . . We postponed further discussion on this delicate subject until we reached Palestine."[11]

MARSEILLES, SPRING 1947

In mid-June, as the UNSCOP delegates arrived in Jerusalem, the Mossad moved the *President Warfield*, which had been denied permission to sail from either Italy and Yugoslavia, to Port-de-Bouc, near Marseilles. Foreign Secretary Bevin requested that the French government prevent it from leaving port. When the French refused, declaring only that they would obey international laws, British officials warned that illegal immigrants who landed in Palestine after departing from a French port would be apprehended, arrested, and returned to that port.

The Mossad, which was monitoring the negotiations between the French and British, assured that the French were not going to block the departure of the *President Warfield*, directed its representatives in Germany to assemble and transport five thousand displaced persons to Marseilles.

"For better or worse," Aviva Halamish, the author of *The* Exodus *Affair*, has written, the displaced persons chosen for the journey

represented an accurate cross-section of the Jewish DP population in the American zone of Germany in spring 1947, not only from the point of view of the division between "pioneers" [members of the Zionist kibbutzim] and "individuals," but also the various "generations" in the camps; the diversity of the countries of origin—Poland, Russia, Lithuania, Czechoslovakia, Hungary, Rumania; and the experience of the Jews during the war years. Some of them had lived under Nazi occupation—in ghettos, concentration and death camps, forced labor camps, in

hiding places in towns and forests, or as partisans and underground fighters. Others had spent the war years in places out of
the Nazis' reach, especially in Asiatic Russia. Many of them
were lonely people, who had no kin alive in the whole world, and
there were others who came aboard ship with their families—in
some cases, these were old established families, mainly of repa-
triates who had come back to their countries of origin, after having spent the war years in Russia, bringing with them children
of various ages. And there were families who had been established after the war—men and women who had met and formed
unions and were coming on board with small babies.[12]

They left their camps and Germany on June 29 and July 6, Sundays,
when the military, police, and border guards could be counted on to be
"less alert than usual." Mossad had secured a collective visa issued by
the consul in Marseilles for seventeen hundred people to enter France
on their way to Colombia; additional visas were forged.

The seventeen hundred on the legal visa arrived in France by train
and were housed in IRO facilities. Those exiting Germany on the
forged visas were driven in sealed trucks to the border, then, with the
active assistance or "blind eye" of the American military and French
border officials, smuggled into France and put on trains for Marseilles,
where they were housed in transit camps set up by Mossad. The documents the displaced persons would need to depart port were prepared in
the transit camps. Photographers from Marseilles were brought in to
take passport photographs. In a secret laboratory in Lyons, these photographs were used to produce forty-five hundred personal travel documents.[13]

On July 9, the *President Warfield* left Port-de-Bouc and sailed a short
distance to the smaller port of Sète. On July 10, 1947, a final obstacle to
the operation, a truckers' strike, having been averted with a one-million-
franc donation to the strike fund, forty-five hundred of the Jewish

*Two Jewish DPs walk
in Marseilles before their
departure to Palestine
aboard the* Exodus 1947.

displaced persons in Marseilles were loaded into 150 trucks and driven to Sète. The French officials who early that morning examined the passengers' travel documents and the ship's licenses ignored the fact that the sailing license was for Istanbul while the passengers' visas were for Colombia. Like the American military, the French had to have guessed what was going on, but Marseilles was a Communist-dominated city with little sympathy for the British and neither inclination nor incentive to help them block the Jewish displaced persons from leaving Europe for Palestine.

The *President Warfield* was ready to sail on July 11, but prevented from doing so when the French, acceding to British pressure, refused to assign a trained pilot to steer it out of port and onto the open seas. The ship's captain and crew decided to leave on their own, and at 4 a.m. on the morning of July 12 disengaged the cables that secured the *President*

Warfield to the dock and set sail. The ship crashed into a sandbar. With its engines at high speed, it reversed power, freed itself, and at 6 a.m. cleared the port.

From the moment it left port, the *President Warfield* was under British surveillance, by plane until it reached the high seas, then by British destroyers. Three days out, British naval officers by loudspeaker informed the passengers of what was now known as *Exodus 1947* that they would not be permitted to land in Palestine.

At 2 a.m. on July 18, 1947, twenty miles west of Gaza, eight British destroyers approached the ship, flooded the sky and water with giant beams of light, and demanded over loudspeakers that the ship "halt" at once. Two destroyers came alongside with soldiers prepared to jump on board. The destroyers rammed the ship and the British sailors hurled smoke bombs and tear gas grenades onto the decks. A bloody battle ensued between the British sailors who had boarded the ship and Jewish passengers, resulting in the deaths of three Jews, with another two hundred injured, dozens of them laid out in the open air on the ship's decks. Though the British failed to seize control of the ship, the Jewish commanders on board, informed by the doctors that the wounded needed immediate medical assistance, several of them transfusions, ordered an end to the resistance.

JERUSALEM, JULY 1947

The UNSCOP delegates had meanwhile arrived in Jerusalem and begun taking testimony from Jewish leaders there.

In his testimony on July 16, Zalman Rubashov, head of the Histadrut, the General Federation of Jewish Labour, urged committee members to take into account, in making their recommendations for the future of Palestine, the "hundreds of thousands" of Jewish displaced persons "who, fortunately for our nation, have survived the mass murder. The surviving Jews of Europe have seen cruelty, savagery; yes, and miracles beyond belief, such as no man ever saw before them. They long for life and, with their ample experience, they are struggling for their future. About a quarter of a million of these surviving Jews are still kept in internment camps, without any status, without any rights, without any hope for the morrow." Rubashov pleaded with the committee to "demand that the gates of this country be opened wide to the Jews beating upon it. Help to deliver the refugees from inevitable degeneration and destruction."[14]

A week later, in Lebanon, Hamid Frangié, Lebanon's minister of foreign affairs, answered Rubashov's plea—and those of the other Jewish witnesses—by demanding that "the problem of refugees and displaced persons be dealt with apart from the Palestine problem and settled on the basis of international co-operation and solidarity. There cannot be any question of transferring these refugees to Palestine en masse. The alleviation of the sufferings of one nation must not and cannot be sought in the aggravation of the sufferings of another nation and in its annihilation."[15]

On July 18, 1947, as the UNSCOP delegates were coming to the close of their visit to Palestine, *Exodus 1947* limped into the port of Haifa at four o'clock in the afternoon, "escorted by eight warships of the British Royal Naval Fleet." Moshe Shertok,* chief of the Jewish Agency political department and its principal ambassador and negotiator with the United States, the UK, and the UN, alerted UNSCOP chairman Emil Sandström of Sweden, who was nearby in Haifa, of the ship's arrival. The chairman, with Vladimir Simic, the Yugoslav delegate, arrived at the port as the Jewish passengers were being removed. "They looked very tired, very poor," Sandström later reported to the other committee members.[16]

"From somewhere on the dock," wrote Ruth Gruber of the *New York*

---

* Shertok, who would later change his name to Sharett, would serve as Israel's second prime minister.

Herald Tribune, who had accompanied the UNSCOP delegation to Palestine and witnessed the disembarkation of the *Exodus 1947* passengers,

> a loudspeaker began to address the people, who now crowded every hole and porthole on our side. The loudspeaker said in Hebrew: "The commanding officer wishes you to come off quietly, women and children first." Soldiers placed gangways . . . and then ran up to take charge. Several stretchers were carried aboard. The first person to come down was a pale, sick woman, holding the arm of her husband. She wore a huge army raincoat that made her look like a scarecrow. She carried no bundles, no bags at all. Her face was white and sunken; her eyes were sunken; her lips trembled. She looked like a thousand years of misery. A child came off, with large, frightened eyes. He carried a potato sack with his belongings; a blanket was strapped across his back. A man and a child came down, hand in hand. The child broke away and ran back up the gangway, looking for his mother. He was sobbing with fright. . . . A man with the dark look of hunger came down, carrying a brief case. . . . Soldiers followed, carrying the dead body of a sixteen-year-old orphan, Hirsch Yakubovich, who had come from the DP orphanage in Indersdorf, Bavaria. He had been killed in the battle. . . . The people trickled down the gangways in little groups and milled on the dock like frightened animals. They looked weary and shattered, mourning their dead and hundreds wounded.[17]

As they exited the ship, the passengers were escorted, with rows of British soldiers on either side of them, down the pier. Their luggage or whatever they carried with them was searched, their identity cards taken. The heat grew more intense, near suffocating. British soldiers separated male and female passengers into two separate pens where their bodies were searched. Told that they were going to be transported to Cyprus, which they had expected all along, they boarded the three ships that were awaiting them at the pier.

Only once on board did they learn that the ships were bound not for Cyprus, but for France. On July 29, after another ten days at sea, they arrived back at Port-de-Bouc. One hundred and thirty to 150 of the passengers, the sick, the elderly, and a few pregnant women near delivery, disembarked voluntarily. The remainder refused to.

GENEVA, JULY–AUGUST 1947

The week after the return of the *Exodus 1947* passengers to France, UNSCOP members, having concluded their hearings in the Middle East, flew to Geneva for their final round of deliberations. At their first meeting, according to UNSCOP records, "the committee received a number of petitions asking intervention on behalf of a group of illegal immigrants who had been apprehended and transported in British ships from Palestine to Port-de-Bouc, France, where they refused to disembark. The Committee agreed that it had no authority to intervene."

In Geneva, the committee took up again the question of whether it should visit the camps and interview the Jewish displaced persons. After another heated discussion, the question was put to a vote and, by a vote of six to four, with one abstention, a compromise was reached. A subcommittee of delegates and alternates was assigned to visit "selected representative assembly centres for Jewish refugees and displaced persons . . . with a view to ascertaining and reporting to the Committee on the attitude of the inmates of the assembly centers regarding resettlement."[18]

The subcommittee visited the camps, interviewed about a hundred residents, met with military authorities and IRO officials, received a briefing from Rabbi Bernstein, the U.S. military adviser on Jewish affairs, and reported its conclusions and recommendations to the full committee.

> Taken over all, it seems to us fair to say that practically all the persons in the Jewish assembly centres . . . wish, more or less determinedly, to go to Palestine. . . . We got the impression that any large-scale absorption of the Jewish displaced persons into the German or Austrian communities was impossible. The feeling of anti-Semitism is strong among the native population, especially towards the Jews now living in assembly centers.[19]

The subcommittee's findings impelled the full committee to recommend in its final report that "the General Assembly undertake immediately the initiation and execution of an international arrangement whereby the problem of the distressed European Jews, of whom approximately 250,000 are in assembly centers . . . will be dealt with as a matter of extreme urgency for the alleviation of their plight and of the Palestine problem."[20]

PORT-DE-BOUC, JULY–AUGUST 1947

While UNSCOP deliberated in Geneva, the *Exodus 1947* passengers remained on board their ships in Port-de-Bouc. The British had convinced themselves that the overcrowding, lack of water and sanitary facilities, stifling heat, claustrophobia, boredom, and threat of illness would take its toll and the passengers would disembark voluntarily. But they did not.

Days, then weeks passed without any change, as rumors continued to fly: the passengers would be taken to Cyprus, Kenya, Australia, Colombia, or—and this was the rumor that was whispered most often—returned to displaced persons camps in Germany.

Finally, on August 21, British officials informed the passengers, in person and in writing, in English and in French, that if they did not leave the ships by six o'clock the following day, they would be transported to Hamburg on them. The response remained the same as it had always been: the passengers would not voluntarily disembark anywhere but Palestine.

WASHINGTON, JULY–AUGUST 1947

President Harry Truman received hundreds of letters and calls urging him to do something to resolve the crisis, but he refused to act. On July 21, he wrote in his diary that he had "had ten minutes conversation with Henry Morgenthau about Jewish ship in Palistine [*sic*]. Told him I would talk to Gen Marshall about it. He'd no business, whatever to call me. The Jews have no sense of proportion nor do they have any judgment on world affairs. . . . The Jews, I find are very, very selfish. They care not how many Estonians, Latvians, Finns, Poles, Yugoslavs or Greeks gets murdered or mistreated as DP as long as the Jews get special treatment."[21]

As angry as he was at the Jews, he was angrier still at the British. On the morning of August 22, he questioned Under Secretary of State Robert A. Lovett about the "harsh action" by the British that "has caused a storm of protest in this country." Lovett informed him that the State Department had "communicated informally with the British Embassy" and expressed its concern, but that a formal protest had not been contemplated as it "would have had an almost certain effect of freezing the British in their position because of Bevin's great sensitivity on this point."

After meeting with Truman, Lovett cabled new instructions to the American embassy in London.

We are deeply disturbed at reports which have been reaching us that Brit Govt is planning to return Jewish refugees on *Exodus* to camps in Germany. Action of this kind would profoundly shock large sections of American public opinion and would injure Brit position in US. . . . We appreciate difficulties encountered by Brit in endeavoring to maintain *status quo* Palestine pending outcome of UN decision. We also realize Brit irritation with US on ground that illegal immigration to large extent planned, financed and organized in this country. Nevertheless return of Jewish refugees to Germany will serve only to arouse bitterness and to aggravate situation.[22]

Informed that the British planned to proceed with returning the *Exodus 1947* passengers to Germany, Lovett directed the U.S. ambassador, Lewis W. Douglas, to "take up matter at once with Brit Govt at high level."

Ambassador Douglas was unable to meet with either Foreign Secretary Bevin or his under secretary, but reached the British assistant under secretary, who acknowledged that returning the *Exodus 1947* passengers to Germany was going to cause distress in the United States, but that there was no alternative to landing them in Hamburg, where there were "good facilities . . . for taking care of [them]. . . . He hoped that Jews could be persuaded to disembark quietly at Hamburg and said that all possible measures are being taken to see that they are handled as gently as possible."[23]

The British would not back down. And the Truman administration was, in the end, not willing to do anything other than complain. Though the forty-five hundred *Exodus* passengers had begun their journeys in the American zone of occupation, their fate was now in the hands of the British government.

The Jews in Palestine, in the displaced persons camps, and in the United States were astounded and distressed by the timid response of

*Jews in New York demonstrate against the American
government's reluctance to push Britain harder to allow
the emigration of the Jewish DPs from Germany.*

the American government, and indeed, by the rest of the world. The news that the Jewish DPs after disembarking in Hamburg were going to be "sent to a displaced persons camp less than a mile from the site of the infamous Nazi Bergen-Belsen concentration camp" was, Eleanor Roosevelt wrote in her *My Day* column on August 23, too ghastly to contemplate. "I find it hard to see how the present situation can seem fair and right to anyone."[24]

"The most shocking thing," Golda Myerson (Meir) declared in a speech in Jerusalem in late August, "is not what is happening to the thousands aboard those ships, but the fact that not a single country has come forth to cry out against this horrible injustice."[25]

GERMANY, FALL 1947 TO FALL 1948

On the morning of September 8, the *Exodus 1947* passengers, hungry, anxious, angry, and exhausted, arrived in Hamburg. It had been nearly two months since they had departed from France for Palestine. Hundreds of militants and some of the children refused to disembark; they were subdued, sometimes with hoses and leather belts, dragged from their holds onto the decks and down the gangplanks; pushed, pulled, and loaded onto trains to their next destination, two newly constructed DP camps, a mile apart. Journalists and photographers stood on shore to record the event, as did a sizable delegation of displaced persons from the Belsen camp who had come to express their solidarity and to mourn the return of those who had attempted but failed to escape Germany.

"It can be said," a Joint Distribution Committee research report in November 1947 concluded,

> that the morale of the Jewish DPs in Germany can be traced on a graph, varying according to emigration possibilities and actual emigration. At the beginning of July, there was a sharp rise in morale throughout the camps for they knew and had heard of a good number of people who had apparently left for the "Exodus 1947." . . . When the news of ensuing events came through and it was learned that the migrants were being returned to Germany, the camps and the Jewish communities became centers of gloom and desperation. Morale dipped to the lowest ebb since last winter.[26]

The camps to which the *Exodus 1947* passengers were delivered, one a former POW facility, were ringed by barbed wire, with watchtowers and spotlights that blazed through the night. The fear was not that the former passengers would escape—the British would have welcomed that—but that they would be joined inside by other displaced persons protesting their forced return to Germany.

The detainees refused to cooperate in any way. Having touched ground, if ever so slightly, in Haifa, they regarded themselves as displaced persons no longer, but exiles from Palestine. They refused to register for IRO assistance, forcing the British to pay for their food, shelter, and upkeep, and answered only to randomly chosen names—Greta Garbo, Charlie Chaplin. When asked, they gave their birthplaces as Haifa, their nationality as Palestinian.

The displaced persons who had followed and cheered their progress from Marseilles to Palestine back to Marseilles, then to Hamburg and into the camps, donated food and supplies so that the former passengers would be less dependent on the British for minimal sustenance. "Appeals for emergency assistance were received and allocations of substantial amounts of supplies have been made to meet the needs of the migrants. Sixty tons of foodstuffs were delivered during the month of October," JDC representatives in Europe reported.

> This does not include the amount volunteered as a contribution by the Central Committee of Liberated Jews, which voted to transfer considerable quantities of food normally allocated to it by the JDC to the aid of its brethren in distress. . . . The American Zone organized a team of doctors and nurses to proceed to the British Zone to care for the medical welfare of the Exodus passengers, but it was refused clearance by the British Military authorities. Only the Zone Nurse was permitted to enter the British Zone to aid in organizing the nursing service. Later a mobile dental unit was also given authorization.[27]

Mossad assumed responsibility for the *Exodus 1947* passengers and used every trick it possessed to smuggle them into the American zone and from there to ships that would return them to Palestine. By early March 1948, a thousand *Exodus 1947* passengers were already in Palestine, with another thousand awaiting passage in France. By the fall of 1948, the last of the *Exodus* survivors would be returned to what was now the nation of Israel.[28]

18.

"JEWISH IMMIGRATION IS THE CENTRAL ISSUE IN PALESTINE TODAY"

The Debate over Partition, Independence, and the Future of the Jewish DPs

FLUSHING MEADOWS, NEW YORK, SEPTEMBER 26 TO NOVEMBER 29, 1947

In early September, UNSCOP delivered its final report to the UN General Assembly. The stark differences between UNSCOP committee members were such that the report outlined two separate plans for the future of Palestine. The majority plan approved by nine of the twelve delegates called for a two-year transition period leading to the partition of Palestine into two states, one Jewish and one Arab, bound together in an economic union, with Jerusalem designated an international zone and protection guaranteed for minorities, religions, and holy sites in each state. The minority plan, which was backed by India, Iran, and Yugoslavia, recommended the establishment of a unitary "federal state" with an elected constituent assembly.

On the question of the displaced persons, the majority plan acknowledged that "Jewish immigration is the central issue in Palestine today and is the one factor, above all, that rules out the necessary co-operation between the Arab and Jewish communities in a single state." It rejected the Jewish Agency demand for unlimited, uncontrolled immigration, but recommended the admission "into the borders of the proposed Jewish State of 150,000 Jewish immigrants at a uniform monthly rate" during a two-year transitional period, followed, should the transitional period be extended, by 60,000 annually. "The responsibility for the selection and care of Jewish immigrants and for the organizing of Jewish immigration during the transitional period shall be placed in the Jewish Agency."[1]

The Arab Higher Committee, representing Arab Palestinians, rejected both the majority partition plan and the minority federal-state plan. The British denounced the partition plan as "so manifestly unjust to the Arabs that it is difficult to see how we could reconcile it with our conscience." Arthur Creech-Jones, the colonial secretary, predicted that should it be passed, "Palestine would be overtaken by 'a state of chaos.'"[2]

The Americans remained virtually silent. Secretary of State George Marshall, speaking before the General Assembly on September 17, commended UNSCOP "for its contribution to the solution of the problem," but refused to endorse either the majority or the minority plan. Two days earlier he had explained to General Hilldring and Mrs. Roosevelt, his colleagues on the American delegation, that if the United States endorsed the majority plan it would be committing itself to implementing it, and this he was unwilling to do.[3]

Senator Robert Taft, on the other hand, called on the Truman administration to endorse the partition plan at once. "Mr. Taft," the *New York Times* reported, "now seeking to determine whether he has the grass roots support that would justify his seeking the Presidency, called attention to the recommendation in the report for the admission of 150,000 Jews into Palestine. He said such immigration 'will remove a sore spot in the economy of Europe and reduce seriousness of the problem of displaced persons in Europe.'" If, as Taft expected, his colleagues in the Senate were not going to report out a DP bill that authorized the immigration of a significant number of Jewish DPs to the United States, the only way to remove them from Germany without incurring the permanent wrath of Jewish voters would be to relocate them to a Jewish state in Palestine.[4]

On October 11, 1947, more than three weeks after Senator Taft had come out in favor of partition, the Truman administration signaled its support for the basic principles of the UNSCOP majority plan, while suggesting that the plan needed further modifications and amendments. After an extended round of debate, discussions, and the appointment of yet another subcommittee, the American and the Soviet representatives announced on November 11, 1947, that they had agreed on a modified partition plan under which the British would end their mandate and begin withdrawing troops and administrators on May 1, 1948. A three-to-five-member UN commission, chosen by the General Assembly but responsible to the Security Council, would oversee the transition to and establishment, not later than July 1, 1948, of two independent states, one Arab, one Jewish.[5]

The British government waited only three days before it responded to the U.S.-Soviet proposal, declaring that it would not accept "the role that would be required of it . . . for carrying out the partition of Palestine." Sir Alexander Cadogan, the British permanent representative to the United Nations, announced "that he had been instructed by his Government to make it clear that British troops would not be available to enforce a settlement in Palestine against either the Arabs or the Jews." The British government, he went on, would not obstruct the work of the proposed UN commission on Palestine, but it was not committed to supporting or assisting it in any way. Its priority was to safely remove its troops from Palestine, nothing more, nothing less.[6]

The British announcement appeared at first to have derailed passage of the partition plan. Without the British army in place to maintain the peace until the arrival of a UN commission, it was feared that civil war would engulf the region and prevent the peaceful implementation of the General Assembly resolutions. Fearful of such an outcome, some of the nations that had signaled their support for partition began to draw back.

The Jewish Agency, Jewish leaders in the United States, and influential politicians lobbied Truman to pressure the wavering nations to vote yes on partition. Though Truman would later deny doing so, there is substantial evidence that the American delegation applied considerable pressure to get the votes necessary to pass the resolution.[7]

On November 29, 1947, the General Assembly by a vote of 33–13–11 approved Resolution 181 establishing a five-nation Commission on Palestine that, on the departure of the British, would assume transitional authority and prepare the way for the implementation of partition. The resolution directed the British "to ensure that an area situated in the territory of the Jewish State, including a seaport and hinterland adequate to provide facilities for a substantial immigration, shall be evacuated at the earliest possible date and in any event not later than 1 February 1948." The area in question would include the port of Haifa, the only suitable entryway for the European displaced persons.[8]

THE JEWISH CAMPS, GERMANY, NOVEMBER 1947

"Sunday, the thirtieth, was a radiant day," Leo Schwarz, the former Joint Distribution Committee director in the U.S. zone of Germany, would later write.

> The German radio had been silent, but in the early hours of the morning BBC broadcast the first announcement of the news. From all sides the people streamed [into the public squares in Munich]. The stars and stripes waved from flagpoles at the headquarters of the Center Committee [of Liberated Jews]. The streets resounded with congratulations. An ethereal joy imbued the very air. Happy faces were everywhere; people kissed and embraced. *Mazel tov.* On the corners where the people usually

hunted for a pat of butter, an egg, an apple, there was a festive
spirit. "Well, we lived to see it! This calls for a drink!" . . . Bot-
tles pass around. The ancient benediction, rich with new meaning. "Blessed be our God who has allowed us to live to see this
day." A marvelous moment to be alive.[9]

PALESTINE, NOVEMBER TO DECEMBER 1947

"We had only one single night of rejoicing," David Horowitz, director
of the economic department of the Jewish Agency, recalled.[10]

The Arab Higher Committee responded to the passage of the partition resolution by calling a three-day general strike. "On 2 December a
large Arab mob, armed with clubs and knives, burst out of Jerusalem's
Old City," writes Benny Morris in *1948: The First Arab-Israeli War*.
"Small Haganah units fired above and into the mob as Mandate police
and troops generally looked on. . . . The mob eventually turned back
and dispersed. But the war had begun. Yet that day, and for the next few
weeks, no one really understood this."

The Arab nations that had threatened war did not send troops into
Palestine and would not do so as long as the British army remained in
place, which it would until May 1948. Instead, the Arab League* organized, trained, and equipped an all-volunteer Arab Liberation Army
that began to infiltrate into Palestine in support of local irregular
forces.[11]

Most of the fighting took place in the territories that the UN had
designated as part of the Jewish state, in and around Jerusalem, Tel
Aviv, Jaffa, and Haifa. Though the loss of life was not great, no one on
either side felt secure. The Jews had no safe havens to flee to. The

* Founded in 1945 with Egypt, Iraq, Lebanon, Saudi Arabia, Syria, Transjordan, and North Yemen.

Palestinian Arabs abandoned their homes, villages, and settlements by the thousands, the elites for their winter residences across the borders, peasants and workers and shopkeepers to the villages their families had come from, in the hope and expectation that when hostilities ceased, they would be able to return to their homes.

THE JEWISH CAMPS, GERMANY, DECEMBER 1947 TO FEBRUARY 1948

The exhilaration experienced at the announcement that the partition plan had been approved lasted through the Hanukkah holidays in mid-December, then collapsed as reports of hostilities in Palestine reverberated through the camps. The Central Committee of Liberated Jews in Munich and the camp committees agreed to work with the Jewish Agency and Haganah emissaries to recruit and train displaced persons between the ages of seventeen and thirty-five for eventual military service in Palestine. It was imperative, the Zionists in the camps argued, that the displaced persons identify and conduct themselves as citizens of the Jewish homeland, responsible to and for its future, its survival, and its security.

LONDON, DECEMBER 1947 TO FEBRUARY 1, 1948

As the British had given no clear sign that they were going to provide the displaced persons with visas or adhere to the UN partition plan that obligated them to evacuate the port of Haifa, the illegal immigration to Palestine continued. The British government redoubled its efforts to halt it. Foreign Secretary Bevin in a December 6 meeting in

London with Secretary of State Marshall lectured him "on the importance of stopping any further illegal immigration. It was bound to lead
to bloodshed, since the Arabs would undoubtedly be incited to massacre the Jews, and the situation might then require the use of force. The
U.S. Government might then find themselves required to provide
forces and the Soviet Government might press to provide a force.
Would the U.S. Government like this?" Marshall admitted that the
United States did not want Soviet forces in the Middle East.

Bevin replied that if Jewish immigration was halted until the British
had left, bloodshed would be avoided, as would the need for an American or Soviet peacekeeping force. Marshall's response was that he "could
not believe that the Jews would any longer proceed with illegal immigration, since it must be a dead loss to them and would be of no pressure
value. Bevin questioned this. He had no confidence in the Jewish
Agency, to whom illegal immigration would still seem to have a pressure value; their object would be to cause incidents and keep their cause
alive. He urged that the U.S. Government should restrain the Jewish
Agency from these conditions." Marshall agreed to "send a message to
Washington in the general sense advocated by Bevin."[12]

Two days later, on December 8, 1947, Moshe Shertok, who represented the Jewish Agency in Washington, called on Loy Henderson,
the director of the State Department's Near East Division, to discuss,
among other issues, the immigration of Jewish displaced persons, legal
and illegal. The UN, Shertok reminded Henderson, had directed the
British to evacuate "a port and hinterland in Palestine to receive immigrants." He reminded Henderson as well that the UN resolution on
Palestine had declared "that the UN Commission, which was expected
to leave for Palestine in December 1947, would have general control of
immigration. Mr. Shertok concluded that unless a seaport were available in the near future and unless the UN Commission arrived in Palestine at an early date, it would probably be difficult for the Jewish
Agency to restrain illegal immigration."[13]

The Jewish Agency did attempt to limit illegal immigration, in the expectation that legal immigration procedures would soon be put into place. But Mossad operatives in Europe who had for months been preparing a rescue mission of tens of thousands of Romanian Jews insisted it was too late to cancel their plans. Earlier that spring, Mossad had purchased two huge banana freighters, the *Pan York* and the *Pan Crescent*, with a combined capacity of 16,500 passengers, nearly four times that of the *Exodus 1947*.[14]

The British government, which had been monitoring the movement of the refitted banana freighters, authorized MI6 to sabotage the *Pan Crescent* while it was moored in Venice for refitting. Mines were attached to the underside of the hull and detonated, but the damage was repaired and on December 26 both freighters sailed from the Bulgarian port of Burgas for Haifa, fully loaded with Romanian Jews and displaced persons. The ships were intercepted by British destroyers in the Mediterranean, but this time around, neither the British nor the Haganah commanders on board were willing to risk a battle like that on the *Exodus 1947*. An agreement was reached to sail the ships directly to Cyprus, where the passengers were interned.[15]

Desperate now to enlist American assistance in halting the illegal immigration, the British attempted to frighten Washington into taking action by charging that the banana freighters were "full of potential 'fifth columnists.'" The *New York Times* reported from London on December 31 the British claim that their sources indicated that the twelve thousand "visaless Jews" on the freighters were "mostly hand-picked Communists or fellow travelers, with links to the Stern Gang. . . . The British realize that whenever they say anything like this or think aloud on the subject of Palestine they are suspected of unnatural bias. They are wondering tonight whether officials in Washington are not as worried as they are about these new immigrants."[16]

As it became apparent that the Americans were indeed not particularly worried about the "new immigrants," the British doubled down on their claims of Soviet subversion by releasing to *New York Times* correspondent Herbert Matthews material which, they maintained, proved that the Soviets had demanded that the *Pan Crescent* and *Pan York* include a thousand Jewish Communists among the fifteen thousand passengers as a condition for letting the ships sail from Bulgaria. Although the officer in charge of the camps in Cyprus where the passengers had been detained claimed to have no knowledge that "there were Communist agents among his charges," the Foreign Office, at a press conference in London, insisted that "security officers of the Palestine Government," after interrogating the new immigrants, had discovered large numbers of Communist agents among them. Matthews was so suspicious of the British claims that he ended his February 1 article with a disclaimer. "Every statement in this dispatch is based on British official reports. None is made on the authority of this correspondent or of the *New York Times*."[17]

LAKE SUCCESS, JANUARY TO MARCH 1948

The British had made it clear, through their words and actions, that they intended to block or at least delay implementation of the majority partition plan. On January 29, 1948, the UN Palestine Commission issued its first progress report to the Security Council, in which it prominently cited a series of exchanges with Sir Alexander Cadogan, the British permanent representative to the United Nations.

Asked about the UK's "plans . . . regarding immigration," Cadogan had responded that "it is my government's intention to maintain its present policy in regard to Jewish immigration into Palestine, under which 1500 Jews are admitted monthly."

Asked if his government intended to comply with the resolution that required it to evacuate "a seaport and hinterland adequate to provide facilities for a substantial immigration," Cadogan declared that the British government could not do so "because the opening of a Jewish seaport to the introduction of unlimited numbers of Jewish immigrants and possibly to the unregulated importation of arms, would undoubt-edly produce a most serious deterioration of the security situation."

Asked if the British intended to prevent the landing of "ships carry-ing unauthorized Jewish immigrants . . . between 1 February and the termination of the Mandate," Cadogan responded with an emphatic "Yes, in accordance with my Government's decision that the existing immigration policy [fifteen hundred a month] is to be maintained until the termination of the Mandate."[18]

With the British refraining from any significant peacekeeping activ-ities, conditions on the ground in Palestine continued to worsen. As the Palestine Commission reported to the Security Council on February 16, 1948, the only way to prevent the situation "from deteriorating com-pletely into open warfare on an organized basis" was the immediate organization of an armed, non-Palestinian military force. Without such an "armed force" in place, the commission predicted that "the period immediately following the termination of the Mandate will be a period of uncontrolled, wide-spread strife and bloodshed in Palestine, includ-ing the City of Jerusalem. This would be a catastrophic conclusion to an era of international concern for that territory." It would also mark the end of current attempts to resettle Europe's displaced persons in a new Jewish state.[19]

At a February 24 Security Council meeting called to consider the Palestine Commission's request, Warren Austin, the American repre-sentative, declared that any action by an international armed force au-thorized by the Security Council "must be directed solely to keeping the peace and 'not to enforcing partition.'" Three weeks later, on March 19, Austin signaled that the United States was rethinking its support for partition by recommending that "a temporary trusteeship for Palestine should be established" and that "the Security Council should instruct the Palestine Commission to suspend its efforts to implement the pro-posed partition plan."[20]

"Shock was the reaction and gloom the mood at the United Nations today after the announcement by the United States of its abandonment of the Palestine partition plan," the *New York Times* reported. "Zionist leaders seemed stunned; some seemed near tears. . . . The Arabs indicated openly that they thought partition was dead and the victory theirs."[21]

President Truman was furious. He had seen and apparently approved Austin's speech, but had not given explicit permission for it to be delivered. On March 25, in an attempt to undo the damage, he read a brief statement at a press conference that succeeded only in muddying the waters. He was still in favor of the partition plan, he declared, but because it could not "be carried out at this time by peaceful means," and because he was not going to send troops to Palestine as the British were withdrawing theirs, he was proposing "a temporary United Nations trusteeship for Palestine to provide a government to keep the peace. . . . If we are to avert tragedy in Palestine an immediate truce must be reached between the Arabs and Jews of that country." Asked whether he still favored "conditional immigration into Palestine," he responded that his "position hasn't changed with regard to immigration in Palestine." It was unclear, however, how, absent the establishment of a Jewish state, that was going to happen.[22]

GERMANY, MARCH TO MAY 1948

"Is it necessary to tell you how shocked and depressed all of us have been in the past week as a result of the announcement that the U.S. is reversing its position on partition of Palestine?" William Haber, the Jewish liaison to the American military in Germany, wrote to Rabbi Wise on March 25. "It has made our people feel trapped and complicated the task of constructive work in the camps."

Not only was immigration to Palestine in danger, but it appeared that the possibilities for the Jewish DPs resettling elsewhere were rapidly diminishing. "If you believe that the outlook for large scale migration to Palestine is dark," Haber warned the delegates to the Third Congress of the Central Committee of Liberated Jews, "may I tell you that I am even less optimistic about migration to other countries and particularly to the United States." Some progress had been made in Congress, but the bill that was emerging was not at all favorable to the Jewish survivors.

> The single group that stands least to profit by the proposed legislation are the Jews stranded in Central Europe. . . . Not only is this picture not encouraging but it is even more bleak when you consider that the immigration opportunities to other countries, for all practical purposes, do not exist. . . . I believe that under existing circumstances the only country in the world to which the Jews of Central Europe may go in any but the most meagre numbers is Palestine. . . . The alternatives presented . . . seem to be these: either take the risk of joining in the struggle for survival in Palestine or take the risk of being again trapped in Europe.[23]

Nearly three years after liberation, every avenue of escape from Europe appeared to be closing down. At a Joint Distribution Committee conference of European country directors held in Paris in early April 1948, Samuel Haber, William's brother and director of the Joint's operations in Germany, reported that

> the morale of the DPs today in Germany is at its lowest point since liberation. . . . It is difficult to describe the horror which exists in Germany today in terms of the terrible urgency to get out. People now come to my office all of the time, pleading for special attention, pleading to be included in special groups, and for any assistance to get out. And it is not easy to sit as Joint director in a miserable place like Germany and listen to these pleas

and know the all abiding fear of the people, and also to be unable
to do very much for these people who have suffered so very
much. . . . You get to the point where you feel like throwing the
people out of the office. But when the day is over and you think
about the people who come to see you, you cannot help but have
a terrific feeling of respect and admiration for them. They are
looking for an "aitze" [advice] and the "aitze" is emigration; to
get out of Germany at any cost. No matter where you take them.
I have heard a Jewish leader for whom I have great respect say to
me: "Take us to Madagascar until you can take us to some other
place."[24]

For the first time since liberation, the Jewish displaced persons were
forced to entertain the possibility that the only place on earth where
they were welcome might not survive the year. The battle of two peoples for one land was just beginning. It was feared that the situation in
Palestine would only deteriorate, that once the British departed, the
Arab nations would launch a full-scale invasion. "The prospects of war,"
William Haber wrote in his report to the American Jewish agencies in
early April,

are responsible for a depression of spirit, difficult to exaggerate.
Many expressed themselves in the most despairing terms, indicating that those few who escaped the last holocaust will be fin-
ished in the one which they consider just around the corner. . . .
It is my impression that the fighting in Palestine and the doubts
about the United States position on support of partition . . . may
compel us to revise our impressions as to the proportion of Jewish DPs who "intend" to go to Palestine. . . . Frankly, I have been
told by responsible officials in the work here that, in spite of the
hardships and the ominous outlook, many, perhaps a very large
number of Jewish DPs, have accommodated themselves to the

prevailing situation here and are not inclined to go places where the risks are very great.[25]

This apparent change of attitude regarding Palestine came at the worst possible moment. Haganah soldiers and officers had for the past year been training young DPs for military duty. Thousands had already departed Europe as part of the illegal immigration, but many thousands more were needed. "The war depends on immigration, because the manpower in Israel will not suffice," Ben-Gurion had on March 18 written the head of the Mossad in Europe. "The Arabs have huge reserves and we need people from overseas for the war now. Immigration that is not directed entirely, from start to finish, to the war's needs is no blessing. You must understand that your operation . . . must accommodate itself to those needs, and this means sending only people from the ages of 18 to 35 or, in exceptional cases, to 40, trained to carry arms."[26]

Mossad was ordered to pull back on its attempts to remove orphans and the *Exodus 1947* survivors from Germany, and to prioritize the movement of young men and women ready to join the war effort. In some of the camps, Jewish Agency emissaries attempted to institute a sort of compulsory draft, much as in Palestine. Additional resources were directed to recruiting and training boys, girls, men, and women from eighteen to thirty-five. The Central Committee of Liberated Jews in Frankfurt passed resolutions at its Third Congress in late March 1948 declaring all single men between seventeen and thirty-five "eligible for military service. . . . Those who failed to comply would be considered beyond the pale of the Sheerith Hapletah." With the call for enlistment came a demand for monetary contributions from all displaced persons "for the purchase of weapons and munitions to support the Haganah forces in Palestine."[27]

Zionist youth groups joined together to "persuade" every young person in camp to "volunteer" for service. "In yet another unprecedented manifestation of the strange new nationalism born in the DP camps

Parents at Bergen-Belsen, Germany, say goodbye to their son, who is leaving the camp for Israel, probably to fight in the war for independence.

and out of the cataclysm of the Holocaust, the Haganah, first as the Yishuv's underground army and then as a fledgling Israeli defense force, undertook a draft for a nation that did not yet exist or had just been founded, in order to conscript soldiers who had never seen the land for which they would be fighting."[28]

Enlistment was to be regarded as a duty, not an option. "Every camp established its own Giyus [mobilization] department," William Haber reported to his contacts in the United States, "and, through posters and other propaganda media, issued a general call to the people. When this means was exhausted, the Giyus leaders examined the cases of those who had not responded and used 'persuasive' measures of different degrees to get the men to enlist."[29]

Despite such efforts, there remained a disturbingly high number of shirkers in the camps. "The notion of national duty," youth movement historian Avinoam Patt concluded, "was not always successful in garnering full support for the campaign. Camp committees employed coercive measures such as denial of additional food rations and dismissal from work [and the wages it brought in] to encourage those who were reluctant to participate in the draft."[30]

Samuel Haber decried the measures employed to force young men to undergo military training, particularly when they involved denying rations or supplies contributed by the Joint. He warned camp officials and Jewish Agency representatives that the Joint could not countenance the withholding of supplies. Even Chaim Hoffman, the representative of the Jewish Agency in Germany, urged camp leaders not to deny food or work or wages to the shirkers. Social pressure was acceptable, but not financial pressure. The local committees dismissed Hoffman's warnings and worked their way around Haber's.[31]

With the situation in Palestine deteriorating and hope dwindling for a change in America's restrictive immigration laws, the displaced persons were left to live their lives, as best they could, in the displaced persons camps. The children went to school, the young to German universities, the camp committees kept order, the historical commissions collected testimonies from survivors, the black marketeers did their business, the sports teams trained and competed against one another, newspapers and journals were published, and the cultural events, so important to the morale of the displaced persons, continued to lift the spirits of all who were trapped in Germany.[32]

On May 10, 1948, twenty-nine-year-old Leonard Bernstein, who was touring Europe and appearing with the Bavarian State Opera orchestra, conducted two concerts, a matinee at Feldafing and an evening concert at Landsberg. "I was received by parades of kids with flowers, and the greatest honors," Bernstein wrote home. "I conducted a twenty piece concentration camp orchestra (*Freischütz* [a German opera by Karl Maria von Weber] of all things) and cried my heart out."[33]

Leonard Bernstein conducts members of the Bavarian State Opera
orchestra at either Feldafing or Landsberg, May 1948.

PALESTINE, APRIL TO MAY 1948

Conditions in Palestine changed dramatically in early April after the
Haganah went on the offensive, fearing that all would be lost if it had
not gained the upper hand by May 15, when the British were to give up
their mandate and withdraw the last of their troops. The military objective was to secure "the emergent state's territory and borders and the
lines of communication between the Jewish centers of population and
the border areas." Operationally, this meant clearing the land of Palestinian militants and Arab Liberation Army infiltrees, and evacuating Palestinian villages that lay along the roadways connecting the
Jewish cities, blocs of settlements outside the cities, and the new nation's
borders.[34]

On April 9, 1948, members of the Irgun and the Stern Gang attacked Deir Yassin, an Arab village of cut stone houses on the high
ground between Tel Aviv and Jerusalem. "The figures given for the

number of victims ranged from the contemporary Red Cross estimate of 254 to a high of 350, but the most detailed and careful study of the massacre," historian Rashid Khalidi has written, "gives the names of 100 persons killed, 75 of them children, women, and the elderly. Some of the survivors were paraded through Jerusalem before being taken back to the village and shot."[35]

Whatever the numbers, the atrocities were so horrific that the Executive of the Jewish Agency felt obligated to express its "'horror and disgust' at the 'barbarous manner in which this action had been carried out.'" News of the attack sparked "fear and future panic flight from Palestine's villages and towns." Palestinian Arabs who might before Deir Yassin have attempted to remain in their homes now fled, frightened that their villages might be next.[36]

There is and will always be controversy over whether the eviction of the Palestinian Arabs was part of a premeditated "ethnic cleansing" plan, a strategy born of military necessity, or an unintended outcome of the war. For the Palestinians who were evacuated from their homes, the intent was and remains less important than the consequences. By early May, between 250,000 and 350,000 Palestinian Arabs had been evicted or fled from their homes. Some had left out of fear of future hostilities or because of shortages of food and water; many more were driven out by the Haganah, or more violently by the Irgun or Stern Gang. As the Palestinians departed, the Jewish military systematically demolished their villages and towns to remove any possibility that they might return or that Arab militias might use them as bases to launch their own attacks.[37]

JERUSALEM AND WASHINGTON, MAY 1948

On May 7, eight days prior to the end of the British Mandate and the Jewish Agency's anticipated declaration of independence, the American

State Department cobbled together a tentative truce proposal in the hope that it might forestall the Arab invasion that would trigger full-scale war. In return for a cease-fire and an Arab promise to call off the invasion, the Jewish Agency was asked to postpone its declaration of independence, permit the return of the displaced Palestinians, and cede control over immigration to a Security Council Truce Commission. For the three months the truce was in effect, fifteen hundred immigrants a month would be permitted to enter Palestine from Europe, with perhaps a few thousand more entering from British camps in Cyprus. As Dean Rusk, who had put together the proposal, explained to Secretary of State Marshall, the truce agreement would maintain the status quo on immigration. It was for precisely this reason, and the fact that it required the Israelis to delay their declaration of independence, that Ben-Gurion rejected it.[38]

At midnight, on May 15, the British mandate elapsed. At one minute past midnight, Jerusalem time, "the state of Israel [was] proclaimed as an independent republic." Ten minutes later, at 6:11 p.m. on May 14 in Washington, D.C., President Harry Truman issued a brief two-sentence statement. "This Government has been informed that a Jewish state has been proclaimed in Palestine, and recognition has been requested by the provisional government thereof. The United States recognizes the provisional government as the de facto authority of the new State of Israel."[39]

On May 16, combat troops from Egypt, Transjordan, Syria, and Iraq invaded Israel, launching the second phase of what the Israelis would call the war of independence and the Palestinians al-Nakba (the catastrophe).

There were multiple, interlocking reasons behind Truman's decision to recognize the new state. Important, but not decisive, was the political one. Truman was running for election in six months and would need to hold on to the Jewish vote in New York City and elsewhere to win. There were humanitarian and personal reasons as well. "From his youth," according to Clark Clifford, Harry Truman "had detested intolerance and discrimination. He had been deeply moved by the plight of the millions of homeless of World War II, and felt that alone among the homeless, the Jews had no homeland of their own to which they could return." Truman's early reading in ancient history and the Bible had convinced him that that homeland had to be Palestine. "The president had repeatedly made clear to us that only through the partition of Palestine into viable Jewish and Arab states could the fate of the Jewish survivors be solved in a decent and enlightened way."[40]

Fortunately for the president, the political, personal, and humanitarian rationales for recognizing Israel were aligned with geopolitical ones. In the context of the Cold War rivalry with the Soviet Union, heated up that spring by Soviet actions in Czechoslovakia and Berlin, the president dared not allow the USSR to recognize Israel before the United States and gain a foothold in the Middle East.

There was another imperative for recognizing the state of Israel. A place for the Jewish DPs had to be found prior to the establishment of the sovereign West German state that the British and the Americans believed to be a necessary element in the restoration of economic prosperity and the fortification of Western Europe against Communist influence and/or Soviet aggression.

Germany was by the spring of 1948 "the nerve center of American world policy and the front line of American defense," Samuel Gringauz, survivor of the Kovno Ghetto and Dachau, leader of the Landsberg displaced persons camp, and former president of the Council of Liberated Jews explained in *Commentary*. "Germany is no longer our foe in a war not yet concluded, but a potential ally in a war that has not yet begun. . . . Germany is to be transformed from a defeated enemy into the guardian of our European front line. The Jewish survivors in the occupied zone of Western Germany are an obstacle to this development." They could not possibly be integrated into a sovereign German nation. Nor could they remain an independent island nation, sustained by American or international assistance in camps outside the reach of German law. Their removal from Germany was a precondition to the establishment of a sovereign, self-ruling West Germany, without which the coming Cold War could not be won and economic stability returned to Europe. "The resettlement of the Jewish DP's from West Germany must be seen as an integral part of our new American security policy, if not the very basis of its application in Germany."[41]

GERMANY, MAY TO JUNE 1948

Truman's recognition of the Israeli state had with the stroke of a pen ended the U.S. Army's nightmare that it would be compelled for the foreseeable future to provision and police the displaced persons camps. In a private and "unusually warm conference" with William Haber, General Lucius Clay, military governor of the U.S. occupation zone in Germany, "expressed his profound interest in the new State, was happy that it had come into being, and stated that he was always for an independent national homeland for the Jewish people." Clay assured Haber that he and "his subordinates . . . would do everything within their power to assist in the migration of Jewish DP's to Palestine."[42]

The first priority was getting the displaced persons out of Germany, which General Clay declared the Army would assist in. It had been assumed that the IRO would cover the cost and use its own fleet of ships to transport the DPs to Israel, as it had for every other group of displaced persons in Germany. To the surprise, however, of the Israelis, the U.S. government, and the American Jewish community, William Hallam Tuck, IRO director general, announced on May 18 that "the IRO could not sponsor migration to Palestine until it could negotiate an agreement with 'a properly constituted authority set up with the approval of the United Nations.' The IRO also made clear that its facilities could not be used to send persons anywhere to join armed forces that 'are or may be engaged in active warfare.'"[43]

The Israelis refused to be deterred. "A speed-up of immigration to Israel is a primary aim of the new state," Israeli officials told the *New York Times* after the IRO announcement.

> Immigration Minister Moshe Shapiro has declared that the influx would be at the rate of at least 125,000 a year. The first two years' program for absorbing at least 250,000 immigrants had already been set up. . . . The Government plans to organize the Mediterranean crossing of about 10,000 immigrants a month. For this purpose all ships flying Israel's flag will be mobilized, others will be chartered and vessels of regular shipping lines will be used.[44]

In the absence of IRO support, it was left to the voluntary agencies, the Joint Distribution Committee in particular, to assist the new Israeli government in covering the costs of transporting the displaced persons. "We are very much handicapped by the attitude of the IRO in not meeting the transportation costs of DPs to Palestine," Moses Levitt, JDC executive vice chairman, wrote Haber in Frankfurt on June 10. "For the JDC to take on that responsibility and relieve the IRO of its just obligation, is a very difficult decision for us to make. The situation in Washington, however, is so delicate that we may not be able to put as much pressure on a change in the IRO point of view at the moment as we would like."[45]

While the Israelis were committed as a matter of public policy to accepting every Jewish displaced person who wanted to immigrate, they were constrained for the immediate future to moving Haganah recruits and those who could directly aid the war effort. Those who were neither capable nor desirous of living in a war-torn land and aiding the war effort would for now have to be left behind in Germany.

With funds allocated by the Joint Distribution Committee and Mossad and the full cooperation of the American army, thousands of young Jewish displaced persons left the camps for reception centers in

France and Italy, where they were given Israeli passports, then transported to Italian ports or to Marseilles. Arriving at Haifa, some were given additional military training; others were sent directly to the front. There was a war to be fought; any but the most basic training was a luxury the Haganah, or, as it was now known, the Israel Defense Forces (IDF), could not afford.

As Zionist leaders and those of military age left for Israel, life inside the camps was transformed. "During the past few months," William Haber reported on June 10, 1948, "the leadership in many camps has been seriously weakened because the most capable and disciplined people have left for Palestine. There had been a substantial turnover in camp committee membership, in camp police and in camp administration. In some camps, most of the nurses have left for Palestine. The same is true of many doctors. . . . Most of the young men are already gone and . . . such 'reserves' as remain will go in the next four to six weeks."[46]

ISRAEL, MAY TO OCTOBER 1948

The mass exodus of the Jewish DPs out of Germany and into Israel was nearly blocked as soon as it began, not by the war, but by the terms of the truce agreement negotiated by Count Folke Bernadotte of Sweden and his deputy, American Ralph Bunche, which prohibited each side from introducing "fighting personnel" into the region or mobilizing or training "men of military age."

The Israelis, fully aware that success in a long-term military conflict with the Arabs required an increase in the size of their military and support forces, signed on to the truce agreement only after Count Bernadotte assured them that he had no intention of interfering with their right to regulate immigration. Jewish "men of military age" would be permitted to enter the country, but not in "big numbers." On arrival, they would be prohibited from enlisting in the army and consigned to special camps under UN surveillance.[47]

The June truce lasted four weeks. A second three-month truce took effect from July 18 to October 15, during which each side expanded its armed forces. Between June and December the IDF recruited 17,400 "overseas" volunteers and DPs. In the end, some 22,000 Jewish DPs would take part in the war, comprising one-third of the Israeli combat soldiers and one-third of the casualties.[48]

This increase—by immigration—in the Israeli armed forces violated the terms of the truce, but Count Bernadotte, with never enough "observers," was unable to do anything about it. There were no port inspections, and whereas in the first weeks of the first truce men of military age had been concentrated in a single camp under UN surveillance, they were now dispersed throughout the country, supposedly subject to periodic checks that were rare to nonexistent.

Count Bernadotte pressed Israel during the second truce, as he had during the first, to permit the return of the Palestinian Arab refugees, or at least a portion of them, but the Israelis refused to do so. "By late summer 1948," Benny Morris has written, "a consensus had formed that the refugees were not to be allowed back during the war, and a majority—led by Ben-Gurion and Shertok—believed that it was best that they not return after the war, either. The Israelis argued that a discussion of refugee repatriation must await the end of hostilities: in wartime, returnees would constitute a fifth column. But, in private, they added that after the war, too, if allowed back, returnees would constitute a demographic and political time bomb, with the potential to destabilize the Jewish state." In September 1948, the cabinet declared that it would agree to the return of the refugees only "as part of a general settlement when peace comes. . . . But peace never came—and the refugees never returned."[49]

In early 1949, James McDonald, who had been a member of the Anglo-American Committee of Inquiry on Palestine and was appointed by President Truman as America's first ambassador to Israel, raised the

question of the Palestinian refugees with Prime Minister Ben-Gurion, as
he had several times in the past. "The Israel attitude was clear. . . . So long
as there was a threat of war, the refugees could not be readmitted to
Israel as a potential fifth column. The refugee question would have to
be worked out within the context of peace treaties. In addition, new
Jewish immigrants had already been settled in the deserted Arab towns
and villages of Israel."[50]

ISRAEL, 1949 TO 1951

The magnitude and pace of the immigration of the Jewish DPs from
Germany to Israel was nothing less than miraculous. Next to the United
States and Australia, more displaced persons would resettle in Israel
than anywhere else, almost 100,000 during the first year of independence, 132,109 by December 31, 1951. To put these numbers in some
perspective, the U.S. population in 1948 was about 147 million, that of
Israel about 800,000. The displaced persons would add 0.02 percent to
the total U.S. population, 16.5 percent to the Israeli population.[51]

For many of the Jewish displaced persons who immigrated to Israel,
the exhilaration of leaving Germany and arriving in their new homes
was followed rather quickly by disappointment, approaching despera-
tion. They had miraculously survived one war in Europe. They were
now entering another war zone. The young adjusted more quickly, the
adults more slowly; some would never feel secure or at peace in their
new homes. They tried to forget their past—were told over and over
again that they were Israelis now, not Europeans, that they must learn
and speak Hebrew, not Yiddish or Polish or German or Russian. Aharon
Appelfeld, who had spent the war years "in many places" in Europe,
was brought to Israel in 1946 and placed in a youth village. Without
friends, family, parents, or a language he could speak and own, he was

lost. "My first year in Israel was not an opening out to the world for me, but an even more extreme withdrawal into myself. . . . Memories of home and the sounds of its language faded away, but the new language would not take root easily."[52]

On arrival at Haifa, the displaced persons were placed in reception camps, clothed, examined, and, when necessary, as it too often was, given the medical care they required. The reception centers were over-crowded, dirty, and damp; many of the arrivals were forced to live in tents. In April 1949, Yossel Rosensaft visited Israel and inspected one of the camps that housed Jewish survivors, including several recently ar-rived from Belsen. He found the conditions deplorable, with people "living in water-logged huts." Several former Belsen DPs told him that they wanted to go back to Germany with him. According to his wife, Hadassah,

> this experience had such an impact on Yossel that he decided he could not live in Israel. . . . After his return from Israel, Yossel delivered a powerful speech to the Jews of Belsen. He told them that Israel was a wonderful but difficult country and urged them to make aliyah (that is, to go to Israel), as long as they were pre-pared for the harsh conditions they would encounter there. He also told them that they would be on their own. "Ben-Gurion will not meet you at the boat," he said, "and Eliezer Kaplan [Israel's first finance minister] will not present you with a check."

Rosensaft and his wife remained "devoted Zionists," but they would not make aliyah. They would, after a brief stay in Switzerland, emigrate to the United States.[53]

Many of the displaced persons were placed in homes and on land where Arabs had once lived and worked. About two in ten were sent to agricultural settlements, though only 2 percent of the Jewish DPs had farm experience. They had not chosen to live in isolated settlements on the land, but without resources of their own, they had no choice but to follow the directions of Israeli officials.

By 1949, areas of Palestine that were now part of the Jewish state were pockmarked by farms, fields, agricultural settlements, towns, villages, and entire city neighborhoods that had been abandoned by Palestinians and settled by displaced persons.[54] The ironies are inescapable—and tragic. Tens of thousands of displaced Jews from World War II Europe and from Arab nations were resettled in dwellings that were vacant because 750,000 Palestinians had been displaced during the 1948 war. Whether the Palestinians fled voluntarily in panic, as the Israelis would claim, or were violently evicted by Israeli militias and the army, they were forbidden to return. They and their descendants were consigned to exile, large numbers of them to refugee camps in Jordan, Lebanon, Syria, the Gaza Strip, and the West Bank, administered and serviced by the United Nations Relief and Works Agency for Palestine Refugees.[55]

Part Five

AMERICA'S
FAIR SHARE

19.

"A NOXIOUS MESS WHICH
DEFIES DIGESTION"

Congress Passes a Displaced Persons Act

WASHINGTON, MARCH TO MAY 1948

On his return to Washington from his fact-finding trip to Europe, Senator Revercomb, chairman of the Senate Judiciary Committee's Subcommittee on Immigration, drafted a new displaced persons bill. On March 1, 1948, his bill was approved by the full Senate Judiciary Committee by a vote of 6 to 5. Rather than bring the bill to the Senate floor, Revercomb asked and received permission to hold it back until after his primary election in West Virginia. The bill would, as a result, not reach the Senate floor until May 20, leaving little time for debate or a vote before Congress adjourned for summer recess.

The bill Revercomb had written, to which Senator Alexander Wiley, Republican from Wisconsin and chairman of the Judiciary Committee, affixed his name, reduced the number of DP visas from one hundred thousand a year for four years, as authorized by the Stratton bill, to fifty thousand DPs a year for two years. As significantly, it reserved 50 percent of the fifty thousand annual visas for displaced persons from nations that had been annexed by a foreign power—that is, Latvians,

Lithuanians, Estonians, and Ukrainians who had resided east of the Curzon Line—and 50 percent for DPs who had previously worked in agricultural pursuits and agreed to do so in the United States. These provisions, if written into law, would have dealt a virtual death blow to the immigration of Jewish displaced persons. Only a handful of the surviving Jewish DPs were from Ukraine, Lithuania, Latvia, and Estonia, and fewer than 3.7 percent in the American zone and 6 percent in the British were agricultural workers.[1]

To make matters worse for the Jewish DPs, the Wiley-Revercomb bill mandated that only those displaced persons who had entered Germany, Austria, or Italy prior to December 22, 1945, were eligible for visas. This provision effectively rendered ineligible 90 percent of the Jewish displaced persons who had crossed into Germany in 1946, including the survivors who had after liberation returned to Poland or Lithuania in search of family members and those who had spent the war in hiding or with the partisans or in the USSR.

Though the Wiley-Revercomb bill, as historian Leonard Dinnerstein has written, "reflected the lawmakers' desire to exclude Jews," there was nothing explicitly antisemitic in the bill's language. This was 1948 and no sitting congressman dared attack Jews as Jews. It was more expedient and effective to craft a bill that reduced the number of Jewish immigrants by bowing to Cold War anxieties by focusing attention on the nation's need to admit displaced persons who were reliably and vocally anti-Communist (i.e., the Balts and Ukrainians) and keep out those who might not be (i.e., the Polish Jewish survivors).[2]

The December 22, 1945, cutoff date, which had the effect of excluding 90 percent of the Jewish DPs, it would be argued, was necessary to bar the admission of displaced persons who had spent time in the Soviet Union or Communist-dominated Eastern Europe and might have been brainwashed or converted to support or sympathy for the Soviets. That the only DPs who had entered the camps after this date happened to be Polish Jews was rarely, if ever, acknowledged.

The 50 percent preference for persons from "annexed" countries was another deliberately and visibly anti-Communist measure designed to reward Estonian, Latvian, Lithuanian, and Ukrainian DPs who had demonstrated their opposition to Communism in refusing to be repatriated to Soviet-dominated or -annexed nations. The 50 percent preference for "agricultural laborers" could also be defended as an anti-Communist measure, as it brought farmers into the nation—and everyone knew that Communism was an urban, not a rural, disease.

As William S. White of the *New York Times* reported, in an April 11 article on congressional efforts to pass a displaced persons bill, "whatever legislation is finally enacted, it will provide the most fine-meshed screen against persons with Communist backgrounds or leanings."[3]

Anne O'Hare McCormick noted in her *New York Times* column that the displaced persons bills under discussion were "hedged around with as many restrictions and priorities as if this little group of homeless people—exactly the same human material of which this nation is made—were cargoes of dynamite intended to blow up the economy of the United States."[4]

SENATOR CHAPMAN REVERCOMB made it clear from the onset that the bill he had written would protect the nation from Communist intruders who were planning to seek entry as displaced persons. "In this day of great Communist expansion and infiltration throughout the world America must be alerted and on guard not to invite into her midst those who would bring to her the disease of government which originated in Europe."

To bolster his case, Revercomb cited findings from his recent trip to Europe, including the claim "that 6,000 known Communists have been spotted in and around the displaced-persons camps at Stuttgart, Germany. They constitute a constant threat and menace to this country." On further questioning, he acknowledged that he did not know how many or if any of these "known Communists" were displaced persons.[5]

As the debate proceeded, Revercomb's charges were backed by other southern Democrats, including Richard Russell of Georgia and James Eastland of Mississippi.[6]

Eastland, in a long-winded speech on June 2, 1948, which he insisted he had shortened because "the hour is late," railed against any liberalization of the immigration laws that might increase the number of Eastern Europeans who brought with them subversive, anti-American, left-wing ideas.

> Mr. EASTLAND. . . . I say that we are getting away from American ideals when we admit to this country from eastern Europe people with an Oriental philosophy, a philosophy not compatible with that of the people of the United States. . . . Let us not increase the power of those forces already making a dangerous onslaught against the foundations of American institutions. Let us not admit even 200,000 as an opening wedge. The conquest of America by communism which Stalin recently predicted would occur within 5 years. It can be facilitated in no better way than by the lowering of our immigration borders.[7]

Had such arguments been presented only by Revercomb and the southern Democrats, they might have carried less weight. But they were voiced by others, including the genial midwesterner Alexander Wiley of Wisconsin, who was not known as an extremist on immigration, claimed to be a descendant of immigrants, and came from a state with a large immigrant population.

> Mr. WILEY. This is America, our home. We want good blood to come to this country. But we do not want any "rats"—we have enough of them. We want to be careful how we handle the problem, because it is dynamite. Every time we have fooled around with Joe Stalin, as the facts show, we have generally been

taken for a ride. There is no need of our opening up the gates, in this world crisis, to an influx of immigrants, if there is any question about their character and their ability to be absorbed into our way of life.[8]

At one of the many low points during the debate, Senator Revercomb, indulging in a time-honored antisemitic slur about money-grubbing Jews, claimed that the displaced persons who had entered the camps after the war (again, only the Polish Jews fit this description) had not been "compelled to flee" but had "migrated and moved simply because they felt they could improve their economic condition."

Republican senator Leverett Saltonstall, the former governor of Massachusetts whose family roots extended back to the *Mayflower,* disagreed emphatically. The Polish Jews, he corrected Revercomb, had left Poland because of the violence directed against them. "It will be recalled that there was a pogrom in May, 1946. Many people were pushed westward by fear of that pogrom."

Revercomb brushed aside Saltonstall's reference to the Kielce pogrom. "Horrible as it was, it was not a wide-spread, terrible general pogrom, and no incident like it has occurred since."

Saltonstall responded that "if the Senator were a person of Jewish faith he certainly would not have any feeling of security if he went back to the general vicinity where those 35 people were killed, or anywhere near that vicinity."[9]

On June 2, 1948, the Wiley-Revercomb bill, amended to increase the number of displaced persons from fifty thousand to one hundred thousand a year over two years, but with the December 22, 1945, cutoff date and the "annexed nations" and agricultural worker preferences intact, was approved by a vote of 63 yeas and 13 nays.[10]

Eight days later, on June 10, the House opened hearings on a very different bill drafted by Republican congressman Frank Fellows from Maine.* The Fellows bill eliminated the "annexed" nations and agricultural experience provisions, and moved the cutoff date for eligibility from December 1945 to April 1947.[11]

The debate in the House over the Fellows bill was many times more vituperative and vicious than the one in the Senate. There was no overlay of decorum, no southern gentlemanly tradition of watching one's words and avoiding hyperbole. Within minutes of the opening of debate, Eugene "Goober" Cox of Georgia, the senior Democrat on the Rules Committee, a committed segregationist and a man so combative that in 1949, at age sixty-nine, he would take a swing at eighty-three-year-old Jewish congressman Adolph Sabath of Chicago, rose to express his opposition.

> Mr. COX. . . . I have been in some of these camps, and I say to you that while there are undoubtedly many who would be acceptable and suitable as immigrants to this country as a whole, these camps are hotbeds of revolutionists who, if they came here, would join those who now are gnawing away night and day like termites at the foundation of our constitutional government. . . . They are the least desirable people of the whole of Europe. They do not want to work and will not work. Russia has conditioned the most of them to do her work wherever they may go. . . . You should remember that these camps have been stuffed with so-called displaced persons with the view of having them admitted to the United States.[12]

Congressman Ed Lee Gossett of Texas opposed the current DP bill, as he had the Stratton bill the year before.

---

* There was no attempt made to reintroduce the Stratton bill, which had been debated in committee in the first session of the 80th Congress but never brought to the House for a vote.

Mr. GOSSETT. . . . Our camps are literally filled with bums, criminals, subversives, revolutionists, crackpots, and human wreckage. . . . There can be no doubt but many of those registered as DP's awaiting passage to America have been schooled in subversive activities, and seek entry here to serve foreign ideologies. . . . You have 100,000 who came into our camps in 1946 and 1947 from behind the iron curtain, and probably 50 percent of them are Communists. . . . To enact DP legislation will be to lose another battle in the cold war—to inject more poison into the national bloodstream. . . . Congress should refuse these selfish, destructive appeals to American generosity and American gullibility.[13]

Congressman William Jennings Bryan Dorn of South Carolina was, like Gossett, "opposed to any legislation."

Mr. DORN. . . . One of the favorite devices of the dictators and would-be world conquerors is to employ a fifth column. . . . Gentlemen of the Committee, listen—I am told [by whom he did not say] that there are more Communists in New York City today than there are in the entire country of Holland. . . . No great country was ever destroyed, or at least it has happened very seldom—from without. It was always from within. Most of the time it was by political demagogues taking advantage of political expediency at such times as this.[14]

As in the Senate, the rabble-rousing voice of the southern Democrats was augmented by northern Republicans like Robert F. Rich of Pennsylvania.

Mr. RICH. Mr. Speaker, I am unalterably opposed to the opening of the doors of this country to everyone who wants to come to America from some foreign country. . . . I am not going to throw the doors wide open and permit America to be the dumping place for all humanity. That would mean a haven for Communists and every other person who would be unacceptable to our citizenship.[15]

Ethnic and religious tensions that had remained sub rosa in the Senate debate came to the surface in the House and disrupted party loyalties after an amendment to admit Polish soldiers now resident in Great Britain was voted down. Democratic congressman John Lesinski from Michigan protested that this was part of a Jewish conspiracy. "When there was an amendment brought in here to recognize certain Polish soldiers, every man of Jewish faith in this House voted against it."

Congressman Adolph Sabath of Chicago, also a Democrat, rose at once to contradict Lesinski's blanket condemnation of his Jewish colleagues for being anti-Christian. "I was here and I voted for the amendment."[16]

Lesinski apologized, but it was too late. He had opened the floodgates by mentioning the Jews by name. Francis Walter, the aggressively anti-Communist Democratic congressman from Pennsylvania, strongly rebuked his colleague from Michigan.

Mr. Chairman, I never thought the day would come when any Member of the House would make the kind of appeal that has just been made by the Representative from Michigan. Certainly, this is the last place in the world where anything even resembling an appeal to religious prejudice should even be whispered. . . . When, therefore, the Representative from Michigan talks about the number of Jews who came into this country he is doing it for the deliberate purpose of appealing to the baser instincts of people who do not sit in the halls of the Congress of the United States.

Despite Walter's warning and one like it that followed from Congressman Celler, the debate on the displaced persons bill would from this point on be transparently focused on ethnic group politics. Members rose, one after another, to argue for the admission of national and ethnic groups that just happened to comprise large portions of their electorates.

Republican John Davis Lodge of Connecticut—a state with a large Polish population—proposed an amendment to admit eighteen thousand Polish veterans now living in Great Britain. George MacKinnon, Republican from St. Paul, Minnesota—which also had a large Polish population—spoke in favor of the Lodge amendment, as did Alvin O'Konski, a Republican congressman from northern Wisconsin, with a large Polish population. Newly elected congressman John Fitzgerald Kennedy and veteran John McCormack, whose Boston districts had sizable Polish American populations, also supported the amendment.[17]

Freshman congressman Charles Kersten of Wisconsin offered an amendment to include the *Volksdeutsche* within the definition of displaced persons, claiming that their exclusion was an act of racial discrimination. Congressman Mitchell Jenkins of Pennsylvania disagreed.

> Mr. JENKINS. . . . Is it not a fact that the people who would be covered by this amendment are the so-called Sudeten Germans? . . . Their exclusion from the definition [of displaced persons] under IRO was because of the fact that they had been considered quislings of the Nazis, therefore outside of the IRO set-up. . . . Is it not likewise true that they are the same people who were sent into Czechoslovakia by Hitler to assist in taking over Czechoslovakia? . . .
>
> Mr. KERSTEN. The gentleman knows that that is not true as to the great bulk of these people.

The debate was interrupted by John Rankin of Mississippi, who supported the *Volksdeutsche* amendment but focused his remarks on the threat posed by other Eastern European displaced persons.

> Mr. RANKIN. . . . I believe you are getting ready to bring into this country, through these concentration camps [he was referring to the DP camps], a gang of well-trained Communists, and representatives of the Comintern, who will spread out over this country for the purpose of plotting the overthrow of this Government. . . . Ninety percent of the members of the Communist Party in this country are members of racial-minority groups. Sixty percent of them are immigrants who have come here from Europe and are spending untold millions of dollars in every State in the Union plotting the overthrow of the Government of the United States. The Communists have men right now in these concentration camps for the purpose of getting them in here as spies. . . . What they want to do is to come here and tear down America.

Responding to the charge that the *Volksdeutsche* were Hitler followers and admirers, Rankin asked, "Whom did you expect them to follow? They had to follow either Hitler or Stalin."[18]

Congressman Abraham Multer of New York City, convinced that Rankin's diatribe against Eastern Europeans was directed at the Jews, felt obligated to answer his charges.

> Mr. MULTER. . . . Mr. Chairman, I detect an undercurrent of feeling being stirred up, unfairly, by some Members of this House in an effort to sabotage this bill. It is best typified by the statement inserted in the remarks of the Representative from Mississippi on May 19, 1948. . . . He said that his information is that 75 percent of the members of the Communist Party in this country are Yiddish and that 60 percent of them were born in

foreign countries and that the FBI files will bear that out. If the statement had been made on the floor, I would have challenged it then and there. The statement is as libelous as the forged and fraudulent Protocols of Zion. . . . The fact is that in the over-all Communist movement Jews are outnumbered 50 to 1. . . . If you must think along religious lines, remember that 80 percent of the persons to be helped by this bill are good, decent Christians.[19]

No one came to Rankin's defense.

After discussion of a few other amendments—which were also defeated—the House, on June 11, 1948, passed a displaced persons bill by a vote of 289 to 91. Two of the three future presidents sitting in the house, John Fitzgerald Kennedy and Richard Milhous Nixon, voted for the bill; Lyndon Johnson was recorded as "Not Voting." Fifty southern Democrats, two non-southern Democrats, and thirty-nine Republicans voted "No."[20]

THE NEXT STEP in the legislative process was the convening of a conference committee to reconcile the very different bills passed by the Senate and the House. The reconciled bill would then be resubmitted to each chamber for approval, and if passed, forwarded to the president for his signature—or veto.

Time was exceedingly short—eight days to summer recess—to have a full debate in the conference committee or, following that, in either chamber. Senator Revercomb had no doubt realized as much when he asked that his bill not be brought to the floor until May 20.

On several differences between the two bills, compromise was quickly arrived at. Senate members agreed to reduce the percentage of visas reserved for displaced persons from "annexed" countries from 50 percent to 40 percent and for agricultural workers from 50 percent to 30 percent. They accepted, without debate, the most regressive of the provisions in the House bill, the mortgage arrangement under which half of the number of DPs admitted each year would be subtracted from the quotas for future years. Both sides agreed to add to the two hundred thousand number in the original bills two thousand Czechs who had fled after the 1948 coup.

"The real bone of contention," Congressman Fellows reported back to the House, was the cutoff date for eligibility. The Senate bill had fixed it as December 22, 1945, which would have excluded 90 percent of the Jewish DPs, including the two hundred thousand Polish Jews who had entered the American zones of occupation in 1946. The House cutoff date was April 21, 1947, which would have included them.

Led by Senator Revercomb, who had been added to the conference committee at the last minute, the Senate conferees refused to extend the December 22 deadline by a day, much less by the sixteen months the House asked for. They demanded as well that the reconciled bill include a version of Senator William Langer's *Volksdeutsche* amendment that directed INS to reserve 50 percent of the German and Austrian quotas for "persons of German ethnic origin" born outside Germany or Austria.[21]

The Senate conferees refused to compromise. And the House members gave in. "We had a gun barrel at our heads," Democrat Frank Chelf of Kentucky reported to the full House.

> That gun barrel was the element of time. . . . Had it not been for the time element and immediate adjournment slapping us in the face I would have hung the jury until Gabriel blew taps on his trumpet. I would have never compromised. . . . But my colleagues, 200,000 poor, miserable, pathetic people were hanging in the balance, their fate was in our hands—with this upon my conscience and in my heart—I therefore reluctantly signed the conference report—for it was better than no bill at all.[22]

The congressmen who opposed the reconciled bill were trapped. They could pass it and admit two hundred thousand DPs and two thousand Czech refugees, few of whom would be Jews, or reject it and start all over again after the 1948 elections, which might very well result in a new president, Senate, and House. Few were willing to take that chance.

The most vocal advocates for a no vote on the reconciled bill were Jewish members of the New York City House delegation.

Mr. JAVITS. . . . Have we not taken the worst features of the Senate bill and the most onerous features of the House bill and put them together and brought in this conference report?

Mr. MULTER. . . . The bill in its present form is worse than no bill. It is viciously discriminatory. It is hard for me to believe that, in a country that fought Nazism so successfully, and is now attempting to stop communism, any Member of Congress can consider voting in favor of a bill that would grant priorities to prospective immigrants [the *Volksdeutsche*] who were part and parcel, if not the backbone, of the Hitler regime during its worst days. Rather than give them priorities in seeking admission to this country, Congress should bar them forever. No bill is better than a bill in the form now before us.

Mr. KLEIN. Mr. Speaker, the displaced persons bill as finally shaped by this conference report is a noxious mess which defies digestion. It is compounded of large portions of fear, hate, and suspicion, faintly flavored with shame. I cannot vote for this bitter gruel of legislation.

Congressman Arthur Klein was the last speaker to take the floor before a vote was called. Though it was a foregone conclusion that the

House would approve the bill, nearly one-third voted to recommit it, including every member of the New York City delegation, James Fulton of Pittsburgh, and McCormack and Kennedy of Boston. Congressmen Johnson and Nixon voted to accept the reconciled bill.[23]

The day after the House approved the reconciled bill and one day before the scheduled summer recess, the Senate convened to debate and vote on it. Senator Wiley defended himself and his colleagues on the conference committee, Senators McCarran, Forrest C. Donnell of Missouri, and Revercomb, from any imputation that these "Christian, honorable men, Members of the Senate, permitted bigotry and religious bias to dictate their judgment. . . . Knowing these men as I know them, working with some of them in Christian relationship, I know that what was said is not only wrong, but false. These men have no prejudice against Jews or against Catholics."[24]

Senator Claude Pepper, the loud-voiced, sometimes fiery, independent Democratic senator from Florida, while refraining from accusing his colleagues of intentional bigotry, noted that the "practical" effect of setting the cutoff date for eligibility on December 22, 1945, was "to deny to the most wretched people of all, the Jews, the sanctuary which this bill was intended to afford." But that was not, Pepper warned his colleagues, the only atrocity in the bill they were about to pass.

> Mr. PEPPER. . . . What does the bill do? . . . It denies eligibility to those . . . miserable Jews who fled from the pogrom of Poland. . . . They have been factually excluded, whether by design or not. They are not permitted to be counted in the displaced persons group, and for some strange reason the date has been tenaciously held to December 22, 1945, in spite of every effort of the House and of Senators who shared the opinion of Members of the House who wished the date moved up to April 21, 1947. . . . Mr. President, I would hardly believe it possible that anyone who has been to the displaced-persons camps

of Europe, anyone who has been to Dachau, Nuremberg, and to the other concentration camps under the evil Nazis, to see what the Jewish people have suffered, would ever countenance the possibility that they should be denied their proportionate share of eligible persons to seek sanctuary under this legislation. . . . The bill provides that those who may have been quislings or Nazi fifth columnists . . . are included in the eligible class. We exclude the Jews fleeing from the Polish pogroms, but we reach out and extend the tender hand of welcome and sympathy and inclusion to the quislings and the Nazi fifth columnists who . . . prepared the field for the Nazi aggression. . . . Is that the solution of the displaced-persons question?

Senator Revercomb had the last word, which he used to defend his integrity, his colleagues, and his bill. He closed by attacking Earl Harrison and the Citizens Committee on Displaced Persons. Mr. Harrison, he reminded his colleagues, had in April 1943 been honored by the American Committee for the Protection of the Foreign Born, which a year later was "listed as subversive by the House Un-American Activities Committee."

Following Revercomb's final speech on the subject, the Senate approved the conference committee report and the reconciled bill by voice vote.[25]

"A SHAMEFUL VICTORY FOR [THE] SCHOOL OF BIGOTRY"

T HE DISASTER THAT HAD once been unimaginable had come to pass.

The *New York Times,* in a powerful editorial, condemned the reconciled displaced persons bill as "a shameful victory for [the] school of bigotry." Governor Herbert Lehman, the former head of UNRRA and now a candidate for the Senate from New York, declared it "a shock and a disappointment." Judge Joseph M. Proskauer, the AJC president, a mild-mannered, even-tempered man who did not indulge in histrionics, characterized it as "a betrayal of our basic American traditions. Through ignorance or design, this legislation in effect aims at the deliberate exclusion of Jews, and to a lesser extent, of Catholics, now languishing in displaced persons camps in Europe. It places on the statute books discriminatory legislation of a type for which there is no precedent in our history."[1]

Drew Pearson, who had criticized Revercomb for the past year, charged that the West Virginia senator had earlier told colleagues on the Judiciary Subcommittee on Immigration that "we could solve this DP problem all right if we could work out some bill that would keep out the Jews." That, Pearson declared in his July 20 column, was "exactly what he did."[2]

NEW YORK, JUNE TO AUGUST 1948

There was complete agreement among the Jewish organizations and the Citizens Committee on Displaced Persons that the bill passed by both houses was an abomination, but profound disagreement on what should be done about it. Should the president be pressured to veto it? Would it not be better to start over again in the next Congress than to allow this disgrace of a bill to become law?

On June 21, 1948, at 3:30 in the afternoon, Jewish leaders gathered at the National Community Relations Advisory Council offices to decide on a unified strategy. In attendance were representatives from the Hebrew Immigrant Aid Society, the Citizens Committee on Displaced Persons, the Jewish Labor Committee, the American Jewish Committee, the American Jewish Congress, the Anti-Defamation League of B'nai B'rith, the American Jewish War Veterans, the National Council of Jewish Women, and the United Service for New Americans, the agency charged with the resettlement of Jewish refugees.

The American Jewish Congress delegate proposed that "the Jewish agencies call upon the president to veto the Displaced Persons Bill alone or jointly with non-Jewish groups and . . . try to get the Citizens Committee on Displaced Persons to do likewise." The HIAS delegate agreed. George Hexter and Irving Engel of the American Jewish Committee argued, to the contrary, that the Jewish groups refrain from asking the president to veto the legislation. To do so would open them to the charge that they were "casting aside humanitarian principles in saving non-Jewish DP's because Jewish DP's are excluded."[3]

Here was the crux of the problem. The bill discriminated against Jews, but in so doing it privileged Protestants and Catholics. As the

leadership of the National Catholic Welfare Conference informed diocesan leaders, 80 percent of the displaced persons who had resided in
Polish territory now annexed by the Soviet Union were Catholic, as
were 95 percent of the Lithuanians and 20 percent of the Latvians.[4]

While the Jewish organizations debated whether to ask for a
veto, the Catholic leadership urged Truman to sign the bill.

"BILL NOT PERFECT BUT BEST THAT CAN BE OB-
TAINED NOW. PRESSURE NOW BEING EXERTED BY CER-
TAIN GROUPS FOR PRESIDENTIAL VETO," Monsignor
Swanstrom of the National Catholic Welfare Conference telegrammed
General Secretary Howard Carroll, the day the bill was passed by the
Senate. "URGE YOU YOUR GROUPS AND OTHERS WIRE
APPROVAL OF THIS BILL DIRECTLY TO PRESIDENT TRU-
MAN. REPEAT APPROVAL."[5]

John T. McNicholas, the archbishop of Cincinnati and chairman of
the administration board of the NCWS, cabled the president: "I VEN-
TURE TO HOPE THAT YOUR EXCELLENCY WILL AP-
PROVE THE LEGISLATION FOR DISPLACED PERSONS
DESPITE ITS LIMITATIONS AND DISCRIMINATION." Car-
dinal Spellman wired the president with the same message.[6]

WASHINGTON, JUNE TO JULY 1948

Harry Truman waited six days before announcing that he was "with
very great reluctance" signing the bill. "If the Congress were still in
session, I would return this bill without my approval and urge that a
fairer, more humane bill be passed. In its present form this bill is fla-
grantly discriminatory. It mocks the American tradition of fair play.
Unfortunately . . . if I refused to sign this bill now, there would be no
legislation on behalf of displaced persons until the next session of the
Congress."

Truman could not in good conscience, he believed, block the immigration of two hundred thousand displaced persons, the vast majority of them Christians, because the bill discriminated against Jews. To do so would have been morally wrong and politically suicidal. So he signed the bill, while publicly acknowledging that it

> discriminates in callous fashion against displaced persons of the Jewish faith. This brutal fact cannot be obscured by the maze of technicalities in the bill or by the protestations of some of its sponsors. . . . More than 90 per cent of the remaining Jewish displaced persons are definitely excluded. Even the eligible 10 per cent are beset by numerous additional restrictions written into the bill. For all practical purposes, it must be frankly recognized . . . that this bill excludes Jewish displaced persons, rather than accepting a fair proportion of them along with other faiths.[7]

Like the seasoned politician he was, the president had found a way to gesture to both sides of the debate. By signing the bill, he met the demands of the Catholics, Protestants, and Eastern European ethnics. By condemning it as he signed it, he placated Jewish organizations and voters and offered them a bit of hope for the future.

That Congress had passed and the president had signed a bill so blatantly antisemitic led to a great deal of second-guessing within the Jewish community. The day Truman signed the bill, Tzvion, the pen name of Dr. Ben-Zion Hoffman, who had immigrated from Latvia in 1908 and whose *Forward* columns had become near-compulsory reading for left-wing Jews, responded to a reader who criticized him for not having opposed the bill from the very beginning.

The "reader" was correct, he admitted. He should have opposed the bill before it became law. "Amongst the . . . displaced persons that will be able to come to America, according to the adopted legislation, there will be many Nazis and fascists, but few Jews. . . . As the bill stands, it is more concerned with Hitler's allies than with his victims."[8]

The organized American Jewish community had taken a calculated gamble in not arguing for the admission of Jews as a privileged category of displaced persons and not warning the public and Congress of the danger in admitting large numbers of Baltic nationals and Ukrainians, when it was common knowledge among UNRRA and IRO officials, military officers, journalists, and nearly everyone who had had contact with the camps that significant numbers of them were antisemites or suspected collaborators, Waffen-SS soldiers, and war criminals.

During the congressional debate, Joseph Horowitz, a New York City businessman, had written "Tex & Jinx," Tex McCrary and Jinx Falkenburg, the married couple who hosted one of New York City's and the nation's most popular morning radio programs, that he had listened to their discussions with guests who supported the bill.

> I'm against it—the bill that is—and my mother isn't a D.A.R.* either. I'm a Jew—and against the "bill"; surprising? And I'm not a communist. . . . To say—as your first guest said—"that these people have an aversion towards 'totalitarian dictatorship'"—is both stupid and ridiculous! . . . The reason these people (the 80% of them)† don't want to go back is because they have <u>Blood on their Hands</u>! The Germans were very sporting! When they entered the respective lands of the Lithuanians, the Poles, the Letts, the Ukrainians, etc., they gave the honor of killing the Jews—to the Nazi sympathizers of these lands! . . . In the town of Lida—Lithuania—where my people come from, and have lived for centuries!—the entire Jewish population was slaughtered! I remember them—my aunts and uncles—cousins and nieces—hard working people—good people—peaceful people—slaughtered in cold blood—like sheep—by these self-same people![9]

---

* Daughters of the American Revolution, the conservative group, which had opposed any change in immigration legislation, including emergency displaced persons laws.
† The reference was probably to the 80 percent of DPs who were not Jewish.

McCrary forwarded the letter to Irving Engel of the American Jewish Committee, who confirmed Horowitz's charges.

> What Mr. Horowitz has to say, unfortunately, has a substantial basis in the facts. However, we took those facts into consideration and decided to go ahead nevertheless. It was our feeling that, not only for the benefit of the displaced persons but for the good of its own soul, America must take a leading part in solving this problem. We also felt that with most of the people to whom Mr. Horowitz refers life in America would bring about a change in their viewpoint.[10]

"All of us realized," Engel admitted in a letter to Dr. Jacob Billikopf, a transplanted Lithuanian Jew who had become an influential labor organizer and Jewish philanthropist, that "it was inherent in the situation that the result of our campaign might be the admission of more fascists and anti-Semites than liberals and Jews. Nevertheless, we had no choice but to make the fight."[11]

The most damning critique was that of Abraham Duker, whose integrity, experience, and educational training made it even more compelling. Duker had been born in Poland and educated at City College of New York and Columbia, where he had studied Jewish history under Professor Salo Baron. He had taught at the Jewish Theological Seminary and been a research consultant for the American Jewish Congress and the American Jewish Committee. During the war years, he had served as a political analyst in the Foreign National Division of the Office of Strategic Services and as a member of the research staff that had assisted Justice Robert Jackson* in the preparation of evidence to be offered at the Nuremberg trials. On returning to New York City after

---

* Associate Supreme Court justice Robert Jackson was appointed by President Truman as the chief U.S. prosecutor at the Nuremberg trials.

the war, he edited the English supplement of the Yiddish daily *Der Tog* (*The Day*).[12]

On June 1, 1948, Duker published a sixteen-page report, "On the Need for Screening Displaced Persons Applying for Entry into the U.S.," and forwarded it to American Jewish organizations and to every U.S. senator and congressman. Duker anticipated that Congress would pass and the president sign a bill that would bring into the United States "large numbers of Lithuanians, Latvians, Estonians, White Ruthenians, Ukrainians, Poles, Hungarians, Croats, and Slovaks, who voluntarily joined the Nazis and loyally and devoted served them during the period of occupation." His major concern were the Balts and Ukrainians who would be admitted under the "annexed nations" provision of the legislation.

"Contrary to popular opinion," he wrote in a one-page summary of his findings,

> the Balts constituted the closest of Nazi collaborators and received favorable attention at the hands of their masters to the very end. Balts willingly served in the German police and formed large volunteer detachments of their own which were responsible for the slaughter of tens of thousands of Jews and partisans. Second only to the Balts were the Ukrainians who butchered Jew and Pole alike. . . . When the tide of battle turned and the Nazis began their retreat from the East, they allowed these collaborationists <u>and their families</u>, in mortal fear for their lives, to return to Germany with them. Untold thousands of these quislings fled to escape the just wrath of their countrymen who knew their guilt. In Germany they sought anonymity, hoping to escape identification and prosecution for murder and treason.
>
> It is one of the cruel ironies of our day that . . . the oppressors and tormentors and exploiters, they who enjoyed the good life

under the Nazis, have been acclaimed as apostles of freedom, the living embodiment of the spirit of liberty, and are to be given the supreme boon of admission to the United States by special legislation, which gives them every priority over the real victims.

It was too late, Duker recognized, to change the basic focus of the legislation, which had "been drafted with a view toward favoring the perpetrators rather than the victims of persecution," but it was not too late to add to the bill "an effective screening procedure" that might serve to separate out and deny admission to Nazi collaborators and war criminals who were hiding in the camps. Such screening, he admitted, would require "thorough studies of the Nazi reports and records, as well as depositions of Jewish DPs and residents of the localities from which the pogromists hail. A special body ought to be established for this purpose, with representatives attached to our consular bodies."[13]

Five days after he had released his memorandum, Duker, under the pseudonym Ben Asher, published an article, "Of Bagels, Votes and Pogromists," in the English-language supplement to *Der Tog*. The celebratory meeting of Presidents Truman and Weizmann at Blair House over bagels did nothing "for the struggling state of Israel [but was] good public relations" for both sides, Duker commented. "And speaking of public relations," he continued, shifting the subject,

the Jewish defense and other organizations have done a beautiful bang-up job on behalf of the Baltic pogromists. As we are writing these lines it looks like the DP bill admitting 200,000 D.P.'s, with preference for Baltics and farmers will pass. It so happens that a good proportion, if not the majority of the Estonians, Lithuanians and Latvians on the preferred list are Nazi collaborationists and participants in the massacres against the Jews. . . . The tragedy is that most of the money which went for the propaganda to sell to the American public the idea that

all the D.P.'s are "political refugees" came from Jewish organizations.[14]

Duker was not the only critic to attack the Jewish establishment in
this way. In early July, *Der Yidisher Kempfer,* a left Zionist labor journal,
published an article that excoriated Jewish leaders for "relying completely" on the Citizens Committee on Displaced Persons. "It is time
that Jewish leaders should have learned from experience how front organizations operate. But they have learned nothing." Hundreds of thousands of dollars from Jewish sources had been employed "to propagandize
for the benefit of the Baltic and Ukrainian murderers and pogrom-
makers" who were now going to enter the United States under the DP
Act of 1948.[15]

What particularly galled the critics was that the Jewish leaders and
organizations that had supported the bill failed to acknowledge the error
of their ways. Duker was aghast to discover that before the ink had even
dried on the June 1948 bill, the American Jewish Committee was lobbying for an amended DP bill that would increase the number of displaced
persons from two hundred thousand to four hundred thousand.

> In other words, they are asking for more fascists, which will
> make it even more difficult to thoroughly screen these peo-
> ple. . . . Some day Jewish historians will try to interpret the mass
> psychosis of communal leaders who invested so enthusiastically
> their organizations' time and money to bring to the U.S. the
> mass-killers of their own brethren in Europe. It is our belief that
> the excuse that this was done in order to bring in Jewish DP's
> will not be accepted as erasing the sin of short-sightedness and
> lack of Jewish dignity.[16]

Duker's attacks could not go unanswered, but neither could they be
dismissed. On July 28, George Hexter of the AJC wrote Jacob Billikopf
that it was

not true that none of us realized that we would be admitting considerable numbers of DP's who do not like Jews along with Jewish DP's. This fact was brought out at the very first meeting of our Administrative Committee . . . and it was the consensus that if this country could not absorb and neutralize some thousands, or perhaps tens of thousands, of anti-Semites, then it was already later than we thought. In this case it was felt that this was a calculated risk that should be taken since it was unavoidable if a haven were to be found in this country for any real significant number of displaced Jews.[17]

The most cogent analysis of the June 1948 Displaced Persons Act might have been that of Tzvion in *The Forward*, who declared that while there was "absolutely no doubt that the law discriminates extremely harshly against Jewish DPs . . . that particular discrimination is, according to my understanding, not the result of calculated anti-Semitic motives." It was necessary, declared Tzvion, that the Jews, instead of crying antisemitism, look at the political environment in which the bill was drafted, passed, and signed into law. A sizable majority of congressmen and senators had voted for it not because they were antisemites, but because they were anti-Soviet.

The true motive of the DP legislation is to ensure that the displaced who will be allowed to immigrate to America will be politically "kosher." Our legislative bodies, with this aim in mind, have correctly approximated that the DPs who will most surely fulfill this objective must be from the three small Baltic regions that Soviet Russia has annexed; from the eastern region of Poland occupied by Soviet Russia; from the population of Sudeten Germans and Austrians, and from the newly displaced Czech population. Our legislative bodies have supposed that these specific DPs will certainly be the enemies of Soviet Russia, and that makes them politically kosher by default.

It was incumbent on Jewish activists, leaders of the major organizations, politicians, and elected officials to write a new DP bill that would accomplish two distinct purposes.

> First that a larger number of Jewish DPs will be able to immigrate to America. Secondly, no fascists will be able to immigrate. The second point is possibly more important than the first. We Jews in America must take very strong interest to ensure that the defeated fascists from Europe do not get across to us in America. We are doubly invested, both as Americans and as Jews, because in addition to the fact that a fascist carries with him reactionism, he also carries antisemitism. It would have been possible for a lot more Jews to escape from Hitler's murderous hands into Lithuania and Latvia if not for the fascist Lithuanians and fascist Latvians. In these two lands, Hitler found ready and willing accomplices for the extermination of the Jewish people. They have gladly carried out his evil work.[18]

"GET THESE PEOPLE MOVING"

"Pro-Nazis Entering U.S. Under DP Law That Keeps Out Jews"

A FTER THREE YEARS OF WAITING, the news that the United States was now ready to accept displaced persons for resettlement was greeted with cautious enthusiasm by the Last Million in Germany.

"Over the whole of the DP world an unnatural quiet settled," Kate Hulme, formerly of UNRRA but now an IRO officer, recalled in her memoir.

> The allocation of . . . visas, for example, specified forty percent go to DP's "whose place of origin or country of nationality has been *de facto* annexed by a foreign power." When you penetrated that *de facto* and realized that it meant that almost half the total visas were reserved for Balts, you saw many of your Poles, the great majority of your DP world, possibly shut out because their country had not been *de facto* annexed, but only secretly stolen. Then there was the trap we called the "farmer clause"—thirty per cent of all visas must be given to persons who had been "previously engaged in agricultural pursuits."

Worriedly you thought of your DP doctors, nurses, professionals
and engineers.[1]

In the Baltic camps, the news was greeted with greater enthusiasm.
Those who had collaborated with the Nazi occupiers were delighted to
learn that they might now get to spend the rest of their lives in an anti-
Communist nation that would never surrender them to the Soviets.
Those who had not were delighted to be given the opportunity to re-
settle in the richest country on earth.

The only downside to the passing of the legislation was its timing.
By the time Congress approved the bill and the president signed it in
the early summer of 1948, tens of thousands of Balts who might have
preferred to resettle in the United States had already departed for Great
Britain, Belgium, Canada, Australia, and South America. IRO regulations forbade them from receiving assistance to resettle in a second
country.

Twelve-year-old Agate Nesaule from Latvia remembered the pain in
her family as some of her relatives, but not all of them, accepted resettlement in faraway places. "My cousin Astrida, at age eighteen, went to
Canada by herself, to work as a maid. . . . Another cousin left to work
in the coal mines in England." She and her family were distressed that,
whatever happened, family members would be separated from one another by thousands of miles. They worried as well that they might not
be accepted by the American authorities.

> When the United States opened its doors, it was again only
> to the most desirable workers, that is, the young and vigorous,
> those unencumbered by children, illness and old people. Ōmite
> [her grandmother], who had finally rejoined our family, was not
> allowed to emigrate with us, since America would admit only
> one dependent per worker. . . . The future in the camps looked
> meaningless and bleak, and my parents struggled silently with
> the guilt of even thinking of leaving Ōmite behind.

Only when relatives in the United States agreed to send for Ōmite could her parents even contemplate leaving the camp.

And so the Nesaules began the arduous task of applying for visas under the 1948 law.

> Before being allowed to go to America, everyone had to have a sponsor who would guarantee that the newcomers would have a job and a place to live so that we would not become public wards. . . . The tension in the camps became close to unbearable. Having to separate from family and friends yet again was part of the anxiety, and so were the various tests that we were undergoing, most often without being told the results. Reading and math ability, teeth, eyes, ears, skin and bodily cavities were checked and checked again, and again. A dark spot on a lung or partial deafness in one ear meant the person was condemned to the camps forever. "We treated our horses with more dignity," said one of the camp leaders.[2]

Harry Kapeikis's Latvian parents had listed Australia as their first choice, Canada second, but when Harry's father was notified that the Lutheran World Federation had found him a position in Tacoma, Washington, he accepted it. In February 1949, Harry said goodbye to his friends and his aunt and cousin, who were bound for Australia. "Tears were flowing everywhere. Once more I made the rounds, saying my goodbyes and hearing well wishes. Then, like in a dream, I climbed into the truck."[3]

Andrejs Eglitis, the Latvian pilot for the Luftwaffe, who had been working on "guard and engineering duties" for the U.S. Third Army, on learning that the IRO had begun to resettle displaced persons from his former camp, sought and received his discharge papers, returned to the camp, applied for an American visa, found a sponsor, and a year later was on a ship to the United States.[4]

The Jewish displaced persons accepted with stoic indifference the news that a DP bill had been signed in Washington but that it would bar most of them from receiving visas. "The reaction of the Jewish DPs to this bill is interesting," William Haber wrote the American Jewish organizations on August 31, 1948.

> Although it must be assumed that many who entertained hopes of migrating to the United States were saddened and disheartened, the disappointment took no articulate form. . . . The Jewish DPs have a very realistic attitude towards the world. They were not surprised to learn that they were not wanted in our country. A significant and not altogether unanticipated by-product of the U.S. immigration law is that it has helped the DPs to resolve their personal doubts about where their future lies. Our Congress did for many what they could not do for themselves. It made them make up their minds to think in terms of one possibility, instead of in terms of alternatives.

Even those who had been hesitant about going to Israel recognized now that they had no alternative.[5]

As Tzvion had written, no one, certainly not he, could predict what would now "happen with the Jewish DPs, but it was safe to say that "their condition will continue to worsen. . . . We must wait until the situation becomes stabilized. The prospects for America are currently as good as settled. Less Jews will be able to immigrate."[6]

GERMANY, AUGUST TO SEPTEMBER 1948

Fortunately for the Jewish DPs in Germany, the "situation" in Palestine that Tzvion had worried about "stabilized" much sooner than he had expected. "The phenomenal success of Israel in maintaining itself as a 'going concern,'" William Haber observed on August 31, 1948, has had a "definite impact" on the DPs. "I believe that the morale of the people is, on the whole, higher than it has been at any time since my arrival. All reports that reach me indicate that, despite the disappointment in their emigration, imposed by the truces, the people have confidence in their future. The recognition of Israel's representative in the Zone and the visaed legal movement of people from the camps* has given the DPs the feeling that the solution of their individual problems is in sight."[7]

The British evacuation, the IDF's military successes, and the occupation of Haifa and its seaport on the Mediterranean made possible the immigration of large numbers of displaced Jews. "We are really making some progress in the last few months and the movement of people to Israel is proceeding at a good pace," Haber wrote Jacob Billikopf of the AJC on August 29. "About 3,500 will leave during August, about the same number left in June and July, and 4,000 are scheduled to leave for September. If open warfare does not break out or the Mediator does not tighten his restrictions, this progress should continue."[8]

The State Department, still smarting over Truman's decisions, first to support partition, then to recognize Israeli independence, did its best to impede the migration of military-age men from the DP camps to Israel, ostensibly because it believed America should do its part to enforce Count Bernadotte's truce efforts. "The striped-pants boys of the State Department have crossed swords again with Gen. Lucius Clay, this time over the tragic DP problem," Robert S. Allen reported for Drew Pearson on September 3, 1948.

> In an effort to get the thousands of Jewish DP's out of their squalid camps, the U.S. occupation commander authorized transportation to the German border for all desiring to migrate to Palestine. He took this stand because it was humane and also would help reduce occupation costs. But the State Department is now demanding that Clay lock the DP's in their camps; that

---

* The occupation government had permitted the Israelis to establish a visa office in the American zone.

is, to make these camps, in effect, concentration camps. At the bottom of this move is the British Foreign Office. The British are refusing to allow any Jewish DP's under their control to go to Palestine. . . . The British are pursuing this policy as part of their pro-Arab tactics. And the State Department, over Clay's vehement protests, appears to be playing the British game.[9]

Pearson was exaggerating, as he often did. The State Department was not attempting to block all movement out of the camps but only that of men of military age, and it was failing rather miserably at that. DPs refused exit visas simply left the camps without them. The exodus from Germany to Marseilles to Haifa continued at an accelerated rate.

Given the decreasing number of Jews left behind in Germany, Abraham Hyman, acting liaison to the military, and Louis Barish, a Jewish chaplain who worked with him, asked in their February 1949 report to the American Jewish organizations whether it still made sense for them to campaign for new legislation to expand the number of DP visas from two hundred thousand to four hundred thousand. Hyman and Barish urged them to focus their energies instead on encouraging the remaining displaced persons to resettle in Israel. "Our responsibility to the DPs has been to deliver them from their homelessness and to restore them to normal living at the earliest possible moment. That responsibility is now being met. The state of Israel is accepting the DPs en masse and is prepared to absorb all the Jews in the DP countries. While the struggle for a U.S. DP immigration bill was urgently needed [when there was no possibility of immigration to Israel], the struggle for an improved bill has much less to commend it today." Hyman and Barish estimated that the amended law the Jewish organizations were campaigning for would accommodate no more than 10,000 Jewish DPs. The cost of getting visas for these 10,000 Jews* was the admission of

---

* Hyman and Barish's estimates were low. More than twenty-five thousand Jews, not ten thousand, would be admitted under the proposed amendments.

190,000 non-Jewish displaced persons. "It must be remembered that the non-Jewish DPs are, at very best, a potentially anti-Semitic element and certainly not worthy of even an ounce of Jewish effort on their behalf."[10]

WASHINGTON, AUGUST TO
NOVEMBER 1948

President Truman had signed the Displaced Persons Act on June 25, 1948, "in the hope," as he put it, "that its injustices will be rectified by the Congress at the first opportunity." He then tried, but failed, to get the bill amended during a brief special session in July.

Recognizing that there was no more he could do for the time being, he requested $2 million for a Displaced Persons Commission (DPC) to administer the law, and nominated as his three commissioners Ugo Carusi, a Protestant and a former U.S. commissioner of immigration; Edward O'Connor, a Catholic, who had been the director of War Relief Services of the National Catholic Welfare Conference; and Harry Rosenfield, a Jew and a delegate to the UN Economic and Social Council in Geneva. The commissioners' appointments were subject to Senate confirmation, but when the Senate adjourned without acting, Truman offered his three nominees recess appointments.

From the moment they took office, the commissioners recognized that they had been given a flawed, sloppily written, ill-conceived act to administer. They were tasked with bringing into the nation two hundred thousand DPs, but 40 percent of these had to be from annexed nations, and another 30 percent with agricultural experience.

Unfortunately, there were not enough eligible DPs from annexed nations to make up the 40 percent requirement (only 19 percent of the DP population were from the Baltic nations), nor sufficient numbers of farmers to reach the 30 percent requirement (only 25 percent of men, 16 percent of women). If the DPC fell short in either category, which was highly likely, it would have to proportionally reduce the number of displaced persons admitted from other than annexed nations or without agricultural experience.[11]

There were other difficulties as well that would have to be overcome if the commissioners were to meet their goal of bringing two hundred thousand displaced persons into the United States within the next two years. The act stated that no displaced person could be admitted without written "assurances" from designated sponsors that there were jobs and housing awaiting them, that they would not become "public charges," and that all the members of their families were of good health and character and would not pose a "security risk." Getting these "assurances" would not be easy.

The commissioners delegated the work of securing sponsors and assurances to a selected group of voluntary organizations. The most important of these were the sectarian ones, funded by the three major faith groups: the Church World Service and Lutheran Resettlement Service for Protestants and Eastern Orthodox, the National Catholic Resettlement Council for Catholics, and the Hebrew Sheltering and Immigrant Aid Society (HIAS) and the United Service for New Americans (USNA) for the Jews. Each organization worked with smaller, locally based ethnic and national societies: the Protestant Church World Service with the Serbian National Defense Council, the Mennonite Central Committee, the Tolstoy Foundation (for Russian DPs); the Lutheran Resettlement Service with Estonian Relief; the National Catholic Resettlement Council with Polish, Lithuanian, and Ukrainian agencies; USNA with its dozens of local chapters.

The commissioners set out to make it as easy as possible for the voluntary organizations to secure sponsors and assurances by writing regulations that liberally interpreted the law's requirements. Meeting with representatives of the voluntary agencies in September 1948, Commissioner Harry Rosenfield declared that to meet the requirement that the displaced person have a job and housing waiting for him or her, the sponsor had only "to indicate where the job has been obtained . . . that is, name of employer is not needed nor is it necessary to indicate the exact place where the immigrant will reside. The assurance should indicate that a job has been provided in a certain field or skill [and] that housing has been provided." Regarding inland transportation, which the sponsors were obligated to provide, it was "not necessary to indicate who will provide the inland transportation or the route to be taken; a simple statement that inland transportation will be provided is sufficient."[12]

To make it possible for Jewish displaced persons to enter the country with their adopted children and stepchildren, the DPC changed the definition of "child," which under the 1924 immigration law had excluded stepchildren and adopted children. For Jewish survivors whose biological children had been murdered during the war and who had formed new families in the DP camps, this regulation was of critical importance. When the State Department overruled the DPC and, in accordance with the 1924 laws, denied visas to adopted children and stepchildren, the DPC countered by directing the voluntary agencies to secure "individual assurances" for the excluded children. It then wrote a regulation declaring that a "person coming to undertake studies in the United States shall be determined to have suitable employment."

Questioned as to why the commissioners had altered the definition of "child," Commissioner Rosenfield answered that they had done so because they believed "the obvious intent of the Congress" in writing the displaced persons law had been "to maintain family unity and integrity and not to break up families, and in view of the fact that there were so many marriages among people in the camps whose spouse had died or had been killed under the terrifying circumstances under which they lived; in view of the fact that there were so many step-children within families and adoptive children, the Commission felt that that was an appropriate way of carrying out the functions allotted to the Commission by the Congress."[13]

Another regulation drafted by the commissioners expanded the number of DPs eligible for visas by providing that if written documentation was not available to establish that they had been in Germany, Italy, or Austria on or before December 22, 1945, and then again on January 1, 1948, "other documentation, including personal records, . . . the statements and affidavits of applicants and of other persons, and . . . any other pertinent evidence" would suffice. Under this regulation, all a displaced person had to do to establish eligibility was to have another resident of the camp or a German civilian open to a bribe vouch for him or her. Though not quite an invitation to commit fraud, the regulation made it much easier to do so for those who had no other way of securing visas to America.[14]

On October 4, President Truman, clearly pleased with the work of his commissioners, extended the DPC's powers in an executive order that designated it, not the INS or the FBI, "as the agency" responsible for investigating "the character, history, and eligibility . . . of displaced persons seeking admission into the United States." To counter the criticism that they were ill-prepared to keep out "security risks and persons of other undesirable traits," the commissioners designed "security protections" that, they claimed, were more numerous and exacting than those "in the normal immigration laws." In a direct bow to congressmen who had intimated that Jewish DPs who had spent the war in the Soviet Union or returned to Poland after liberation might be security risks, the DPC included a "special additional investigation in connection with displaced persons whose country of origin has been overrun by the Communists."[15]

Section 13 of the Displaced Persons Act of 1948 directed that "no visas shall be issued to any person who is or has been a member of, or participated in any movement which is or has been hostile to the United States or the form of government of the United States." The DPC accordingly wrote a regulation barring from entry members of Communist, Nazi, or fascist parties or movements associated with them. To identify these entities, it compiled a list of "inimical organizations" that it forwarded for "advice and guidance" to the CIA, FBI, State Department, attorney general, and Army Counter-Intelligence.

Rear Admiral Roscoe H. Hillenkoetter, the first director of the CIA, responded to the DPC request with a paragraph on each of the organizations the DPC had identified as being "hostile to the United States." He then qualified his remarks by adding that he believed it was

> definitely worth pointing out, in connection with many of the organizations listed, that a curious anomaly has developed since the end of the war. Several of these organizations [he included here the fiercely nationalist, fascist, and antisemitic Ukrainian OUN] sided with the Germans during the war not on the basis of a pro-German or pro-Fascist orientation, but from a strong anti-Soviet bias. In many cases their motivation was primarily nationalistic and patriotic with their espousal of the German cause determined by their national interests. . . . These opportunistically pro-German groups remain strongly anti-Soviet and, accordingly, find a common ground with new partners. The position of similar groups with a highly fascist, rather than middle-of-the-road, political program presents an even more subtle problem. They similarly array themselves on the anti-Soviet side, but the degree or nature of their actual hostility to the United States or its form of government will continually vary with conditions in their own country and with the changing international situation.

Members of these "highly fascist" groups, the CIA director seemed to be suggesting, should not automatically be barred from entering the United States. The fact that they were and had been only "opportunistically pro-German" and remained strongly anti-Soviet had to be taken into account.[16]

GERMANY, FALL 1948 TO WINTER 1950

The race was on among the Jewish, Protestant, and Catholic voluntary organizations to get as many of their people into the United States as possible before the Displaced Persons Act expired on July 1, 1950. The Catholic and the Jewish agencies and their local affiliates had no difficulties recruiting individuals and groups to sponsor DPs. The Protestant organizations, without established networks to call upon, started out at a disadvantage. "More sponsors are needed!" the *Church World Service News* appealed to its readers in its January 1949 issue. "Sponsorship can be divided so one person or group guarantees housing, another provides a job, and a third guarantees that the DP will not become a public charge. If you, your church or your organization can help an American-to-be, write to the Displaced Persons Committee of Church World Service."[17]

The DPC authorized the voluntaries to request "blanket assurances," with no names attached, for as many DPs as they thought they could secure sponsors for in a specified locality: twenty-five single domestic workers for New Jersey or seventy-five agricultural laborer families for Louisiana. Having secured the blanket assurances, the voluntaries directed their representatives in the camps to select displaced persons who matched the descriptions outlined in the assurances.

"The undertaking is a complicated one," William Haber wrote to his contacts in the United States on December 20, 1948. "The commission is apparently following a policy which seeks to maintain a balance among the various national and religious groups. Accordingly, I learn that Catholic and Jewish cases are being held back because there are an inadequate number of Protestant cases." By December 31, 1948, more than three months after the DPC had begun operations, only 2,507 displaced persons "had emigrated to the United States."[18]

The commissioners recognized quickly that they were never going to reach the goal set by Congress of bringing two hundred thousand

DPs into the country within two years if they adhered, on a week-by-week basis, to the 40 percent quota for former residents of annexed nations and 30 percent for agricultural workers. They decided instead to process all the displaced persons for whom assurances had been attained regardless of where they came from or whether they had ever been farmers. They would worry later about meeting the quota requirements.

"The logjam on U.S. emigration has finally burst!" Samuel Haber of the JDC noted in his report for February 1949. "During the month of February approximately 1,700 Jewish Displaced Persons left from Bremen for the United States. Our immigration officers predict that movement to the United States will henceforth continue at an accelerated pace."[19]

"The voluntary agency people swarmed into the field with thousands of unnamed assurances and began the greatest matching operation ever seen in human affairs—a veritable man-hunt to find in the flesh the exact type of worker described on each affidavit, with a family of specified size that would fit into the house or rooms held in readiness," wrote Kate Hulme in her narrative of life with displaced persons.

At last we could see the usefulness of the exhaustive studies we had done on our DP—mountains of descriptive paper beneath which we thought we had buried him. Under the main categories of nationality, age, skill, creed and family composition, we had him "broken down" practically to color of eyes, so that if any voluntary agency wanted, say fifty blue-eyed Balts in a hurry, each with a family of no more than six and no dependents over sixty-five years of age, we could produce people from our statistical Himalayas in nothing flat. You want a Lithuanian skilled in violin repair?—We have him. You want a hundred tractor drivers?—We have them. Fifty Poles for work in the tobacco fields?—We have five thousand. A neat clean old lady agile enough to be an invalid's companion?—Here she is. We had everything the employer-citizens of the States were asking for and thousands more besides.[20]

Hulme and the voluntary agency, IRO, and DPC representatives in the camps were so committed to the resettlement of the Last Million that they were willing to stretch the truth a bit to make the right matches. "Was there much mismatching in so stupendous [a] task?" Eileen Egan of Catholic Relief Services asked rhetorically in her memoir.

> Of course there was. The chief reason—compassion. A field staff worker, knowing the needs of refugees in nearby camps from frequent visiting and long-term material aid programs, was often moved by pity and love. . . . In his hand was a paper with a blank space that needed a name; a person with a name desperately needed to be inserted in that piece of paper. The simple act of filling in his name gave him release from the bondage of camp, gave him a shelter, a country. A Polish forester became a farmer; a Lithuanian bookkeeper became a lumberman; a Ukrainian peasant who knew his wheat fields became a dairyman—all on paper. . . . From the mail sacks of assurances delivered regularly by plane, boatloads of D.P.'s materialized at U.S. ports.[21]

Friends, neighbors, sometimes strangers were willing to testify that DPs who lacked documentation had been in the camps on December 22, 1945. They had seen them, talked to them, eaten with them on and before that date. "The D.P.s, a people who get along without official papers to prove anything," Janet Flanner observed during her several visits to camps in Germany, "and who have lied splendidly for years as a *modus vivendi*, have recently lied about their names, nationalities, and birthplaces to prevent repatriation to Communist lands and to save their families from punishments. If lying could help, they would lie in order to live in their dreamed-of America."[22]

Ella Schneider Hilton and her family had been evacuated by the German army from Kiev in Ukraine in 1943. As *Volksdeutsche*, they were clearly ineligible for UNRRA or IRO assistance, but they passed through every screening process, claiming that they were Polish.

> We all lied about where we came from. We lied wherever we went. In most instances, the lies were for self-preservation. . . . Our identification papers were full of lies. Every time we moved, we reinvented our family and ourselves. Whenever we registered in a new city, we Refugees invariably had lost, misplaced or thrown away our original papers and could make up any story we felt like. Many people did just that. Where would the authorities check? The identification cards the Nazis had given us in Berlin were worthless and disposed of long ago. The heavy bomb- ings . . . took care of any questions about the loss of identifica- tion papers. No one could prove anything. Everyone made things up as time went by. Since most people had lost their papers during the evacuation and bombing and new official papers were made, you could be anybody, with any name, any believable age, from anywhere, with whatever occupation you wanted. Most ref- ugees took advantage of this by changing names, citizenship, birthplaces, even marital status. . . . All of us children were drilled in what we should say. We always claimed we came from Poland.[23]

For large numbers of DPs, lying was a necessity, because they had arrived in the camps after December 22, 1945, because their children had once suffered from whooping cough, because they had never really worked on a farm, because their marriages were not officially sanc- tioned, because their youngest child was not their own but a dead relative's, because they had once in the distant past belonged to a Com- munist or socialist party or youth group, because they had spent the war in the Soviet Union and feared being labeled as Communist sympathizers or agents, because they were German citizens or *Volksdeutsche* and ineligible for IRO assistance, because they had collaborated with the Nazi occupiers or joined the auxiliary police forces or enlisted or been conscripted into Waffen-SS divisions.

The Jewish DPs had the most difficult time producing the documentation required by the DPC. Fortunately, there were German officials who were more than willing, for a fee, to forge or backdate residency papers. HIAS advised those who lacked written documents "to request that their sponsoring relatives submit sworn affidavits attesting to the DPs' parents' names and their places and dates of birth. German authorities granted the Central Committee [of Liberated Jews] in Munich the power to issue replacement documents."

Marriage certificates were a problem, because German officials did not recognize marriages performed by rabbis, and the DPs refused to go before a German registrar. To get around this problem, the British military government designated Belsen as a "registration district" and appointed German Jews as registrars. In the American zone, UNRRA staff had provided certificates attesting to the couples' religious marriages and pressured the German authorities to recognize them. To meet the requirement that all documents be translated into English, Jewish displaced persons in the camps started up small businesses and, for a fee, not only translated documents but took passport photos.[24]

Once the requisite documents had been secured and translated, the applicant was screened by DPC officers, and the files of those found eligible were sent to the IRO, which certified that each was a "displaced person within the meaning of the IRO constitution." There followed an interview with Army Counter-Intelligence Corps (CIC) as to the DP's "character and history." If no problems were discovered at this stage— and they seldom were, as the CIC had neither the staffing, the skill set, the languages, nor the will to do any sort of thorough investigation— the IRO scheduled a medical examination, chest X-rays, and a blood test. The results were forwarded to the Public Health Service office at the nearest U.S. consulate, which did its own examination.[25]

It was at these final stages, during the medical examinations, that the largest numbers of otherwise eligible displaced persons were rejected: for a spot on their lungs or because they might once have been or might currently be infected with syphilis, smallpox, or measles, or because they limped or missed a limb or had high blood pressure or exhibited signs of being retarded or feeble-minded. Jewish survivor Rose Minsky's departure was delayed because her infant son, born in the DP camp, was undernourished. The departure of the Bertulis family from Lithuania was postponed—for how long they did not know—because Ina, a young teenager, was found to have tuberculosis. The family could have left without her but waited until the doctors decided the disease had been contained. Not all such stories had happy endings. Families with children or aged parents or relatives whom the doctors deemed feeble-minded or impossibly frail or suffering from communicable diseases or epilepsy were offered the impossible choice of staying behind in Germany with their loved ones or leaving for the United States without them.[26]

Those who cleared medical were sent forward, with their IRO, DPC, CIC, and medical clearances, to the consulate offices, where they were interviewed once again as to their eligibility under both the DP Act and the immigration laws that preceded it and remained in force. If the consular office issued a visa, the displaced persons were interviewed a final time by an INS officer, often one recently transferred from Ellis Island, to determine whether they were morally and politically fit to enter the United States.

The DPs who had the most to fear, at every stage of the process, were not those who had collaborated with occupation authorities but those who might be suspected of harboring Communist sympathies because they had spent the war years in the Soviet Union. Joseph Berger, the future *New York Times* reporter and editor, had until he was twenty-one years of age believed he had been born in Poland. That was what the small laminated card that served as his entry into the United States had said. That was what his parents had told him. Only much later, when he began looking through family records for the proof of citizenship he needed to apply to graduate school at Columbia University, did his mother, after pledging him to secrecy, confess that the identity card was a lie. He had been born in the Soviet Union, not in Poland.

"You even had a birth certificate, but we had to destroy it. We made up the story about hiding in Poland because we had to tell the American officials how we survived."

Berger was incredulous. "'I don't understand,' I said. 'Why couldn't you tell the Americans I was born in Russia?'"

"If the Americans knew we had been in Russia during the war," his mother responded, "they would not have let us come here. . . . You know already in 1950 there were—how you say it—suspicions, suspicions of communists, and the Americans did not trust anyone who had been in Russia. A lot of the greeners [new immigrants to the United States] ran to Russia when the war broke out. That's how they survived the war. Who survived in Poland? Hitler killed almost everyone. Only the skeletons left in the *lager*—the concentration camps. But nobody could tell the Americans they were in Russia. We all made up false documents. That's why you can't tell."

The lie about Joseph's birthplace was one of many the Bergers had to tell to gain admission to the United States. Father, mother, and young Joe had not left the Soviet Union until 1946 and were therefore far from occupied Germany on December 22, 1945, the cutoff date for eligibility. That had not prevented them from claiming—and having that claim accepted—that they were in Germany on December 22 and then applying for admission to the United States under a law that they knew had been "written in such a way that it rejected most people who had spent the war in the Soviet Union. We got rid of our Soviet papers," Joe's mother recalled, "and were easily able to get false documents that said we were married in Germany. . . . The American authorities questioned us closely to see if we were spies or communist infiltrators. . . . At the end we were all approved for a voyage to America. We left behind the DP camp at Landsberg and made our way to the port of Bremerhaven."[27]

NEW YORK, FALL AND WINTER 1948

Seasick, weary, sleep-deprived, frightened, exhilarated, weighed down by their baggage, clutching their children's hands, the first contingent of 813 displaced persons arrived in New York Harbor on October 30, 1948. They were greeted by "national, state and city officials and representatives of the Roman Catholic Protestant and Jewish faiths" and a small army of photographers and newspapermen. Almost as if ashamed at the unconscionable delay in providing homes for the war victims, the Americans now overwhelmed them with good wishes.

"Everybody was pleasant to the newcomers," the *New York Times* reported the next morning.

> Nobody pushed them around or made them line up. . . . The welcoming ceremonies were held on the upper deck of the transport. Ugo Carusi, representing the Federal Displaced Persons Commission, presided. The newcomers were crowded on another section of the upper deck where they were photographed until their heads swam. The ceremonies were in English, which only a few of the new arrivals could understand. They waved and cheered and expressed their thanks at what seemed to them to be the proper moments.

First to speak was Attorney General Tom Clark, representing the president, who congratulated the American people on providing such a warm reception for the newcomers. "The fact that you are being admitted to our land is evidence that our people have not forgotten that our

USS General Black *departs Bremerhaven, Germany, with 813 displaced persons bound for the United States, October 1948.*

nation was founded by immigrants." Clark did not allude to the fact that the war that had displaced them had ended in May 1945 and it was now October 31, 1948. Edward Corsi, chairman of the New York State Commission on Displaced Persons, read a message from Governor Dewey. Mayor William O'Dwyer welcomed them on behalf of all New Yorkers. "Victor Fediai, a young White Russian, spoke on behalf of the new arrivals. . . . 'This is the miracle of our second birth. We have come here to enjoy the benefits of democracy and freedom.'"[28]

The IRO and the DPC stage-managed the arrival with an endless supply of heartwarming vignettes for the newspapers. Among the displaced persons pointed out to reporters was "nineteen-month-old Marie Irena Bronny, who had been practicing the difficult name 'Wisconsin' throughout the trip, [as she] toddled around the deck in a Polish national costume." She and her mother and father, a doctor, were bound for Fairchild, a small town in Wisconsin with the perfect name for the occasion, which had not had a doctor for ten years. The story, of course, was too good to be true. When the Wisconsin State Board of Medical Officers refused to grant Dr. Bronny a license, the National Catholic Welfare Conference pledged to find him a position in Chicago instead, "either as a laboratory assistant or a hospital intern."[29]

Newspapers large and small, encouraged by the voluntary organizations and the Displaced Persons Commission, inundated the public with heartwarming human interest stories about freedom-loving foreigners who had escaped from Communist tyranny. Only occasionally did the English-language press report on the minority of displaced persons who had come to America for another reason: to escape punishment for possible war crimes.

Buried on page 17 of the *New York Times* on March 30, 1949, was a report on passengers of the *Marine Falcon,* which had just arrived from Hamburg with 550 passengers, one of whom, Herman Borenkraut, a Polish Jew, had accused another, Albertas Bauras, a Lithuanian DP, of having been among "a group of Nazi storm troopers who incarcerated him in a concentration camp."[30]

INS officials, acting on Borenkraut's accusation, convened a "board of special inquiry" and, after a brief investigation, denied admission to Bauras and his alien wife and two minor children. Bauras appealed to the Board of Immigration Appeals, which permitted his wife and children to enter the country, but confirmed that he should be excluded because he had "willfully made misrepresentations for the purpose of gaining admission into the United States as an eligible displaced person."

Bauras had told UNRRA, IRO, and DPC officers that he had entered Germany in October 1944. The truth was that, claiming to be an ethnic German, which he was not, he had been "repatriated" in 1941, joined the Waffen-SS, and served as a guard at a concentration camp in Radom, Poland. The Board of Immigration Appeals, in denying Bauras admission to the United States, "stated that in no case which has come before it involving displaced persons has there been such flagrant and intentional misrepresentation as in the case of this alien."[31]

Had the chance encounter on a ship with 550 passengers not

THE LAST MILLION

occurred between Borenkraut and Bauras, he and his family, having secured their DP visas in Germany by lying about their wartime collaboration, would have entered the country and probably escaped detection for the rest of their lives. The inevitable conclusion to be drawn from this incident, submerged in the *New York Times* item, was that had Jewish displaced persons, like Herman Borenkraut, been involved in the screening process, many more former concentration camp guards, Nazi collaborators, and war criminals would have been denied admission to the United States and perhaps brought to justice for their crimes.

To PROVIDE MAXIMUM positive publicity to mark the sailing and landing of the first boatloads of displaced persons, the IRO and the DPC invited several American journalists to travel to Germany to meet the DPs in the camps and accompany them on their journey. Among the journalists invited was David Nussbaum of the Overseas News Service (ONS).* On his return to the United States, Nussbaum prepared a two-part article that was subsequently published in a number of newspapers, including the *Cleveland Plain Dealer* and the left-leaning *New York Post*, owned by Dorothy Schiff of the Schiff family.

The first installment of Nussbaum's article appeared on November 19, 1948, on page 2 of the *New York Post* under the headline "Pro-Nazis Entering U.S. Under DP Law That Keeps Out Jews."[32] Two days later, part two, "DP Camps Swarm with Pro-Nazis; IRO Shrugs It Off," was published, also on page 2. The article opened inauspiciously. "The first shiploads of European refugees are in. Under the terms of the Displaced Persons law, 203,385 will follow, a community of no small proportions to be introduced into American society. Who are these new

---

* ONS was a syndication agency founded by the British during the war to get favorable articles into the American press. After the war, it became an ongoing enterprise with a distinguished set of officers, most of them Jewish publishing executives, and an even more distinguished board of advisers, most of them non-Jewish college presidents, academics, and writers. It had no known political agenda or ideological leanings; its articles were syndicated in a variety of newspapers across the country.

and future Americans? What kind of citizens can be expected from among them?"

Nussbaum then answered his own questions. "Most of the non-Jewish refugees who had elected to remain behind" in the camps rather than accept repatriation and were now entering the United States as displaced persons had not been

> displaced by the war, but voluntarily joined the Nazis in their retreat from Eastern Europe in late 1944. They are not victims of Nazism, but as one IRO official put it, "victims of the Allied victory." . . . The DP camps today are shot through with collaborators, with those who actively co-operated in the Nazi design, with former members of the SS and the Wehrmacht, and with men who played a role in the extermination of tens of thousands of Jews. This is the story unfolded in talks with numerous officials of the IRO and others close to the refugee problem. It was borne out in interviews with the refugees themselves.[33]

In the second part of his article, Nussbaum elaborated on his charges, claiming that there were in the camps and on the way into the United States refugees who, according to an IRO informant, "don't want to return home because they have something to conceal. . . . A document expert in Austria told me: 'The DP camps are the hiding-place for many war criminals.'"[34]

Nussbaum, who provided no hard evidence, but only anecdotes from unnamed sources, was immediately attacked for false reporting, for fanning the flames of religious bigotry, for parroting "Soviet thinking," and for setting Jews against Christians. At a press conference held a little more than a week after the articles were published, Monsignor Edward Swanstrom, director of Catholic resettlement, announced that the National Catholic Resettlement Council (NCRC) had adopted a resolution disputing "allegations that residents of the Baltic States coming into the United States under the Displaced Persons Act aided the

Nazis." Swanstrom "termed the charges 'the opening gun in an attempt
to discredit the whole program. . . . My answer to the critics is to go
down to one of these boats and see the DP's come in. I have been there.
I'll guarantee that those who go will find the finest kind of people. To
see them, and to know what America means to them, will bring tears to
the eyes, not once but many times.'"

"From the early days after the war," the NCRC resolution read, "when
resettlement of bona-fide refugees and displaced persons was recognized
for the problem that it is, representatives of Soviet thinking wished all
irrepatriables to be considered as Fascists and traitors. It would be unfortunate if such thinking were to lead Americans to believe that all persons
seeking resettlement in our shores are in these categories."[35]

A week after Swanstrom's press conference, the National Catholic
Welfare Conference news service published an extended two-part re-
buttal of Nussbaum's charges. Joseph Shepard of the *Indianapolis Star*
claimed that he had interviewed the same people as Nussbaum "and
came out with observations" diametrically opposed.

> I was filled with pride at these intense people bravely starting
> life anew. When they sang "God Bless America" I believe they
> meant it. Mr. Nussbaum apparently spent his shipboard nights
> livid with horror over a nazi plot to populate American with
> criminal underground quislings, collaborators and saboteurs and
> to siphon them in on IRO ships. I think the IRO screening pro-
> cess and the U.S. consular and immigration bureau investiga-
> tions are ample, safe and effective. I was impressed not frightened,
> on viewing our new future citizens.[36]

The attacks on Nussbaum were unrelenting and ecumenical. Irving
Engel, chair of the AJC Immigration Committee, was blindsided by a
cable from the United States Zone Council of Voluntary Agencies in
Germany formally dissociating its members from Nussbaum's charges.
"THE MEMBER AGENCIES OF THE COUNCIL ARE ABLE

TO STATE VERY DEFINITELY FROM THEIR OWN IN-
VESTIGATION THAT THE MAJORITY OF THESE PEOPLE
HAVE NOT BEEN COLLABORATORS."

Engel, disturbed that the Jewish agency leaders had signed off on
this statement, when they had to have known, as he did, that there was
more than a grain of truth in Nussbaum's accusations, asked Sidney
Liskofsky to investigate. "I am not clear as to whether this cablegram
came from the IRO or from U.S. Army Headquarters in Germany. . . .
In particular I would like to know the extent to which the European
representatives of JDC and HIAS actually joined in the sentiments expressed in the cablegram quoted above."

The AJC and other American Jewish organizations were not prepared to dismiss Nussbaum's accusations out of hand, but neither could
they endorse them without provoking an irrevocable break with Protestant and Catholic voluntaries and politicians.[37]

On December 28, Father William J. Gibbons, a Jesuit who informally
represented Cardinal Spellman and formally the National Catholic Resettlement Council, cautioned Engel that if Catholics and Jews were to
be able to work together in the future,

> everything possible must be done to counteract the bad feeling
> toward non-Jewish refugees which has been stimulated by the
> Nussbaum attacks. Before U.S. entry into the war many of us
> were sincerely grieved at the anti-Semitic feeling stirred up by
> the followers of Father Coughlin and America First. We did
> what we could to neutralize that group and to counteract that
> sentiment. Today some of the Christian group and the various
> nationality groups feel that ONS, the *Post* and such commenta-
> tors as Nussbaum are creating the same problem in reverse. It is
> our sincere hope that responsible Jewish leaders will not allow
> their people to be confused by such racial thinking or by foreign
> forces eager to split the American democratic front. We have
> nothing to gain and everything to lose by such a development.[38]

Gibbons was hinting—and not too subtly—that if the Jewish organizations wanted Christian support for an amended nondiscriminatory displaced persons act, they would have to disavow Nussbaum's charges that non-Jewish DPs might be Nazi collaborators.

Representatives from the American Jewish Committee, the American Jewish Congress, the Anti-Defamation League of B'nai B'rith, the Jewish Labor Committee, the Jewish War Veterans, and the National Community Relations Advisory Council came together to formulate a united response to Nussbaum's articles. Their statement, published as a letter to the editor in the *New York Times* on January 12, 1949, in a rebuke to Nussbaum and to assuage his critics, condemned "as irresponsible and indefensible any effort to cast blanket aspersions upon any national or religious group of displaced persons." They acknowledged nonetheless, as Nussbaum had, that "in view of the chaotic conditions existing in Germany at the war's end" and despite the best efforts of UNRRA and IRO, some collaborators had "succeeded in entering the camps" and were now entering the United States.

> We should be remiss in our duty as American citizens . . . if we failed to exert our best efforts to prevent the settlement in this country of those whose infamous performance towards the hapless people of Europe makes them dangerous to America and unworthy of the high privilege of American citizenship. . . . We are therefore convinced that American public opinion generally will demand screening techniques to bar Nazis, their collaborators and all others contaminated with racism and totalitarianism as rigorous as those now properly being used to bar Communists.[39]

Designing and putting into operation an effective screening plan would, the Jewish leaders realized, for financial, political, and logistical reasons, require the full cooperation of the American government. In the summer and fall of 1948, the Jewish organizations assembled a committee, led by Sidney Liskofsky of the AJC, to draft a comprehensive screening plan. Under this proposed plan, the DPC would forward the names of all applicants for visas to a screening agency in Paris, organized, funded, and operated jointly by the Jewish agencies. The Paris agency would then check applicant names against "a central index file on all suspected collaborators."

The sources from which this "central index file" would be assembled were voluminous and accessible. Among those identified by the Liskofsky committee were the archives of the Polish Historical Commission and the Centre de Documentation Juive Contemporaine in France; the Jewish Historical Institute and the Polish Ministry of Information in Poland; the Polish War Criminals Committee and the British Section of the World Jewish Congress in London; the Historical Commission of Bratislava in Czechoslovakia; the Jewish Historical Museum in Vilna; Simon Wiesenthal's Jewish Historical Documentation Center in Austria; the seventy-five historical commissions in the DP camps, including the Central Historical Commission in Munich, the War Criminals Division of the Central Committee of Liberated Jews, and the Federation of Lithuanian Jews; and in the United States, the materials assembled by the American Jewish Committee, which had hired Dr. Samuel Gringauz, the former leader of the Landsberg DP camp, to research "the YIVO and World Jewish Congress archives, the New York Public Library, the Library of Congress in Washington, D.C., and several other sources."

Additional evidence was available in the Soviet Union, but Liskofsky, recognizing the political difficulties inherent in utilizing documents assembled by the Soviets or seized by them from the Germans, cautioned that "information from behind the 'Iron Curtain' will have to be carefully evaluated before submission to any official government screening body."[40]

The Liskofsky committee proposed as an additional screening

technique that six to seven teams of investigators "representing various national origin groups" be organized to enter the DP camps "and contact and interview the people there with a view to getting all possible information about applicants for visas."[41]

Because large numbers of collaborators had taken on new paper identities, photographs would have to be scrutinized to identify suspected collaborators and war criminals. Fortunately, every refugee who had sought DP status from the IRO had had his or her photograph taken. "Whatever the applicant can hide, one thing about him is sure—his origin. Therefore, the applications with the pictures must be made available to as many reliable persons of the same geographical origin as possible [including] Jewish DP's who know many of them from their experience [and] democratic elements of the same ethnical group (Lithuanian, Latvians, Poles, etc.)."[42]

In late November 1948, representatives of the major American Jewish organizations met with Displaced Persons Commissioner Harry Rosenfield to discuss their screening plan. They recommended that the DPC, instead of relying on the Army CIC to screen the visa applicants, establish its own procedures, work together with the Paris agency that the Jewish organizations intended to establish, and make full use of the numerous sources of evidence they had identified.

"Rosenfield disclosed that Carusi [the DPC chairman] was opposed to such a unit," Will Maslow of the American Jewish Congress reported in his notes on the meeting. "What may be motivating Carusi, Rosenfield had intimated, is that the screening process would be directed principally against Protestants," while the commission was "attempting desperately to get more Protestants on the DP boats." Edward O'Connor, the Catholic commissioner, Rosenfield added, "is likewise opposed to a special screening unit." Rosenfield did not argue against the need for the type of screening outlined in the plan Liskofsky had drafted, but "pointed out the difficulties" involved in getting government agencies involved in the visa process to cooperate with the "Jewish agencies in screening."

CIC does not like information from private organizations; the Army of Occupation is antagonistic to all Jewish organizations; . . . the DPC can not and will not submit the names of the DP visa applicants to any private organizations. It is unlikely that the IRO will submit to the Jewish groups a list of the DP inmates. It will be necessary to obtain Army approval before resource people or liaison officers of the Jewish Agency are permitted to enter Germany.

Rosenfield ended the meeting by suggesting "that the Jewish agencies request a formal hearing before the DPC to bring all of their recommendations on screening to their attention."[43]

The WJC, following up on Rosenfield's recommendation, passed a resolution calling on the Displaced Persons Commission "to establish a division within the agency charged with the exclusive duty of screening Nazi collaborators from the ranks of the displaced persons seeking admission to these shores." The Jewish organizations, in their *New York Times* letter to the editor in January, also called for enhanced screening. The DPC did not respond to any of these requests.[44]

Unsure of how to proceed, but unwilling to drop the issue entirely, Irving Engel of the AJC, in late December 1948, proposed that Rabbi Joseph Baron of Milwaukee organize a letter-writing campaign in Wisconsin to urge Senator Alexander Wiley to include in an amended DP Act a provision that screening be enhanced and directed not only against Communists, but against Nazis and fascists as well. "As you know," Engel wrote Rabbi Baron, "there is a great deal of controversy raging at the present time on the latter point. Many people are convinced that American officials are not sufficiently alert to the danger that many former active Hitler sympathizers may come in as displaced persons. Senator Wiley's failure to mention this possibility is further evidence of the lack of awareness of many Americans on this point."[45]

It is not known whether the rabbi followed through on the suggestion. If he did, it was to no avail. Wiley would continue in the next session, as he had in the previous one, to warn his colleagues and constituents about the threat posed by Communist infiltrators, with nary a word about Nazis or fascists.

The Jewish organizations, clearly disheartened by their failure to get anyone in Congress or the DPC to take their screening plans seriously, eventually abandoned their efforts. After January 1949, there were no further press releases, no articles in the newspapers or magazines, no campaigns in Congress alerting Americans to the possibility that among the DPs on their way might be large numbers of former Nazis.

The list of suspected collaborators that the American Jewish Committee had compiled would remain in its offices unexamined until August 1949, when the chairman of the Board of Special Inquiry at Ellis Island inquired whether it had any "data regarding persons who collaborated with Nazis." Executive Vice President John Slawson responded that the AJC had identified

> approximately 1,200 individual collaborators . . . from eye witness accounts, from reports of German authorities, from newspapers published in the occupied countries during the War and from official collections of laws and ordinances. . . . The names are arranged by country. . . . In many cases alternate spelling of the name is given. Where possible, the place of most recent residence is indicated, as well as offices and positions held, incriminating activities and original sources of information.

Slawson forwarded the AJC files on collaborators to Mr. Watson B. Miller, commissioner of Immigration and Naturalization. There is no evidence that the INS made use of or even consulted the files.[46]

On May 31, 1950, John Slawson wrote Displaced Persons commissioner Harry Rosenfield to inform him that since delivering its file to INS nine months earlier, the AJC researchers had refined and bound it in individual volumes for each country in question. The names in each volume are arranged alphabetically, and in some, are divided into two parts—those culled from official documents and those based on eye-witness accounts of victims. . . . Inasmuch as there is a strong likelihood that some of the individuals listed have made or will make efforts to immigrate to this country, you may find this file—which is being sent you under separate cover—useful in identifying them.[47]

A notation on Slawson's letter archived with the DPC papers at the National Archives indicates that the "big box" was received and stored with Rosenfield's other files. There is no evidence that it was ever consulted or used to identify potential collaborators and bar them from entry.[48]

WHILE THE AMERICAN JEWISH organizations tried but failed to push the DPC to institute its own screening process to weed out Nazi collaborators, a small, near-obsessively dedicated group of "Nazi hunters," most of them Jewish, was conducting its own independent investigations of Nazis hiding in plain sight in the DP camps.

On October 20, 1948, Simon Wiesenthal wrote to a Mr. Bedo, IRO chief eligibility officer in Salzburg, calling his attention to a Latvian war criminal, apprehended in Brazil, who had immigrated there "with the help of I.R.O." "I take the opportunity of this little, but not infrequent incident to touch the whole problem of the 'Eligibility.' Therefore I like to speak frankly about this matter."

Wiesenthal informed Bedo that "on the basis of statements of a few survivors we listed about 200 Lithuanians who are responsible for the death and torture of thousands of Jews . . . and sent this list to the eligibility officers in Linz, Salzburg and Innsbruck." Wiesenthal hoped that IRO officers would cooperate with his Jewish Historical

Documentation Center in identifying and helping to bring to justice the Lithuanian war criminals still in the camps or about to be resettled. "Dear Mr. Bedo, in your capacity as chief of Eligibility Division for Austria I like to draw special attention to this problem. I, as chairman of the Committee of former Jewish Concentration Camp Inmates, feel as my duty not only to represent the interests of the survivors, but even more of our killed parents, wives, children, who were murdered by some of the present 'United Nations DPs.' Therefore we will do everything within our possibilities to prevent this outrageous injustice."[49]

Wiesenthal and his group, in the course of assembling evidence on Nazi collaborators and war criminals, placed an article in the January 7, 1949, issue of *Aufbau*, the German-language New York–based weekly, read in Jewish communities throughout the world—and in the DP camps in Germany. The article was headlined "Witnesses Sought: A List of War Criminals Currently Situated in DP-camps in Germany." Beneath the headline was a list of thirty-four suspected Latvian war criminals, thirty-two of whom were living in DP camps in Germany, one in Switzerland, and one in the United Kingdom, who had been recruited by the "Westward Ho!" labor program.

The list included several members of the Arājs Kommando and Latvian auxiliary police who had participated in the murder of Jews in Riga, in Rēzekne, in Liepāja, and elsewhere in Latvia. Wiesenthal identified them by name, DP camp, and their particular war crimes. At the bottom of the article was a brief note.

> We are in a difficult situation in that usually we have one or two testimonies against these persons, [but none in the case of the Latvian war criminals,] as the Latvian Jews, in some areas of Latvia, were completely destroyed. We would be extremely grateful if, through the mediation of your newspaper, we could obtain testimonies from Latvian Jews now in the USA. If that does not work, we would at least like to make the public aware of the . . . DP's who will soon be seeking hospitality and citizenship.[50]

Among the names on the *Aufbau* list were several men who would within the next few years be resettled by the IRO in Brazil, Canada, and the United States.

Haralds Puntulis was resettled in Willowdale, Ontario, where he lived peacefully until 1965, when he was tried and convicted, in absentia, by a Latvian court for participation in the mass killing of Jews and others in the town of Rēzekne in July and August 1941. Sentenced with Puntulis for the killings at Rēzekne was Albert Eichelis, also on the list, who was at the time living in the Esslingen DP camp in Germany. Puntulis would die of natural causes in 1982; Eichelis would in 1984 be sentenced to six years' imprisonment in Germany.[51]

Vilis Hāzners, also identified as a war criminal by Wiesenthal in 1949, had been a member of the Latvian auxiliary police, police chief in the Abrene (Pytalovsky) district, and an officer in the Latvian Waffen-SS. He immigrated to the United States in 1956, settled in East Orange, New Jersey, and became active at once in Latvian American politics as chairman of the Committee for a Free Latvia, an organization funded by the CIA. Though there was extensive, well-documented evidence that Hāzners had committed war crimes, he was, in 1960, put on the CIA payroll. He would, after turning back attempts to deport him, die a free man in the United States in 1989.[52]

Whether the other names on Wiesenthal's list were war criminals or not, and if so, whether they were ever brought to justice, is unclear. What is clear is that every one of them should have been thoroughly screened by the IRO before being declared eligible for resettlement. In the years to come, excuses would be made that it had been impossible to screen out suspected war criminals and collaborators without the participation of the Soviet Union. But that was not entirely true. Too many of the crimes committed during the war were committed in public; many victims had survived; evidence had been gathered and archived in Poland, Germany, the United States, and elsewhere.

22.

"THE UTILIZATION OF REFUGEES
FROM THE SOVIET UNION IN THE
U.S. NATIONAL INTEREST"

I N AN HISTORICAL IRONY almost too grotesque to be true, American government agencies were already, unbeknownst to the American Jewish organizations or Wiesenthal and the Nazi hunters, investigating individuals who had collaborated with the Nazi war machine and occupation forces, not for the purpose of punishing or denying them entrance to the country, but to enlist them in intensifying Cold War battles with the Soviet Union.

There was a new war to be fought, intelligence to be gathered, propaganda to be produced and distributed, and a home front to be mobilized. In all of these areas, formerly pro-Nazi, now anti-Communist, anti-Soviet DPs could be invaluable assets. They spoke the language, knew the history, had experienced Soviet tyranny firsthand, or claimed they had, and maintained or could establish active contacts with compatriots in Germany, in their homelands, and around the world. The British had well-established intelligence networks in the Baltic states and the Soviet Union; the Americans would have to construct their own. The military had already, under a program code-named Operation Paperclip, imported Nazi scientists to the United States, including a contingent of rocket scientists, led by Wernher von Braun, to engage in research and development on a variety of military-based space and weapons programs. The State Department would now do the same with nonscientists it required for its own purposes.[1]

In early February 1948, the State Department's Policy Planning Staff, directed by George Kennan, produced a "study" entitled "The Utilization of Refugees from the Soviet Union in the U.S. National Interest," which outlined a series of projects that required the participation of anti-Communist displaced persons. In a tone infused equally with self-righteous outrage and wearied dismay, "The Utilization of Refugees from the Soviet Union in the U.S. National Interest" bemoaned the failure of the State Department and other government agencies to make use of these valuable assets.

> There has thus far been no systematic and concerted effort on the part of this Government to utilize refugees from the Soviet World in the furtherance of U.S. national interests. No combined effort has been made to screen the elite among the refugees for information regarding the Soviet World. No overall study has been made of the possibility of utilizing either the elite or the mass of these refugees in U.S. national interests.
>
> We are ill-equipped to engage in the political and psychological conflict with the Soviet World, now forced upon us. Our information program, for example, is suffering from an acute shortage of personnel who have specialized knowledge of the target areas of the Soviet World. Among the refugees in this country and Western Europe are political leaders from the Soviet World. . . . These men and lesser political figures among the refugees are the potential nucleus of possible Freedom Committees encouraging resistance movements in the Soviet World and providing contacts with an underground. No systematic study

has been made by this Government of whether these political leaders might, by private or official means, in this country or elsewhere, be enabled to further U.S. national interests.

The displaced persons represented a vital asset in another way as well. Not only could they provide information to the government about the "Soviet World," they could also educate the American public and the world about the evils of Soviet Communism. Kennan proposed as an element in the "Utilization of Refugees" project the organization of an Institute for the Study of the Soviet World, based in Washington, that would bring together in a government-sponsored think tank American scholars and graduate fellows with refugee scholars and "consultants . . . who, while not having the qualifications of scholars, possess nevertheless special knowledge. Falling within this category would be former Communist Party and government officials, engineers, technicians, journalists, etc." Kennan recommended that, to safeguard the institute's "reputation for complete objectivity and academic freedom, it should be financed by private rather than government funds. . . . The Social Science Research Council and individual American scholars . . . are at present studying the question of the organization and programs."[2]

Kennan's institute met with opposition from those whose support it would require, including Captain Alan McCracken, CIA deputy assistant director for special operations, who regarded it as "nothing but expensive hot air. . . . I do not think any 'social science scholars' will do us a particle of good—we have too damned many of this type of faker in the U.S. already." The leaders of the Russian studies programs at Columbia and Harvard were also unenthusiastic, as were the foundations that were needed to fund the operation.[3]

In November 1948, Kennan, in an attempt to gather support for his institute, leaked his proposal to Joseph and Stewart Alsop, his Georgetown friends, who endorsed it in their nationally syndicated column. "Tens of thousands of Soviet citizens outside the Soviet Union constitute a gold mine of information," the Alsops reported on November 2, 1948. "And the fact is that the gold mine has hardly been worked at all." The best way to unlock its riches, "according to those who have studied the matter, including the State Department planners," the Alsops declared, was "to establish the proposed 'Institute of Russian studies.' . . . American policy toward the Soviet Union could then be based on fact rather than on intelligent guesswork."[4]

The Alsops' endorsement was not enough to save Kennan's institute. "The gold mine of information" in the possession of the displaced persons would, however, be dug up and utilized in other ways. A Russian Research Center was organized at Harvard in 1948, and, with Air Force funding, scholars and researchers were dispatched to displaced persons camps, provided with military clearance, and instructed to fill in rather extensive questionnaires with information gathered from the DPs. "These mountains of information provided the basis for air force reports as well as scholarly monographs." In 1950, the Research Program on the USSR, similar to Kennan's in design, was established at Columbia University.[5]

The "Utilization of Refugees" proposal (minus the Institute section) was approved by the State–Army–Navy–Air Force Coordinating Committee (SANACC) and given the code name BLOODSTONE by the Joint Chiefs of Staff, with instructions that "the word itself should be handled as Top Secret."[6]

Under Operation BLOODSTONE, the Department of State, the Army, the Navy, the Air Force, and the CIA were authorized to "promptly begin in Europe a systematic and combined program of screening refugees from the Soviet World and acquiring documentary material regarding the Soviet World . . . with a view of obtaining intelligence regarding the U.S.S.R. and its satellites." SANACC, with the assistance of a Justice Department representative, was "charged with studying the security and legal problems involved in bringing these . . . selected refugees to the U.S. and with recommending measures necessary to facilitate their movement into and residence in the U.S." On

August 2, 1948, it was determined that "to extent possible these aliens would be brought in under the DP Act."[7]

Though congressional approval was not believed to be required for the implementation of BLOODSTONE, SANACC members agreed that key members of the Congress should be informed "on a confidential basis, [of] the general purport of this program." The Justice Department, in particular, felt "very strongly" that congressional leaders be briefed "so that when the inevitable undesirable alien brought in under these programs appears in the U.S., the Congress will have been forewarned and undue criticism of the Departments of State and Justice should thereby by minimized."

Charles Bohlen of the State Department disagreed. "I feel that some leading members of Congress might rather resent being cut in on something over which they have no decision or control but which they would be expected to defend if any undesirable publicity arises during the course of this operation."[8]

On Kennan's suggestion, Frank Wisner, a former OSS operative in Romania who had visited and was familiar with the DP camps, was appointed director of the Office of Special Projects within the Central Intelligence Agency, delegated with the planning and execution of covert operations like BLOODSTONE. To protect the top secrecy of the program, the Office of Special Projects was, eight days after it had been approved by the National Security Council, renamed the Office of Policy Coordination (OPC).[9]

The first step in putting the BLOODSTONE programs into operation was the screening, selection, and recruitment of displaced persons to staff them. Fortunately, Army CIC had been monitoring political activities in the camps and identifying potential informants and intelligence sources. On October 1, 1948, Under Secretary of State Lovett requested of Defense Secretary James Forrestal that CIC make available to Wisner whatever information the Army in Germany had "concerning (a) political activity among refugees from the Soviet world and (b) handling of bona fide political refugees and deserters from the Soviet Zone. There may be other requests of this nature which will have to be made."[10]

The CIA's and OPC's appetite for Eastern European refugees and displaced persons to assist in fighting the Cold War, abroad and at home, was limitless. Displaced persons could serve multiple, essential tasks, covert and overt: intelligence gathering; identification, recruitment, and clandestine funding of resistance networks in the former Baltic nations and Ukraine; selection of individuals who might, when the time came, serve in governments-in-exile; provision of support for CIA-funded organizations in the United States like the Committee for a Free Latvia and the National Committee for a Free Europe; publication and dissemination of anti-Communist propaganda, pamphlets, leaflets, books, magazine articles, and scholarly studies; scripting, translating, and broadcasting radio programs for transmission into Eastern Europe and the Soviet Union.

To facilitate the entry of the displaced persons it required, the State Department, military, and CIA in the spring of 1949 approached Congressman Emanuel Celler, chairman of the House Judiciary Committee, and asked him to include among the amendments to the 1948 DP Act he planned to introduce a provision that provided fifteen thousand visas to refugees "whose admission . . . is recommended by or on behalf of the Secretary of State and the Secretary of Defense." Celler agreed to do so.

Questioned later on the House floor, Celler defended the amendment on both humanitarian and geopolitical grounds. "The State Department says, 'Give encouragement to at least 15,000 of these anti-Communists who will be able to escape, so that you can give them some surcease from their travail. They will make worthy citizens, and they will aid our intelligence and our counterintelligence departments of the Army and the State Department.'" The amendment was approved, without debate, though the number of displaced persons permitted under it was reduced, again without public debate, from fifteen thousand to five hundred. Though Celler had agreed to the amendment, his colleagues in Congress were reluctant to cede their authority over immigration policy to the executive branch.[11]

On June 1, 1949, another step in the implementation of BLOODSTONE was taken with the formation of the National Committee for a Free Europe (NCFE), an ostensibly "independent organization spontaneously formed by private American citizens," but in fact a CIA front that provided guidance and distributed paychecks to the hundreds of formerly displaced persons who worked for it as publicists, journalists, broadcasters, translators, and speechwriters. Dwight Eisenhower, Lucius Clay, William J. Donovan, corporate leaders Peter Grace, H. J. Heinz, and Henry Ford II, Hollywood notables Darryl Zanuck and Cecil B. DeMille, a handful of labor leaders, and a large contingent of Wall Street lawyers were among NCFE's initial sponsors. Allen Dulles would be named executive secretary.

In 1949, NCFE organized Radio Free Europe, and in 1953, Radio Liberation, to broadcast programs written, translated, produced, and narrated by former displaced persons to Eastern Europe and the Soviet Union.[12]

The long arm of the CIA continued to reach out to and make use of former displaced persons. Among those brought into the United States with CIA assistance were two Lithuanian displaced persons, Aleksandras Lileikis and Kazys Gimzauskas.

In 1947, Army CIC had investigated allegations that Lileikis, who had taken up residence in UNRRA Camp #6 in Bamberg, had been "chief of the political Lithuanian Security Police in Vilna during the German occupation." Lileikis had indeed, as the *New York Times* would later report, "led a Lithuanian secret police unit that collaborated in anti-Jewish atrocities [and] handed over dozens of Jews . . . to Nazi execution squads."

Lileikis applied for admission to the United States under the DP

Act, but was rejected because of his work with the Nazi security police in Vilna. He remained in Munich, where he was contacted by CIA officers who, in August 1952, asked for and were granted permission to use him to recruit other Lithuanians. In 1955, Lileikis again applied for entry to the United States and was given a visa. He was resettled in Norwood, Massachusetts, a Boston suburb, worked for the CIA for a few years, then for the next quarter century for a Lithuanian publishing company in the United States that may have been funded by the agency.

In 1982, the Justice Department opened an investigation of Lileikis as a possible war criminal. Fourteen years later, his citizenship was revoked and he returned voluntarily to Lithuania. In 1998, a Lithuanian court charged him with genocide, but his trial was suspended a day after it opened because of his ill health. The trial resumed in 2000, but was suspended again after thirty minutes, this time indefinitely. Lileikis died two months later at age ninety-three, a free man.[13]

Kazys Gimzauskas, who was Lileikis's second in command in Vilna during the war, followed the same path into Germany and a displaced persons camp. He too was initially denied a DP visa, but though Army CIC, consular officials, and the IRO all had sufficient evidence of his wartime activities to keep him out of the United States, he was, like Lileikis, rewarded for having assisted the CIA in Europe and granted an American visa. In 1955, Gimzauskas was resettled with his wife in St. Petersburg, Florida, where he took up work as a mechanic. When his past crimes were revealed decades later, he fled the United States for Lithuania. Charged and found guilty by a Lithuanian court for war crimes, he was spared imprisonment because of poor health, and died in Lithuania in February 2001. He was ninety-three years of age.[14]

Among the most notorious of the displaced persons recruited by the CIA was the Ukrainian Mykola Lebed. In 1941, Lebed had assumed command of the OUN-B when its leader, Stepan Bandera, was arrested by the Germans after declaring Ukrainian independence. As a commander of the OUN-B guerrillas, then the Ukrainian Insurgent Army

(UPA), Lebed organized the slaughter of thousands of Ukrainian Jews and Polish civilians.

At war's end, having taken up residence in Rome, Lebed contacted the American military and offered, in return for its protection, his files on Communist agents in Ukraine, his contacts with anti-Communist resistance fighters behind the Iron Curtain, and information about and assessments of the reliability of Ukrainian exiles in the displaced persons camps. The Americans accepted Lebed's offer, even though "a CIC report from July 1947 cited sources that called Lebed a 'well-known sadist and collaborator for the Germans.'"

Lebed was so valuable as an informer and as a leader of the Ukrainian "Liberation Council" of anti-Communist resisters that when Soviet agents discovered his presence in Italy, the American army moved him and his family to Munich, where Frank Wisner recruited him to work on several projects, including the organization of underground resistance groups in Ukraine.[15]

In the fall of 1949, with a false name, false papers, a concocted past, and Army CIC clearance that was obtained with the assistance of the CIA, Lebed secured a visa as a displaced person. Once in the United States, he took back his name and, with CIA funding, embarked on a national speaking tour, wrote pamphlets and articles, and assumed a leadership role within the Ukrainian nationalist community. When the INS, acting on multiple tips from Ukrainians in the United States, looked into the circumstances under which Lebed had been given a visa, the CIA declared that the charges against him were false and warned that his deportation "would create serious political repercussions among the anti-Soviet Ukrainian groups all over the world [and] create certain security hazards affecting United States government intelligence activities."[16]

On May 5, 1952, Allen Dulles, CIA deputy director, notified Argyle R. Mackey, INS commissioner, that because it was "urgently necessary that [Lebed] be able to travel in Western Europe" in his capacity as "Foreign Minister of the Ukrainian Supreme Council of Liberation," the CIA intended to invoke the "Admission of Essential Aliens; Limitation on Number" section of the CIA Act of 1949 and provide Lebed with "permanent resident" status so that he could travel overseas and return without INS investigation or impediment. Dulles asked INS to "record the subject's admission for permanent residence as of the date of his original entry, 4 October 1949." In 1957, Lebed freed himself entirely from INS scrutiny by becoming a naturalized citizen.

Mykola Lebed would spend the next three decades working for the CIA on a number of projects, the most important of which was running a front organization, Prolog Research and Publishing Association, which, with offices in London, Paris, Munich, and New York, produced radio programs and published books, pamphlets, articles, and leaflets for distribution in the West and airdrop into Ukraine. He continued to maintain his contacts with Ukrainian nationalists in Europe, gather intelligence for the CIA, and distribute his propaganda materials.[17]

In 1975, Lebed's CIA contact met with the president of Prolog Research and Publishing to discuss Lebed's "proposed retirement. . . . It was pointed out that Government employees must retire at age 60, and that Headquarters believes that age 65 is appropriate for retirement in any outside activity receiving our support." Lebed would in retirement "be entitled to about $300 per month Social Security. He has a [CIA] pension totaling about $30,000 which he may take as a lump sum or as an annuity."

When, a decade later, articles appeared in the *Village Voice* and the *New York Times* accusing Lebed of war crimes, he was visited by CIA representatives who urged him not to respond or let anyone else respond to the allegations. "Our main objective," the CIA "update on Mykola Lebed's Situation" reported on April 10, 1986, "has been to avoid any legal action which could jeopardize the current Agency relationship with the [front] organization [with which Lebed had worked and now advised.]"[18]

Protected by the CIA, Mykola Lebed, whose war crimes had been exposed by Ukrainians in the United States, reported to the INS, and widely covered in American newspapers, would die, a free man, in Pittsburgh in 1998, almost four decades after he had arrived in the United States with his displaced persons visa.

23.

THE DISPLACED PERSONS
ACT OF 1950

T HE REPUBLICANS HAD TAKEN back both houses of Congress
in the midterm elections of 1946. The consensus of party professionals, press, and pundits was that they would in 1948 take
back the White House as well. But the experts, not for the first or last
time, got it wrong. Truman won the popular vote by more than two
million votes and the electoral college by 303 to 189;* the Democrats
regained the House and the Senate by sizable margins.

For the advocates of an amended Displaced Persons Act that would
increase the number of DP visas and eliminate the discriminatory provisions of the 1948 law, the most striking and positive election result
was the defeat of Chapman Revercomb of West Virginia.

"The Democrats," Drew Pearson reported in his January 30, 1949,
column, had gone

> to all sorts of trouble to defeat Chapman Revercomb as Senator
> from West Virginia, because of religious discrimination in his

---

* Strom Thurmond, running for a States' Rights Party, won 39 electoral votes.

Displaced Persons Bill. Even Governor Dewey refused to make
a speech for Revercomb in West Virginia because of the charge
that he had discriminated against Catholics and Jews. But now
it looks as if Revercomb's defeat was in vain. The new Democratic Chairman of the Judiciary Committee, Senator Pat Mc-
Carran of Nevada, is just as bad as Revercomb—possibly worse.
It is the Judiciary Committee which passes on displaced-persons
legislation, and to handle it McCarran has carefully appointed a
subcommittee guaranteed to make no important changes in the
Displaced Persons Bill. . . . It is unusual for the chairman of a
full committee to sit on a subcommittee, but McCarran is so
anxious to block liberalization of the Displaced Persons Act that
he appointed himself on the subcommittee.[1]

Pat McCarran of Nevada, the short, stocky, unsmiling seventy-two-
year-old "Silver Fox" of the Senate, had been a fierce opponent of the
New Deal and a hardened isolationist who advocated a near-total disas-
sociation of the United States from Europe and Europeans. He had
opposed the draft, Lend-Lease, aid to Britain and France, and any measure that might have increased the number of immigrants permitted to
enter the United States. He was also a dedicated anti-Communist whose
major objection to letting displaced persons into the country was that
they might be Communist sympathizers or subversives. First elected in
1932, McCarran had seniority, standing, and a working knowledge of
Senate rules and traditions that made him nearly invincible when he set
his mind for or against a piece of legislation. He was intensely proud of
the fact that he was not a compromiser. "'I never compromise with
principle,' he says, 'but almost everything is principle to me.'"[2]

NEW YORK CITY AND WASHINGTON,
JANUARY TO MARCH 1949

Buoyed by Revercomb's defeat and undeterred by McCarran's accession to Judiciary chair, the advocates for an expanded and nondiscriminatory DP bill assembled their forces for the new campaign. Catholic, Protestant, and Jewish organizations were all agreed that the December 22, 1945, cutoff date for eligibility should be pushed forward to April 1947 or later; that the number of displaced persons admitted be increased from 200,000 to 350,000 or 400,000; and that the 40 percent Baltic preference be eliminated. The Jews additionally proposed provisions for enhanced screening, the Catholics an amendment requiring that visas "be made available to each group and element of the DPs in the proportion each bears to the over-all total of Displaced Persons," and the Catholics and Lutherans a provision for the admission of large numbers of *Volksdeutsche* expellees.[3]

In a December 28, 1948, letter to Irving Engel of the AJC, Father William J. Gibbons emphasized how important the *Volksdeutsche* issue was to the Christians. "No Christian group could go along with the anti-*Volksdeutsche* amendment which apparently has the blessing of the American Jewish Congress. To us it seems based on racial discrimination, the kind of thing which so revolted decent people in the Nazi ideology. I am well aware that the majority of the Jewish community, opposed as they are to group-guilt ideas, feel the same way."[4]

Gibbons had effectively turned the tables on Engel and the Jewish organizations, cautioning that in the future the Catholic and Protestant voluntaries, churches, and their spokesmen would not hesitate to brand as discriminatory, extremist, hateful, and racist any attempt to bar *Volksdeutsche* expellees from the country.

Oswald C. J. Hoffman of the Lutheran Church–Missouri Synod, which claimed to represent 1.5 million Lutherans, in a letter to Democratic congressman Francis Walter of the House Judiciary Commit-

tee, echoed Father Gibbons's concern that "because of racial prejudice
a certain group of genuine displaced persons may be overlooked. We
refer to the people of German ethnic origin who have been rooted up
from their homes, sometimes after centuries of residence." Hoffman
urged Walter to support "the inclusion of a generous number of these
unfortunate people in the help to be extended by the American
people."[5]

The *Volksdeutsche* issue was not the only one dividing Jewish and
Catholic organizations. The Catholics proposed—and the Jewish
groups opposed—an amendment to the 1948 DP Act under which the
numbers of displaced persons admitted to the country from each DP
"group and element" would be based on their proportion in the overall
DP population.

The Catholics feared that without such an amendment, the better-
organized and -funded Jewish organizations would secure more than
their fair share of visas. The Jewish organizations opposed the "group
and element" amendment because mass immigration to Israel had lowered the percentage of Jews in the DP population, to the point that such
a provision would result in a drastically reduced number of visas available
to them. There was a matter of basic principle at play as well. Jewish
organizations opposed quotas of any sort: for entrance to schools, col-
leges, and every other institution. As Irving Engel explained in a letter
to Judge Proskauer, he and his colleagues had "already pointed out to
some of our Catholic friends [that] their promotion of this provision will
inevitably be interpreted by the Jewish community as unfriendly, particularly since it will doubtless be picked up by members of Congress who
are known to have anti-Semitic leanings." Engel asked Judge Proskauer
to "meet with Cardinal Spellman . . . for some discussion on the amended
DP Bill. . . . You would be performing another notable service if you
could work out something on this which would meet the legitimate
needs of the Catholic groups without bringing on another Catholic-
Jewish fight."[6]

Proskauer contacted Spellman and, as Engel had recommended,

requested "a few minutes of your time to discuss certain phases of the amendment to the DP Immigration Law, as to which there has developed some difference of opinion between a Catholic group and a Jewish group. . . . What I want is just an off-the-record talk to get the benefit of your always sound and fair judgment."[7]

Spellman did not meet with Proskauer, but arranged for him and his colleagues "to consult with some gentlemen who have more knowledge and experience than I have in the matter." The subsequent meetings between Jewish and Catholic leaders—Engel, Proskauer, and Will Maslow of the American Jewish Congress on one side of the table; Father Gibbons, Monsignor Swanstrom of the National Catholic Resettlement Council, and Catherine O'Brien, their legal adviser, on the other—went splendidly.[8]

The Catholics agreed not to insist upon a "group and element" clause in an amended DP bill. The Jewish leaders agreed not to oppose the entry of *Volksdeutsche* into the country, but asked that they be designated as "persons who have been deported into Germany and Austria . . . for religious, political, racial, cultural or linguistic reasons" rather than "persons of German ethnic origin." The later designation, by identifying them by blood and breeding rather than country of birth, would, the Jews argued, affirm Hitler's claims that there existed an Aryan nation which transcended national borders. The Catholics approved the Jewish request, but to no avail. Politicians from districts with large German American populations much preferred the original wording that identified the objects of their largesse as ethnic Germans.[9]

WASHINGTON, JUNE TO AUGUST 1949

In early June, the House passed an amended DP bill that authorized the admission of an additional 179,000 displaced persons and 56,623 *Volksdeutsche,* removed the preferences for DPs from annexed territories and with agricultural experience, and changed the cutoff date from December 22, 1945, to January 1, 1949.[10]

The amended House bill was delivered to the Senate Judiciary Committee, where Chairman McCarran refused to either schedule hearings on it or draft a Senate version. The Democratic leadership, concerned that McCarran's obstructionism was handing the Republicans a golden opportunity to rebrand themselves as the party of immigrants, ethnics, Catholics, and Jews, called for a closed-door meeting of the Judiciary Committee.

"Neither side," according to columnist Drew Pearson, "minced words in the closed-door meeting . . . when Senator Pat McCarran, D., Nev., refused to budge on his blockade of the House-passed bill" and insisted there was no need for an amended bill.

> "Charges that this Act is discriminatory are hokum," McCarran snapped. "I worked with Senator Revercomb on this Act when it was drafted, and I know that the charges are untrue." . . . "What will you do if the Republicans take the initiative and move to discharge this committee?" asked [West Virginia Democratic senator Matthew M.] Neely.
>
> "I'll do plenty," retorted McCarran. . . . "I will not stand for any shoving around."
>
> That ended the meeting.[11]

Senator Scott Lucas, Democrat of Illinois and now majority leader, was exhausted, enraged, and humiliated by McCarran, who, though nominally a Democrat, was doing everything he could to bottle up a bill written and supported by President Truman and a majority of Democrats in both houses. The only way to get a displaced persons bill to the Senate floor over McCarran's objection was for the Democrats to join with Republicans in support of a "discharge motion" to remove the bill from the Judiciary Committee and bring it to the floor for a vote.

Support for the motion increased by the day. On September 5, a joint appeal signed by leaders of the Federal Council of Churches of Christ in America, the Lutheran Resettlement Service, the National Catholic Resettlement Council, and the Jewish National Community Relations Council "respectfully urge[d] 'prompt adoption.'"[12]

McCarran, realizing he could no longer block the motion, found a way to delay a vote on it. On September 12, 1949, he announced on the floor of the Senate that he had decided to travel to Europe to investigate the displaced persons matter firsthand. He asked that no action on any bill be taken during his absence.[13]

Two days later, he sailed for Europe on the *Queen Mary*. From abroad, McCarran cabled his colleagues on the progress of his investigation. On October 7, 1949, he reported "that he had found fraud in the workings of the present Displaced Persons Law and said that its proposed liberalization would be a 'serious mistake.' He suggested deferring still further Senate action on the proposed bill."[14]

His intended three-week absence was extended more than once. He did not return to the United States until December 7, almost three months after he had departed.

GERMANY, JULY TO NOVEMBER 1949

In the fall of 1949, Janet Flanner of the *New Yorker* paid a visit to two of the displaced persons camps in the American zone of occupation. "The D.P.'s dwell, eat, breed, wait, and ponder their futures, living a simulacrum of life that has no connection with the world outside except through the world's callousness and charity."

To her surprise, she found that "of all those now homeless in this foreign land the Jews are the cheeriest—a situation without precedent in the Jewish people's sad, roving history. Ninety per cent of the

Jewish D.P.'s in the American Zone have signed up to go to Israel."
Their cheeriness was a result of their knowing where they were going,
if not quite when. The non-Jews, on the contrary, remained in limbo.
Those still in the camps, having turned down offers of resettlement,
had through delay lost their sense of choice in regard to what remains
of life. "Except for the Jews, whose faces are finally turned again toward Israel, the D.P's are indeed unconnected with reality. . . . They
want to go to the America of their dreams; they fear that the Argentine is too far, Morocco too hot, Canada too cold, England too harsh,
Australia too full of horned toads—which it is, according to a startled
convoy of D.P. Lithuanians who lately arrived there. And Sweden is
too close to Moscow. . . . What these D.P.s most fear is insecurity and
Russia."[15]

That insecurity was exacerbated by the fear that they would soon be
thrown out of the camps. The IRO was scheduled to cease all assistance
to refugees by June 30, 1950, the same day that the 1948 Displaced
Persons Act would expire. Barring an amended resolution keeping IRO
functioning or an amended Displaced Persons Act, the camps would be
closed.

"Never in our roughest days in the field had there been such a time
of anxiety," Kate Hulme recalled.

> In early 1950 there was no hint that there might be an exten-
> sion of the DP Act. There was only the stark fact to face that
> after nearly a year and a half of operation under the Act we had
> managed to get just about half the authorized DP's to the States
> and that we had less than six months to get the remainder across,
> if we were to fill the quota. Every one of us knew that this was
> an impossibility and that by June 30 we would have more than
> fifty thousand ready-to-go DP's left over in the camps, all cov-
> ered by assurances of jobs and housing in a land they would
> never see.[16]

The difficulties faced in getting eligible displaced persons out of Germany and into the United States had been exacerbated when, in November 1949, the DPC sharply scaled back the number of visas offered to nonagricultural workers. The commissioners had no other choice if they were going to meet the congressional mandate that 30 percent of all visas go to agricultural workers. Commissioner O'Connor notified state resettlement agencies at a conference in St. Paul that the DPC would have to cease processing nonagricultural workers "until we get the requisite number of farmers." Thousands of displaced persons who had expected to be sent across the Atlantic within days were informed they would have to wait—for how long, no one knew.[17]

Ignatz, one of the Polish displaced persons with whom Kate Hulme worked, "was caught in this trap. All set again to be called forward on his new assurance, which was for work in a Pittsburgh mill, he now had to sit back and wait until we could find enough farmers to carry not only him, but the thousands of other nonfarmer assurance-holders as well. . . . Watching the machinery of the U.S. program in early 1950 was like watching an enormous merry-go-round without music, on which all the DP's you had ever known seemed to be permanently stuck."[18]

WASHINGTON, JANUARY TO JUNE 1950

On January 3, 1950, six months before the expiration of the 1948 DP Act, the second session of the 81st Congress was convened. On February 22, 1950, "ten prominent Americans—Democrats and Republicans representing the Protestant, Catholic and Jewish faiths," publicly appealed to the United States Senate to pass a new, amended displaced persons bill before the old one expired. Included among the ten were General Lucius Clay, Mrs. Franklin D. Roosevelt, James Farley, Major General William

J. Donovan, Judge Proskauer, and several prominent businessmen. Representatives of the National Catholic Welfare Conference, the Federal Council of Churches of Christ in America, and the National Lutheran Council signed similar appeals on behalf of their agencies.[19]

Senator McCarran fought back, citing the results of his recent in-person investigations in Europe.[20] America's efforts on behalf of the displaced persons in Europe, he charged, were

> being used by the Soviet Government as a method of infiltrating into this country those who would destroy the very government which affords them the opportunity to come here and obtain shelter after they do come here. Is it any wonder that some of us are given pause when we think of this? Is it any wonder that some of us are resolved and determined that so long as we have breath in our body the law should not again be so written that under the guise of being a humanitarian movement it can be used by those who would destroy our form of government?[21]

Neither McCarran, nor Revercomb and Gossett before him, explicitly identified these subversive, communistic agents as Jewish displaced persons. Still, when names were provided of those who had fraudulently been admitted to the United States, they turned out to be Jewish names. When names were provided of officials who had assisted the entry of subversives, they too turned out to be Jewish.

John Wilson Cutler Jr., formerly an employee of the Displaced Persons Commission in Germany, accused Ben Kaplan, the executive assistant to the DPC coordinator in Frankfurt, who had previously been employed by the Joint, of having engaged in the fraudulent admission of subversive displaced persons. Displaced Persons Commissioner Harry Rosenfield, Major Abraham Hyman, and officials of the HIAS and the JDC were among those charged with having facilitated the entry of suspected Communists. Senator McCarran cited a letter from an

"American Consulate General" in Munich that listed the names of in-
dividuals who should have been denied but were given visas by the
DPC, every one of them with a recognizably Jewish name: Lea Boltuch,
Simon and Taube Haber, Daniel and Anna Brafman, Israel and Irena
Dreier, Solomon Albert, Juda and Perla Apfelbaum, Leib Taffel.[22]

Richard Arens, McCarran's chief lieutenant, never failed to make
connections between Communists and Jews and Jews and forged papers. On Friday, February 3, 1949, Arens, questioning Edward M.
Glazek, a former employee of the Displaced Persons Commission,
asked him about the "percentage of the people who have been brought
to this country . . . illegally or pursuant to fraud."

> Mr. GLAZEK. The non-Jewish might be estimated to be
> about 15 to 20 percent. The Jewish is over half.[23]

Following Glazek to the witness stand, John Wilson Cutler Jr. was
asked the same question.

> Mr. ARENS. Is there any particular element or group among
> the displaced persons which has a greater percent, proportion-
> ately, of the fraud and false documents as compared to the other
> groups?
> Mr. CUTLER. Yes. These cases I gave you referred com-
> pletely to all, I would say, over 95 percent to one group.
> Mr. ARENS. What group is that?
> Mr. CUTLER. That was the Jewish group.[24]

A large number of the Jewish DPs had indeed forged documents, but
not because, as McCarran and Arens accused them, they were part of a
Soviet conspiracy to infiltrate the United States. They forged passports
and travel and other documents because the 1948 law had made it impossible for them to get visas without these papers.

The Jewish DPs were not the only ones who resorted to forged papers and perjured testimony. Edward Glazek made it clear that former Baltic and Ukrainian SS men also presented forged documents. The Ukrainians, in fact, had their own printing presses to produce them. But fraud committed by the non-Jews was of little concern to McCarran and his supporters because they were not suspected of being subversives smuggled by the Soviets into the United States.

McCarran continued to issue dire warnings, charge conspiracy, lambaste the Displaced Persons commissioners, Harry Rosenfield in particular, and garner headlines every time he opened his mouth. But he was fighting a losing battle—and he knew it.

He managed to delay a vote for another six weeks. Finally, on June 1, 1950, a month before the 1948 DP Act was set to expire, the Senate and the House passed a new displaced persons bill. On June 16, 1950, President Truman signed it into law.

The amended Displaced Persons Act of 1950 was pockmarked with giveaways and compromises that had been necessary to push it through Congress. Among the most glaring was a provision for the issuance of up to eighteen thousand visas to "members of the armed forces of the Republic of Poland" currently residing in the "British Isles." Because the Polish soldiers had been resettled in England and Scotland, they were not technically DPs. Hence the need for a special provision to accommodate them. Primary among the reasons advanced for admitting them, even though they were no longer displaced, was that, as anti-Communists, they would stiffen the spine of Americans who, the recent world war now over, were hesitant to fight another. As Connecticut congressman John Davis Lodge pointed out in testimony before the House Judiciary Committee, "These men are anti-Communists down to the ground. There is no question about that. I am sure you understand that. I have talked to them. They certainly understand the Communist menace. They have had abundant reason to know what it is all about." Leo J. Michalowski, representing the Polish American Congress, declared,

"Their love of freedom would be a worth-while instrument for the future security of America. I think that is all I have to say."[25]

To alleviate the fears of congressmen that the amended bill might let into the country Communist sympathizers and subversives, Section 13, the security provision, was revised and extended to explicitly deny visas "to any person who is or has been a member of the Communist Party, or to any person who adheres to, advocates, or follows, or who has adhered to, advocated, or followed, the principles of any political or economic system or philosophy directed toward the destruction of free competitive enterprise and the revolutionary overthrow of representative governments, or to any person who is or has been a member of any organization which has been designated by the Attorney General of the United States as a Communist organization." Displaced persons who secured visas were required "upon arrival at the port of entry in the United States . . . to take and subscribe an oath or affirmation" that they were not and had never been members "of any organization or movement named in this section."[26]

With all its flaws, the amended DP Act of 1950 represented a triumph for the coalition of religious and ethnic groups that had lobbied for it. The new act more than doubled the number of persons to be admitted to the United States, removed the obstacles that had kept out the Jewish DPs, and extended the deadline for issuing visas to June 30, 1951.* Still, if we look closely at the numbers, we see that only half of those eligible for visas under the new act were displaced persons as defined by the IRO and the DPC. The remaining 95,000 included German expellees (54,744), Polish veterans (18,000), and Greek refugees (10,000) who had been "forcibly removed or forced to flee from their former habitual residence in Greece as a direct result of military operations in Greece by the Nazi government [or] by Communist Guerrillas."[27]

The Jewish organizations had won a victory in securing the removal

---

* On June 28, 1951, the president signed a bill extending the deadline to December 31, 1951.

of the discriminatory provisions of the 1948 Act, but it had come too late to have much of an effect. By the time the amended law took effect, on September 30, 1950, 142,000 Jewish DPs had already departed for Israel and only 35,761 Jewish displaced persons remained in the British and American zones of occupation.* The Jewish organizations' victory in getting their amended bill through Congress was, in the end, a hollow one. Fewer than 17,000 of the 56,736 Jewish DPs who immigrated to the United States under the Displaced Persons Acts were able to do so as a result of the amended law.[28]

---

* This figure is from September 1, 1950.

24.

MCCARRAN'S INTERNAL SECURITY ACT RESTRICTS THE ENTRY OF COMMUNIST SUBVERSIVES

The Ban Is Lifted on the Immigration of the Waffen–SS Veterans

GERMANY, JUNE TO NOVEMBER 1950

Eleven days after Truman signed the amended DP Act, he ordered American air and sea forces to Korea. Ground forces would soon follow.

Added pressure was now put on Army counterintelligence officers and consular officials in Germany to scrupulously enforce the tightened security requirements written into the amended displaced persons act.

"The cases of some fifty thousand documented, cleared and ready-for-visa DP's, whom we had innocently thought would flood the Resettlement Centers," Kate Hulme recalled,

> were pulled from processing and bucked back for a second check
> by Counter-Intelligence, to find out among other things if any
> of those assurance-holders advocated the overthrow of the cor-
> ner grocery store. . . . Our Polish countess from Wildflecken was
> one of the scores of people suddenly put in peril by a university

degree. She had a Ph.D. from Leningrad University listed in her seventeen yards of paper, under the heading "educational background." . . . How could any non-Russian receive one of their degrees, she was asked, if he or she were not friendly to the regime? . . . The agent, she said, kept talking about "the regime," and because she thought it would be tactless to educate an American on his history, she did not stress the fact that in 1910, when she took her degree, the czar was still the ruler of all the Russias. Her case was filed for further investigation.[1]

Jewish displaced persons who had lived in the Soviet Union or in Communist-dominated Poland were, once again, scrutinized for Communist affiliations or sympathies. Commissioner Harry Rosenfield, worried that Jewish DPs were being denied visas because of suspicions that they were Communists, forwarded to Robert Corkery, a DPC official in Europe, a copy of two CIC investigative reports and their conclusions.

Case number one concerned Pinchas Miodoweik, a Jewish Pole who had been a member of the First Polish Army and had served under Russian officers. Although Miodoweik "denied membership in or sympathy with any of the Polish organizations considered inimical to the Security of the United States," he was denied a visa because the Army investigator determined that "based on sources available to this organization at this time, it appears that subject adheres to or advocates, or followed the principles of [a] political or economic system or philosophy directed towards the destruction of free competitive enterprise and the revolutionary overthrow of representative governments."

Case number two concerned Teodor Ziubreckyj, a non-Jew who had also served in the Polish army under Russian officers but had, unlike Miodoweik, presented the investigator with what appeared to be a forged "work card." Asked about the forged document, Ziubreckyj "denied any knowledge of alterations being made on the card or that the card was falsified." He was approved for a visa.

Corkery could not, he wrote Rosenfield, "reconcile these two finds." The only possible explanation was that the Jewish veteran was denied a visa because he was a Jew—and therefore suspected of being a Communist—while the non-Jewish veteran was given a visa, though his papers had probably been forged.[2]

WASHINGTON, SEPTEMBER 1950

The Korean War provided Senator McCarran with a new opportunity, which he seized, to block the immigration of displaced persons whom he suspected might be Communist agents.

On August 10, 1950, Senator McCarran introduced in the Senate "An Act to protect the United States against certain un-American and subversive activities. . . . This Act may be cited as the 'Internal Security Act of 1950.'" "There exists a world Communist movement," the preamble to the act asserted, "which, in its origins, its development, and its present practice, is a world-wide revolutionary movement whose purpose it is to . . . establish a Communist totalitarian dictatorship in the countries throughout the world." One of the key methods by which the Communists intended to infiltrate American society and government was "by procuring naturalization for disloyal aliens who use their citizenship as a badge for admission into the fabric of our society." To safeguard the nation, it was necessary to tighten its immigration laws.

Section 22 of the Internal Security Act excluded several classes of aliens from immigrating, including those

> who seek to enter the United States whether solely, principally, or incidentally, to engage in activities which would be prejudicial to the public interest, or would endanger the welfare or safety of the United States . . . ; who are members of or affiliated with the Communist Party of the United States [or] any totalitarian

party . . . or any section, subsidiary branch, affiliate, or subdivision of any such association or party; . . . who write or publish, or cause to be written or published, or who knowingly circulate, distribute, print, or display, or knowingly cause to be circulated or distributed or printed or have in their possession written or printed matter, advocating . . . the economic, international, and government doctrines of world communism; . . . who [might after entry] engage in activities which would be prohibited by the laws of the United States relating to espionage, sabotage, public disorder, or in other activity subversive to the national security.[3]

Truman vetoed the bill, with a long section-by-section commentary that attacked it as unworkable and an assault on long-held and cherished American principles. Among the reasons he gave for his veto was that the act, as written, "would deprive us of the great assistance of many aliens in intelligence matters," including, though he did not explicitly mention it, the displaced persons who were working for the CIA and Frank Wisner's OPC.[4]

The House waited but an hour to pass McCarran's Internal Security Act over his veto; the Senate did so after a twenty-two-hour filibuster.

GERMANY, SEPTEMBER 1950

The McCarran Act played havoc with the displaced persons still in Germany. "More than 100,000 refugees," the DPC declared in its final report, "were estimated to be adversely effected."

The revised and tightened security requirements, Kate Hulme wrote in her memoirs, set off an avalanche of accusations, rumors, and denunciations. "A new indoor sport had been born among the waiting DP's—the sinister game of denunciation. There had always been a little of this, an occasional denunciation of a DP by a DP, sent to the investigating agents to pay off an old grudge cheaply or to get even for some fancied sight which, in their years of living so closely together, had built itself up from nothing to a towering injustice. Now we saw the mean blight spreading."

Untold numbers of DPs were denounced for being soft on Communism or sympathetic to the Soviets. Consular and INS officials charged with enforcing the McCarran Act were obligated by law to take every denunciation seriously. And they did.

"The passage of the Internal Security Act of September 1950," according to Hulme,

> seemed to paralyze the security agents on our side of the water, making them fearful to recommend a single alien for entry to the States unless he appeared before them shining white like an angel. Any denunciation—oral, written, signed or anonymous—was seized upon and treated like top-secret business, as if every gray filament in the web could be traced straight back to the Kremlin. Even we field people . . . were no longer trusted. Inquiry on our accumulating cases of delay received the stock answer—"Held for security reasons not to be divulged under the law." We were wrestling with ghosts when we tried to trace the writers of the anonymous denunciations.[5]

This was precisely what McCarran and the supporters of his bill had intended. Their goal was to unleash a worldwide manhunt for subversives to employ ordinary citizens as investigators, to shine a spotlight not only on members of Communist parties and affiliated groups, but also on those who might now or at some time in the future be sympathetic to their cause. The act paid scant attention to Nazis and fascists, who received one mention each in the text of the bill; "Communists" were referenced 146 times.[6]

WASHINGTON, FALL AND WINTER 1950

Advocates for the Baltic and Ukrainian displaced persons took advantage of heightened Cold War anxieties to make the case once again that former members of the Waffen-SS should be admitted to the United States. That they had fought in German uniforms and under Nazi command was immaterial. What was infinitely more important was that they had taken up arms against the Soviets during the recent world war and remained virulently anti-Communist.

There were two impediments to the issuance of visas to the Waffen-SS members: they had "borne arms against the United States," and they had belonged to "movements hostile to the United States." On each ground, they were, under current laws and regulations, prohibited from entering the United States as displaced persons.

On February 17, 1950, the leaders of the National Lutheran Council, the Latvian and Estonian relief committees, and Father Gibbons of Catholic War Relief Services met with the Displaced Persons commissioners to deliver "a joint petition . . . on behalf of Latvian and Estonian displaced persons who are former members of German military units. . . . The petition," R. E. Van Deusen of the National Lutheran Council noted, "seemed to present conclusive evidence that the Latvian and Estonian Legions were . . . engaged in fighting only against Russia and did not participate in political activities."[7]

The NLC leadership followed up with a letter to forty-one senators from every region of the nation calling on them to support a one-word change in Section 13 of the amended DP Act by adding "voluntarily" to the phrase that now read "no visas shall be issued . . . to any person who has borne arms against the United States during World War II." The addition of the adverb "voluntarily," which was incorporated into the final bill, meant that Estonian and Latvian Waffen-SS soldiers who claimed, as they all did, that they had not volunteered but been forcibly conscripted into service would now be able to apply for visas.[8]

They could still, however, be rejected because they had belonged to movements "hostile to the United States." The National Lutheran Council and the Latvian and Estonian relief committees petitioned the DPC and the State Department once again, this time to ask them to declare that the Baltic Waffen-SS divisions should not be considered such movements.

When there was no immediate response to their petition, Cordelia Cox, the director of resettlement for the National Lutheran Council, wrote Paul Empie, executive director, and C. E. Krumbholz, executive secretary, to suggest that they apply more pressure on the State Department. She questioned as well the prevailing assumption that the major obstacle to admitting the Waffen-SS men was opposition from Jewish organizations.

> It does not seem reasonable to assume that in a country where so much anti-Semitism exists a Jewish group could influence a State Department decision against the largest group of Protestants among the displaced persons. So far, we do not know from the State Department why they are excluding the Baltics, nor who is responsible for the decision. Could we not approach this thing now with an open and direct inquiry to the State Department, asking for full information on what has happened and why questions have been raised. . . . I just cannot understand how a Jewish group could carry such influence.[9]

Empie, on Cox's recommendation, set up another meeting with State Department officials at which he assured them that the National Lutheran Council "would under no circumstances advocate the entrance of any Nazi collaborators into the United States but that the Council had strong evidence that most members of the Baltic Legions had been impressed into service by the Germans. . . . Dr. Empie referred to the fact that the members of the Baltic Legions were intensely anti-Communist and stated that their participation in the war had been limited almost entirely to the Eastern Front."[10]

Secretary of State Acheson had already sought the counsel of John J. McCloy, who had succeeded General Lucius Clay as American high commissioner for occupied Germany, on the question of whether the Baltic Waffen-SS veterans should be permitted to immigrate to the United States under the terms of the Displaced Persons Act. "Dept. urgently considering questions whether Baltic DP's who were former members Baltic Legions (under GERs) or Waffen SS during yrs 1941–1944 may qualify for visas under U.S. DP Act. Specific question is whether these organizations in Baltic countries shld be considered as having been 'movements' as the term is used in Sec. 13, DP Act. . . . Info available to dept. indicates that organizations in Baltic countries . . . were exclusively military in character and purpose" and should therefore not be considered "movements" per se. McCloy's response was that, in his opinion and that of the military in Germany, the Baltic legions were not "'movements' as term is used in Section 13 of the Displaced Persons Act."[11]

On May 8, following McCloy's recommendation, the State Department formally notified consular officers in Germany that it had determined that the Baltic Waffen-SS divisions were "military organizations," not "movements," and that their members should therefore not be automatically barred from receiving DP visas. Because it was possible that some of the Waffen-SS divisions might have "contained regular German SS cadre, war criminals, traitors, and collaborators," the department recommended that from this point forward, consular officials consider each application for a visa "on its merits."[12]

The DPC, which had the final say in the matter, delayed making any determination, despite the State Department's finding. Commissioners Carusi and O'Connor were in favor of lifting the ban on the admission of former Baltic Waffen-SS members; Commissioner Harry Rosenfield was opposed. In a memorandum dated August 11, 1950, Rosenfield reminded his fellow commissioners that the International Military Tribunal at Nuremberg had determined that the "Waffen-SS was a criminal organization and that it had committed War Crimes and Crimes against Humanity."[13]

Rosenfield's brief was dismissed by his colleagues. By a vote of two to one, they voted to lift restrictions on the admission of former Waffen-SS members to the United States.[14]

There remained one more obstacle in their path. Section 22 of the McCarran Internal Security Act explicitly denied admission to aliens who had been members of Communist or totalitarian parties or "any section, subsidiary, branch, affiliate, or subdivision" of these parties. Because the Waffen-SS was an organization of the "totalitarian" Nazi Party, its members were thereby automatically barred from admission to the United States.[15]

With startling alacrity, Congress sprang into action and passed "AN ACT to clarify the immigration status of certain aliens." The new legislation specified that the terms "members of" and "affiliated with" as employed in the Internal Security Act "shall include only membership or affiliation which is or was voluntary, and shall not include membership or affiliation which is or was solely (a) when under sixteen years of age, (b) by operation of law, or (c) for purposes of obtaining employment, food rations, or other essentials of living." To make absolutely sure that this new law did not provide loopholes through which Communists might enter, the DPC, the State Department, and INS stipulated in "a joint instruction" that "membership in the Communist Party, regardless of its nature would in every case be an automatic bar" to immigration. President Truman signed the "Act to Clarify" into law on March 28, 1951.[16]

At the stroke of a pen, the members of the Baltic Waffen-SS legions and others who had collaborated with the Nazi occupation could now exempt themselves from the requirements of the Internal Security Act by claiming that they had been compelled to do so by law or to get a job, food rations, or other "essentials of living." The new law had an immediate effect not only on Estonian and Latvian Waffen-SS members, but on thousands of other potential immigrants, including Germans and *Volksdeutsche* who could now claim—and did—that their enrollment in Nazi and fascist organizations had been involuntary.

In July 1951, the DPC further eased the way into the country for suspected collaborators and war criminals when it revised its list of "inimical organizations" and "deleted 90 of the 200 organizations" originally placed on it, including the Waffen-SS in Latvia and Estonia; the "quisling government" in Estonia; the Aizsargi, a fascist paramilitary "Home Guard" organization in Latvia; the Iron Wolf, an extremist, paramilitary, pro-Nazi fascist organization in Lithuania; and dozens more.[17]

Albertas Bauras had been held in custody since the Board of Immigration Appeals had confirmed the accusation of a Jewish DP who had accused him of being a concentration camp guard. Following the DPC's determination that Waffen-SS members should no longer be barred from applying for visas, Bauras appealed his "exclusion," was paroled to the home his wife and children lived at in Bridgeport, Connecticut, and subsequently, under Private Law 702, sponsored by Connecticut congressman Albert Moreno, was granted admission to the United States, not as a displaced person—the law having expired—but under the Lithuanian quota.[18]

Boleslavs Maikovskis, the auxiliary police precinct commander in Rēzekne, who had participated in, if not led, the burning of the village of Audriņi and the shooting of villagers in the town square, had originally been denied a visa because he had admitted to being a member of the Aizsargi, the Latvian paramilitary organization, before the war. His appeal, like that of Bauras, was "favorably reconsidered on July 26, 1951, when the Civic Guard was deleted from the list of subversive organizations." Sponsored by War Relief Services of the National Catholic

Welfare Conference, with "eighteen letters of recommendations predominantly from Catholic clergy," he was admitted to the United States.[19]

The change in regulations regarding the Baltic Waffen-SS members was but one of the measures that opened wide the gates of America to suspected collaborators and war criminals. Almanza Tripp, an INS officer stationed in Germany, questioned by a congressional committee in 1978 about why so many Nazi collaborators and war criminals had been able to enter the country, put the blame directly on the laxity of DPC, IRO, and voluntary agency officers, who were "interested mostly in the quantity of the DP's—displaced persons—they would bring to the United States. . . . As a result of the desire to bring in as large a number as possible in a short period of time, I am afraid that some of those agencies cut corners a bit."[20]

Mario de Capua, who had been chief of security and investigations for the DPC, testified that every aspect of the screening process had been rushed.

> From the moment we got there, there was pressure particularly from the voluntary agencies to get these people moving. I don't think . . . that the voluntary agencies wanted to aid and abet any war criminals, but they were interested in moving people. There was pressure also from various Members of the Congress who were intervening in behalf of displaced persons at the urging of their constituents. We also were under pressure of filling ships, we had ships tied up. We had to get them to the dock within a certain period of time, at least we would try to keep the pipelines moving. . . . I think we ought to recognize that given the tumult in Europe, the wholesale destruction of documentation, records, ID's, the dislocation of millions of people, it was darned difficult for us to really get a handle on what these people may have done before. . . . I am not aware of the number of people who may have gotten in who were Nazis, but . . . I will be the first to say it was possible because of the circumstances.[21]

Algimantas Dailide, a Lithuanian, who had been a high-ranking member of the Nazi-sponsored Saugumas, or Security Police, and was responsible for the arrest of Jews attempting to escape from the Vilna Ghetto, was one of the war criminals who should have been but was not barred from entering the country as a displaced person. Dailide, claiming on his application that he had been a "forester" during the war, received his visa and entered the United States in 1950. Only in 2004 was he ordered to be deported by an American court—based on evidence that had been available when he applied for a DP visa, fifty-four years earlier. Dailide left the country of his own accord for Germany, where he lived out his life in a small town. He died, a free man, in 2015.[22]

John Demjanjuk, a Ukrainian, who had been drafted into the Red Army, taken as a prisoner of war, then released from a German POW camp and sent to Trawniki, an SS training camp, had worked as a guard at several concentration and death camps. The war over, he destroyed his papers, attempted to remove the Waffen-SS tattoo he had received at Trawniki, then, claiming he had spent the war as a farmer in Poland, sought and attained displaced persons status and protections, married, had a child, and worked as a truck driver in Germany for the U.S. Army.

Demjanjuk's first choice for resettlement had been Canada or Argentina, but after the passage of the Displaced Persons Act, which gave preference to farmers and to displaced persons from lands annexed by the Soviet Union, including Ukraine, he applied for a visa to the United States. Despite the fact that on his visa application he had listed Sobibór, the Polish hamlet that was the site of one of the most notorious of the death camps where he had served as a guard, as his place of residence from 1934 to 1943, he was given a visa when a Decatur farmer agreed to sponsor him and his family. Demjanjuk, his wife, and their child departed from Bremerhaven, arrived in New York on February 9, 1952, and settled in Cleveland, where he found employment as an autoworker.

In 1981, Demjanjuk's citizenship was revoked, and in 1983 he was extradited to Israel, where he was convicted of crimes against humanity and sentenced to be hanged. Five years later, when evidence emerged from the Soviet Union that he was not the "Ivan the Terrible" who had committed the crimes he had been charged with, Demjanjuk was reprieved and returned to the United States. In 2002, his citizenship was revoked again by a Cleveland court on charges he had worked as a guard in the death camps. In 2009, he was extradited to Germany, where he was tried for war crimes. He was found guilty, sentenced to five years in jail, then released to a nursing home because of ill health to await a decision on his appeal of the guilty verdict. He died in that nursing home in 2012 at age ninety-one.[23]

Feodor Fedorenko was, like John Demjanjuk, a Ukrainian who had been drafted into the Red Army, captured by the Germans, and then released from POW camp to be trained as a concentration camp guard at Trawniki. From Trawniki, he was assigned to Treblinka, a death camp where he worked in 1942–43. He ended the war as a warehouse guard in Hamburg. When British forces entered the city, Fedorenko took off his uniform and successfully presented himself as a civilian. He was admitted to a DP camp outside of Hamburg. In 1949, he applied for a visa to the United States, claiming on his application that he had been a farmer in Poland before being deported as a forced laborer to Germany. He received his visa and sailed for the United States in late 1949. Fedorenko was deported to the Soviet Union in December 1984. He was subsequently found guilty of treason and mass murder by a court in Crimea, sentenced to death, and executed by shooting in July 1987.[24]

Pranas Puronas, Rita Gabis's grandfather, police chief in Švenčionys, and a participant in the mass shooting of eight thousand Jews, had included "on the extensive form for the DP Commission . . . his service as chief of security police in Švenčionys." Despite his admission, he too was given a visa for America. His granddaughter, years later, trying to understand how a Lithuanian police chief who had participated in the massacre of Jews and Poles had "slipped through the cracks and became a United States citizen," speculated that at the time he was "interviewed at the DP camp, the main interest was in the Communist threat, not the Jewish dead or those who had helped kill them." Puronas would live and work in the United States, undetected by anyone save his granddaughter. He would die, a free man, at the age of ninety-three.[25]

One of the most notorious of the war criminals to gain entrance as a displaced person and hide in plain sight for decades was Viorel Trifa, a leader of the Romanian fascist Iron Guard, who in 1941, during a failed coup attempt against the Romanian dictator, Ion Antonescu, had incited a pogrom that lasted four days and resulted in the destruction of synagogues and the murder of hundreds of Jews. Trifa had spent the war years in Germany under protective custody, then after his release in 1944 made his way to Italy, where in 1948 he applied for and was granted a visa. Under the sponsorship of the Church World Service, he immigrated to the United States on July 19, 1950. A year after his arrival, the Romanian Orthodox Church in America elected Trifa as its bishop, though he had no prior training or experience and had not been ordained as a priest.*

Trifa's past membership in the Iron Guard and his antisemitic speeches, manifestos, and actions were well known to members of the Romanian American community, who denounced him almost as soon as he arrived in the United States. In August 1950, evidence that Trifa had fomented the 1941 pogrom that resulted in the murder of hundreds of Jews in Bucharest reached the Buffalo, New York, office of the INS, which contacted the Displaced Persons Commission for further information. The DPC reported back that in granting Trifa a visa, it had followed standard procedures and admitted him because he had been sponsored by a "reliable" organization.

In February 1951, Senator Homer Ferguson of Michigan asked the DPC to look further into the Trifa case. On September 9, 1951, Walter Winchell in his syndicated radio show charged that Trifa had been a fascist leader in Romania. Drew Pearson accused the bishop of war

---

* On his ordination, he would change his first name from Viorel to Valerian.

crimes. So too did Milton Friedman in a March 1952 article in *The Nation*, "The Nazis Come In."

On being elected bishop, Trifa relocated from Cleveland, his first home in America, to the Romanian American episcopate headquarters in Grass Lake, Michigan, outside Detroit, reinvented himself as a religious leader, became a governor of the National Council of Churches board, and was invited by Richard Nixon to deliver the opening prayer at the convening of the 1955 Senate session.[26]

Though the FBI, INS, and DPC had substantial evidence that he had been a leader of the Iron Guard, Valerian Trifa would remain in the United States, a free man, for the next three and a half decades.

Part Six

THE LAST ACT

25.

"THE NAZIS COME IN"

The Office of Special Investigations

THE CUMULATIVE EFFECT OF the Displaced Persons Acts, McCarran's Internal Security Act, and the "Act to Clarify" was that, from late 1948 through the early 1950s, suspected Communists were denied visas while untold numbers of antisemites, Nazi collaborators, and war criminals gained entrance to the United States.

The capture, in May 1960, of Adolf Eichmann and his subsequent trial and execution brought worldwide attention to the issue of Nazi war criminals, but because Eichmann had never been in America and had not survived the immediate postwar period by posing as a displaced person, the trial did not lead to the investigation of war criminals at large in the United States. "Eichmann's capture," as *New York Times* reporter Eric Lichtblau put it in *The Nazis Next Door*, "proved more a blip than a turning point."[1]

That was not the case in the USSR. To demonstrate to their citizens and to the world that, unlike the Americans, they were intent on bringing to justice former Nazi collaborators, including those the Americans and their allies were protecting, the Soviets, beginning in 1961 and continuing over the next four years, staged a series of show trials. The primary objective was not the conviction and punishment of war crim-inals. It was to provoke, humiliate, and call attention to the West's harboring of Nazi collaborators, to incite dissension within émigré communities, like the Romanian American one, and to issue a warning to anti-Soviet activists in the United States, the United Kingdom, Canada, and Australia that the long arm of Soviet justice was about to corral those who had collaborated with the Nazis.

Victims were rounded up and put on the stand to testify against the accused collaborators. Further testimony was taken from "accomplices" who had been released from hard labor and exile and allowed to return to their homes in the general amnesty for collaborators proclaimed in September 1955.[2]

In one of the first show trials, held in Estonia on March 11, 1961, two of the four defendants were displaced persons tried in absentia: Ain-Ervin Mere, who lived in Leicester, England, and Aleksander Laak, who lived outside Winnipeg, Canada.

Ain-Ervin Mere, the former chief of the Estonian Security Police, was charged with participating in the murder of two trainloads of Jews who had been transported from Czechoslovakia and Germany to the Jägala labor camp near Tallinn and executed at a nearby artillery range. When the Jägala camp was closed in August 1943, Mere joined the Estonian Waffen-SS legion, was imprisoned after the war in a POW camp in the British zone, released, given DP status, and, in 1947, left for Britain as part of their "Westward Ho!" program. He settled in Leicester, where he worked in a local textile factory. The Soviets requested that he be extradited to stand trial, but the British refused. He would remain in Leicester. He died, a free man, in 1969.[3]

Aleksander Laak was the commandant of the Jägala camp. After fleeing Estonia at the end of the war, he too sought and received DP status, and was resettled and naturalized in Canada. Laak denied the Soviet charges as "99 percent lies. . . . it is only Communist propaganda," then a week later hanged himself in the garage behind his home in suburban Winnipeg.[4]

In a second Estonian show trial, held in January 1962, two of the three defendants were former displaced persons who were charged in absentia with taking part in the mass murder of four thousand Jews and Roma at a "correctional labor camp" in Tartu. Ervin Viks was living in Sydney, Australia, having been resettled there by the IRO in 1950 after a stint as a "Westward Ho!" laborer in England. The Soviets requested his extradition, but the Australian attorney general refused because Australia had no formal extradition treaty with the Soviet Union and the Soviets no business intervening in Australian immigration policy. "There is the right of this nation, by receiving people into this country to enable men to turn their backs on past bitternesses and to make a new life for themselves and for their families in a happier community. . . . The time has come to close this chapter." Viks was sentenced to death for his crimes in Estonia, but remained in Australia where he died, a free man, in 1983.[5]

Karl Linnas, who succeeded Viks as commandant of the Tartu concentration camp, was charged with him. During the three years of his command, thousands of Jews and Roma had been loaded into buses, transported outside the city, beaten, and shot. In 1944, after the Tartu camp was liquidated in advance of the Red Army's arrival, Linnas served with the Estonian Waffen-SS legion until he was wounded and evacuated to a hospital in Germany.

At war's end, he sought and received displaced persons status and in 1951 applied for a visa to the United States. On his application questionnaires, he stated that he had been a student and draftsman in Estonia until May 1943, when he was conscripted into the Estonian army. This should have raised questions, as there was no Estonian army in 1943, only the German-directed Estonian Waffen-SS division. Linnas nonetheless was given a visa for entry to the United States.[6]

In October 1962, the Soviet Ministry of Foreign Affairs requested

Linnas's extradition to stand trial in Estonia, his former homeland. The State Department refused the request. Linnas was convicted in absentia and sentenced to death.[7]

The most spectacular of the Soviet war criminal show trials was held in the fall of 1965 before live television cameras on the stage of the House of Culture of Riga's "electric factory." Six former Latvian policemen from the Rēzekne district, three of them displaced persons— Haralds Puntulis, who was living in Toronto; Boleslavs Maikovskis, in Mineola, New York; and Albert Eichelis, still in Karlsruhe, Germany— were charged with the razing of the village of Audriņi and the shooting of dozens in the town square.

"Three defendants guarded by two soldiers with tommy guns solemnly sat in the prisoners dock on the stage before 800 invited guests in the audience," Steven Nordlinger of the *Baltimore Sun,* one of the foreign journalists invited to witness the trial, reported on October 12, 1965. "There were also three empty chairs in the dock. They were set aside from the absent defendants. . . . Judge Valfried Kauke complained to the courtroom that the countries involved refused to extradite the three missing defendants so they could be tried."[8]

The refusal of the Americans, the British, the Australians, the West Germans, and the Canadians to extradite the accused or investigate them played into Soviet hands, offering what they claimed was clear evidence that the Americans and their allies had forgotten the horrors of the past war, forgiven the crimes committed, and welcomed war criminals. Documentary films were produced; court records, firsthand testimony of victims and accomplices, and other evidence made available to the press; books, articles, and pamphlets written, translated into English, Swedish, and German, and widely distributed.

The campaign bore little fruit in the United States. There were a few newspaper articles, a column by Drew Pearson, scattered remarks and queries in Congress by representatives from New York and California, and some calls for government investigation. The most extensive coverage of the show trials was by Charles Allen, a freelance journalist who wrote three articles for *Jewish Currents,* a journal with a tiny circulation affiliated with and funded by the Communist Party USA (CPUSA).

In the course of his reporting, Allen contacted Karl Linnas, who had been sentenced to death in Estonia but continued to live and work as land surveyor in Greenlawn, Long Island, with his wife and three daughters. Linnas admitted that he had served as a reservist at a Nazi camp, but denied having anything to do with the killings. "They are Communist lies, rotten lies! You want to do some more Communist propaganda work, is that right? . . . I can tell from your questions that you are nothing but a paid Communist agent."[9]

Boleslavs Maikovskis, also sentenced to death in Riga, was living at 232 Grant Street in Mineola on Long Island and working as a carpenter. He admitted in a telephone interview with a *New York Times* reporter to being a Latvian, but denied everything else. The Soviet charges were "propaganda, of which 'not 1 percent is right.'"

Maikovskis remained in the United States, where he was active in Latvian anti-Communist organizations. In 1972, he was invited to serve "on a subcommittee of the Committee to Re-elect the President during Richard M. Nixon's 1972 campaign." More than a decade later, after an extensive investigation and prosecution by the Justice Department, Maikovskis in 1984 was ordered to be deported. When Switzerland, his first choice, then Germany refused to accept him, U.S. officials asked that he be deported to the USSR. In 1987, while that request was being considered, Maikovskis sought and received a West German visa. He was tried for mass murder in Germany in 1988, but after years of delay let free when the court ruled he was too frail to stand trial. He died in Münster, Germany, at age ninety-two, a free man.[10]

THE SUBJECT OF NAZI war criminals hiding in plain sight remained dormant for much of the 1960s. The State Department refused to extradite the displaced persons sought by the Soviets; the DPC had years before been dissolved; the INS showed little interest in revisiting any of the cases brought to its attention. The Nazi hunters—and a handful of newspaper reporters for Yiddish papers and the mainstream press— kept the story alive.

On February 2, 1964, Clyde A. Farnsworth of the *New York Times* published a long feature on Simon Wiesenthal, "Sleuth with 6 Million Clients." In July, Wiesenthal, after investigating the case of a particularly loathsome camp guard at Majdanek and discovering that she now lived in Queens, New York, called Farnsworth. Joseph Lelyveld, a young metro reporter, was sent to investigate.[11]

On July 14, 1964, buried deep in the *New York Times* on page 10, Lelyveld reported that Hermine Braunsteiner-Ryan, who had been convicted in Austria of infanticide, assassination, and manslaughter, was alive and well in Maspeth, Queens. After an early release from prison, she had married an American soldier, Russell Ryan, immigrated to Canada, then moved to 72nd Street in Maspeth, where Lelyveld found her. "Mrs. Ryan was doing some painting in the home she and her husband, a construction worker, recently acquired . . . when she was interviewed about the report of her wartime activities. . . . 'All I did is what guards do in camps now,' she said in heavily accented English. . . . 'I was punished enough. . . . And now they want something again from me.'"[12]

In 1971, seven years after Lelyveld's article appeared, Braunsteiner was stripped of her citizenship and ordered deported. The order of deportation was executed in August 1973. Another eight years would pass before, in mid-1981, she was sentenced by a West German court to life in prison. She was released for health reasons in 1996 and died in 1999, at age seventy-nine.[13]

The Lelyveld article prompted the INS to open an investigation "into the circumstances" of Braunsteiner's entry into the United States, but it did not lead to further news stories or government investigations. In 1973, Congresswoman Elizabeth Holtzman, who had defeated Emanuel Celler in a primary election and been named a member of the Judiciary Committee and the Subcommittee on Immigration, Citizenship, and International Law, was contacted by "a mid-level official with the Immigration and Naturalization Service [who] made a confidential appointment to see me."* Holtzman's visitor, courteous, mild-mannered, forthcoming, told the congresswoman that INS had a list of fifty-three Nazi war criminals but was doing nothing to investigate or bring them to justice. "You have to do something," he told her. Holtzman listened politely, but was incredulous. These so-called Nazi war criminals had been in the country for a quarter century and, aside from the Ryan case, this was the first she had heard of them.[14]

The list of Nazi war criminals that Holtzman's informant had referred to had most likely been compiled by Otto Karbach of the World Jewish Congress, who had for years been keeping track of accounts of war atrocities that had appeared in Yiddish-language newspapers. Karbach had given his list to Anthony DeVito, the chief investigator in the INS deportation case against Braunsteiner. DeVito had passed the list on to his superiors, but kept a copy for himself.[15]

Simon Wiesenthal also had a list of Nazi war criminals in the United States. One of the names on his list, he told *New York Times* reporter Ralph Blumenthal in late 1972, was Bishop Trifa, who had entered the United States as a displaced person in 1951 and whom Walter Winchell, Drew Pearson, and others had accused of being a former Iron Guard leader two decades earlier. Blumenthal was intrigued, got the go-ahead from his editors, and began his research in the YIVO Institute for Jewish Research in New York City, where a YIVO associate translated articles from Romanian newspapers that contained incendiary antisemitic speeches made by Trifa, as well as a photograph of him in an Iron Guard uniform.

Blumenthal traveled to Michigan, showed up at Trifa's residence without advance notice, and asked if he had been a member of the fascist Iron Guard. Trifa denied it. Blumenthal then showed him the photograph and Trifa replied that he had indeed worn an Iron Guard

* We do not know her visitor's name.

uniform, but had never been a member. Blumenthal asked about the antisemitic speech that had provoked the Bucharest pogrom. Trifa denied having made it; then, after Blumenthal showed him articles from Romanian newspapers that described him giving the speech, confessed that he had made it, but hadn't written it. "It was given to me to deliver."[16]

On December 26, 1973, one of the slowest news days of the year, Blumenthal's article on Trifa appeared on the front page of the *New York Times*. Four days later, he reported, again on the front page, that the INS had assigned investigators to "a new countrywide effort to resolve the long-dormant cases of suspected Nazi war criminals living in the United States." Thirty-eight different people, most of whom had entered the country as displaced persons, were under investigation. The names had all come from the list Oscar Karbach had given Anthony DeVito.

Sol Marks, district director, had, as part of the INS investigation, Blumenthal reported, "asked the Soviet Union for depositions by five eye-witnesses . . . [to] wartime atrocities in the Western Ukraine." Prior to this, no American government would have dared ask for Soviet cooperation in investigating war criminals, but with "détente" in bloom after visits by President Nixon to Moscow and Secretary-General Leonid Brezhnev to Washington and the signing of the Paris Peace Accords ending U.S. military involvement in Vietnam, the climate was right to reach out across the Iron Curtain.[17]

On April 3, 1974, Congresswoman Holtzman, during a regularly scheduled INS oversight hearing, pursuing the tip she had received, which had now been confirmed by Blumenthal, asked Commissioner Leonard Chapman about allegations that the INS had a list of Nazi war criminals currently in the United States. "The *Times* mentioned there were 38 persons whose names have been submitted to the Immigration Service. Can you tell me whether any of these 38 persons have been deported since this article appeared last December?" Holtzman was stunned when the commissioner did not deny that INS had such a list, but declared that no one on it had been deported, there were no plans to commence deportation hearings, and no witnesses had been interviewed.[18]

Holtzman subsequently held a press conference and charged that the "appalling laxness and superficiality" of INS investigations had turned the United States into a "haven for . . . Nazi war criminals over the last 25 years." Among the alleged war criminals whom INS had not satisfactorily investigated were "Boleslavs Maikovskis, who is under a Latvian death sentence for an alleged role in wartime exterminations . . . and Bishop Valerian D. Trifa of the Rumanian Orthodox Episcopate of America, outside Detroit, former student leader of fascist Rumania."[19]

Two weeks later, the INS released the names of the thirty-seven persons who were under investigation. Included among them were Karl Linnas, Boleslavs Maikovskis, and Bishop Trifa.

Questioned at a second oversight hearing as to why INS had not completed its investigations, Commissioner Chapman answered that it could not proceed further without documentation and eyewitness testimony from the Soviet Union. Because INS was not authorized to contact foreign governments on its own, it had requested that the State Department do so, but there had as yet been no response.[20]

Congressman Joshua Eilberg, chairman of the Subcommittee on Immigration, Citizenship and International Law, wrote Secretary of State Henry Kissinger to register his "deep concern" that the State Department had not yet assisted the INS in "obtaining statements abroad from eye witnesses to reported atrocities."[21] There was no substantive response from Secretary Kissinger and the State Department.

Members of a Judiciary subcommittee visiting the Soviet Union in the spring of 1975 to discuss the immigration of Soviet Jews asked Soviet officials directly if they were prepared to assist the American government in compiling evidence against alleged war criminals. The officials responded that they would be happy to cooperate in the matter.[22]

And still there was no forward movement. In August 1975, Congresswoman Holtzman accused the State Department of "'continuing failure' to get in touch with officials in the Soviet Union and Eastern European nations for information" on suspected war criminals. The State Department's actions were "'plainly dilatory' and 'utterly incomprehensible.'"[23]

Another fourteen months passed, until, on October 3, 1976, Ralph Blumenthal reported that the State Department had contacted Soviet officials and that INS investigators had been dispatched to Israel to interview eyewitnesses and gather documentary evidence. The question that had to be asked—and Blumenthal asked it in a subsequent article—was, "Why has it taken until now, 31 years after the end of World War II, to step up or resolve the investigations? Many of the names were first provided to the Immigration Service more than a decade ago by Jewish groups and other war crimes archivists."[24]

On January 13, 1977, Congressman Eilberg, looking for answers to the question Blumenthal had asked, requested that the General Accounting Office (GAO) undertake a formal investigation into whether "INS personnel [had] deliberately obstructed active prosecution of alleged Nazi war criminal cases or engaged in a conspiracy to withhold or quash any information in its possession."[25]

The GAO submitted its report in May 1978. While it had found no evidence of "widespread conspiracy," it could not "absolutely rule out the possibility of undetected, isolated instances of deliberate obstruction of investigations of some alleged Nazi war criminals." The GAO had reviewed forty of the fifty-seven cases of suspected war criminals brought to INS's attention before 1973 and discovered that only twenty of these had been investigated, that "inquiries were made with overseas sources" in only nine cases, that only five of these inquiries "appeared to be thorough," and that three of the nine had been closed "because the Department of State had precluded INS from obtaining information from communist countries," and without such information, no evidence of guilt could be obtained.

The GAO discovered as well that the CIA had been in contact with twenty-two of the suspected war criminals. "The CIA stated its contacts with these individuals came at a time when there was an acute shortage of intelligence on Soviet intentions and developments in Eastern Europe in general. . . . The individuals concerned were all strongly anti-Communist and their willingness to cooperate and their knowledgeability were the definitive factors leading to their use by CIA."[26]

IN AUGUST 1977, in response to congressional pressure and the mounting crescendo of revelations in the press, the Justice Department created a special unit within INS to investigate charges that Nazi collaborators and war criminals had entered the United States under the cover of the Displaced Persons Acts. When after a year and a half the special unit had failed to accomplish much of anything, Justice, in 1979, responding to a demand from Congresswoman Elizabeth Holtzman, now chair of the Subcommittee on Immigration, Citizenship, and International Law, transferred the unit, newly renamed the Office of Special Investigations (OSI), to the Criminal Division.[27]

With dramatically enhanced funding from Congress, the Office of Special Investigations hired lawyers and prosecutors, researchers, historians, and support staff to review and substantiate documents that had been collected and archived more than three decades earlier but never consulted. Alan Ryan, OSI deputy, then director, from 1980 to 1983, secured an agreement with the Soviet Union that permitted American historians and lawyers to view and videotape depositions from Soviet witnesses.[28]

OSI staff traveled to Germany, Eastern Europe, and Israel, where they examined "concentration camp rosters, transfer orders, incident reports, personnel records, and similar documentation, often written in German or in East European languages, and collected data on individuals mentioned in each document," OSI historian Peter Black later recalled. "We understood, as historians what kinds of documentation bore what weight of reliability. We'd gather documentation on the institutions that were relevant to the charges in the complaint. We'd gather information on the individual, but we'd also gather information on the comrades of the individuals."[29]

One of the first cases OSI took up was that of Karl Linnas of Greenlawn, Long Island, the Estonian camp commandant admitted to the United States as a displaced person in 1951 and naturalized in 1960. OSI brought action to revoke Linnas's "naturalization on the grounds that it had been 'illegally procured' and 'procured by concealment of a material fact or by willful misrepresentation.'" Historian Raul Hilberg, testifying before the U.S. District Court for the Eastern District of New York, introduced into evidence documents about the Tartu camp and the participation of Estonians, under the direction of Germans, in the murder of Jews. Videotaped testimony from eyewitnesses was presented. The defense attorney, Ivars Berzins, who was active in the Latvian American community and had defended other alleged Nazi offenders, dismissed the evidence because, having originated in the Soviet Union, it "was all prima facie unreliable." The courts found otherwise. Linnas's citizenship was revoked on June 30, 1981. He appealed, but the ruling was upheld. In 1983 he was ordered deported to Estonia, his country of birth. Linnas appealed to the U.S. Court of Appeals for the Second Circuit, which on May 8, 1986, affirmed the deportation order.[30]

The criticism of OSI's pursuit of and use of evidence from the Soviet Union was widespread and well organized. Jay Matthews of the *Washington Post* reported on March 23, 1985:

A coalition of American ethnic organizations, alarmed by the Justice Department's hunt for war criminals among Eastern European emigrants, today launched a protest against use of Soviet-collected evidence. . . . Current and former department officials said the 10-group alliance, which claims potentially strong support in Congress and the backing of 35 million Americans of Eastern European descent, could cripple the recently revived effort to find former Nazis and Nazi collaborators in the United States. . . . Moscow "has infiltrated the American justice system to get even with former refugees, defectors and 'anti-Soviet' activists," Anthony B. Mazelka, vice president of the Los Angeles–based Baltic American Freedom League, said in an interview.[31]

It was not only Baltic anti-Communist activists who protested against the Linnas deportation order. William F. Buckley and Patrick Buchanan, President Reagan's communications director, joined the campaign. Buckley took to the "letters to the editor" page of the *New York Daily News* to lambaste Soviet justice and American obeisance to it. "The entire episode is judicially revolting. How is it possible to try someone on the basis of Soviet testimony—which was written before the trial was actually conducted? Even if someone had films showing Linnas as a guard at a concentration camp in the early '40s, what is the appropriate penalty in 1986?"[32]

Buchanan and Buckley were joined by former attorney general Ramsay Clark, who also defended Linnas, in part, he declared, because he opposed "the idea of regenerating hatreds and pursuits 40 years after the fact." Clark also questioned the Soviet 1962 show trial proceedings that had generated much of the evidence against Linnas. Amnesty International opposed deportation because it opposed the death penalty.[33]

OSI investigators, historians, and attorneys fought back, insisting that the evidence gathered from the Soviet Union was authentic. The documents were originals, the signatures on them authenticated by the FBI. The eyewitness testimony showed no signs of having been coerced or being unreliable. "Not once in 40 years has anyone proved a case of Soviet forgery or perjury by a Soviet-supplied witness," Eli Rosenbaum, a former OSI prosecutor, but at the time World Jewish Congress general counsel, declared.[34]

Some commentators, including Buchanan, demanded that Linnas be tried in the United States, which was not possible as his crimes had been committed outside the country. After Menachem Rosensaft, the child of survivors and an attorney, wrote an op-ed for the *New*

York Times, "Deport Karl Linnas to the Soviet Union," criticizing him, Buchanan responded by attacking Rosensaft and other "revenge-obsessed Nazi hunters" for slandering "their fellow Americans simply because we do not wish to collaborate with a brutalitarian and anti-Semitic regime." The Reagan State Department, much as it hated to deport anyone, even a convicted war criminal, to the Soviet Union, had in the end no choice but to recommend this course. The State Department had tried to find another country willing to take Linnas, but failed. Panama had volunteered, but backed down after protests organized and led by Congresswoman Holtzman.[35]

On April 20, 1987, Linnas, handcuffed, in a brown fedora and suit and tie, was put on a plane to Prague. "'Tell the American people what they are doing is murder and kidnaping,' he yelled. . . . As Linnas' plane was taxiing down the runway, Chief Justice William H. Rehnquist rejected a last-minute bid from Linnas' daughter for a temporary stay." In Prague, Linnas was transferred to a Soviet Aeroflot jet. He landed in Tallinn, Estonia, where he was imprisoned. While awaiting a decision on the appeal of his 1962 show trial death sentence, Linnas took ill and was transferred to a Leningrad hospital, where he died in July 1987.[36]

OSI also pursued denaturalization proceedings against Bishop Trifa, who voluntarily surrendered his certificate of naturalization two months before he was ordered to appear in court. When OSI filed deportation papers against him, Trifa "appealed the voluntary surrender of his certificate." A deportation hearing was scheduled for October 1982.

At the hearing, Trifa admitted that he had been a leader of the Iron Guard and that he had lied to get a visa under the DP Act. He volunteered to leave the United States within sixty days after arrangements were made for another country to accept him. Two years later, he left his home in Grass Lake, Michigan, for Portugal.

"I am a man who happened to get put in a moment of history when some people wanted to make a point," he declared in an interview just before he departed. "The point was to revive the Holocaust. But all this talk by the Jews about the Holocaust is going to backfire." Trifa died in

*Karl Linnas is escorted to the plane that will return
him to Estonia in April 1987, after thirty-six
years in the United States.*

a Portuguese hospital after a heart attack in 1987. He was seventy-two
years of age and a free man.[37]

The OSI investigations focused the attention of print and broadcast
outlets and government agencies on the Nazi war criminals who had
entered the country decades earlier as displaced persons. On May 16,
1982, a *60 Minutes* segment, "The Nazi Connection," reported on the
claims of John Loftus, a former OSI staff member, that the State
Department, the CIA, and the Displaced Persons Commission had
clandestinely smuggled Nazi collaborators and war criminals into the
United States and organized secret armies of refugees and DPs to fight
Communism behind the Iron Curtain. The charges were incendiary
and the evidence soft to nonexistent, but they had the ring of truth.

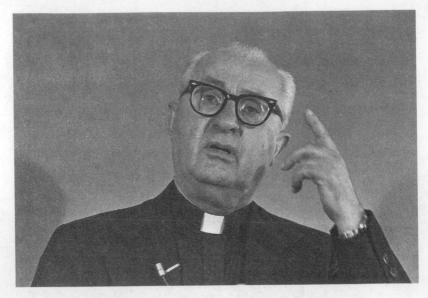

Viorel Trifa speaks at a conference in Detroit, the day after he was ordered to be deported from the United States.

The GAO in 1985 launched another investigation and found "some evidence that intelligence agencies aided Nazis and Axis collaborators to immigrate on an individual basis." According to one former intelligence officer, the utilization of "members of East European Fascist organizations . . . was a matter of weighing their present value versus their past history. . . . If a person was a war criminal, the decision of whether or not to use him depended on what he could do for you."[38]

THE OSI PROSECUTIONS and GAO reports, the findings of print and broadcast journalists, the ongoing campaigns of the Simon Wiesenthal Center, now in Los Angeles, and affiliated "Nazi hunters" in the United States, Europe, Canada, Australia, and Israel had a direct effect on activists, journalists, and politicians outside the United States who inquired of their own governments whether Nazi collaborators and war criminals had been admitted as displaced persons after the Second World War.

In February 1985, in response to the accusation by a representative of the Wiesenthal Center that Joseph Mengele, the so-called Angel of Death from Auschwitz-Birkenau, was in Canada (he was not),* the Canadian minister of justice announced the creation of a special, independent Commission of Inquiry on War Criminals to determine whether Nazi war criminals were resident in Canada, and if so, how they had obtained entry and what action should be taken to bring them to justice.

After a series of contentious hearings and press battles between representatives of the Jewish and Ukrainian communities, the commission, led by Jules Deschênes of the Superior Court of Quebec, concluded that while there were not as many war criminals in Canada as Simon Wiesenthal had charged, there were some, and to bring them to justice, amendments should be made to Canada's Criminal Code and the Extradition Act to make it easier to deport them. In a rather backhanded exculpation of government policy, the commission concluded that though there had been no investigation of war crimes "for a third of a century" after the end of the war, "Canadian policy on war crimes . . . was not worse than that of several Western countries which displayed an equal lack of interest."[39]

Almost simultaneously with the Canadian inquiry, the Australian acting special minister of state, in June 1986, directed Andrew Menzies, a retired deputy secretary in the Attorney General's office, to conduct a "Review of Material Relating to the Entry of Suspected War Criminals into Australia." The inquiry had been prompted by a series of programs broadcast by Australia's national radio and television networks, which had charged "that substantial numbers of Nazi war criminals [had been] allowed to enter Australia." The inquiry, completed on November 28, 1986, concluded that there was sufficient evidence that war criminals had entered Australia and were still living there to warrant further investigation.[40]

---

* Wiesenthal had for years raised false alarms about Mengele. Mengele was not and had never been in Canada.

In Great Britain, in response to charges from the Simon Wiesenthal Center that significant numbers of Nazi war criminals were living in the country, an unofficial All-Party Parliamentary War Crimes Group was organized in November 1986 "to consider the available evidence." Newspapers published by Robert Maxwell, whose Jewish relatives had been murdered by the Nazis, ran several reports on the subject. A 1987 television documentary produced in Scotland but screened nationally focused additional attention.[41]

The pressure was such that on February 8, 1988, the British home secretary announced the appointment of an official government "War Crimes Inquiry." In July 1989, the *Report of the War Crimes Inquiry* was presented to Parliament by the secretary of state for the Home Department. One of its principal conclusions was that "some" of the two hundred thousand displaced persons who entered Britain after the world war had not only "fought for the Germans against the Russians, mostly in what were nominally SS units," but had previous to joining the German military "been members of auxiliary units which were responsible for mass killings of Jews, partisans and whole villages of peasants, as well as other categories of people the Germans disliked. There is no doubt that the screening methods employed were ineffective at identifying such people."

The commission recommended that "some action should be taken in respect of alleged war criminals who are now British citizens or resident in this country where the evidence is sufficient to justify such action" and that "adequate resources should be made available in England and Scotland to the respective investigating and prosecuting authorities and to the courts to allow war crimes to be fully investigated and, where appropriate, prosecutions to take place."[42]

While every one of these inquiries—in Canada, Australia, and the UK—recommended that government agencies pursue further investigations of suspected collaborators, none of these investigations resulted in more than a handful of prosecutions, punishments, or deportations.

Nearly a half century after the war crimes had been committed and forty years since the DPs had been allowed to resettle, it was difficult, if not impossible, to assembly the necessary evidence to convict those who were still alive and could be located.

In Canada, three criminal prosecutions were undertaken, with no convictions. By 2017, eight Canadian citizens found guilty of war crimes and/or making false statements to enter the country had been denaturalized. Two of them had voluntarily left the country, but not a "single person stripped of his Canadian citizenship had been successfully deported."[43]

In the UK, the War Crimes Inquiry examined a total of 301 allegations, but found only "two cases in which we consider that there is already evidence sufficient to give a realistic prospect of conviction and one further case where sufficient evidence exists but the subject of the allegation is in ill-health."[44]

In Australia, the Special Investigations Unit, organized in response to the initial inquiry, was shut down in 1992, after five years of operation, with three cases referred to the courts and none successfully prosecuted.[45]

Only in the United States did the hunt for Nazi war criminals continue, with some success. By 2018, OSI had "taken law enforcement action" on 137 persons, the majority of whom had entered the country as displaced persons, and won cases against 108 of them. Eighty-six had been denaturalized and 68 "removed, extradited, or otherwise expelled/departed."[46]

The last displaced person to be tried, convicted, and deported was Jakiw Palij, a Ukrainian who had served as a guard in several concentration camps. Palij had applied for a visa in 1949 and been screened by a Displaced Persons Commission case analyst who accepted his contention, corroborated by a witness who had served with him in the SS, that he had spent the war years in Ukraine as a joiner from 1940 to 1942, on his father's farm from 1942 to 1944, and during the final year of the war at a factory in Germany.[47]

The truth, which was developed by OSI historians from masses of documentary evidence, and later confessed to by Palij, was that he had been recruited by the SS and the German police in early 1943 and sent to Trawniki training camp, where, while being trained for future SS assignments, he served as a guard at the attached labor camp. In late 1944, he had joined the SS Battalion Streibel, where his assignment was to guard the forced laborers. When in the final weeks of the war the battalion disbanded, he made his way into Germany. In July 1949, having falsified his DPC application and erased any reference to his SS service, Palij entered the United States as a displaced person. In early 1957, he became a U.S. citizen and with his wife bought a house in Queens, New York.[48]

In 1990, OSI opened its investigation into Palij, after being tipped off by Canadian officials who were investigating a man who claimed he had worked alongside him. In 2002, OSI began denaturalization proceedings. In 2003, the U.S. District Court for the Eastern District of New York, having found that Jakiw Palij had made material misrepresentations on his application for a visa to immigrate to the United States, revoked his citizenship. A year later he was ordered deported, but, as had been the case with more than a dozen other Nazi collaborators, he was permitted to remain in the United States when no country was willing to accept him. It would take another fourteen years and extraordinary pressure from the White House before German officials agreed to his extradition.[49]

On Monday, August 20, 2018, nearly seventy years after he had lied his way into the United States, INS officials removed Palij from his Jackson Heights home, placed him on a stretcher, drove him to the airport, and put him on a government air ambulance to Düsseldorf, Germany. When German investigators determined that there was not enough evidence to bring charges against him, Palij was placed in a retirement facility in Ahlen, where on January 9, 2019, he died, a free man. He was ninety-five years old.[50]

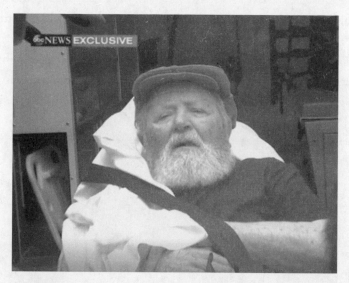

Jakiw Palij, a former Nazi camp guard who illegally immigrated to America after the war, is deported to Germany in August 2018.

At the press call on the morning after Palij had been deported, Eli Rosenbaum, an OSI attorney from 1980 to 1984 and thereafter OSI deputy director, then director, expressed satisfaction that Palij had finally been brought to justice. "Palij's removal cannot, of course, undo the devastation and the tragedy he helped make possible," Rosenbaum admitted. Still, he hoped that the deportation might serve "as a warning to the would-be perpetrators of future human rights crimes that the civilized world will never cease pursuing them."[51]

The legacy of OSI and the war criminal investigations pursued in the United States, Canada, Australia, and Great Britain is found not in the convictions obtained or the collaborators and war criminals deported and punished, but in the contribution made to the recovery of a history that had been lost. The material assembled, scrutinized, and synthesized by historians, researchers, government investigators, and lawyers reached the public in a variety of ways. Headlines were made, journalists prompted to undertake their own inquiries, and an historical record constructed that revealed how postwar governments had protected some war criminals and allowed others to hide in plain sight.

It was thirty to fifty years too late to right the wrongs of the past, but it was not too late to set the record straight. Justice might not have been served, but history was.

THE GATES OPEN WIDE

T HE DISPLACED PERSONS COMMISSION had gotten off to a slow start, but by the end of 1951, when the amended DP Act of 1950 expired, some 328,851 displaced persons had been re-settled in the United States: 77,454, according to IRO figures, from Estonia, Latvia, and Lithuania, almost all of them Lutherans or Catholics; 110,566 from Poland, with another 45,044 identified as Ukrainian.* Though neither the IRO nor the DPC compiled figures on Jewish immigration, the United Service for New Americans, which did, estimated that they totaled just under 57,000 of the almost 330,000 who entered the country with DP visas.[1]

Proponents of legislation to permit the Last Million to immigrate to the United States had argued that once America opened its doors, other nations would as well. And that was precisely what occurred. The in-crease in worldwide resettlements after the June 1948 passage of the first Displaced Persons Act was extraordinary. Just over 61,000 DPs had been resettled outside Europe prior to June 1948. More than

---

* The DPC figures, which combine Poles and Ukrainians, vary slightly (U.S. Displaced Persons Commission, *Memo to America: The DP Story* [Washington, DC: Government Printing Office, 1958], 376).

560,000 would be resettled in the next two years. By December 31, 1951, the Last Million (or to be exact, the last 1,038,759) had been removed from the camps: 328,851 to the United States, 182,000 to Australia, 150,000 to western and northern European nations, 132,000 to Israel, 123,000 to Canada, almost 100,000 to South America, Central America, and the Caribbean.[2]

For the overwhelming majority of displaced persons who were not guilty of war crimes, who had neither collaborated with nor aided the Nazis in murdering Jews or suspected partisans, but who had rejected repatriation for other reasons, resettlement was a blessing, but a mixed one. It meant leaving countrymen behind and entering foreign lands where few understood your language, knew your recent history, or could locate your birthplace on a map of the world. It meant taking on a job you were probably unprepared for. It meant giving up the dream of return to a "liberated" Estonia, Latvia, Lithuania, or Ukraine; to an independent Poland not dominated by the Soviets; to a Yugoslavia not ruled by Tito. It meant putting thousands of miles and an ocean between you and your loved ones.

For the younger children from Estonia, Latvia, Lithuania, and Ukraine who had arrived with their extended families in the last year of the war, and for the Polish Jews who had arrived in 1946, the displaced persons camp was the only home they had known or remembered. Leaving it was at one and the same time exciting, frightening, and disheartening.

It was not easy for the Last Million to start over again, but they had to and they did. They packed their belongings, said their goodbyes, boarded trains or trucks to Bremerhaven, and set sail for Boston, New York, and New Orleans, for Haifa, Halifax, Melbourne, Sydney, and Fremantle. On arrival, they were greeted by relatives or by government officials or volunteers from immigrant relief societies, taken to transit camps or hostels, hotels, and boardinghouses, then put on trains to their new homes. The men found jobs; most of the women kept house, put food on the table, and raised the children. The young went off to school and, as their parents watched with equal measures of awe and dismay, left Eastern Europe behind and became something else entirely: hyphenated Americans, Australians, Canadians.

The Jewish DPs who had suffered the most during the war had the easiest time leaving Germany, the land of their murderers, and arriving in America, where sponsoring organizations and family members had the resources available to assist them until they were on their feet.

Both the Displaced Persons Commission and the Jewish resettlement agencies tried to settle as many Jewish DPs as possible outside New York City, in accordance with the dictates of the DP legislation, but met with enormous resistance from the displaced persons, more than 60 percent of whom remained where they had landed. Others initially placed elsewhere eventually made their way back to New York.[3]

Though newspaper and magazine stories and promotional pamphlets distributed by the immigrant relief organizations were almost uniformly positive about the ease with which the DPs adjusted to their new lives in America, that was seldom the case. The executive director of the United Service for New Americans, in his annual report for 1952, described with rare honesty the difficulties the newly arrived Jewish displaced persons encountered. "Some have been slow to learn English; some have been ill from malnutrition or other deprivations over the years; most are tired from their years of hiding, of living in camps, of frustrations at every turn, of waiting for the cherished visa; some have been idle too long before arriving here or have mistaken ideas of what skills they may have retained. And some are just old and infirm."[4]

Still, they made their way. They were, as a group, defined by their resiliency, their refusal to surrender. If one path forward was closed, they would find another.

Joe Berger's mother had been against coming to America from the beginning but had been overruled, she told her son decades later.

> I wanted to go to Israel. It had just declared its independence. . . . I wanted my children to grow up in a Jewish

country. . . . But Daddy's friend Moshe Granas advised him not to go there. "In Israel the new immigrants sleep in tents," he said. "There is not enough milk for the children. There are no jobs for tailors like myself." Daddy listened to him, and I was too scared about Israel to argue. I was afraid there would be another war with the Arabs. . . . Daddy had an uncle in New York City. Before the war he had sent over money for his oldest sister's dowry. Maybe we would have a little something to start our lives in America. I was tired of struggle. Israel would be more struggle.

Soon after their arrival in New York, Marcus went looking for his uncle Morris in Brooklyn, only to discover that he had died three years earlier.

After several months, Joe's mother located a vacant apartment on 102nd Street on the West Side of Manhattan. A week later, a neighbor found a job for Marcus in Newark in a factory that manufactured asbestos cloth for ironing board covers. It was not what Marcus had had in mind, but he took it. He would work there for the next twenty-five years.[5]

Henry Goteiner, after traveling from Germany to Łódź to look for family members, had returned to Germany, married, and had a child in the camps. He and his half brother wanted to immigrate to the United States, where they had relatives who could sponsor them, but they didn't know their addresses. Henry's half brother wrote a letter to *The Forward*, asking for assistance. A relatively short time afterward, he received word from an uncle in Paterson, New Jersey, who offered to sponsor him, his wife, and their six-month-old daughter. They arrived at Boston Harbor in March 1949 and boarded the train to Penn Station, where they were met by Henry's uncle and aunt, who escorted them to Paterson. They would soon move to the Lower East Side, where Henry found work as a butcher. He had, he explained at the union office, made bologna in Europe and was sure he could learn to do the same in America, though he didn't yet speak English.[6]

Seventy years after he had arrived in the United States, tears came to Itsik Lachman's eyes when he recalled the kindness of his American cousins who had sponsored him, his wife, and his child. His entire Polish family, including his parents, three brothers, and three sisters, had been murdered by the Nazis. When he told an American rabbi in the Feldafing DP camp that he had cousins in America, the rabbi contacted the cousins, who, joyous to find that someone in the family had survived, wrote back at once. "They took us with both hands," and found work for Itsik, who was a skilled carpenter and locksmith.[7]

Once settled in America, the survivors were advised to forget their pasts and start life anew. But even the most successful, the most prosperous, the most outwardly content could not obliterate memories of the war years. The camp survivors had spoken out in the immediate aftermath of liberation, but when no one listened, they had decided that the best way forward was to keep their suffering to themselves. That was what happened in their new homes as well. They learned rapidly that no one wanted to hear about the loss of their loved ones, about their lives in Auschwitz or Mauthausen or Dachau or Bergen-Belsen or in hiding, about their years in limbo in Landsberg or Feldafing or Föhrenwald waiting to immigrate to Israel or for the gates of America to be opened to them.

Polish Jews who had spent the war in the Soviet Union were reluctant to speak of their pasts for fear that they would be labeled Communist sympathizers or worse. They kept their stories to themselves or shared them with family or other survivors. Because they believed they owed it to the dead to keep their memories alive, they did so, but among one another, rarely with those who had not experienced what they had. Some survivors could not speak at all of what they had endured. In the Lachman family, Itsik would answer his sons' questions about the war and the camps, but his wife, Lola, whose twin sister had died of typhus at Dachau, only wept.[8]

LIKE THE JEWISH displaced persons, the Poles, who comprised 37 percent of the total DP population, were assisted in resettlement by an active Polish American community, led in this endeavor by Polish American women who raised money, sponsored or sought sponsors for the DPs, arranged for someone to meet them on their arrival and send them on their way by train.[9]

The majority of Polish displaced persons were sponsored by Polish Americans in urban centers like Chicago, but large numbers were resettled in rural areas. Polish American farmers working with the Polish American Congress arranged for the "resettlement of 735 young, single Polish men, mostly former members of the Polish Guards [who had performed security and police work for the Americans in Germany], on farms in Long Island." Other large-scale agricultural projects were organized in Texas, Connecticut, Nebraska, Florida, and Montana. The most fortunate of the Polish displaced persons were those who were resettled by Poles, with other Poles. Many, regrettably, were taken advantage of by sponsors who looked at them as a cheap, pliant source of labor.[10]

But there were others who thrived in their new homes. Tadeusz Piotrowski's Polish family had been sponsored by the John Thompson family in Kentucky. "After receiving our clearance and our papers, we were all greeted by Catholic Relief Services volunteers, who poured us cups of steaming coffee, stuffed us with doughnuts, and gave us two dollars each." They were then placed on a train with a one-way ticket to Owensboro, Kentucky, and the Thompson farm. Arriving, they were taken to a five-room wooden cabin, without plumbing or heating, but with a garden outside. "The homestead was rather rustic, but what did it matter to us? It was, after all, our very own, and we made the most of it. . . . For as long as it lasted, life was good to us down on the farm."

Tadeusz's father and two older brothers worked the land "from sunrise to sunset for two dollars and fifty cents a day." His mother tended the house and garden. And Tadeusz went off to school.[11]

The displaced persons from Estonia, Latvia, and Lithuania were comparatively disadvantaged by the relatively small size, disorganization, and lack of resources in the ethnic communities that welcomed them to the United States. Still, they too found their way in America.

Mirdza Labrencis, from Latvia, with her husband, Janis, and their baby, had been placed on a large farm in Hopeton, Oklahoma, where they were given their own small house, and where her husband could make "use of his carpentry and mechanical skills." They arrived with debts, but once they had paid them off, moved to Oklahoma City. With assistance from the Lutheran Resettlement Service, Janis found a job in a steel plant and Mirdza as a janitor of sorts at a women's club. "We stayed in Oklahoma City until the summer of 1952. Janis had received a letter . . . from a cousin who had settled in New England [where] there was a growing Latvian community. . . . With a new car, we headed northeast across America looking for a modern piece of Latvia."[12]

Andrejs Eglitis had been sponsored by the Sterling Steel & Wire Co. of Sterling, Illinois, two hours west of Chicago. He would eventually secure for himself a Department of Defense security clearance and a position with NASA in Huntsville, Alabama, where he met another refugee who had served the German military, Wernher von Braun, whom the American military had secreted out of Germany as part of Operation Paperclip in early 1946. "Several times Wernher von Braun came to see our laboratory and shook hands with us. This was very exciting to me, as I consider him one of the greatest minds of our time." The two, we can assume, did not discuss their wartime work for the Nazis.[13]

The younger the displaced persons, like Mirdza Labrencis and her husband, Janis, and Andrejs Eglitis, the better their chances of adjusting to their new worlds, learning English, and getting jobs that made use of the skills they had acquired in the old one. The middle-aged and

elderly had more difficulty with the new language and with transition-
ing to their new lives.

Petras Stakė, who was in his forties when he arrived, had been a
legal professional in Lithuania. He and his family were sponsored and
welcomed by Lithuanians and the Lithuanian community in Bingham-
ton, New York. The only work Petras could find "in the beginning," his
daughter recalled in an oral interview, was "carrying coal into people's
houses. Then, he got a job at Johnson Shoe Factory doing piecework."
After a few years, the family moved to Chicago, where her father got "a
better-paying job at a screw factory, until he lost two fingers of his right
hand."

Juozas Bertulis, who was in his fifties when he emigrated, had been
a composer and educator in Lithuania, but in Los Angeles, he and his
wife worked in the flight kitchens of United Airlines.[14]

The displaced persons who had the most difficult time finding their
way in America were the minority families who were resettled in the
South and put to work as sharecroppers, tenant farmers, and field hands
by sponsors who hoped that they might prove a suitably compliant, diligent, low-paid substitute for the black families who had worked the
land for decades, if not generations.

In Flannery O'Connor's 1954 short story "The Displaced Person,"
the Guizacs, a Polish family of four, remarkably like the one that arrived on the O'Connor family farm in Milledgeville, Georgia, are escorted onto the McIntyre land by the local priest. Mrs. Shortley, the
white foreman's wife, and the Negro workers, including the elderly
Astor, look on as the newcomers appear.

> The old man, Astor, raised himself. . . . "Who they now?"
>   "They come from over the water," Mrs. Shortley said with a
> wave of her arm. "They're what is called Displaced Persons."
>   "Displaced Persons," he said. "Well now. I declare. What do
> that mean?"

"It means they ain't where they were born at and there's no-where for them to go—like if you was run out of here and wouldn't nobody have you." . . .

"They ain't where they belong to be at," she said. "They belong to be back over yonder where everything is still like they been used to. . . . But yawl better look out now," she said and nodded her head. "There's about ten million billion just like them and I know what Mrs. McIntyre said. . . . I heard her say, 'This is going to put the Fear of the Lord into those shiftless niggers!'" . . .

She was having an inner vision. . . . She was seeing the ten million billion of them pushing their way into new places over here and herself, a giant angel with wings as wide as a house, telling the Negroes that they would have to find another place.[15]

To meet the demand of southern landowners for white sharecroppers and tenant farmers, the IRO and the DPC routed ships directly to New Orleans. The DPs were offloaded and large numbers of them were transported to local sugarcane plantations. The *New York Times* in a May 4, 1949, story reported that the Catholic priest Carl Schutten, of New Orleans, who had made a visit to the new arrivals, had found that "150 displaced persons resettled on Louisiana sugar cane plantations were so ill-paid their babies are crying for food and milk." They were living and working, Father Schutten remarked, in "semi-servitude."[16]

The *Times* followed up with a report, this time from a Lithuanian clergyman, the Reverend Joseph B. Koncius, that more than 600 of the 844 Lithuanian and Latvian displaced persons who had arrived in New Orleans on the Army transport *General Omar Bundy* had been put to work as sharecroppers. "'I drove over here from Alabama, where I talked to a priest who was familiar with the displaced persons situation in his state,' Father Koncius said. 'He told me that he would almost rather see these people die in their camps in Europe than to have them come to America as sharecroppers.'"

When Father Koncius questioned S. L. Davenport, the vice president of the Delta and Pine Land Company of Scott, Mississippi, which had sponsored 144 of the displaced persons, Davenport informed him that in the preceding year his company had employed 603 Negro families under the same conditions. "At the end of the year, after the cotton was sold and their accounts to us paid, we paid those families $537,000." The *New York Times* commented that this came to "an average of about $890 per family." Using the Consumer Price Index as a basis for comparison, $890 in 1949 would be worth $9,150 in 2017.[17]

Conditions in the South were so intolerable that in April 1949, Cordelia Cox, director of resettlement for the Lutheran National Council, felt obligated to contact Displaced Persons Commissioner Harry Rosenfield with

> some unverified information concerning the Mississippi situation. . . . Among the things we have heard which have caused us concern is that [one of the farmers who had sponsored the Latvian DPs was] charging a fee of $30.00 to neighborhood employers for securing other displaced families as employees. . . . It also seems that the conditions of the share-crop contracts under which the group of Latvians are operating may be difficult. . . . As in all share-crop arrangements we understand the cash settlement will be made when the crops are marketed. . . . This, I believe, is the usual share-crop arrangement. However, under such an arrangement it may be quite difficult for these people to establish themselves.[18]

No one denied the allegations, which were investigated and confirmed by the Displaced Persons Commission, the Mississippi Displaced Persons Commission, the U.S. Department of Agriculture, the U.S. Employment Service, and the Catholic and Lutheran Resettlement Councils. The Baltic DPs, mostly Latvians, and some Poles, were indeed working under onerous sharecropper contracts. But because, as DPC chairman

Ugo Carusi wrote the head of Latvian Relief, who had protested conditions in Mississippi, those conditions were standard for the region, the "Commission feels that no action need be taken under the circumstances."

When the DPC refused to act because, according to the law, it could not, the National Catholic Resettlement Council, which had sponsored the Louisiana DPs, transferred 150 families elsewhere and rerouted future displaced persons bound for the state to other locations. Sharecropping might have been acceptable for African American families, but not for white Eastern European displaced persons.[19]

Fortunately for the displaced persons, they were not required to remain with their sponsors. Many left as soon as they had accumulated enough money. So many displaced persons, in fact, left their sponsors that the state commissions and some of the voluntary organizations warned that a near epidemic of "job hopping" endangered the future of the program.

"The major movements," the DPC affirmed in its final report, "were out of the South and into the North Central regions." By December 1950, the 30 percent of the DP population that had been "sponsored" for farm work had fallen to less than 6 percent still working in agriculture; the percentage of craftsmen, foremen, and "semiskilled" workers had increased from 14 percent to nearly 40 percent; the percentage of professionals had nearly doubled; "proprietors and managers" had more than doubled. As the American economy expanded through the 1950s, so too would the opportunities for the displaced persons and their children, especially those who had mastered English.[20]

THE MAJOR UNIFYING force among the non-Jewish displaced persons in America, wherever they settled, was a visceral anti-Communism and an abiding anger at the Roosevelt/Truman Democratic Party for allowing the Soviet Union to take hold of their nations. The displaced persons who had refused to return to homelands annexed or dominated by the Soviet Union carried their anti-Communism with them to their new homes. It remained an essential element in their self-definition, a second skin that they proudly wore and called attention to. Inese Kaufman remembers to this day how much her Latvian father "hated the Communists."[21]

"Uncompromising anti-communism," Ieva Zake has written of the Latvian displaced persons in America, "served . . . as an expression of their loyalty to the host country, as a way to oppose the Soviet Union, as an instrument for maintaining connections to their lost homelands, and as a set of ideas that could unify the émigré community." The same was true of the Poles. "The Polish displaced persons and other European refugees," according to Anna Jaroszyńska-Kirchmann, "saw themselves—and were seen by others—as a symbol of the anticommunist opposition and as leaders in the struggle for freedom."[22]

In the United States, anti-Communists in both political parties facilitated the displaced persons' political assimilation by actively and enthusiastically courting their support. The newcomers responded by opposing accommodation and peaceful coexistence and calling for liberation. They published, in their own languages and in English, pamphlets, books, broadsides, newspaper opinion pieces, and magazine articles about Communist treachery and barbarism. They joined the CIA-sponsored and -funded National Committee for a Free Europe and the Assembly of Captive European Nations. They celebrated Captive Nations Week and played an indispensable role in the formation and operation of Radio Free Europe. They protested against what they believed to be the false distinctions too many Americans held between Nazism and Communism—both, they insisted, were brutal, murderous ideologies. They pushed the unions to which they belonged toward adopting a straightforward, almost militant anti-Communist position. And they lobbied and voted for those who saw the world through the same anti-Communist lens that they did.[23]

The Polish vote, which had been solidly Democratic, came into play for the first time in decades. The displaced persons were not solely responsible for this shift, though their voices and votes gravitated in the direction of the Republicans, who, recognizing the political utility of blaming Roosevelt and Yalta for the loss of Poland and Eastern Europe to the Communists, organized an Ethnic Origins Division and a Foreign Language Group Activities Unit. In 1952, more than half of Polish American voters, including untold numbers of newly naturalized DPs, voted for Eisenhower.[24]

The Democratic Party quickly realized that to hold on to the so-called ethnic vote it had once owned, it too had to parade its anti-Communist sympathies. John F. Kennedy repeated the ethnic anti-Communist arguments so effectively that he was awarded a special citation from the Council of Latvian Organizations of Boston. The Democratic Party platform in 1960, on which he ran for office, included a plank that could have been written by the Eastern European ethnic organizations. "We look forward to the day when the men and women of Albania, Bulgaria, Czechoslovakia, East Germany, Estonia, Hungary, Latvia, Lithuania, Poland, Rumania, and the other captive nations will stand again in freedom and justice. We will hasten, by every honorable and responsible means, the arrival of the day. We shall never accept any deal or arrangement which acquiesces in the present subjugation of these peoples."

Kennedy won the Eastern European ethnic vote in 1960.

In 1964, Latvian exiles supported Barry Goldwater because he was more vocal and less restrained in his anti-Communism than his opponent, Lyndon Johnson. Eastern European immigrants, Polish Americans in particular, would vote for both Nixon in 1968 and Reagan in 1980. They would have done so for Ford in 1976 had he not made the mistake of "denying that Poland was under Communist domination."[25]

AFTERMATHS

AS THE LAST MILLION departed Germany, the camps they had inhabited since liberation were largely emptied. Left behind were the elderly, the lame, the incurably ill and invalid.

"To be old and unwanted is a sad enough fate in one's own country," Margaret McNeill recalled. "Against the background of an unfriendly foreign country, the plight of the aged D.P.'s was heartrending. . . . No country seemed prepared to give asylum to the aged and helpless D.P.'s who were now conveniently termed in official jargon the 'hard core'—a singularly inept phrase to apply to shaky old women, patients wilting away with T.B., and haggard armless or legless youths."[1]

Among the "hard-core" DPs were fifty-four thousand non-Jewish Poles who, according to Gertrude Samuels of the *New York Times*, were in 1956 "living under the same primitive conditions" she had observed ten years earlier in the UNRRA DP camps. The camps she visited were populated with "old people, invalided prisoners of war, post-tuberculosis cases, and survivors of the concentration camps, and slave labor gangs." They survived on stipends from the West German government, assistance from private voluntary organizations, and whatever employment they could find. In the years to come, some would emigrate; many more would be imperfectly integrated into the bottom rungs of the German economy and society.[2]

A minority of the "hard-core" left behind in Germany were Jews. The Joint, with funding from the United Jewish Appeal and in cooperation with the Jewish Agency, had organized MALBEN, a Hebrew acronym for "Institutions for the Care of Handicapped Immigrants," which had managed to remove most of the infirm, elderly, and invalid from Germany to Israeli hospitals, TB sanitaria, rehabilitation centers, old age homes, and a Village for the Blind.[3]

By June 1950, there remained in the Jewish camps in Germany a few thousand displaced persons, including the so-called returnees, some of them war veterans who had returned to Germany from Israel in the hope that they might get visas under the Displaced Persons Act to emigrate to the United States. Because, under IRO rules, having been resettled once, they were no longer eligible for assistance in Germany, the JDC was saddled with the responsibility of resettling them.[4]

The returnees and those who voluntarily remained behind proved something of an embarrassment to the Jewish agencies. The World Jewish Congress called on the remaining Jews to leave Germany, and virtually disowned those who refused to. "If Jews in small or larger groups choose to continue to live among the people who are responsible for the slaughter of six millions of our brothers, that is their affair. The World Jewish Congress is no longer concerned with these Jews."[5]

As the Jewish displaced persons left Germany, most of them for Israel, the IRO closed their camps one after the other. In September 1950, Bergen-Belsen in the British zone was closed; in October, the Landsberg camp was shut down; in May 1951, Feldafing was closed and its 1,585 residents transferred to Föhrenwald. On December 1, 1951, when responsibility for administering Föhrenwald was officially transferred from the IRO to West German authorities, only 3,100 residents remained in the camp.[6]

"Some 400 were chest clinic cases. Many were chronically ill, some

were blind or amputated or physically handicapped," Charles Jordan, a
JDC correspondent, reported from Germany. "They constituted themselves a small, independent community—as somebody once said, a Jewish 'shtetl'—where life became routinized, where a roof, food, clothing
and other necessities of life were guaranteed them, where they felt secure
in their own group, however abnormal that group was when measured
against the usual criteria of normal people in an accepted society."

The JDC, with the help of national and local Jewish organizations,
succeeded in removing large numbers of them to the United States,
Brazil, Argentina, Canada, Uruguay, and Australia. Sweden accepted
54 TB cases, Norway 104. In 1955, anticipating that the last Jewish
DPs would soon be removed, German authorities sold the Föhrenwald
land and buildings to the local archdiocese and the Catholic Settlement
Works, which planned to renovate the camp and house *Volksdeutsche*
expellees where the Jewish DPs had once lived.[7]

The 891 Jews who remained at Föhrenwald rejected all offers of resettlement, some because they had German relatives or lovers. The
West Germans found or built apartments for them and the majority
moved out, many reluctantly. Three hundred Orthodox Jews, however,
refused to leave until the West German authorities provided them with
a block of apartments "in central Munich, within walking distance of a
synagogue, a mikvah, religious schools, and other religious institutions."
West German, Bavarian, and JDC officials tried to meet their demands,
but were reluctant to give the Orthodox all that they asked for, fearful
that doing so would result in the establishment of a state-sanctioned
Jewish ghetto. The United Nations High Commissioner for Refugees,
which had been created when the IRO was dissolved, was enlisted to
broker an agreement. Finally, in the spring of 1956, the Ministry of the
Interior came up with a plan acceptable to the Orthodox leadership.[8]

The last of the Last Million departed Föhrenwald, eleven and a
half years after it had been designated as a camp for Jewish displaced
persons. "When Alter Haimowitz moved out of Camp Föhrenwald on
February 28, 1957," Charles Jordan reported from Germany, "he had

completed 17 years of living in camps, but for this he received no diploma. There were only speeches. Officials of the German Government, the American Joint Distribution Committee and the United HIAS Service were on hand to witness and commemorate the closing of the last Jewish Camp in Germany. An era, Alter was told, had come to an end."[9]

THE LAST MILLION could not escape the past, but neither could they permit themselves to be buried in it. Inese Kaufman's father, who had worked for and with the Germans in a hospital in Latvia before escaping with the Wehrmacht in the last year of the war, had on arriving in the United States retrained and found work as a doctor with the U.S. Army. He and his wife raised their children and lived a good, middle-class life in upstate New York, but, as their daughter remembered, never ceased mourning what they had lost and would never regain. "Their hearts were broken."[10] And, still, they pushed on from a broken past into an unknowable future.

Itsik Lachman had lost his family and countless friends and comrades in the Warsaw Ghetto and in Majdanek, Birkenau, Buchenwald, and Dachau. At war's end, he was transported by train from Dachau to Feldafing. "I wasn't so happy because I found out nobody alive." But he felt safe for the first time, was treated well by the American soldiers and the JDC, and remembered his elation when General Eisenhower visited the camp.

A day after his arrival at Feldafing, Lachman was, to his delight, put to work constructing room dividers in a women's dormitory. There he saw a young girl, Lola, whom he had first glimpsed years before at a lake near his hometown of Grodzisk Mazowiecki, Poland, which she was visiting with her girlfriends. Itsik and Lola were married at Feldafing, had a child, then two more in Brooklyn, where they resettled under the sponsorship of his cousins. Now, ninety-eight years old, sitting beside his wife of seventy-three years, who, her leg amputated, was in a wheelchair and unable to communicate after a stroke, Itsik alternately tearful and smiling, told his visitor, "Couldn't be a better life—a good wife, everything good."[11]

IN EVERY NEW HOME where the formerly displaced were resettled, there were secrets, silences, stories that could not be told. "The language and stories of my childhood were always referencing hidden places," Inara Verzemnieks, the daughter, granddaughter, and great-granddaughter of Latvian displaced persons, recalled in her memoir. Joe Berger did not know until he was twenty-one years of age that he had been born in the Soviet Union, not in Poland.[12]

In some homes, the secrets withheld were of war crimes committed, secrets that, revealed, would lead to denaturalization, deportation, imprisonment, execution. In others, they were of suffering, of injuries, and pain so intense it could not be spoken. As Elie Wiesel remarked at a gathering of the children of the Jewish survivors, "a tortured person remains tortured. . . . There are wounds that don't heal."[13]

The children of the Last Million were burdened with their own guilt and shame. Try as they might to fit in, they too were different. Their parents and the displaced adults they grew up with spoke broken English and were overprotective, haunted by fears, possessed by singular hatreds, and comfortable, it appeared, only with fellow survivors. A Latvian daughter could not understand her father's antisemitism; a Canadian Ukrainian son viewed his parents' generation as "'too political,' too fragmented against itself, too out of touch with North American realities, too right-wing."[14]

The Last Million had carried with them to their new worlds their wounds, their fears, their hatreds, their pasts, and their hopes for a different future. The non-Jewish Eastern Europeans were admonished to do all they could to remember their parents' homelands, the Nazi and Soviet invasions, the tyrannical rule of the Soviet usurpers. They were pledged to carry on their parents' cause, to dedicate themselves to restoring an independent Latvia, Estonia, Lithuania, Ukraine, and Poland freed of Soviet domination.

The burden placed on the children of the Jewish DPs was greater still. They took on the responsibility of reconstituting a Jewish nation, of protecting Israel, and of keeping alive their parents' memories, which encompassed not only displacement, but incomparable suffering, violence, and the murder of the six million.

The Last Million and their children could not escape history, nor will they let the rest of us do so. They stand as living testimony to the inescapable truth that the dislocations and displacements of the war in Europe did not magically end with the cessation of hostilities, but bled into the postwar period and the Cold War that followed. We cannot understand the madness of that war or any war without considering its aftereffects, its aftermaths, how the past haunts the present.

We must take heed of the stories of the Last Million, the stories they told and the stories they withheld; their lived experiences, visions, heartaches, losses, and loves; their uneasy dialogue with the world outside their camps; their struggle to be more than pawns in the global conflict that followed directly on the world war. We must write their history and, having done so, recognize that it is our history as well.

Acknowledgments

Historians do not recreate or represent the past, but construct it through the stories we tell. While we are the authors—and responsible—for our stories, they do not belong to us, but to the once-living souls who left behind records of their daily lives, with one eye on the future and the hope that someone, somewhere would care enough to remember them. From the ghettos and the concentration camps, on the death marches, in the displaced persons camps, and in the homes in which they were resettled, they wrote of and recalled the worst—and the best—of times and left a record for us to transcribe and make sense of. I am grateful not only to those who contributed their stories but to those who collected and preserved them: at the USC Shoah Foundation in Los Angeles; the Immigrant History Research Center in Minneapolis; the Imperial War Museum in London; the Balzekas Museum of Lithuanian Culture in Chicago; the Museum of the Occupation of Latvia in Riga; Yad Vashem in Jerusalem; the Center for Jewish History in New York City; and the United States Holocaust Memorial Museum in Washington, D.C.

Among those who made special efforts on my behalf and whom I want to single out for thanks are the staff of the National Archives of the United States, College Park, Maryland, and the National Archives of the United Kingdom, Kew, Richmond; the Manuscript Division of the Library of Congress; the Center for Jewish History; Elizabeth Anthony, Ron Coleman, and Judith Cohen at the United States Holocaust

Memorial Museum; Misha Mitsel at the Joint Distribution Committee archives; Michael Swanson at the Elwyn B. Robinson Department of Special Collections, Chester Fritz Library, University of North Dakota; Deborah Basham at the West Virginia Division of Culture and History; Matthew Schaefer at the Herbert Hoover Presidential Library; David Clark at the Harry S. Truman Presidential Library; Joel Thoreson at the Evangelical Lutheran Church Archives; Shane MacDonald at the Catholic University of America Archives; Joe Weber and Steve Collins at the American Jewish Archives; Ostap Kim at the Shevchenko Scientific Society; Mary Baumann at the United States Senate Historical Office; Desiree Guillermo at the American Jewish Committee; Melinda Wallington at the Department of Rare Books, Special Collections, and Preservation, River Campus Libraries, University of Rochester; John Balow, Librarian for Business, Economics, and Politics at the York Public Library; Matthew Baker at the Burke Library, Special Collections, Union Theological Seminary; Jamie L. Hoehn at the Migration and Social Services Collections, Immigration History Research Center Archives, Elmer L. Andersen Library, University of Minnesota; Stephen Klein and the interlibrary loan staff at the Mina Rees Library at the CUNY Graduate Center.

Joshua Freeman, Thomas Kessner, and Steve Brier, my colleagues at the Graduate Center, and Joseph Berger, Ralph Blumenthal, and Menachem Rosensaft read an earlier draft and provided me with valuable suggestions and commentary. My thanks also to Benjamin C. Hett, Steven P. Remy, and Dagmar Herzog at the Graduate Center and Atina Grossman, Robert Edelman, and Stephen Kotkin for answering my many questions about German, Jewish, and Soviet history.

Interviews with Ralph Blumenthal, Alan Ryan, Elizabeth Holtzman, Rita Gabis, and Eli Rosenbaum provided a new and added perspective on the search for and prosecution of collaborators and war criminals.

Thank you to the displaced persons and their children who took the time to speak to me: Menachem Rosensaft; Samuel Norich; Joseph

Berger; Rita Gabis; Inese Kaufman; Herbert Lachman and his parents, Itsik and Lola; and Sharone and Anna Ornstein.

My travels to and in Eastern Europe were arranged by Daniel Gurevich of Jerulita Travel in Vilnius, Lithuania. William Žitkauskas guided me, with patience and a good deal of historical knowledge, through Lithuania and Latvia. I profited from conversations with Viktorija Juse of the World Jewish Congress in Vilnius.

My students at the CUNY Graduate Center assisted me in numerous tasks including fact- and reference-checking and translations from Yiddish, Russian, Hebrew, Italian, and German. Thank you to Yuliya Barycheuskaya, Arinn Amer, Davide Giuseppe Colasanto, Alex Galling, Ky Woltering, Adam Kocurek, Sarah Litvin, Israel Ben-Porat, Esther Adair, Stephanie Makowski, Maayan Brodsky, Carli Snyder, and Miranda Brethour.

It has been my great good fortune to be represented by Andrew Wylie, published by Penguin Press, and edited by Ann Godoff. I am grateful to Andrew for his help in shaping the project and his careful reading and commentary on the final draft. Ann remains the consummate editor: generous, enthusiastic, scrupulously honest, and accessible. Thank you also to Will Heyward for his editorial advice, to Casey Denis for steering the manuscript into book form, to Juliana Kiyan for publicity, and to Danielle Plafsky for marketing. Jeffrey L. Ward did a remarkable job on the maps.

My sons, Daniel and Peter, my daughter-in-law Layla Moughari, and my dear friends Annie and Victor Navasky have cheered me on every step of this long trip. As always I find myself at a loss of words when it comes to thanking my wife, Dinitia Smith. With good grace and good humor, she has listened to me for hours on end as I laid out my research agenda and my endlessly evolving interpretive questions and conclusions. No one could have been more supportive or a better or tougher reader and editor. I do not exaggerate when I say that this book could not have been conceived or written without her as my partner.

Abbreviations

Libraries, Archival Collections, and Online Depositories

ACHRC   American Catholic History Research Center and University Archives, Catholic University of America, Washington, D.C.

ACJ   American Council for Judaism, CJH

AELCA   Archives of the Evangelical Lutheran Church of America, Elk Grove Village, Illinois

AJA   Jacob Rader Marcus Center of the American Jewish Archives, Hebrew Union College, Cincinnati, Ohio

AJC   American Jewish Committee Archive, CJH; American Jewish Committee Records, CJH

AJC ONLINE   American Jewish Committee Archives, New York, New York

AUDRA   American University, Digital Research Archive

BEVIN   Papers of Ernest Bevin, NAUK

CABINET   Cabinet Papers, NAUK

CATHOLIC CHARITIES   Catholic Charities, USA Archives, ACHRC

CCDP   Citizens Committee on Displaced Persons Collection, IHRC and USHMM

CELLER   Emanuel Celler Papers, LC

CJH   Center for Jewish History, New York, New York

CO   Colonial Office Records, NAUK

CONNALLY   Tom Connally Papers, LC

CU   Columbia University Library, Rare Book and Manuscript Library, New York, New York

CWS   Church World Service, UTS

DDEPL   Dwight D. Eisenhower Presidential Library, Abilene, Kansas

DEWEY   Thomas E. Dewey Papers, River Campus Library, University of Rochester

DORR   Goldthwaite Higginson Dorr Oral History, 1962, CU

DPC   Displaced Persons Commission, NACP

ELSEY   George M. Elsey Papers, HSTPL

ESTONIANS   Displaced Persons from Estonia Records, IHCR

FDRPL   Franklin D. Roosevelt Presidential Library, Hyde Park, New York

FIAERR   Freedom of Information Act Electronic Reading Room

FO   Foreign Office and Foreign and Commonwealth Office Records, NAUK

FRANKFURTER   Felix Frankfurter Papers, LC

GCMF   George C. Marshall Foundation Digital Archive, Lexington, Virginia

GRIFFITHS   Bishop James Griffiths Papers, Archdiocese of New York Archives,
    Yonkers, New York

HARRISON   Earl G. Harrison Papers, USHMM

HASELKORN   Rabbi Abraham Haselkorn World War II Collection, CJH

HEATH   Private Papers of Mr. and Mrs. H. Heath, IWM

HEYMONT   Irving Heymont Papers, USHMM

HHPL   Herbert Hoover Presidential Library, West Branch, Iowa

HSTPL   Harry S. Truman Presidential Library, Independence, Missouri

HUTLER   Albert A. Hutler Papers, CJH

IHRC   Immigration History Research Center, University of Minnesota, St. Paul,
    Minnesota

ITS   International Tracking Service, ITS Digital Archive, USHMM

IWM   Imperial War Museum, London

JACKSON   Robert G. A. Jackson Papers, CU

JAREMKO   Christina Jaremko Papers, IHRC

JC-USARMY   Jewish Chaplains in the U.S. Army, Oral History Division, Avraham
    Harman Institute of Contemporary Jewry, Hebrew University

JDC   Joint Distribution Committee Archives, AJA, CJH, and online

KAULS   Kauls Family Papers, IHCR

KLAUSNER   Abraham Klausner Papers, CJH

LC   Manuscript Division, Library of Congress, Washington, D.C.

LEHMAN   Herbert H. Lehman Papers, CU

MORGENTHAU   Diaries of Henry Morgenthau, Jr., FDRPL

NACP   National Archives, College Park, Maryland

NAUK   National Archives, United Kingdom, Kew, Richmond

NCJW   National Council of Jewish Women, LC

NJWB   National Jewish Welfare Board Military Chaplaincy Records, CJH

NLC   National Lutheran Council Papers, AELCA

NTP   Nuremberg Trials Project, Harvard Law School Library, Cambridge, Massachusetts

O'BOYLE   Memoir of Patrick Cardinal O'Boyle, Archbishop of Washington, Archives of the Archdiocese of Washington, Washington, D.C.

PAC   Polish American Congress Archives, Piłsudski

PIŁSUDSKI   Józef Piłsudski Institute of America, New York, New York

PREM   Prime Minister's Office Files, NAUK

REVERCOMB   Chapman Revercomb Collection, West Virginia State Archives, Charleston, West Virginia

ROSENFIELD   Harry N. Rosenfield Papers, HSTPL

ROSENWALD   Lessing J. Rosenwald Papers, LC

SCHWARTZ   Leo Schwartz Papers, YIVO

SPELLMAN   Francis Cardinal Spellman Collection, Archdiocese of New York Archives, Yonkers, New York

TAFT, CHARLES   Charles Taft Papers, LC

TAFT, ROBERT   Robert A. Taft Papers, LC

TUCK   William Hallam Tuck Papers, HHPL

UNRRA   United Nations Archives, New York, New York

USCCB   United States Conference of Catholic Bishops, ACHRC

USHMM   United States Holocaust Memorial Museum, Washington, D.C.

UTS   Union Theological Seminary, New York, New York

UUARC   United Ukrainian American Relief Committee, IHRC

VHA   Visual History Archives, USC Shoah Foundation, Los Angeles, California

WC   Wilson Center, Digital Archive, Washington, D.C.

WJC   World Jewish Congress Papers, AJA

WRB   War Refugee Board, FDRPL

YIVO   YIVO Institute for Jewish Research, New York, New York

YVA   Yad Vashem Archives, Jerusalem, Israel

Organizations

AJC   American Jewish Committee

CIC   Counter-Intelligence Corps, United States Army

CCDP   Citizens Committee on Displaced Persons

CJHC   Central Jewish Historical Commission
(Lublin and Łódź, Poland)

CROWCAS   Central Registry of War Criminals and Security Suspects

DPC   Displaced Persons Commission

EUCOM   United States European Command

HIAS   Hebrew Sheltering and Immigrant Aid Society

IDF   Israel Defense Forces

IGCR   Intergovernmental Committee on Refugees

INS   Immigration and Nationalization Service

IRO   International Refugee Organization

JDC   Joint Distribution Committee

NCFE   National Committee for a Free Europe

NCRAC   National Community Relations Advisory Council

NCRC   National Catholic Resettlement Council

NCWS   National Catholic Welfare Conference

NLC   National Lutheran Council

OMGUS   Office of Military Government, United States

ONS   Overseas News Service

OPC   Office of Policy Coordination

OSI   Office of Special Investigations

OSS   Office of Strategic Services

OUN   Organization of Ukrainian Nationalists

OUN-B   OUN faction, loyal to Stepan Bandera

P&A   (Army) Personnel and Administration

P&O   (Army) Plans and Operations

PCIRO   Preparatory Commission of the International Refugee Organization

RCMP   Royal Canadian Mounted Police

SANACC   State–Army–Navy–Air Force Coordinating Committee

SHAEF   Supreme Headquarters Allied Expeditionary Force

SNWCC   State-War-Navy Coordinating Committee

UN   United Nations

UNHCR   United Nations High Commissioner for Refugees

UNRRA   United Nations Relief and Rehabilitation Administration

UNRWA   United Nations Relief and Work Agency for Palestine Refugees

UNSCOP   United Nations Special Committee on Palestine

UNWCC   United Nations War Criminal Commission (London)

UPA   Ukrainian Insurgent Army

USFA   United States Forces, Austria

USFET   United States Forces European Theater

USNA   United Service for New Americans

WRB   War Refugee Board

WRS   War Relief Services

Newspapers and Periodicals

CDT   *Chicago Daily Tribune*

CR   *Congressional Record*

FRUS   *Foreign Relations of the United States*

LAT   *Los Angeles Times*

NYP   *New York Post*

NYT   *New York Times*

WP   *Washington Post*

Individuals and Titles

AGWAR   Adjutant General, War Department

BERCOMB   Commander in Chief in Berlin

DDE   Dwight D. Eisenhower

ER   Eleanor Roosevelt

FDR   Franklin Delano Roosevelt

HICOG   United States High Commissioner for Germany

HST   Harry S. Truman

WARCOS   War Department Chief of Staff

Notes

Introduction: The War's "Living Wreckage"

1. John MacCormac, "Wandering Hordes," *NYT,* April 7, 1945, 1.
2. Joel Sayre, "Letter from Germany," *New Yorker,* May 12, 1945, 48.
3. W. B. Courtney, "Europe's Hangover," *Collier's,* July 28, 1945, 18.
4. Herbert Eskin, oral history, 16–19, JC-USARMY.
5. Dan Stone, *The Liberation of the Camps: The End of the Holocaust and Its Aftermath* (New Haven, CT: Yale University Press, 2015), 71–72; "Buchenwald," *Holocaust Encyclopedia,* USHMM.
6. Herschel Schacter, oral history, JC-USARMY. I have elided here portions of two different interviews.
7. Henry Aizenman, Interview 16345, VHA, USC Shoah Foundation, 1996.
8. Albert Hutler, "weekly report," May 5 to May 11, 1945, box 1, folder 2, Hutler, CJH.
9. Courtney, "Europe's Hangover," 60.
10. Henriette Roosenburg, *The Walls Came Tumbling Down* (New York: Akadine Press, 2000). Originally published 1957.
11. "DP's Return: A Frenchman Goes Home," *Life,* May 14, 1945, 88–91.
12. Malcolm Proudfoot, "The Anglo-American Displaced Persons Program," *American Journal of Economics and Sociology* 6, no. 1 (October 1946): 48.

Chapter 1: From Poland and Ukraine: Forced Laborers, 1941–45

1. Ian Kershaw, *Hitler, 1936–1945: Nemesis* (New York: Norton, 2000), xxxviii.
2. Mark Mazower, *Hitler's Empire: How the Nazis Ruled Europe* (New York: Penguin, 2008), 294–95.
3. Mazower, *Hitler's Empire,* 296–97.
4. Walter Kempowski, *Swansong 1945: A Collective Diary of the Last Days of the Third Reich,* trans. Shaun Whiteside (New York: Norton, 2015), 29.
5. Richard J. Evans, *The Third Reich at War* (New York: Penguin, 2008), 350.
6. Frank Golczewski, "Shades of Grey: Reflections on Jewish-Ukrainian and German-Ukrainian Relations in Galicia," in *The Shoah in Ukraine: History, Testimony, Memorialization,* ed. Ray Brandon and Wendy Lower (Bloomington: Indiana

University Press, 2008), 139–40; Lawrence Douglas, *The Right Wrong Man: John Demjanjuk and the Last Great Nazi War Crimes Trial* (Princeton, NJ: Princeton University Press, 2016), 127–28.

7. Mazower, *Hitler's Empire,* 297; Evans, *Third Reich at War,* 349.

8. Karel C. Berkhoff, *Harvest of Despair: Life and Death in Ukraine Under Nazi Rule* (Cambridge, MA: Harvard University Press, 2008), 253–54.

9. Paul Raab, "Concerning: Burning of Houses in the Wasilkow District," June 7, 1944, trial document, USA v. Erhard Milch, HLSL Item No. 2963, NTP.

10. Evans, *Third Reich at War,* 361.

11. Julia Alexandrow with Tommy French, *Flight from Novaa Salow* (Jefferson, NC: McFarland, 1994), 58–60, 68, 73–74, 79–81.

12. Tadeusz Piotrowski, *Vengeance of the Swallows: Memoir of a Polish Family's Ordeal* (Jefferson, NC: McFarland, 1995), 116–19.

13. Adam Tooze, *The Wages of Destruction: The Making and Breaking of the Nazi Economy* (New York: Penguin, 2006), 517.

14. Piotrowski, *Vengeance of the Swallows,* 123.

15. Piotrowski, *Vengeance of the Swallows,* 134–35, 137–38.

Chapter 2: From Latvia, Lithuania, Estonia, and Western Ukraine

1. Piotr Łossowski, "The Resettlement of the Germans from the Baltic States in 1939/1941," *Acta Poloniae Historica* 92 (2005): 87, 93; "The Resettlement of the Germans from Lithuania During World War II," *Acta Poloniae Historica* 93 (2006): 128; Andrejs Plakans, *A Concise History of the Baltic States* (New York: Cambridge University Press, 2011), 339–40.

2. Plakans, *A Concise History of the Baltic States,* 344–45.

3. Romauld J. Misiunas and Rein Taagepera, *The Baltic States: Years of Dependence, 1940–1990,* expanded and updated ed. (Berkeley and Los Angeles: University of California Press, 1993), 43.

4. Valdis O. Lumans, *Latvia in World War II* (New York: Fordham University Press, 2006), 183.

5. Markus Eikel, "Division of Labor and Cooperation: The Local Administration Under German Occupation in Central and Eastern Ukraine, 1941–1944," in *The Holocaust in Ukraine: New Sources and Perspectives* (Washington, DC: Center for Advanced Holocaust Studies, USHMM, 2013), 105.

6. Yitzhak Arad, *The Holocaust in the Soviet Union* (Lincoln: University of Nebraska Press; Jerusalem: Yad Vashem, 2009), 104.

7. Jan T. Gross, "Themes for a Social History of War Experience and Collaboration," in *The Politics of Retribution in Europe,* ed. István Deák, Jan T. Gross, and Tony Judt (Princeton, NJ: Princeton University Press, 2000), 25.

8. Toomas Hiio, Meelis Maripuu, and Indrek Paavle, eds., *Estonia 1940–1945: Reports of the Estonian International Commission for the Investigation of Crimes Against Humanity* (Tallinn: Estonian Foundation for the Investigation of Crimes Against Humanity, 2006), 542–67; Voldemārs Salnais, "Report of First Year of the German Occupation, 1942," in *Stockholm Documents: The German Occupation of Latvia, 1941–1945,* ed. Andrew Ezergailis (Riga: Historical Institute of Latvia, 2002), 16–29.

9. Paul Hanebrink, *A Specter Haunting Europe: The Myth of Judeo-Bolshevism* (Cambridge, MA: Harvard University Press, 2018), 139.

10. Vita Steinhardt oral history, February 21, 1982, Jaremko, IHRC.
11. Timothy Snyder, *Black Earth: The Holocaust as History and Warning* (New York: Tim Duggan Books, 2015), 152–53.
12. Jürgen Matthäus, "Key Aspects of German Anti-Jewish Policy," in *Lithuania and the Jews: The Holocaust Chapter* (Washington, DC: Center for Advanced Holocaust Studies, USHMM, 2004), 17–18.
13. Richard Breitman and Norman J. W. Goda, *Hitler's Shadow: Nazi War Criminals, U.S. Intelligence, and the Cold War* (Washington, DC: National Archives, 2010), 74–75.
14. Mark Levene, *The Crisis of Genocide*, vol. 2, *Annihilation: The European Rimlands, 1939–1954* (Oxford: Oxford University Press, 2013), 191.
15. David Cesarani, *Final Solution: The Fate of the Jews, 1933–1949* (New York: St. Martin's, 2016), 364.
16. Jack Arnel, Interview 19111, VHA, USC Shoah Foundation, 1996.
17. Yakob Basner, Interview 6277, VHA, USC Shoah Foundation, 1995.
18. Snyder, *Black Earth*, 168.
19. Matthew Kott, Arūnas Bubnys, and Ülle Kraft, "The Baltic States," in Jochen Böhler and Robert Gerwarth, *The Waffen-SS: A European History* (Oxford: Oxford Univerity Press, 2017), 125–26, 142–43, 149–53; Dieter Pohl, "The Murder of Ukraine's Jews," in *The Shoah in Ukraine*, ed. Brandon and Lower, 54–55.
20. Kott et al., "Baltic States," 124.
21. Anton Weiss-Wendt, *On the Margins: Essays on the History of Jews in Estonia* (Budapest: Central European University Press, 2017), 145–46, 176–80, 230.
22. "Vilna," *Holocaust Encyclopedia*, USHMM; United States v. Dailide, January 13, 2003, caselaw.findlaw.com/us-6th-circuit/1213793.html; U.S. Department of Justice, "Nazi Collaborator Who Helped Lure Jews for Execution Departs United States," news release no. 04-017, January 14, 2004, www.justice.gov/archive/opa/pr/2004/January/04_crm_017.htm.
23. Rita Gabis, *A Guest at the Shooters' Banquet: My Grandfather's SS Past, My Jewish Family, a Search for the Truth* (New York: Bloomsbury, 2015), 215, 243–44.
24. Boleslavs Maikovskis v. Immigration and Naturalization Service, 773 F.2d 435 (2d Cir. 1985), www.courtlistener.com/opinion/458682/boleslavs-maikovskis-v-immigration-naturalization-service/.
25. Christoph Dieckmann, "Holocaust in the Lithuanian Provinces: Case Studies of Jurbarkas and Utena," in *Facing the Catastrophe: Jews and Non-Jews in Europe During World War II*, ed. Beate Kosmala and Georgi Verbeeck (Oxford: Berg, 2011), 73, 80.
26. Jürgen Matthäus, "Operation Barbarossa and the Onset of the Holocaust, June–December 1941," in Christopher R. Browning with contributions by Jürgen Matthäus, *The Origins of the Final Solution* (Lincoln and Jerusalem: University of Nebraska Press and Yad Vashem, 2004), 274–75.
27. Michael MacQueen, "Lithuanian Collaboration in the 'Final Solution': Motivations and Case Studies," in *Lithuania and the Jews: The Holocaust Chapter. Symposium Presentations* (Washington, DC: Center for Advanced Holocaust Studies, USHMM, 2004), 1; Saul Friedländer, *The Years of Extermination: Nazi Germany and the Jews* (New York: HarperCollins, 2008), 223; Father Patrick Desbois, "The Witnesses of Ukraine . . . ," in *The Holocaust in Ukraine: New Sources and Perspectives* (Washington, DC: Center for Advanced Holocaust Studies, USHMM, 2013), 91; Arad, *The Holocaust in the Soviet Union*, 525.

28. Evans, *Third Reich at War*, 214, 350; Peter Black and Martin Gutmann, "Racial Theory and Realities of Conquest in the Occupied East," and Kott et al., "Baltic States," in Böhler and Gerwarth, *The Waffen-SS*, 1-18, 122-23.

29. Lumans, *Latvia in World War II*, 197; Rolf-Dieter Müller, *The Unknown Eastern Front: The Wehrmacht and Hitler's Foreign Soldiers*, trans. David Burnett (London: I. B. Tauris, 2012), 166.

30. Misiunas and Taagepera, *Baltic States*, 58–59; Müller, *The Unknown Eastern Front*, 182.

31. Inara Verzemnieks, *Among the Living and the Dead: A Tale of Exile and Homecoming on the War Roads of Europe* (New York: Norton, 2017), 161–62.

32. Jacek Andrzej Młynarczyk, Leonid Rein, Andrii Bolianovskyi, and Oleg Romanko, "Eastern Europe," in Böhler and Gerwarth, *The Waffen-SS*, 198–200, 208.

33. Aleksandr Reent and Aleksandr Lysenko, "Ukrainians in Armed Formations of the Warring Sides During World War II," trans. Harold Orenstein, *Journal of Slavic Military Studies* 10, no. 1 (March 1997): 219.

34. Müller, *The Unknown Eastern Front*, 168, 176, 182, 212; Museum of the Occupation of Latvia, *1940–1991: Latvia Under the Rule of the Soviet Union and National Socialist Germany* (Riga, 2018), 76.

35. Tanja Penter, "Local Collaborators on Trial: Soviet War Crimes Trials Under Stalin (1943–1953)," *Cahiers du Monde Russe* 49, no. 2/3 (April–September 2008): 341–42.

36. Pohl, "Murder of Ukraine's Jews," 58.

37. Michael James Melnyk, *To Battle: The Formation and History of the 14th Galician Waffen-SS Division* (West Midlands, England: Helion & Company, 2002), 276.

38. "Evald Mätas: Born 1921," in *Estonian Life Stories*, ed. and trans. Tiina Kirss, comp. Rutt Hinrikus (New York: Central European University Press, 2009), 107–24.

39. Andrejs Eglitis, *A Man from Latvia* (West Conshohocken, PA: Infinity, 2009), 91–94, 122–31.

40. Plakans, *A Concise History of the Balkan States*, 358–59; Orest Subtelny, "Ukrainian Political Refugees: An Historical Overview," in *The Refugee Experience: Ukrainian Displaced Persons After World War II*, ed. Wsevolod Isajiw, Yury Boshyk, and Roman Senkus (Edmonton: Canadian Institute of Ukrainian Studies Press, 1992), 13.

41. Subtelny, "Ukrainian Political Refugees," 14.

42. Povilas Burneikis, "A Glimpse into My Life Under Nazi 'Care,' 1944–45," trans. Zita Petkus, *Lithuanian Museum Review*, no. 247 (July–September 2014): 16–21; no. 248 (October–December 2014): 12–16.

43. Rita Gabis, personal communication, April 30, 2018.

44. Lumans, *Latvia in World War II*, 338.

45. "Riga Radio Reports," in *Stockholm Documents*, 315–16.

46. "Riga Radio Reports," in *Stockholm Documents*, 309–10.

47. Author interview with Inese Kaufman, July 31, 2019.

48. Verzemnieks, *Among the Living and the Dead*, 172–73, 177.

49. Jon-Hinnerk Antons, "Leaving with the Enemy? The Flight of Soviet Citizens into the 'Third Reich' 1944/45," web.hsu-hh.de/fak/geiso/fach/his-ost/forschung/zuflucht-im-dritten-reich.

50. Linda McDowell, *Hard Labour: The Forgotten Voices of Latvian Migrant "Volunteer" Workers* (London: UCL Press, 2005), 60.

51. Ventis Plume and John Plume, eds., *Insula: Island of Hope* (Morgan Hill, CA: Bookstand Publishing, 2013), Part One: "Leaving Home," 15–92.

52. Acting Lithuanian chargé d'affaires to the Lithuanian minister in London, May 15, 1945, FO 371/47039, NAUK.

53. Barbara Zawkiewicz Conaty, "The Zavkevičius/Zawkiewicz Family Story," *No Home to Go To: The Story of Baltic Displaced Persons, 1944–1952*, exhibition, Balzekas Museum of Lithuanian Culture, balzekasmuseum.org/displacedpersons /zavkevicius-zawkiewicz.

54. Agate Nesaule, *A Woman in Amber: Healing the Trauma of War and Exile* (New York: Penguin, 1995), 37–48.

55. Jane E. Cunningham, *The Rings of My Tree: A Latvian Woman's Journey* (Coral Springs, FL: Llumina Press, 2004), 25, 29–30.

Chapter 3: From the Concentration and Death Camps

1. Levene, *The Crisis of Genocide*, 2:119–21.

2. Nikolaus Wachsmann, *KL: A History of the Nazi Concentration Camps* (New York: Farrar, Straus & Giroux, 2015).

3. Ian Kershaw, *The End: The Defiance and Destruction of Hitler's Germany, 1944–1945* (New York: Penguin, 2011), 228.

4. Jack Arnel, Interview 19111, VHA, USC Shoah Foundation, 1996.

5. Martin Gilbert, *The Routledge Atlas of the Holocaust*, 4th ed. (London: Routledge, 2009), 181–82; Friedländer, *The Years of Extermination*, 646; Daniel Blatman, *The Death Marches: The Final Phase of Nazi Genocide*, trans. Chaya Galai (Cambridge, MA: Harvard University Press, 2011), 81.

6. Henry Aizenman, Interview 16345, VHA, USC Shoah Foundation, 1996.

7. Martin Aaron, Interview 28325, VHA, USC Shoah Foundation, 1997.

8. Wachsmann, *KL*, 444–45.

9. Göran Rosenberg, *A Brief Stop on the Road from Auschwitz*, trans. Sarah Death (New York: Other Press, 2012), 106.

10. Henry Aizenman, Interview 16345, VHA, USC Shoah Foundation, 1996.

11. Wachsmann, *KL*, 575, 583–84.

12. Henry Aizenman, Interview 16345, VHA, USC Shoah Foundation, 1996.

13. Jack Arnel, Interview 19111, VHA, USC Shoah Foundation, 1996.

14. Robert L. Hilliard, *Surviving the Americans: The Continued Struggle of the Jews After Liberation* (New York: Seven Stories Press, 1997), 43–50; Zeev W. Mankowitz, *Life Between Memory and Hope: The Survivors of the Holocaust in Occupied Germany* (London: Cambridge University Press, 2002), 30.

Chapter 4: Alone, Abandoned, Determined, the She'erit Hapletah Organizes

1. "From the Testimony of Edward R. Murrow About the Liberation of Buchenwald," YVA, www.yadvashem.org/odot_pdf/Microsoft%20Word%20-%203978.pdf.

2. "Dachau," *Time*, May 7, 1945; "Dachau," *Holocaust Encyclopedia*, USHMM.

3. Jeffrey Shandler, *While America Watches: Televising the Holocaust* (New York: Oxford University Press, 1999), 11; "Nazi Murder Mills, April 26, 1945 Universal Newsreel," YouTube, www.youtube.com/watch?v=8jdefO0Dxhc&bpctr=1577134762.

4. Mankowitz, *Life Between Memory and Hope*, 13.

5. Menachem Z. Rosensaft, "Bergen-Belsen: The End and the Beginning," in *Children of the Holocaust: Symposium Presentations* (Washington, DC: Center for Advanced Holocaust Studies, USHMM, 2004), 119.

6. Menachem Z. Rosensaft, "Reclaiming a National Jewish Identity After the Holocaust," *Tablet*, September 14, 2016, www.tabletmag.com/scroll/213331/reclaiming-a-national -jewish-identity-after-the-holocaust.

7. Marcus, "Memo," May 12, 1945, box D64, folder 3, WJC, AJA.

8. Adam R. Seipp, *Strangers in the Wild Place: Refugees, Americans, and a German Town, 1945–1952* (Bloomington: Indiana University Press, 2013), 59–60.

9. Alex Grobman, *Rekindling the Flame: American Jewish Chaplains and the Survivors of European Jewry, 1944–1948* (Detroit: Wayne State University Press, 1993), 38–39; Eichhorn to Jewish Welfare Board, May 17, 1945, in *The GI's Rabbi: World War II Letters of David Max Eichhorn*, ed. Greg Palmer and Mark S. Zaid (Lawrence: University Press of Kansas, 2004), 184–88.

10. *The GI's Rabbi*, 186, 188–89.

11. Eli Rock, oral history, RG-50.030.0386, 12, USHMM.

12. Hadassah Rosensaft, *Yesterday: My Story* (New York and Jerusalem: Yad Vashem and the Holocaust Survivors' Memoirs Project, 2004), 54–55.

13. H. Rosensaft, *Yesterday*, 58.

14. Marcus to Wise, June 26, 1945, box D64, folder 3, WJC, AJA.

15. Klausner to Bob, August 1, 1945, box 1, folder 6, Klausner, CJH.

16. Irving Heymont to Joan Heymont, November 5, 1945, Series 1, folder Joan Heymont, November 1945, Heymont, USHMM.

17. Eugene Lipman, oral history, 2, JC-USARMY.

18. Klausner, "A Detailed Report . . . ," June 24, 1945, box D63, folder 9, WJC, AJA.

19. Klausner to Bernstein, n.d., cited in Grobman, *Rekindling the Flame*, 65–66.

20. Herschel Schacter, oral history, 5, 7; Herbert Eskin, oral history, 15, JC-USARMY; Grobman, *Rekindling the Flame*, 56–58.

21. Hilliard, *Surviving the Americans*, 9–10.

22. "Speech given by Z. Grinberg," May 27, 1945, box 2, folder 9, Klausner, CJH.

23. Hilliard, *Surviving the Americans*, 79.

24. Schacter, oral history, 12, JC-USARMY.

25. Abraham J. Klausner, *A Letter to My Children: From the Edge of the Holocaust* (San Francisco: Holocaust Center of Northern California, 2002), 22–23.

26. Klausner, *A Letter to My Children*, 33; Mankowitz, *Life Between Memory and Hope*, 47–48.

27. Marcus to WJC, July 1945, box D64, folder 3, WJC, AJA.

28. Pinkusewitz, "Minutes of the Business Session of the Conference of the Liberated Jews in Germany," box 1, folder 23, Klausner, CJH.

29. Nabriski, "Minutes of the Business Session of the Conference of the Liberated Jews in Germany," box 1, folder 23, Klausner, CJH.

30. Mankowitz, *Life Between Memory and Hope*, 50.

31. Idith Zertal, *From Catastrophe to Power: Holocaust Survivors and the Emergence of Israel* (Berkeley: University of California Press, 1998), 31–32.

32. Yehuda Bauer, *Flight and Rescue: Brichah* (New York: Random House, 1970), 97–99.

33. Lucjan Dobroszycki, *Survivors of the Holocaust in Poland: A Portrait Based on Jewish Community Records, 1944–1947* (Armonk, NY: M. E. Sharpe, 1994), 9.

34. Dobroszycki, *Survivors of the Holocaust in Poland*, 10–11, 13.

35. Henry Goteiner, Interview 24346, VHA, USC Shoah Foundation, 1996.
36. Bluma Doman, Interview 9908, VHA, USC Shoah Foundation, 1996.
37. Masza Rosenroth, Interview 198, VHA, USC Shoah Foundation, 1994.

Chapter 5: The Harrison Report

1. Zorach Warhaftig, *Relief and Rehabilitation: Implications of the UNRRA Program for Jewish Needs* (New York: Institute of Jewish Affairs, 1944), 16–17, 162–63.
2. Wise and Goldmann, "Memorandum," September 1944, box C96, folder 6, WJC, AJA.
3. Tartakower to Hilldring, November 13, 1944, box C119, folder 11, WJC, AJA.
4. SHAEF, Office of the Chief of Staff, *Handbook for Military Government in Germany Prior to Defeat or Surrender,* December 1944, paragraph 710.
5. Grossman to Lipsky, May 11, 1945, box 15, Celler, LC.
6. Celler et al. to Eisenhower, n.d. [May 1945]; Ulio to Celler, May 29, 1945, box 15, Celler, LC.
7. JDC Archives, New York Office, 1945–1954, folder 1498, Lipsky to Cooley, June 12, 15, 1945.
8. M. Grossman, notes on "Meeting with Governor Lehman . . . June 28, 1945," box D11, folder 2, WJC, AJA; for UNRRA nondiscrimination directive, see "Resolution 2: Non discrimination," November 1943, in George Woodbridge, *UNRRA: The History of the United Nations Relief and Rehabilitation Administration* (New York: Columbia University Press, 1950), 3:46.
9. JDC Archives, New York Office, 1945–1954, folder 1498, Lipsky to Lehman, July 5, 1945.
10. JDC Archives, New York Office, 1945–1954, folder 1025, Lord Reading, "Memorandum," May 29, 1945.
11. Arieh J. Kochavi, *Post-Holocaust Politics: Britain, the United States, and Jewish Refugees, 1945–1948* (Chapel Hill: University of North Carolina Press, 2004), 33–34; Winant to Secretary of State, July 25, 1945, *FRUS,* 1945, 2:1178.
12. Wise to DDE, n.d. [August 3, 1945], box D59, folder 4, WJC, AJA.
13. DDE to UK Base for UK Embassy, August 10, 1945, box D59, folder 4, WJC, AJA.
14. Morgenthau, "Memorandum for the president," May 23, 1945, Book 848, May 19–24, 1945, 346–47, Morgenthau, FDRPL.
15. "Memorandum for the president," June 8, 1945 [in draft, both "Memorandum to the president" and "8 June 1945" are crossed out], "Harrison File," WRB, FDRPL.
16. Lewis M. Stevens, "The Life and Character of Earl G. Harrison," *University of Pennsylvania Law Review* 104, no. 5 (March 1956): 591–602.
17. Grew to Murphy, cable, June 11, 1945; Paris to Sec. State, June 18, 1945, "Harrison File," WRB, FDRPL.
18. Grew to HST, June 21, 1945; HST to Harrison, June 21, 1945, "Harrison File," WRB, FDRPL.
19. Pehle, "Memorandum," June 12, 1945, "Harrison File," WRB, FDRPL.
20. Weisgal to Harrison, June 25, 1945, in *Political Documents of the Jewish Agency,* vol. 1, ed. Yehoshua Freundlich (Jerusalem: Hasifriya Hazionit, pub. House of the World Zionist Organization, 1996), 67–72.
21. Weisgal to Morgenthau, cable, June 27, 1945, "Harrison File," WRB, FDRPL; JDC Archives, New York Office, 1945–1954, folder 1025, Grew to Schwartz, July 2, 1945.

22. Grew to HST, June 21, 1945; HST to Harrison, June 21, 1945, "Harrison File," WRB, FDRPL.

23. Sec. State to HST, April 18, 1945, *FRUS*, 1945, 8:704–5.

24. Acting Sec. State to HST, "Memorandum," May 1, 1945, *FRUS*, 1945, 8:705–6.

25. Harry S. Truman, *Memoirs*, vol. 1, *Year of Decisions* (Garden City, NY: Doubleday, 1955), 68–69.

26. HST to Churchill, July 24, 1945, *FRUS*, 1945, 8:716–17.

27. Attlee to HST, July 31, 1945, *FRUS*, 1945, 8:719.

28. HST, press conference, August 16, 1945, www.presidency.ucsb.edu/ws/index .php?pid=12389.

29. Harrison, "Journal," Earl G. Harrison Papers, Series 1, 105, USHMM.

30. Harrison to Sec. State, Sec. Treasury, July 28, 1945; Vinson to Grew, August 1, 1945, WRB, FDRPL.

31. Harry S. Truman, *Memoirs*, vol. 2, *Years of Trial and Hope* (Garden City, NY: Doubleday, 1956), 138–39.

32. JDC Archives, New York Office, 1945–1954, folder 1025, Report of J. J. Schwartz, Paris, August 9, 1945, 1, 3.

33. Harrison Report, in Leonard Dinnerstein, *America and the Survivors of the Holocaust* (New York: Columbia University Press, 1982), Appendix B, 292, 294–95.

34. Harrison Report, 300–301.

35. Harrison Report, 305.

36. Harrison Report, 291, 296.

37. Harrison Report, 298–99, 305.

38. Rendel to Strang, August 24, 1945, FO 371/51120, NAUK.

39. HST to Attlee, August 31, 1945, *FRUS*, 1945, 8:737–39.

40. Attlee to HST, September 14, 1945, *FRUS*, 1945, 8:739.

41. Attlee to HST, September 16, 1945, *FRUS*, 1945, 8:740–41.

42. HST to Attlee, September 17, 1945, *FRUS*, 1945, 8:741.

43. Goldmann to Ben-Gurion, September 18, 1945, *Political Documents of the Jewish Agency*, 1:115–17.

44. Meetings of the Jewish Agency Executive in London, September 20, 1945, *Political Documents of the Jewish Agency*, 1:125–26.

45. Dinnerstein, *America and the Survivors of the Holocaust*, 44.

46. DDE to Stimson, August 10, 1945, *The Papers of Dwight David Eisenhower*, ed. Alfred D. Chandler Jr., Louis Galambos et al. (Baltimore: Johns Hopkins University Press, 1978), 266–67; H. H. Newman, by Command of General Eisenhower, to Headquarters, United States Forces, August 22, 1945, *FRUS*, 1945, 2:1186.

47. JDC Archives, New York Office, 1945–1954, Folder: General, IX–XII, 1945, Nadich, "Report on Conditions in Assembly Centers for Jewish Displaced Persons," September 16, 1945.

48. HST to DDE, August 31, 1945, released September 29, 1945, Public Papers, Harry S. Truman, 1945–1953, HSTPL.

49. DDE to HST, September 14, 1945, Dwight D. Eisenhower Pre-presidential Papers, Principal File, box 116, Truman Harry S. (4); NAID #12007685, DDEPL.

50. Patton, "Diary," September 15, in *The Patton Papers, 1940–1945*, ed. Martin Blumenson (Boston: Houghton Mifflin, 1974), 751–52.

51. Patton, "Diary," September 17, 1945, *Patton Papers*, 753–54.

NOTES TO PAGES 117–134

52. Dwight D. Eisenhower, *Crusade in Europe* (Garden City, NY: Doubleday, 1948), 439–40.
53. Eli Rock, oral history, RG-50.030.0386, 15–16, USHMM.
54. Patton, "Diary," September 17, *Patton Papers,* 754.
55. JDC Archives, New York Office, 1945–1954, folder 1024, Jointfund, Paris, to JointDisco, NY, September 20, 1945; Rock, oral history, 22–23.
56. DDE to HST, September 18, 1945, Dwight D. Eisenhower Pre-presidential Papers, Principal File, box 116, Truman Harry S. (4) NAID #12007674, DDEPL.
57. "Truman Said to Aid . . .," *NYT,* September 23, 1945, 17; Cable Distribution. From Foreign Office to Washington, October 5, 1945, FO 371/51124, NAUK.
58. Halifax to Foreign Office (FO), October 4, 1945, FO 371/45380, NAUK.
59. Halifax to FO, October 11, 1945, FO 371/51125, NAUK.
60. Bevin to ambassadors, October 12, 1945, FO 800/484, NAUK.
61. Brit. Amb. to Sec. State, October 19, 1945, *FRUS,* 1945, 8:771–73.
62. Brit. Embassy to Dept. of State, "Informal Record of Conversation," October 19, 1945, *FRUS,* 1945, 8:773–76.
63. Memorandum of a Conversation between the Sec. State and the British Ambassador, October 22, 1945, *FRUS,* 1945, 8:779–83.
64. Herbert Matthews, "U.S., Britain Share Palestine Inquiry, Shape Trusteeship," *NYT,* November 14, 1945, 1; John H. Crider, "Truman Discloses U.S. Palestine Role," *NYT,* November 14, 1945, 13; "U.S. in British Trap, Zionists Here Say," *NYT,* November 15, 1945, 4.
65. *Undzer Veg,* November 16, 1945, 1, in Mankowitz, *Life Between Memory and Hope,* 77.
66. Dinnerstein, *America and the Survivors of the Holocaust,* 119, 163; "Truman Statement on Displaced Persons," *NYT,* December 23, 1945, 9.

Chapter 6: The U.S., the UK, USSR, and UNRRA

1. Dean Acheson, *Present at the Creation: My Years in the State Department* (New York: Norton, 1969), 69; George Woodridge, *UNRRA: The History of the United Nations Relief and Rehabilitation Administration* (New York: Columbia University Press, 1950), 3:42, 135.
2. Keith Lowe, *Savage Continent: Europe in the Aftermath of World War II* (New York: St. Martin's, 2012), 9–10.
3. Telegram, FO to Halifax, May 22, 1945, *FRUS,* 1945, 2:982–83.
4. Acting Secretary of State to Ambassador in Italy, May 19, 1945, *FRUS,* 1945, 2:1163.
5. Wilcox to Clayton, July 10, 1945, *FRUS,* 1945, 2:995–97.
6. "Discussion with United States Delegation . . . ," August 3, 1945; "Memorandum for the Soviet Foreign Minister," August 1, 1945, FO 371/51098, NAUK.
7. "Discussion with Soviet Delegates . . . ," August 4, 1945, FO 371/51098, NAUK.
8. Woodbridge, *UNRRA,* 3:428.
9. C. P. Trussell, "Senate Bill for $1,135,000,000 to UNRRA Sent to White House," *NYT,* December 18, 1945, 1.
10. Gerhard P. Bassler, *Alfred Valdmanis and the Politics of Survival* (Toronto: University of Toronto Press, 2000), 176–77; "SHAEF FWD, SIGNED SCAEF to EXFOR A REAR," May 21, 1945, RG 331, box 88, NACP.
11. "United States Delegation Minutes of the 19th Meeting of the Council of Foreign Ministers," September 24, 1945, *FRUS,* 1945, 2:350, 352.

12. Gabis, *A Guest at the Shooters' Banquet*, 382.
13. Mrs. Heath, "Some Afterthoughts," Heath, IWM.
14. Mrs. Heath's diary, August 5, 1945, Heath, IWM.
15. Dariusz Rogut, "Estonians in Soviet Filtration Camps After World War II," in *The Baltic States Under Stalinist Rule*, ed. Olaf Mertelsmann (Cologne and Weimar: Böhlau Verlag, 2016), 87–97; Pavel Polian, "Soviet Prisoners of War . . . ," in *Beyond Camps and Forced Labour: Current International Research on Survivors of Nazi Persecution*, ed. Johannes-Dieter Steinert and Inge Weber-Newth. Proceedings of the First International Multidisciplinary Conference at the Imperial War Museum, London, January 29–31, 2003 (Osnabrück: Secolo, 2005), 181.
16. Bilmanis to Adjutant General, September 25, 1945, SWNCC 238, NACP.
17. State Department, October 17, 1945, SWNCC 238, NACP.
18. Brimelow to King, October 31, 1945, FO 945/368, NAUK.
19. Eglitis, *A Man from Latvia*, 132–34, 147.
20. Marta Dyczok, *The Grand Alliance and Ukrainian Refugees* (New York: St. Martin's, 2000), 42, 45.
21. Alexandrow, with French, *Flight from Novaa Salow*, 114–17.

Chapter 7: Inside the DP Camps

1. Woodbridge, *UNRRA*, 1:488.
2. Irving Heymont to Joan Heymont, October 22 and November 5, 1945, Series 1, Heymont, USHMM.
3. UNRRA, *Monthly Review*, no. 16, December 1945, 23.
4. Atina Grossmann, *Jews, Germans, and Allies: Close Encounters in Occupied Germany* (Princeton, NJ: Princeton University Press, 2007), 176; Giles MacDonogh, *After the Reich: The Brutal History of the Allied Occupation* (New York: Basic Books, 2007), 372–80.
5. Lucy S. Dawidowicz, *From That Place and Time: A Memoir, 1938–1947* (New York: Bantam, 1991), 292–93.
6. Irving Heymont to Joan Heymont, November 8, 1945, Series 1, Heymont, USHMM.
7. Margarete Myers Feinstein, *Holocaust Survivors in Postwar Germany, 1945–1957* (New York: Cambridge University Press, 2010), 24–28; Anna D. Jaroszyńska-Kirchmann, *The Exile Mission: The Polish Political Diaspora and Polish Americans* (Athens: Ohio University Press, 2004), 154–55; Seipp, *Strangers in the Wild Place*, 56–67.
8. Theodor W. Adorno, *Guilt and Defense: On the Legacies of National Socialism in Postwar Germany*, trans., ed., and with an introduction by Jeffrey K. Olick and Andrew J. Perrin (Cambridge, MA: Harvard University Press, 2010), 128–33.
9. Ben Shephard, *The Long Road Home: The Aftermath of the Second World War* (New York: Anchor Books, 2012), 349–50.
10. Jaroszyńska-Kirchmann, *The Exile Mission*, 95; Feinstein, *Holocaust Survivors in Postwar Germany*, 81–82; Museum of the Occupation of Latvia, *1940–1991: Latvia Under the Rule of the Soviet Union and National Socialist Germany*, 9.
11. Laura Jockusch, *Collect and Record! Jewish Holocaust Documentation in Early Postwar Europe* (New York: Oxford University Press, 2012), 146–47; Ferdinand Kool, *DP Chronicle: Estonian Refugees in Germany, 1944–1951* (Lakewood, NJ: Estonian Archives in the U.S., Inc., 2014), xv, xix–xx.

12. Mr. Heath's diary, July 23, 1945, IWM.

13. Kool, *DP Chronicle,* 105; Balzekas Museum of Lithuanian Culture, *No Home to Go To: The Story of Baltic Displaced Persons, 1944–1952* (Chicago, 2014), 34.

14. Eileen Egan, *For Whom There Is No Room: Scenes from the Refugee World* (Mahwah, NJ: Paulist Press, 1995), 150–51.

15. Robert McFadden, "Kathryn C. Hulme, Author Who Wrote 'Nun's Story,' Dead," *NYT,* August 28, 1981; Kathryn Hulme, *The Wild Place* (Boston: Little, Brown, 1953), 166–67.

16. "Situation of Displaced Lithuanians in Western Germany Up to the Middle of October, 1945," *Lithuanian Bulletin* 3, no. 5 (October–November 1945): 13.

17. Brimelow to King, October 31, 1945, FO 945/368, NAUK.

18. See, for example, oral histories, in *Insula: Island of Hope;* and *No Home to Go To: The Story of Baltic Displaced Persons, 1944–1952,* exhibition, Balzekas Museum of Lithuanian Culture, balzekasmuseum.org/displacedpersons/.

19. Kool, *DP Chronicle,* 19, 103.

20. Margaret McNeill, *By the Rivers of Babylon: A Story of Relief Work Among the Displaced Persons of Europe* (London: Bannisdale Press, 1950), 40; Grigor McClelland, *Embers of War: Letters from a Quaker Relief Worker in War-Torn Germany* (London: British Academic Press, 1997), 47; British Chargé (Balfour) to Sec. State, August 22, 1945; *FRUS,* 1945, 2:1187.

21. Ambassador in Poland to Sec. State, August 28, 1945; Acting Sec. State to Chargé in Poland, September 14, 1945, *FRUS,* 1945, 2:1191.

22. Malcolm Proudfoot, *European Refugees: 1939–52: A Study in Population Movement* (Evanston, IL: Northwestern University Press, 1956), Table 25, 283.

23. Hugh Service, *Germans to Poles: Communism, Nationalism and Ethnic Cleansing After the Second World War* (Cambridge: Cambridge University Press, 2013), 40; Jan T. Gross, *Neighbors: The Destruction of the Jewish Community in Jedwabne, Poland* (Princeton, NJ: Princeton University Press, 2001), 26; Tony Judt, *Postwar: A History of Europe Since 1945* (New York: Penguin, 2005), 82; Norman Davies, *God's Playground: A History of Poland,* vol. 2, *1795 to the Present,* rev. 2nd ed. (New York: Columbia University Press, 2005), 365.

24. Norman M. Naimark, *Stalin and the Fate of Europe: The Postwar Struggle for Sovereignty* (Cambridge, MA: Harvard University Press, 2019), 204–5; Halik Kochanski, *The Eagle Unbowed: Poland and the Poles in the Second World War* (Cambridge, MA: Harvard University Press, 2012), 572.

25. Jaroszyńska-Kirchmann, *The Exile Mission,* 1.

26. Seipp, *Strangers in the Wild Place,* 66–67.

27. Marvin Klemme, *The Inside Story of UNRRA: An Experience in Internationalism: A First Hand Report on the Displaced People of Europe* (New York: Lifetime Editions, 1949), 140, 142.

28. Francesca Wilson, *Aftermath* (London: Penguin, 1947), 76.

29. Naimark, *Stalin and the Fate of Europe,* 208; Service, *Germans to Poles,* 54–57.

30. Klemme, *The Inside Story of UNRRA,* 141.

31. Hulme, *The Wild Place,* 46–47.

32. Piotrowski, *Vengeance of the Swallows,* 156.

33. Jaroszyńska-Kirchmann, *The Exile Mission,* 62, 76.

34. Albert A. Hutler, diary entries of August 29, September 5 and 12, 1945, Hutler, CJH. On Russian DPs, see Benjamin Tromly, *Cold War Exiles and the CIA: Plotting to Free Russia* (Oxford: Oxford University Press, 2019), 36–37.

35. McFarland to State-War-Navy Coordinating Committee, September 6, 1945, SWNCC 46, NACP.

36. Dyczok, *The Grand Alliance and Ukrainian Refugees*, 77.

37. Dyczok, *The Grand Alliance and Ukrainian Refugees*, 145.

38. "Ukrainian Resistance Groups Escaping to American Zone," *Ukrainian Weekly*, September 15, 1947.

39. McNeill, *By the Rivers of Babylon*, 60.

40. "Agreement Relating to Prisoners of War and Civilians Liberated by Forces Operating Under Soviet Command and Forces Operating Under United States of America Command, February 11, 1945," Avalon Project, Yale Law School, avalon.law .yale.edu/20th_century/sov007.asp.

41. Angelika Königseder and Juliane Wetzel, *Waiting for Hope: Jewish Displaced Persons in Post–World War II Germany* (Evanston, IL: Northwestern University Press, 1994), 97–98.

42. Königseder and Wetzel, *Waiting for Hope*, 188–95.

43. Koppel S. Pinson, "Jewish Life in Liberated Germany: A Study of the Jewish DP's," *Jewish Social Studies* 9, no. 2 (April 1947): 114.

44. Susan Pettiss and Lynne Taylor, *After the Shooting Stopped: The Story of an UNRRA Welfare Worker in Germany 1945–1947* (Cheshire, UK: Trafford, 2004), 126–27.

45. Wilson, *Aftermath*, 44–45.

46. JDC Archives, New York Office, 1945–1954, Folder: General, IX–XII, 1945, Nadich, "Report on Conditions in Assembly Centers for Jewish Displaced Persons," September 16, 1945, Michael Brenner, *After the Holocaust: Rebuilding Jewish Lives in Postwar Germany*, trans. Barbara Harshav (Princeton, NJ: Princeton University Press, 1997), 23.

47. Dawidowicz, *From That Place and Time*, 279, 285, 288–95.

48. Tom Segev, *A State at Any Cost: The Life of David Ben-Gurion*, trans. Haim Watzman (New York: Farrar, Straus & Giroux, 2019), 369–71; Irving Heymont to Joan Heymont, October 22, 1945, Series 1, Heymont, USHMM.

49. "Report by D. Ben-Gurion," November 6, 1945, *Political Documents of the Jewish Agency*, 1:196.

50. Feinstein, *Holocaust Survivors in Postwar Germany*, 244–45.

51. Laura Jockusch, "Rehabilitating the Past? Jewish Honor Courts in Allied-Occupied Germany," in *Jewish Honor Courts: Revenge, Retribution, and Reconciliation in Europe and Israel after the Holocaust*, ed. Laura Jockusch and Gabriel N. Finder (Detroit: Wayne State University Press, 2015), 54–58, 68–69, 75–77, 84, 89.

52. Samuel D. Kassow, *Who Will Write Our History? Rediscovering a Hidden Archive from the Warsaw Ghetto* (New York: Vintage, 2009), 3. Originally published 2007.

53. Jockusch, *Collect and Record!*, 117, 119.

54. Mankowitz, *Life Between Memory and Hope*, 215.

55. Jockusch, *Collect and Record!*, 130–31.

56. Pinson, "Jewish Life in Liberated Germany," 109.

57. Dawidowicz, *From That Place and Time*, 303–4.

58. Jockusch, *Collect and Record!*, 152.
59. Jockusch, *Collect and Record!*, 146–47, 149, 155.

Chapter 8: "The War Department Is Very Anxious"

1. Sec. State to Amb. UK, November 8, 1945, *FRUS*, 1945, 2:1196–99, 1206–7.
2. Shephard, *The Long Road Home*, 154.
3. Sec. War to Sec. State, November 29, 1945, *FRUS*, 1945, 2:1208–9.
4. Lowe, *Savage Continent*, 7.
5. Jacques Vernant, *The Refugee in the Post-War World* (London: George Allen & Unwin, 1959), 94–96.
6. Potsdam agreement, cited in R. M. Douglas, *Orderly and Humane: The Expulsion of the Germans After the Second World War* (New Haven, CT: Yale University Press, 2012), 90.
7. Seipp, *Strangers in the Wild Place*, 98–100, 104–5, 118–20.
8. Hulme diary, October 3, 1945, in Seipp, *Strangers in the Wild Place*, 65.
9. Simon to Ward, "Policy on Ex-Prisoners of War," December 4, 1945, S 0400 0003 06, UNRRA.
10. Bercomb to Troopers, December 21, 1945, FO 945/368, NAUK.
11. MacKillop to Gottlieb, December 22, 1945, FO 371/51128, NAUK.
12. Chief of staff to district headquarters, January 28, 1946, FO 1049/612, NAUK; Telegram, FO to Berlin, February 4, 1946, FO 1049/629, NAUK.
13. Sir Thomas Hetherington and William Chalmers, *War Crimes: Report of the War Crimes Inquiry* (London: Her Majesty's Stationery Office, 1989), ii, 38.
14. Joint Chiefs of Staff to occupying military commanders in Berlin, Frankfurt, Vienna, March 9, 1946, SWNCC 238, NACP.
15. UNRRA U.S. Zone to UNRRA Liaison Office, Headquarters Third U.S. Army, [April 27, 1946], rec. May 6, 1946, S 0437 0024 7, UNRRA.
16. Andreas Lembeck, "'—to set up a Polish enclave in Germany': Displaced Persons in the Emsland, 1945–50," Kleine Reihe/Dokumentations-und Informationszentrum, Heft 4, 2001, 21.
17. Sec. State to Sec. War, January 7, 1946, SWNCC 222, NACP.
18. Hull to Chief of Staff, Secretary of War, January 24, 1946; "Memorandum for the State-War-Navy Coordinating Committee, January 30, 1946; Sec. War to Sec. State, January 30, 1946; "Memorandum to Holders of SWNCC 222/2," February 11, 1946, SWNCC 222, NACP.
19. Raymond Daniell, "Army Enlistment of Foes of Russia Stirs Slav States," *NYT,* February 4, 1946, 1.
20. Marek Jan Chodakiewicz, "All That Ruckus About the Holy Cross Brigade," Polonia Institute, April 25, 2018, www.poloniainstitute.net/history-of-poland/all-that-ruckus-about-the-holy-cross-brigade/; Władysław Anders, *An Army in Exile: The Story of the Second Polish Corps* (London: Macmillan, 1949), 283.
21. Daniell, "Army Enlistment," 1, 8.
22. Eglitis, *A Man from Latvia*, 148, 153; "Soldiers in Germany," in National Archives of Estonia, Latvia, Lithuania, *Camps in Germany 1944–1951 for Refugees from Baltic Countries,* www.archiv.org.lv/baltic_dp_germany/index.php?lang=en&id=215.

Chapter 9: "U.S. Begins Purge in German Camps. Will Weed Out Nazis, Fascist Sympathizers and Criminals Among Displaced Persons," The New York Times, *March 10, 1946*

1. Drew Middleton, "Displaced Balts Studied by Allies," *NYT,* October 19, 1945, 9.
2. Kendall Foss, "UNRRA Has Baltic Fascists on Its Hands," *NYP,* October 26, 1945.
3. "Disorders Ascribed to Displaced Balts," *NYT,* December 31, 1945, 5.
4. AGWAR to USFET, OMGUS, January 9, 1946, RG 165, box 831, NACP.
5. *WP,* February 18, 1946, 4; *Los Angeles Examiner,* February 18, 1946, 9.
6. "U.S. Won't Make Balt D.P.'s Return," *New York Herald Tribune,* February 22, 1946.
7. Strang to FO, March 9, 1946, FO 371/55975, NAUK.
8. Sydney Gruson, "U.S. Begins Purge in German Camps," *NYT,* March 10, 1946, 5.
9. Susan Carruthers, *The Good Occupation: American Soldiers and the Hazards of Peace* (Cambridge, MA: Harvard University Press, 2016), 170.
10. Thomas J. Hamilton, "Wives of Soldiers Query Eisenhower," *NYT,* January 23, 1946, 1.
11. Patterson, "Memorandum for General Hilldring," February 8, 1946, RG 165, box 831; USFET, Frankfurt, to War Dept., February 25, 1946, RG 165, box 827; Patterson to Byrnes, March 14, 1946, RG 165, box 829, NACP.
12. Penrose to MacKillop, February 25, 1946; MacKillop to Penrose, March 1, 1946, FO 371/57759, NAUK.
13. "U.S. Studies Closing DP Camps . . . ," *NYT,* March 16, 1946, 8.
14. Egan, *For Whom There Is No Room,* 130.
15. Morris J. MacGregor, *Steadfast in the Faith: The Life of Patrick Cardinal O'Boyle* (Washington, DC: Catholic University of America Press, 2006), 113–14.
16. "Memorandum Re: American Policy on Displaced Persons," in O'Boyle to Byrnes, March 20, 1946, box 36, File 34, General Secretary Records, USCCB, ACHRC.
17. Stritch to Murray et al., March 30, 1946; Spellman to Stritch, April 13, 1946, box 36, file 34, General Secretary Records, USCCB, ACHRC.
18. Bishop of Fort Wayne to Stritch, April 1, 1946, box 36, file 34, General Secretary Records, USCCB, ACHRC.
19. Swanstrom to Carroll, April 8, 1946, box 36, file 34, General Secretary Records, USCCB, ACHCR; Egan, *For Whom There Is No Room,* 131.
20. Sec. State to HST, April 12, 1946, *FRUS,* 1946, 5:153–54.
21. War Department, Outgoing Classified Message, April 22, 1946, RG 165, box 827; BYRNES, April 4, 1946, PPF, box 2287, HSTPL.
22. Petersen, "Memorandum for the Secretary of War," May 27, 1946; Patterson, "Memorandum for Mr. Petersen," May 28, 1946; War Department to USFET, June 3, 1946, RG 165, box 827, NACP.
23. MacKillop, "Minute," July 4, 1946, FO 371/57764, NAUK.
24. AGWAR to USFET, USFA, April 27, 1946, S 0401 0008 07, UNRRA.
25. Hammer to Henderson, March 1946, FO 371/55975, NAUK.
26. Kool, *DP Chronicle,* 612–15.
27. Central Committee, Report, June 1, 1946, Appendix B, S1280 0000 0026, 18–22, UNRRA.
28. "Record of Special Meeting on Displaced Persons Held at Geneva 14/15 August 1946," S1261 0000 0007, UNRRA.

Chapter 10: The Anglo-American Committee of Inquiry Issues Its Report

1. Anglo-American Committee of Inquiry, *Report to the United States Government and His Majesty's Government in the United Kingdom, Lausanne, Switzerland, April 20, 1946* (Washington, DC: Government Printing Office, 1946), vii.
2. James G. McDonald, *To the Gates of Jerusalem: The Diaries and Papers of James G. McDonald, 1945–1947*, ed. Norman J. W. Goda et al. (Bloomington: Indiana University Press, 2014), 20.
3. Bartley C. Crum, *Behind the Silken Curtain: A Personal Account of Anglo-American Diplomacy in Palestine and the Middle East* (New York: Simon & Schuster, 1947), 8.
4. Crum, *Behind the Silken Curtain*, 20–22.
5. Mankowitz, *Life Between Memory and Hope*, 124; Crum, *Behind the Silken Curtain*, 75, 100–101.
6. Jewish Telegraphic Agency, "Weizmann Outlines His Views on Palestine at Hearings of Anglo-American Committee," March 10, 1946, www.jta.org/1946/03/10/archive /weizmann-outlines-his-views-on-palestine-at-hearings-of-anglo-american -committee/.
7. Segev, *A State at Any Cost*, 376–79; Statement of David Ben-Gurion, "Public Hearings Before Anglo-American Committee of Inquiry—Mar. 11, 1946," cojs.org /public_hearings_before_anglo-american_committee_of_inquiry_-_mar-_11th_1946/.
8. Albert Hourani, "The Case Against a Jewish State in Palestine: Albert Hourani's Statement to the Anglo-American Committee of Enquiry of 1946," *Journal of Palestine Studies* 35, no. 1 (Autumn 2005): 80–90.
9. Norman J. W. Goda, "Surviving Survival: James G. McDonald and the Fate of Holocaust Survivors," Monna and Otto Weinmann Annual Lecture, June 11, 2015, 12, USHMM.
10. Anglo-American Committee of Inquiry, *Report*, 2, 4, 5, 12.
11. Richard Crossman, *Palestine Mission: A Personal Record* (New York: Harper & Brothers, 1947), 75, 79.
12. HST, "Statement by the President on Receiving Report of the Anglo-American Committee of Inquiry," April 30, 1946, Public Papers, Harry S. Truman, 1945–53, HSTPL.
13. Amb. in the UK to Sec. State, May 1, 1946, *FRUS*, 1946, 7:589–90.
14. Ben-Gurion to Laski, May 2, 1946, *Political Documents of the Jewish Agency*, 1:386.
15. Asst. Sec. State to Under Sec. State, May 3, 1946, *FRUS*, 1946, 7:591–92.
16. Acheson to HST, May 6, 1946; Truman to Attlee, May 8, 1946, *FRUS*, 1946, 7:595–97.
17. Attlee to HST, May 9, 1946, *FRUS*, 1946, 7:603–4.
18. HST to Attlee, May 16, 1946 *FRUS*, 1946, 7:607–8.
19. "Meeting: D. Ben-Gurion and E. Epstein-D. Niles," June 15, 1946 [date of meeting: May 17, 1946], *Political Documents of the Jewish Agency*, 1:403, 660.
20. Sec. State to Truman, May 9, 1946, *FRUS*, 1946, 7:601–3.
21. Herbert L. Matthews, "Bevin Unwilling to Open Palestine for 100,000 Jews," *NYT*, June 13, 1946, 1.
22. "Criticism of Bevin Soars Here," *NYT*, June 14, 1946, 6.
23. Washington to FO, June 13, 1946, FO 800/485, NAUK.
24. Byrnes to Truman, July 29, 1946, *FRUS*, 1946, 7:671–73.
25. McDonald, *To the Gates of Jerusalem*, 246–49.
26. John D. Morris, "Truman 'Rebuffs' Palestine Plea," *NYT*, July 31, 1946, 5.

27. "Memorandum of Conversation, by the Acting Sec. of State," July 30, 1946, *FRUS,* 1946, 7:673–74.
28. Inverchapel to FO, July 31, 1946, PREM 8/627, Part 3, NAUK.
29. "Truman Bars Shift in Law to Aid Jews," *NYT,* June 15, 1946, 8.
30. Mankowitz, *Life Between Memory and Hope,* 261.
31. Grossmann, *Jews, Germans, and Allies,* 179.

Chapter 11: The Polish Jews Escape into Germany

1. Letter from unnamed chaplain, January 19, 1946, Folder 1564, Reel 113, RG 294.9, YIVO.
2. Naimark, *Stalin and the Fate of Europe,* 213–16; Bauer, *Flight and Rescue,* 114.
3. JDC Archives, New York Office, 1945–1954, Folder: General, IX–XII, 1945, Trobe to Rifkind, "Report written by Eli Rock," November 8, 1945.
4. Klausner to Stein, December 8, 1945, box D 63, folder 9, WJC, AJA.
5. Pettiss and Taylor, *After the Shooting Stopped,* 138, 140.
6. Hilldring, "Memorandum for the Secretary of War," November 30, 1945, RG 165, box 827, NACP.
7. Patterson to Acheson, December 19, 1945, *FRUS,* 1945, 2:1215–16.
8. Amb. Poland to Sec. State, December 16, 1945, *FRUS,* 1945, 2:1214.
9. Byrnes to Patterson, January 7, 1946, RG 165, box 827, NACP.
10. WARCOS to USFET, January 13, 1946; RG 165, box 827, NACP.
11. Cable from Bercomb to War Office, December 9, 1945, FO 371/51128/WR3648, NAUK.
12. Gladwin Hill, "Polish Jews Face Hunger in Berlin," *NYT,* December 9, 1945, 39.
13. Henderson minute, December 11, 1945, FO 371/51128/WR3648, NAUK.
14. Cavendish-Bentinck to Bevin, December 18, 1945, FO 371/57684/WR15, NAUK.
15. Hankey to Young, December 18, 1945, FO 371/57684, NAUK.
16. Bauer, *Flight and Rescue,* 194–96.
17. Ruth Milman, Interview 4131, VHA, USC Shoah Foundation, 1995.
18. Joseph Berger, *Displaced Persons: Growing Up American After the Holocaust* (New York: Washington Square Press, 2001), 142–43, 218–36, 291–94.
19. Berger, *Displaced Persons,* 298–301.
20. Edith Milman, Interview 36999, VHA, USC Shoah Foundation, 1998.
21. Acheson to HST, May 2, 1946, *FRUS,* 1946, 5:156–58.
22. Bernstein to Kennan, June 28, 1946, box D63, folder2, WJC, AJA.
23. Bauer, *Flight and Rescue,* 206–7; Baruch Goldman, cited in Jan T. Gross, *Fear: Anti-Semitism in Poland After Auschwitz* (New York: Random House, 2007), 89; Kielce Pogrom, *Holocaust Encyclopedia,* USHMM.
24. Dwork to Kubowitski, July 22, 1946, box D59, folder 11, WJC, AJA.
25. JDC Archives, New York Office, 1945–1954, Folder General 1.-VII, 1946, Wahl to Grossman, July 23, 1946.
26. Byrnes to Truman, July 26, 1946, *FRUS,* 1946, 5:175.
27. Whiting to Flynn, July 11, 1946, Flynn to McNarney, July 14, 1946, box 36, folder 35, General Secretary Records, USCCB, ACHRC.
28. McNarney to Flynn, August 22, 1946, box 36, folder 35, General Secretary Records, USCCB, ACHRC.

29. JDC Archives, New York Office, 1945–1954, Folder Gen VII-X, 1946, Bernstein to McNarney, August 2, 1946.
30. Philip Bernstein, "Address," October 1, 1946, box D66, folder 2, 6, WJC, AJA.
31. Berger, *Displaced Persons,* 303–6.
32. Ruth Milman, Interview 4131, VHA, USC Shoah Foundation, 1995.
33. Bernstein, "Address."
34. Coville to Baxter; Ian L. Henderson, "Proposed Transfer," August 15, 1946, FO 371/57694, NAUK.
35. Deputy Military Governor, Berlin, to Control Commission for Germany, London, July 23, 1946, and Appendix A, FO 945/400, NAUK.
36. Bercomb to Confolk, August 3, 1946, FO 945/400, NAUK.
37. "Note of Mr. La Guardia's Interview with the Prime Minister on 5th September, 1946," FO 371/57769, NAUK.
38. FO to Washington, September 26, 1946, FO 371/57773; New York to FO, October 1, 1946, FO 371/57696, NAUK.
39. Jessica Reinisch, "Relief in the Aftermath of War," *Journal of Contemporary History* 43, no. 3 (July 2008): 393–95.
40. Bauer, *Flight and Rescue,* 274.
41. Grossmann, *Jews, Germans, and Allies,* 184, 189.
42. Philip Bernstein, "Displaced Persons," *American Jewish Year Book* 49 (1947–48): 526; Leo Schwartz, Report No. 391, January 13, 1947, Leo Schwartz Papers, Reel 9, folder 59, YIVO.
43. Tara Zahra, *The Lost Children: Reconstructing Europe's Families After World War II* (Cambridge, MA: Harvard University Press, 2011), 132–37.
44. "Resolutions of the Jewish Agency Executive," August 5, 1946, *Political Documents of the Jewish Agency,* 1:500–501.
45. HST to Attlee, August 12, 1946, *FRUS,* 1946, 7:682.
46. "White House Statement on Palestine and on the Problem of Displaced Persons in General," August 16, 1946, HSTPL.
47. "Congressmen Found Cool to Truman's Plan . . . ," *NYT,* August 18, 1946, 7.
48. HST, "Statement by the President Following the Adjournment of the Palestine Conference in London," October 3, 1946, Public Papers, Harry S. Truman, 1945–1953, HSTPL.
49. Attlee to HST, 8:55 p.m., October 4, 1946, PREM 8/627, Part 5, NAUK.
50. E. Epstein to N. Goldmann, October 9, 1946, Epstein to Jewish Agency Executive, October 17, 1946, *Political Documents of the Jewish Agency,* 1:683, 696–97; HST to Attlee, October 10, 1946, PREM 8/627, Part 5, NAUK.
51. Bromley report, in Balfour to Bevin, November 22, 1946, CO 537/1737, NAUK.
52. "Meeting: D. Ben-Gurion—Lord Jowitt," February 13, 1947, *Political Documents of the Jewish Agency,* 2:207.
53. Cabinet minutes, February 14, 1947, PREM 8/627, Part 6, NAUK.
54. Acheson to Henderson, February 15, 1947, *FRUS,* 1947, 5:1048–49.
55. "Memorandum of Telephone Conversation," Acheson to Balfour, February 15, 1947; Gallman to Sec. State, February 19, 1947, *FRUS,* 1947, 5:1049–50, 1053–54.
56. Sec. State to Bevin, February 21, 1947, *FRUS,* 1947, 5:1054–55.
57. *Parliamentary Debates,* Commons, February 25, 1947, 433 cc1901–10.

Chapter 12: Fiorello La Guardia to the Rescue

1. European Regional Order No. 40.E, September 12, 1946, S 0411 0003 06, UNRRA.
2. Ralph Price, U.S. Zone Germany, "History Report No. 28," May 1947, S 1021 0081 03, 22–23, UNRRA.
3. Hulme, *The Wild Place*, 150–51.
4. Shephard, *The Long Road Home*, 242.
5. "U.S. Bids Refugees Study Repatriation," *NYT,* September 20, 1946, 12.
6. Proudfoot, *European Refugees: 1939–52*, Table 25, 291.
7. "American Poles Ask Congress Probe of UNRRA," *CDT,* October 12, 1946, 4.
8. Polish American Congress, "A Factual Report on the Plight of Displaced Persons in Germany," January, 1947, box 6, folder 1, 1947, Piłsudski; Rozmarek, Nurkiewicz to Byrnes et al., October 11, 1946, attachment to "Investigation by Ira A. Hirschmann of the Specific Points . . . ," January 4, 1947, S 1304 0000 0255, UNRRA.
9. Youdin to Wood, December 12, 1946, S 1261 0000 0018, UNRRA.
10. Robert Howard, "G.O.P. Assails Betrayal of Poles to Reds," *CDT,* September 29, 1946, W1; *CDT,* October 6, 1946, 16; October 12, 1946, 4; October 20, 1946, 30; November 6, 1946, 22.
11. "UNRRA and Displaced Persons," *America,* November 16, 1946, 174.
12. *CDT,* December 2, 1946, 2; December 9, 1946, 5.
13. U.S. Zone Headquarters, Heidelberg, "Administrative Order No. 199," November 11, 1946, S 0402 0004 03, UNRRA.
14. Ralph Price, U.S. Zone Germany, "History Report No. 28," May 1947, S 1021 0081 03, 3, UNRRA.
15. Mayers to Whiting, December 8, 1946, box 34, folder 2, UUARC, IHRC.
16. Rozmarek and Nurkiewicz to Byrnes, October 11, 1946, attachment to "Investigation by Ira A. Hirschmann . . . ," S 1304 0000 0255, UNRRA; *CDT,* December 9, 1946, 5.

Chapter 13: The Death of UNRRA

1. Louise W. Holborn, *The International Refugee Organization: A Specialized Agency of the United Nations: Its History and Work, 1946–1952* (London: Oxford University Press, 1956), 31.
2. UN General Assembly, Committee 3, "Delegation of Yugoslavia Proposal on the Question of Refugees," January 25, 1946, A/C.3/7.
3. UN General Assembly, "Speech by the Yugoslav Delegate," January 29, 1946, A/C/.3/12, 7–9.
4. UN General Assembly, Committee 3, "Delegation of the Soviet Union Proposal," February 4, 1946, A/C.3/19; Vyshinsky, February 12, 1946, United Nations, *Plenary Meetings of the General Assembly, Verbatim Record,* January 10–February 14, 1946, 413–15.
5. ER, February 12, 1946, United Nations, "Verbatim Record," 418–21.
6. Eleanor Roosevelt, *On My Own* (New York: Harper & Brothers, 1958), 51; Vyshinsky, February 12, 1946, United Nations, "Verbatim Record," 426–28.
7. Belehradek, February 12, 1946, United Nations, "Verbatim Record," 423.
8. Telegram, Kennan to Byrnes, February 22, 1946, Harry S. Truman Administration File, 9, HSTPL.
9. UN General Assembly, *Resolutions Adopted on the Reports of the Third Committee,* 62 (1), December 15, 1946, Annex 1, part 1, section A.

10. Andrew Paul Janco, "'Unwilling': The One-Word Revolution in Refugee Status, 1940–51," *Contemporary European History* 23, no. 3 (August 2014): 429–31.

11. UN Economic and Social Council, *Report of the Special Committee on Refugees and Displaced Persons,* June 1, 1946, E/REF/75, chapter 3, part 2.

12. UN Economic and Social Council, *Report of the Special Committee on Refugees and Displaced Persons,* Annex 2, "Statement by the United Kingdom Delegate," 2–4.

13. AJC, *Memorandum on Refugees and Displaced Persons, Submitted to the Special Committee on Refugees and Displaced Persons of the United Nations Organization,* April 8, 1946, subject files: Immigration/Refugees, 1946–8, AJC online.

14. "Mrs. Roosevelt Assails . . . ," *NYT,* November 9, 1946, 7.

15. Abraham Duker, under pseudonym Ben Asher, "Mrs. Roosevelt vs. Comrade Vyshinsky," *The Day,* November 24, 1946, 1.

16. Text of amendments in UN General Assembly, 3rd Committee, Amendments proposed by the Yugoslav Delegation, A/C.3/59, November 11, 1946; summary of debate on amendment, in UN General Assembly, Official Records, 1946–47, 213–17.

17. Mrs. Roosevelt, Official Records, UN General Assembly, 66th Plenary Meeting, December 15, 1946, 1420–24.

18. Gromyko, Official Records, UN General Assembly, 66th Plenary Meeting, 1429.

19. Medved, Official Records, UN General Assembly, 66th Plenary Meeting, 1440.

20. James Reston, "Negotiating with the Russians," *Harper's Magazine* 195, no. 1167 (August 1947): 104.

Chapter 14: "Send Them Here," Life Magazine, September 23, 1946

1. "Text of Secretary Byrnes' Speech on U.S. Policy in Germany," *NYT,* September 7, 1946, 5.

2. Dinnerstein, *America and the Survivors of the Holocaust,* 114–15.

3. "DP's in One World," *America,* August 31, 1946, 527; "Our Own Open Door," *The Commonweal,* August 30, 1946, 468.

4. "Church Group Urges U.S. Admit Refugees," *NYT,* September 29, 1946, 13.

5. "Send Them Here," *Life,* September 23, 1946, 36.

6. Proskauer to members, October 7, 1946, Gen-10, box 116, folder 1, AJC, CJH.

7. Celler to Proskauer, October 11, 1946, box A8, folder 28, AJC, AJA.

8. AJC, Immigration Sub-Committee Luncheon, "Minutes," November 5, 1946, AJC online.

9. AJC, Immigration Committee, "Minutes," December 17, 1946, AJC online.

10. Hexter to Rosenwald, December 31, 1946, Gen-12, box 28, folder 20, AJC, CJH.

11. AJC, Immigration Committee, "Minutes," November 25, 1946, AJC online; Swanstrom to Carroll, January 22, 1947, box 36, folder 35, Office of General Services, USCCB, ACHRC.

12. AJC, Memorandum, December 20, 1946, box 1, folder 1, AJC, AJA.

13. AJC, Immigration Committee, "Minutes," November 25, 1946, box 1, folder 1, AJC online.

14. Revercomb, *Report to the Senate Republican Steering Committee, on the Possible Admission of Displaced Persons to the United States,* December 30, 1946, 58.

15. Revercomb, *Report to the Senate Republican Steering Committee,* 58.

16. Isaiah M. Minkoff, "Inter-Group Relations," *American Jewish Year Book* 49 (1947–48): 189.
17. William S. Bernard, "Not Sympathy, but Action," *Survey Graphic,* February 1947, 133, 137.
18. Citizens Committee, "The Displaced Persons 'What's What,'" n.p., n.d.
19. Aristide R. Zolberg, *A Nation by Design: Immigration Policy in the Fashioning of America* (Cambridge, MA: Harvard University Press, 2006), 303.
20. Citizens Committee, Executive Committee, Minutes, January 31, February 14, 21, March 28, 1947, box 1, folder 2, IHRC.
21. 93 *CR,* S2485, S250–7, 2521 (daily ed., March 25, 1947).
22. Samuel A. Tower, "Proposal to Admit DP's Meets Many Obstacles," *NYT,* June 8, 1947, E8.
23. Goldthwaite Higginson Dorr, oral history, 375–76, CU.
24. House Committee on the Judiciary, *Permitting Admission of 400,000 Displaced Persons into the United States: Hearings . . . on H.R. 2910,* 80th Congress, 1st Session, 1947, 2, 19.
25. House Committee on the Judiciary, *Permitting,* 233.
26. House Committee on the Judiciary, *Permitting,* 321–33.
27. House Committee on the Judiciary, *Permitting,* 82.
28. House Committee on the Judiciary, *Permitting,* 511–12.
29. House Committee on the Judiciary, *Permitting,* 140, 144–45, 511–12.
30. Dinnerstein, *America and the Survivors of the Holocaust,* 148; AJC, minutes, September 30, 1947, Subject file: Immigration, 1948–50, AJC online.
31. "Text of Truman Message on Admission of D.P.'s to U.S.," *NYT,* July 8, 1947, 16.
32. Drew Pearson, "Washington Merry-Go-Round," July 18, 1947, AUDRA.
33. House Committee on the Judiciary, *Permitting,* 572, 576.

Chapter 15: Fact-Finding in Europe

1. AJC, Immigration Committee, Engel to "Dear Member," August 26, 1947, AJC online.
2. Senate Committee on the Judiciary, *Displaced Persons in Europe: Report of the Committee on the Judiciary Pursuant to S. Res. 137,* 80th Congress, 2nd Session, Report no. 950, 1948, 1.
3. Citizens Committee to Slawson, July 17, 1947, Gen-10, box 127, folder 4, AJC, CJH.
4. Dorr to Tuck, July 31, 1947, box 2, folder 5, Tuck, HHPL.
5. Dorr to Clay, July 24, 1947, box 2, folder 5, Tuck, HHPL.
6. Paul H. Griffith, "On Hallowed Ground," *American Legion Magazine* 43, no. 3 (September 1947): 38; American Legion, National Executive Committee Meeting, "Digest of Minutes," Indianapolis, October 30–November 1, 1947, 164; HST, handwritten note, Vaughan to Clay, September 1, 1947, OF 127 (September 1947–1948), box 674, HSTPL.
7. American Legion, National Executive Committee Meeting, "Digest of Minutes," Indianapolis, October 31–November 1, 1947, 165–66, 189–91.
8. American Legion, "Digest of Minutes," 166, 190.
9. House Committee on Foreign Affairs and the Committee on the Judiciary, 80th Congress, 1st Session, *Displaced Persons and the International Refugee Organization* [Fulton Report], 80th Congress, 1st Session, November 16, 1947, 69, 81–82.
10. Tuck to Dorr, November 8, 1947, box 2, folder 5, Tuck, HHPL.
11. Senate Committee on the Judiciary, *Displaced Persons in Europe,* 15–16.

12. Senate Committee on the Judiciary, *Displaced Persons in Europe*, 27.
13. Senate Committee on the Judiciary, *Displaced Persons in Europe*, 20.
14. Excerpt from Taft address and discussion at Corvallis, Oregon, September 27, 1947, in Alderson, "Memo for Mr. Wilson (Office of Senator Taft)," November 3, 1947, box 519, folder: displaced persons, 1946–48, Taft, LC.
15. "Summary of meeting at the Yale Club, Wednesday, Oct. 29, 1947," box A8, folder 28, AJC, AJA.
16. Swanstrom to Carroll, with attachment marked "Personal and Confidential," January 27, 1948, box 37, folder 9, Office of General Secretary, USCCB, ACHRC.
17. Spellman to McNicholas, with attachment, January 3, 1948, box 36, folder 36, Office of General Secretary, USCCB, ACHRC.
18. Swanstrom to Carroll, with attachment, January 27, 1948, box 37, folder 9, Office of General Secretary, USCCB, ACHRC.
19. Assorted pamphlets, box 37, folder 10, Office of General Secretary, USCCB, ACHRC.
20. Church World Service, Inc., Board of Directors Meeting, January 14, 1948, Series 1, box 2, folder 2, Burke Library, CWS, UTS.
21. AJC, Refugees, Imm/Refugees 1946–48, Phillips to Bennett, December 11, 1947, AJC online.
22. Citizens Committee, Executive Committee, Minutes, March 25, 1948, box B2, folder 15, AJC, AJA; J. E. Smyth, *Fred Zinnemann and the Cinema of Resistance* (Jackson: University Press of Mississippi, 2014), 78–84.
23. Busch to Atkinson, December 18, 1947, box B2, folder 15, AJC, AJA.
24. Hexter to Feldman, March 10, 1948, box B2, folder 15, AJC, AJA.

Chapter 16: "The Best Migrant Types"

1. Hulme, *The Wild Place*, 190.
2. On camps occupying sites that the Germans and Americans coveted, see Seipp, *Strangers in the Wild Place*.
3. Noce to Kaif, June 3, 1947, box 9, folder 3, Estonians, IHRC.
4. Ieva Zake, *American Latvians: Politics of a Refugee Community* (New Brunswick, NJ: Transaction Publishers, 2010), 31.
5. Dyczok, *The Grand Alliance and Ukrainian Refugees*, 152.
6. Estonian, Latvian, and Lithuanian DPs in Augsburg to W. H. Tuck, November 1947; John S. Wood to Mr. N. Berg, Camp Leader, December 2, 1947, box 9, folder 3, Estonians, IHRC.
7. IRO, *Manual for Eligibility Officers*, n.d., 6.
8. IRO, *Manual*, 7–8.
9. IRO, *Manual*, 32; Hetherington and Chalmers, *War Crimes*, 39.
10. Holborn, *The International Refugee Organization*, 586; IRO, *Manual*, 33, 57.
11. Holborn, *The International Refugee Organization*, 210.
12. IRO, Decision of Review Board on case of Pabijans, Osvalds, May 19, 1949, ITS, USHMM.
13. IRO, Decision of Review Board on case of Paegle, Janis, May 13, 1950, ITS, USHMM.
14. IRO, Decision of Review Board on case of Palaitis, Gustaves, April 20, 1950, ITS, USHMM.
15. Michael L. Hoffman, "Two Million War Prisoners . . . ," *NYT,* September 7, 1947, E5.

16. Holborn, *The International Refugee Organization*, chapter 20.
17. House Committee on Foreign Affairs and the Committee on the Judiciary, *Displaced Persons and the International Refugee Organization*, 68–69.
18. Hulme, *The Wild Place*, 199–200.
19. McNeill, *By the Rivers of Babylon*, 204–5.
20. Hulme, *The Wild Place*, 206–8.
21. McNeill, *By the Rivers of Babylon*, 216.
22. Egan, *For Whom There Is No Room*, 141, 151–52.
23. U.S. State Department to FO, April 16, 1947, FO 371/66660, NAUK; U.S. State Department to FO, May 20, 1947, FO 371/66662, NAUK.
24. Linda McDowell, "Narratives of Family, Community and Waged Work: Latvian European Volunteer Worker Women in Post-war Britain," *Women's History Review* 13, no. 1 (2004): 24, 27–28.
25. Diana Kay and Robert Miles, *Refugees or Migrant Workers: European Volunteer Workers in Britain 1946–1951* (London: Routledge, 1992), 34–35.
26. Kay and Miles, *Refugees or Migrant Workers*, 49–50.
27. Kanty Cooper, *The Uprooted: Agony and Triumph Among the Debris of War* (London: Quartet Books, 1979), 121–22.
28. Kay and Miles, *Refugees or Migrant Workers*, 50–51; Mary Applebey to Control Office for Germany, December 20, 1946, FO 1049/61, NAUK.
29. Johannes-Dieter Steinert, "British Post-War Migration Policy and Displaced Persons in Europe," in *The Disentanglement of Populations*, ed. J. Reinisch et al. (London: Palgrave Macmillan, 2011), 234.
30. *Parliamentary Debates*, Commons, February 14, 1947, cc749.
31. Rucker to Edmonds, September 26, 1947, Chitty to Wilkinson, October 13, 1947, FO 371/66714, NAUK.
32. Holborn, *The International Refugee Organization*, Annex 41, 440.
33. Zarine to Brimelow, October 22, 1947, FO 371/66714, NAUK.
34. IRO, *Manual*, 115; Brimelow minute, October 22, 1947, FO 371/66714, NAUK.
35. Burger to Wyatt, November 17, 1947, FO 371/66714, NAUK.
36. Boothby to Rouse, January 2, 1947, FO 371/66714, NAUK.
37. David Cesarani, *Justice Delayed: How Britain Became a Refuge for Nazi War Criminals* (London: Phoenix Press, 2001), 98–100.
38. Vernant, *The Refugee in the Post-War World*, 365.
39. Stephen Dorril, *MI6: Inside the Covert World of Her Majesty's Secret Intelligence Service* (New York: Free Press, 2000), 268–99. On Soviet intelligence's penetration of British and American spy rings, see Tromly, *Cold War Exiles and the CIA*, 59–65.
40. UN Economic and Social Council, *Report of the Special Committee on Refugees and Displaced Persons*, June 1, 1946, E/REF/75, chapter 5, section 2, 12; Vernant, *The Refugee in the Post-War World*, 622.
41. Holborn, *The International Refugee Organization*, 402; Sidney Liskofsky, "Immigration Prospects," *American Jewish Year Book* 49 (1947–48): 551.
42. Holborn, *The International Refugee Organization*, 404.
43. Calwell to Chifley, July 18, 1947, in Department of the Special Minister of State, *Review of Material Relating to the Entry of Suspected War Criminals into Australia* (Canberra: Australian Government Publishing Service, 1987), 37.
44. Jayne Persian, "'Chifley Liked Them Blond,'" *History Australia* 12, no. 2 (2015): 93.

45. Vernant, *The Refugee in the Post-War World,* 705, 712–14.
46. Department of the Special Minister of State, *Review of Material,* 70; Mark Aarons, *War Criminals Welcome* (Melbourne: Black Inc., 2001), 250–58.
47. Mark Aarons, *Sanctuary: Nazi Fugitives in Australia* (Melbourne: William Heinemann Australia, 1989), 89–101; Konrads Kalejs v. Immigration and Naturalization Service, 10 F.3d 441 (7th Cir. 1993), www.refworld.org/cases,USA_CA_7,3ae6b70d10.html; Department of the Special Minister of State, *Review of Material,* 50, 70–71.
48. Vernant, *The Refugee in the Post-War World,* 721; Suzanne Rutland, "Postwar Anti-Jewish Refugee Hysteria: A Case of Racial or Religious Bigotry," *Journal of Australian Studies* 27, no. 77 (2003): 71, 77.
49. Rutland, "Postwar Anti-Jewish Refugee Hysteria," 75, 77.
50. Vernant, *The Refugee in the Post-War World,* 721.
51. Mackenzie, May 1, 1947, House of Commons Debates, 20th Parliament, 3rd Session, 3:2244–46.
52. Howard Margolian, *Unauthorized Entry: The Truth About Nazi War Criminals in Canada, 1946–1956* (Toronto: University of Toronto Press, 2000), 79.
53. Holborn, *The International Refugee Organization,* 438–39, 442; Vernant, *The Refugee in the Post-War World,* 563–64.
54. Margolian, *Unauthorized Entry,* 97.
55. Margolian, *Unauthorized Entry,* 92–93, 107; Commission of Inquiry on War Criminals, Honourable Jules Deschênes, Commissioner, *Report* (Ottawa, December 30, 1986); Vernant, *The Refugee in the Post-War World,* 562.
56. Königseder and Wetzel, *Waiting for Hope,* 207; Sidney Liskofsky, "Canada," *American Jewish Year Book* 51 (1950): 277; Vernant, *The Refugee in the Post-War World,* 562.
57. Anthony Leviero, "Army Recruiting Shows Sharp Drop," *NYT,* May 22, 1947, 14.
58. Paul, "Memorandum for the Director of Plans & Operations," May 28, 1947; Schow, "Enlistment of Alien Personnel," June 19, 1947, RG319, Decimal File 1946–48, box 29, folder 091.714, NACP.
59. P&A, "Reconsideration of Nonconcurrence by Intelligence Division," n.d., RG 319, Decimal File 1946–48, box 29, folder 091.714, NACP.
60. Paul, "Recruitment of White Non-Enemy Aliens," November 6, 1947, RG 319, Decimal File 1946–48, box 29, folder 091.714, NACP; P&O, "Possible Enlistment of Displaced Persons in U.S. Army," November 21, 1947, RG319, Decimal File 1946–48, box 29, folder 091.714, NACP.
61. Laurin L. Williams, Colonel, GSC, "Analysis of Available DP Manpower," February 25, 1948; Lt. Col. Lawlor, "Analysis of Available DP Manpower," March 3, 1948, RG319, box 29, folder 091.714, NACP.
62. James Jay Carafano, "Mobilizing Europe's Stateless: America's Plan for a Cold War Army," *Journal of Cold War Studies* 1, no. 2 (May 1, 1999): 67–69.

Chapter 17: "So Difficult of Solution": Jewish Displaced Persons

1. Sidney Liskofsky, "Immigration Prospects," 542–43.
2. "Interview with Rae Kushner," Oral History Interviews of the Kean College of New Jersey Holocaust Resource Center, 32, USHMM.

3. United Nations, *Report on the Progress and Prospect of Repatriation, Resettlement and Immigration of Refugees and Displaced Persons,* 7th Session, June 10, 1948, E/816, 31.
4. Zev Birger, *No Time for Patience: My Road from Kaunas to Jerusalem* (New York: Newmarket Press, 1999), 108–9.
5. Egan, *For Whom There Is No Room,* 146–48.
6. Imre Rochlitz, Interview 32300, VHA, USC Shoah Foundation, 1996.
7. I. F. Stone, *Underground to Palestine* (New York: Pantheon, 1976), 141–43. Originally published 1946.
8. Jon and David Kimche, *The Secret Roads: The "Illegal" Migration of a People, 1938–1948* (New York: Farrar, Straus & Cudahy, 1955), 158–63.
9. Kochavi, *Post-Holocaust Politics,* 78.
10. Abram L. Sachar, *The Redemption of the Unwanted: From the Liberation of the Death Camps to the Founding of Israel* (New York: St. Martin's, 1983), 211–13.
11. Jorge García-Granados, *The Birth of Israel: The Drama as I Saw It* (New York: Knopf, 1948), 8, 24–26.
12. Aviva Halamish, *The* Exodus *Affair: Holocaust Survivors and the Struggle for Palestine,* trans. Ora Cummings (Syracuse, NY: Syracuse University Press, 1998), 45–46.
13. Halamish, *The* Exodus *Affair,* 46–47, 49; Zertal, *From Catastrophe to Power,* 67.
14. United Nations, Official Records of the Second Session of the General Assembly, Supplement 11, UNSCOP, Report of the General Assembly III, "Verbatim Record of the Thirty-Third Meeting," Jerusalem, Palestine, A/364/Add.2 PV.33, July 26, 1947, Testimony of Mr. Zalman Rubashov.
15. Special Committee on Palestine, Official Records of the Second Session of the General Assembly, Supplement no. 11, UNSCOP, Report of the General Assembly III, "Verbatim Record of the Thirty-Eighth Meeting (Public), Held at the Ministry of Foreign Affairs," Beirut, Lebanon, July 22, 1947, Testimony of Mr. Hamid Frangie.
16. García-Granados, *The Birth of Israel,* 172–73.
17. Ruth Gruber, *Destination Palestine: The Story of the Haganah Ship* Exodus 1947 (New York: Current Books, 1948), 25–27.
18. UN General Assembly, Official Records of the Second Session, Supplement no. 11, UNSCOP, A/364, September 3, 1947, vol. 1, chapter 1, paragraph 64–69.
19. UN General Assembly, UNSCOP, A/364 Add. 1, September 3, 1947, Annex 18.
20. UN General Assembly, UNSCOP, chapter 5, Section A, Recommendation 6.
21. HST diary entry, July 21, President's Secretary's Files, HSTPL.
22. Memorandum by Under Sec. State, August 22, 1947; Acting Sec. State to Embassy in UK, August 22, 1947, *FRUS,* 1947, 5:1138–40.
23. Acting Sec. State to Embassy in UK, August 22, 1947; Amb. in the UK to Sec. State, August 26, 1947, *FRUS,* 1947, 5:1141.
24. ER, *My Day,* August 23, 1947, FDRPL.
25. Myerson, cited in Halamish, *The* Exodus *Affair,* 186.
26. JDC Archives, 1945–1954, New York Office, Countries, Germany, Displaced Persons, 11–12, 1947, "Research Department Report No. 36," November 13, 1947, 2.

27. JDC Archives, "Research Department Report No. 36," November 13, 1947, 3.
28. Halamish, *The* Exodus *Affair,* 248, 251.

Chapter 18: "Jewish Immigration Is the Central Issue in Palestine Today"

1. UN General Assembly, Official Records of the Second Session, Supplement no. 11, UNSCOP, A/364, September 3, 1947, chapter 6, Part 1, Recommendations, Section B.
2. Benny Morris, *1948: A History of the First Arab-Israeli War* (New Haven, CT: Yale University Press, 2008), 51.
3. George C. Marshall, "Speech to the United Nations General Assembly," September 17, 1947; "Minutes of the U.S. Delegation to the United Nations, September 15, 1947," GCMF.
4. Clayton Knowles, "Palestine Division Approved by Taft," *NYT,* September 22, 1947, 5.
5. George Barrett, "U.S.-Soviet Accord on Palestine . . . ," *NYT,* November 11, 1947, 1.
6. Frank Adams, "Britain Mystifies U.N. on Palestine," *NYT,* November 14, 1947, 1, 10.
7. Allis Radosh and Ronald Radosh, *A Safe Haven: Harry S. Truman and the Founding of Israel* (New York: HarperCollins, 2009), 271–72.
8. UN General Assembly, Resolution 181: The future of Palestine, November 29, 1947, A/RES/181 (2).
9. Leo W. Schwarz, *The Redeemers: A Saga of the Years 1945–1952* (New York: Farrar, Straus & Young, 1953), 266.
10. David Horowitz, *State in the Making* (New York: Knopf, 1953), 312.
11. Morris, *1948,* 76–78.
12. Sec. State to Acting Sec. State, December 6, 1947, *FRUS,* 1947, 5:1301–2.
13. "Memorandum of Conversation, by the Director of the Office of Near Eastern and African Affairs," December 8, 1947, *FRUS,* 1947, 5:1302–4.
14. Kochavi, *Post-Holocaust Politics,* 149.
15. Joseph M. Hochstein and Murray S. Greenfield, *The Jews' Secret Fleet: The Untold Story of North American Volunteers Who Smashed the British Blockade* (Jerusalem: Gefen, 1987), 149–58.
16. "Red 'Fifth Column' for Palestine Fears . . . ," *NYT,* January 1, 1948, 1.
17. Herbert L. Matthews, "London Insists Communists . . . ," *NYT,* February 1, 1948, 1; "Britain Confirms Smuggling of Reds," *NYT,* February 5, 1948, 3.
18. UN General Assembly, United Nations Palestine Commission, "First Monthly Progress Report to the Security Council," A/AC.21/7, January 29, 1948, paragraph 11.
19. UN General Assembly, United Nations Palestine Commission, "First Special Report to the Security Council," A/AC.21/9 S/676, February 16, 1948, 18–19.
20. Mallory Browne, "Asks Big 5 Action," *NYT,* February 25, 1948, 1; "Declaration by Austin . . . ," *NYT,* March 20, 1948, 2.
21. "Zionists Here Pledge Fight," *NYT,* March 20, 1948, 1.
22. The President's News Conference, March 25, 1948, Public Papers, Harry S. Truman, 1945–1953, HSTPL.
23. W. Haber to Wise, March 25, 1948; "Speech delivered by Dr. William Haber at the opening session of the Third Congress of Liberated Jews in U.S. Zone," March 30, 1948, box D65, folder 7, WJC, AJA.

24. Minutes of JDC conference, Paris, April 5–10, 1948, JDC, RG 294.1, reel 1, folder 3, YIVO.

25. W. Haber to Meir Grossman et al., April 7, 1948, box D66, folder 2, 3, 8, WJC, AJA.

26. Cited in Tom Segev, *The Seventh Million: The Israelis and the Holocaust* (New York: Henry Holt, 2000), 177.

27. Schwarz, *The Redeemers*, 278.

28. Grossmann, *Jews, Germans, and Allies*, 250.

29. W. Haber to Grossman, June 10, 1948, box D66, folder 2, 7, WJC, AJA.

30. Avinoam J. Patt, *Finding Home and Homeland: Jewish Youth and Zionism in the Aftermath of the Holocaust* (Detroit: Wayne State University Press, 2009), 252.

31. JDC Archives, New York Office, 1945–1954, Countries, Germany, Displaced Persons, 5–6, 1948, S. Haber to Beckelman, June 2, 1948; Patt, *Finding Home,* 252.

32. W. Haber to Meir Grossman et al., April 7, 1948, box D66, folder 2, WJC, AJA.

33. Image of letter from Leonard Bernstein to Helen Coates, May 11, 1948, in www.loc .gov/resource/lbcorr.00567.0/?sp=2&st=single; JDC Archives, New York Office, 1945–1954, Countries, Germany, Displaced Persons, 5–6, 1948, "Report of the Executive Vice-Chairman," June 15, 1948.

34. Morris, *1948*, 120.

35. Rashid Khalidi, *The Iron Cage: The Story of the Palestinian Struggle for Statehood* (Boston: Beacon, 2006), 133.

36. Dana Adams Schmidt, "Arabs Say Kastel Has Been Retaken . . . ," *NYT,* April 12, 1948, 1; Morris, *1948,* 127.

37. Ilan Pappe, *The Ethnic Cleansing of Palestine* (London: Oneworld, 2006), chapter 5; Khalidi, *Iron Cage,* 131; Morris, *1948,* 132.

38. Sec. State to Certain Diplomatic and Consular Office, May 7, 1948; Memorandum from Rusk to Sec. State, May 8, 1948, *FRUS,* 1948, vol. 5, part 2, 927–29, 932–33; Morris, *1948*, 173–4.

39. Eliahu Epstein to the President, May 14, 1948; "Statement by the president, May 14, 1948, Truman papers, OF 917 Jewish State 1948–49, box 2043, HSTPL.

40. Clark Clifford, *Counsel to the President: A Memoir* (New York: Random House, 1991), 7; Clark M. Clifford, "Recognizing Israel," *American Heritage* 28, no. 3 (April 1977).

41. Samuel Gringauz, "Our New German Policy and the DP's," *Commentary,* June 1948, 508, 514.

42. W. Haber to Grossman et al., June 10, 1948, box D66, folder 2, 2, WJC, AJA.

43. "IRO Suspends Help for DP's to Israel," *NYT,* May 19, 1948, 3.

44. "Israel to Speed Up Immigration," *NYT,* May 23, 1948, E4.

45. JDC Archives, New York Office, 1945–1954, file 1019, Levitt to Haber, June 10, 1948.

46. W. Haber to Grossman et al., June 10, 1948, box D66, folder 2, 2, WJC, AJA.

47. Morris, *1948*, 266–67; Amitzur Ilan, *Bernadotte in Palestine, 1948* (New York: St. Martin's, 1989), 90–91.

48. Segev, *The Seventh Million,* 177; Hanna Yablonka, *Survivors of the Holocaust: Israel After the War,* trans. Ora Cummings (London: Macmillan, 1999), 82.

49. Morris, *1948,* 298–99, 301.

50. James G. McDonald, *My Mission in Israel, 1948–1951* (New York: Simon & Schuster, 1951), 175.

51. Holborn, *The International Refugee Organization,* Annex 43, 442; Vernant, *The Refugee in the Post-War World,* 488.
52. Aharon Appelfeld, *The Story of a Life,* trans. Aloma Halter (2004; New York: Knopf, 2009), 109.
53. H. Rosensaft, *Yesterday,* 120–21.
54. H. B. M. Murphy, "The Resettlement of Jewish Refugees in Israel, with Special Reference to Those Known as Displaced Persons," *Population Studies* 5, no. 2 (November 1951): 163, 168–69.
55. "Palestinian Refugees," UNRWA, www.unrwa.org/palestine-refugees.

Chapter 19: "A Noxious Mess Which Defies Digestion"

1. Dinnerstein, *America and the Survivors of the Holocaust,* 167.
2. Dinnerstein, *America and the Survivors of the Holocaust,* 166.
3. William S. White, "Bitter Fight . . . ," *NYT,* April 11, 1948, E7.
4. Anne O'Hare McCormick, "Abroad: The DP's and Palestine . . . ," *NYT,* May 3, 1948, 20.
5. 94 *CR,* part 5, 6180–81 (daily ed., May 20, 1948).
6. 94 *CR,* part 5, 6864 (daily ed., June 2, 1948).
7. 94 *CR,* part 5, 6901–4 (daily ed., June 2, 1948).
8. 94 *CR,* part 5, 6544–48 (daily ed., May 26, 1948).
9. 94 *CR,* part 5, 6806–8 (daily ed., June 1, 1948).
10. 94 *CR,* part 5, 6916 (daily ed., June 2, 1948).
11. Samuel Tower, "Group Would Let 200,000 DP's Enter," *NYT,* April 30, 1948, 9.
12. 94 *CR,* part 6, 7732 (daily ed., June 10, 1948).
13. 94 *CR,* part 6, 7746–47 (daily ed., June 10, 1948).
14. 94 *CR,* part 6, 7774 (daily ed., June 10, 1948).
15. 94 *CR,* part 6, 7733 (daily ed., June 10, 1948).
16. 94 *CR,* part 6, 7861 (daily ed., June 11, 1948).
17. 94 *CR,* part 6, 7860–64 (daily ed., June 11, 1948).
18. 94 *CR,* part 6, 7871–74 (daily ed., June 11, 1948).
19. 94 *CR,* part 6, 7875 (daily ed., June 11, 1948).
20. 94 *CR,* part 6, 7887 (daily ed., June 11, 1948).
21. 94 *CR,* part 7, 8856 (daily ed., June 18, 1948).
22. 94 *CR,* part 7, 8859 (daily ed., June 18, 1948).
23. 94 *CR,* part 7, 8860–63 (daily ed., June 18, 1948).
24. 24 *CR,* part 7, 9008 (daily ed., June 19, 1948).
25. 94 *CR,* part 7, 9019–23 (daily ed., June 19, 1948).

Chapter 20: "A Shameful Victory for [the] School of Bigotry"

1. "A Shameful DP Bill," *NYT,* June 19, 1948, 14; "DP Compromise Denounced," *NYT,* June 19, 1948, 13; AJC, Press Releases, 1948, June 19, 1948, AJC online.
2. Drew Pearson, "Washington Merry-Go-Round," July 20, 1948, AUDRA.
3. Minutes of Special Meeting of Legislative Information Committee . . . ," June 23, 1948, Rosenfield Papers, box 3, folder Displaced Persons Commission, chronological file, 1948, HSTPL.

4. Swanstrom to Carroll, July 2, 1948; Swanstrom to Diocesan Resettlement Director, January 24, 1949, with attachment, box 37, folder 9, Office of General Secretary, USCCB, ACHRC.

5. Swanstrom to Carroll, June 19, 1948, box 37, folder 9, Office of General Secretary, USCCB, ACHRC.

6. McNicholas to Truman, June 21, 1948, box 37, folder 9, Office of General Secretary, USCCB, ACHRC; Spellman to Truman, June 21, 1948, PPF 214, folder Spellman, HSTPL.

7. HST, "Statement by the president upon Signing the Displaced Persons Act," June 25, 1948, Public Papers, Harry S. Truman, 1945–1953, HSTPL.

8. Tzvion, *The Forward,* trans. Esther Adaire, June 26, 1948, 6.

9. Horowitz to Tex & Jinx, March 9, 1948, box B2, folder 15, AJC, AJA.

10. Engel to McCrary, March 13, 1948, box B2, folder 15, AJC, AJA.

11. Engel to Billikopf, June 29, 1948, box B2, folder 17, AJC, AJA.

12. Lloyd P. Gartner, "In Memoriam: Abraham G. Duker," *Jewish Social Studies* 49, no. 3/4 (Summer–Autumn 1987): 189–90.

13. JDC Archives, New York Office, 1945–1954, Folder: Immigration to U.S., 1948, Abraham Duker, "Statement of the Need for Screening Displaced Persons Applying for Entry into the United States," with "Summary" attached, June 1, 1948, 1–2, 13–14, 17.

14. Ben Asher, "Of Bagels, Votes and Pogromists," *The Day,* June 6, 1948, 1.

15. E. Greenberg to John Slawson, July 9, 1948; Gen-12, box 229, folder 2, AJC, CJH.

16. Duker, "The DP Scandal Reviewed," *The Day,* July 25, 1948, 1.

17. Hexter to Billikopf, July 28, 1948, box B2, folder 18, AJC, AJA.

18. Tzvion, *The Forward,* trans. Esther Adaire, July 24, 1948, 6.

Chapter 21: *"Get These People Moving"*

1. Hulme, *The Wild Place,* 224–25.

2. Nesaule, *A Woman in Amber,* 134–35.

3. Harry G. Kapeikis, *Exile from Latvia: My WWII Childhood—From Survival to Opportunity* (Victoria, BC: Trafford Publishing, 2007), 262, 264, 269.

4. Eglitis, *A Man from Latvia,* 157–59, 161, 181.

5. W. Haber to Rothfeld, August 31, 1948, box D66, folder 10, WJC, AJA.

6. Tzvion, *The Forward,* trans. Esther Adaire, June 26, 1948, 6.

7. W. Haber to Rothfeld et al., August 31, 1948, box D66, folder 10, WJC, AJA.

8. W. Haber to Billikopf, August 29, 1948, box B2, folder 19, AJC, AJA.

9. Drew Pearson, "Washington Merry-Go-Round," September 3, 1948, AUDRA.

10. JDC Archives, Geneva Office, 1945–1954, Folder: Countries, Germany, DPs/Survivors/Refugees, Abraham S. Hyman, Louis Barish to American Jewish Committee et al., February 28, 1949.

11. U.S. DPC, "Second Semi-Annual Report to the President and Congress," August 1, 1949, 12, 15; Holborn, *The International Refugee Organization,* 306.

12. JDC Archives, New York Office, 1945–1954, Folder: General, VIII–XII, 1948, "Meeting of DP Executive Committee of ACVAFS (American Council of Voluntary Agencies for Foreign Service) with DP Commissioners," September 17, 1948.

13. Senate Committee on the Judiciary, "Displaced Persons," *Hearings Before the Subcommittee on Amendments to the Displaced Persons Act,* 81st Congress, 1st and 2nd Sessions, 1950, 5–6, 133–38.
14. U.S. DPC, *Memo to America: The DP Story* (Washington, DC: Government Printing Office, 1952), 52.
15. HST, Executive Order 10003, 1948, in Executive Orders, Public Papers, Harry S. Truman, 1945–1953, HSTPL; U.S. DPC, "Second Semi-Annual Report," 40–41.
16. Hillenkoetter to Carusi, April 7, 1949, RG 278, box 45, folder CIA, DPC, NACP.
17. "A Place for the Displaced," *Church World Service News* 4, no. 1 (January 1949): 1.
18. William Haber to World Jewish Congress et al., December 20, 1948, box D67, folder 7, 17–19, WJC, AJA; U.S. DPC, "First Semi-Annual Report," February 1, 1949, 35.
19. JDC Archives, New York Office, 1945–1954, Folder: Germany, Displaced Persons, 1–6, 1949, S. Haber, "Report on Activities . . . During the Month of February, 1949," March 22, 1949.
20. Hulme, *The Wild Place,* 228–29.
21. Egan, *For Whom There Is No Room,* 183.
22. Janet Flanner, "Letter from Würzburg," *New Yorker,* November 6, 1948, 121.
23. Ella E. Schneider Hilton, *Displaced Person: A Girl's Life in Russia, Germany, and America* (Baton Rouge: Louisiana State University Press, 2004), 121–22.
24. Feinstein, *Holocaust Survivors in Postwar Germany,* 285–86.
25. Testimony of Almanza Tripp, INS, Munich, Germany, in Senate Committee on the Judiciary, "Displaced Persons," *Hearings Before the Subcommittee on Amendments to the Displaced Persons Act,* 81st Congress, 1st and 2nd Sessions, 1950, 691, 693, 695–96.
26. Rose Minsky, Interview 422, VHA, USC Shoah Foundation, 1994; "The Bertulis Family," *No Home to Go To,* Balzekas Museum, balzekasmuseum.org /displacedpersons/bertulis_questionnaire; Hulme, *The Wild Place,* 251–52.
27. Berger, *Displaced Persons,* 279, 310–11.
28. Kenneth Campbell, "U.S., City Welcome Ship . . . ," *NYT,* October 31, 1948, 1.
29. Harold Faber, "DP's Rise in Dark for Sight of City," *NYT,* October 31, 1948, 41; "Wisconsin Board Bars DP Doctor," *NYT,* October 30, 1948, 10.
30. "Accuses Fellow-Refugee," *NYT,* March 30, 1949, 17.
31. U.S. Congress, House, "Albertas Bauras, Report no. 1529, to accompany H.R. 4248," 83rd Congress, 2nd Session.
32. David Nussbaum, "Pro-Nazis Entering U.S. Under DP Law That Keeps Out Jews," *NYP,* November 19, 1948, 2.
33. Nussbaum, "Pro-Nazis Entering U.S. Under DP Law That Keeps Out Jews," 2, 28.
34. Nussbaum, "DP Camps Shelter Nazi Collaborators," *NYP,* November 21, 1948, 2, 16.
35. Bess Furman, "Catholics Assail 'Nazi' Gibe at DP's," *NYT,* December 1, 1948, 15.
36. William E. Ring, N.C.W.S. News Service, December 8, 1948, 1–3; December 13, 1948, 1–2A.
37. Engel to Liskofsky, December 18, 1948, box B2, folder 20, AJC, AJA.
38. Gibbons to Engel, December 28, 1948, box B2, folder 28, AJC, AJA.
39. Jules Cohen to Louis Bennett et al., December 30, 1948, box B1, folder 3, AJC, AJA, "Screening of DP's," *NYT,* January 12, 1949, 26.
40. "Plan for Screening Project," in Liskofsky to Bennett, October 19, 1948, box B1, folder 3, AJC, AJA.

41. AJC, Subj Files: Immigration: Displaced Persons, Staff Policy Committee Meeting, November 24, 1948, AJC online.
42. "Observations concerning the American Jewish Committee's plan . . ." [November 1948], box H350, folder 1, WJC, AJA.
43. Maslow to Petegorsky, November 24, 1948, box H350, folder 1, WJC, AJA.
44. Resolution, November 26, 1948, box H350, folder 1, WJC, AJA.
45. Engel to Baron, December 28, 1948, box B2, folder 20, AJC, AJA.
46. Slawson to Miller, August 16, 1949, box B2, folder 23, AJC, AJA.
47. Slawson to Rosenfield, May 31, 1950, box 44, folder AJC, RG 278, DPC, NACP.
48. "Handwritten notation," box 44, folder AJC, RG 278, DPC, NACP.
49. Wiesenthal to Bedo, October 20, 1948, box H349, folder 13, WJC, AJA.
50. "Zeugen gesucht," *Aufbau*, trans. Esther Adaire, January 7, 1949, 1.
51. Margolian, *Unauthorized Entry*, 131, 294, note 58; Andrew Ezergailis, "Holocaust's Soviet Legacies in Latvia," Holocaust Archive of Latvia USA, haolusa.org/index.php?en/Soviet/sov-050-Soviet-Legacies.ssi; UPI archives, "A Court Sentenced a 72-Year-Old Man to Six . . . ," June 26, 1984, www.upi.com/Archives/1984/06/26/A-court-sentenced-a-72-year-old-man-to-six/3373457070400/.
52. "Hāzners, Vilis," vols. 1, 3, FIAERR, www.cia.gov/library/readingroom/search/site/Hazners.

Chapter 22: "The Utilization of Refugees from the Soviet Union in the U.S. National Interest"

1. Tromly, *Cold War Exiles and the CIA*, 95–102; Annie Jacobsen, *Operation Paperclip: The Secret Intelligence Program That Brought Nazi Scientists to America* (New York: Little, Brown, 2014), 219.
2. Department of State, Policy Planning Staff, "The Utilization of Refugees from the Soviet Union in the U.S. National Interest," SANACC 395, box 22, folder 1, NACP; also in *The State Department Policy Planning Staff Papers, 1948*, vol. 2 (New York: Garland, 1983), PPS 22/1, 99–102.
3. Kevin C. Ruffner, "Cold War Allies," 35, FIAERR, www.cia.gov/library/readingroom/docs/STUDIES%20IN%20INTELLIGENCE%20NAZI%20-%20RELATED%20ARTICLES_0015.pdf; David C. Engerman, *Know Your Enemy: The Rise and Fall of America's Soviet Experts* (New York: Oxford University Press, 2009), 40.
4. Joseph and Stewart Alsop, "Refugees from Russia Could Tell Us a Lot," *LAT*, November 2, 1948, A5.
5. Engerman, *Know Your Enemy*, 40–41, 51–52, 61, 65.
6. H. W. Moseley, "Memorandum for the Secretary, Joint Chiefs of Staff, June 10, 1948," "Enclosure 'A,' BLOODSTONE," SANACC 395, NACP.
7. "Utilization"; Kirlin to Bohlen, August 2, 1948, SANACC 395, NACP.
8. Saltzman to Lovett, May 27, 1948; Bohlen to Saltzman, July 3, 1948, SANACC 395, NACP.
9. "National Security Council Directive on Office of Special Projects," Document 292, June 18, 1948; "Memorandum for the President of Discussion at the 19th Meeting of the National Security Council," Document 299, August 19, 1948; "Central Intelligence Agency General Order No. 10," Document 300, August 27, 1948, *FRUS, 1945–1950, Emergence of the Intelligence Establishment*.

10. Lovett to Forrestal, October 1, 1948, Document 301, *FRUS, 1945–50, Emergence of the Intelligence Establishment.*

11. 95 *CR,* part 6, 7186 (daily ed., June 2, 1949).

12. "Policy Planning Staff Memorandum," Document 269, May 4, 1948, *FRUS, 1945–1950, Emergence of the Intelligence Establishment;* "George F. Kennan on Organizing Political Warfare," April 30, 1948, WC, digitalarchive .wilsoncenter.org/document/114320.pdf?v=94; Hugh Wilford, *The Mighty Wurlitzer: How the CIA Played America* (Cambridge, MA: Harvard University Press, 2008), 31; "A Look Back . . . The National Committee for Free Europe, 1949," News & Information, CIA, www.cia.gov/news-information/featured-story-archive /2007-featured-story-archive/a-look-back.html.

13. Timothy Naftali, "The CIA and Eichmann's Associates," in Richard Breitman, Norman J. W. Goda, Timothy Naftali, and Robert Wolfe, *U.S. Intelligence and the Nazis* (New York: Cambridge University Press, 2004), 363–65; Eric Lichtblau, *The Nazis Next Door: How America Became a Safe Haven for Hitler's Men* (Boston: Houghton Mifflin, 2014), 217–19; David Johnston, "U.S. Seeks to Deport Man Accused of Collaborating with Nazis," *NYT,* September 22, 1994; Maura Reynolds, "Nazi Collaborator Aleksandras Lileikis Dies at 93 in Lithuania," *WP,* September 30, 2000.

14. Gimzauskas files, FIAERR, www.cia.gov/library/readingroom /document/519a6b24993294098d510b79.

15. Breitman and Goda, *Hitler's Shadow,* 85–91; Richard Rashke, *Useful Enemies: America's Open-Door Policy for Nazi War Criminals* (Harrison, NY: Delphinium Books, 2013), 442–51; James Riley, INS to Director, CIA, June 7, 1951, in FIAERR, www.cia.gov /library/readingroom/docs/LEBED%2C%20MYKOLA_0016.pdf.

16. Norman J. W. Goda, "Nazi Collaborators in the United States: What the FBI Knew," in Breitman, Goda, Naftali, and Wolfe, *U.S. Intelligence and the Nazis,* 252–53; Sheffield Edwards to W. W. Wiggins, October 3, 1951, FIAERR, www.cia.gov /library/readingroom/docs/LEBED%2C%20MYKOLA_0018.pdf.

17. Goda, "Nazi Collaborators in the United States: What the FBI Knew," 249–55; CIA Acting Chief, Political and Psychological Staff to Deputy Director for Operations, April 10, 1986, FIAERR, www.cia.gov/library/readingroom/docs /LEBED%2C%20MYKOLA_0060.pdf.

18. CIA, "Memorandum for the Record, Subject: Retirement of Mykola Lebed, February 19, 1975, FIAERR, www.cia.gov/library/readingroom/docs /LEBED%2C%20MYKOLA_0035.pdf.

Chapter 23: The Displaced Persons Act of 1950

1. Drew Pearson, "Washington Merry-Go-Round," January 30, 1949, AUDRA.

2. Alfred Steinberg, "McCarran, Lone Wolf of the Senate," *Harper's Magazine,* November 1950, 93.

3. NCRC, Statement released by Executive Committee [January 26, 1949], box 37, folder 9, USCCB, ACHRC.

4. Gibbons to Engel, December 28, 1948, box B2, folder 28, AJC, AJA.

5. Subcommittee No. 1 of the Committee on the Judiciary, *Amending the Displaced Persons Act of 1948,* 81st Congress, 1st Session, 1949, 222.

6. Engel to Proskauer, February 18, 1949, box B2, folder 21, AJC, AJA.

7. Proskauer to Spellman, February 23, 1949, box B8, folder 28, AJC, AJA.

8. Spellman to Proskauer, February 26, 1949; Proskauer to Engel, March 9, 1949, box B2, folder 28, AJC, AJA.

9. Catherine O'Brien to Engel, March 8, 1949; Engel, "In Re: Displaced Persons Legislation," March 8, 1949, box B2, folder 28, AJC, AJA.

10. Dinnerstein, *America and the Survivors of the Holocaust*, 225–26.

11. Robert Allen, "Washington Merry-Go-Round," August 18, 1949, AUDRA.

12. "Groups Ask Passage of Liberal DP Laws," *NYT*, September 6, 1949, 44.

13. 95 *CR*, part 10, 12769 (daily ed., September 12, 1949).

14. "M'Carran Charges Fraud in DP Set-Up," *NYT*, October 8, 1949, 3.

15. Janet Flanner, "Letter from Aschaffenburg," *New Yorker*, October 30, 1948.

16. Hulme, *The Wild Place*, 248–49.

17. George Eckel, "Cut in D.P. Entry Feared by Board," *NYT*, November 1, 1949, 20.

18. Hulme, *The Wild Place*, 242, 245.

19. "U.S. Leaders Urge DP Quota Increase," *NYT*, February 23, 1950, 15.

20. 96 *CR*, part 1, 113 (daily ed., January 6, 1950, part 2, 2459, 2470 (daily ed., February 28, 1950).

21. 96 *CR*, part 2, 2470 (daily ed., February 28, 1950).

22. 96 *CR*, part 1, 323 (daily ed., Jan. 11, 1950); 96, part 2, 2473 (daily ed., Feb. 28, 1950).

23. Senate Committee on the Judiciary, "Displaced Persons," *Hearings Before the Subcommittee on Amendments to the Displaced Persons Act*, 81st Congress, 1st and 2nd Sessions, 1950, 497.

24. Senate Committee on the Judiciary, "Displaced Persons," 553.

25. Subcommittee No. 1 of the Committee on the Judiciary, *Amending the Displaced Persons Act of 1948*, 81st Congress, 2nd Session, 1949, 125; Senate Committee on the Judiciary, "Displaced Persons," 421.

26. "An Act to authorize for a limited period of time the admission into the United States of certain European displaced persons . . . ," Public Law 774, 80th Congress, 2nd Session, June 25, 1948; "An Act to amend the Displaced Persons Act of 1948," Public Law 555, 81st Congress, 2nd Session, June 16, 1950.

27. U.S. DPC, "Fifth Semi-Annual Report to the President and the Congress," February 1, 1951, Table 10, 22.

28. U.S. DPC, *Memo to America*, Table 2, 366; Table 30, 376. Because the DPC did not include figures for Ukrainians or Jews, I have taken the Ukrainian figure from Myron Kuropas, "Ukrainian-American Resettlement Efforts, 1944–54," in *The Refugee Experience: Ukrainian Displaced Persons After World War II*, 399, and the number of Jews from Vernant, *The Refugee in the Post-War World*, 535.

Chapter 24: McCarran's Internal Security Act Restricts the Entry of Communist Subversives

1. Hulme, *The Wild Place*, 255–56.

2. Rosenfield to Corkery, November 17, 1950, box 53, folder Memo to Squadrilli, RG 278, DPC, NACP.

3. "An Act to protect the United States against certain un-American and subversive activities . . . ," Public Law 831, 81st Congress, 2nd Session, chapter 1024, 987, 989, 1006–7.

4. HST, "Speech on the Veto of the Internal Security Act," September 23, 1950, Public Papers, Harry S. Truman, 1945–1953, HSTPL.

5. Hulme, *The Wild Place*, 256–57.
6. "An Act to protect the United States against certain un-American and subversive activities . . . ," chapter 1024, 991.
7. "Meeting with DP Commission About Baltic Legion," February 17, 1950, NLC, 5/3/2, box 1, folder 5, AELCA.
8. Empie to Senators, February 25, 1950, NLC, 5/3/2, box 1, folder 5, AELCA.
9. Cox to Empie, Krumbholz, April 22, 1950, NLC, 5/3/2, box 1, folder 5, AELCA.
10. Department of State, Memorandum of Conversation, May 19, 1950, RG 59, DP Subject File, 1944–52, box 4, NACP.
11. Sec. State to HICOG, Frankfurt, April 1, 1950; HICOG to Sec. State, April 13, 1950, RG 165, Civil Affairs Division, box 814, NACP.
12. "To HICOG, Frankfurt, for Consular Section," May 8, 1950, RG 59, DP Subject File, 1944–52, box 4, NACP.
13. Rosenfield to Carusi, O'Connor, "The Baltic Legions," RG 59, DP Subject File, 1944–52, box 4, NACP.
14. Oral History Interview with Harry N. Rosenfield, July 23, 1980, 26–27, HSTPL.
15. McGrath to Acheson, October 20, 1950, RG 59, DP subject File, 1944–1952, box 3, NACP.
16. "An Act to clarify the immigration status of certain aliens," Public Law 14, 81st Congress, 2nd Session, March 28, 1951, chapter 1024, 28.
17. "Inimical Organizations" list, September 27, 1950, in McTigue to Dawson, RG 59, box 26, folder "inimical list"; Inimical organizations list, June 21, 1951, Harry Rosenfield papers, box 21, HSTPL; "Memorandum of Conversation" by Laurence Dawson, April 13, 1951, *FRUS*, 1951, vol. 4, part 2, 1242–44.
18. U.S. Congress, House, "Albertas Bauraus, Report no. 1529, to accompany H.R. 4248," 83rd Congress, 2nd Session.
19. Maikovskis FBI file, April 19, 1966, in FIAERR, www.cia.gov/library/readingroom/docs/MAIKOVSKIS%2C%20BOLESLAVS_0006.pdf.
20. House Committee on the Judiciary, "Alleged Nazi War Criminals," *Hearings Before the Subcommittee on Immigration, Citizenship, and International Law*, Part 2, July 19, 20 and 21, 1978, 103.
21. House, "Alleged Nazi War Criminals," Part 2, 151–52.
22. Department of Justice, news release, "Nazi Collaborator Who Helped Lure Jews for Execution Departs United States," January 14, 2004, www.justice.gov/archive/opa/pr/2004/January/04_crm_017.htm.
23. "Expert Report of Charles W. Sydnor, Jr.," United States v. John Demjanjuk, 518 F. Supp. 1362 (N.D. Ohio, 1981), 98; Douglas, *The Right Wrong Man*, 28–29, 34.
24. Douglas, *The Right Wrong Man*, 43–44.
25. Gabis, *A Guest at the Shooters' Banquet*, 382–84.
26. Milton Friedman, "The Nazis Come In," *The Nation*, March 1, 1952, 200–201; FBI Report, December 4, 1951, FIAERR, www.cia.gov/library/readingroom/docs/TRIFA,%20VIOREL%20DONISE_0011.pdf; Rashke, *Useful Enemies*, 61–62; Lichtblau, *The Nazis Next Door*, 39–40, 69.

Chapter 25: "The Nazis Come In"

1. Lichtblau, *The Nazis Next Door*, 77.

2. Meelis Maripuu, "Cold War Show Trials in Estonia: Justice and Propaganda in the Balance," in *Behind the Iron Curtain: Soviet Estonia in the Era of the Cold War*, ed. Tõnu Tannberg (Frankfurt am Main: Peter Lang, 2015), 13–22, www.mnemosyne.ee/old /wp-content/uploads/2015/04/Meelis_Maripuu_-_Cold_War_Show_Trials_in _Estonia.pdf; Weiss-Wendt, *On the Margins*, 233–37.

3. Maripuu, "Cold War Show Trials," 13–14; All-Party Parliamentary War Crimes Group, *Report on the Entry of Nazi War Criminals and Collaborators into the UK, 1945–1950* (London: House of Commons, November 1988), 78.

4. "Canada Checks on Immigrant Who Took Life," *Ottawa Citizen*, September 7, 1960.

5. David Fraser, *Daviborshch's Cart: Narrating the Holocaust in Australian War Crimes* (Lincoln, University of Nebraska Press, 2010), 57–58; Klaus Neumann, *Across the Seas: Australia's Response to Refugees; A History* (Collingwood, Victoria: Black Inc., 2015), 118–19.

6. Rashke *Useful Enemies*, 253; "Moscow Bids U.S. Extradite Estonian," *NYT*, October 13, 1961, 9.

7. Ministry of Foreign Affairs to U.S. Embassy in Moscow, February 20, 1962, FIAERR, www.cia.gov/library/readingroom/docs/LINNAS%2C%20KARL_0022 .pdf.

8. Steven E. Nordlinger, "Latvia Opens War Crimes Trial," *Baltimore Sun*, October 12, 1965, in "The Holocaust in Occupied Latvia, 1941–1944: The Scholarship of Professor Andrew Ezergailis," haolusa.org/index.php?en/Soviet/sov-200-Soviet-Show.ssi.

9. "Soviet Condemns Three," *NYT*, January 21, 1962, 16; Charles R. Allen Jr., *Nazi War Criminals Among Us* (New York: Jewish Currents, 1963), 31–32.

10. "Soviet Demands U.S. Extradite L.I. Man," *NYT*, June 12, 1965, 9; Rashke, *Useful Enemies*, 45–48, 160; Robert Thomas Jr., "Boleslavs Maikovskis, 92," *NYT*, May 8, 1996, D21.

11. Clyde A. Farnsworth, "Sleuth with 6 Million Clients," *NYT*, February 2, 1964, SM11; Tom Segev, *Simon Wiesenthal: The Life and Legends* (New York: Schocken, 2010), 180–81.

12. Joseph Lelyveld, "Former Nazi Camp Guard Is Now a Housewife in Queens," *NYT*, July 14, 1964, 10.

13. Douglas Martin, "A Nazi Past, a Queens Home Life, an Overlooked Death," *NYT*, December 2, 2005.

14. Elizabeth Holtzman with Cynthia L. Cooper, *Who Said It Would Be Easy? One Woman's Life in the Political Arena* (New York: Arcade Publishing, 1996), 91; author interview with Elizabeth Holtzman, July 29, 2019.

15. Rashke, *Useful Enemies*, 41–44, 52.

16. Author interview with Ralph Blumenthal, June 24, 2019.

17. Ralph Blumenthal, "Bishop Under Inquiry on Atrocity Link," *NYT*, December 26, 1973, 1; Ralph Blumenthal, "U.S. Opens New Drive on Former Nazis," *NYT*, December 30, 1973, 1.

18. House Committee on the Judiciary, *Hearings Before the Subcommittee on Immigration, Citizenship, and International Law*, 93rd Congress, 2nd Session, April 3 and June 25, 1974, 22–29.

19. Ralph Blumenthal, "Rep. Holtzman Calls U.S. Lax on Nazi Inquiries," *NYT*, May 21, 1974, 8.

20. House Committee on the Judiciary, *Hearings Before the Subcommittee on Immigration, Citizenship, and International Law,* 50–53.

21. Eilberg to Kissinger, June 26, 1974, in House Committee on the Judiciary, *Alleged Nazi War Criminals, Hearings Before the Subcommittee on Immigration, Citizenship, and International Law,* August 3, 1977, vol. 1, Appendix I, 69.

22. Friedersdorf to Eilberg, November 21, 1974; McCloskey to Eilberg, July 29, 1975, *Alleged Nazi War Criminals,* Appendix 1, 72–73, 75–76; House Committee on the Judiciary, *Emigration of Soviet Jews: Report of a Special Study Subcommittee of the Committee on the Judiciary on Its Trip to the Soviet Union, May 24–June 1, 1975,* 94th Congress, 2nd Session, January 1976, 1–2; author interview with Elizabeth Holtzman, July 29, 2019.

23. Ralph Blumenthal, "Inquiry of Nazis Called Lagging," *NYT,* August 25, 1975, 11.

24. Blumenthal, "Nazi War-Criminal Suspects in U.S. Face Deportation as Drive Widens," *NYT,* October 3, 1976, 1; "Some Suspected of Nazi War Crimes Are Known as Model Citizens," *NYT,* October 18, 1976, 16.

25. House Committee on the Judiciary, *Alleged Nazi War Criminals,* 1:2.

26. U.S. General Accounting Office, Report by the Comptroller General of the United States, "Widespread Conspiracy to Obstruct Probes of Alleged Nazi War Criminals Not Supported by Available Evidence—Controversy May Continue," May 15, 1978, i, 8, 33–34.

27. A. O. Sulzberger Jr., "Agency Studying Nazis Is Upgraded," *NYT,* March 29, 1979, A18.

28. Alan A. Ryan Jr., *Quiet Neighbors: Prosecuting Nazi War Criminals in America* (San Diego: Harcourt Brace Jovanovich, 1984), 87–88.

29. Adam Fels, "OSI's Prosecution of World War II Nazi Persecutor Cases," *United States Attorneys' Bulletin* 54, no. 1 (January 2006): 9; "Interview with Peter Black," September 21, 2000, RG-50.030.0409, 32, USHMM.

30. Karl Linnas v. Immigration and Naturalization Service, 790 F.2d 1024 (2nd Cir., 1986), in *Justia,* law.justia.com/cases/federal/appellate-courts /F2/790/1024/8258/; Jerome S. Legge Jr., "The Karl Linnas Deportation Case, the Office of Special Investigations, and American Ethnic Politics," *Holocaust and Genocide Studies* 24, no. 1 (Spring 2010): 26–46.

31. Jay Matthews, "Nazi-Hunt Methods Protested," *WP,* March 23, 1985.

32. William F. Buckley, "In U.S.S.R., the Verdict Comes Before Trial," *New York Daily News,* December 12, 1986, in Judy Feigin, *The Office of Special Investigations: Striving for Accountability in the Aftermath of the Holocaust,* ed. Mark M. Richard (December 2, 2008), 281.

33. Kenneth B. Noble, "Lobbying the Office That Hunts Nazi Suspects," *NYT,* March 3, 1987, A20.

34. Andrew Rosenthal, "The U.S. Case Against the Estonian," *NYT,* April 24, 1987; Richard Lacayo, Anne Constable, and Jeanne McDowell, "Problems of Crime and Punishment . . . ," *Time* 129, issue 16 (April 20, 1987): 60.

35. Menachem Rosensaft, "Deport Karl Linnas to the Soviet Union," *NYT,* March 31, 1987; Patrick Buchanan, "Dr. Hammer's Role in 'Ivan the Terrible' Trial," *NYT,* April 7, 1987.

36. Al Kamen and Mary Thornton, "Accused War Criminal Deported to Soviet Union," *WP,* April 21, 1987; Thom Shanker, "Linnas Dies in Soviet Union," *CDT,* July 3, 1987.

37. Ryan, *Quiet Neighbors*, 240–42; Ari Goldman, "Valerian Trifa, an Archbishop with a Fascist Past, Dies at 72," *NYT,* January 29, 1987.
38. United States Government Accounting Office, Report by the Comptroller General of the United States, "Nazis and Axis Collaborators Were Used . . . ," June 28, 1985, ii, 19.
39. Commission of Inquiry on War Criminals, *Report*, 3.
40. Department of the Special Minister of State, *Review of Material*, 177, 180.
41. The All-Party Parliamentary War Crimes Group, "Report," iii.
42. Hetherington and Chalmers, *War Crimes,* 90–91, 106–7.
43. Efraim Zuroff, "Worldwide Investigation and Prosecution of Nazi War Criminals," Simon Wiesenthal Center—Israel Office, December 2017, 12.
44. Hetherington and Chalmers, *War Crimes,* 92–93; Tim Luckhurst, "Why Won't Britain Jail This War Criminal," *Guardian,* September 2, 2001.
45. "Unit Failed to Nail War Criminals," *The Australian,* January 1, 2014.
46. Eli Rosenbaum to author, October 24, 2018, in author's possession.
47. United States v. Jakiw Palij, "Opinion and Order" (E.D. N.Y., July 31, 2003), 22.
48. Document 1, filed May 9, 2002, in United States v. Jakiw Palij, "Opinion and Order" (E.D. N.Y., July 31, 2003), 2–7, 9.
49. United States v. Jakiw Palij, "Opinion and Order" (E.D. N.Y., July 31, 2003), 25.
50. David Rising, *WP,* January 10, 2019.
51. Eli Rosenbaum, "Statement for Palij Removal Case Press Briefer at White House," August 21, 2018, in author's possession.

Chapter 26: The Gates Open Wide

1. Holborn, *The International Refugee Organization*, 438–39, 442, Vernant, *The Refugee in the Post-War World*, 535.
2. Figures derived from Holborn, *The International Refugee Organization*, Annex 43, 442.
3. Beth B. Cohen, *Case Closed: Holocaust Survivors in Postwar America* (New Brunswick, NJ: Rutgers University Press, 2007), 33.
4. USNA, "Report of the Executive Director," in "Reports to the Annual Meeting," January 19–20, 1952.
5. Berger, *Displaced Persons,* 31, 35, 44–45.
6. Henry Goteiner, Interview 24346, VHA, USC Shoah Foundation, 1996.
7. Author interview with Itsik Lachman, July 29, 2019.
8. Author interview with Herbert Lachman, July 29, 2019.
9. Jaroszyńska-Kirchmann, *The Exile Mission,* 134.
10. Jaroszyńska-Kirchmann, *The Exile Mission,* 121–24.
11. Piotrowski, *Vengeance of the Swallows,* 175, 177–78.
12. Cunningham, *The Rings of My Tree,* 133–34, 139.
13. Eglitis, *A Man from Latvia,* 161, 201–2.
14. "Stakė-Užgiris Family," *No Home to Go To,* Balzekas Museum, balzekasmuseum.org /displacedpersons/stake-uzgiris-family; "The Bertulis Family," *No Home to Go To,* balzekasmuseum.org/displacedpersons/bertulis_questionnaire.
15. Flannery O'Connor, "The Displaced Person," in *The Complete Stories* (New York: Farrar, Straus & Giroux, 1971), 199–200; Brad Gooch, *Flannery: A Life of Flannery O'Connor* (New York: Little, Brown, 2009), 239–46.
16. "Priest Finds DP's Work in 'Semi-Servitude' in South . . . ," *NYT,* May 4, 1949, 13.
17. "DP Sharecroppers Brought to South," *NYT,* May 14, 1949, 11.

18. Cox to Rosenfield, April 13, 1949, NLC, 5/3/2, box 4, folder 12, AELCA.
19. Carusi to Sudduth, May 12,1949, NLC, 5/3/2, box 4, folder 12, AELCA; Jaroszyńska-Kirchmann, *The Exile Mission,* 125.
20. U.S. DPC, *Memo to America,* 248, Table 15, 372.
21. Author interview with Inese Kaufman, July 31, 2019.
22. Ieva Zake, "Multiple Fronts of the Cold War: Ethnic Anti-Communism of Latvian Emigres," in *Anti-Communist Minorities in the U.S.,* ed. Ieva Zake (New York: Palgrave Macmillan, 2009), 129; Jaroszyńska-Kirchmann, *The Exile Mission,* 109.
23. John Radzilowski, "Ethnic Anti-Communism in the United States," in *Anti-Communist Minorities in the U.S.,* ed. Ieva Zake, 12.
24. Jaroszyńska-Kirchmann, *The Exile Mission,* 201.
25. Donald Pienkos, "The Polish American Congress, Polish Americans, and the Politics of Anti-Communism," in *Anti-Communist Minorities in the U.S.,* ed. Ieva Zake, 36–37; Jaroszyńska-Kirchmann, *The Exile Mission,* 308, note 22.

Chapter 27: Aftermaths

1. McNeill, *By the Rivers of Babylon,* 219.
2. Gertrude Samuels, "People in Search of Identity," *NYT,* September 23, 1956, 39, 42
3. JDC Archives, New York Office, 1945–1954, Folder: Germany, Displaced Persons, 1950, "Report of the Executive Vice-Chairman," April 18, 1950; "Minutes of the Meeting of the Executive Committee," June 20, 1950; Holborn, *The International Refugee Organization,* 486.
4. JDC Archives, New York Office, 1945–1954, Folder: Germany, Displaced Persons, 1950, "Report for April–June, 1950."
5. WJC letter to Executive Committee, June 16, 1950, cited in Grossmann, *Jews, Germans, and Allies,* 263.
6. Grossmann, *Jews, Germans, and Allies,* 256, 260; Königseder and Wetzel, *Waiting for Hope,* 149.
7. JDC Archives, Jerusalem Office, 1944–1952, folder c45.072.2, Legal Aid, Charles Jordan, "The Story of Föhrenwald," May 1957, 2–4, 6.
8. Kierra Mikaila Crago-Schneider, "A Community of Will: The Resettlement of Orthodox Jewish DPs from Föhrenwald," *Holocaust and Genocide Studies* 32, no. 1 (Spring 2018): 99–106; Königseder and Wetzel, *Waiting for Hope,* 165.
9. Jordan, "The Story of Föhrenwald," 1.
10. Author interview with Inese Kaufman, July 31, 2019.
11. Author interview with Itsik Lachman, July 29, 2019.
12. Verzemnieks, *Among the Living and the Dead,* 19.
13. Elie Wiesel, "Keynote Address," *Life Reborn: Jewish Displaced Persons, 1945–1951; Conference Proceedings, Washington, D.C., January 14–17, 2000* (Washington, DC: USHMM, 2001), 84.
14. Author interview with Inese Kaufman, July 31, 2019; Lubomyr Luciuk, *Searching for Place: Ukrainian Displaced Persons, Canada, and the Migration of Memory* (Toronto: University of Toronto Press, 2000), 274.

Bibliography

Aarons, Mark. *Sanctuary: Nazi Fugitives in Australia*. Melbourne: William Heinemann Australia, 1989.

———. *War Criminals Welcome*. Melbourne: Black Inc., 2001.

Acheson, Dean. *Present at the Creation: My Years in the State Department*. New York: Norton, 1969.

Adorno, Theodor W. *Guilt and Defense: On the Legacies of National Socialism in Postwar Germany*. Translated, edited, and with an introduction by Jeffrey K. Olick and Andrew J. Perrin. Cambridge, MA: Harvard University Press, 2010.

Alexandrow, Julia, and Tommy French. *Flight from Novaa Salow*. Jefferson, NC: McFarland, 1994.

All-Party Parliamentary War Crimes Group. *Report on the Entry of Nazi War Criminals and Collaborators into the U.K., 1945–1950*. London: House of Commons, November 1988.

Allen, Charles R., Jr. *Nazi War Criminals Among Us: A Documented Exposé*. New York: Jewish Currents, 1963.

AJC. *American Jewish Year Book*. Vols. 45–54.

———. *Memorandum on Refugees and Displaced Persons, Submitted to the Special Committee on Refugees and Displaced Persons of the United Nations Organization*. April 8, 1946.

Anders, Władysław. *An Army in Exile: The Story of the Second Polish Corps*. London: Macmillan, 1949.

Appelfeld, Aharon. *The Story of a Life*. Translated by Aloma Halter, 2004. New York: Knopf, 2009.

Arad, Yitzhak. *The Holocaust in the Soviet Union*. Lincoln: University of Nebraska Press; Jerusalem: Yad Vashem, 2009.

Arendt, Hannah. *The Origins of Totalitarianism*. New York: Harcourt, 1951.

Bailey, Stephen K., and Howard D. Samuel. *Congress at Work*. New York: Henry Holt, 1952.

Bartov, Omer. *Anatomy of a Genocide: The Life and Death of a Town Called Buczacz*. New York: Simon & Schuster, 2018.

Bauer, Yehuda. *Flight and Rescue: Brichah*. New York: Random House, 1970.

———. "The DP Legacy." In *Life Reborn: Jewish Displaced Persons, 1945–1951: Conference Proceedings*, USHMM. Washington, DC, January 14–17, 2000.

Bazyler, Michael J., and Frank M. Tuerkheimer. *Forgotten Trials of the Holocaust*. New York: New York University Press, 2014.

Berger, Joseph. *Displaced Persons: Growing Up American After the Holocaust*. New York: Washington Square Press, 2001.

Berkhoff, Karel C. *Harvest of Despair: Life and Death in Ukraine Under Nazi Rule*. Cambridge, MA: Harvard University Press, 2008.

Berkovits, Annette Libeskind. *In the Unlikeliest of Places: How Nachman Libeskind Survived the Nazis, Gulags, and Soviet Communism*. Waterloo, ON: Wilfrid Laurier University Press, 2014.

Bernard, William S. "Not Sympathy, but Action." *Survey Graphic*, February 1947.

———. "Homeless, Tempest-Tossed." *Survey Graphic*, April 1948.

Bessel, Richard. *Germany 1945: From War to Peace*. New York: Harper, 2009.

Bessel, Richard, and Claudia B. Haake, eds. *Removing Peoples: Forced Removal in the Modern World*. Oxford: Oxford University Press, 2009.

Blatman, Daniel. *The Death Marches: The Final Phase of Nazi Genocide*. Translated by Chaya Galai. Cambridge, MA: Harvard University Press, 2011.

Bikont, Anna. *The Crime and the Silence: Confronting the Massacre of Jews in Wartime Jedwabne*. Translated by Alissa Valles. New York: Farrar, Straus & Giroux, 2015.

Bird, Kai. *The Chairman: John J. McCloy, The Making of the American Establishment*. New York: Simon & Schuster, 1992.

Birger, Zev. *No Time for Patience: My Road from Kaunas to Jerusalem*. New York: Newmarket Press, 1999.

Blumenson, Martin, ed. *The Patton Papers, 1940–1945*. Boston: Houghton Mifflin, 1974.

Bosworth, Patricia. *Anything Your Little Heart Desires: An American Family Story*. New York: Simon & Schuster, 1997.

Böhler, Jochen, and Robert Gerwarth. *The Waffen-SS: A European History*. Oxford: Oxford University Press, 2017.

Bower, Tom. *The Red Web: MI6 and the KGB MasterCoup*. London: Aurum Press, 1989.

———. *Blind Eye to Murder: Britain, America, and the Purging of Nazi Germany—A Pledge Betrayed*. London: Warner Books, 1997.

Brandon, Ray, and Wendy Lower, eds. *The Shoah in Ukraine: History, Testimony, Memorialization*. Bloomington: Indiana University Press, 2008.

Breitman, Richard, and Norman J. W. Goda. *Hitler's Shadow: Nazi War Criminals, U.S. Intelligence, and the Cold War*. Washington, DC: National Archives, 2011.

Breitman, Richard, Norman J. W. Goda, Timothy Naftali, and Robert Wolfe. *U.S. Intelligence and the Nazis*. New York: Cambridge University Press, 2004.

Brenner, Michael. *After the Holocaust: Rebuilding Jewish Lives in Postwar Germany*. Translated by Barbara Harshav. Princeton, NJ: Princeton University Press, 1997.

Browning, Christopher R., with contributions by Jürgen Matthäus. *The Origins of the Final Solution*. Lincoln: University of Nebraska Press; Jerusalem: Yad Vashem, 2004.

Buruma, Ian. *Year Zero: A History of 1945*. New York: Penguin Press, 2013.

Carafano, James Jay. "Mobilizing Europe's Stateless: America's Plan for a Cold War Army." *Journal of Cold War Studies* 1, no. 2 (May 1, 1999): 61–85.

Carruthers, Susan. *The Good Occupation: American Soldiers and the Hazards of Peace.* Cambridge, MA: Harvard University Press, 2016.

Cesarani, David. *Justice Delayed: How Britain Became a Refuge for Nazi War Criminals.* London: Phoenix Press, 2001.

———. *Final Solution: The Fate of the Jews, 1933–1949.* New York: St. Martin's, 2016.

Citizens Committee on Displaced Persons. "The Displaced Persons 'What's What.'" N.p., n.d.

Clare, George. *Before the Wall: Berlin Days, 1946–1948.* New York: Dutton, 1989.

Clay, Lucius D. *Decision in Germany.* Garden City, NY: Doubleday, 1950.

Clifford, Clark. "Recognizing Israel." *American Heritage* 28, no. 3 (April 1977).

———. *Counsel to the President: A Memoir.* New York: Random House, 1991.

Close, Kathryn. "They Want to Be People." *Survey Graphic,* November 1946.

Cohen, Beth. *Case Closed: Holocaust Survivors in Postwar America.* New Brunswick, NJ: Rutgers University Press, 2007.

Cohen, Gerard Daniel. *In War's Wake: Europe's Displaced Persons in the Postwar Order.* New York: Oxford University Press, 2012.

Cohen, Michael J. *Truman and Israel.* Berkeley: University of California Press, 1990.

Commission of Inquiry on War Criminals, Honourable Jules Deschênes, Commissioner. *Report.* Ottawa, December 30, 1986.

Cooper, Kanty. *The Uprooted: Agony and Triumph Among the Debris of War.* London: Quartet Books, 1979.

Costigliola, Frank. "The Creation of Memory and Myth: Stalin's 1946 Election Speech and the Soviet Threat." In *Critical Reflections on the Cold War,* ed. Martin Medhurst and H. W. Brands, 38–54. College Station: Texas A&M University Press, 2000.

Courtney, W. B. "Europe's Hangover," *Collier's* 116 (July 28, 1945).

Crossman, Richard. *Palestine Mission: A Personal Record.* New York: Harper & Brothers, 1947.

Crum, Bartley C. *Behind the Silken Curtain: A Personal Account of Anglo-American Diplomacy in Palestine and the Middle East.* New York: Simon & Schuster, 1947.

Cunningham, Jane E. *The Rings of My Tree: A Latvian Woman's Journey.* Coral Springs, FL: Llumina Press, 2004.

David-Fox, Michael, Peter Holquist, and Alexander M. Martin. *The Holocaust in the East: Local Perpetrators and Soviet Responses.* Pittsburgh: University of Pittsburgh Press, 2014.

Davies, Norman. *God's Playground: A History of Poland.* Vol. 2, *1795 to the Present.* Rev. 2nd ed. New York: Columbia University Press, 2005.

Dawidowicz, Lucy. *From That Place and Time: A Memoir, 1938–1947.* New York: Bantam, 1991.

Deák, István. *Essays on Hitler's Europe.* Lincoln: University of Nebraska Press, 2001.

Deák, István, Jan T. Gross, and Tony Judt, eds. *The Politics of Retribution in Europe.* Princeton, NJ: Princeton University Press, 2000.

Deane, John R. *The Strange Alliance: The Story of Our Efforts at Wartime Co-operation with Russia.* New York: Viking, 1947.

Dekel, Mikhal. *Tehran Children: A Holocaust Refugee Odyssey.* New York: Norton, 2019.

Department of the Special Minister of State. *Review of Material Relating to the Entry of Suspected War Criminals into Australia.* Canberra: Australian Government Publishing Service, 1987.

Dieckmann, Christoph. "Holocaust in the Lithuanian Provinces: Case Studies of Jurbarkas and Utena." In Beate Kosmala and George Verbeeck, eds., *Facing the Catastrophe: Jews and Non-Jews in Europe During World War II.* Oxford: Berg, 2011.

———. "Killing Sites in 1941: History and Memory." In *As Mass Murder Began: Identifying and Remembering the Killing Sites of Summer–Fall 1941.* Vilnius, Lithuania, April 2017. www.youtube.com/watch?v=VFHohfrVOjI.

Dinnerstein, Leonard. *America and the Survivors of the Holocaust.* New York: Columbia University Press, 1982.

———. *Anti-Semitism in America.* New York: Oxford University Press, 1994.

Dobroszycki, Lucjan. *Survivors of the Holocaust in Poland: A Portrait Based on Jewish Community Records, 1944–1947.* Armonk, NY: M. E. Sharpe, 1994.

Dorril, Stephen. *MI6: Inside the Covert World of Her Majesty's Secret Intelligence Service.* New York: Free Press, 2000.

Douglas, Lawrence. *The Right Wrong Man: John Demjanjuk and the Last Great Nazi War Crimes Trial.* Princeton, NJ: Princeton University Press, 2016.

Douglas, R. M. *Orderly and Humane: The Expulsion of the Germans After the Second World War.* New Haven, CT: Yale University Press, 2012.

Duchesne-Cripps, Audrey. *The Mental Outlook of the Displaced Person as Seen through Welfare Work in Displaced Persons Camps.* Cambridge: self-published, 1955.

Dyczok, Marta. *The Grand Alliance and Ukrainian Refugees.* New York: St. Martin's, 2000.

Edele, Mark, Sheila Fitzpatrick, and Atina Grossmann, eds. *Shelter from the Holocaust: Rethinking Jewish Survival in the Soviet Union.* Detroit: Wayne State University Press, 2017.

Egan, Eileen. *For Whom There Is No Room: Scenes from the Refugee World.* Mahwah, NJ: Paulist Press, 1995.

Eglitis, Andrejs. *A Man from Latvia.* West Conshohocken, PA: Infinity, 2009.

Eisenhower, Dwight D. *Crusade in Europe.* Garden City, NY: Doubleday, 1948.

Elliott, Mark. R. *Pawns of Yalta: Soviet Refugees and America's Role in Their Repatriation.* Urbana: University of Illinois Press, 1982.

Engerman, David C. *Know Your Enemy: The Rise and Fall of America's Soviet Experts.* New York: Oxford University Press, 2009.

Evans, Richard J. *The Third Reich at War.* New York: Penguin, 2009.

Ezergailis, Andrew. *The Holocaust in Latvia, 1941–1944: The Missing Center.* Riga, Latvia: Historical Institute of Latvia, 1996.

———. "The Holocaust in Occupied Latvia, 1941–1944: The Scholarship of Professor Andrew Ezergailis." haolusa.org/.

Fay, Sidney B. "Displaced Persons in Europe." *Current History,* March 1946.

Feigin, Judy. *The Office of Special Investigations: Striving for Accountability in the Aftermath of the Holocaust.* Edited by Mark M. Richard. Washington, DC: Office of Special Investigations, December 2, 2006.

Feingold, Henry. *The Politics of Rescue: The Roosevelt Administration and the Holocaust, 1938–1945.* New Brunswick, NJ: Rutgers University Press, 1970.

Feinstein, Margarete Myers. *Holocaust Survivors in Postwar Germany, 1945–1957.* New York: Cambridge University Press, 2010.

Fishman, David E. *The Book Smugglers: Partisans, Poets, and the Race to Save Jewish Treasures from the Nazis.* Lebanon, NH: ForeEdge, 2017.

Fitzpatrick, Sheila. *Mischka's War: A Story of Survival from War-Torn Europe to New York.* New York: I. B. Tauris, 2017.

Flanner, Janet. "Letter from Paris." *New Yorker,* June 16, 1945.

———. "Letter from Heidelberg." *New Yorker,* July 21, 1945.

———. "Letter from Aschaffenburg." *New Yorker,* October 30, 1948.

———. "Letter from Würzburg." *New Yorker,* November 6, 1948.

Fousek, John. *To Lead the Free World: American Nationalism and the Cultural Roots of the Cold War.* Chapel Hill: University of North Carolina Press, 2000.

Fraser, David. *Daviborshch's Cart: Narrating the Holocaust in Australian War Crimes.* Lincoln: University of Nebraska Press, 2010.

Friedländer, Saul. *The Years of Extermination: Nazi Germany and the Jews.* New York: Harper Collins, 2008.

Fritz, Stephen. *Endkampf: Soldiers, Civilians, and the Death of the Third Reich.* Lexington. University Press of Kentucky, 2004.

Fuerch, Richard E. *Displaced Persons: An Immigrant Journey to America.* Bloomington, IN: AuthorHouse, 2014.

Gabis, Rita. *A Guest at the Shooters' Banquet: My Grandfather's SS Past, My Jewish Family, a Search for the Truth.* New York: Bloomsbury, 2015.

Gaddis, John Lewis. *George F. Kennan.* New York: Penguin, 2011.

García-Granados, Jorge. *The Birth of Israel: The Drama as I Saw It.* New York: Knopf, 1948.

Gartner, Lloyd P. "In Memoriam: Abraham G. Duker." *Jewish Social Studies* 49, no. 3/4 (Summer–Autumn 1987): 189–94.

Genizi, Haim. *America's Fair Share: The Admission and Resettlement of Displaced Persons, 1945–1952.* Detroit: Wayne State University Press, 1993.

Gessen, Masha. *Where the Jews Aren't: The Sad and Absurd Story of Birobidzhan, Russia's Jewish Autonomous Region.* New York: Schocken, 2013.

Gilbert, Emily. *Rebuilding Postwar Britain: Latvian, Lithuanian and Estonian Refugees in Britain, 1946–51.* South Yorkshire: Pen & Sword History, 2017.

Gilbert, Martin. *The Routledge Atlas of the Holocaust.* 4th ed. London: Routledge, 2009.

Goda, Norman J. W. "Surviving Survival: James G. McDonald and the Fate of Holocaust Survivors." Monna and Otto Weinmann Annual Lecture, Jack, Joseph and Morton Mandel Center for Advanced Holocaust Studies. Washington, DC: USHMM, 2015.

Gooch, Brad. *Flannery: A Life of Flannery O'Connor.* New York: Little, Brown, 2009.

Gringauz, Samuel. "Jewish Destiny as the DP's See It." *Commentary,* December 1947.

———. "Our New German Policy and the DP's," *Commentary,* June 1948.

Grobman, Alex. *Rekindling the Flame: American Jewish Chaplains and the Survivors of European Jewry, 1944–1948.* Detroit: Wayne State University Press, 1993.

Grose, Peter. *Operation Rollback: America's Secret War Behind the Iron Curtain.* Boston: Houghton Mifflin, 2000.

Gross, Jan T. *Neighbors: The Destruction of the Jewish Community in Jedwabne, Poland.* Princeton, NJ: Princeton University Press, 2001.

———. *Fear: Anti-Semitism in Poland After Auschwitz.* New York: Random House, 2007.

Grossmann, Atina. *Jews, Germans, and Allies: Close Encounters in Occupied Germany.* Princeton, NJ: Princeton University Press, 2007.

Gruber, Ruth. *Destination Palestine: The Story of the Haganah Ship* Exodus 1947. New York: Current Books, 1948.

Halamish, Aviva. *The* Exodus *Affair: Holocaust Survivors and the Struggle for Palestine.* Translated by Ora Cummings. Syracuse: Syracuse University Press, 1998.

Hanebrink, Paul. *A Specter Haunting Europe: The Myth of Judeo-Bolshevism.* Cambridge, MA: Harvard University Press, 2018.

Hayes, Peter. *Why? Explaining the Holocaust.* New York: Norton, 2017.

Herbert, Ulrich. *Hitler's Foreign Workers: Enforced Foreign Labor in Germany Under the Third Reich.* Cambridge: Cambridge University Press, 1997.

Herken, Gregg. *The Georgetown Set: Friends and Rivals in Cold War Washington.* New York: Vintage, 2014.

Hersh, Burton. *The Old Boys: The American Elite and the Origins of the CIA.* New York: Scribner's, 1992.

Hetherington, Sir Thomas, and William Chalmers. *War Crimes: Report of the War Crimes Inquiry.* London: Her Majesty's Stationery Office, 1989.

Hilliard, Robert L. *Surviving the Americans: The Continued Struggle of the Jews After Liberation.* New York: Seven Stories Press, 1997.

Hilton, Ella E. Schneider. *Displaced Person: A Girl's Life in Russia, Germany, and America.* Baton Rouge: Louisiana State University Press, 2004.

Hiio, Toomas, Meelis Maripuu, and Indrek Paavle, eds. *Estonia 1940–1945: Reports of the Estonian International Commission for the Investigation of Crimes Against Humanity.* Tallinn: Estonian Foundation for the Investigation of Crimes Against Humanity, 2006.

Hirschmann, Ira. *The Embers Still Burn: An Eye-Witness View of the Postwar Ferment in Europe and the Middle East and Our Disastrous Get-Soft-with-Germany Policy.* New York: Simon & Schuster, 1949.

Hitchcock, William I. *The Bitter Road to Freedom: The Human Cost of Allied Victory in World War II.* New York: Free Press, 2008.

Hochstein, Joseph M., and Murray S. Greenfield. *The Jews' Secret Fleet: The Untold Story of North American Volunteers Who Smashed the British Blockade.* Jerusalem: Gefen, 1987.

Holborn, Louise W. *The International Refugee Organization: A Specialized Agency of the United Nations; Its History and Work, 1946–1952.* London: Oxford University Press, 1956.

Holian, Anna. *Between National Socialism and Soviet Communism: Displaced Persons in Postwar Germany.* Ann Arbor: University of Michigan Press, 2011.

Holtzman, Elizabeth, with Cynthia L. Cooper. *Who Said It Would Be Easy? One Woman's Life in the Political Arena.* New York: Arcade Publishing, 1996.

Horowitz, David. *State in the Making.* New York: Knopf, 1953.

Hulme, Kathryn. *The Wild Place.* Boston: Little, Brown, 1953.

Hutler, Albert, with Marvin J. Folkertsma Jr. *Agony of Survival.* Macomb, IL: Glenbridge, 1989.

Hyman, Abraham S. *The Undefeated.* Jerusalem: Gefen, 1993.

Ilan, Amitzur. *Bernadotte in Palestine, 1948.* New York: St. Martin's, 1989.

International Refugee Organization. *Manual for Eligibility Officers.* N.d.

———. *Migration from Europe.* Geneva, 1951.

Isajiw, Wsevolod, Yury Boshyk, and Roman Senkus, eds. *The Refugee Experience: Ukrainian Displaced Persons After World War II.* Edmonton: Canadian Institute of Ukrainian Studies Press, 1992.

Jacobsen, Annie. *Operation Paperclip: The Secret Intelligence Program That Brought Nazi Scientists to America.* New York: Little, Brown, 2014.

Janco, Andrew Paul. "'Unwilling': The One-Word Revolution in Refugee Status, 1940–51." *Contemporary European History* 23, no. 3 (August 2014): 429–46.

Jaroszyńska-Kirchmann, Anna D. *The Exile Mission: The Polish Political Diaspora and Polish Americans.* Athens: Ohio University Press, 2004.

Jockusch, Laura. *Collect and Record! Jewish Holocaust Documentation in Early Postwar Europe.* New York: Oxford University Press, 2012.

Jockusch, Laura, and Gabriel N. Finder, eds. *Jewish Honor Courts: Revenge, Retribution, and Reconciliation in Europe and Israel After the Holocaust.* Detroit: Wayne State University Press, 2015.

Judis, John D. *Genesis: Truman, American Jews, and the Origins of the Arab/Israeli Conflict.* New York: Farrar, Straus & Giroux, 2014.

Judt, Tony. *Postwar: A History of Europe Since 1945.* New York: Penguin, 2005.

Kacel, Boris. *From Hell to Redemption: A Memoir of the Holocaust.* Niwot: University Press of Colorado, 1998.

Kapeikis, Harry G. *Exile from Latvia: My WWII Childhood—From Survival to Opportunity.* Victoria, BC: Trafford Publishing, 2007.

Karabell, Zachary. *The Last Campaign: How Harry Truman Won the 1948 Election.* New York: Knopf, 2000.

Kassow, Samuel D. *Who Will Write Our History? Rediscovering a Hidden Archive from the Warsaw Ghetto.* New York: Vintage, 2009. Originally published 2007.

Kay, Diana, and Robert Miles. *Refugees or Migrant Workers? European Volunteer Workers in Britain 1946–1951.* London: Routledge, 1992.

Keegan, John. *The Second World War.* New York: Penguin, 1989.

Kempowski, Walter. *Swansong 1945: A Collective Diary of the Last Days of the Third Reich.* Translated by Shaun Whiteside. New York: Norton, 2015.

Kershaw, Ian. *Hitler, 1936–1945: Nemesis.* New York: Norton, 2000.

———. *The End: The Defiance and Destruction of Hitler's Germany, 1944–1945.* New York: Penguin, 2011.

Kertzer, David I. *The Pope and Mussolini: The Secret History of Pius XI and the Rise of Fascism in Europe.* New York: Random House, 2014.

Khalidi, Rashid. *The Iron Cage: The Story of the Palestinian Struggle for Statehood.* Boston: Beacon, 2006.

Kimche, Jon, and David Kimche. *The Secret Roads: The "Illegal" Migration of a People, 1938–1948*. New York: Farrar, Straus & Cudahy, 1955.

Kirby, Dianne, ed. *Religion and the Cold War*. New York: Palgrave, 2013.

Klausner, Abraham J. *A Letter to My Children: From the Edge of the Holocaust*. San Francisco: Holocaust Center of Northern California, 2002.

Klemme, Marvin. *The Inside Story of UNRRA: An Experience in Internationalism: A First Hand Report on the Displaced People of Europe*. New York: Lifetime Editions, 1949.

Knowles, Christopher. *Winning the Peace: The British in Occupied Germany, 1945–1948*. London: Bloomsbury, 2017.

Kochavi, Arieh J. *Post-Holocaust Politics: Britain, the United States, and Jewish Refugees, 1945–1948*. Chapel Hill: University of North Carolina Press, 2004.

Königseder, Angelika, and Juliane Wetzel. *Waiting for Hope: Jewish Displaced Persons in Post–World War II Germany*. Evanston, IL: Northwestern University Press, 1994.

Kool, Ferdinand. *DP Chronicle: Estonian Refugees in Germany, 1944–1951*. Lakewood, NJ: Estonian Archives in the U.S., Inc., 2014.

Kotkin, Stephen. *Stalin: Waiting for Hitler, 1929–1941*. New York: Penguin Press, 2017.

Legge, Jerome S., Jr. "The Karl Linnas Deportation Case, the Office of Special Investigations, and American Ethnic Politics." *Holocaust and Genocide Studies* 24, no. 1 (Spring 2010): 26–55.

Levene, Mark. *The Crisis of Genocide*. Vol. 2, *Annihilation: The European Rimlands, 1939–1954*. Oxford: Oxford University Press, 2013.

Levi, Primo. *The Reawakening*. Translated by Stuart Woolf. New York: Simon & Schuster, 1995.

———. *Survival in Auschwitz*. New York: Touchstone, 1996.

Lichtblau, Eric. *The Nazis Next Door: How America Became a Safe Haven for Hitler's Men*. Boston: Houghton Mifflin, 2014.

Lipstadt, Deborah. *Beyond Belief: The American Press and the Coming of the Holocaust, 1933–1945*. New York: Free Press, 1985.

Litvak, Yosef. "Jewish Refugees from Poland in the USSR, 1939–1946." In *Bitter Legacy: Confronting the Holocaust in the USSR*, ed. Zvi Gitelman, 123–50. Bloomington: Indiana University Press, 1997.

Loftus, John. *America's Nazi Secret: An Insider's History*. Walterville, OR: TrineDay, 2011.

Łossowski, Piotr. "The Resettlement of the Germans from the Baltic States in 1939/1941." *Acta Poloniae Historica* 92 (2005).

Lowe, Keith. *Savage Continent: Europe in the Aftermath of World War II*. New York: St. Martin's, 2012.

Luciuk, Lubomyr. *Searching for Place: Ukrainian Displaced Persons, Canada, and the Migration of Memory*. Toronto: University of Toronto Press, 2000.

Lukas, Richard C. *Bitter Legacy: Polish-American Relations in the Wake of World War II*. Lexington: University Press of Kentucky, 2009.

Lumans, Valdis O. *Latvia in World War II*. New York: Fordham University Press, 2006.

MacDonogh, Giles. *After the Reich: The Brutal History of the Allied Occupation*. New York: Basic Books, 2007.

MacGregor, Morris J. *Steadfast in the Faith: The Life of Patrick Cardinal O'Boyle.* Washington, DC: Catholic University of America Press, 2006.

Mankowitz, Zeev W. *Life Between Memory and Hope: The Survivors of the Holocaust in Occupied Germany.* New York: Cambridge University Press, 2002.

Margolian, Howard. *Unauthorized Entry: The Truth About Nazi War Criminals in Canada, 1946–1956.* Toronto: University of Toronto Press, 2000.

Marrus, Michael R. *The Unwanted: European Refugees in the Twentieth Century.* New York: Oxford University Press, 1985.

Mazower, Mark. *Hitler's Empire: How the Nazis Ruled Europe.* New York: Penguin, 2008.

McClelland, Grigor. *Embers of War: Letters from a Quaker Relief Worker in War-Torn Germany.* London: British Academic Press, 1997.

McDonald, James G. *My Mission in Israel, 1948–1951.* New York: Simon & Schuster, 1951.

———. *To the Gates of Jerusalem: The Diaries and Papers of James G. McDonald, 1945–1947.* Edited by Norman J. W. Goda et al. Bloomington: Indiana University Press, 2014.

McDowell, Linda. "Narratives of Family, Community and Waged Work: Latvian European Volunteer Worker Women in Post-war Britain." *Women's History Review* 13, no. 1 (2004): 23–55.

———. *Hard Labour: The Forgotten Voices of Latvian Migrant "Volunteer" Workers.* London: UCL Press, 2005.

McNeill, Margaret. *By the Rivers of Babylon: A Story of Relief Work Among the Displaced Persons of Europe.* London: Bannisdale Press, 1950.

Melnyk, Michael James. *To Battle: The Formation and History of the 14th Galician Waffen-SS Division.* West Midlands, England: Helion & Company, 2002.

Merritt, Richard L. *Democracy Imposed: U.S. Occupation Policy and the German Public, 1945–1949.* New Haven, CT: Yale University Press, 1995.

Mertelsmann, Olaf, ed. *The Baltic States Under Stalinist Rule.* Cologne and Weimar: Böhlau Verlag, 2016.

Misiunas, Romuald J., and Rein Taagepera. *The Baltic States: Years of Dependence, 1940–1990.* Expanded and updated edition. Berkeley and Los Angeles: University of California Press, 1993.

Moorehead, Alan. *Eclipse.* New York: Harper & Row, 1968. Originally published 1945.

Morris, Benny. *1948: A History of the First Arab-Israeli War.* New Haven, CT: Yale University Press, 2008.

Müller, Rolf-Dieter. *The Unknown Eastern Front: The Wehrmacht and Hitler's Foreign Soldiers.* Translated by David Burnett. London: I. B. Tauris, 2012.

Murphy, H. B. M. "The Resettlement of Jewish Refugees in Israel, with Special Reference to Those Known as Displaced Persons." *Population Studies* 5, no. 2 (November 1951): 153–74.

Museum of the Occupation of Latvia. *1940–1991: Latvia Under the Rule of the Soviet Union and National Socialist Germany.* Riga, 2018.

Muszyński, Wojciech Jerzy. "The Polish Guards Companies of the U.S. Army After World War II." *Polish Review* 57, no. 4 (2012): 75–86.

Nadich, Judah. *Eisenhower and the Jews.* New York: Twayne, 1953.

Nagorski, Andrew. *The Nazi Hunters.* New York: Simon & Schuster, 2016.

Naimark, Norman M. *Stalin and the Fate of Europe: The Postwar Struggle for Sovereignty.* Cambridge, MA: Harvard University Press, 2019.

Nesaule, Agate. *A Woman in Amber: Healing the Trauma of War and Exile.* New York: Penguin, 1995.

Neumann, Klaus. *Across the Seas: Australia's Response to Refugees; A History.* Collingwood, Victoria: Black Inc., 2015.

Novick, Peter. *The Holocaust in American Life.* New York: Houghton Mifflin, 2000.

O'Connor, Flannery. "The Displaced Person." In *The Complete Stories,* 194–235. New York: Farrar, Straus & Giroux, 1971.

Palmer, Greg, and Mark S. Zaid, eds. *The GI's Rabbi: World War II Letters of David Max Eichhorn.* Lawrence: University Press of Kansas, 2004.

Pappe, Ilan. *The Ethnic Cleansing of Palestine.* London: Oneworld, 2006.

Patt, Avinoam J. *Finding Home and Homeland: Jewish Youth and Zionism in the Aftermath of the Holocaust.* Detroit: Wayne State University Press, 2009.

Persian, Jayne. "'Chifley Liked Them Blond.'" *History Australia* 12, no. 2 (2015): 80–101.

Pettiss, Susan T., and Lynne Taylor. *After the Shooting Stopped: The Story of an UNRRA Welfare Worker in Germany 1945–1947.* Cheshire, UK: Trafford, 2004.

Piotrowski, Tadeusz. *Vengeance of the Swallows: Memoir of a Polish Family's Ordeal.* Jefferson, NC: McFarland, 1995.

Plakans, Andrejs. *The Latvians: A Short History.* Stanford, CA: Hoover Institution Press, 1995.

———. *A Concise History of the Baltic States.* New York: Cambridge University Press, 2011.

Plavnieks, Richard. "Nazi Collaborators on Trial During the Cold War: The Cases Against Viktors Arājs and the Latvian Auxiliary Security Police." PhD dissertation, University of North Carolina, 2013.

Plume, Ventis, and John Plume, eds. *Insula: Island of Hope.* Morgan Hill, CA: Bookstand Publishing, 2013.

Political Documents of the Jewish Agency. Vols. 1, 2. Edited by Yehoshua Freundlich. Jerusalem: Hassifriya Hažionit, Publishing House of the World Zionist Organization, 1996.

Proudfoot, Malcolm. "The Anglo-American Displaced Persons Program for Germany and Austria." *American Journal of Economics and Sociology* 6, no. 1 (October 1946): 33–54.

———. *European Refugees: 1939–52: A Study in Forced Population Movement.* Evanston, IL: Northwestern University Press, 1956.

Piirimäe, Kaarel. *Roosevelt, Churchill, and the Baltic Question: Allied Relations During the Second World War.* New York: Palgrave, 2014.

Radosh, Allis, and Ronald Radosh. *A Safe Haven: Harry S. Truman and the Founding of Israel.* New York: HarperCollins, 2009.

Rashke, Richard. *Useful Enemies: America's Open-Door Policy for Nazi War Criminals.* Harrison, NY: Delphinium Books, 2013.

Remy, Steven P. *The Malmedy Massacre: The War Crimes Trial Controversy.* Cambridge, MA: Harvard University Press, 2017.

Reston, James. "Negotiating with the Russians." *Harper's Magazine* 195, no. 1167 (August 1947).

Revercomb, Chapman. *Report to the Senate Republican Steering Committee on the Possible Admission of Displaced Persons to the United States.* December 30, 1946.

Roosenburg, Henriette. *The Walls Came Tumbling Down.* New York: Akadine Press, 2000. Originally published 1957.

Rosenberg, Göran. *A Brief Stop on the Road from Auschwitz.* Translated by Sarah Death. New York: Other Press, 2012.

Rosensaft, Hadassah. *Yesterday: My Story.* New York: Yad Vashem and the Holocaust Survivors Memoirs Project, 2004.

Rosensaft, Menacham Z. "Bergen-Belsen: The End and the Beginning." In *Children of the Holocaust: Symposium Presentations.* Washington, DC: Center for Advanced Holocaust Studies, USHMM, 2004.

———. "Children Born in Displaced Persons Camps . . ." *Tablet,* December 21, 2015.

———. "Reclaiming a National Jewish Identity After the Holocaust." *Tablet,* September 14, 2016.

Roosevelt, Eleanor. *On My Own.* New York: Harper & Brothers, 1958.

Rowinski, Leokadia. *That the Nightingale Return: Memoir of the Polish Resistance, the Warsaw Uprising and German P.O.W. Camps.* Jefferson, NC: McFarland, 1999.

Ruffner, Kevin C. "Cold War Allies: The Origins of CIA's Relationship with Ukrainian Nationalists," www.cia.gov/library/readingroom/docs/STUDIES%20IN%20INTELLIGENCE%20NAZI%20%-20RELATED%20ARTICLES_0015.pdf.

Rutland, Suzanne. "Subtle Exclusions: Postwar Jewish Emigration to Australia and the Impact of the IRO Scheme." *Journal of Holocaust Education* 10, no. 1 (Summer 2001): 50–66.

———. "Postwar Anti-Jewish Refugee Hysteria: A Case of Racial or Religious Bigotry." *Journal of Australian Studies* 27, no. 77 (2003): 69–79.

———. "Jewish Immigration After the Second World War." *Israel and Judaism Studies,* 2006. www.ijs.org.au/Jewish-Immigration-after-the-Second-World-War/default.aspx.

Rutland, Suzanne, and Sol Encel. "Three 'Rich Uncles in America': The Australian Immigration Project and American Jewry." *American Jewish History* 95, no. 1 (March 2009): 79–115.

Ryan, Alan A., Jr. *Quiet Neighbors: Prosecuting Nazi War Criminals in America.* San Diego: Harcourt Brace Jovanovich, 1984.

Sachar, Abram L. *The Redemption of the Unwanted: From the Liberation of the Death Camps to the Founding of Israel.* New York: St. Martin's, 1983.

Saidel, Rochelle G. *The Outraged Conscience: Seekers of Justice for Nazi War Criminals in America.* Albany: State University of New York Press, 1984.

Salnais, Voldemārs. "Report of First Year of the German Occupation, 1942." In *Stockholm Documents: The German Occupation of Latvia, 1941–1945,* ed. Andrew Ezergailis. Riga: Historical Institute of Latvia, 2002.

Sanua, Marianne R. *Let Us Prove Strong: The American Jewish Committee, 1945–2006.* Lebanon, NH: Brandeis University Press, 2007.

Sayre, Joel. "Letter from Germany." *New Yorker,* May 12, 1945.

———. "Letter from Munich." *New Yorker,* May 19, 1945.

Schiessl, Christopher. "The Search for Nazi Collaborators in the United States." PhD dissertation, Wayne State University, 2009.

Schwarz, Leo W. *The Redeemers: A Saga of the Years 1945–1952.* New York: Farrar, Straus & Young, 1953.

Segev, Tom. *1949: The First Israelis.* New York: Henry Holt, 1999.

———. *The Seventh Million: The Israelis and the Holocaust.* Translated by Haim Watzman. New York: Henry Holt, 2000.

———. *Simon Wiesenthal: The Life and Legends.* New York: Schocken, 2010.

———. *A State at Any Cost: The Life of David Ben-Gurion.* Translated by Haim Watzman. New York: Farrar, Straus & Giroux, 2019.

Seipp, Adam R. *Strangers in the Wild Place: Refugees, Americans, and a German Town, 1945–1952.* Bloomington: Indiana University Press, 2013.

Service, Hugh. *Germans to Poles: Communism, Nationalism and Ethnic Cleansing After the Second World War.* Cambridge: Cambridge University Press, 2013.

SHAEF, Office of the Chief of Staff. *Handbook for Military Government in Germany Prior to Defeat or Surrender.* 1944.

Shandler, Jeffrey. *While America Watches: Televising the Holocaust.* New York: Oxford University Press, 1999.

Shapell, Nathan. *Witness to the Truth.* New York: David McKay, 1974.

Shephard, Ben. *The Long Road Home: The Aftermath of the Second World War.* New York: Anchor Books, 2012.

Simpson, Christopher. *Blowback: America's Recruitment of Nazis and Its Effects on the Cold War.* New York: Weidenfeld & Nicolson, 1988.

Smyth, J. E. *Fred Zinnemann and the Cinema of Resistance.* Jackson: University Press of Mississippi, 2014.

Snyder, Timothy. *Bloodlands: Europe Between Hitler and Stalin.* New York: Basic Books, 2010.

———. *Black Earth: The Holocaust as History and Warning.* New York: Tim Duggan Books, 2015.

———. *The Road to Unfreedom.* New York: Tim Duggan Books, 2018.

Sollors, Werner. *The Temptation to Despair: Tales of the 1940s.* Cambridge, MA: Harvard University Press, 2014.

Somers, Erik, and René Kok. *Jewish Displaced Persons in Camp Bergen-Belsen, 1945–1950: The Unique Photo Album of Zippy Orlin.* Seattle: University of Washington Press, n.d.

Steel, Ronald. *Walter Lippmann and the American Century.* New York: Atlantic Monthly Press, 1980.

Steinert, Johannes-Dieter. "British Post-War Migration Policy and Displaced Persons in Europe." In *The Disentanglement of Populations,* ed. J. Reinisch et al., 229–50. London: Palgrave Macmillan, 2011.

Steinert, Johannes-Dieter, and Inge Weber-Newth, eds. *Beyond Camps and Forced Labour: Current International Research on Survivors of Nazi Persecution.* Proceedings of the First International Multidisciplinary Conference at the Imperial War Museum, London, January 29–31, 2003. Osnabrück: Secolo, 2005.

Stevens, Lewis M. "The Life and Character of Earl G. Harrison." *University of Pennsylvania Law Review* 104, no. 5 (March 1956): 591–602.

Stone, Dan. *The Liberation of the Camps: The End of the Holocaust and Its Aftermath.* New Haven, CT: Yale University Press, 2015.

Stone, I. F. *Underground to Palestine.* New York: Pantheon, 1976. Originally published 1946.

Tannberg, Tõnu, ed. *Behind the Iron Curtain: Soviet Estonia in the Era of the Cold War.* Frankfurt am Main: Peter Lang, 2015.

Tooze, Adam. *The Wages of Destruction: The Making and Breaking of the Nazi Economy.* New York: Penguin, 2006.

Traverso, Enzo. *Fire and Blood: The European Civil War, 1914–1945.* Translated by David Fernbach. London: Verso, 2016.

Tromly, Benjamin. *Cold War Exiles and the CIA: Plotting to Free Russia.* Oxford: Oxford University Press, 2019.

Truman, Harry S. *Memoirs.* Vol. 1, *Year of Decisions.* Garden City, NY: Doubleday, 1955.

———. *Memoirs.* Vol. 2, *Years of Trial and Hope.* Garden City, NY: Doubleday, 1956.

Tuchman, Marcel. *Remember: My Stories of Survival and Beyond.* New York: Holocaust Survivors' Memoirs Project and Yad Vashem, 2010.

UN Economic and Social Council. *Report of the Special Committee on Refugees and Displaced Persons.* London, April 8–June 1, 1946.

———. Official Records. *Special Supplement: Report of the Special Committee on Refugees and Displaced Persons.* 2nd Year. Second Session. June 1, 1946.

UN General Assembly. Official Records. UN Official Records of the 1st Part of the 1st Session of the General Assembly. *Plenary Meetings of the General Assembly. Verbatim Record.* Session 1–2. 1946–47, 1947–48. January 10 February 14, 1946.

———. Official Records of the Second Session of the General Assembly. Supplement no. 11. United Nations Special Committee on Palestine. *Report to the General Assembly. Vol. 3. 1947.*

———. Third Committee: Social, Humanitarian and Cultural Questions. Official Records of the 1st Part of the 1st Session. *Summary Record of Meetings.* January 11–February 10, 1947.

———. Third Committee: Social, Humanitarian and Cultural Questions. *Resolutions Adopted on the Reports of the Third Committee.* December 15, 1946.

———. *Report on the Progress and Prospect of Repatriation, Resettlement and Immigration of Refugees and Displaced Persons.* 7th Session. June 10, 1948.

U.S. Congress. House. Committee on Foreign Affairs and the Committee on the Judiciary. *Displaced Persons and the International Refugee Organization.* 80th Congress, 1st Session, November 16, 1947.

———. Subcommittee No. 1 of the Committee on the Judiciary. *Amending the Displaced Persons Act of 1948.* 81st Congress, 1st Session, 1949.

———. Committee on the Judiciary. *Permitting Admission of 400,000 Displaced Persons into the United States: Hearings Before Subcommittee on Immigration and Naturalization.* 80th Congress, 1st Session, 1947.

————. Committee on the Judiciary. *Hearings Before the Subcommittee on Immigration, Citizenship and International Law.* 93rd Congress, 2nd Session, April 3 and June 25, 1974.

————. Committee on the Judiciary. *Emigration of Soviet Jews: Report of a Special Study Subcommittee, May 24–June 1, 1975.* 94th Congress, 2nd Session, January 1, 1976.

————. Committee on the Judiciary. *Alleged Nazi War Criminals: Hearing Before the Subcommittee on Immigration, Citizenship, and International Law.* 95th Congress, 1st Session, 1978.

U.S. Congress. Senate. *Atrocities and Other Conditions in Concentration Camps in Germany: Report of the Committee Requested by Gen. Dwight D. Eisenhower. . . .* 79th Congress, 1st Session, 1945.

————. *Displaced Persons in Europe: Report of the Committee on the Judiciary Pursuant to S. Res. 137.* 80th Congress, 2nd Session, Report no. 950. 1948.

————. Committee on the Judiciary. *Displaced Persons: Hearings Before the Subcommittee on Amendments to the Displaced Persons Act.* 81st Congress, 1st and 2nd Sessions, 1950.

U.S. Department of Justice. United States Attorneys' Bulletin. *Office of Special Investigations* 54, no. 1 (January 2006).

U.S. Displaced Persons Commission. *[First through Sixth] Semi-Annual Report to the President and the Congress.* Washington, DC: Government Printing Office, 1949–52.

————. *Memo to America: The DP Story.* Washington, DC: Government Printing Office, 1958.

U.S. Government Accounting Office. Report by the Comptroller General of the United States. "Widespread Conspiracy to Obstruct Probes of Alleged Nazi War Criminals Not Supported by Available Evidence—Controversy May Continue." May 15, 1978.

————. Report by the Comptroller General of the United States, "Nazis and Axis Collaborators Were Used . . . ," June 28, 1985.

USHMM. *Life Reborn: Jewish Displaced Persons 1945–1951: Conference Proceedings.* Washington, DC, January 14–17, 2000.

————. *Children of the Holocaust: Symposium Presentations.* Washington, DC: Center for Advanced Holocaust Studies, 2004.

————. *Lithuania and the Jews: The Holocaust Chapter. Symposium Presentations.* Washington, DC: Center for Advanced Holocaust Studies, 2004.

————. *The Holocaust in Ukraine: New Sources and Perspectives. Conference Presentations.* Washington, DC: Center for Advanced Holocaust Studies, 2013.

Veidemanis, Juris. "Latvian Settlers in Wisconsin: A Comparative View." *The Wisconsin Magazine of History* 45, no. 4 (Summer 1962): 251–55.

Vernant, Jacques. *The Refugee in the Post-War World.* London: George Allen & Unwin, 1953.

Verzemnieks, Inara. *Among the Living and the Dead: A Tale of Exile and Homecoming on the War Roads of Europe.* New York: Norton, 2017.

Vida, George. *From Doom to Dawn: A Jewish Chaplain's Story of Displaced Persons.* New York: Jonathan David, 1967.

von Plato, Alexander, Almut Leh, and Christoph Thonfeld. *Hitler's Slaves: Life Stories of Forced Labourers in Nazi-Occupied Europe.* New York: Berghahn Books, 2010.

Wachsmann, Nikolaus. *KL: A History of the Nazi Concentration Camps*. New York: Farrar, Straus & Giroux, 2015.

Walosik, Henry. *My DP Story*. XLibris: 2013.

Warhaftig, Zorach. *Relief and Rehabilitation: Implications of the UNRRA Program for Jewish Needs*. New York: Institute of Jewish Affairs, 1944.

———. *Uprooted: Jewish Refugees and Displaced Persons After Liberation*. New York: Institute of Jewish Affairs, 1946.

Weinberg, Gerhard L. *A World at Arms: A Global History of World War II*. 2nd ed. Cambridge: Cambridge University Press, 2005.

Weisbrode, Kenneth. *The Year of Indecision, 1946: A Tour Through the Crucible of Harry Truman's America*. New York: Viking, 2016.

Weisgal, Meyer. *So Far: An Autobiography*. New York: Random House, 1971.

Weiss-Wendt, Anton. *On the Margins: Essays on the History of Jews in Estonia*. Budapest: Central European University Press, 2017.

Wiesel, Elie. "Keynote Address." *In Life Reborn: Jewish Displaced Persons, 1945–1951; Conference Proceedings, Washington, D.C., January 14–17, 2000*. Washington, DC: United States Holocaust Memorial Museum, 2001.

Wilford, Hugh. *The Mighty Wurlitzer: How the CIA Played America*. Cambridge, MA: Harvard University Press, 2008.

Wilson, Francesca. *Aftermath*. London: Penguin, 1947.

Woodbridge, George. *UNRRA: The History of the United Nations Relief and Rehabilitation Administration*. 3 vols. New York: Columbia University Press, 1950.

Wyman, Mark. *DPs: Europe's Displaced Persons, 1945–51*. Ithaca, NY: Cornell University Press, 1998.

Yablonka, Hanna. *Survivors of the Holocaust: Israel After the War*. Translated by Ora Cummings. London: Macmillan, 1999.

Zahra, Tara. *The Lost Children: Reconstructing Europe's Families After World War II*. Cambridge, MA: Harvard University Press, 2011.

———. *The Great Departure: Mass Migration from Eastern Europe and the Making of the Free World*. New York: Norton, 2016.

Zake, Ieva. *American Latvians: Politics of a Refugee Community*. New Brunswick, NJ: Transaction Publishers, 2010.

———, ed. *Anti-Communist Minorities in the U.S.* New York: Palgrave Macmillan, 2009.

Zertal, Idith. *From Catastrophe to Power: Holocaust Survivors and the Emergence of Israel*. Berkeley: University of California Press, 1998.

Zolberg, Aristide R. *A Nation by Design: Immigration Policy in the Fashioning of America*. Cambridge, MA: Harvard University Press, 2006.

Zuroff, Efraim. *Operation Last Chance: One Man's Quest to Bring Nazi Criminals to Justice*. New York: Palgrave, 2009.

Image Credits

Page 25: United States Holocaust Memorial Museum, courtesy of M. Dognon Schmitt

Page 48: Courtesy of Bundesarchiv-Bildarchiv

Page 68: Courtesy of Yad Vashem, The World Holocaust Remembrance Center

Page 69: United States Holocaust Memorial Museum, courtesy of Morris and Lala Fishman

Page 77: United States Holocaust Memorial Museum, courtesy of Lilo, Jack, and Micha Plaschkes

Page 118: United States Holocaust Memorial Museum, courtesy of Saul Sorrin

Page 143: AP Photo

Page 146: United States Holocaust Memorial Museum, courtesy of Jack Sutin

Page 151: Courtesy of the Lithuanian Cultural Institute

Page 157: A Polish family registering at No. 17 Displaced Persons Assembly Centre in Hamburg Zoological Gardens, 18 May 1945, No. 5 Army Film & Photographic Unit, Mapham J (Sgt). War Office Second World War Official Collection, Imperial War Museums

Page 159: AP Photo

Page 176: United States Holocaust Memorial Museum, courtesy of Alice Lev

Page 240: United States Holocaust Memorial Museum, courtesy of Leah Lahav

Page 248: DP Camp Internees Salzburg, ca. 1945–1951, the Louis Rittenberg Archive of Yeshiva University Museum

Page 252: United States Holocaust Memorial Museum, courtesy of Ruchana Medine White

Page 335: United States Holocaust Memorial Museum, courtesy of Saul Sorrin

Page 368: United States Holocaust Memorial Museum, courtesy of Benny Guinossar

Page 376: © Beth Hatefutsoth

Page 394: Courtesy of Yad Vashem, The World Holocaust Remembrance Center

Page 396: Courtesy of the American Jewish Joint Distribution Committee

Page 454: United States Holocaust Memorial Museum, courtesy of National Archives and Records Administration, College Park

Page 525: AP Photo/Rick Maiman

Page 526: AP Photo/Richard Sheinwald

Page 531: ABC via AP, file

Index

Note: The abbreviation "DP" refers to "displaced persons." Page numbers in *italics* indicate photographs and illustrations.

and cultural preservation in DP camps, 152
destruction of, *68*
and DP resettlement in U.S., 450
and the "hard core" DPs, 547
and the Harrison Report, 103
and illegal immigration to Palestine, 376
liberation of, 65, 67
and migration of Jewish DPs to Israel, 405
public awareness of, 65, 72
and recruits into Israeli defense forces, *394*
Berger, Joseph, 236, 245, 451–52, 535–36, 550
Berger, Marcus, 236, 245–46, 536
Bernadotte, Folke , 402–3
Bernard, William S., 302–3
Bernstein, Leonard, 395, *396*
Bernstein, Philip, 75–76, 238, 244, 245, 247,
   307, 372
Bertulis, Juozas, 540
Berzins, Ivars, 522
Bevin, Ernest
   and Anglo-American Committee
      negotiations, 217–18, 221–22, 226
   and conflicts over UNRRA's mandate, 134
   and the Harrison Report, 111
   and illegal immigration to Palestine, 366,
      374–75, 385–86
   and migration of Polish Jews into Germany,
      232–33, 234
   and U.S. pressure on Palestine issue,
      122–25, 255, 257–59
Bierut, Bolesław, 158
Billikopf, Jacob, 429, 432–33, 439
Bilmanis, Alfred, 139
Birger, Zev, 360–61
Birkenau concentration camp, 67, 549. *See also*
   Auschwitz-Birkenau
Black, Peter, 521–22
black market, 10, 148–49, 164, 177
BLOODSTONE, 471–72, 474
Blumenthal, Ralph, 517–18, 520
Board of Deputies of British Jews, 93
Board of Immigration Appeals, Immigration
   and National Service, 455
Board of Special Inquiry, Immigration and
   Naturalization Service, 464
Bohlen, Charles, 357, 472
Bolsheviks, 12, 20–21, 32–33, 35–36, 40,
   46–47, 228
Boltuch, Lea, 489
bomb damage, 5–6, 50, 54–56, 60–61

Boothby, E. B., 345
Borenkraut, Herman, 455–56
Boston, Massachusetts, *xiv–xv*, 417, 475, 534,
   536, 545
boxing in DP camps, 146, *146*, 150, 170
Boy Scouts, 155
Brafman, Anna, 489
Brafman, Daniel, 489
Braunschweig, Germany, 56–57, 60
Braunsteiner-Ryan, Hermine, 516–17
Brazil, 206, 318, 334, 347, 465, 467, 548
Bremerhaven, Germany, xv, 453, *454*, 504, 535
Bresinuk, Helen, 22–23
Bresinuk, Ivan, 22–23
Bresinuk, Julia, 22–23, 141
Breslau (Wrocław), Poland, 247
Brezhnev, Leonid, 518
Brichah, 244–45, 244n
Brimelow, Thomas, 155, 343–44
British Dominions, 340, 340n. *See also* Great
   Britain and the United Kingdom
British Foreign Office
   and Anglo-American Committee
      negotiations, 213, 217, 218, 221–22, 226
   and conflicts over UNRRA's mandate,
      131–32
   and deliberations on camp closures, 200,
      206–7
   and deliberations on special status for
      Jewish DPs, 93
   and the Harrison Report, 105, 109, 111,
      121–25
   and migration of Polish Jews into Germany,
      232–33, 247, 249–50
   and political activities in DP camps, 155
   and purge of suspected Nazi collaborators
      from DP camps, 197
   and resettlement of non-Jewish DPs, 341,
      342, 343–46
   and screening of camp residents, 207
   and status of POWs held in Germany, 140,
      188–89
   and U.S. pressure on Jewish immigration to
      Palestine, 257–59
British Home Office, 342, 528
British House of Commons, 123, 125,
   218–19, 259
British Ministry of Labour, 336, 341–42
British Parliament, 110. *See also* British House
   of Commons

0
0

Clifford, Clark, 398–99
Clift, Montgomery, 325
CM/1 (Care and Maintenance)
  questionnaires, 329
Cold War
  and Anglo-American Committee
    negotiations, 213, 213n
  and Cold War activities involving DPs, 12,
    467, 468–78
  and deliberations on DP bill, 299–303, 305,
    308–9, 309n, 312–13, 317, 320, 325–26,
    410–11, 411–19
  and deliberations on replacing UNRRA,
    283, 290–91
  and discriminatory immigration laws,
    12–13
  and Israeli declaration of independence,
    399–400
  and legacy of Last Million DPs, 551
  and refugees from Soviet Union in the U.S.,
    468–78
  See also anti-Communism; anti-Soviet
    sentiment
Collier's, 1–2
Cologne, Germany, 185
Colombia, 373
Columbia University, 452, 470–71
Come to Lovely Germany (propaganda film), 21
Comintern, 418
Commentary, 399
Commission of Inquiry on War Criminals
  (Canada), 527
Committee for a Free Latvia, 467, 473
Committee of former Jewish Concentration
  Camp Inmates, 466
Committee on Army and Navy Religious
  Activities, 75–76
Commonweal, 295
Commonwealth Investigation Service
  (Australia), 349
Commonwealth of Nations (British
  Commonwealth), 277, 349. See also Great
  Britain and the United Kingdom
Communist Party, 470, 491
Communist Party USA (CPUSA), 515
concentration camps
  and Baltic POWs, 139
  and deliberations on DP bill, 423
  and DPs retreating from Soviet advance, 9
  and forced labor in Germany, 25

and the Harrison Report, 106–7,
  110–11, 119
and IRO resettlement of DPs, 11
public awareness of, 65–67, 72, 75, 79
and Soviet-German conflict over Baltic
  states, 36–37
See also specific camp names
Congress of Industrial Organizations (CIO),
  203, 303
conspiracy theories regarding DPs, 116,
  233–34, 244, 319–20, 419
Consultant on Jewish Activities, U.S.
  Army, 114
Cooley, Thomas M., II, 91–92
Cooper, Kanty, 340–41
Corkery, Robert, 494–95
Corsi, Edward, 454
Coughlin, Charles, 459
Council of Foreign Ministers, 110, 134
Council of Latvian Organizations, 545
Counter-Intelligence (CIC), U.S. Army, 444,
  450–51, 462, 472, 474–76
Courtney, W. B., 2, 6–7
Court of Honor (Central Committee of
  Liberated Jews), 178
Cox, Cordelia, 499
Cox, Eugene "Goober," 414
Creech-Jones, Arthur, 381
Crossman, Richard, 218
Crum, Bartley, 213, 215
Crusade in Europe (Eisenhower), 117
Curzon Line, 141, 410
Cutler, John Wilson, Jr., 488–89
Cyprus
  and DP movements to and from Germany,
    xiv–xv
  and illegal immigration to Palestine,
    363–64, 387
  and international tensions on Palestine
    issue, 387–88
  and Israeli declaration of independence, 398
  and resettlement of Jewish DPs, 372, 373
Czechoslovakia
  and criticisms of DP bill, 433
  and deliberations on DP bill, 303, 309, 417,
    420, 421
  and deliberations on replacing UNRRA, 280
  and establishment of IRO, 292
  and expulsions of Volksdeutsche, 185, 186
  and illegal immigration to Palestine, 366

Operation Barbarossa, 29
Operation Carrot, 263, 265–67
Operation Paperclip, 468–69, 539
Operation Swallow, 249
Organization of Ukrainian Nationalists
  (OUN), 33, 33n, 41, 168, 445, 475–76
Orloff (Russian major), 136–37
orphans, 199, 251, 342, 371, 393
ORT, 173
Orthodox Jews, 548
Otwock, Poland, 236–37
Overseas News Service (ONS), 456,
  456n, 459
Ozorków, Poland, 86

Pabijans, Osvalds, 332
Paegle, Janis, 332
Pakistan, 380
Palaitis, Gustaves, 332–33
Palestine
  and Anglo-American Committee
    negotiations, 212–18, 218–23, 223–25,
    225–26
  and antisemitism, 309n
  and Brichah, 244n
  and deliberations on camp closures, 207
  and deliberations on DP bill, 293, 294, 318,
    319, 321
  and deliberations on replacing UNRRA,
    284–85
  and deliberations on special status for
    Jewish DPs, 93
  and discriminatory immigration laws, 13
  and DP movements to and from Germany,
    xiv–xv
  and the Harrison Report, 98–102, 103, 107,
    110–12, 115–16, 120, 121–26
  illegal immigration to, 12, 359–79,
    385–88, 393
  and migration of Polish Jews into Germany,
    232, 238, 247–48, 249–50, 251–52
  and Morgenthau's influence on policy, 97
  and organization of camp committees,
    82–83
  and political organization in DP
    camps, 150
  and status of Jewish DPs, 169, 175–77
  and ultimate destination of Jewish DPs, 9
  U.S. pressure on Palestine issue, 12,
    253–56, 257–60

and withdrawal of IGCR, 183
  See also Israel
Palij, Jakiw, 20, 529–31, *531*
Palmach, 214, 360
Panama, 292, 524
Pan Crescent (ship), 387–88
Pankivsky, Kost, 46
Pan York (ship), 387–88
paramilitary units, 41, 44, 192–93. *See also*
  underground fighters
"Parish Resettlement Kits," 324
partisans, 21, 84, 168, 244–45, 244n
partition plans (Palestine), 255, 257, 381–92
passports, 44, 235, 367, 402, 450, 489
Paterson, New Jersey, 536
patriotism, 150–51
Patt, Avinoam, 394–95
Patterson, Robert, 184, 191–92, 200, 205,
  231, 240, 242
Patton, George S., 65, 81, 116–20, 316–17
Paul, W. S., 354, 355–56
peacekeeping missions to Palestine, 389–90
Pearson, Drew
  on amendments to DP bill, 484
  on Cold War conspiracy narratives, 299
  on criticisms of DP bill, 424–25
  on deliberations for DP bill, 312
  on migration of Jewish DPs to Israel,
    439–40
  on Nazi war criminals in the U.S.,
    506–7, 517
  on political implications of DP bills, 479–80
  on Soviet trials of Nazi collaborators,
    514–15
Peenemünde, Germany, 54
Pegler, Westbrook, 299
Pehle, John, 97
Pepper, Claude, 422–23
"persecuted persons" status, 200–204, 230,
  242, 242n
Persian, Jayne, 349
Peru, 335
Petain, Marshal, 277–78
Petersen, Howard, 204–5
Pettiss, Susan, 171, 229–30
Pinson, Koppel, 171, 180
Piotrowski, Anna, 24
Piotrowski, Franek, 24
Piotrowski, Janek, 24
Piotrowski, Tadeusz, 24–26, 164, 538–39

Special Committee on Refugees and
Displaced Persons, 281–86, 288
Special Investigations Unit (Australia), 529
Spellman, Francis, 201, 297, 323, 459, 482–83
sports clubs and events in DP camps, 146,
150, 170
Stakė, Petras, 540
Stalin, Joseph, 27, 95, 235, 283, 412–13
St. André, August, 7
Star (London), 234
State–Army–Navy–Air Force Coordinating
Committee (SANACC), 139n, 471–72
"stateless person" designation
and creation of IRO, 282
and cultural preservation in DP camps, 150
and deliberations on camp closures, 202
and DPs retreating from Soviet
advance, 44
and the Harrison Report, 108, 114, 117
and IRO assumption of camp
administration, 331
and migration of Polish Jews into
Germany, 243
and organization of camp committees, 81
and resettlement of non-Jewish
DPs, 356
and survivors of concentration and death
camps, 73, 76
and withdrawal of IGCR, 183–84
State–War–Navy Coordinating Committee
(SWNCC), 139, 139n
Steinhardt, Vita, 32
Stettin (Szczecin), Poland, 244–46
Stettinius, Edward, Jr., 98–99, 298
Stevens, George, 70
Stimson, Henry, 114, 115
Stokes, Richard Rapier, 342
Stone, I. F., 362–63
St. Ottilien hospital, 60–61, 78, 81
Strang, William, 109
Stratton, William, 304–7, 310–13, 317, 326,
409, 414, 414n
Stritch, Samuel Alphonsius, 201–3, 204
Stutthof (Sztutowo) concentration camp,
55–56
Supreme Headquarters Allied Expeditionary
Force (SHAEF)
and conflicts over UNRRA's mandate,
134, 137
described, 93n

and the Harrison Report, 102, 104
Survey Graphic, 303
Švenčionys, Lithuania, *xiii*, 37, 136, 505
Swanstrom, Edward E., 297–98, 322–23,
457–58, 483
Sweden, 290, 370, 486
Switzerland, 83
Syria, 398, 406

Taagepera, Rein, 29
Tablet, 267
Taffel, Leib, 489
Taft, Charles P., 298, 322
Taft, Robert A., 122, 224, 300–301, 304, 315,
320, 381–82
tailors and garment workers, 298, 308, 320,
335–36, 352–54, 536
Tajikistan, 235, 237
Tartakower, Arieh, 89–90
Tartu concentration camp, *xiii*, 36–37,
513, 522
tattoos, SS
attempts to remove, 44
blood type of SS members, 9, 20, 44,
343–44, 345
and Internal Security Act, 504
and Polish laborers, *159*
and resettlement of non-Jewish DPs,
343–45, 349
and Trawniki guards, 20
and Waffen-SS initiation, 9
Tel Aviv, 384
tenant farming and DPs, 540–41
Thompson, John, 538
Tilsit (Sovetsk), 47
Time, 66
Tito, Josip Broz, 130–31, 193, 279, 534
Tolstoy Foundation, 442
Torah services in DP camps, 70–71
Tower, Samuel A., 306
trade unions in UK and DPs, 341
transit centers, 229–30, 349, 534
Transjordan, 398
Trawniki, Poland, 20, 504–5, 530
Treaty of Riga, 27
Treaty of Versailles, 17
Treblinka extermination camp, 55,
237, 505
Trifa, Viorel, 506, 517–19, 524–25, *528*
Tripp, Almanza, 503